What the veterans said ... praise for *A Long Long War*

"A superb job. This story had to be told. What's so important is that he galvanised the many of us to tell our stories – before we got too old and forgot the details – in the memory of our lost comrades and those permantently affected by that long forgotten war. I doubt if any of our politicans will read this book – but they ought to. Ken – thanks from the active and silent voices from *A Long Long War*."

"When Ken contacted me to ask me to publicise what was then a project only little did I know what an excellent read the book would be. One of the few books to tell of "the troubles" from the soldiers point of view, remarkably frank, a compelling read, politicians should read this before committing soldiers to the front line anywhere."

"Over the years the voices of the main protagonists of 'The Troubles' were very often heard. The voice perhaps heard least of all was that of the ordinary British soldier, the guy sent over there to try and keep the peace, in what at times was an almost impossible situation. A thankless task for scant reward. What Ken has achieved is a testimony to those who walked the streets and more importantly to those who never came back. Essential Reading !!!!"

"Awesome – a stunning read. I was one of the 300,000 that served in N.I. and this book is long overdue. If you are going to read one book on the troubles in N.I. then it has to be this one, you will feel the fear, the pain, the worry, the heartache, the joy and the bond of brotherhood felt by of all who served their friends and families."

"An excellent and weighty book with stories well worth telling – how it really was for and from those on the ground. Long overdue as memories are already beginning to blur and fade and those that were left behind deserve better. Thanks Ken."

"My Dad was a soldier in Ulster and I bought the book for him. He says that it was so real that it brought back the smells and fears of Belfast. He says that it is, without doubt, the best book on the troubles and he has read a few. Good stuff."

"Excellent piece of work from a true gentleman. Conveys the professionalism and courage of soldiers working in impossible conditions. Down to earth stories compiled in a practical and interesting manner. First class read."

BULLETS, BOMBS AND CUPS OF TEA

Further Voices from the British
Army in Northern Ireland 1969–98
Including Voices of their Loved Ones

Written and compiled by

Ken M. Wharton

Helion & Company Ltd

Helion & Company Limited
26 Willow Road
Solihull
West Midlands
B91 1UE
England
Tel. 0121 705 3393
Fax 0121 711 4075
Email: info@helion.co.uk
Website: www.helion.co.uk

Published by Helion & Company 2009
Designed and typeset by Farr out Publications, Wokingham, Berkshire
Cover designed by Farr out Publications, Wokingham, Berkshire
Printed by Cromwell Press Group, Trowbridge, Wiltshire

The opinions expressed in the book are those of the individuals quoted and do not necessarily accord with views held by the author or publisher.

ISBN 978-1906033-34-7

British Library Cataloguing-in-Publication Data.
A catalogue record for this book is available from the British Library.

For details of other military history titles published by Helion & Company Limited contact the above address, or visit our website: http://www.helion.co.uk.

We always welcome receiving book proposals from prospective authors.

This book is dedicated to Nell Webster, Mo Norton, Carol Richards, Doreen Gilchrist, Patsy Hurst, Annie Bowman, Marie Hale, Tracey Butcher, Kathleen Gillespie and to Karen and Stevie Rumble. They are eleven remarkable ladies who shared the pain and grief of the soldiers who served in Northern Ireland

To Anne-Marie, Anna-Martina, Jonathan, Jenny, Robbie, Alex and Nathan, my seven wonderful children

To Sherriden, Kelsey and William; my three incredible grandchildren

To my lovely lady, Helen, the Navy brat who turned my life around

To my Jacket mates, Dave Hallam & Darren Ware

To all my many mates in the 'Jackets'

To Colour Sergeant Ken Ambrose from the best Regiment in the British Army

To my Kings mate, George Prosser who did so much and still continues to give himself to help others

To all those who mastered the art of walking backwards on the streets and lanes of Northern Ireland and especially to those who did it with such style and bravery

To every 'bullet catcher' and 'tail end Charlie'

To every Regiment but a special dedication to the men and women of the U.D.R.

The people at NIVA who do so much for every Northern Ireland veteran

To the memory of Lieutenant Commander Joseph Geraghty, R.N. (Who would have been my Father-in-Law)

and
To my late mother, Irene Wharton (1929–99) and my father, Mark Clifford Wharton (1927–2009)

The Death of Robert Curtis

Ask the family not to hate the Irish; neither I nor my daughter chose to be born there; we just were. This is the baby I crawled with, up Hillman Street with the bullets flying; this was the baby born from love; her mum and dad fed Robert Curtis (officially the first British soldier to die in N.I.) his last meal, fish and chips from the Silver Key Chip shop on Duncairn Gardens; with fun, laughter, love and total respect. This was before the IRA took him from this world, so unfairly before he could see his own daughter Jasmine born, 6 months after he was murdered.

Please let the family know we care, and there were others who did, and held her son as a hero in our hearts. He was there to protect us, he made the world a better place for our daughter to be born in, and may God hold him in the Palm of His Hands.

Thank you to all you wonderful boys, who we depended on for some sort of freedom and safety. Your sacrifices were never taken for granted; I know; I have two beautiful grandchildren to prove it.
Doreen Gilchrist, Belfast Resident

❧

Although it is clear that the politicians and policy makers were clueless it is evident that the people on the 'frontline' knew the situation. It's a pity they were not listened to at the time; a lot of hurt could have been avoided.
James Henderson, Ulster Defence Regiment

❧

I loved the man I sent to Belfast; I didn't much like the man who came back.
Ruby Hill, former wife of a soldier

The author gratefully acknowledges and endorses the words of the following contributors:

'To our Members of Parliament, who, through their mismanagement and failure to understand the problems of Northern Ireland, by not allowing the security forces to fight the war, in the way soldiers were trained to do. They gave us 'yellow cards', bad equipment, disgusting accommodation, long eighteen hour days for four months, with a mere four days R&R; also to insult us by giving us fifty pence danger money, per day (which was taxable). Thank you, you weak, sniffling, desk-ridden rodents.'

'To the soldiers who were severely wounded and lost limbs, sight and were severely disfigured, the Government gave you nothing for your suffering. They, the Government, would give thousands of pounds to typists for sitting too long at a computer. Finally, you the politician are detested by 95% of the population and 100% by the soldiers, for whom you have neither respect nor regard for.'
Senior NCO, Royal Highland Fusiliers

ℰℐ

'To all of those who say that Northern Ireland was not a war, try telling those of us who served there. We will tell you different; to us it was, and still is, a war, because it lives with us every day of our lives.'

'It is a war which still goes on inside of us; try telling the loved ones of those who never came home that it wasn't a war. Try telling any Northern Ireland vet that it wasn't a war; try telling us not to cry when we are on our own. Try telling us not to remember the things that happened; just try for God's sake, to understand. I am a Northern Ireland vet and proud of it.'
Rifleman David Hallam, Royal Green Jackets

ℰℐ

'I have the greatest admiration for the modern soldier who is serving now in Iraq etc, one of them being my next door neighbour, but I think the British Public have forgotten how bad Northern Ireland was and the amount of casualties suffered. I told friends in Liverpool that my daughter was thinking of joining up and the lady was horrified about her going to Iraq, her husband said but her Dad knows all about that having served in Ulster and she then says but that was nothing compared to Iraq. She was speechless when I told her how may had died in Northern Ireland, she thought it had been about 50.'
Mark Chapman, Royal Artillery

ℰℐ

'Looking back now it is quite remarkable, though not surprising in the circumstances, how naïve and ill-prepared we were. But, who could have thought that we were involved in what Ken Wharton has so rightly titled his book *A Long Long War* and in part of the United Kingdom. If someone had said to me in 1969, that the Army would be on operations in Northern Ireland for almost 40 years, I would have thought them barking mad.'
Major Peter Oakley, King's Regiment

જ

'I think every day about the lads that didn't come back, and I will never let their names fade; not while I'm alive. I raise a glass on the anniversary of their deaths every year. God Bless You Lads.'
Eddie Atkinson, Green Howards

જ

'I have always thought that 95% of the people in Northern Ireland were normal law abiding citizens who just wanted to live their lives in peace, terrorised by that remaining 5% percent whose sole pleasure in life was maiming and killing them.
My religion is pure heathen but I always had a great deal of sympathy for the downtrodden Catholic minority in Northern Ireland until the IRA took over. It then took me a while to realise what a small minority they were and I would say the same about the so-called loyalist terrorists. Both groups did their best to fan the flames of hatred and keep the war going for as long as it did.'
Ken Ambrose, Royal Green Jackets

Contents

List of Photos and Maps

Maps of Belfast and Londonderry originally appeared in *The British Army in Northern Ireland* by Michael Dewar (1985) and are © Weidenfeld & Nicolson, a divi sion of The Orion Publishing Group (London)

Foreword

It is always a pleasure, not often given to me, to write a Foreword for a book written by a former colleague in the same regiment. Ken Wharton and I both served in the late 1960s and early 1970s but we were never in the same battalion. His service in Northern Ireland also ended before mine began in Belfast in 1973. I am hesitant, though, about writing this Foreword as this book and its predecessor *A Long Long War* are clearly intended to provide an opportunity and outlet for the more junior ranks to tell of their experiences and voice their opinions on service in the Province from 1969-98. It is humbling to read them, not least because it shows that all soldiers, regardless of rank, have hearts, souls and feelings, and that pity and compassion rarely lie far beneath the surface of the seemingly hard exterior that soldiers often misguidedly seek to cultivate. My reservation, however, arises from a fear that a Foreword by a more senior officer may be misplaced. The eloquence with which some contributors have recounted their stories is remarkable and I would not wish in any way to dilute their raw impact with trite comments from a 'Rupert'.

But it is not just the eloquence of the contributors that is remarkable. It is also the extraordinary single-mindedness and commitment with which Ken Wharton has undertaken a self-imposed task from which others would quickly have shied. I sense that what may have started as a good intention has developed into something bordering upon an obsession. Two volumes so far and I know Ken has plans for more and, as his books become more widely read, no doubt many more willing contributors will step forward seeking to add their voices, new stories and different angles to those already recorded.

Historians, of course, will have every reason to be grateful to Ken in future years. Whether the present peace in Northern Ireland turns out to be lasting or just another punctuation mark in over 300 years of recurring Troubles will not become apparent for very many decades. But what Ken has done is to ensure that the views and experiences of those who served at the sharp end during the 30 years of conflict in Northern Ireland from 1969-98 are recorded for posterity, warts and all. As each year passes and as old soldiers fade away, the significance and value of these accounts will become increasingly important in adding colour to, and often, I suspect, contradicting official histories.

The campaign in Northern Ireland from 1969-98 is often said to have been neither fought nor shaped by senior officers but by corporals, lance-corporals and riflemen. And it was. It was the junior ranks who bore the brunt of the dangers and discomforts which formed a part of the daily diet of military service in the Province, and the taunts and provocations of a population in which it was rarely possible to be sure who was friend or foe. It is unsurprising, therefore, that, as is evident in *Bullets, Bombs and Cups of Tea*, some resent the lack of reward and recognition accorded their efforts. But for Tommy Atkins it was ever thus. Ours has never been to reason why, but to do and die – a sentiment which sits uncomfortably alongside the long-standing promotion in my regiment of the thinking rifleman. *Bullets, Bombs and Cups of Tea* and its predecessor A Long

Long War suggest that there are and always have been plenty of brave, thinking riflemen in the British Army and, however they may express themselves, there can be no disguising their fears and feelings. Testimony to the fact lies within the 500 pages of this admirable book.

Lieutenant-General Sir Christopher Wallace
January 2009

Author's Personal Notes

I received many letters of praise and thanks from readers and contributors to the first book *A Long Long War* and I also received other, less than complimentary remarks. The latter I noted and then filed away, but the former, as I write in the introduction to this book, made me feel proud and honoured. The first was from the mother of a soldier, killed, indirectly, by the IRA after the 'final' ceasefire and the other was from an Infantry Captain. I reprint them below in no particular order.

Hi, I am Private Andrew Richardson's mam, I have just been looking at your great book and I would just like to say thank you to all involved in reporting the true facts of Andrew's death/murder, and getting him the honour that he so rightly deserved. He was a dedicated soldier and loved every minute of his army life. He is such a great loss to our family; I can't thank everyone enough.
Gloria Richardson, Mother of Private Andrew Richardson

My wife read my contribution and commented that she was very proud of me – which in a way is all the recognition I really wanted. I have to say that the Roll of Honour is the finest of all your achievements in this book. It is an absolute disgrace that the current government, so seduced by paramilitaries, and so focused on 'peace at any price' have attempted to dumb down the sacrifice of so many people who gave their lives between and since ceasefires, on operational duty in Northern Ireland

Finally you have made such an important contribution to the process for all of us (as veterans) in recognising for ourselves, the importance of our own achievement. This is just my view, but I would say that in the British Army people do not openly welcome recognition. There is a culture of doing a fantastic job and then outwardly deliberately not talking about it. Its not considered 'cool' to either seek or be recognised for a job well done.

This is a culture that the Army would do well to change. The current generation of soldier is, I suspect, needier of recognition and public praise than ever before, and the current conflicts represent challenges and sacrifices which are unprecedented. Don't stop now Ken, crack on and cover Bosnia, Kosovo, Sierra Leone, Iraq and Afghanistan. The veterans have found a voice in your work, and I think that's such a fabulous achievement.
An Infantry Captain

Jon Pilger, the famed Australian journalist, twice wrote to me, in the 1970s, and to echo his own eloquent words, it is support like this, which gives me new heart.

Acknowledgements

Where can I possibly begin in order to correctly thank all those who helped me, encouraged me, and even praised me? How can I possibly prioritise the legions of both former soldiers and civvies without whose help, I couldn't have written my second book on the history of the troubles? I can't; so I won't; the following list is random and suggests no order of seniority whatsoever.

Miss Boothroyd was my teacher at East Ardsley Secondary Modern from 1960-64; she was a martinet, she was rude, she was a disciplinarian of the 'old school' but she honed my writing skills and though I hated her at the time, I owe her much. She taught me the word 'euphemism' and if ever there was a euphemism, the term 'troubles' is one. After I came out of the Army and went to University as a mature student, my next mentor was Zyg Layton-Henry my personal tutor at Warwick University; I was a lazy sod and at a time of turmoil in my life and he helped me so much.

I am sorry that my late mother, Irene Wharton wasn't around when my first book was published because, although a Jehovah's Witness with an absolute abhorrence of violence, she would have been so proud of me.

I have to say profound thanks to Mike Day a photographer extraordinaire for his boundless energy, skills behind the lens and for the non-stop encouragement; Mike was a helper who became a mate and I am pleased to class him as both. George Prosser is a an ex-Kingsman who, even all these years after his last tour of Northern Ireland, tirelessly works himself into the ground as a families' officer for the Independent King's Regimental Association; I am proud to call him a friend and a comrade.

For obvious reasons, the Royal Green Jackets are my favourite Regiment, and I have to say thank you to Darren Ware – now, I can add, proudly – a published author like myself. He is a cop, but we love you anyway, mate. Lots of Jackets wrote for the book and amongst those who patiently helped me were Ken Ambrose, Kevin Stevens, John Moore, Mick Copp, Tim Marsh and many others. Bless you guys for your support and the trust you have placed in me. Another Jacket, Dave Hallam and his wife Cindy, now happily ensconced in sunny Western Australia have become dear friends and Dave's energy, like Mike Day's, knows no bounds. One day though, mark my words, I will have my revenge on Cindy for dunking me in the Indian Ocean!

Paddy Lenaghan, another bloody Aussie and his wife Josie; thank you for your friendship and all your help; you did so much for me and both books. Thanks to Tommy Clarke, a former member of the Rogues, Cutthroats and Thieves; Tommy, when it came to help and support, you were never found wanting.

To June and 'Tiny' Rose; thank you for all your help and kindness. 'Tiny' was shot by the IRA in the Royal Victoria Hospital in Belfast, eventually discharged and then put on the growing list of wounded ex-soldiers forgotten by the Government which sent them to fight and be wounded or die.

Mick 'Benny' Hill because the troubles cost you more than physical pain and because your enthusiasm for getting our story out knows no ends. Emma

Beaumont, for her work on the AFM wall at the National Arboretum, and for being a source of inspiration for her dedication to preserving the memories of those who fell, and for her selflessness in helping me compile the Roll of Honour in both books.

To Andrew MacDonald of the KORB, a gentleman and a friend and a constant source of new information about the troubles. To Andy, Keith, 'Onion,' 'Big Stevie' all of NIVA for their help, contributions and support in both books. Also to my Aldershot Concrete Company comrade, Dave Langston for admitting that he could take good food and turn it into shit in 10 minutes.

Dave Langston, Keith Hudson, Von Slaps, 'Big Stevie', 'Onion' and Andy Bennett of NIVA; I cannot thank you enough.

James Henderson for his vast contributions to my hitherto limited knowledge of Irish history and the myriad precursors to the troubles. To Roger Payne – another bloody Aussie – for his encouragement and constant offers to rewrite the book. To Arfon Williams and Celia and Martin and Carmel at the RRW museum in Brecon; has any museum done more for me than them? To Ray Gascoyne and Eddie Atkinson of the Green Howards for all their support and encouragement. To my friend, Phil Winstanley, a Medic who survived the IRA's cowardly attack at the Musgrave Park Hospital; thank you.

Geoff Smith; what more can I say about you that was not written in a dozen Army discipline books; his site at www.lightinfantryreunited.co.uk is one of the finest on the Internet. To David Dews, a former Fusilier terribly injured in a helicopter crash in South Armagh; ignored by his Government and his country; you will never be ignored by me, mate.

To a 'drop short', John Swaine; John, you may be a Bradford lad but I am honoured to know you, my friend. Kev Wright, a 'Brummie' who did so much for this book as well as his mum, Iris, as the Wrights tried to commandeer the second volume!

To Mo Norton; a lady who lost her brother, murdered with others by the IRA on the M62 in Yorkshire in 1974. Mo, you are my friend for life. Mick Pickford, another 'drop short' who became a friend and a prolific contributor to the book. To Richard Peacocke a bomb disposal 'nutter.' I couldn't have done your job, mate for the entire world; many thanks for all you did. Richard Nettleton, a 'woodentop' from Suffolk who never stopped helping me.

To all my friends in beautiful Canada, but especially to my best friend in God's country, Sandie Blair who encouraged me from the first day I met her and to Helen Cheshire for believing in me.

I gratefully acknowledge Jackie Chappell for her kind permission to use 'Dear Mum; We Kip With Our Boots On' from the July 30, 1971 edition of *The Bath & Wilts Evening Chronicle* which is reprinted on page 193.

To Helen MacDonald, my partner, for life – I trust – for her endless patience in helping me proof-read contributions to the book and for being an 'Author's widow.'

At a lecture in Chelsea, I told my audience that former soldiers were not ex-comrades; they are just 'comrades' and always will be; for life. Thank you to all of you who have contributed and helped with this book and for all the love given to me by my family and friends.

The Voices

(In no special order from first to last)

John Swaine	Andy Bennett
Dave Hallam	Lawrence Bowman
Eddie Atkinson	Lawrence Jagger
Darren Ware	Jim Ward
Andrew MacDonald	Jason Benn
George Prosser	Paul Hazelwood
Arfon Williams	Frank Jones
Tommy Clarke	Dave Bradwell
Tim Francis	Colin (Argylls)
Terry Friend	Mickey Lee
Doreen Gilchrist	Kev Flynn
Bob Gallagher	David Wilson
Dave Langston	Gloria Richardson
David Dews	Bill Jones
James Henderson	Lee Sansum
Billy Fitzgerald	Steve Burke
Tony Procter	Haydn Davies
General Sir Peter Graham	Simon Richardson
Mick Pickford	Tony Yarwood
Ray Mitchell	Hugh Heap
Kevin Stevens	Tim Marsh
Stephen Corbett	'Taff' Fitzgerald
John Rafferty	Bob Davies
Jim Parker	D.C.
Keith Hazelwood	Neil Evans
Ian Mitchell	Joe Jurkiewicz
Malcolm Patinson	Paul Weston
Ross Saxby	Mick Copp
Steven Larne	Steve Clarke
Richard Nettleton	Ray Mitchell
Eddie Dixon	Ted Edwards
Barry Lovell	Gerry Butcher
Kevin Chatfield	Jimmy Mac
Paddy Larkin	Mike Day
Tim Castle	Bill Jones
Nick Bagle	Rob Colley
Darren Croucher	Mo Norton
Alan Borthwick	Big Stevie
Alan Bolton	Mike Davies
Harry Knight	John Black
Phil Hutchinson	Laura Speers

Annie Bowman
Marie Hale
Geoff Moore
Dave Maltby
Iris Wright
Kevin Wright
Richard Smith
Ken Ambrose
Hilary Reynolds
Mick Hill
Ruby Hill
Bill Callaghan
Lee Wilkins
Peter & Felicity Townend
Stuart Corns
Mr Peter Briscoe
Mrs Sandra Briscoe
Pat Moir
Ken W
'Bugle'
Jim ('Argylls')
Andy Wood
John Girdler
Ian Jones
Peter Oakley

Mark Chapman
David Henley
David Creese
Brian Baskerville
Brian Smith
Gareth Dyer
Graham 'Onion'
    (Well, that's what he says!)
Roy Banwell
Von Slap
Tracy Abraham
Kevin Gorman
Liz Burns
Sue Hanisch
Alan Holborough
Carney Lake
Dougie Durrant
Simon Hodges
Gary Smith
Brian Aitken
Kathleen Gillespie
Gary 'A'
And the twenty who wanted to be
anonymous

Glossary of Terms

2IC	Second in com mand
Angle Iron	Soldier of Royal Anglians
ASU	IRA Active Service Unit
ATO	Army Technical Officer (bomb-disposal)
Bandit Country	South Armagh and especially the area around Crossmaglen
Barrett.50	High velocity sniper's rifle (US-made)
Brick	4 men under a Corporal (4 bricks under a Sergeant)
B-Special	Part-time Police auxiliaries
Btn/ Bn	Battalion (generally 480 – 600 men in an infantry unit)
Bullet Catcher	Either the lead man or the tail-end Charlie in a foot patrol
Bullshit	The expression for the rigorous spit 'n' polishing routine
Casevac	Casualty evacuation
Cas-Rep	Casualty Report
CGM	Conspicuous Gallantry Medal
CO	Commanding Officer (Lieutenant-Colonel)
GOC	General Officer Commanding
Contact	Shot fired by enemy
COP	Close Observation Platoon
CP	Check Point
CPC	Civilianised Patrol Car
Crap Hat	To a Para, this meant any other Regiment
CSM	Company Sergeant-Major
CSU	Civilian Search Unit
DERR	Duke of Edinburgh's Royal Regiment (see also DoE)
Det 14/The Det	Undercover British Army unit (also 14th Detachment)
Dicking	Being observed by gunman's helpers prior to a shot being set up. Also: being dicked
ECM	Electronic counter measure (to block radio signals intended to detonate bombs by remote control)
FP	Foot Patrol. Also firing point; the reader needs to check the context of the incidents.
Full Screw	Full Corporal
GC	George Cross
GOC	General Officer Commanding
GPMG	("Jimpy") General Purpose Machine-Gun (1960s successor to LMG or Bren)
Green Bottles	Term used by soldiers to describe the RUC

GS	Garda Síochána (Irish Republic Police Service)
GSM	General Service Medal (awarded to British soldiers who have served a tour of active service)
HED	High explosive device
Hen patrol	Women looking out for soldiers and then alerting others by usually banging dustbin lids noisily.
IA	Immediate action
IC	In command
ICP	Incident Command Post
IED	Improvised Explosive Device
INIBA	Improved Northern Ireland Body Armour
INLA	Irish National Liberation Army
Int	Army Intelligence (thought to be a contradiction in terms)
IRA	Irish Republican Army (Óglaigh na hÉireann)
Irish Cocktail	Petrol Bomb
IRSP	Irish Republican Socialist Party (political wing of INLA)
IWS	Individual Weapons Sight (sniper scope)
Lance-Jack	Lance Corporal
Left-footer	Catholic (see also 'Taig')
Lift	To arrest
LMG	Light Machine Gun
LVF	Loyalist Volunteer Force
MC	Military Cross
MiD	Mentioned in Dispatches
MM	Military Medal
Mob	Usually a reference to the Army as a whole, used by soldiers
Multiple	12 man grouping (3 x 4 man teams) 2 multiples = a platoon
MQs	Married Quarters
ND	Negligent Discharge (premature or unnecessary firing of a weapon)
NIFSL	Northern Ireland Forensic Science Laboratory
NITAT	Northern Ireland Training Advisory Team
NORAID	American fund raising organisation which financed the IRA
NTH	Newtownhamilton
OC	Officer Commanding
Officials	Volunteer in the Official wing of the IRA (see also 'Stickies')
OP	Observation Post
Operation Motorman	Army operation in 1972 to forcibly end the "no go" areas of the province
Ops	Operations
ORBAT	Order of Battle

Overwatch	One unit giving support or protection to another (esp at VCPs)
Own Goal	Where a terrorist bomb might explode prematurely killing the bomber
PIG	Armoured personnel carrier (Patrol Infantry Group) produced by Humber
PIRA	Provisional IRA
Player	Army slang for known or suspected terrorist.
PPW	Personal Protection Weapon
Prod	Protestant
Provie / Provo	Member of the Provisional IRA as the Nationalists would call them
Proxy	Bomb carried to point of detonation by a person under duress.
PTI	Physical Training Instructor (also known as the 'SS')
PVCP	Permanent vehicle checkpoint
QCB	Queen's Commendation for Bravery
QRF	Quick Reaction Force
RCIED	Remote controlled Improvised Explosive Device
RIRA	"Real" IRA (behind the Omagh atrocity)
RMC	Royal Marine Commando
RMO	Regimental Medical Officer
RN	Republican News (*An Phoblacht*) Republican newspaper
RPG	Rocket-propelled grenade
RT	Radio Transmitter
RUC	Royal Ulster Constabulary
RVH	Royal Victoria Hospital, Belfast
Rupert	An unofficial British Army term for Officer
SA80	Current British Army standard assault rifle
Sangar	Heavily fortified protective guard post
Sarry	Saracen Armoured Vehicle
SD	Suspect device
SDLP	Social and Democratic Labour Party (Páirtí Sóisialta Daonlathach an Lucht Oibre)
SF	Security Forces
Sf	Sustained fire (automatic weapons firing on fixed lines)
Shankhill Butchers	A Protestant murder gang who targeted only Catholics
Shebeen	Illegal drinking dens run on sectarian lines and offering all hours drinking
Sinn Fein	"We Alone / Us Alone" (so-called political wing of the IRA)
Slot	To kill

SLR	Self Loading Rifle. 7.62mm standard British Army rifle
SMG	Sub Machine Gun
SOPS	Standard operating procedures
SOTAT	Security Operations Training Unit; N.I. street training in Germany
Squaddie	British soldier
Stag	Period of guard duty (i.e. a 2 hour stag)
Stickies	The derisive nickname for an Official IRA volunteer
Storno	Radio transmitter
SUSAT	Sight Unit, Small Arms Trilux
Taig	Protestant term to describe a Catholic (see also Left-footer)
The 'Murph'	The Ballymurphy estate in West Belfast
The Badge	Regimental Sergeant Major
The Bog	Northern Ireland or Ireland as a whole
Tom	Another word for squaddie
Tout	IRA term for an informer or spy
UCBT	Under car booby trap (see also UVBT)
UDA	Ulster Defence Association (Protestant paramilitary force)
UFF	Ulster Freedom Fighters (see also UVF)
US	Useless! Unserviceable
UVBT	Under Vehicle Booby Trap
UVF	Ulster Volunteer Force
VBIED	Vehicle-borne improvised explosive device
VCP	Vehicle Checkpoint
VISA	Vehicle Incendiary: South Armagh
Wad	Sandwich
WO	Warrant Officer (Sergeant Major)
Woodentop	Soldier in the Guards Brigade
Wriggly Tin	Corrugated iron
XMG	Crossmaglen

Regimental Abbreviations

17/21 L.	17th/21st Lancers
A. & S.H.	Argyll & Sutherland Highlanders
A.C.C.	Army Catering Corps*
A.P.T.C.	Army Physical Training Corps
B. & R.	Blues and Royals
B.W.	Black Watch
C.G.	Coldstream Guards
C.R.	Cheshire Regiment
D & D.	Devon & Dorsets
D.O.E.	Duke of Edinburgh's Regiment
D.W.R.	Duke of Wellington's Regiment

G.G.	Grenadier Guards
G.H.	Gordon Highlanders
G.Hr./XIX	Green Howards
GLOS	Gloucestershire Regiment
K.H.	King's Hussars
K.O.B.	King's Own Border Regiment
K.O.S.B.	King's Own Scottish Borderers
K.R.	King's Rifles
L.I.	Light Infantry
P.O.W.	Prince of Wales' Own Regiment of Yorkshire
P.W.R.R.	Princess of Wales' Royal Regiment
PARA	Parachute Regiment
Q.D.G.	Queen's Dragoon Guards
Q.L.R.	Queen's Lancashire Regiment
Q.O.H.	Queen's Own Highlanders
Q.O.H.	Queen's Own Hussars
Q.R.	Queen's Regiment
Q.R.L.	Queen's Royal Lancers
R.A.	Royal Artillery
R.A.F.	Royal Airforce
R.A.M.C.	Royal Army Medical Corps
R.A.O.C.	Royal Army Ordnance Corps *
R.A.R.	Royal Anglian Regiment
R.A.V.C.	Royal Army Veterinary Corps
R.C.S.	Royal Corps of Signals
R.C.T.	Royal Corps of Transport*
R.D.G.	Royal Dragoon Guards
R.E.	Royal Engineers
R.E.M.E.	Royal Electrical & Mechanical Engineers
R.G.B.W.	Royal Gloucester Berkshire & Wiltshire Regiment
R.G.J.	Royal Green Jackets
R.H.F.	Royal Highland Fusiliers
R.H.R.	Royal Highland Rifles
R.I.R.	Royal Irish Rangers
R.L.	Royal Lancers
R.L.C.	Royal Logistics Corps
R.M.	Royal Marines
R.M.P.	Royal Military Police
R.N.	Royal Navy
R.P.C.	Royal Pioneer Corps*
R.R.W.	Royal Regiment of Wales
R.S.D.G.	Royal Scots Dragoon Guards
R.T.R.	Royal Tank Regiment
R.W.F.	Royal Welsh Fusiliers
S.G	Scots Guards
Staffs	Staffordshire Regiment
T.A.V.R.	Territorial Army & Volunteer Reserve

U.D.R.	Ulster Defence Regiment (Northern Ireland's T.A.)
W. & S.F.	Worcestershire & Sherwood Foresters
W.G.	Welsh Guards
W.R.A.C.	Women's Royal Army Corps

* Merged into R.L.C. 1993

Army Chain of Command (Infantry)

Brick	4 men under a Lance-Corporal
Section	Generally 8 men led by a Sergeant
Platoon	Generally 30 men led by a Lieutenant
Company	120–160 men, led by a Captain or Major
Battalion	600 men led by a Lieutenant-Colonel
Brigade/ Regiment	1800 men led by a full Colonel or Brigadier

Maps

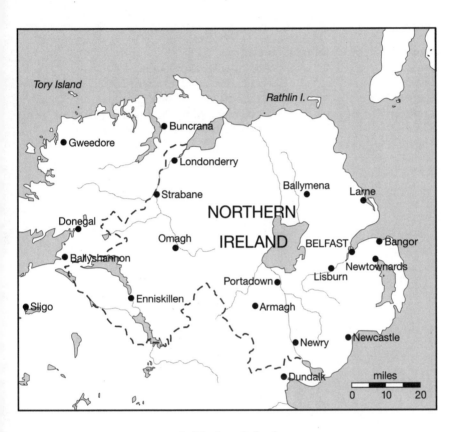

1. Northern Ireland

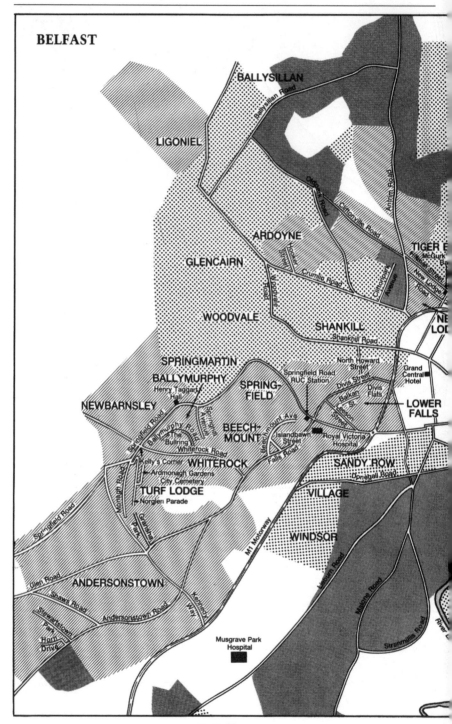

2. Belfast

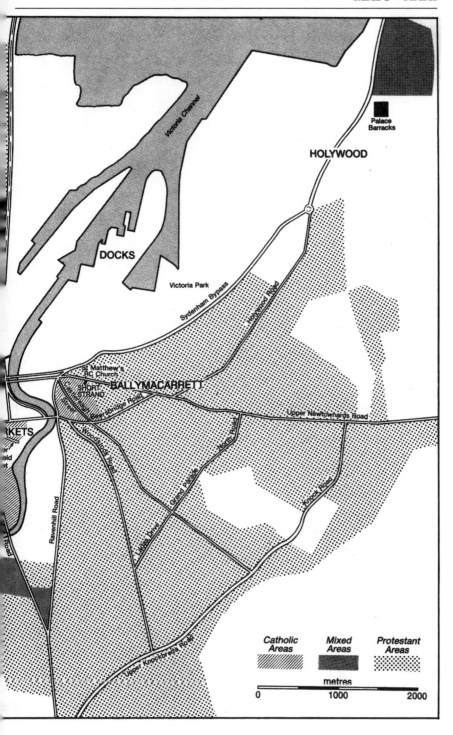

HOLYWOOD

Palace
Barracks

Victoria Channel

DOCKS

Victoria Park

Sydenham Bypass

Holywood Road

St Matthew's
RC Church

SHORT
STRAND

BALLYMACARRETT

Ballybridge Road

Upper Newtownards Road

North Road

RKETS

Knock Road

Woodstock Road

Ravenhill Road

Island Drive

Grand Parade

Upper Knockbreda Road

| Catholic Areas | Mixed Areas | Protestant Areas |

metres

0   1000   2000

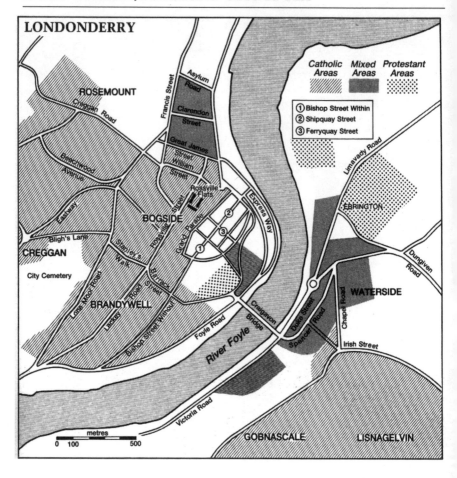

3. Londonderry

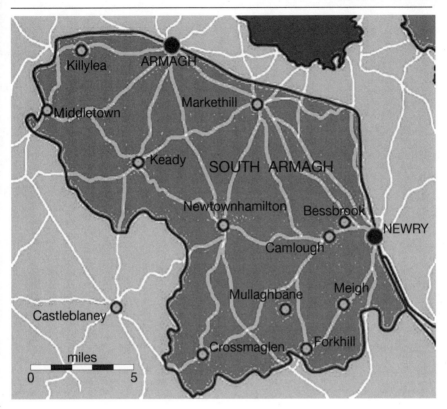

4. South Armagh ('bandit country')

Introduction

Some time ago – it feels like a lifetime now – I began writing a book about the role and experiences of the British soldier in Northern Ireland during the course of the somewhat euphemistically named 'troubles.' This book – like that one – will be a collection of voices from the soldiers who fought in Britain's forgotten war.

During the lifespan of 'Operation Banner' some 300,000 squaddies served in the Province. The numbers of those killed in, or as a result of, the events connected with the troubles were comparatively low; officially 731, unofficially, well over 1,300. Indeed, the admirable Northern Ireland Veterans Association (NIVA) lists the names of 1300 military personnel who died in, or as a result of, the troubles. It is my intention, my goal, to one day, produce a definitive Roll of Honour thus showing the scale of deaths, indeed, what the late writer, Charles Whiting referred to, with a tired irreverence as the 'butcher's bill.' Comparatively low, as I said, that is, to the mandarins of Whitehall, to the compilers of such statistics, but agonisingly high to ladies like Carol Richards, Mo Norton, Karen Rumble or Nell Webster. Too high, in fact, to the wives and mothers, the fathers and lovers and the brothers and sisters of those 1,300 plus men and women.

Remember this also; during the long and bloody course run by the troubles, in Ulster, one family in six had a close relative killed or injured. One person in every eleven actually witnessed a shooting.

In the grand scheme of things, the casualty figures for the British Army during the course of the troubles were indeed low, certainly, that is, compared with the unprecedented and almost casual slaughter on the Western Front. Take one day in isolation – admittedly the worst day – and look at the figures on July 1, 1916. On the first day of Haig's Somme offensive, British and Empire forces (British, Canadian, and ANZAC) suffered a sickening 57,470 losses. These figures include a staggering 19,240 soldiers killed and 35,493 wounded, with 2,739 missing; in a single day! On D-Day, in 1944, on a single beach, the Americans lost over 2,000 men and at Gallipoli in 1915, the Australians alone suffered the loss of almost 1,000 men on the first day alone.

Viewed in the context of those figures, losses over the period of fewer than 30 years seem light. Light that is, until we remember the grief suffered by the families of those c. 1,300 men and women, light until we remember that, other than the Falklands campaign, Britain was not at war with anyone. Light also, when we remember that they were sustained a few dozen miles away from the mainland on the streets of the United Kingdom.

Almost 6,000 of my former comrades were injured; many physically, but many emotionally. During the course of the research for the first volume, I had the honour of meeting many ex-squaddies and some of them were injured in explosions and shootings. But I also met those who had been damaged psychologically and within seconds of meeting them, I could sense this and my respect for them grew exponentially. Several of them told me that it was an honour to meet me and that they were honoured to be included in my book. Gentlemen, the honour was mine; it was all mine.

That first book dealt with a squaddie's eye view of the events on a year by year basis and it told the story in strict chronological order from 1969 through to 1998. Each year unfolded through their stories and were linked by one factor: the timeline in which their stories took place. This volume deals with specific events, specific places and specific experiences but again, the men of Britain's forgotten war will tell their story. A common thread throughout, was the complaint, or possibly, observation, that we fought this war like no other; in that, we fought it with one hand tied behind our backs. We knew who the IRA/INLA 'players' were and they knew that we knew, but we couldn't do anything.

One Infantry officer wrote to me and expressed the frustration felt by virtually all who served in the Province. Namely, that had we been the SS or some tin pot South American military junta, we would have been ruthless and soon destroyed the terrorists. That we weren't – and didn't – is a tribute to our integrity, honour and professionalism. As always, the politicians of all major parties sat back and watched soldiers die with a monotonous and tragic regularity and did nothing. I name no specific party, because with varying degrees, British troops were sent over the Irish Sea to fight and die by Harold Wilson, Edward Heath, James Callaghan, Margaret Thatcher, John Major and Tony Blair.

During my childhood, I was raised on a diet of war stories – both First and Second World Wars – and the occasional black and white movie which led me to appreciate that the British soldier was the finest in the world. Not so numerous as the Red Armies of the USSR and China, not so bitter and back-to-the-wall as the Israelis and nothing like as well equipped as the American. But, nonetheless; the finest Army on this globe. I joined the British Army as a 17 year old in 1967 and none of my experiences subsequent to that event have dissuaded me from that assertion; that assertion being that the Tom, the squaddie, the 'nig', as the Royal Green Jackets call their new recruits, right before they eat them, has no match on the face of this Earth. I interviewed men from Regiments with long and proud histories; the aforementioned 'Jackets' the Parachute Regiment, the Black Watch, King's Own Borderers, the Guards Regiments, the Royal Regiment of Wales, the Green Howards, the Glosters, the Kings, the Cheshires et al with far too many to mention.

These were all proud, county regiments which tended to recruit from specific geographical areas, thus retaining that 'local' feel, almost as emotional as the 'Pals' battalions of the so-called 'Great War' as groups of lads enlisted together, trained together, fought together and, in their droves, died together. In that quite excellent BBC comedy 'Black Adder Goes Forth' written by Ben Elton, one of the characters, the diminutive and unspeakably filthy 'Baldrick' proudly relates how he joined up with the 'workhouse Pals.' Whilst this was pure comedy – or was it, for, how many of you have wiped tears from your eyes at that final, poignant scene – the reality was starker. The Hull Pals, the Leeds Pals, the Hunslet Pals, the Accrington Pals et al, cheerfully marched off to the slaughter of the Somme, Ypres and dozens of unpronounceable French towns and villages. Our county regiments were the envy of the world and were copied by our colonial cousins in Canada and other countries.

When one looks at the bland, colourless names of the fighting regiments of the United States – the 1st, the 2nd, the 3rd, etc – and then compares them with the names of our long gone regiments, there is an abyss of difference. Imagine the pride of lads who had served with The King's Own Yorkshire Light Infantry, the West Kents, the Devon and Dorsets, the Argyll and Sutherlands, the Royal Anglians and the South Wales Borderers? These were Regiments of the line whose battle honours reflected a myriad number of campaigns over many centuries over parts of the globe from Québec to Singapore. On my own first day in the Army, I was informed, proudly, that men from my Regiment had fought with Wolfe and had stormed the Heights of Québec in his vanguard. Never forget our Corps; Corps of Pioneers, Signals, Transport et al, because in Northern Ireland, we were ALL front-line troops. In Belfast there were no 'tail' troops; only those with teeth.

Successive British Governments in their *wisdom* (author's own italics) saw fit to reduce the Army, to 'slim' it down and destroy our wonderful County identities. In the opening to this book, a Scottish Sergeant – a man I met personally and sat in awe as he recounted his story – describes politicians as being 'weak, sniffling, desk-ridden rodents.' I wholeheartedly and absolutely endorse his words.

In August, 1969, having sat on their collective hands, the weak and prevaricating British government led by Harold Wilson sent troops onto the streets of Northern Ireland for the first time. Its role was to keep the warring sectarian factions apart, restore law and order to the streets where anarchy ruled and to protect the downtrodden Catholic population. One Welsh soldier told his wife, when greeted by the news that troops were going in, that it would never happen. But if it did, it would be all over by Christmas. Where did we hear those words before? 1914? 1939? 1950 perhaps, as Britain's National Servicemen sailed off to Korea? Major Hardy, when you used those words to me in a museum in Brecon, several lifetimes ago, you were almost 40 years out, but, sir, you were there and you did your part and I am honoured to have met you.

Initially, the troops were greeted by a relieved Catholic community, a community held down by years of Protestant and Unionist domination. Second best in housing, in education, in jobs and even in the voting arena. Rioting and lawlessness and the brutality of the infamous 'B' Specials had left a violent vacuum of power; law and order had ceased to function. Once order was restored, thanks to the professional impartiality of the squaddies, the Catholics relaxed and out came the tea cups and sandwiches and plates of biscuits. The Protestants watched in sullen silence and trouble was brewing. Within months, those same Catholic women had swapped cups of tea for buckets of urine and used sanitary towels thrown from upstairs windows and the sandwiches were replaced with rocks and petrol bombs; and, before too long, by the .303, the Armalite and, soon enough, the .50 calibre bullet.

British soldiers began to die and continued to die at an alarming rate and, from being the first item on the BBC and ITV nightly news, the death of a soldier soon rated no more than a brief mention just before the latest sports news as the programme drew to an end. When the three young 'Jocks' of the Royal Highland Fusiliers were murdered at Ligoniel in 1971, proudly resplendent in their No 1 dress uniforms, their innocent faces were splashed across most dailies of the time. The photos of the increasing number of fallen soon began to be relegated to the inner and central pages and soon, the death of a soldier in Northern Ireland would merit merely a small paragraph or two, well away from the 'acceptable' news of the day.

During the early days of the Great War, the *Times* ran a daily obituary listing the dead of the trenches; very soon, the lists became untenable and morale on the Home front was being eroded so they ceased. On a less grand a scale, the lists of Ulster dead soon took on the same, albeit smaller, dimensions.

This series of accounts will look at the life and death struggles of the soldiers on the streets of Belfast and Londonderry; on the country lanes around Crossmaglen, Belleek, Lisnaskea, and Bessbrook Mill. It will look at their experiences on the vast sprawling Republican estates of the 'Murph, Turf Lodge, Andersonstown, the Ardoyne, Shankhill, in Belfast and the terrorists' breeding grounds of the Bogside and the Creggan in Londonderry. It will examine the roles and the dangers of being a member of that magnificent fighting force, the Ulster Defence Regiment. To some of the readers, the very mention of the words 'Murph, Turf Lodge, Derrybeg, Creggan et al will mean much to them both emotionally and probably physically; to others they are just 'areas.' But imagine if you lived in Leeds and the Turf Lodge was replaced by Gipton, or to a Mancunian and we substitute Andersonstown for Moss Side, or a Bristolian and St Pauls replaces the Creggan Estate; get the picture? We were fighting a war on our own streets and the British Government didn't seem to give a tinker's cuss for all that was happening there.

It will also look at attacks by the IRA on soldiers, airmen and their families on the streets of England and on the European mainland. It will, for the first time, feature the unseen victims, the loved ones of the men just a few dozen miles away across the Irish Sea. Those who waited for the Casualty Visiting Officers (CVOs) to draw up outside their house, generally flanked by the local policeman and a neighbour 'to make a cup of tea' and deliver the news which they didn't want to hear, refused to hear; that their son or husband had been killed in Belfast or Londonderry or Crossmaglen. Those of us who served can never begin to understand the anguish in the hearts of those who loved us as we bade farewell for possibly the last time. During the last war, it was the GPO Telegram boy who delivered the shocking news in an inoffensive-looking brown envelope; during the troubles we had 'progressed' to the CVO.

Had Mrs Rachel Hardy a clue of what would happen to her Light Infantry son David as he returned to Ireland from leave and would catch a bus for Omagh, a bus which was destined to go no further than Ballygawley? Did Mo Norton know that she would never see her beloved brother Terrence again as he went off to catch a bus over the M62? Did Carol Richards, then Ware, know that she would only have one, albeit glorious, year with her Coldstream Guards husband, Simon Ware? The pain in their hearts is reflected in the pages of the book which deals with the loved ones.

This section will show the human tragedy, the emotional cost and grief which the newspapers or the television news could not portray which lay behind the simple words: 'In Northern Ireland, another British soldier has been killed.'

Let us not forget also, that there were and still are, some lovely people in Northern Ireland; to this day, I will never forget the mainly women who brought us cups of tea, sandwiches and biscuits and the people who shed tears not only at the death of a young soldier, but also at the destruction of their country. If peace lasts – and I pray that it does – then this will be for all those decent, law abiding citizens whose blood was spilt alongside three generations of soldiers.

The IRA was not a motley crew of red-haired, country bumpkins, with charming picture book Irish accents and armed with obsolete World War I weapons. They were an implacable, increasingly professional, terrorist organisation, backed in the main by the Irish-Americans and they were very good at doing what they did best; killing us. They had no qualms, no consciences and they thought that a pious apology after an innocent civilian had been caught in the crossfire would suffice. They were a very difficult enemy to take on and overcome because they didn't care who got in the way. Make no mistake; they were amongst the most difficult foe that the British Army has ever had to take on.

The British Army went into Ulster on August 14, 1969 and they were greeted by cups of tea and biscuits. Hopefully this book will help bridge the gap between those welcoming cups of tea and biscuits and the eventual bombs, bullets and, ultimately, coffins.

At the Peace centre in Warrington during the writing of this second book, I had the honour of meeting some UDR/RUC men and their families from Co Tyrone and they told me much about their experiences of the troubles. I said to one of them that Ulster and the troubles had been like a dream – albeit one of the nightmare variety – but one which had lasted for most of my life. I was 19 when it started and almost 50 when it ended; if it was a dream, I was thanking God when I finally woke up. Andrew Edwards of BBC Radio Leeds who interviewed me just before I went to St Pauls Cathedral, for the Commemoration of Op Banner said something interesting to me. He said of the troubles: 'Sometimes, Ken, I have to pinch myself that it's all over.' Andrew, sometimes I have to pinch myself that it ever started.

This book will continue to pay tributes to the squaddie which began in volume one. It will continue, as before, to be unashamedly pro-Squaddie; I couldn't possibly write anything which wasn't. I think that I might have to bite off my own right arm before I could be negative about my magnificent comrades.

Ken Wharton, North Yorkshire June, 2008

I think it's great that the boys coming back from Iraq, Afghanistan are getting the recognition they so deserve, but what about us? We when came back, nobody ever gave a f*ck about us. When I saw the cold blooded, evil murderers walk free from jail thanks to the Good Friday agreement, I thought, that's it for them, it's over, and they can start fresh. But what about me, what about us? I still bear the scars and I won't ever be freed from that.

When I got to the Regiment, I was allocated to John Watson's team. I didn't know who John was, but he had a great reputation. John was a quiet man; he kept himself to himself and enjoyed a laugh just like the rest of us. Now, John took on lot of responsibility by having a new guy to the Regiment put in his team. I'd like to think I never let him down as he certainly never let me down. Besides, you would know if you did, as

I have previously mentioned, John was a quiet man. And a man like John would put the fear of God in you by the 'John Watson' look. That was his thing; he only had to look at you.

I was blessed by being part of his team in Belfast and there is not one day I regret by not keeping in touch with him. Something that I know now is impossible. John was taken by cancer 2004. So, John; thanks big man. I would like to dedicate all my words that I contribute in this book to you.
Mick Pickford, Royal Artillery

The bloody Government made us fight the IRA with one hand tied behind our backs and then both hands and then, eventually they blindfolded us as well.
Rifleman, Royal Green Jackets

To the civvie with whom I worked, whom the libel laws prohibit my naming; the one who sneered at our efforts in Ulster; just thank God you never had to go.
Ken Wharton

Part One: Belfast

Belfast: from the Irish: Béal Feirste meaning 'Mouth of the (River) Farset' is the seat of government in Northern Ireland. It is the largest urban area in Northern Ireland and the province of Ulster. To many of the troops who served there, it was known as 'Bloody Belfast.'

Although in this section we will re-walk the same streets that countless soldiers walked, we will not have to dodge the hurled urine and excrement, the lobbed nail and petrol bomb or the aimed round from the Armalite, but we will visit the main hotspots of this once great shipbuilding city. This was the city which the IRA and INLA and the UVF and UFF chose as their main battleground and the city where most blood was spilt during the long, tortuous and murderous troubles. The major areas of violence were to be found in the west of the city, to the north and around the city centre. Walk with me around the city where so many fell.

Chapter 1

The 'Murph

The Ballymurphy Estate, or the 'Murph as it was known to a succession of squaddies posted to the west part of Belfast, is a moderately large, sprawling, post war council estate. It was a rundown area of the box-style housing favoured by countless city councils throughout the British Isles. George Prosser (ex-King's Regiment) described it as a 'rabbit warren of houses' as it was full of bolt holes for the fleeing gunman and the like.

Rather like the through houses on the Falls, where a gunman could enter through an unlocked front door and disappear through the back into the next street, with the co-operation of the householder. Those same doors would then be locked and it would cost precious seconds for the pursuing soldiers to enter. Or, as an ex-Royal Green Jacket said, 'kick the door in as it was easier.' Even then, a pram or an item of furniture would somehow block their paths. And it was, probably still is, a fertile and productive breeding ground for the Republican movement. Over twenty members of the Security Forces were killed on this estate.

To the north of the 'Murph is Springmartin, and to the east and North east is the Falls. It is separated from the Turf Lodge area by the length of the Whiterock Road and Andersonstown is next. Further to the south there is easy access to the Falls Road and to Milltown and Penny Lane. Penny Lane is the site where two

IRA mural, Ballymurphy Estate (Ken Wharton)

Corporals from the Signals Corps were murdered by the IRA after almost being lynched by a crazed, hate-filled mob of mourners at a Republican funeral in 1988.

Many squaddies will remember the Henry Taggart Memorial Hall –yet nobody seems to remember who Henry Taggart was – which was soon fortified and thereafter occupied by a succession of touring regiments, including the Scots Guards who lost two men there in 1971. They will remember Vere Foster school and the fact that they had to share it with schoolchildren and their hateful teachers. Maybe 'hateful' is too strong an epithet to tar the educators with, but they certainly had no love for the soldiers who occupied the school. For the Kingos, it will be the place they remember with dread, losing two of their young lads there.

There is the odd patch of green, then at its western extremity, Springfield Heights and New Barnsley Crescent back onto the Ballygomartin Road and then to the vast expanse of land on which sits the Black Mountain.

Today, the estate has changed; windows have been renewed, the wooden gates to the dreary gardens repaired and even the old Ford Anglias or Vauxhall Vivas, once up on bricks, are now cubed metal in some Belfast scrap yard. There is the odd palm tree, decorative pillars, stone-cladding and the old killing ground looks a nice place to live; that is, until one sees the plaques remembering IRA and INLA dead and the graphic murals to their terrorist heroes. The three generations of kids who threw rocks and bricks and petrol bombs at the squaddies will be older, perhaps even wiser. Then again, perhaps not wiser; the sectarian hatred will still be there, bubbling at the surface, awaiting a spark which will bring it to

ATO detonate a bomb, Ballygomartin Road (Mark Campbell)

the boil. The Republican graffiti still adorns the walls and gable ends and even though the open top buses with German and Japanese and no doubt, American, tourists trundle around the hot spots of the troubles, the underlying attitudes will be much the same.

The place which saw 19 British soldiers and 2 RUC men killed by bomb or by bullet might have had a cosmetic refit, a face-lift, but it will be forever the 'Murph where King's Regiment man, Steve Rumble was shot and fatally wounded by an IRA sniper on April 11, 1979 and where his comrade, Christopher Shanley fell in the same attack.

ON THE 'MURPH

Brian Smith, 1st Devon & Dorsets

During the General Election of May 1983 we had to guard the election polling stations. I was with a section from 8 platoon at a prominent church near the Ballymurphy Estate, using the church tower as an O.P. When a bomb went off at the local Police station, you could feel the tower move through the shock waves. When we were there the local priest came and visited us mainly I think because he was worried and checking that the Brits were not desecrating his church. We at this time had run out of water from our water bottles so Mike Devlin Lurch Shears and I improvised and made a cup of tea for him from the water in the baptism font. Let's say the priest enjoyed his blessed tea.

The first soldier to be killed on the 'Murph was Guardsman George Hamilton (21) who was shot as he carried out the 'tail-end Charlie' role on foot patrol. The patrol from the Scots Guards was on Glenalina Road when he was fatally wounded, on October 17, 1971. Just 18 days later, a fellow Scots Guard, Stephen McGuire (19) died of his wounds after being shot at the Henry Taggart army base on September 14. These two young members of the Scots Guards thus became the first soldiers to fall on the infamous Ballymurphy Estate. On December 8, UDR member, Sean Russell (30) was shot dead at his home in the New Barnsley area which touches the 'Murph; the modern idiomatic expression is 'sectarian interface.' Masked gunmen from the IRA burst into his home and killed him and, in the same attack, wounded his young daughter.

The army base was also the scene of the shooting of Lance Corporal Peter Sime (22) of the King's Own Scottish Borderers (KOSB) who was killed by an IRA sniper on April 7, 1972. This was followed by the killing of Kingsman Private Eustace Hanley (20) on Springhill Avenue as he stood guard over comrades from the King's Regiment who were removing barricades. It is thought, that Eustace Hanley became the first black soldier to be killed in Northern Ireland.

Just two months later, on the 28th anniversary of the Allied landings in Normandy, a 22 year old Leeds boy, Private George Lee (22) of the Duke of Wellington's Regiment was shot and killed by the IRA who had taken over a house in Whitecliffe Parade.

The following month, 18 year old James Jones of the King's Regiment was shot and killed at the Vere Foster school on the edge of the Ballymurphy Estate. This famous and proud Regiment then lost 20 year old Kingsman Brian Thomas who was also killed whilst on duty at Vere Foster.

On September 17, in the same year, Private Frank Bell of the Parachute Regiment was shot and fatally wounded in the Springhills area of the 'Murph. Private Bell, who was only 18, died of his wounds three days later. The year ended with another shooting in the Ballymurphy area on December 8, when Rifleman Raymond Joesbury also 18, of the Royal Green Jackets was hit. Sadly, Rifleman Joesbury died of his wounds two days later.

So, in just 14 months, no less than six British soldiers had been killed on the 'Murph and its reputation for being a run down, modern slum estate was now surpassed as being one of the most dangerous places in Belfast, if not, in the entire Province.

Just 7 weeks into the New Year, Guardsman Michael Doyle of the Coldstream Guards was shot and killed in an alleyway close to the Ballymurphy Estate; he was the third Coldstreamer to die that day. A Roman Catholic Nun attending a patient nearby rushed to his aid, but despite her brave, frantic efforts, the young Guardsman died.

On July 1, on his 25th birthday, Private Reginald Roberts of the Light Infantry was shot and killed whilst on routine protection duty. His pregnant wife, expecting twins lost both after going into early labour. That day, the IRA could 'celebrate' as they had taken three lives.

Glenlina Crescent, Ballymurphy, where King's Regiment soldiers Shanley and Rumble were killed by the IRA, 11 April 1979 (Ken Wharton)

It would be some nine months later, in the March of the following year when another Coldstreamer, Guardsman Anton Brown who was 20 was shot and killed on Whitecliffe Crescent. The pattern continued and on July 4, the only Cheshire soldier to die in actual combat during the troubles – eight men from this Regiment were murdered at the Droppin' Well Inn, Ballykelly – Corporal Arthur Smith died of his wounds. He had been shot 5 days earlier on the edge of the estate.

Two and a half years would pass before another soldier was killed in this place of inherent hatred, thanks in the main to the superb work the Army was doing in conjunction with the RUC. Intelligence was also improving and informers were making the Security Force's (SF) role much easier and the PVCPs (permanent vehicle checkpoints) were making the movement of arms next to impossible. But, one got through the net when, on November 24, 1976, Fusilier Andrew Crocker (18) was shot by an INLA gunman near Ardmonagh Gardens. The incident had been observed from an Army helicopter and the pilot was able to direct an Army patrol to the house where the gunman was hiding and he was arrested. It is thought that this was among the first instance of an aerial observer helping in the arrest of a gunman.

A further 30 months would pass without fatalities among the soldiers who patrolled and controlled the 'Murph, but, on April 11, a mobile patrol of the King's Regiment was attacked by the IRA. The Kingsmen are drawn, in the main from Merseyside and the Manchester area and are a tight knit bunch of lads – like many of the old 'County' regiments – and it was a terrible blow for this unit to lose two popular men almost in one fell swoop. Men from the Regiment were travelling in a Saracen armoured vehicle when they were attacked by gunmen in Glenalina Crescent, close to the Whiterock Road. Much controversy surrounds the fact that the vehicle had a broken door and that it wouldn't close properly, leaving an IRA sniper a gap into which to fire a round. From a bedroom window, the gunman fired into the back of the 'Sarra' and the round hit the first 'Kingo', killing him instantly and then ricocheted into his comrade. Kingsman Christopher Shanley (21) an unmarried soldier and footballer from Liverpool was killed and his comrade, Lance Corporal Stephen Rumble was badly wounded. After a desperate fight for life, Stephen died of his wounds, eight days later on April 19. A Liverpool boy, he left a pregnant widow, whom the author had the honour of meeting during the unveiling of the Armed Forces Memorial in 2007.

THE 'MURPH

Sergeant-Major 'W' Royal Highland Fusiliers

Now back in Belfast and it was a busy first two weeks with lots of searches and getting to know our area. This was made difficult as all the street names had been removed and so we had to memorise their name; and, as most of our searches were in the early hours of the morning, this made things even more difficult.

On one occasion, our base was attacked by a number of gunmen, firing from different positions, and ten in fact, as we were to find out later.

During the contact, we could not identify any, as they were firing from windows with coal bags in front, so that we could not see the flashes.

My tour was mixed and included the anniversary of 'Internment' which had its own all night riot. There were petrol bombs, shootings; a real hairy night. I was called out to what turned out to be a hoax bomb call and had to search the grounds of the school on a Sunday afternoon and found nothing. At 1am, I was called out again to the same school and again, this time with the help of sniffer dogs, found nothing. The next day, it was reported that all our movements were being watched by the IRA; this was no surprise, as they often did this, to see the way we did our searches.

The following day, I was on search training with the Bomb Disposal unit, in an all day event to bring us up to date with new methods of training. On my return to base, I was told that my Company Commander had been seriously wounded by a booby trap at the school; the same school which we had twice searched! What had happened was that another bomb warning had been called in and, as I was not available, my OC decided to investigate. The school was evacuated and he was looking at a suspicious object when he triggered the booby trap, containing approximately 3lbs of Semtex with nails and nuts and bolts. The IRA bomb makers packed this stuff in, in order to cause maximum damage.

He was badly wounded and lost several fingers, but worst of all, some nails were embedded in his head causing brain damage. He was, and is a tough cookie and after the tour, met us all in Glasgow to welcome us home; to this day, he is still not fully recovered. He learned to write with his left hand and he is a remarkable man whom I still see often.

The IRA, with no regard for the children, placed a booby trap where they played; what depths of depravity they stooped to! It was bad luck that my OC tripped the bomb, and had it not been him, the children would have tripped it. So much for 'looking after' their own people; like in many other incidents, they just didn't care who they killed.

VERE FOSTER SCHOOL, BALLYMURPHY ESTATE

Major Peter Oakley, King's Regiment

I was back in Belfast in 1972, as CSM 'B' Company, deployed to the Vere Foster School where the Ballymurphy and Turf Lodge estates comprised the greater part of our TAOR. The school was in daily use and we occupied some classrooms and shared the kitchen. By day when the school children were in, we were safe. Here I must emphasise that we never took advantage of that and never moved about where we might have endangered the children or staff. But at night, weekends and during school holidays we were much of a target. This was to be the troubles at their most dangerous and I lost five men when we occupied that school and had many men wounded and some of those were badly hurt.

My memories of that time are of being always very tired, coping with continuous night operations and daytime administration; sleeping fully clothed with weapons at our sides, and meals left uneaten as we coped with yet another shooting or bombing. It was relentless but the Kingsmen never faltered, never complained, looked out for each other and just got on with the job. We consistently took so much fire that I believe that we were the first company to break out the GPMGs (*General Purpose Machine Guns or 'Jimpy'*) for the sangars and the first to get Saracen armoured vehicles mounted with the .30 Browning.

Here it must be noted that it was a 'convention' if not an unspoken rule that the Army would not use automatic weapons in West Belfast; there was, however, no such restraints on the IRA.

Peter Oakley

No sooner had we arrived that the IRA decided to 'have a go' at us and we had been briefed to expect that to happen. The details of my company's losses in Northern Ireland are well documented in *A Long Long War* and numerous other histories so I won't record them in much detail here. For readers who have not read that book what follows is just a brief resume of things that lie deep in my memory and which I keep well buttoned down.

- Corporal Alan Buckley was shot and killed opposite the Whiterock flats where a platoon had come under very heavy and sustained rifle fire. Eventually we were rescued by two very brave Ferret Scout Car commanders and our MO won an MC for running to help that dying man under intense fire.
- Kingsman James Jones shot and killed by a sniper in the school yard; the 100th soldier to die in Belfast.
- Kingsman Brian Thomas shot and killed by a sniper whilst in the school roof sangar.
- Kingsman Rennie Layfield killed by a sniper whilst on a VCP.
- Kingsman Eustace Hanley killed by a sniper whilst on foot patrol.
- Corporal Joe Horrobin survived a bullet going through one thigh and into the other.
- Kingsman Elliott survived being shot in the neck.
- Kingsman Michael 'Popeye' Hughes received a very serious head wound in an OP on Black Mountain.
- Colour Sergeant Bertie Durkin shot in the thigh by a sniper eventually losing his leg above the knee.
- Four others wounded whilst taking cover by the side of a PIG and hit by automatic fire.

There were too many, but no less serious, injuries to record here.

Also killed during that tour were Kingsman Marcel Doglay, following an IRA bomb explosion at Springfield Road RUC station and Kingsman Roy Christopher who died of the wounds he received following an explosion at Cupar Street in the Falls area of Belfast.

Peter Oakley

I trust that that record of my soldiers being shot by snipers will give some idea of the constant danger of the accurate sniper fire we had to cope with. To 'switch off' after patrols could, and would be, fatal. You could never assess where the fire might come from, and it was even more difficult finding where the firing point was due to the noise echoing around buildings and houses. Men had to move quickly and have continuous all round observation; vigilance was the watchword. Never crossing open ground without cover from the others and finding 'hard' cover at all times were paramount.

We watched the net curtains for signs of movement that might be a gunman taking aim and noted areas which might suddenly become devoid of people and sound as that might indicate that there was a gunman or a bomber about. And if fired at, run as fast as possible to where you thought that the fire came from. You might get lucky and surprise the gunman but at least you were moving out of the killing zone and doing something positive.

ON THE 'MURPH AFTER 'BLOODY SUNDAY'

Corporal 'B' King's Own Scottish Borderers

January's action was heating up, the shooting increased with the base receiving some incoming almost daily. Hijackings of buses increased as part of the escalation which was designed to invite us in to clear the burning wreckage and get shot whilst doing so! Ulster geared up for a mass civil rights protest at this time which was to take place in Derry at the end of the month. Protests locally increased with more mini riots and hijackings and bomb hoaxes with the occasional real device being planted in parked cars. On the weekend of the civil rights march it went fairly quiet in the area. Then the news of disturbances in Derry started coming in to our base. It sounded bad and then got worse as the day went on. Paras had shot a couple; then it was six; then it was nine. Standby all patrols and sentries, things could go mental yet on this thus far quiet Sunday in the 'Murph. My last bit of information was that the death toll was twelve. There was going to be a backlash; it duly arrived on Monday.

Later on the Monday morning after earlier gatherings of angry protesting crowds of women, children and youths were denied aggravated entry to the Henry Taggart base; a bigger and even more hostile crowd came and ripped off the front gates. Simultaneously two hijacked buses appeared on the Springfield Road in front of the base. Kids ran into the front apron of the base hurling stones and bottles as older people carried away the gates. An order came from the base commander to go out there and retrieve the gates! Did this warrant a reply? It got one, unrepeatable in print. I primed my section quickly to prevent what I saw as a disaster happening. Although two sections had gone out the back entrance with the intention of getting behind the crowd and attempt to draw them away and break up the mass effort, they were not succeeding. The hostiles were trying to draw us out of cover as the stone throwers kept the usual gap between themselves and us; the killing zone. This whole thing was being orchestrated from the back of the now sizeable gathering. We had to do some quick-thinking to retrieve a dangerous situation - fortunately, my section was up to the task, and did just that!

Attitudes hardened after Bloody Sunday. Things were bad enough before then but we found that the Provos were on to a recruiting winner with the Derry debacle. Combining this gift with political aggravation and manipulation of the human rights issues in the new European situation—a real bonus to terrorists—the situation for troops on the ground began to worsen. Secretary of State Whitelaw came under real pressure to end internment and grant 'Political Prisoner' status to those sentenced. They got to him, attacking his residence and then shooting up his official vehicle; he capitulated. The enemy's wishes were granted. They could not believe their luck and neither could we. There was no Special Powers Act in force, only the rule of law viz a viz independent witnesses needed to prove crimes committed etc, et al.

Hard core Provos fearing jail or internment prior to the ending of the Act came streaming back into our area from their Irish Republic hideouts free to roam the streets in front of us; we could do nothing. This situation was unbelievably stressful. I felt completely unprotected now as there was no way that under ordinary civil law could we deal with this situation. Some other powers would have to be granted.

The Police and legal teams took three weeks to come up with a scheme to replace internment; detention without trial if two witnesses could confirm the person detained was an insurgent. All of a sudden there seemed to be a lot of witnesses! We had survived an uncertain patch during which time a variety of incidents took place.

NEW BARNSLEY, ON THE 'MURPH

Private Richard Smith, Duke of Wellingtons

All this happened a long time ago and I could never talk to civvies about it because they just can't - or won't - understand; this is so much easier, talking to you as an ex-squaddie.

It was on General Election day in 1987 and Maggie Thatcher was going for a third win a row and we were based at the New Barnsley RUC station just on the edge of the Ballymurphy Estate. The polling station was a school near the station and we were sent in the night before, once it had been cleared and checked as night and day guards. Our intention was to stag it some of the time and kip the rest of the time, but the locals on the 'Murph had seen us come out in full gear and they weren't about to let us have a quiet night. Our escort, the Queen's Lancashire Fusiliers (QLF) had left us to get on with things and we were on our own.

The locals boyos, alerted to our presence, then started, despite mesh over all the windows, to stone us and it went all night; crash, bang, wallop as they threw everything that they could get their hands on. Some of the bastards even climbed onto a flat roof and stoned us from there! We were protected by the mesh but, because of it, we couldn't fire the baton rounds and they knew it! Anyway, the day dawned, they all went home to sleep it off and the first voters – including one Gerry Adams – began to turn up to vote. It was the first time that I had seen him in the flesh and I had him in the sights of my SLR. I turned to a nearby RUC officer and whispered: 'What do you think I'd get if I fired now?' He just smiled and replied: 'Five years....and a f*****g medal!' As posterity has recorded, I desisted.

That night, after the voting had finished, a senior RUC man came in and said: 'There's an escort lined up for you boys' and out we went to see our 'escort.' The QLF were short of bodies and they had sent out mess waiters and clerks, i.e. lads not used to front line stuff. This probably wouldn't have happened had the QLF not been so stretched.

Then, all of a sudden, I saw one of their lads literally, just lift up and fly over a hedge and then I heard the crack of the round which had hit him. The mess lads were not used to this type of situation and we were tired and loaded down with gear. The shot lad was dragged into a doorway by his mates and me and another lad dived in there and got our first aid kits and went to work on him. One thing which I really remember, is the sight and the smell of blood; sort of a coppery smell. Lots of guys were milling around, and I could see that he had two small holes in his shoulder – the round had split on impact – and he didn't look right healthy! We turned him over and I could see a massive exit wound in his back; I could have fitted my clenched fist into it. None of my training prepared me for that sight; it couldn't possibly have.

By now, their QRF (*Quick Reaction Force*) had crashed out and they took over, leaving us to return to base. I am pleased to say that the wounded lad recovered and I later bumped into him at Musgrave Park Hospital. That same night, when I was alone, I tried to light a cig' but my hands were shaking so much, I couldn't light the match!

WHITEROCK ROAD INCIDENT

Rob Colley, Green Howards

Another incident happened one night towards the end of one of my tours, when my brick was on QRF and we were sent out to have a wander up and down the Whiterock Road as reports had come in of possible activity in the graveyard. It was thought it was either petrol bombers or a shooter. So we went down the Falls Road towards Whiterock and all seemed quiet; myself and 'Smudge' were on top cover of a mobile. We turned right into Whiterock Road and drove along it quite slowly, keeping a beady eye on the cemetery wall. After about 20 seconds or so, this hooded figure appeared from behind the wall with a lit petrol bomb in his hand. Then he launched it towards our Land Rover and disappeared back behind the wall, and the petrol bomb landed on the roof of the cab and exploded.

A huge ball of fire engulfed the vehicle and swept backwards towards 'Smudge' and I; instinct and training kicked in and we both broke the world ducking-down record and hit the floor. I looked up and saw the fireball as it swept over the hatch and down into the interior of the rover; it was quite warm for a few seconds then it was gone as quickly as it appeared. A quick inspection of each other and the vehicle revealed no serious damage with only a few scorch marks here and there. At that, we drove up the road a bit, turned round and went back to see if we could find the git responsible; wisely we didn't go into the cemetrey as it was a bit dark and we could see no sign of anyone. After a while we left the area and went back to NHSM (*North Howard Street Mill*) for an egg banjo, tea and to tell war stories and show off singe marks. The feelings were fear, excitement, relief and anger that we never got the bastard!

Later that year, a soldier from the Royal Anglians, 21 year old Private Paul Wright was ambushed and killed on the edge of the estate as he was driving towards Fort Monagh. The IRA claimed that he was an undercover soldier, whereas the Army maintained that he was acting as a courier. Another soldier, also in plain clothes was wounded in the attack.

On June 10, 1983 as the first day of a new summer approached, 20 year old Light Infantry Private Geoffrey Curtis, a Lancashire boy, was killed by a bomb attached to a lamppost as his patrol from the Light Infantry passed by. Two other soldiers and two RUC men were also injured, by the bomb, callously detonated by the IRA whilst children were nearby.

With the ending of the 'troubles' still some 14 or more years away, no further soldier would be killed on the estate after Curtis; the 'Murph had claimed its final victim amongst the British Army. The RUC too, suffered and they lost two of their officers there; in 1981 Constable Samuel Vallely was killed in an IRA rocket blast, and in 1986, Reserve Constable John Dobbin was killed in a mortar bomb attack.

PADDY LARKIN

On the 'Murph

As I was in the O.C.'s rover group, we got called out to all shootings in our area. It just so happened that Gerry Adams and his side kick Martin McGuiness were always there if it took place in Ballymurphy. I was on top cover in the rear Land Rover and was eying up Adams thinking to myself would it be worth it if I just pulled the trigger, think of all the cheers and flags that would go up.

Then I heard a shout '... stop pointing that weapon at me!' The OC told the top covers to get down as he was outside on foot. The O.C. was Major Robin Brims, now Lt Gen R V Brims.

BALLYMURPHY: DECEMBER 1971

Corporal 'B' King's Own Scottish Borderers

We underwent a lot of training for this trip. Officers were trying hard to interpret information coming in from Ulster, arranging lectures by prominent police officers and those military personnel with recent relevant experience on the ground. Tactical training had to change. We were facing a developing situation. The pure rage of 1970s' riots accompanied by wild shootings was now becoming more orchestrated, more organised. More soldiers were dying from planned urban ambushes using what seemed to be well trained snipers. Rumours abounded. We knew this was going to be a bad one. Still, the Jocks maintained morale and got on with preparations laid before them.

December 27th, we disembarked from *Sir Galahad* (I think!) onto Belfast dock. A convoy of three tonners from the Scots Guards ferried us to our destinations between 2am and 4am. Mine was with Charlie Company. The combined Henry Taggart Memorial Hall and Vere Foster Primary School temporary base. There was the Upper Springfield Road and Ballymurphy facing us; New Barnsley to the sides and rear; Dermott Hill and Turf Lodge just up the road a bit.

We had a quiet New Year as I recall. Strange, considering the fatalities and woundings in the ranks of the regiment we had just relieved. My new base was one of the most shot at in Belfast at the time. Were things changing? We went about our patrols, ever alert, learning to find our way around the streets on our new patch. Rumours of activity elsewhere. Our base in the Falls had been shot at. A couple of bombs had gone off in the City centre. We heard them; the tension was building. Some stone throwing incidents occurred and the abuse was building up. Then, one frosty day in early January 1972, the sound of a 'Chicago Piano', the old drum-fed Thomson machine gun was heard loud and clear. One of our 'squirrel patrols' was shot at on the Whiterock Road. A lingering burst of about 20 rounds was directed at them; no casualties. The IRA had opened its account with us in Ballymurphy; the waiting was over. The beginning of one of the most turbulent tours of duty was underway. The shit-storm that was to follow over the next four months must have deeply affected all of us; it did me.

Being a walking target all the time had its mental strains. It was the waiting I found worst, because I knew if it had been quiet for a day or two, that something was about to break. The relief came when an incident erupted, the mental tension then eased. Strange that, when shots are incoming we, or I, should feel relieved but the incident focused attention and our activities became positively directed, the adrenalin pumping. We also felt that after one incident it could be a little while before the next one as our adversaries weren't so brave that they would hang around for long enough for us to locate them or stop them in a roadblock. They had to be quick. The pattern just then was to let off a few shots at a patrol or a standing roadblock and either disappear quickly down a pre-planned escape route to another part of the city or move quickly to a nearby safe house whilst someone else would dispose of the weapon used. Women with prams were a favourite method used to transport weapons out of the zone, at least for a while, as were women wearing long heavy coats.

I also remained deeply suspicious of the Catholic clergy in these matters; Ballymurphy's new round chapel we suspected of providing sanctuary for gunmen. The smell of bacon and eggs wafted regularly from the building. One classic occasion whilst surveying a known area of regular sniper fire from a secret hide we did espy the local priest, Father 'X' 'spotting' our base with binoculars in classic military fashion. Standing 5 feet back from an open window and half open curtains he was both watching our base and talking to someone else hidden in the room. Was he helping to spot for a sniper? I got my section sniper to locate and fix his sights on him. We knew Father 'X' to be a shit stirrer who did not like soldiers and this was a suspicious situation. My order was first to break radio silence and alert the sentries to a possible impending attack and then told my sniper to hold his aim and if a shot was fired into the base the Holy See would be one priest less. After ten tense minutes Father 'X' aborted, and that responsibility was lifted from me.

IN THE 'MURPH.

Major Peter Oakley, King's Regiment

We had an RC Padre who regularly came to Vere Foster School where we were stationed; I have no idea which unit he was from. He always travelled regularly in a black 'Mini' in civilian clothes and, whilst often stopped at illegal road blocks by the IRA, was never hindered because he was an RC Priest. He had a wonderful calming manner and would gather all denominations for a few moments of prayer and reflection. I am not religious, but I attended those sessions, as did many of my soldiers, and we got a great deal from his quiet and reassuring words. I don't know who he was but he gave my men a few minutes of peace and reflection which was support which was of great value. If he reads this, we will forever be grateful for his pastoral care.

Later on, we warned of a visit by some high ranking officer, but who he was, I cannot recall; if he is reading this, I hope that he does! Bear in mind that when the children were not in school, we were often under fire so we only moved about at night. Clearly not aware of this situation, two Land Rovers arrived just before lunch; the officer had a peaked cap with red band around it and red tabs on his collar and no flak jacket! The escort of RMP was resplendent in red caps and pistols and it was a bright and sunny morning and you just knew that were would be many pairs of eyes upon us. I invited them to move along the long path across the schoolyard to the entrance suggesting that they had a little more haste to their step; not sure if they heard me as I was long gone!

Visit over and, needless to say, as they left, all hell broke loose, with one gunman around the corner firing a pistol at us until it was empty. I ordered the front sangar to let off the smoke pots positioned about the yard and paths for such an attack; this happened and probably covered the whole of Belfast! We then fired some shots into the air hoping to put the gunmen off. At last the danger sunk in and the VIP's party moved with commendable speed never to be seen again. I am convinced that this group had no idea of what a dangerous place that school was or, more importantly, how they had compromised our safety.

Later on, one of the Kingsmen was shot and killed, and the platoon commander brought the platoon back into the base. I told him that he needed to get back out and continue his task and not allow his men to sit about after such a serious incident. Some years later, I met one of these soldiers at a reunion and he recalled the incident and, the booze having loosened his tongue and brain, said that he thought that I was a right callous bastard for making them go out again after losing one of their own. He went on to say that he knew that I had very little concern for any of them. If only he knew just how concerned and worried I was for them all, and that I was often on patrol with them.

I tried to explain to him that if, when soldiers are afraid, and we often are, and go to ground, it is a mighty difficult task to get them up again and move on. Plus, if the platoon had stayed on the base, then the opposition had gained the upper hand and initiative and we would soon cease to dominate our area. We would have been seen to run away and that would do our morale no good at all. We didn't have the luxury of time to grieve, I told him; that would come later and we had our task and hard thought that it was, we had to keep going. I don't think that he heard a word and I don't suppose that he sees things any different.

By this stage, my company was utterly exhausted after constantly being in action for three months. I was sorely tested as the CSM keeping the Kingsmen motivated and forever being concerned for their safety and well being. I make no apologies for driving them hard and constantly nagging them about fastening their flak jackets, being switched on at all times, stopping them gossiping to get some rest, keeping the place clean so that they had somewhere pleasant to rest and making them aware of never, never relaxing their guard.

Moving everything at night, rations, rubbish, mail etc and only in armoured vehicles, we continued to do daily battle with the IRA. Thankfully, we eventually got out of that school because of Operation Motorman.

We were packed up and ready to go and after leaving the Ballymurphy and Turf Lodge estates and cursing the benighted places, we ended up in another school, the name of which I cannot recall. My memory of that short period was one of patrolling and of foul-mouthed people at the school gates telling us that we were trespassing and that we should get out. We did get out after a short time and ended up on HMS *Maidstone* moored in Belfast harbor. 'Maidstone' was a military base and a prison for internees, including Gerry Adams and some of whom managed to escape

FORT WHITEROCK

Private Kevin Chatfield, Light Infantry

Between 1st May and 18th September 1983, as a young Private soldier I was with 'C' Company, 1st Battalion Light Infantry in West Belfast. Amongst my duties, I was also Company Clerk, with two hour daily super sangar stags and five hour daily Ops Room stags. I was in the OC's Rover Group, as rear hatch sentry in the rear vehicle, and the other lad in the hatch with me was Private Steve Brown; his brother Peter was in the other vehicle commanded by CSM Ray Grainger.

For the first few months of the tour Company HQ and one rifle platoon were based at Fort Whiterock on the Springfield Road next to Turf Lodge and close to the Ballymurphy Estate. Private Geoffrey Curtis was killed in the 'Murph on 10th June. The rest of the Company was based at Macrory Park. Fort Whiterock was known locally as 'Fort Jericho' as the wriggly tin perimetre used to have a habit of falling down in the wind. If you took a wander around the base you would have seen a number of bullet holes in the perimetre, all coming in. As bases in Northern Ireland go it was quite comfortable and the accommodation blocks looked fairly new.

One sunny day, we were returning to our base at Fort Whiterock from a mobile patrol and were turning left onto the Springfield Road at Kelly's Corner, the cross-roads in front of the base, from Whiterock Road. Usually at this point or just before, the kids would have been chucking rocks and bricks at us which was generally fine by us as it meant that nothing worse was about to happen. As we slowed to take the left turn there was an explosion, everything went very dark and very quiet and for a moment I thought I was dead; although, never having been killed before I didn't know if you still had conscious thought or not. After what seemed to me like quite a long time, sight and sound returned to me and I took a look around; I could see paint on the hatch cover, paint on me and my equipment. Poor Steve was absolutely covered in orange paint from head to toe; he'd obviously taken most of the 'blast.' While all this was happening the vehicle just kept on going and never altered its normal travelling speed, and I suppose the vehicle commander (Major Mitchell Philp) and the driver just thought it was another stone bouncing off the vehicle as they did every time we went out on patrol and there was nothing to worry about. Fortunately we were both wearing motorcycle crash helmets with visors down otherwise it could have been somewhat more serious for us with all that flying glass from the bottle containing the paint. The paint bomb had hit the lid of the hatch which didn't quite lay flat on the vehicle roof making it smack against the roof which made the bang sound even louder. It made me realise just how easy it would have been for someone to take the both of us out with one grenade.

Again, the thin gossamer thread of fate had spared the lives and health of a soldier; on another day, it could have been a petrol bomb or a blast bomb and the consequences might have been catastrophic. This thin thread could just as capriciously have taken life as easily as in this instance it spared it. That was the capricious, almost whimsical nature of the conflict in Northern Ireland; a patrol of soldiers could be passing a gap in wall and at the firing point, an IRA sniper could have taken a bead on the first man through and then decided to shoot the second man. At the moment he took pressure on the trigger, he might have blinked or heard noises nearby or simply been too slow and shot the third man instead. Thus the patrol's Regimental CVO took a trip to deliver the news of yet another tragedy to a house in Leeds instead of making the trip to a house in York.

BUSINESS AS USUAL ON THE 'MURPH

Corporal 'B' King's Own Scottish Borderers

The shootings in our patch did not lessen. There were regular pot shots at the base in Ballymurphy and at patrols and vehicle checkpoints. We eventually worked out the positions which we suspected as being the most used. Increased criss-cross patrolling around these positions at irregular intervals began to make life more difficult for would-be snipers trying to pick off the base at least, and made it less comfortable for would-be ambushers by creating uncertainty regarding our patrol directions and numbers. Regular 24 hour surveillance on a couple of these positions to back up patrols nearly paid a big dividend one sunny day in February 1972. On a bend on the Springfield road approaching Ballymurphy, was a cottage on its own with a big garden backing on to the Springhill Estate. A hedge separated the garden from Springhill, and a long wooden fence between the cottage and hedge secluded the garden. Through a wooden door in the fence pulled slightly ajar, we believed several sniper attacks had been launched. A patrol found the casings of previously discharged bullets one day and our suspicions were confirmed.

On the day in question, I lay up in a disused flat overlooking this cottage and garden with three others. Half dozing in the afternoon sun, we were jolted by three high velocity shots across our front. I gave the order to the sniper, 'gate.' He had previously fixed his sight on the converted Lee Enfield and I told him to scan closely for movement in that narrow area. Target! Our man was on his way through a hole in the hedge to Springhill Avenue, verified by another patrol member looking through binoculars. I told the sniper to finish him. He fired, but in his excitement he had touched the sight drum on the telescope raising the sight from 300 metres to 600. Instead of hitting our Provo we hit the local ice cream van nearly causing a tragedy, although the biggest tragedy was missing the sniper.

We believed, upon later information, it was James Bryson, a notorious gunman who had killed several soldiers before this day and would go on to kill more before suffering his own demise in an ambush. To have shot him that day may have saved several men's lives and damaged the PIRA ASU (active service units) in Ballymurphy to the point where they would have needed quite a bit of time to re-organise; Bryson being a catalyst for them. The shots fired that day badly wounded a policeman arriving for duty. Not two weeks later 'C' company lost L/Cpl Sime, shot dead from or very near to the position of the aforesaid garden gate. No one was covering that position on that day. His hallmark three shots, one well aimed and two for luck had struck the target again. Myself and a Private in my section recovered the prostate body and dragged him into cover. From the angle he was lying and the entry of the bullet there was no doubt in my mind where the shot came from. He had been drawn out of position by a bus driver seeking assistance after his bus was attacked by a gang of school kids. It was not random. As soon as the driver left the bus to seek help at the Henry Taggart base and the soldier was drawn out to the open apron between the sandbags and the gate, they disappeared. Another successful set-up killing for the Provos and I suspected Bryson again was the gunman.

Peter Deacon Sime (22) and the father of a young child was killed by an IRA gunman on 7 April, 1972; he lived in the Edinburgh area. Bryson, a 'Captain' in the IRA and known to have murdered at least 6 members of the Security Forces was shot dead by the Army in the Ballymurphy Estate on September 22, 1973. In that same incident, two other IRA men were shot, one of whom was also killed.

Gunner John Swaine, Divis Mountain (John Swaine)

Sergeant 'B' continues

From the many and various violent incidents of that tour I will recall one more, the spectacular shoot-out at the Wake of a leading Provo, Joe McCann, nicknamed 'the baker' from an incident that made his name notorious in Belfast. He had been shot by the Paras in the Markets area of Belfast. McCann had been a Para once and was recognised by a former colleague who just happened to be on patrol that day, or so the story goes. He (McCann) was from our patch, Turf Lodge. He was to 'lie in state' for a few days. Acceding to his families wishes and via an agreement between our base commander and the local Provo hierarchy, we sent no patrols into the immediate area. Mistakenly, as we know from hindsight. They were planning a major send off for McCann and the moratorium on patrolling allowed the Provos time to organise it. First, hi-jack your buses and your lorries. Then re-arrange them into handy staggered road blocks and disable by burning. Pretending you are only doing this to protect the area from intrusion while the Wake proceeds. During this time, deploy your newly re-enforced ASU's before inviting the security forces in to remove said road blocks as Wake is now coming to an end. 'There will be no trouble' said the Provo hierarchy. We were just to move the stuff at our leisure; and the band played 'Believe it if you like!'

Approaching the road blocks with caution, a ticking clock was heard from the first vehicle, a truck, so a tactical withdrawal to covered positions was advised. Charlie Company threw a cordon round the zone blocking off all approaches to Turf Lodge from Ballymurphy and the Whiterock cemetrey up to Falls park and from New Barnsley through Dermott Hill. The 'squirrel patrols' closed on the road blocks then, using one man, one risk policy, sent a man forward to check the ticking noise. It appeared to be a bomb attached to a truck chassis. Retiring to a safe distance a single rifleman opened fire on the device with the intent of exploding it. It turned out to be a hoax, an empty box with a clock. After the initial shots though, a volley came back in our general direction. Thus began a major exchange of gunfire. We estimated the Provos had at least twelve, and some say up to thirty, armed men out and about in the area as we engaged targets in various locations. They had located the 'squirrels' position and tried to bring more accurate fire on to them. One of them moved on to the roof of a block of flats in Norglen Parade to get a better shot but was spotted by one of our men on the Falls park side positioned in the cemetrey. A single shot knocked him off the roof and he was thought to have fallen on to railings in the nearby schoolyard; he would not have survived that. Gunmen flitted in and out of the flats using the vehicle road blocks as cover and as the 'squirrel' section was closest to them, they engaged them more intensely. Several Provos were thought to be hit in this exchange. My position was to the right of the squirrels' and we covered their right flank. As expected the Provos tried to outflank the 'squirrels' position so then it was our turn to engage as some of them tried to pick their way round a field towards us using a hedge as cover. They returned our fire and some of their shots landed around us; they had guessed our position. We continued to shoot using single shots when they presented a target and this dissuaded them from coming on to us and they faded back into the estate. We think we hit one and this would have had an influence on their intentions. We had image enhancing night sights, they did not.

By this time, the Sappers were called forward with the armour plated 'Scooby-doo' to begin clearing the road. Both 'Scooby-doo' and their armoured Ferret support came under fire and we continued engaging targets as we located their positions. As the road blocks were cleared the Ferret shone its powerful searchlight on the flats and between them and around the general area counted seven bodies in various states of distress; one or two looking lifeless. They were now on the back foot having bitten off more than they could chew, so a street by street clearance would have delivered a final and telling blow, but it was not to be. HQ Northern Ireland ordered our immediate withdrawal, concerned about all the shooting in the area. Simultaneously the Paras had been involved in a lot of shooting at Divis Flats in the Falls area where six casualties were reported. It was going to be a setback for community relations between the Army and the Republican communities and HQ maybe wanted to go down a less confrontational road perhaps in an earlier effort to engage in dialogue. We know in hindsight that things were working towards Sunningdale but what is the poor squaddie to do when faced with naked hostility? They talked to us in bullets and bombs and on such occasions as McCann's Wake, a solid result would have worked wonders for morale in the ranks. As it was we delivered a bloody nose to them so we had to settle for that.

Upon withdrawing towards our base we were obliged to go through a narrow path between gardens as the returning patrols split into different directions. Entering the path and about to go in single file we came under fire again. A gunman had positioned himself at the far end of the lane and let fly with a few rounds of high velocity. He nearly got lucky-I had smarting eyes from a round that passed too close to my face for comfort – but we quickly took evasive action and went around the gardens adjacent to the path to try and head him off. He did not hang around. Returning to base, we were all as high as kites after the action in Turf Lodge and felt ready to do it all over again without a break. However the adrenalin stopped pumping and after a couple of hours those that were not required for extra base guard duties crashed out with all their kit still on. After McCann's' burial, Turf Lodge was quiet again for a while with the action switching back to Ballymurphy and the Springhill estates. We took a few gunshot casualties in random incidents but we generally kept a tight lid on the area up until the handover to the Kings Regiment.

People right across that area, including those living on the other side of the Lagan river, talked long after, about their fears and anxiety at the events of tho night of McCann's Wake. With all the shooting echoing everywhere on a still and frosty night more people thought that they were a lot closer to events than was the case. I heard years later from someone living a mile away from events on that night that they actually hid under their beds for fear of being shot! Such was the disturbing effect of these actions on ordinary citizens. Belfast was on that occasion more like Beirut. It was very interesting for me to hear both Catholic and Protestant views on this event so long after it occurred as I had given no extra thought to it. Residents of Turf Lodge in particular were not chuffed at the events and had been quite frightened by the shooting. Protestant communities east of the Lagan shared similar thoughts even though they were further away.

Civil order then had gone completely at that time but the Jocks ploughed on with their daily tasks trying to find humour amongst the stresses of the day. We managed, but I would say that many of us were changed people in ways not imagined and new patterns of behaviour entered our lives as Northern Ireland was never to be out of our minds again with all that that entailed. The situation was set to worsen further over the next few years, giving us not a lot to look forward to and the psychological outlook was one of gloom, as far as I was concerned. Too many close shaves with death and violent injury to be repeated at regular intervals could mean that on one occasion there is a bullet with my name on it or a bomb just made for my personal demise. I was deployed for a total of three years and five months between 1970 and 1976, the worst years of the 'Troubles', and I do not have many happy memories of the whole shebang. It was endured and not enjoyed and I often looked back with mixed feelings about what the collective experience did to my mental outlook on life and wonder if I should have chosen a different career path! It certainly ended my first marriage as well as altering my daily behaviour patterns and led to a sort of estrangement from ordinary life which can only be noted in hindsight after many years of rediscovering what ordinary life is. Yes, along with other campaigns I took part in, I lived a life unknown to ordinary civilians, taking part in some unbelievable events with huge adrenalin rushes and having to make critical decisions in the face of hostility and uncertainty. That had to be balanced against the losses during the gaining of these experiences. Did it make a better person of me? I do not know. Perhaps the experiences were meant to unfold as they did to further my own personal development. I keep telling myself that anyway!

WEST OF BELFAST

Gareth Dyer, Royal Corps of Signals/Royal Irish Regiment

While serving with the Royal Irish Regiment I was doing chat-up at a VCP on a quiet rural road on the edge of Belfast I stopped and spoke with a man, travelling on his own. While waiting for him to find his licence I asked him where he was coming from. He replied that he was 'Just coming from a meeting at a wee hall up the road.' While talking with him I had a nosey inside his car. On the back seat was an orange coloured length of sash. 'Lodge meeting was it?' I asked. He seemed quite affronted and asked what I meant. 'Orange lodge meeting tonight?' I asked him again. By now he had found his licence and as he handed it to me retorted, 'I don't think so!'

I opened the licence and read the name and address. "Father xxxxx, of xxxxx Parochial House. I had another look, a better one, at the "sash" on the back seat. It was his priests stole, folded inside out replete with silken orange lining on show. 'Sorry about that father, away you go.' The complaint was waiting for me by the time I finished the next morning. No doubt a tale spread amongst the local congregation of an example of the institutionalised sectarianism inherent within the regiment!

WEST BELFAST

Mark 'C', Royal Artillery and UDR

During my tour with the RA, the first signs of the hunger strikes were beginning, by the first 3 weeks of my UDR employment the 2nd hunger strike was in full flow and, when Bobby Sands died on the 5th March all hell broke loose across Belfast.

During this period we were deployed to the interface at Areema Drive Dunmurry and Twinbrook. Republican rioters from Twinbrook had been attacking the Protestant houses in Areema and hijacking vehicles coming into the estate. PIRA was also shooting at the security forces on duty there. As the UDR were not allowed into Republican West Belfast we were deployed along a hedgerow running opposite Twinbrook, and there was a field with long grass between us and the first houses, which the rioters had been using as cover.

The rioters then hijacked a post office van and set it alight, and so a section of Fusiliers were sent forward in PIGs to deal with that. Meanwhile, the RUC in armoured Land Rovers came from the opposite direction. Both were attacked heavily by petrol bombers, some of whom were hidden in the long grass. The security forces responded with baton rounds, but I can still hear the rioters cheer when they had direct hits with their petrol bombs.

I was on the right flank, scanning the windows for gunmen when I spotted movement in the long grass about 25 yards in front of me, I could make out a mask and they had something in their hands. I did not shout out to my nearest colleague as I did not want to give away my position, but cocked my weapon and took aim. I was just about to shout the obligatory warning when they either heard the rifle getting cocked or spotted me. A child of about 10 or 11 stood up with a stick in his hand; he must have had the sense to see what was happening, so he took off his mask, dropped his stick and ran back towards the houses and the continuing riot.

I have woken up many times thinking about that incident and how close the lad was to being shot; in fact as we were moving out of the area, several shots hit the houses in Areema fired from across the field.

DOG HANDLING ON THE 'MURPH

Warrant Officer Dougie Durrant, Royal Pioneer Corps

I was possibly the youngest soldier in the Army dog Unit at the time (1976) and my Sergeant (Hobson) told me to take over one of the biggest dogs there at this time. A guard dog called 'Cabre' weighed over 120lbs; we got on well; he did not bite me so I did not bite him.

Later I trained as a search dog handler and left the Maze prison leaving Cabre behind and with my new search dog Bluce went onto 39 Bde Specialist Dog section and quickly settled in; my first find was not long in coming; a pistol at the back of Queens Street RUC station. I would spend most of my time in the 'Murph, and, at 05.30hrs on a cold January morning I was with the King's Regiment who were to conduct a planned search of a house in the centre of the notorious estate. The briefing was given, and the information was that a weapon was there and the old woman who lived in the house was a real bitch of a Republican. However she was confined to her bed due to illness.

We moved into the house with the police leading the way; her son was there, shouting abuse at us. I went upstairs after the procedures had been sorted, and there in the bed, in the main room, was the old lady of the house, calling me every name that she could think of. The search team commander asked me if I could search the loft; no problem, I thought. I lifted 'Bluce' into the loft and climbed up with him; seek it on son. With this, he stopped and assumed the 'dumping' position and crapped on the loft floor. There was steam pouring from it and, although there was a smell that would kill, we just ignored it and continued searching. The dog searched away around the loft and then, with an almighty crash disappeared from view. I crawled forward to see where he had fallen, and, looking through the hole in the floor, I could see 'Bluce' sitting on the bed, wagging his tail next to the old woman. Only, this time she could not talk as she was covered in dog shit and plaster; we had to leave the house as we could not stop laughing.

Chapter 2

The Turf Lodge

Turf Lodge, or the 'Turf' as the soldiers were wont to call it, was not dissimilar, physically to the 'Murph and certainly in terms of the hatred and violence and Republicanism; very much a sibling to its sister just across the Whiterock Road. Much of the physical side is identical to the 'Murph, with those same depressing post-war council house boxes.

It has the same 'rabbit warren' of housing and doors always unlocked to IRA and INLA men, the archetypal 'safe' houses. It had perhaps, more of the council flat blocks than its sister to the north, and it was in one of those tenement-like buildings, that Kingsman Andy Webster was killed by an IRA IED (improvised explosive device) in mid-1979.

It includes the vast swathes of Milltown cemetrey, a place as infamous as it is both beautiful and mournful. It encompasses a huge, general plot as well as a Republican plot where the IRA and INLA have traditionally buried their dead, their 'fallen' as they call them, each time, with all the paramilitary trappings and the firing of a volley of shots over the coffin by men in masks and black berets.

It was here in 1988 that the mad dog, Michael Stone, attacked and killed mourners attending the funerals of three IRA members. The three – two men and a woman – had been killed in Gibraltar by the SAS, in the process of bombing a British Army parade there. It was also the scene, just a few days later, where two soldiers were seized by a mob, beaten half to death, and then handed over to IRA gunmen who then murdered them.

Altogether, eight soldiers were killed on the Turf Lodge, half of the number killed in the 'Murph, but the words 'O.k., boys, foot patrol on the Turf, tonight' could still strike dread into the hearts of soldiers chosen for such a duty.

The gunmen of the Turf Lodge claimed their first SF victim on May 13, 1972, when the King's Regiment lost their first man in Northern Ireland. 22 year old Corporal Alan Buckley, a married man from the North East with a young son, was shot by an IRA gunman, as he sat in the turret of an armoured vehicle. He was one of six men to be shot in the Province on that day, five of whom were killed in Belfast alone.

Later on in the year, with Christmas approaching, Colour Sergeant Henry Middlemass (33) of the King's Own Scottish Borderers (KOSB) a married man with 3 children was killed instantly when examining an abandoned IRA bomb. He was killed in Fort Monagh, a fortified Army position in the Turf Lodge area. It has been accepted that the device was booby-trapped by the IRA but there is now a school of thought that the device – a rocket fin – might have been a piece of British Army ordnance which was unsafe. That the IRA had it in their possession is undoubted; the question is: did they abandon it as unsafe or was it booby-trapped? At the time of writing, the author was unable to be given a definitive answer.

Almost five years would pass, before another member of the SF was killed in this area. On August 12, 1977, Royal Marine Neil Bewley (19) from Shropshire was on foot patrol in Norglen Drive when they were attacked by the IRA. Shots were fired and a blast bomb thrown at the patrol; Marine Bewley was killed and two other Marines were badly injured.

The next fatality occurred just 4 months later, when Corporal Paul Harman (27) nominally of 16/5 Queen's Royal Lancers, but understood to be with Army Intelligence was ambushed at Monagh Road. His car was attacked and he was shot and killed by IRA gunmen; he was in plain clothes at the time of the attack.

On May 9, 1979, Lance Corporal Andrew Webster (20) of the King's Regiment was patrolling inside one of the blocks of flats on Ardmonagh Gardens. As he passed in front of a window, in full view of watching terrorists, a hidden IED was remote detonated and this young man from the Merseyside area was killed. Another soldier with him was injured but recovered after hospital treatment. The author met several people who knew Lance Corporal Webster [*a detailed account of this incident can be found in* A Long Long War *by the same author*] and he was described as a '... fine lad... ' '... a decent human being and a good soldier ...'

AFTER THE DEATH OF ANDY WEBSTER

George Prosser, King's Regiment

After an hour or two, we returned to Fort Monagh and, as we expected, the atmosphere was one of great sadness and a feeling of emptiness hung over the place. Words cannot describe the scenes that I witnessed inside the Platoon accommodation; many lads were in tears, others just stood or sat in silence trying to make sense of it all. Nobody knew quite what to say to each other, so few words were exchanged. Members of other platoons seemed embarrassed to say anything to us for fear of causing distress. I suppose I would have felt the same, not knowing whether to approach for fear of intruding in their grief.

The soldier who had been injured and was now in the Royal Victoria Hospital (RVH) was not as seriously hurt as first thought, and physically, at least, he would recover. Psychologically though, none of us knew how it would affect him. Can anyone experience what he had and not be affected in some way? He had survived, apparently, because as the explosion occurred, he was standing under a stairwell between the second and third floors, and was therefore, protected from the full force of the blast. He had been lucky; if the bomb had gone off just seconds later, then he too, might have been killed.

I did something that some people might find strange soon after arriving back at camp. I went over to the cookhouse for dinner and was joined, surprisingly, by one of the other members of 23 Alpha, who had been in the block at the time of the incident. Did I feel guilty about this; to be frank, I do not know what I felt at the time. Both of us talked about what had happened, but did not stay to finish our meals.

On arriving back at the accommodation, the Sergeant-Major instructed the both of us to empty the locker containing Andy Webster's personal effects. This was one of the hardest things I have ever had to do in my life, and a task that I did not enjoy. There I was, about to empty the locker of a man I had laughed and joked with only hours earlier; but somebody had to do it. After removing all his military-issue clothing, we then sorted through his personal stuff; civilian clothes, toiletries and many other items that were on the shelves.

I came across a handful of letters, probably from family and his girlfriend and put them, neatly, with everything else into a large cardboard box. The last two items I removed from the locker were two cassettes that Andy had played constantly through the tour; these were 'The Best of the Commodores' and 'Marvin Gaye's Greatest Hits.'

Each time we had been on guard duty or in the Standby room, one would always be able to hear these tapes playing in the background. Then, after ensuring that nothing had been left behind, I closed the locker doors, and, in essence, the door to Andy Webster's life, at least in the physical sense.

Five and a half years would pass, and, whilst British troops and RUC personnel would continue to die throughout the Province, the Turf Lodge, for all the fears, despite continued rioting and continued attacks by both IRA and INLA, would not claim any SF lives. That all changed, on October 19, 1984, when IRA gunmen held a family hostage in their house in Downfire Gardens and opened fire at a Royal Green Jackets' foot patrol. Gunner Timothy Utteridge, a 19 year old soldier from Lincolnshire, attached to the RGJ, was shot and killed instantly as he walked along Norglen Gardens past a shop.

TURF LODGE BAPTISM

Barrie Lovell, C Company, 2nd Battalion, The Queen's Regiment

We reported for duty on the Monday morning, when we were issued with a travel warrant for Belfast via British Rail and the Liverpool – Belfast ferry. The journey started off normally enough, and we travelled in civilian clothes, albeit carrying army issue kitbags and suitcases. However by the time we approached Liverpool we were becoming nervous. Boarding the ferry was easy enough, although I remember staring suspiciously at our fellow passengers, wondering how many were IRA gunmen or sympathisers.

The voyage passed peacefully but, by the time the ship docked at Belfast Lough, we were all very much aware that our haircuts, suitcases and kit bags clearly identified us as soldiers. We disembarked and sat on the quayside, nervously watching the crowds around us and hoping that the transport would arrive soon to collect us. We didn't have to wait long. Two men in civilian clothes approached and showed us their military ID cards. They confirmed our identities and told us to follow them. Our transport was waiting not far away, a civilian laundry van. Once in the vehicle the driver and his mate produced a sub-machine gun and a 9mm pistol, and kept them handy during the trip to the battalion echelon at Musgrave Park. These 'covert' vans were used for many routine administrative duties as well as a few other clandestine operations.

We didn't get to see much of the scenery during the trip. The windows in the rear doors of the van had been covered over for security. Somehow it seemed a bit of an anti-climax. None of us really knew what to expect but we thought that we'd at least hear some shooting or explosions. Instead, apart from the armed men in the front of the van, everything seemed normal. In due course we would learn that there were areas that were extremely quiet, and that in any case most of the shootings took place in the evenings or the hours of darkness. Eventually however we would become so used to the sound of gunfire that, as long as the fire wasn't aimed at us, we would hardly notice it.

We arrived on a Wednesday morning and were marched straight in to meet the Rear Party OC. He wasted no time in welcoming us to the Regiment and informed us that we would be joining the battalion in a matter of days. He told us that the Battalion was currently deployed in West Belfast, in one of the most dangerous hard line Republican areas of Northern Ireland. Of the four companies in the battalion: 'C' Company was in the roughest spot in the battalion Tactical Area of Operations (TAOR), a particularly nasty piece of real estate known as Turf Lodge. Almost as an afterthought he added that the three of us were reinforcements for C Company, replacements for several casualties sustained over the past few weeks.

Barrie Lovell, Queen's Regiment, Belfast 1977 (Barrie Lovell)

Turf Lodge was a Catholic council housing estate sandwiched between the Andersonstown, Whiterock and Ballymurphy Districts of Belfast. The Turf, as it was known by the troops, was a run-down council estate, with a few streets of private houses, the Granshas, surrounding it. It did not appear to be a nice place to live. Those families that tried to make something of their lives and to improve their conditions were dragged down to the lowest common denominator by a mixture of poverty, terrorist threats, extortion and apathy. The IRA was very active in the area and the level of anti-Army feeling was high.

The Turf was bordered on the North by the lower slopes of the Black Mountain, and the New Barnsley and Ballymurphy districts, and to the south by the Falls Road and the M1 motorway. The whole area was a violently Republican area of West Belfast and, during the 1970s, it was virtually ruled by the IRA's Belfast Brigade. The police didn't even enter the Turf unless given an Army escort. Our patch was regarded by the army as Indian country, a place to enter only if you were ready for trouble. The impression of danger and isolation was enhanced by the fact that our base on the patch was officially known as Fort Monagh, like one of the US army forts in Indian country in a Holywood western film.

The TAOR (Tactical Area of Operational Responsibility) also included the Falls Road and Milltown Cemetrey, the scene of many Republican funerals and demonstrations and the Falls Road police station. The Falls Road Police Station was only a short distance away and, at this time, boasted of being the most shot at police station in the world.

10 Platoon, C Company, 2nd Battalion The Queen's
Regiment, Belfast 1977 (Barrie Lovell)

Anyway, once inside the base, we were dropped off at the Ops Room. Our escorts vanished, leaving us uncertain as to what would happen next. We were still in our civilian clothes and felt out of place surrounded by armed troops, most of whom were wearing flak jackets. After a while we were told to stay put as C Company were sending transport for us. Our next lift arrived shortly afterwards; two Makralon armoured Land Rovers accompanied by a Bedford truck. We shared the back of the truck with some stores destined for Fort Monagh.

It was only a short journey across the motorway to Fort Monagh. This time, sitting by the tailgate of the truck, we had a much better view of our surroundings. The area around Musgrave Park had looked like a typical 1970's London suburb, the sort I was familiar with at home. As we crossed the M1 however we entered another world altogether. Pro-IRA and anti-British graffiti began to appear, the buildings appeared scruffier and there was more litter in the streets. The occasional burnt out building or car could be seen, and the windows of shops and bars were protected by steel or wire mesh screens. Concrete filled oil drums, welded together with steel pipes, were placed outside many bars to prevent vehicles from being parked too close to the walls, a necessary precaution against car bombs. Bars and pubs were often favourite targets for sectarian attacks and this was reflected in the lengths to which the owners would go to protect their business and their customers.

Turning off the Falls Road at the Monagh Road roundabout we finally had our first glimpse of our home for the next few months, Fort Monagh. From the outside it looked like any other SF base, all wriggly tin and sangars. Completely surrounding the wall was a high wire mesh fence. The top part of the fence sloped inward. It stood about 10-15 feet out from the wall and was designed to prevent anyone placing grenades or blast bombs next to the flimsy wriggly tin. It was also high enough to prevent grenades being thrown over the top. Behind the main tin wall was a second one. The clear space between the walls allowed troops access to the sangars and provided a clear path for patrols around the perimetre. Inside the base it was a smaller version of the Musgrave Park base, portacabins, breezeblocks and yet more wriggly tin. Monagh was the temporary home of the battalion HQ, as well as C Company. In addition we had the battalion medics, and a detachment of RCT drivers for the Humber armoured personnel carriers. The fort itself was about 200 metres long and about 150 metres wide.

14th Intelligence Company or the 'Det', although rarely acknowledged in official circles is reputed to have been an integral, albeit secret, part of the British Army Intelligence Corps which operated in Northern Ireland from the 1970s onwards. The unit conducted undercover surveillance operations against suspected members of Irish Republican and loyalist paramilitary groups.

COVERT OP ON THE TURF LODGE

Soldier, RAOC Attached to the Det

Pictures were required to ID a key player who had moved into the North from the South, and I was given sole use with a minder of an OP overlooking a street below in which was a well know Sinn Fein (SF) club that included the membership of well known senior key players.

This was to be a 24hr 'obbo' and once in, we were not leaving until the job finished; therefore, alongside the non standard equipment of a specialist firearm plus specialist rations such as Mars Bars, tins of Coke, banjos and toothbrush; we also had three Pentax SLR cameras and what was known as a bucket lens; the circumference of which was the size of a dustbin lid. Myself and my minder made ourselves comfortable and set ourselves up ready for a 24 hour stint that always felt more like 72. We were looking over towards the street opposite that was around 70 feet below us; the terraced houses that were built around 1920 were drab and needed some tender loving care. Our target was the entrance door to the SF club.

Traffic was quiet as were the streets; the road lights came on (for those still working) and gave that early glow. The arc of light from the lamp was the uniformed soldier's nightmare as entering the light was like going into an arena with a spotlight directly on you; an area where the sniper just waited for his opportunity. The lights came on in the club and the outer security door was opened; the only thing we knew was that our new face would be frequenting the club, because, to the IRA this was like their TA centre where they would go to get training, instructions briefings etc.

It was November and the evenings were now getting colder; the coal fire smoke from the chimneys of the houses produced an early evening mist which partly obscured our view. The street light directly above the club door was working and was now causing me problems, as trying to focus the camera onto the doorway and obtain a head shot of our target was not going to be easy. As the evening moved on, various men and women entered and left the club; the quality of picture was not going to be very good due to this damn street light. I spoke with my minder who said he could solve my problem in a matter of minutes, and he got on the radio and advised the boss of our problem, after giving a very clear and defined location of the guilty lamp he signed off.

The evening was getting colder and another layer of clothing was called for; the house lights were now on and made the streets look warm and inviting. You took in a deep breath but all you could smell was a mixture of gun oil, damp sandbags and the smoke from the coal fires. After putting a jumper on, I turned back to the camera; the doorman was standing just inside the half lit doorway when I heard a familiar sound of a Saracen engine winding up the pre-select gearbox. The sound was coming from my left, and then, an all too familiar sight came down the road; the driver's hatches were down and the back doors closed.

I looked back at the club and the doorman on hearing the vehicle had closed the outer club door and gone inside. The Saracen moved closer to the club end of the street, by now doing around 40mph; he suddenly veered over to the left and we heard this almighty crash. The Saracen had struck the street light outside the SF club and caused it to fall to the ground; with a second loud crash, the glass smashed as it struck the pavement.

The club door remained firmly shut, and the back doors of the Saracen opened and three guys jumped out; two took up defensive fire positions and the third took up an unusual pose of one hand on the hip the other removing his beret and scratching his head. Two minutes later, they mounted; the vehicle reversed off the lamp and drove off. A few minutes after the vehicle had left the area, our radio came to life; the minder responded with our call sign and the originator asked the question: 'Can you see the door ok, now?'

We got our pictures that night including the new face, and we left the next morning, freezing cold with our bags of equipment, still in our less than adequate civvie clothing. Uniformed guys were lining up at the loading bay watching us get back into our car, wondering who the hell we were. Operations such as these took place each and every day; intelligence gathering; being one step ahead of the game; ensuring that our uniformed boys were up to speed. The guy we were after was a gunman and, from what we were told, a very useful gunman. He was nicked by an army patrol and handed over to the RUC three days later, picking up an Armalite; a camera is as powerful as a rifle in the right hands.

TURF LODGE

Private Richard Smith, Duke of Wellingtons

I was 19 at the time and my lot was on duty for an IRA funeral procession; I was in a garden keeping watch, and my back was to the cortège. A door opened and I looked around to see a little lad of about 5 or 6 and as he approached me, I turned my back to him to have a quick glance at the IRA funeral procession.

I was wearing a NIBA vest (Northern Ireland Body Armour) and it had a plate over the heart and a plate in the back also covering the heart. This little bastard knew exactly where the plates were and kicked me right in the back one; it was agonising. Before I could say something, his mother, who had been looking on, called out, proudly: 'Well done, sorn; Youse brother will get him for real, next time.'

I remember thinking: 'What the hell am I doing here?'

TURF LODGE, 1981

Fusilier David Dews, Royal Regiment of Fusiliers

This was my first tour, and every time I went out on those streets on that big estate, my arse was puckering up! I remember so vividly, the smell of sulphar and burned out cars and other vehicles. I do recall that we patrolled in armoured vehicles as at that time, it was just too dangerous to be out on foot and we would be ambushed every time we drove up the Whiterock Road. The little bastards would hide behind the wall of the City Cemetrey on our left and then pelt us with bricks and petrol bombs as we drove by.

I always seemed to be on 'top cover' on one of the Land Rovers and was bricked time and time again by the bastards!

ON THE TURF

Barrie Lovell, C Company, 2nd Battalion, The Queen's Regiment

My first patrol into the Turf was a tense experience for me. It certainly helped that all the others had been carrying out similar patrols for some weeks. I had been warned what to expect, what to do in particular circumstances, and how to behave under others. It was also a great help to know that the others would be watching my back, as I was expected to watch theirs. The belief that your mates will look after you is found in most units in the British Army, although it reaches a particular intensity in the fighting units, and even more so when the opposition is firing live rounds, or otherwise trying to kill you. It was very much a situation of 'us' against 'them' and when we were faced by hostile stone throwing crowds, several hundred strong, it was a great source of strength to know that whatever happened the lads were with you all the way.

My introduction to the Turf took the form of a foot patrol and fortunately it was a relatively quiet one. We left the Fort in the usual fashion. This consisted of walking up to the camp gate and then, once visible to anyone watching from the outside and with two guards in the gate sangar ready to provide covering fire, sprinting for about fifty yards down the road, zigzagging all the way. This was known as hard targeting and the idea was to make it harder for a potential sniper to hit you. Once away from the gate we shook out into our patrol formation, each brick forming an irregular square with the troops about ten to fifteen yards apart.

The Monagh Road, outside the camp, ran downhill to the right to the roundabout on the Falls Road, about two hundred yards away. On the other side of the road, directly opposite the camp, some two hundred yards away on the far side of a stretch of waste ground, stood a row of houses. To the left it sloped uphill, then gently curved to the right before entering the Turf Lodge housing estate about four or five hundred yards from the camp. To the left of the road was waste ground while on the other side it was a mixture of waste ground and building site. On the edge of the estate, to the right of the road and directly in line with the fort, stood a row of partially built shops. These were always referred to as the New Shops, although they had remained in a semi-completed state for some time and, as far as I can tell, they were never actually completed before the estate was demolished.

Due to the excellent view of the camp obtained from the New Shops they were a popular location for the IRA to shoot at the Fort. Spent cartridge cases were found there on a number of occasions but, with the main estate right behind them, it was very easy for the gunmen to disappear immediately after firing. Whenever I was on guard duty in the sangars facing the Turf I would spend hours staring through the binoculars, rifle at the ready, hoping to spot a gunman taking up a firing position in the shops. It was everyone's ambition to get themselves a gunman, and I thought that my best opportunity would be to shoot one in the process of setting up a shoot at the camp, poetic justice I suppose.

The walk up the road towards the New Shops took about five minutes. The Turf's early warning system was on full alert as usual and the warning that we were on our way was passed round the estate like lightning. This became evident once we deployed past the New Shops, and crossed the pedestrian area which, had it been completed, would have fronted the small parade of shops. As we entered the estate we were met with a desultory shower of half bricks, stone and bottles. The throwers kept well out of the way, hiding in gardens and alleyways, and I don't think I actually saw anyone throwing stones for about five or ten minutes. The patrol advanced further into the estate in two columns, each composed of three bricks. My brick was in the centre of the right hand column, led by Dave B the Platoon Sergeant. The leading brick was bearing the brunt of the stoning, and this allowed me to watch and try and figure out what was happening. By this time I was buzzing with adrenalin, simultaneously trying to take in the activity around me and to keep my position in the patrol. It all appeared totally confusing to my inexperienced eyes but everyone seemed to accept this as normal. There was no shouting or fuss from the troops. Orders were given quietly and concisely. When a brick commander wished to do something, or to redeploy his men, he would call them by their forename or nickname and indicate what he wanted them to do: 'Barney, on the corner; watch the left, Frank; check out the blue Ford.' It all seemed to be going smoothly.

In contrast to the soldiers, the inhabitants of the Turf were not a pleasant sight. This was my first close look at them and I was not impressed with what I saw. The overall impression was of a badly run down council estate occupied mostly by ugly, foul mouthed women and scruffy teenagers of both sexes. Adult males would usually keep out the way during our patrols, as they were likely to be stopped and searched. To avoid the troops, and the risk of arrest, they would stay indoors or use another road. The women were not so cautious however. Once the presence of a patrol became known they would commence to warn their immediate neighbours, and anyone else within earshot, by blowing whistles and banging steel dustbin lids on the ground. The result was a raucous din which could be heard across the estate. As others took up the warning the noise level would continue to grow. They would persist in the noisemaking even while we were walking past them, presumably to antagonise us and to make hearing radio messages difficult. Each brick commander carried a small Pye radio. These radios used a combined microphone and speaker, usually worn clipped to front of the flak jacket, and sometimes it could be extremely difficult to hear the messages above the noise of the crowd. In addition to the whistle blowing and bin lid banging we were subject to a constant stream of verbal abuse. Any ideas about women being the gentle sex were dispelled by the level of obscenities which they used. I was used to the way in which soldiers swore, but I was surprised by the language used by the women. More unsettling was the obvious hatred with which they shouted their abuse at us. For the first time in my life I realised that these were people who would like to see me dead. It is not a pleasant feeling, and I think that my dislike of the Irish stems from the impressions I formed of that Republican mob.

The teenagers also tended to keep away from us. This was to allow them to throw stones at us while giving them sufficient time to run should we attempt to arrest any of them. Numbering up to several hundred at a time, although the average was usually a lot less, and dressed in jeans and training shoes, they made a dangerous and fast moving hazard for patrols. The crowds were usually large enough to keep up a constant barrage of missiles; bricks, stones, bottles, lump of metal, masonry chisels and, on one occasion, even an axe. Of course, with the close proximity of the building site adjacent to the New Shops there was no shortage of suitable throwing materials. Despite wearing flak jackets and helmets whenever we deployed to the Turf such missiles could cause surprisingly severe injuries and, during the course of the tour, the company had over a hundred riot injuries recorded in the medical centre log book. As we generally only had about ninety troops in the company at any one time this meant that some men were injured several times. I still carry two scars from wounds caused by flying bricks. The most common wounds were cuts and bruises, but they could result in broken bones, concussion or, in one case, temporary blindness due to broken glass in the face. It was accepted that if you were hit, it was important not to show any pain and not to let the crowd know that they had hurt you. This meant gritting your teeth and carrying on, often limping and with tears in your eyes due to the pain.

We learnt how to dodge the bricks and stones, but it was skill that took time to acquire. Failure to learn resulted in more bruises and more pain. Eventually however it became second nature, and by using our peripheral vision could spot an incoming rock before it struck, while at the same time watching what was happening further up the street. Most people could cope well with three or four bricks at a time, sidestepping or dodging them in a kind of "one step forward, stop, one step sideways, two steps forward, one step backwards" walk. We must have looked like a bunch of idiots practicing a parody of the Monty Python Silly Walk. There were times however when the sheer numbers of missiles in the air overwhelmed us and, despite the most energetic dodging, we would be hit repeatedly. Under these circumstances any attempt at standing around was abandoned. We would take what cover was available and open spaces were crossed running flat out.

Our usual defence against the stone throwers was to threaten to use the baton guns but, after we had called their bluff several times, we either had to use them for real or back down. The baton guns were really only to be used in emergencies and permission to fire was supposed to be given by Company Headquarters. In practice we fired when we felt that we needed to, particularly if we had injured lads to look after or, as in my own experience, the risk of personal injury was getting too high.

If the crowd began pressing closer, and on occasions the rioters would approach within ten yards of the troops before letting fly, we would be forced to make short charges into the crowd. As soon as we drew the batons and ran towards the crowd they would run away, under no illusions as to what would happen to them if they got caught. We rarely bothered to arrest them because of the time consuming legal procedures involved and also because the courts would do little more than fine them. The fines were usually paid from collections organised, often with a little persuasion, by the IRA. In any case the culprit would be back on the streets within hours of being handed over to the civilian police, the Royal Ulster Constabulary. Instead of arrest therefore, we would simply deal out a few blows with batons or rifle butts and let them go. The ensuing melees were not one sided affairs however, we were usually outnumbered and the rioters were on ground they knew intimately. As a result we took great care that no one got separated from their patrol during a riot, as the threat of being beaten up, or worse, was ever present. Most soldiers who have been caught out like this in the past have been beaten by the mob before their mates could rescue them. In the worst case, as happened to two Royal Signals soldiers several years ago, they could be beaten up, dragged away and shot with their own weapon. Such close encounters were not all that common however, as a lightly dressed teenager wearing a pair of training shoes is a lot faster off the mark than a soldier weighed down with a 20 or 30 pounds of flak jacket, helmet, boots, weapons, ammunition and radio. Still, it was some satisfaction that that we could put the fear of God into them even if we couldn't catch them.

GERRY ADAMS AND FORT WHITEROCK

Eddie Dixon, Light Infantry

In 1991, the Gulf War had kicked off and as usual 3LI were not invited and our booby prize was to take over the Paras' tour of Belfast whilst they went to Iraq. When it finally came around, anti tank platoon was attached to 'C' company at 'Fort Whiterock.' 'Fort Whiterock' was built on the hillside overlooking the Turf Lodge and Ballymurphy estates in west Belfast, both staunch Catholic areas. Getting a cup of tea off the locals here was very, very rare indeed!

I had done two tours of Ireland, previously; in Fermanagh where, sometimes you didn't see people for days on end. Belfast was different altogether, and the day we arrived was the day those two poor signalers were captured and murdered at Penny Lane.

The company itself had more than its share of incidents; the camp was shot at; patrols were shot at, with a shot just missing Corporal Young by mm. Then there was a rocket attack which missed the Land Rover and the top cover man, missing them, again by mm. As Davie Shaw was aiming at the RPG firer, myself 'Jap' and 'Zorro' gave as much support as we could. Later, we had a coffee jar bomb thrown at our vehicle, but it hit the RUC Land Rover instead and nobody was hurt; however, a change of underwear was needed that day.

One of the memories which stands out for me, was when we were on our way to Springfield Road RUC station and we were patrolling past the house of Gerry Adams' mother. His driver was outside in the car, so the boss (Mike Thornton) decided to search the car as he was known to us. After a while, Adams himself came out of the house and was ranting and raving and the boss told me: 'Watch him, Dixie.' For the next 5 minutes, he (Gerry Adams) kept saying: 'You all right, Dixie?' He was really getting on my nerves and in the end I stood up and asked: 'Can I ask you a personal question, Mr. Adams; what do you think of the Anglo Irish agreement?' He went ballistic, ordered his driver to get in the car and drove off and he went to the RUC station to complain.

Anyway, the shit had hit the fan, and I was interviewed by senior officers. They wanted to know what was said and as a consequence, I was taken off the streets; it was like being in prison; sweeping the camp, painting this, and painting that; denied the right to do my job. Then about 2 weeks later, the General visited the camp and walked around like Generals do with all his henchmen behind him.

I was introduced as Private Dixon, 'the one who had had the Gerry Adams incident.' The General then kicked everyone out the room and there was just me and him; he explained the incident had by-passed him and went to the Minister for Northern Ireland. All he wanted to know was what was said in those 3 minutes. I told him what was said by both and I was then asked why I asked him that question.

I then produced my 'get out of jail free' card, because, on the way out of camp was a board with questions to ask, in order to break the ice with the locals. As it happened, the question of the day was 'WHAT DO YOU THINK OF THE ANGLO IRISH AGREEMENT?'

The General agreed with me and I was allowed back out on the streets; I was like a kid with a new toy! All in all a very successful tour, with no one lost In Platoon, Company, or Battalion and I came back a wiser man.

TURF LODGE PATROL

Barrie Lovell, 'C' Company, 2nd Battalion, The Queen's Regiment

I remember one particular patrol which took place on a Saturday evening. The patrol consisted of Percy Thrower, Barney, Frank and myself, and the boss had decided to come with us. It was a beautiful warm, early summer evening and we decided to visit the area of the Falls Park, a surprisingly pleasant park just off the Falls Road near the Turf. While crossing the park Lieutenant 'X' stopped and lay down on the grass; motioning us to do likewise he removed his beret and suggested that we all take a break. We set ourselves down in all-round defence, so that we could watch all around us, and the five of us simply lay in the sunshine and watched the world go by. The conversation drifted along, finally settling on what we were all going to do on leave when we returned to the UK. For a while rank was forgotten, as we discussed the best way to spend our leave, usually involving the consumption of large quantities of alcohol and the company of nubile young ladies. After a while however the real world intruded, in the form of a radio message and a new task, and we were back on our feet and working again.

Sergeant Dave B, the platoon sergeant, was a complete contrast to the officer. and was in many ways an ideal platoon sergeant. He was a tall, quietly spoken man with a typical cynical army sense of humour, and got things done with a minimum of fuss and bother. Like most of the senior NCOs Sgt 'B' had already completed several tours in the province and he knew what he was doing, and under him the platoon seemed to run very smoothly. He and the boss made a good team and their confidence and assurance communicated itself to the rest of the platoon. Although life in an infantry platoon is generally noisy I don't think that there was ever any unnecessary shouting in 10 Platoon.

The rest of the platoon was made up of the mixture of characters typical in any military unit. The battalion's recruiting area was London and

Private Ali (RRW)
meets a local on
the Turf Lodge
(Royal Regiment of
Wales Museum)

the South East although most of the lads were from London or the Medway Towns.

The three Corporals were all in their late twenties or early thirties and, like Sgt B, had all served in Northern Ireland before. Of the corporals Mick V was a real old sweat. In addition to his GSM for earlier tours in Ireland he also had a clasp for service in the Far East. These were far and few between by the mid-Seventies and it showed that he had a lot of experience. Keith? was our second corporal. Basically he was a nice enough guy but he was not as aggressive as the younger NCOs and soldiers. He was one of those people who wanted a quiet life and, as a result he often took a fair bit of ribbing from his lads. He also had a dated taste in clothes and would often wear a brown overcoat with a high turned up collar, like those worn by spies in a 'fifties movie. What with the coat and his slightly pinched face he bore a striking resemblance to Secret Squirrel, a character in a popular children's TV cartoon series. The junior members of the platoon used to refer to him as Secret Squirrel, but generally only behind his back. The last corporal was very quiet and unfortunately I can't even remember his name now.

We also had three lance Corporals, Percy Thrower, Bob 'S' and Pete 'C'. The Lance Corporals were all younger, but with at least one tour in the province behind them. All three of them were also very aggressive, and they expected their soldiers to behave in the same way. Bob S was a powerfully built man, with an extremely boisterous sense of humour. He worked as hard as he played however, and was always in the thick of the action. As with many soldiers he came across as a work hard, play hard type of guy but would revert to a gentle giant when with his wife and children.

The other soldiers were, with one notable exception, mostly younger lads in their late teens or early twenties. Few had any academic qualifications and I was regarded as a bit of a smart Alec for having five 'O' levels. On the whole however they were a sound bunch of guys and could always be relied upon in emergencies.

My closest friend in the Platoon was Andy C. We shared a mutual interest in motorbikes and rock music and in due course became regular drinking companions.

Our main role in Ireland at this time was controlling our patch, with the aim of making life difficult for the terrorist. This involved patrolling the streets and estates, carrying out searches, placing road blocks, manning observation posts and checking the identity of passers-by, the usual activity of anti-terrorist operations.

There were two basic types of patrol, foot and vehicle. The tactics for each varied, usually depending on whether we were operating in the Turf itself, or in one of the quieter parts of the patch. Vehicle patrols were carried out in Land rovers, although we tended to stay out of the Turf in these as they were vulnerable to bricks and petrol bombs, despite being protected by Makralon armour plates. For operations in the Turf we would use the Humber PIGs. Each could carry two bricks, and with the hatches locked shut we were safe from bricks and bottles but could still be attacked with bottles of paint, which splashed across the vision blocks and could effectively blind the crew.

When on any operation, whether an OP, patrol or search, we normally wore a flak jacket. Helmets were always worn when patrolling the Turf, but berets would be worn in the quieter areas. Most helmets were decorated with some form of graffiti. The wearer's blood group was most common. Other examples were 'Do not remove, head attached!' or 'Baby Crusher', which was worn by one of the attached RCT drivers. Dave Kelly played safe drew a red cross on his helmet and added the caption 'Don't shoot – Medic.' The flak jackets looked like a sleeveless body warmer and comprised a series of nylon plates sewn into a nylon outer jacket. They were heavy to wear and, although fairly comfortable, could cause the wearer to overheat on hot days or during periods of physical activity. Most of the lads would therefore just wear a combat jacket and t-shirt underneath the flak jacket. During the summer, on hot days, even the t-shirt would go. Most of the troops marked their blood group on their flak jacket, in the belief that it would assist the medics in the event of their being hit. Frank L's blood group was 'A Negative and he wrote this, using a large black marker pen, along with his name, on the left side of his jacket just below the protective shoulder pad. The words 'FRANK: A NEG' were picked up by the locals. Perhaps the Irish in the Turf really were stupid, but it amused us to hear them shouting after Frank 'We'll get you Aneg, we'll find out where you live and we'll fuckin' get you!'

When on patrol every member of the brick would usually carry an SLR. When there was a likelihood of crowd violence or a riot, the baton gunner would also carry a 1.5" baton gun. The baton gun fired a solid plastic bullet, which resembled an oversized shotgun cartridge, to a distance of 50 to 75 yards. The plastic bullet was designed to administer a non-lethal blow to the target, which would either stun him long enough for the troops to arrest him, or else would inflict sufficient pain to act as deterrent. The baton gun was not supposed to be fired at targets closer than 30 yards. Used correctly the crowd would have time to dodge the slowly travelling bullet, it was easy to spot one coming, and as such it was more of a nuisance weapon as opposed to a deterrent one. Needless to say we didn't use them as instructed. The idea was to keep the weapon loaded and ready to fire, and to fire it as close to the target as possible, so that they would not have time to leap out of the way. A good range was 30 feet. The gun itself could be lethal at close range, as shown by the death of a teenager from the Turf who was shot in the back of the head as he turned to run, by one of the lads from 9 Platoon.

I have often heard stories of soldiers tampering with the baton rounds, cutting down the rounds and filling the vacated space with U2 torch batteries or sharpened pennies. Both methods reputedly increased the damage inflicted on the target, however I never actually saw this in practice. We simply relied on firing fast at close range to get a good solid hit on the target. As most patrols into Turf Lodge seemed to result in a confrontation with a crowd of stone throwers the baton gun was mandatory for such patrols. Invariably the baton gunner's rifle was left behind; however it carried the risk of being caught in a fire fight with the opposition without the means to fire back; this happened to me on one occasion.

As a last resort weapon each soldier also carried an 18" long wooden baton. This was used to apply non-lethal force when necessary, and was usually carried tucked inside the flak jacket. Not everyone used the standard issue baton however. Some of the lads had removed the compressed gas cylinders from the fire extinguishers in the accommodation blocks back in the camp. These were about 12" long and, when emptied, fitted with a leather carrying strap and suitably disguised with black masking tape, proved to particularly effective as clubs. Needless to say their use was illegal and no doubt highly dangerous to the victim. Our own safety came first however and the general attitude was 'If they can throw bricks at me then fuck 'em; they can take what's coming when I catch 'em.'

The tail-end Charlie was the guy who brought up the rear of a patrol. Inevitably the baton gunners were at the back of the patrol in order to discourage the stone throwers from getting too close. In addition, when the patrol was moving towards a hostile crowd, or even just entering the Turf, the baton gunners would move to the front. The order 'gunners to the front' or 'gunners to the rear' became standard procedure. As a result of this job I found myself in a number of hazardous situations. Fortunately I survived them with no more than cuts, bruises and mild concussion, but there was one beneficial side effect when the battalion returned to our barracks in the UK. New recruits were often mercilessly teased or harassed when they first joined the battalion. This was done to amuse the old sweats, and to find out if the new lads had a sense of humour and could cope with a bit of abuse. Eventually a newer recruit would arrive and the previous recipient of the harassment would be left alone, having become one of the boys. In my case the platoon was invariably too busy, or too tired, to carry out this punitive bullying and by the time we returned to the UK I was just one of the boys. On return to the UK the practice picked up again, but I was never bothered by anyone.

INJURED IN THE TURF

Barrie Lovell, 'C' Company, 2nd Battalion, The Queen's Regiment

Eventually my luck ran out and, despite all my precautions, I was injured. On this particular morning we were deployed in the Turf for a routine patrol. As usual I was carrying a baton gun and bringing up the rear of the patrol as tail end Charlie. The PC (Platoon Commander) had arranged for us to RV (rendezvous) with the PIGs at one of the junctions near Norglen Parade. The usual crowd was harassing us but, as we approached the vehicles, I could see that the drivers were under pressure from another crowd. After a while we found ourselves deployed along the street while the crowd had coalesced into a single mob near the vehicles. As I was the tail end Charlie for the rearmost brick I was farthest away from the rioters and was enjoying what was a period of comparative calm until a shout of 'Baton Gunners to the front!' came down the line. I jogged along the street to the Platoon Commander. The crowd was pushing in very close to the vehicles but, for some reason never explained to me we had to hold our position.

The baton gunners were therefore required to keep the crowd at bay with plastic bullets. I eventually found myself standing next to the PIG which was closest to the crowd. With a target that big even the most inept stone thrower couldn't miss and I was soon spending all my time just trying to dodge the missiles aimed at the vehicle. Each hit on the vehicle was accompanied by a metallic clang. It seemed noisy enough outside but must have been deafening for the drivers inside. One missile struck with a resounding bang and, glancing down, I saw that it was a large cold chisel. This I picked up and placed on the vehicle's mudguard, with the intention of keeping it as a souvenir.

I held my position, next to the commanders door, with one of the corporals standing several feet behind me. The crowd pressed in even closer and we found ourselves to be very exposed with the bricks bouncing off the side of the vehicle striking us as well. It was obvious that I needed to open fire in order to drive back the crowd and I turned to the NCO with the intention of telling him that I was going to fire. As I turned, a bottle flew past my shoulder and smashed on the side of the vehicle, the fragments of glass hitting the corporal on the side of his helmet and face. Some of the fragments penetrated the gap between visor and helmet, cutting his face. He put his hands to his face and dropped to his knees, turning away from the crowd for protection.

I suddenly realised that it was all up to me. The nearest soldier was ten or fifteen yards away, and I was the only man between the crowd and the PIG. I turned back and raised the baton gun to fire. Now I should point out that I was wearing a newly issued type of helmet (a prototype model for the current Kevlar plastic helmet). The helmet was equipped with a visor which was excellent in all respects except one. The visor had been designed to protect the face down to a point below the chin but, because of the design of the sights on the baton gun, one couldn't aim the gun properly with the visor fully down. As a result the baton gunners used to take a chance and half raised the visor, allowing them to aim the weapon properly. While this still protected the front of the face it exposed the sides of the jaw to attack. This I now did, raising the visor to an angle of about 45 degrees and bringing the gun up into the aim. I was just about to fire when a rioter ran out of the crowd on my right, closing until he was standing about twenty feet from me. He hurled a chunk of house brick in my direction. The brick missed me by a couple of feet but rebounded from the armoured vehicle and struck me on the side of the chin. The impact of the blow knocked me unconscious, my legs buckled and I fell back against the side of the vehicle before sliding to the ground. As I passed out I put a hand to my jaw, the pain was intense, thinking that it must be broken. I heard the crowd cheer loudly as I fell, and saw them surge towards me before everything went dark.

Soldiers who have been caught by the crowd in similar circumstances have been badly beaten on occasions. I was lucky. Someone, I never found out who, shouted for the platoon to make a baton charge. This they did, sweeping past me and on into the crowd. I came round some moments later as I was being half carried, half dragged away from the crowd towards a PIG further to the rear. I was still very woozy from the blow and, once sat inside, the platoon sergeant gave me the once over. I must have looked a right mess. My face was bleeding and, where one of rescuers had removed my helmet chinstrap, they had smeared the blood across my face. My chin hurt from the cut and my whole jaw ached. Another soldier took my baton gun and, when I was sufficiently conscious to know what I was doing, I was given a rifle to carry. I was deemed to be 'walking wounded,' but apparently not sufficiently hurt to warrant casevac back to Fort Monagh. As a result I spent the remainder of the patrol, some forty five minutes, sitting in the back of the PIG with blood running down my chin, watching for snipers and dodging the occasional brick.

Eventually we pulled out and returned to the fort. After unloading my rifle I reported to the medical centre for examination. The medics cleaned me up and, to everyone's surprise, found only a relatively small cut on my chin. Despite its small size it was very deep, which accounted for the large amount of blood. The Medical Officer checked me for concussion and then decided to stitch the wound on my chin. He was joking nonchalantly all the time and said that the wound really only needed three stitches but that he'd put another one in for me, because under the Criminal Compensation Act, facial wounds received compensation based on the number of stitches required. After about half an hour I walked away from the medical centre, my head aching from the blow and my lower face numb from the local anesthetic. In addition I had been told by the medics to stand down for eight hours, to see if any symptoms of concussion appeared. I was very wary about this as I had been knocked unconscious with a beer mug in a pub fight a year or so earlier. On that occasion I had been affected quite severely, although thankfully the concussion was only temporary. Once back in the platoon accommodation I checked the patrol roster. My next patrol was in exactly eight hours time.

I was feeling pretty low by this stage. My jaw and face hurt too much to eat so I skipped the midday meal. I phoned my parents, simply to hear a familiar voice I think, and then crashed out on my bed for a few hours. When I awoke for the next patrol the pain had subsided to a dull ache, but my chin was badly bruised and tender for some days. The bruising made it uncomfortable to wear a helmet as the chinstrap rubbed against the wound but I eventually became used to it. In any case I was young and extremely fit, with the hefty appetite found only in young men who carry out physically demanding jobs. The wound healed quickly and I bounced back on my feet in no time.

On May 19, 1988, the world witnessed the horrifying abduction, beating and eventual murder of two Corporals from the Royal Corps of Signals. This incident was dealt with extensively in the first volume, but suffice to say, their murder was not only a seminal moment in the history of the troubles but probably the most sickening sight ever shown on British television. It was akin, as one former squaddie told me, to '…watching a hunting pack of Lions tear some poor Antelope to pieces on some natural history programme…' The two men were abducted outside Milltown Cemetrey, savagely beaten, then shot and their bodies dumped at Penny Lane in the Turf Lodge area.

IRA and INLA activity ground to a halt in that part of West Belfast; perhaps the constant patrolling and PVCPs thrown around the area's roads had an effect, perhaps the people of the 'Turf were equally sickened; whatever the reason, the Turf Lodge had claimed its final SF victims.

Chapter 3

Andersonstown

Andersonstown or Andy's Town as the squaddies termed it, with an ironic affection, completes the westward sweep of Republican housing on that side of Belfast. South of both the 'Murph and the 'Turf', it is physically similar to its siblings to the north, but is larger and has more housing than them. When it was designed, no doubt some 'bright spark' in Belfast's Housing Executive thought that it would be a good dumping ground for the poorer (i.e. Catholic) families of the city. Undoubtedly, some Protestant families lived there also, but by the onset of the troubles, they would have been forced out into one of their own enclaves further east or further north towards the Shankhill and Crumlin Road areas.

It is hemmed in on three sides by Kennedy Way, Andersonstown Road, and, to the west, the huge Glen Road. Beyond, like the 'Murph and Turf Lodge, is the vast expanse of open ground dominated by the Black Mountain. High up and further to the west, is the huge Divis transmitter from where the television and communication signals emanate.

Andy's Town was the scene of 22 SF deaths over the period of the troubles and included 16 regular soldiers and no less than 6 RUC officers. It is difficult to imagine a similar Council estate in say, Leeds or Liverpool or Manchester, where the murder of 6 police officers would have been tolerated, as it appeared to have been in Andersonstown.

Between July 14, 1971 and July 23, 1987, a total of almost exactly 16 years, Andersonstown was the place where 22 men, trained to keep the peace and act aggressively when the situation called for it, lost their lives or were to be taken to another place to die of their wounds. It therefore illustrates the dangerous and extraordinary circumstances under which Britain's young men and women and the beleaguered forces of the RUC, found themselves. Extraordinary that, in an area comprising Andersonstown, Turf Lodge and Ballymurphy, equal, possibly, in size to the sprawling Seacroft and Gipton estates in Leeds or Norris Green in Liverpool or Brixton in London, 50 SF men lost their lives. Imagine the outcry had that carnage occurred in any of the aforementioned places?

However, to return to Andy's Town; by the summer of 1971, the second worst year for military deaths in the Province, casualties among the Army were beginning to mount. Immediately prior to July 14 of that year, officially at least, a total of 10 soldiers had been killed, but taking all troubles-related deaths into consideration, the true figure was over 30. On that day, Private Richard Barton (24) of 2 PARA was shot and killed by 3 IRA gunmen who were waiting in ambush in a garden in Killeen Park. He was driving an army vehicle and was approaching the Stewartstown and Andersonstown Road junction, when gunmen opened fire. He attempted to manoeuvre the vehicle into position to provide cover for his comrades when he was hit.

Six weeks later, Barnsley boy, Gunner Clifford Loring (18) was hit by a round fired from the area around Owenvarragh Park, the round having passed through the flak jacket of another soldier first. His wound was mortal and he died in hospital 2 days later on July 31. There were no further fatalities for several months, but as one former soldier, who had patrolled the area for a 4 month period said, all hell broke loose. Three SF personnel were killed in the space of just 2 days.

ANDERSONSTOWN 72/73

Private Eddie Atkinson, 1st Bn The Green Howards

We were stationed in 'silver city' and opposite the camp was a bunker dug into the bank; it resembled something from WW1. I believe it was built because of the amount of RPG attacks from this area. We lived underground for the day; it was self contained and what a hole it was. Everything was on duck boards because of the water and to reach the sangar you had to crouch down and shuffle along a long underground trench. Once in the sangar you couldn't stand up properly and all the time you were in there you could hear the rats running up and down the duck boards behind you.

Gunner Steve Corbett, Royal Artillery

I do recall the events of Saturday 4th March and Sunday 5th March 1972. At the junction of Finaghy Road North and Andersonstown Road, our two PIGs were ambushed by up to four gunmen. I was in the back of the lead PIG with 'Scouse' Cureton; about 15 rounds hit ours – one of which hit the edge of the slit where my head was. The rear one returned fire with 14 rounds, but no hits were recorded. It was rumoured that two of the gunmen were responsible for the ambush on the Police PIG, when Johnny Sutton was shot in the head.

Later that day (Saturday) we went out on op 'Cotton Wool' at the Green Briars Club. The idea was to place a cordon around the building, and then send a phone call to say the Army was on its way to raid the place. Three blokes shot out, and were promptly arrested.

On the 5th March, we were again ambushed at the same spot as Saturday, but I was half-expecting this, and had my rifle ready. As I looked out of the slit, I could see a girl lying in the road, and a man went down as though he had been pole-axed. There was a gunman to the left of us with a 'Thompson' standing on top of a grassy mound; he was firing down at our vehicle. I can't remember if it was Pete or Mick Krasnowski who was in the co-drivers seat, but he couldn't get his rifle pointed at the gunman. He still got sixteen rounds off at him though! Dick Rothwell was in the back with me; he fired two shots – and got a stoppage. I got off twelve rounds, but no hits. None of this is done from memory, I kept diaries on both tours I did in Ireland. Everything was written on the day it happened, and represents what I saw and heard at the time.

ANDERSONSTOWN IN THE LONG HOT SUMMER

Major Andrew Macdonald, 1 King's Own Border Regiment

For those who served on that tour, few will forget that long, hot summer of 1976 which seemed to go on forever; hot, scorching, airless days and the four very hectic months. The Vice President of Sinn Fein – by the name of Marie Drum – threatened to close down all of West Belfast and make life impossible for the Army; her 'long hot summer.' But for those that tangled with the Battalion group, it was not a good time. Sadly for one innocent local family, they paid the ultimate price for the IRA's activity.

I was the Recce Platoon commander at the time and based in Glassmullan Camp in Andersonstown. Our CO made it clear to all of us that she wouldn't succeed and it was 'business as usual.' During that 4 months tour, we had 5 companies deployed in that part of Belfast; Arnhem Coy on the 'Murph, in the Henry Taggart Hall, Burma were at Lenadoon, Chindit were at Fort Whiterock, Somme were at Glassmullan Camp in Andersonstown and we had an attached 'Jock' company from the KOSB in the Turf Lodge.

Fortunately or unfortunately, depending on how you look at it, I missed three of the 'big' four weeks of that August due to being on a course in England. So much of my story recounts the coverage we received of the various incidents in the period as well as the tales from the soldiers on my return. That August was the fifth anniversary of Internment (9th August 1971) and the season traditionally gave rise to a wide range of attacks and violence. I left my platoon in the very capable hands of a Staff Sergeant I shall just call 'Steve.' He and the lads really were in the thick of it in Andersonstown. (*see Chapter 9, pp240 and the 'Case of the Damaged Dresses' in the author's* A Long Long War). They were involved in the incident in which the Maguire children were killed.

On the day of this tragedy, 9th August, there was an IRA 'come on' (*an incident designed to draw troops out onto the streets and walk into ambushes*) disguised as a robbery at the Butcher's shop in Rosareen Avenue, a few minutes away from the base. Two of the platoon's vehicles were sent out to investigate and, although the distance involved was only several hundred metres, they were highly suspicious as the anniversary of internment is always a good day to settle scores with the Army. So they advanced with extreme caution.

It only took a matter of minutes to react to the call and to get to the shops from the base. When the patrol arrived, it was deathly quiet; no one was about and it had the atmosphere that something was about to happen. And it did! The first shot fired was very close – it hit the field dressing which the commander had attached to his helmet in order to keep his visor propped open – sometimes you're lucky! We used open topped Land Rovers in those days – mainly for mobility and speedy deployment; not so good in a riot – and hence helmets with visors for each crew member.

Three gunmen were seen running away, and two attempted to escape by car.

The 'contact' report was sent, possibly by Steve. For those not-in-the-know, the contact report is sent immediately in reaction to an incident to provide everyone with sufficient information and act as a trigger for the reaction forces. I do not know the detail but the report was likely to include 'Contact. No casualties; gunmen seen running in the area of.....; am following up; wait out.' It is the crispest, most succinct way of letting the reaction forces know what was happening. Immediately this was heard, the QRF (*Quick Reaction Force*) deployed to prearranged positions, which, in this instance, were two open-top Land Rovers with 4 men per vehicle. They screamed out of the base to set up pre-planned check points to try to cut off any escape routes.

The IRA shooters were Danny Lennon and Michael Chillingworth and both were well known IRA gunmen from the Andersonstown area. After they had shot at the lads, they made their escape in a blue Ford Cortina – stolen earlier, and a standard getaway car – and headed southwards down the Shaw's Road towards Finaghy Road South. The QRF on hearing the contact report drove quickly to one of the pre-prepared positions – coincidentally along the getaway route.

As Lennon and Chillingworth drove south at speed, the QRF vehicle slotted in behind, unaware that the Cortina in front contained the gunmen. The IRA driver must have panicked and thought that he was being chased and the passenger opened fire at the Land Rovers behind. This, of course, alerted to the soldiers that this was their quarry – big mistake – as all of them were good shots, but one, if I recall correctly, was a Bisley standard marksman. After some confusion about whether to stop and fire or drive on after the getaway car, they returned fire.

The QRF fired four shots altogether. They hit the car, killing the driver. The car then went out of control mounted the pavement and tragically smashed into a mother with her three young children, innocently walking on the pavement fatally injuring the children and seriously injuring the mother. After the car had crashed, the other gunman (carrying his Armalite automatic rifle) tried to run away. He was shot and seriously wounded taking no further part in proceedings for a long while.

There was criticism from some quarters of this incident but it was an accident and it could have been avoided If the IRA's planned 'come on' had not taken place. They opened fire on soldiers twice in the space of minutes and their callousness combined with dreadful planning and ineptitude were primarily responsible for those deaths. One of the things which has been forgotten, is that members of the QRF and our medics from the base not only tried desperately to save the lives of the injured children, but also gave mouth to mouth resuscitation to one of the terrorists (the photographs taken at the scene bear witness to all of this). Can you imagine an IRA gunman doing the same for a wounded Squaddie?

There were many incidents on that tour from each of the 5 companies under command; all of which are complete stories in themselves. These are commemorated on a print commissioned after the tour. Fortunately we suffered no fatalities on that very high octane tour but we did have casualties, one in particular that was very serious, which changed the lives and careers of some very fine NCOs and soldiers.

Of note is that Marie Drum and her like never did close down West Belfast in that long hot summer.

On that fateful day – August 10, 1976 – Joanne Maguire (8) and her little brothers Andrew (just 6 weeks old) and John (2) who died the following day, lost their lives when the out of control Cortina driven by Chillingworth and Lennon ploughed into them. Their injured mother, Anne Maguire (35) and the mother of 3 other children took her own life some 3 years later; her life ruined by the tragedy. From the outpouring of grief and sorrow at this appalling accident came the birth of the 'Peace People.' This group was formed by two Belfast women: Mairead Corrigan and Betty Williams and whilst short-lived (they were despised and threatened by the IRA) won international fame.

Danny Lennon (23) a known player was shot by the Borderers and died at the scene.

SOLDIER, PARACHUTE REGIMENT

Andersonstown Revenge

Besides the obvious, one of the many problems in Northern Ireland during the 'troubles' was the vicious protection rackets that sprung up all over the place. These had absolutely nothing to do with the ongoing political problems; they were simply groups of thugs cashing in on the fears of the innocent people in their area. Many of these gangs ran 'drinking clubs' and extorted money from surrounding businesses and householders under the guise of protecting them from damage to their property or injury to themselves. They often professed to be part of the IRA or Protestant Paramilitary, depending in what area they were in. They may have been loosely aligned with one or the other faction, but in reality they were just lining their own pockets.

One such gang held sway in an area patrolled by one of the Parachute Regiment battalions. Intelligence pointed the finger at them for causing a large number of vicious assaults and property damage yet nobody was willing to say anything for obvious reasons. It all came to a head when a young man and woman were severely bashed outside the club by several men. Both were hospitalised and neither would say why they were assaulted. The 'system' was hamstrung as without a complaint they couldn't go and get whoever did it. What really galled everyone was the brazen insolence of these thugs. They knew they were untouchable and loved to flaunt the fact. So plan 'A' was hatched without the knowledge of the hierarchy. Two weeks of careful observation showed that the head thug had an Achilles' heel; he was a man of habit. At 0200 every morning two of his hooligans would escort him home via the same route. Part of the route saw them walking into a long unlit alley, the ideal place for an ambush.

So used were they to the mobile patrols that they never foresaw a threat slowly cruising up the main street after them. They turned down the lane and were halfway along it when another patrol vehicle blocked their way. Still they didn't understand what was going on, simply halting and watching as three of the crew dismounted and began walking toward them. The two bodyguards went to get out their pistols but an ominous coughing behind them somehow changed their minds. Even a blind man would recognise that they were hemmed in. Now bravado took over and their leader began the usual cocky confrontational abuse they normally spewed out when they saw the patrols. Yet it had no outward response from the advancing patrol members, they all remained quiet. With faces camouflaged up and the darkness of the alleyway providing extra protection there was no way of recognising who each Tom was, but it was obvious they were a threat.

Surrounded by heavily armed men, silent men, the three gangsters finally decided that abuse wasn't having an effect and for the first time in ages they must have felt helpless. Abuse became questions, and when their questions weren't answered it was obvious that something unpleasant was going to happen. It didn't take much to disarm them and tie their hands behind their backs and place gags around their mouths. What came next was a total shock and was extremely humiliating to say the least. Their trousers and underpants were ripped down around their ankles. Gloved hands then removed their wallets and put the contents into smock pockets. Then someone produced a tube of super glue and the wallets were covered in it and quickly jammed between their buttocks. For some unknown reason this clearly upset them and as a consequence a tirade of unintelligible sound came from mouths. But that wasn't the end. Another Tom produced a large grease gun and quickly began pumping the contents into the crotch of each man's underpants. When he was finished the underpants and trousers were hoisted back up and belts redone. As if that wasn't enough, as parting gesture sandbags full of human excrement were placed over their heads and patted down.

Having finished, the assailants quietly walked back to their respective vehicles and vanished. The whole episode took no more than fifteen minutes – it was a well thought out and well executed plan. There was a half-hearted inquiry about the whereabouts of each patrol in that area around the time of the attack, but nobody was officially found to be within a mile of it. Neither did it alter what the gangsters did; but it did make sure that the highly embarrassed leader looked over his shoulder while that particular battalion was in Northern Ireland. What goes around comes around. I should point out, of course, that we confiscated aforementioned illegal weapons!

On October 31, another Royal Artillery man, Gunner Ian Docherty (27) died of his wounds after being shot three days earlier. He was being transported in a military convoy, when he was shot on Stockman's Lane. The following day, two RUC Detectives, Stanley Corry (28) a married man with two children and 31 year old William Russell, also married with a child, were both killed. They had been investigating a robbery at a shop in the Avoca Centre in Andersonstown when they were ambushed by IRA gunmen. As one soldier said at the time 'It was just too bloody easy for the IRA to kill soldiers and cops.'

Andersonstown was reasonably quite, other than the routine riots, until a mad 72 hours in June. On the 7th, Sergeant Charles Coleman (29) of the Royal Artillery was on a mobile patrol near Tullymore Gardens, when a shot fired from Kenard Avenue hit him, fatally wounding him. Just two days later, a UDR soldier, Roy Staunton (27) was murdered in cold blood, as he drove home after finishing work, at a factory in the Andersonstown area.

Gunner Steve Corbett, Royal Artillery

Here's a cutting from the *Belfast Telegraph* ...

'In Belfast, terrorists used a dummy filled with explosives in an attempt to injure troops. A patrol went to Glen Road after reports of a 'body' lying in the road. This turned out to be a dummy and it exploded when the soldiers arrived. Some shots were fired at the troops. One civilian was injured in the blast.'

That incident was on Friday 18th February, 1972. We had gone out on op 'yobbo' at 7.30pm, and then we got reports of a man being tarred and feathered and tied to railings opposite the Ulster Brewery. I was in the lead PIG with Captain 'B' along with Mick Krasnowski, 'Titch' Friel and Albert; Tom McSherry was in charge of the rear vehicle. As we approached the 'body', it was rather obvious to us all (except the Captain) that it was a tailor's dummy. A group of school kids walked past it, and then a drunk came staggering down the path

Tom McSherry called him over and said to him 'Go and see what's wrong with your mate over there.' The drunk ambled over towards the dummy, and all of a sudden there was an almighty whoosh and bright red

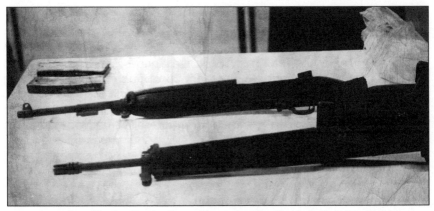

Arms found by Joe Harris, Green Howards, Glen Road, Belfast (Joe Harris)

flash. 'Titch' was thrown to the front of the PIG, and 'Krash' was blinded for a few minutes. I got the force of the blast on the right side of my face which made my ears ring like mad; a problem which I still have after 35 years! The PIG was undamaged, even though we were only 10 feet away from the blast. Captain 'B' was trying to crawl about on the floor of the PIG, and he was in a state of absolute panic. First he was telling us to drive on, and then telling us to reverse. A gunman opened up on us with what sounded like a pistol, but the shots were way off target. When we got ourselves organised, we checked out the poor drunk. Fortunately for him the bomb went off as he staggered against a tree, which saved him from the full force; all he got was a large chunk of railing through his thigh. The actions of the officer were not what you would have expected.

It would be fair to say that we can all have our moments of panic, and he should not be judged badly for his conduct on this particular day. We all react in different ways to moments of extreme danger. I merely relate what I wrote at the time.

August of that year was to prove the bloodiest month in the story of Andersonstown's involvement in the troubles. Four soldiers, all from different regiments were killed in a period of just 19 days. The first to fall was Lance Corporal David Card (21) of the Royal Green Jackets (RGJ) who was shot and killed near Bearnagh Drive. Ten days later, Major Storrey (36) of the Royal Artillery – the most senior SF man to die in the area, and Craftsman Brian Hope (20) of the Royal Electrical and Mechanical Engineers (REME) were both killed by a bomb. The two men were based at Casement Park and were crossing a river near where Army engineers were altering the outside of the park. Nine days later, Fusilier Alan Tingey (25) of the Royal Regiment of Fusiliers (RRF) was shot and killed as Kenard Avenue claimed its second victim. The Fusilier was married and had two children.

ANDERSONSTOWN BUS DEPOT

Fusilier David Dews, Royal Regiment of Fusiliers

At the time that the IRA hunger striker, Bobby Sands was nearing death, my platoon of 3 RRF was billeted at Andersonstown Bus Depot just off the Andersonstown Road. The Belfast Bus Company had closed down the service here because of the high numbers of buses being hijacked and set alight or used as barricades. As the only comfortable seats in the place were on the buses, we slept on them and stretched out as best we could. The best seats were the long bench ones at the back, upstairs.

We had three lads stagging on at the front and 4 roaming guards to give us protection from attack whilst we rested. Conditions were rough with no washing or cooking facilities; we had the odd tea urn brought in but that was it! When we needed food or just a wash, we had to leg it out of the back and up to Woodburn RUC station, about 50 yards up towards where the Andersonstown Road meets Kennedy Way. It was far too dangerous to walk, so we had to run, in full kit and if we dropped anything, eating irons etc., we left them where they fell; we had no wish to die because of a dropped spoon!

Bobby Sands died on the night of May 5, 1981 (*after 66 days of hunger strike in Long Kesh, renamed the 'Maze' where he was serving 14 years for gun-running for the IRA*) and all hell broke loose. Everything kicked off; the noise of screaming, shouting, explosions, banging of dustbin lids, blowing of whistles etc was just too much to take in.

We were ordered out on foot patrol that night, and, little did we know, but it would be 24 hours before we would see what passed for beds again. We dashed out of the rear entrance of the Bus depot and turned left down the Andersonstown Road towards the shops. That night, we were so tired, out for so long and forced to double everywhere, that it was only the adrenaline which kept us going. At one point we were all knelt down, SLRs in the aim, giving all round defence and I fell asleep; only for a millisecond, but I did nod off.

Anyway, the boyos had barricaded the road and had placed about a dozen beer kegs – nicked from the nearby pub – and placed tyres and a burned-out car to stop us. Word got back to us that the kegs were probably booby-trapped so we had to be extremely wary. We just stopped where we were but then got the order to move on and we could see kids of 10 or 11, lifting heavy debris onto the barricades, egged on by the older ones. We were powerless to stop them and we had to remain focused because if you didn't concentrate, it could be fatal. I was so tempted, at the time, to cock my SLR and loose off a full mag of 20 rounds into the ranks of the older men who were watching the younger ones.

Fortunately, we got through that nightmare evening without serious injury or mishaps. We had the odd cuts and bruises and a brick or two (or thirty) flew over our heads, but that was it. After Bobby Sands' funeral, we all felt fucked-in and after that, it was a blur of activity and then we were home; needless to say, I was so pleased to say goodbye to Andersonstown Road.

OPERATION MOTORMAN

Colour Sergeant Ken Ambrose, Royal Green Jackets

Within days we found ourselves at Palace Barracks polishing up the old skills ready for deployment into Andersonstown and it was only a matter of a few days after that we were living in a school, right in the middle of the Andersonstown area. Also billeted in that school were A Company who patrolled the Turf Lodge area to our north. That base came to be known later as Fort Monagh.

The OC believed that you had to use saturation patrolling to control this sort of hard area so we were patrolling in one form or another 24hrs a day. It was just after last light that I assembled with my platoon for a four hour patrol which would take us from 8pm to midnight. We began to walk through the school area which was still occupied by A Company and we were about 20 yards from the front gate when several semi-automatic HV rounds fire cracked overhead through the darkness. I ran forward towards the school gate and as I did so I could see muzzle flashes coming from two positions in the gully which lay in between the houses and about 75 metres forward and half left from the school gate. I saw sparks fly as a couple of incoming rounds hit the ground about two metres to my right and it was at that point that I cocked my Stirling and while still running fired two short bursts in the direction of the muzzle flashes. The first section had caught up with me and arrived at the school fence and gate at the same time as I did. The rest of the platoon had taken cover in rear of us. One or two return rounds were fired by the Riflemen with me and whilst this was going on I had a quick word with Jethro, the section commander and indicated that he and one other, Dave 'R' would move left and cross the road further up from the gully and then left flank it while the remainder gave covering fire. This was all set to happen when the parachute flares started coming up from the B Company Ops Room area.

For the next five minutes I tried to get the flares stopped so that we could move unseen in darkness across the road and eventually had to send a runner to do the job. The radio being too busy and me not being within shouting distance of the Portacabin that served a B Company Ops Room! Suddenly the firing stopped and I knew we were going to have to be quick to catch the retreating gunmen in the gully. I called to Charley 'B', the other section commander, to move across the road and on to the road left of the gully whilst Jethro and Dave 'R' were to clear the gully itself. I with the remainder moved to act as cut off on the road to the right of the gully.

It was not long before we realised that the two gunmen had made good their escape and despite several house searches nothing was found. During the remainder of the patrol only one incident stays in my mind and that was that during moving through a garage area one of the Riflemen, John 'C', reported a strong smell of marzipan coming from one of the garages. Having spoken to the OC on the radio I was told to stay well away from that garage. He informed me that ATO would deal with it first thing in the morning.

When I got back to the Ops Room the OC was waiting for me. We talked about the evenings events and he asked me to get out on the ground before first light because he reckoned that those weapons which had been used to pepper the front gate must have been hidden along the escape route used by the gunmen and that they would still be there. The gully on either side was bordered by gardens which in turn backed on to the houses on either side.

About three and a half hours later with dawn just appearing we left the school and moved silently though the gully with one section providing forward security and the other searching the hedges and garden areas. It was quite a way down that we found the two weapons used against us the previous night and by that time the sun was well up. The weapons, an MI Carbine and a No 4 Lee Enfield, were hidden in a hedge well wrapped up. I spoke to the OC on the radio and he arranged to meet me near the find.

At the place where the weapons were found the gully became a large gap of waste land with 250 metres separating the backs of the houses. For that reason I had posted sentries along the far side of the gully to protect us while we worked at removing the weapons and carrying out a token search of the house in whose back garden they were found.

Within a half hour we had completed the search and were ready to begin moving back. The sentries on the far side of the gully were withdrawn and with Albert 'G', my platoon Sergeant, and Jethro 'S' I began walking towards the road side of the house where the platoon had been assembled in preparation for our move back to base. Major 'J' with his signaller Dave 'C' had started to walk back along the edge of the gully and it was then that the first shot rang out.

The grass in the gully was up to a metre long in most places and I hit the ground and started crawling well away from where I went down. In a few metres I was soaked with the morning dew. There was a silence for a few seconds during which I heard Major 'J' shout that his signaller had been hit. I could hear Albert and Jethro moving through the grass ahead of me as we all three started to look for the OC and Dave 'C'.

The rounds from the unseen gunman continued to thump into the ground around us. As I had been the furthest from Dave 'C' when the first shot arrived I was the last to reach him. He was on his left side and there was a hole the size of a 50p piece in the side of his neck. Every few seconds he moaned but Albert 'G' and Jethro were using everything they could find to stop the bleeding from the entry and exit holes on both sides of his neck. The field dressings we had with us were soaked in seconds, as were our berets. The OC was talking on the radio getting the MO and a cordon in place that would trap the gunman. The radio was still attached to 'C' because to have removed it would have meant presenting the gunman with another easy target.

Looking back towards the house we had so recently searched I could just see the business end of Dave 'R's L42 sniper rifle sticking out from the upstairs window. I gave a 'watch and shoot' fire order to those of my platoon who were in a position to return fire. Within a minute the return fire began. As soon as the first rounds from the platoon started to smack into the hedgerow on the far side of the open ground the incoming fire stopped. Less than a minute later the MO was with us and doing his best to treat our wounded man.

Even after we could see the cordon from Support Company moving into position we were still very concerned about standing up to lift the stretcher with Dave 'C' on it out to the road where the armoured ambulance was waiting for him. After the stretcher with Dave on it was loaded into the ambulance I looked around and took stock of the scene. The whole of the area was packed with the rest of B Company and platoons from A Company and most of them were heavily engaged in house searching. Other platoons from Support Company were providing the cordon to our south.

The OC allocated my Platoon a dozen or so houses and left us to it and we were about half an hour into our house searches when an explosion rocked the whole area. It took me seconds to realise that the bang had come from the area of the garages where we had reported that strong smell of marzipan. As I went round the corner a scene of carnage met my eyes with bodies all over the place and my OC lying in a heap on the other side of the road. Some people remained standing and in the few seconds it had taken me to get there those who were able were already helping those hurt by the explosion. Predictably the reaction from the local population was one of jubilation and several Riflemen were quick to quell this demonstration in the only way that Riflemen know how and the mood soon returned to a state of sullen disapproval.

It turned out that OC 'B' Company had opened the garage door and triggered a small bomb. The door had blown off and in doing so it had injured the OC's arm and anyone standing in its path as it was blown across the road. Several others were suffering ear and burn damage but the most seriously injured was the OC. At about 4pm that day I led my platoon back to our base to get some rest before the next patrol. Tomorrow was another day. On our return that which most of us already knew was confirmed. Dave 'C' had died of his wounds.

I paid the OC a visit at Musgrove Park Hospital the following day and his first words to me were:' That was a bloody silly thing to do wasn't it?' I had the good sense not to reply.

On March 29, the following year, 33 year old Private Michael Marr, a married soldier with one child was shot by an IRA gunman in the Andersonstown Park area. The IRA had held a family hostage and fired the fatal shot from their house in Fruithill Park. Private Marr was a member of the Gordon Highlanders.

It would be 1976, before this notorious area was to claim another SF life. On August 26, RUC Constable James Heaney was visiting his mother's house in Andersonstown, when he was attacked by IRA gunmen. He was shot and killed as he worked on his car.

Fifteen months later, Bernagh Drive, where David Card of the RGJ was murdered in 1971, was the scene of the cold-blooded killing of an off duty soldier. Irish Guardsman Samuel Murphy (21) was visiting his mother's house and he was ambushed by the IRA and shot several times; he died of his wounds, 10 days later.

HATRED AND CREATURE COMFORTS IN ANDERSONSTOWN

WO2 Roy Banwell, Cheshire Regiment

I was one of the lucky ones on this tour; it was the first time I was to come under direct fire. That in itself is not very lucky but at least I am around to tell the tale. Our Section was ordered to set up a vehicle checkpoint (VCP) on Glen road, by the Brewery. I was facing to the west of the VCP, when an almighty bang went off behind me. Something instantly hit me in the left ear; I put my hand up to my ear and pulled out a piece of red brick. I looked round and there was a hole in the brickwork that I could have fitted my fist into. A shot had been fired through the VCP from the east. The bullet had travelled past everyone standing in the road checking vehicles, and hit the wall just behind me.

Working out the trajectory later, the bullet had landed within two inches of my spine, and, on that day I had very nearly became a statistic of Northern Ireland and at the very least a wheel chair case. I was to spend my 21st birthday a few days later, looking out of a sangar window, down the streets of a miserably wet, 16th June in Andersonstown; my morale seemed to match the day to perfection. We were grateful to the public back home and the Newspapers during our tours of NI, because they made life a little more comfortable for us. The media campaigned to provide the troops with TV's, games and small creature comforts, and we will be eternally grateful to all of you. The conditions we had to endure at times were hard, and the overcrowding acute. Our platoon occupied a single portacabin, with bunk beds three high in a room only about eight feet high. This didn't leave much room to move except to lay flat on your back on a bed. There were not enough beds for everyone in the platoon, so someone had to be on duty all the time or you were without anywhere to sleep. When you came off duty you would have to search around to find an empty bed to crawl into and get your head down. Movement and noise was a constant problem along with being woken up in the dark to be asked who you were. Section commanders didn't know where their sections were sleeping and didn't want to put the lights on to find them. This was made worse by the fact that the population that surround you all wanted you dead, preferably by their own hands.

ANDY TOWN

Gunner Stephen Corbett, Royal Artillery

Most guns used against us in the early 70s originated from the good old USA; those were the days when the Mayor of New York actively supported the IRA. Those were the days when most Americans supported the fight against the terrorist British Army, and then came 9/11.

On a lighter note, whilst on patrol in Andersonstown in 71/72 one of our patrols came across a man carrying a large suitcase. Usual procedure took place: 'Where you from?' 'Where you going?' and 'What's your name?' Not satisfied with his answer, they made him open the case and spread the entire contents across the pavement while they checked them over and over again. Next they spread him against a wall; they then proceeded to give him a VERY thorough body search.

Why the hell would a Yank come on vacation to Andersonstown? Revenge is very sweet at times!

In 1979, the IRA showed that it was learning its lessons and that their constant observation of British Army tactics was paying off. Although manned by people who had obvious psychopathic tendencies who might have been gangsters in another era, they had watched and learned. On April 5, having taken over a house and shop opposite Andersonstown RUC station, they waited for an Army mobile patrol to return. As was procedure, two soldiers in a Land Rover dismounted and waited for an armoured vehicle to pull into the courtyard. As they did so, gunmen opened fire on the two soldiers killing them both. The two soldiers, both from the Blues and Royals, were trooper Anthony Dykes (25) and married with two children and 20 year old Anthony Thornett. The two Troopers were from Yorkshire and Coventry, respectively.

It was to be a further 8 years until another soldier died, but almost exactly one year later on April 5, RUC Constable William Magill was killed in a hail of M60 machinegun bullets as he investigated a break – in at Stewartstown Road. He was a married man, aged 24 years, and based at Woodburn RUC station elsewhere in the city. One year later, the INLA killed Constable Gary Martin (28) with a bomb placed in a suspect vehicle in Andersonstown.

On June 15, 1984, Constable Michael Todd (22) was taking part in a raid on a house on Lenadoon Avenue when they, literally, stumbled onto an INLA safe house. During the course of the shoot out, Constable Todd was shot and killed but his colleague shot and killed INLA gunman, Paul McCann. Todd thus became the final RUC member to be killed in the Andersonstown area.

View from the former RUC station at Andersontown; opposite the barbers, which the IRA took over and killed Blues and Royals' soldiers Thornett and Dykes, 5 April 1979 (Ken Wharton)

Andersonstown however, was not finished with the SF and in the June and July of 1987, two SF members were killed. On June 4, Private Joseph Leach (21) of the Queen's Lancashire Regiment (QLR) was shot and died shortly afterwards. He was on a mobile patrol in the Shaw's Road area when attacked by IRA gunmen who had taken over a nearby house, holding the family hostage.

The area claimed its final SF victim on July 23, 1987, when UDR Private, William Megrath (46) was ambushed on the Stewartstown Road, as he drove home from his full-time job at a nearby factory.

MUSGRAVE PARK HOSPITAL

Separated from Andersonstown by the width of the M1 motorway which links Belfast in the north to Dublin in the south, the hospital, especially the military wing, is within easy reach of what RSM Saxby (RAMC) called 'the bad people.'

RSM R.T. Saxby, Royal Army Medical Corps

As we were posted to Northern Ireland for what was supposed to be a two year posting (mine ended up over three years), obviously we were allowed out, to the city centre etc. I 'lived in' the single Sergeants' mess, in what was called the echelon just down from the hospital, a secure fortress as we were situated in West Belfast my wife and son lived back in Yorkshire, we felt it was safer. Life was good, and busy, we were all very close, because of the locality and why we were there.

The military wing was run as a NHS hospital would. But we must remember the 'bad people' were very, very close. As I was the RQMS I dealt with mainly good people in the "civvy" wing, we became good friends. If I said I had been to a certain place over the weekend, they would be the first to tell me not to be so stupid.

In March 1989, our company SGT Major 'MH' was posted and replaced by a man who would become a great friend: Phil Cross. We worked and played hard, Phil lived out with his wife Jan and children Andrew and Richard. We became established thespians at the local Amateur theatre, in fact I was terrible, but that is another story.

One day I remember we both went into the city centre on a Saturday afternoon for some serious 'shopping', well a pint or two. Whilst sitting in a pub enjoying our second pint, a stranger sat opposite us and quietly said: 'Sirs you need to leave; NOW'. I thought it great advice but Phil, being Phil said 'I'm not going f-----g anywhere.' So the stranger said: 'Leave now; I am from 7/10 UDR Intelligence and you have been targeted'. We left lively, as did the guy from 7/10 UDR; as we got round the corner, did we hear a screech of tyres and a slamming of car doors, or was it our imagination? We arrived back at the hospital to be met by the INT officer and others, we had been targeted, bugger!! Me life number two! One for Phil!

Whilst on duty officer at MW MPH, I had a call: 'Helivac incoming', and we went out to the heli pad, which, of course, was now cordoned off by the infantry battalion in station. We had no more news on what to expect.

The helicopter landed; I went to the aircraft to 'triage sort' and could see that there were three casualties. These were two walking wounded and one Sergeant; he was unconscious and bleeding to death from a wound in his stomach. I attempted to stop the bleeding to no avail. So I put my whole fist in the wound, which stopped the bleeding.

We evacuated him on the stretcher, with my fist still in place. We drove back to the hospital, my fist still there. The surgeons and doctors then took over, I retrieved my hand, he was operated on, but he was a very poorly soldier. We attempted to contact his family, as he was sadly dying. He had not regained consciousness and his wife arrived the next morning. We found out he had fallen out with his mother, who lived abroad, just before deployment to N.I. She was contacted; the Sergeant was still alive, but only just. His mother arrived two days after the incident. The doctors said he should have died at least 24 hours ago his injuries were so bad. His mother arrived, walked into the ward held his hand, spoke to him and he silently passed away.

The soldier was Sergeant Michael Matthews (37) from Dorset, an NCO in the Parachute Regiment. He was mortally wounded at Cullyhanna, Armagh by an IRA landmine on July 27, 1988; he died of his terrible wounds two days later.

On November 2, 1991, an IRA 'sympathiser' – a hospital porter – placed a bomb outside the Junior Ranks club at the hospital. It exploded whilst the off duty soldiers were watching television, killing two of them and injuring many.

CSM Philip Cross (33) was married with two children and was from the north east of England. Craig Pantry, RCT Driver, was 20, single and was from the Gwent area of Wales.

A contemporary press report of the time, naturally outraged at this attack read:

'You Evil Cowards.' 'Even the heavens wept as a shocked world witnessed the depths plumbed in the IRA's latest example of man's inhumanity to man.

Rain has washed much of the blood and gore from the scene of yesterday's cowardly attack on the military wing at Belfast's Musgrave Park Hospital. A bomb blast left 2 soldiers dead, dozens hurt, and 8 people seriously wounded including a 7 year old girl. But nothing can erase the stain caused by a nation's shame at a haven for the sick and dying being devastated by cold-hearted killers.'

RSM R.T. Saxby, Royal Army Medical Corps

After a couple more scrapes I was finally posted to Catterick and promoted to WOI (RSM), well deserved of course, in June/July 1991, the last goodbye was from Phil, I didn't know how final it would be! Whilst in my office in Catterick my phone rang it was Phil Cross, all excited because England had got through to the Rugby World Cup Final against Australia and they were having a do in the 'Sin Bin', the unit club.

The day had arrived. I watched the final on television, at half time we were still in the game, NEWSFLASH: the military hospital has been bombed with two fatalities. I knew Phil was one of them!

To this day I have no idea how. But there it is, sadly I was right. They had bombed a hospital, with the bomb timed to go off at half time, killing two – Phil and 'Taff' Pantry. My life number 3; Phil: game over. The IRA thought I was still there, because they sent a wreath to my mother in Kent on the afternoon it happened. When I am asked what my thoughts are of the whole situation and the loss of friends and a great friend, I say 'it is all a total waste'. Phil's funeral was held at Salford Cathedral. I was in charge of the funeral party, at Jan's request, a terrible day, and the saddest one I can think of.

MUSGRAVE PARK HOSPITAL

Eddie Dixon, Light Infantry

I was with 3LI and we were doing a rolling VCP along the Falls Road; it was a dark foggy night and as I remember it, I was the last man as we walked down the middle of the road. I remember turning to look behind me, and, as I turned, I was struck by a car and thrown up in the air and landed on its bonnet. It stopped, and I was tended to and the police turned up, followed by an ambulance; all this took place over a period of time. I recall that my weapon and other equipment were taken from me by my Sgt, Paul Jasper.

I was taken by ambulance to the military wing of Musgrave Park Hospital (MPH), examined and put on a ward. My knee was the major problem and, over the next few days, I was seen by doctors, specialists etc and even had a visit by my CO and RSM, on November 2nd 1991. It was the day of the Rugby World Cup Final and my beloved England were playing Australia. In my ward, there were 6 of us, all from various regiments, all getting on together; 5 were bed bound and I was a walking wounded so to speak

I remember hobbling up to the telly and turning it over onto the Rugby and then went back to my bed to watch the game. At some stage, during the final, timings not known, there was a large explosion; I can remember the windows shattering; the television blew up and a large fireball shot up the whole of the ward. There was also a toilet cubicle next to my bed and the toilet from the upstairs ward came crashing down through the ceiling and smashed off our toilet. There was now smoke and dust everywhere and total confusion. Eventually we were all moved from the ward to a large reception area, just outside the bar, and those in beds were put in corridors etc., with the walking wounded outside.

At first, we were told that there had been a huge gas explosion, then later we found out it had been a bomb. The next bits, I was unaware of at the time but later found out. Apparently, the CO sent the padre over to MPH to find me as the HQ Company of the battalion was over the road at St Angelo. On the Padre's first visit, he was unable to find me as there were people everywhere, inside and outside; he went back and told the CO he could not find me. Allegedly, he was told to get back over and not to return until I had been accounted for. I assume that meant dead or alive!

At the same time my wife at the time was informed by the families' office in Germany what had happened and my father (Thomas Darnton Dixon) was informed by phone from St Angelo.

The next bit I will remember for the rest of my life! There were people being brought out of the bar and one man in particular was covered in blood and screaming that his daughter was still in there. It was not until I read your book, that I found out it was the barman; it was carnage in the bar area, with rubble everywhere. We later found out that two medics had been murdered. At that point, the barman was reunited with his daughter; both covered in dust, the man also in blood. I will cherish that moment, when they were hugging each other, for the rest of my life; it brought a tear to my eye

The two medics who were murdered are gone but not forgotten; I think of you both every Remembrance day.

The two killed that day were Warrant Officer Phillip Cross of the Royal Army Medical Corps and Driver Craig Pantry of the RCT. The details of the cowardly attack on the hospital by the IRA are recounted in the author's earlier book *A Long Long War* and I do not propose to repeat the facts.

Musgrave Park Hospital, these days flanked by a large, modern industrial estate, in the days of the trouble, sat uneasily, less than a kilometre from the fringes of Andersonstown and less than two kilometres from the Falls Road. As it was within easy reach of two major Republican areas, it was an equally easy target for the IRA, and so it proved, as posterity has recorded.

ANDERSONSTOWN ATTACKS

WO2 Roy Banwell, Cheshire Regiment

We were whisked away to our camp in PIGs and Saracen armoured vehicles to Andersonstown in Belfast. There was a high wire fence in the middle of the housing estate, with a corrugated tin sheeted perimetre, surrounding Glassmullan camp. There were sangars at each corner rather like a castle and sand bags everywhere. There were to be many more sandbags by the time we left, after our four months incarceration in that camp. Everyone we came in contact with seemed to abhor us, not that I blame them. We represented the very establishment they wished to be rid of. The fact we would have got on famously had the circumstances been different was neither here nor there. We were there to do a job and they were there because they lived there and couldn't behave themselves. Shootings and explosions, punctuated by a couple of minor riots per day became our life. It was amazing how quickly you adjust to violence. When the violence is absent you tended to miss it, it becomes a way of life. I suppose that is why they cannot give it up now; it becomes like a cancer, it needs cutting out but the cutting out might kill the patient in the process. One of the camp sangars overlooked the house that Bernadette Devlin, later to become Bernadette McAliskey lived in. That must have been most thrilling for her and needless to say the curtains were always closed. I used to wonder what, if any, plans against us were hatched behind those curtains.

The battalion suffered many casualties during this four-month tour. If I can remember rightly, nine soldiers of the 22nd were shot; luckily none fatally. One of the lads was shot from the side, through one arm, through the butt of his rifle, and the bullet carried on through his stomach and out through his other arm. Talk about luck, none of his vital organs were hit, years later he still played football for the Battalion. Unlike another lad who was shot in the stomach, the bullet exited through his back passage, taking all his lower bowels with it; his short time in the Army was over. When he left hospital he was discharged from the forces.

Your life goes on hold in situations like NI. Work is all that matters and the workload is very heavy. It was a continual round of guard duties, patrolling and 'alert' platoons, and any spare time in between was taken up by filling sandbag; thousands upon thousands of sandbags. These were used to build bombproof walls around the camp. Cookhouse fatigues and general camp duties like cleaning the ablutions also played a large part of our daily routine; sadly, only about four hours a day was allocated to the noble art of sleeping.

The camp was later to be on the receiving end of an IRA mortar attack. My patrol was at the loading/unloading bay, just ready to leave camp when I heard the first couple of explosions on the other side of our small camp. We were just leaving camp when the Padre of all people stopped us. A bad choice as far as I was concerned; one, I wanted to be out of the line of fire, (Mortar rounds are pretty indiscriminate whom they kill and maim) and, secondly, we needed to be out on the ground to try and catch the people firing at us. The old saying, 'the best form of defence is attack', springs to mind. It wasn't to be, the Padre refused to let us pass and had the gates locked. God bless him as he was only thinking of us. The fact that we had to stay in the camp and be at the mercy of the incoming exploding and unexploded bombs littering the camp was neither here nor there. One of the lads (Malcolm Lamb) was recording an audio tape to his wife at the time of the attack. It made for interesting listening later, with all the explosions and orders being shouted, I wonder if he has still got the tape. One unexploded Mortar bomb went through the roof of a portacabin and landed on the bed of some lucky person; lucky because he wasn't in at the time. Another unexploded bomb landed on the roof of the operations room. The people inside at the time said they could hear it rolling around on the roof; unsure which way it was rolling, so unsure in which direction to leave the building; all the time wondering if it was going to explode.

TRAGEDY AT TWINBROOK

Warrant Officer Dougie Durrant, Royal Pioneer Corps

I went on location to Woodburn Camp, situated on the outskirts of the city of Belfast; it was home to the RUC and the Blues & Royals who had just started their tour; the area of operation being Andersonstown and Twinbrook.

Two days had passed and I had not been out on ops for some time, so I walked to the ops room and asked if anything was on. They asked who I was and I said: 'I came in on Sunday and introduced myself.' The OC was typical Household Division; privileged and born with silver spoon in his mouth. I left him to it and went off to find the search team advisor, a Corporal-Major Tucker; nice man. I asked him if he needed any help with searches and he told me that he was glad that myself and the dog were there and he gave me a free hand.

Suddenly, there was a burst of automatic gun fire which could be heard in the distance. 'Right Dougie; let's go. Andersonstown Road RUC; wounded; contact still on going.' I arrived with the QRF and there were feathers everywhere. The gunmen had used a mattress to silence the weapon. Across the road was a wounded female Police officer; her hand bleeding from where she had been shot. I had located the firing point so that ATO could move in, and, by this time. 'Moby' had arrived with his tracker dog. 'Which way Doug?' I told him that I didn't know and that he may have got on a bike and fucked off according to the Police.

I got back to Woodburn and put my dog 'Bluce' back in his kennel. The Blues & Royals were planning a disco for the Saturday night and had invited the local girls and I told Corporal-Major Tucker that it might not be a good idea to have a Disco here; but that's what the OC wanted. Saturday came and the disco started; I walked around to take 'Bluce' for a walk before hitting the sack. Just as I got to his kennel, a shot rang out at the front gate, and I thought that someone had had an ND (negligent discharge). Then more shots rang out. I'm thinking: 'what the fuck is going on?' Then three rounds impacted on the kennel; fuck, someone is shooting at me inside the camp. I ran to the ops room where I found two soldiers in shock and Corporal – Major Tucker getting briefed on what was going on. I asked him what was going on and he told me that one of the lads had got drunk on duty and had had an ND at the front gate. He had then shot at the QRF returning to base and he then proceeded to shoot up the camp. 'Where is your pistol, Dougie?' he asked and I told him that I had it with me and he told me to come with him. We walked around to the back of the cookhouse where the QRF had cornered the soldier. We were immediately informed that he had shot a guard in the sangar and someone said: 'Fuck; we need to take him out.' With that, the QRF commander and Tucker went around the wall and then all hell let loose; shots rang out over the base, and the civvies outside must have thought that the IRA were attacking.

It all went quiet and I went around the corner and there was a single shot from a 7.62 SLR. I saw that Tucker and the QRF commander were lying on the floor, with blood pissing from gunshot wounds to their bodies. I gave the medic my field dressings to patch their wounds, but they were both in a bad way and Tucker was to die later that night.

The Soldier – Trooper Maggs – was around the back of the cookhouse; lying there dead. I walked on past; it was not my place to be there. I got to the other side where I spoke to the RUC officer who had tried to shoot Maggs. I just muttered: 'How is he?' and the reply came back: 'Very dead mate!' The following morning I went back to Palace Barracks and they all asked me what had happened, but I was tired so went down to Rhonda's mum and fell asleep. The previous day's events were going through my mind and the big question was: 'WHY?'

Later it came on the news but there was no mention of the soldier who was drunk and the pointless death of an outstanding warrant officer. Maggs' father was on the news saying what a good soldier he was, but I don't think that he was told the truth.

On February 25, 1979, after shooting and killing Staff Corporal-Major John Tucker, whilst in an allegedly drunken state, Trooper Edward Maggs of the Blues and Royals was shot dead by comrades. Many believe – as does the author – that his comrades, tragically, had no other option. A report of the death was printed by both Sinn Fein and by the English-based Troops Out Movement, 'Oliver's Army.' Trooper Maggs' mother said: 'He was a victim of Northern Ireland just as surely as if he'd been shot in the back by a sniper's bullet.'

INCIDENT IN BELFAST

Mark 'C', Royal Artillery and UDR

By 1982 the UDR had taken over the security gates in the city centre, and one by one they stopped being manned until only one was manned throughout shopping times and one at night for access.

The manned gate was in Castle Street and was called X17; it still had a sangar and search area and everyone got searched coming through it. It was important as it was the main route coming in from West Belfast and the soldiers in the Divis Tower OP could inform us if any known players were on their way into the city centre.

It was also our job to open up the gates in the morning, usually between 06:30 and 07:00; this was done by the early patrol brick and they went on to man X17 first thing. Because they were the first ones up, the old army law: I'm awake so everyone is awake was usually in force, and they would make a racket so everyone knew they were up. I wasn't surprised, therefore, to be rudely awakened by my then, and still now, best mate, Norm; I told him to 'F*** ff,' and I had only just got back to sleep, when I was awakened again by my then brother – in – law, Vic. He shouted 'Get up; the Provies have bombed X17.' I shouted: 'F*** off; Norm tried that half an hour ago!' Then the immortal words: 'No Duff!' were spoken and I knew it was for real and serious.

What had happened was that Norm and the rest of the brick had gone to open X17, but the CSU (*Civilian Search Unit*) were running late and they could not open without the searchers being present. As a result, they were just standing close to their Land Rover up the street a bit from the gate when a bomb, which had been hidden in an adjacent shop, was set of by timer. If they had been able to open up on time, they and others would have been undoubtedly killed. Funnily though there were very few civilians around waiting for the gates to open, and we think that the PIRA had probably warned them off, and nobody said anything; that's what we were up against.

All 4 soldiers had been badly shocked and Norm is still deaf in one ear, but it's hard to think that his joke on me could have been his last.

Chapter 4

The Falls Road/Springfield Road

This was the first place most squaddies, in the early days of deployment to the Province would see; it is, perhaps the one place name which springs readily to mind when non-military people on the mainland think about Northern Ireland. Not for nothing did the Falls area acquire the epithet 'Murder Mile' as 36 regular soldiers and 9 RUC men were killed in this part of Belfast. It was, for members of the SF, the most dangerous part of the city. And, with some 95 peace-keepers killed in an area about the size of Wakefield, in this section of west Belfast, even with the benefit of historical observation, the sheer numbers leave one with a feeling of disbelief.

The Falls Road is a continuation of Glen Road which cuts a swathe through the northern part of Andersonstown; it becomes the Falls Road where the Andersonstown Road converges also. It sweeps on and then crosses the Springfield Road and Grosvenor Road and then, further up, becomes part of the notorious Divis Street. At its base, after it is no longer Glen Road, is the south eastern tip of the 'Murph. The Falls Road, especially the Lower Falls where it meets the Springfield Road, was, in the early years of the troubles mainly the blackened stone, two-up, one-down terraced housing so reminiscent of Victorian England. Most had no inside toilets and every so often, was the midden which housed both toilets and dustbin areas. There were few if any gardens and many houses were back-to-back, with no rear entry (or, in the case where a fleeing gunman might seek to pass through, rear exit).

RRW and RUC patrol on the Falls Road (Royal Regiment Wales Museum)

GREEN JACKETS ON THE FALLS

Corporal Frank Jones, Royal Green Jackets

One day. word came through that a leading IRA man would be visiting the Lower Falls; that night I was tasked to set up an OP in a semi-derelict house overlooking a well known bar with the purpose of giving Company HQ early warning to mount a raid and a lift. After a briefing and time to prepare I led half my section out to arrive at the chosen OP location for around 3am. We were escorted by the remainder of the platoon and once at the front door each one of us was given a leg up to the first floor where entry was made through a broken window. Extra equipment was hoisted up via rifle slings and we settled ourselves down for an uncomfortable wait. Our chosen room reeked of stale urine and dampness and the floor being in a particularly bad state of repair made it dangerous to move in the darkness.

At dawn I was able to reorganise our equipment and once again study the photograph of this hairy, bearded top player. His face was pretty familiar to all of us but I worried that if I didn't keep looking at the photograph I might suddenly forget what he looked like, and fail to give warning of his arrival. Despite this self inflicted fear everything seemed to be going well. Without having to hang out the window we had a clear view of the bar and all conversation was kept to a minimum and then only in whispers. The street below, whilst not busy, was used by locals and we simply concentrated on the task in hand and ensured we weren't seen or heard. Yes, all was fine and it was now midmorning. The two gunshots, which sounded from much further up the street, stirred us in to action. Straight away I knew they hadn't been aimed at us and I sent a 'Shots heard' report to Company HQ. However, they did have the affect of bringing crowds of women on to the street, with the obvious intention of providing cover for the gunman and hindering any Army follow-up. It seemed doubtful to me that our top player would turn up in the middle of an incident and I suddenly felt we were quite vulnerable.

Some days earlier whilst involved in cordoning off a street during a company search operation, my platoon had been subjected to a bombardment of blast bombs. One of which had hit the Platoon signaler on the knee. Quite instinctively he had kicked it away. All well and good except it rolled to where I had dived to the ground and exploded some few feet from my outstretched right leg. Fortunately the hard surface of the road directed the blast skywards. Also, during a night patrol, the platoon sergeant had been bowled over by a blast bomb, and probably because he was unhurt we all thought it extremely funny, but we knew that adding nails and Belfast confetti to a blast bomb produces an entirely different beast.

As yet the crowd below our window had not realised our presence so we could probably sit tight. However, it seemed even more unlikely our player would oblige us and turn up during or after an incident and on top of this my concern was that should we be compromised, it probably wouldn't take too long for someone to start lobbing blast or nail bombs in through our broken window. Back at the Mill a section is always kept on 'Immediate Minus'; that is, it is sitting in its armoured PIG ready to respond. Company HQ asked if I wanted to be extracted and I replied in the affirmative.

Only a few minutes later a PIG hurtled in to the street, mounted the pavement and scattered a crowd of about forty women and youths. It shuddered to a halt directly under my broken window. The first riflemen leapt on to the vehicle roof some feet below and assisted as we passed out the A41 radio and a 1 gallon 'tea bomb.' Then my second and third party member joined him. I jumped out last, encouraged by the 'Immediate Minus' section commander and whilst number four and me were still perched on its roof, the section embussed and we sped off with two of us hanging on for dear life. The complete extraction had probably taken less than a minute and it wasn't until we drove off that the crowd woke up to what was happening. I think until that moment no-one could believe what they were seeing; four soldiers with blackened faces jumping out of

Guardroom at a Belfast base (Dave Bradwell)

window of a house within their midst. Away from the crowd the PIG was pulled over and the two of us crammed in to the rear.

The three months from 1RGJ leaving and then 'R' Company following was hectic and full of incident. A rifleman from my section suffered a gunshot wound to his leg inflicted by a sniper from Divis Flats. Fortunately it wasn't too serious and after a few weeks he was back on duty. The day he rejoined the section we were Guard Platoon with my section manning the front ground floor sangar and 'guardroom.' I was standing with him in the sangar when a round hit it. Then a couple of days later during a night search we both saw in absolute slow motion, a hand and pistol appear at the street corner. Three rapid shots ricocheted past us down the street and a quick dash to the corner was unable to prevent the gunman escaping. I looked at Rifleman 'X' and said, 'It's you; you're a bloody magnet.' A semi official nickname of Rifleman 'Bullets' stayed with him for years.

Two female members of the IRA were shot dead when the car they were traveling in deliberately drove through a cordon during the early hours of a company search operation and despite very obvious warnings and signals from us to stop. They would still be alive had the driver not chosen to ignore our signals and try to run over my platoon sergeant. But perhaps what sealed their fate was to open fire at us through the smashed rear window.

Grosvenor Road after rioting (Mark Campbell)

[*On October 23, 1971, two female IRA members, Maura Meehan and Dorothy Maguire, were shot and killed by the British Army in the Lower Falls area of Belfast, in the incident which Frank Jones describes.*]

Despite being involved in numerous other incidents I probably only felt really unnerved on the one occasion. My section had attended a bomb blast at the tax office and just prior to pulling away I spoke to an RUC man standing by his Land rover. I was on my usual soapbox about how I would bet the IRA would never blow up the dole office. Then, there was a soft noise which, whilst puzzling, didn't seem to offer any danger. Then suddenly the rear door of the Land rover was thrown open and a shaken policewoman leapt out yelling that she had nearly been shot. From outside the vehicle she pointed into the rear passenger compartment to a hole in the armour, and sure enough from the outside we pin-pointed the same hole, which was about nine inches from where my head had been when we had heard the noise. The other and less nerving occasion when I honestly thought it was me that had again been singled out; a short burst of fire aimed one night at the section drove me through a house door. I had expected resistance but the door flew open as I shouldered it and I ended up on my back in the middle of the living room floor between a TV and the family sitting on a couch watching it. They simply sat there, probably thinking I was the lead man of a search team. I remember looking at the TV and telling them I knew how it (the film) ended. I apologised, which stunned them, and rejoined my section.

My section was probably the last section to come under fire during this tour. On the last full day, and this time whilst employed searching cars and buses on the Grosvenor Road, a number of shots were fired from a derelict house about two hundred metres away. Obviously the gunman was not concerned with civilian casualties because at that exact time a bus was being searched and I was interviewing the passenger of a car. I ran to cover behind the PIG and was joined by other members of the section. Then low velocity shots passed over our heads from the opposite direction. I remember thinking, 'The bastards; two firing positions.' But I needn't have worried, too much. It was the platoon sergeant firing his pistol into a row of derelicts. We returned fire into the derelict which I reckoned the initial shots had come from, and then we rushed over open ground directly at the firing position. Naturally the sniper had well gone, probably scared off by the platoon sergeant's accurate pistol fire?

At tour's end, on the ferry back to Liverpool with two of my very good mates sharing a bunk we decided to have an hour's sleep then visit the bar. We woke up in Liverpool the next morning having enjoyed our first night of unbroken sleep in months.

MURPHY'S LAW AT WORK ON THE FALLS

Sergeant Mick 'Benny' Hill, 3 Royal Anglians

A march and a demo had been planned for a weekend and was due to start somewhere in 'Andy Town' and go on to the City Centre, via the Falls. Obviously, on a march like that, our sangars at Hasting Street RUC station would come in for some heavy duty 'bricking' and other nasties as it was en-route.

Our plan was, that as soon as the trouble started, we would make some arrests and over the previous few nights we had recce'd all the districts between Hastings Street and Townsend Street. We found a shop that was all boarded up on the Falls Road side and inside we found that the shop had a recessed doorway. The inner door was easily forced and the boarding up of the recess was just held by 4 bolts on the inside. My section would occupy the shop. Watch out for trouble and then burst out and make arrests. Mick's section would get in the upstairs, via a ladder as there were no internal stairs and they would have 2 or 3 Federal Riot Guns (FRGs) and John's section would be in reserve in the back yard.

When the nastiness started, Mick's section would target the instigators and my section would leap out and make the arrests with John's section covering us as we retreated to the RUC station. So, in the early hours, we went into the shop and loosened the bolts on the outer panel. A big lad called 'Dinger' and two others, armed with batons would make the arrests,

This is where the Springfield Road RUC station once stood (Ken Wharton)

covered by three others with shields; Stan, my 2IC and I had rifles. Anyway, in we went and due to an almighty cock-up, several of the lads fell through into the shop, all jammed in the doorway and 'Dinger' found himself all alone in the middle of the Falls Road; armed only with a baton!

The locals must have thought that he was the 'Incredible Hulk' because he didn't bottle it; just stood there in the middle of the road, glaring at the crowd. The only way I could get out to back him up, was to run over all the jammed bodies of the lads in the doorway and when I did so, a mega burst of profanity erupted. Fortunately, the locals were still too shocked to react and Stan kicked some arse – literally – and got everyone on their feet and out into the street and the locals quickly backed off. We just stood there, facing them off and then we withdrew the way we came, securing the doors behind us.

So, was the mission successful? Partly; Hastings Street RUC station was not 'bricked', but we made no arrests. Did the op go as planned? Not in our wildest dreams, although our sangars remained' unbricked' for the rest of the tour. Murphy's Law certainly worked overtime that day and 'he' probably had a good laugh at our expense.

SPRINGFIELD ROAD

Private Richard Smith, Duke of Wellingtons

On another part of the two year posting, we were based at Springfield Road RUC station. It was a quiet period – I was on QRF – and as nothing seemed to be happening, I was bored shitless. Consequently, my mate 'Big Wally' and I decided to volunteer for the next patrol in order to get some relief from the boredom and give a couple of the lads a break. In my brick, there was Sergeant Acklam, 'Wally', me and a lad called Rupert who was 'short' (i.e. Close to the end of his tour).

The routine was one brick out and two outlying bricks and the central one (ours) had an RUC who knew the area well, with them. (*Brick = 4 men*). We came out of the station and turned right and in the direction of the Falls Road. Of course, we had the normal grief; screams, insults and the odd missile thrown in our direction. Then, all of a sudden, it went quiet; we knew that this was the signal for something to happen. In the formation, Sergeant Acklam was on the same side of the Falls Road with me, one of us walking backwards, the other watching his back. 'Wally' and Rupert were on the other side and the RUC was kind of sauntering between us, in the middle of the road.

Sergeant Acklam turned towards me, as if he had wanted to say something, and there was about 10 yards between us when he was shot. He seemed to spin completely around and then went down like a bag of shit! As he did so, I saw the round impact against a wall and then heard the crack. I was the brick medic and reached him just as 'Wally' did likewise. Acklam was conscious and looked at me and said 'Fucking hell, Smudger, I've lost my side.' He had a NIBA vest on (*Northern Ireland Body Armour*) and I ripped that off and saw that the bullet had entered the back of it, travelled around the inside and scorched a bruised and burnt mark around his body and then exited at the front. I simply couldn't believe that he could have been such a lucky bastard; I was so relieved and he knew that from the big grin on our faces.

Rupert was over the other side, and managed to find the only bush on the Falls Road behind which to take cover, and all I could see was this big pair of eyes peering through it!

Richard's Regiment, known universally as the 'Duke of Boots' lost a total of 6 men from 1972 to 1980, but, fortunately, despite the near-misses he reports, none after this time and not on his two year posting. The notorious 'Murph, of which he writes in an earlier chapter, claimed the lives of Private George Lee in 1972 and Corporal Errol Pryce in 1980. The other four losses were Corporal Terrence Graham and Private James Lee, both killed in an IRA landmine attack in Crossmaglen in 1972, and Second Lieutenant Howard Fawley and Private Michael Ryan, both killed in Londonderry in 1974.

SPRINGFIELD ROAD: SLEEPING THE SLEEP OF THE DEAD

Rifleman 'W' 1 RGJ

I was on attachment at the RUC station on Springfield Road in West Belfast in the early days of the troubles. I remember the station was very near the junction with the Falls Road. This ran both ways at the nearby crossroads and to the left as you looked at it, was the bit of the Falls which led up to the Divis. As you might well imagine, being slap bang in the middle of a fiercely Republican area, we came in for a fair bit of stick from the locals.

I felt sorry for the 'green bottles' as we called the RUC as they had to live through this all the time, whereas we, the soldiers, could go home after four months and then not come back for 6, 8, even 12 months. If we thought that we had it tough, spare a thought for those poor bastards being there all the time. This one particular day was a Friday and we had had had a real kicking over the previous week, with the Falls boyos being out on the streets, morning, noon and night with bricks, slabs of concrete, petrol bombs; anything really that they could find to throw. We, in common with most of the other regiments in that part of Ulster, were well under the cosh and suffered a lot of injuries. From memory, we had lads with broken or lacerated ankles – the bastards would skim roof tiles and the like at our feet, ankles and shins – cut faces, bruised heads, bloody noses and lost teeth. It was a rough time for us all and, at times, we gave as good as we got.

Our Company OC, a Major who I liked and don't wish to give his name used to say to us 'Gentlemen; the watchword is restraint.' Sometimes we showed that; sometimes we didn't. When you see a mate go down, white-faced and gasping with pain and you can see the bastard that hurt him, you forgot all about restraint and you reciprocated the pain; if you get my drift?

Anyway, we were kicked out of our pits (*beds*) at around 03:30 and force-fed some ACC crap and then we 'starburst' out of the big gates and in three groups of four men headed right and then left towards the Divis and we went firm near the bad arse tower block a little after 04:30. Our brief was to patrol along there and nip any trouble in the bud. Why so early? Because the boyos liked to get up a bit earlier than normal, get their pre-prepared petrol bombs and piles of rocks ready for the day's 'festivities.' If we could get there early enough and find their stashes of 'weapons' in a derelict house or some lock-up garage, we could prevent some poor squaddie's injuries later in the day.

To cut a long story short; we went back to the RUC station at about 09:00 having seen nothing more dangerous than the packs of dogs which roamed the area and the odd milkman. I was cleaning my SLR and drinking Sarn't Major's brew (an evil concoction of very, very strong tea, heavily sugared and crammed full of condensed milk) when we were crashed out as rioting was taking place in the Divis area. This went on until early evening and then, as mysteriously as it started, it stopped and we left the area, which was covered in bricks and stones and smashed glass and the stench of petrol and returned to base. I was absolutely knackered and just wanted to grab some sleep; I wasn't even hungry as someone had stuffed a corned beef 'doorstop' into my hand during the rioting and I stuffed it into my mouth sideways and gobbled it down. We had all made our weapons 'safe' in the yard and trudged inside with blackened faces and runny eyes and noses.

We can't have been there for longer than thirty minutes when an NCO came in and said something along the lines of: 'The green custards are taking a hammering round the corner; back out in 5, lads.' We called the Green Howards all sorts of names and this was one of them and there was no love lost between the two 'Greens.' We got back to the station for the second time well into Saturday morning and at this stage, we had gone almost 24 hours without sleep. Those 24 hours were hours of constant tension, heightened senses and sheer mayhem. After making my weapon safe in the yard again, I went straight to the sleeping room – declining that evil tea – climbed into the top bunk, loosened my webbing, left my boots on and fell instantly asleep, grimy face and all.

I woke up to the usual blue haze of cigarette smoke, sitting below the ceiling which was close to my face and felt disgustingly knackered and disgustingly filthy and bursting for a piss. I went to the urinals and nearly didn't make it as I fumbled with buttons and all; if I tell you that I was urinating for well over a minute, I exaggerate not! I couldn't believe that I could piss for so long; the relief was absolutely wonderful and I can still smile, 30-odd years later, at the sheer pleasure of relieving myself. I wandered over to where the 'green bottles' had a small tea and snacks area and looked around for the Saturday newspapers. I can remember as though it were yesterday that my team – Leeds United, a fact which got the

London lads taking the piss out of me at every opportunity – were playing West Brom that day. Imagine my shock, when I saw, on the table in front of me, the SUNDAY newspapers! I had slept all through the Saturday and woken up on Sunday morning. Thanks to some act of fate – no riots and no trouble – and some kindly Colour Sergeant, we had been allowed to sleep off the effects of a 24 hour duty.

There weren't many moments of kindness again like that; there were, however, many instances of constant tension and exhaustion.

But then, this was Belfast and this was the troubles.

MARKETS AREA

'Onion' NIVA and Royal Artillery

On 16th October 1976, just after our arrival for another four month emergency tour, the IRA decided to welcome us back to Belfast by way of sending three of their finest 'soldiers' to plant a bomb in the base tucked away in one corner of the gasworks complex on the Ormeau Road. In attempting to do so under cover of darkness, it went off rather earlier than they expected so sending two of them unexpectedly through a wire mesh fence to their makers. We were picking up body parts that night and for days afterwards. The explosion ruptured one of the gasholders and flames ignited the gas sending a huge fireball in to the night sky that was heard and seen for miles. A fellow NIVA member also on the streets that night confirmed to me some years later that they thought a huge bomb had destroyed the entire city centre. Our section had just gone out on foot patrol so were lucky to escape the ensuing chaos of evacuating the base. We did however have to literally pick up the bits of someone's body and in the immediate aftermath we had no idea whose it might be, it could have been a mate, an innocent bystander or a bomber's, we just didn't know.

The three terrorists killed were Paul Marlowe (32), Francis Fitzsimmons (29) and Joseph Surgenor (24). They had been taking several bombs to the Gasworks and had intended to attack an Army post.

After this spectacular own goal and the elation of soon discovering it was the bombers, first two then once the bits were put more or less back together again, three, of them had died, we were left on edge for weeks awaiting the inevitable backlash once the opposition had the chance to regroup. And sure enough, and unbeknown to our 'intelligence', they did indeed plan another major hit. In the meantime we were kept on our toes by the occasional shot at foot and mobile patrols as well as the sangars which over the next few months were unsuccessful. That is, until the night of Sunday, 23rd January 1977.

My section had just come off a 16 hour shift of foot and mobile patrols of 2 hours on, 2 hours standby, 2 hours on etc, and we had grabbed a couple of egg 'banjos' and were off to our pits. For some reason I'd kept the Pye set switched on, probably too 'cream crackered' to care, and just as I was pulling back the sheets came the dreaded word, 'contact,' over the net. Everyone piled back out onto the streets and in the ensuing chaos all hell was let loose in the Markets and Lower Ormeau Road area.

A single high velocity shot fired from Saint Colman's primary school at 22.08 hours hit and killed George, and within minutes, he died in the arms of one of his mates on the corner of Eliza and New Bond Street, only a few hundred yards away from us. The gunman escaped and the firing point discovered the next day, an open window in the school.

Gunner Muncaster (19) of the Royal Artillery was shot by an IRA gunman near Eliza Street, a hundred metres north of Rhoda Park and died within minutes of being wounded; he was a Liverpool boy.

FUN AND GAMES AT SPRINGFIELD ROAD

Steve Larn, Coldstream Guards

During our first tour in Belfast, each company had to take turns to do the guard at Springfield road police station and after a couple of months there, I had to take my turn. Among the main tasks was covering the roof sangars and the front gate. At 2am on a very cold January morning, I was on the front gate looking out of the sangar watching for anything on the road, which included opening up the big gates to let in mobile patrols coming and going.

We had a very heavy modified flak vest to wear which had a big piece of lead in the front and back which, after about half an hour standing around, weighed a ton. After about an hour or so, a mobile patrol arrived, in which a lot of cursing and screaming could be heard. Then, two Land Rovers stopped and the lads inside de-bused; they dragged with them a very scruffy youth aged about 17 or 18. He had long, dirty hair and wearing a black leather jacket and obviously very drunk. He had been arrested for throwing stones at the patrol, but wasn't going to come quietly and wanted to fight everyone. However, as most guardsman are big to start

Private Doyle in
Beechmounts
(Royal Regiment
Wales Museum)

off with, he had picked on the wrong lot in the first place, and was soon dragged off inside by a few lads and some of the RUC coppers.

After about half an hour, the Corporal on duty told me to look out for some people coming to the front gate to get this lad, as, apparently it wasn't his first time being arrested and the RUC who had better things to do had phoned his house and told them to come and get him. Shortly after that, a very angry woman with the most foulest of mouths, wearing her nightdress and dressing gown plus a hair net and thick boots arrived.

At this point, the lad was pushed out the gate, and his mother then proceeded to hit him around the head and to kick his shins all the way down the road shouting that he was, in no uncertain words, a bad son for getting her out of bed at that time in the morning. All he could do was to bleat that it was all the Army's fault and that he hadn't done anything wrong and the last thing we heard as they turned the corner was: 'You wait till you get in; your dad's going to beat the living daylights out of you.

But then, this was just normal family life in Belfast; we all fell about laughing for about 5 minutes then went back to the normal routine of trying to stay alive in Northern Ireland.

This, as Steve described it, was, 'fun and games' as the squaddies had to deal with the minutiae of working class urban life, even during the violence of the troubles. But, there were other, less humorous times and during the two years between 1972 and 1974, this famous battalion of 'wooden tops' as they are known by the rest of the Army, lost 6 men.

On August 27, 1972, Sergeant Anthony Metcalf (28) and a married man from Beverley in Humberside was shot and killed by an IRA sniper inside a base at Creggan Heights in Londonderry. The following year, on February 20, the IRA shot and killed two Guardsmen; Robert Pearson (19) from the author's hometown, Leeds and Malcolm Shaw (23) were killed in a gun and bomb attack in the Falls Road area. The following day, Londoner Michael Doyle (20) was shot and killed by an IRA sniper as he guarded a working party in Fort Whiterock. A little over 12 months later, Guardsman Anton Brown was killed by the IRA on the Ballymurphy estate in West Belfast.

Looking around corners
(Royal Regiment
Wales Museum)

The following month, on April 14, Captain Anthony Pollen (27) from Sonning in Berkshire was shot and killed by an IRA gunman after he was seized by Republican onlookers at a Sinn Fein rally in the Bogside in Londonderry. His retreating comrades saw over a dozen men seize him, wrestle him to the ground and moments later, the shots which took his life rang out. Captain Pollen is considered to have been a member of 14th Int, an undercover organization for intelligence gathering and was photographing the march at the time he was seized and then murdered. There are some observers who have queried the role of this young officer and two other comrades who were also in plain clothes.

Were they trying to pass themselves off as journalists – and here the author has bitter experience of these intrusive gentlemen of the 'fourth estate' – or were they trying to pass themselves off as Sinn Fein supporters? Whatever their rationale – and the notes will be safely filed away in a deep vault under Main Building in Whitehall – there were ominous echoes some years later at Milltown Cemetrey. On March 19, 1988, complete with a watching television audience – 14 years earlier there was no such 'spectators' – two Royal Signals Corporals were seized in similar fashion, beaten half to death and then callously 'executed' by the IRA.

FOGGY NIGHT IN BELFAST

Richard Nettleton, Grenadier Guards

One particular freezing foggy night back in November 1969 we got the call and prepared to leave the relative warmth and safety of the Newtownards Police Barracks and, clambering into the back of our ice covered Saracen A.P.C's, headed out through the gates into a real pea souper. All we'd been told was, that we were going out on a roving V.C.P, and we hoped it wouldn't be similar to the last, where we stopped and searched a convoy of Catholic Clergy, who protested they were men of the cloth and not terrorists; but no matter who they were, everyone received the same treatment.

From the moment we drove through those imposing grey gates, things started to go wrong. The fog was so bad visibility was down to almost zero and finding ourselves lost, ended up on the M1, where our illustrious leader turned the column around and drove the wrong way back towards the approach road, then took another route into the city.

Having spent some considerable time cruising along numerous streets, he eventually admitted to becoming disoriented in the fog and decided that rather than attempt to find the location he'd previously been given, we'd stop some little way further along the road we were on, and set up our checkpoint there.

Once a site had been chosen, everyone sprang into action and quickly formed our vehicles into the familiar positions making it impossible for vehicles to pass then went about our duties. Having stopped and searched what few vehicles were foolish enough to be out in the appalling weather that night, the next to appear along the road was a double decker bus, where in true soldierly fashion we removed everyone on board, lined them up and asked them to place their personal possessions on the ground to their front before physically searching each one in turn prior to allowing them to continue with their journey.

Whilst searching one old man, he commented: 'I wouldn't be doing that here if I were you lads' and thinking it was his way at having a go at us, ignored his comment and carried on searching.

It wasn't until some hour or so later as the fog slowly began lifting I understood the wisdom of his words as there, on the street name screwed to the front of one of the houses across the road for all the world to see, were the words 'FALLS ROAD'! I think that we must have been exceptionally lucky not to have been set upon by the baying mobs that night and, if it wasn't for the fog, which actually caused the problem in the first place, most certainly would have been. Having realized our mistake, we hastily dismantled our check point and moved on to the location we were supposed to be searching vehicles.

I remember at the time thinking oops; how on earth did we end up here? (or similar words) let's get the fuck out of here before the shit really hits the fan! Never had I seen so few soldiers shift so many reels of Dannet wire so quickly (and without the aid of N.I Gloves, which at that time hadn't been issued); breathing, I should add, a heavy sigh of relief.

RECCE PLATOON ON THE LOWER FALLS

Sergeant M.J. 'Benny' Hill, 3 Royal Anglians

In 1972, my battalion was given the dubious responsibility for the Lower Falls area of Belfast; this included the notorious Clonard area and the even more notorious Divis flats. My platoon was located in an old mill behind Hastings Street RUC station on the city end of the Falls Road. Accommodation was basic with just one room for the entire platoon of around 30 blokes; all the others: Signallers, Drivers, Cooks and Clerks – about 100 in total – were crammed into another room. It was a 24 hour operation and with all the constant comings and goings, the only place where you could get any privacy was in the toilets!

Senior NCOs and Officers were a little more fortunate as they had single or shared rooms, large enough for a bed and a chair, with a suitcase to double as a wardrobe; their 'door' was a blanket ! I suppose that my main memories of the tour are of being constantly tired, wet and cold or hot and the awful smells that our flak jackets gave off. The one I had a raised collar to protect the neck and throat and the inside was tacky and stained with dirt and sweat. There were no spares, so they simply were never washed; at least not during the tour.

As a good shot, I was armed with an L42 – a bolt action rifle with a decent telescopic sight – and as a result of my experience and skills, had to spend long hours in sangars, or Ops, especially during demos and marches. They were very tiring, long hours with often nothing to show for it, although, on the odd occasions, I did get to fire. After each incident, I would be met by an RMP wanting a statement of why I had fired, but, after 14 hours of constant vigilance, I was not really interested in the paper war! I have to add that, later on in the tour, after several major gun battles, these kinds of statements just weren't bothered with.

I remember one night, spotting a gunman and following him into an old, dark flax or linen factory, crawling between the machines, trying to locate him, whilst desperately trying, at the same time, to keep in touch with my section. I should point out that this was a pretty good test of my sphincter muscles! On another occasion, we were in a factory overlooking the Falls Road and we came under fire from a gunman in an old, burned out bank. I quickly allocated each member of the section a window of the bank each and told them to fire two rounds each on my order. After we had all fired, I heard 'Titch' giggling and muttering 'Two rounds warmers into the bank; go on.' Old infantry soldiers will probably appreciate that one, even if it is a bit obtuse.

During 'Motorman' (*Army operation to end the no-go areas*) every derelict building in the Lower falls was thoroughly searched and then bricked up by R.E. engineer's teams. My section was doing close protection to one of these teams and somehow, their Officer and I had managed to piss each other off, big style, although I got on well with his Sergeant. Suddenly, from around the corner came a soft-top Rover with only one escort and Dave, the CQMS in the front. He explained that there were so many troops around, that he had great difficulty in not running over 'something green.' We had a great breakfast and I went to ask the RE Rupert if he wanted some egg sandwiches and he just muttered something and walked away. The upshot of it was that the Sergeant and the rest of the sappers had a rare culinary treat and when the Rupert saw us, he had a face like thunder!

On another night, we had just finished an Op' in the Clonard and as I reported in person to company HQ, I was press-ganged into a snap building search and the rest of the section was also roped in. As we began the search, 'rent-a-crowd' appeared and the usual nastiness started to kick-off. I was standing by my vehicle when I was suddenly hit on the head by a heavy, industrial type, galvanized dustbin lid and was knocked unconscious. Half a second relaxed vigilance, half a second to 'head' the dustbin lid and the result: 20 years plus of industrial strength headaches and moods.

Consequently, I caught pneumonia and was bedded down but riddled with guilt and pleasure; guilt because my section were still on the streets, and pleasure because I was in a bed with sheets.

So, all in all, a very busy four months; four killed, Heaven knows how many injured and I think that we all saw things which in a civilized society, we shouldn't have had to see. Of all the types of war, a civil war has got to be the nastiest and cruelest because there is no respite. Everyone is involved and every person to a greater or lesser extent has to take sides.

The saddest thing is that when the war is over, the most savage of terrorists often end up as politicians; am I alone in seeing the irony ?

In an awful six months period, in that year of 1972, this area of Belfast was the scene of the killings of no less than 8 'Angle Irons' from Mick's Battalion and the 2nd battalion of the same Regiment. Second Lieutenant Nicholas Hull (21) from Bedfordshire was killed by an IRA sniper on April 16 and was followed less than a month later by Private John Ballard (18); a Grimsby boy, he was killed by the IRA on Sultan Street, in the Lower Falls. In the space of a few short hours on July 13, two more members of the Regiment fell; Martin Rooney (22) from the Irish Republic was killed by the IRA in the Clonard and then Corporal Kenneth Mogg (29) from Melton Mowbray was shot and died shortly afterwards after a shooting incident at Dunville Park.

Four weeks later, Lance Corporal John Boddy (29) from Peterborough was shot whilst on foot patrol in Selby Street and died two hours later in the RVH. On September 23, whilst on mobile patrol in Cyprus Street, the IRA shot and wounded Corporal John Barry. The Lance Corporal who was (22) and from Lincolnshire died of his wounds two days later. Four days later, in a shootout with members of both wings of the IRA in the Albert Street and Servia Street area, Private Ian Burt who was just 18 and an Essex boy was shot and killed. The final 'Angle Iron' to die in that terrible 6 months was Private Robert Mason (19) from Cambridgeshire; he was shot whilst on foot patrol in the vicinity of Grosvenor Road.

FINDING 'ARMS' ON THE FALLS ROAD

Stephen Larn, Coldstream Guards

I was first posted to the Province in 1974 as a young 18 year old and the Regiment was sent to west Belfast. I was a member of the Mortar platoon and we were attached to one of the Rifle companies for our tour and I found myself in the Whiterock at Macrory Park.

Just before our deployment, we had been undergoing some training and I was sent on a search and detection course with the Royal Engineers. We were sent out in the November, and I remember being very nervous on my first foot patrol; not knowing what to expect. However, the patrol leader was very calm about things and we soon settled down to the day to day routine of things. It was a very tiring time, even for a young lad like me, normally full of get up and go; a combination of fear and long hours and routine, but not knowing what the next hour had in store let alone the next day. On mobile patrols, we would put up snap VCPs on the Falls Road in order to attempt to stop the movement of arms through our area from Andy town and the Murph' and the Turf. As such, it was my job to search the cars and trucks we stopped.

On one of these occasions, we had been targeting black cabs, as Intel had told us they were often used to ferry stuff about. We were looking for ones with FTA stickers in the windows as these were the Falls Taxi Association. After some time, we had stopped about four, and the Sergeant told us one more, then bug out, clearly not wanting to be in any spot for any length of time. Anyway, the next cab along was pulled over and we went into the same routine as all the others; driver and passengers out, to lots of complaints and swearing; bonnet and boot up, in order for me to start searching. I had just about finished, with only the boot to do, so out came the shopping bags and a pram and then the spare wheel, under which was a dirty rag which I thought would hold the tools and jack. But, to my surprise it was a shotgun.

I froze for a minute and my 'oppo watching my back, looked over my shoulder and muttered something like: 'Fuck me!' He then shouted to the Sergeant that we had found a gun, and the driver was arrested on the spot and carted off. After about 20 minutes, an RUC Land Rover arrived to take the cab and the gun away, and we all felt chuffed with ourselves until we where told that the gun was a plastic toy replica.

Anyway, it was all taken off and we didn't hear much more about it until a few weeks later, when an RUC CID Sergeant turned up at our camp with photos of a bank raid. We were told that a plastic shotgun had been used, and so it turned out that we weren't the only ones to be fooled.

HATRED AND HOPE ON THE FALLS ROAD.

Mick 'Benny' Hill, Royal Anglians

Some 35 years on, some of the lasting memories I have are about three different women or sets of women.

The usually middle aged women from the Protestant side of our patrol area baked cakes for us and prayed for our well-being. On the other side of the sectarian divide, their counterparts – the Catholics – who looked and sounded the same but were horrendous and full of vitriol and hatred. I'm sure that they did pray as well, but certainly not for our well-being.

There were three individual women whom I met whilst we were in this part of Belfast; sadly two of their names are now long forgotten. The first was an American reporter; she was plump, motherly and down-to-earth. She wanted to report the war for her newspaper from the Tom's angle. At that time – and probably much later as well – Americans tended to view the troubles through green-coloured spectacles and she wanted to give a more balanced view of the conflict. She was with us for several hours and ate with the 'Toms', interviewed only 'Toms' and generally listened to us and took copious notes.

She made us feel that someone really cared. I don't know if her articles were ever published or even who she worked for, but I hope that she got into print; we all certainly wished her well.

The second woman was a WRAC (*Women's Royal Army Corps*) RMP and she arrived with the RMP arrest team at Hasting Street RUC station early one morning, at about 02:00. She looked absolutely exhausted. In those days the WRAC were thin on the ground and some, especially the RMP, tended to be very overworked. The team had a couple of hours to kill before they had to process the dawn 'lifts' so she asked her Sergeant if he could find her an armchair to doze in.

Gallantly, our guard commander offered her his bed and, even though she discovered that he had to share his sleeping arrangements with over 100 soldiers, gratefully accepted. On being shown to the bed, she took off her blouse and skirt and climbed between the blankets; everyone slept on, blissfully unaware of the sleeping woman in their midst. I don't think that the guard commander changed his pillow case until the last vestige of her perfume had faded away from the pillow. I wonder how many women can claim to have shared a bedroom with 100 plus men and felt perfectly safe.

I should point out that all females deployed to Ulster in those days had to wear skirts so that they were instantly recognizable as female and of course, they were unarmed.

Back in 1972, BBC Ulster ran a programme for the families of the lads serving over there, called 'Ulster Calling' and was presented by the then, little-known Gloria Hunniford. There was a ballot to see who would be interviewed by her and I was lucky enough to win, although, not so lucky on the streets as I had stopped a brick with my knee and could barely walk; at 6' 3" I suppose that I made a good target because I certainly stopped my share of bricks.

Anyway, Gloria came to my bunk to do the interview and shoo-ed away her minders, sat on my bed and for half an hour kept me in fits of laughter through her charm and personality. All that just for a couple of minutes 'air time' but I enjoyed it. She was young, charming, fragrant and completely natural with a way of making you feel completely at ease. She was as big a morale booster as a spot of 'R&R.'

I don't know if she ever got public recognition for her efforts in raising the troops' morale, but she certainly deserved it. When I see her on TV now, I sometimes wonder if she ever remembers those early days of her long career. I'm sure that there are many more like me who won't forget her.

LAUGHING OUR SOCKS OFF ON THE FALLS ROAD

Private Kevin 'Errol' Flynn, 3 Light Infantry

One Sunday morning, we 'bomb burst' out of North Howard Street Mill and made our way through the peace line and on to Springfield road. Gordy Hunter was my brick commander attached to us – bugle platoon – from one of the companies. He was a seasoned Northern Ireland warrior who gained respect from all of us in the brick (call sign 41Bravo) and we would not do anything to upset him. We had a healthy respect and fear towards him. Anyway, we made our way down Springfield road calling in at TAC HQ and turned left at the junction of Falls Road opposite Grosvenor Park. Gordy was at the front, on the left hand side of the road, me next, on the right hand side of the road, and 'Goosey' and 'Spanner' behind us. For some reason on the left hand side of Falls Road, maybe for art reasons or for plain annoyance, there were huge rocks placed along the pavement.

Now as I said we all had a healthy respect for Gordy and did not want to upset him in anyway. At some point, he decided to walk backwards and, a couple of yards later he did a backward somersault over one of the aforementioned rocks. Unfortunately I seen this happen and immediately turned my face away towards the buildings so Gordy could not see me creasing up with mirth. But, at the same time I decided to patrol backwards so Gordy could not see me laughing; straight away, I saw 'Goose' and 'Spanner' walking backwards as well' They were obviously going through the same torture as me because I could see their backs in spasms of laughter. The brick commander on the ground and three of us looking backwards; the Micks missed a great chance of taking us out.

One Saturday afternoon, a week or so later, I was patrolling with another brick and just outside the sports bar on Falls Road, my mate Dicky Reeves did exactly the same thing as Gordy did but in front of a bunch of boyos having a drink outside in the warm afternoon sun. The lot of them broke down; laughing their heads off; it was so loud that you could have heard it in the Clonard. I asked him after how he felt and he told that me that he had wished the ground could have swallowed him up. As I have said, before, it was the misfortunes of others which kept us going.

ALBERT STREET MILL

Corporal Frank Jones, Royal Green Jackets

The news came through that we were to come under command of 1RGJ in Belfast. This brightened me up somewhat; firstly no boggy fields to patrol; secondly, Belfast seemed to be where the action was; and thirdly, working with our own Regiment.

We might have been the same Regiment but I suspect 1RGJ enjoyed housing us on the top floor of Albert Street Mill, Lower Falls. To reach our accommodation that night of the 12th August 1971 meant a climb of some eighty plus steps. Of course it was always going to be a climb of some eighty plus steps but that first night with the whole company sharing one floor of a dusty, smelly and cramped disused mill, the Kesh with its fresh windswept open spaces seemed almost inviting. To make us feel even more at home and before we had unpacked, shots were fired; most definitely at us, we convinced ourselves with excitement and apprehension running high. We hadn't known the roof top OP was only metres from us. Therefore when the sentry returned two rounds, the sound of which echoed and reverberated loudly round the company lines, we knew we had arrived. The lower and more luxurious floors were taken by 'B' and Support Companies. By luxurious I mean the riflemen had fewer steps to climb and each platoon occupied its own segregated, thinly partitioned and therefore certainly not soundproof, but still crowded room.

Over the next few nights some of us accompanied 1RGJ on operations. Mostly officers and SNCO's went out first to assist in clearing barricades from the Falls Road. Those of us left behind could hear the gunfire as the companies, and our 'R' Company guys came under fire. A couple of nights later I got involved in an operation to clear gunmen from Divis Flats, or rather to clear the barricaded stairwells, and to deal with any resistance as necessary. To get to Divis Flats unseen from Albert Street is practically impossible. A foot patrol leaving via the front gate of the mill will certainly provide time for wanted persons or gunmen to either flee or prepare a warm welcome. A company vehicle move, whilst quicker, will give away its intentions by noise and direction.

To overcome this we were led through the bowels of the mill until we reached the outer wall. Here it had been prepared and all that was needed was a hard shove and we emerged on to open ground only fifty or seventy-five metres from the flats. I was probably fourth through and then it was a dash by everyone to predetermined entrances. I had only to keep my eye on one of the 1RGJ section commanders and follow him everywhere, and expecting to come under fire at any moment we crossed open ground and it wasn't but a few seconds before we crashed through what had been blocking our entrance, then up the stairs to secure an alcove and one floor level. One, maybe two gunmen did try to divert our attentions, but the clearing of the barricades went as planned and several hours later I was climbing eighty plus steps to recall my experiences to an all attentive section.

FALLS ROAD

Tony Procter, REME

The patrols did a fantastic job, not only in trying to keep the peace in the main trouble areas of the Shanklin and Falls Road but also guarding heavily fortified police stations. Some patrols were also stationed in certain vulnerable factories. My fellow tradesmen and I were comparatively safe in the sanctuary of our strongly guarded RAF barracks. There were times though when it was necessary for us to go down into Belfast to repair or recover a faulty or damaged vehicle. Every third day we mechanics were on standby duty for twenty-four hours to go out and assist the patrols.

I recall two incidents that had me quite scared. I was called out one Saturday afternoon to repair a Ferret scout car that had a bad engine oil leak. The procedure before leaving the barracks was to draw your weapon and ammunition from the armoury then go to an enclosure by the main gate and load your weapon then board your vehicle. We mechanics always had an accompanying armed guard. On this occasion the disabled Ferret was holed up in a side street near the centre of Belfast. There had been rioting most of the afternoon in the surrounding main streets and I could hear the shouting and the gas canisters being shot. I worked frantically while being guarded by the patrol crew. Suddenly a mob of stone throwing rioters came charging down the side street straight towards us; it seemed that the Ulster Defence Association, (UDA) in order to break up the rioters on the main street had funnelled them down our street not knowing we were there.

The crew commander ordered warning shots to be fired and then radioed for a back up squad. The mob was held off while I finished the repairs and got the Ferret mobile. It was usual for the rioters to break up pavement flagstones and use them for weapons and many of these rocks came hurtling past me at that time. I souvenired one and I still have it to this day although I was tempted to throw it back at the scumbags.

On another occasion I was called out in the middle of the night. There had been some fierce rioting on the Falls Road with many petrol bombs hurled at our vehicles. One of our Saracens was badly burnt and had tyre damage on one side, my job was to winch it onto a suspended tow and recover it back to the barracks. It was a very hairy moment, it was pitch black with gunshots and petrol bombs going off, I felt that I was a sitting target but I was well guarded and I soon had the tow in place and got the hell out of there with the Saracen lurching behind.

FALLS AREA

Private David Wilson, King's Own Royal Borderers

I was nineteen, and it was my first tour of NI which started in December, 1974. I was a Lance Corporal in Recce Platoon. Most of that tour was taken up with covert observation posts in various parts of Belfast. My memory is hazy as it was so long ago but, one covert op does spring to mind as it went tits up because of a bag of piss. There was a fish and chip shop on the Falls Road which was more or less opposite the Provisional Sinn Fein's headquarters.

The shop was owned by a 48 year old Mr. Joe McKearney and one of our patrols had noticed some bricks were missing out of the front wall at attic level. This was passed onto the Int Section who decided it would make a very good covert observation post and, Recce platoon was tasked.

After various recces on the shop it was decided that the best way in was via Clonard Street at the back of the shop. We would place a ladder on the back yard wall and gain access via a window below the attic, then up to the attic. I am certain that there was no one living above the shop. It was decided that we would go in as three or four men teams for a duration of ten days before swapping over. Ten days was a long time to lie still in an attic covered in shit and in winter but, it would minimise the risk of detection when entering or leaving. There was to be no cooking and no lights for obvious reasons. We lived off sandwiches for the first few days then tins of cold compo thereafter, the only drink we had was water and the juice from tinned fruit. We fully tooled up with weaponry, radios, swift scope, pictures of baddies, and of course a fucking good camera. We were to shit and piss in large plastic bags which were taken out with us when we changed over crews. We had a lot of kit which was carried by our protection squad from C Company 1 King's Own Royal Border Regiment.

I was on the first lot of ten days and was quite looking forward to it but after about day two was bored shitless. We photographed everyone and anything entering and leaving the Sinn Fein Headquarters. I even photographed a French twat pulling up in a frog mobile complete with French number plates. I am not sure what the connection was but, can only imagine it was something to do with Basque terrorists. We also radioed in if any of the baddies that we had in our picture book were identified (they all had code words). Our films were collected every 24 hours between 0200hrs and 0400hrs. We simply dropped the roll of film out of the hole in the attic wall to a patrol below after they had given us predetermined code words which changed every 24 hours.

Things were working well; I did my ten days, and then had ten days off. It was on my second lot of ten days in the attic that things went wrong. It was about day four when we heard footsteps coming up to the attic, everyone grabbed their weapon, there was no need to cock it as there was already a round up the spout. The trouble was for me that at the time I was in my sleeping bag with my weapon (a long barreled SLR) the zip on my sleeping bag was fucking stuck, no matter how hard I tried, it wouldn't open. The door to the attic opened and in came Joe McKearney; he froze in abject terror, and at this point I managed to get my sleeping bag open and my weapon out. We all stayed very quite and still for a few moments before we realised he was by himself. We sat him down and asked him what had brought him into the attic. He told us that he thought he had a water leak as water was running down into his chip shop and he had come up to the attic to have a look. It turned out that one of our piss bags was

Grosvenor Road, Belfast after 'H' Block riots (Mark Campbell)

leaking and we hadn't noticed it, so that was it we were compromised, end of op. We did however gain some very useful Intel.

MULLHOUSE/GROSVENOR ROAD

John Girdler, 3rd Bn, the Queen's Regiment

I am a disabled ex-soldier of the Queen's Regiment, (now The Princess of Wales' Royal Regiment). In the early part of 1971, all the under-18s soldiers were ordered to leave the province, as a soldier had been injured and his parents said that he should never have been sent to Northern Ireland at that age. So, as there were nine soldiers under age in the battalion, they had to be replaced with nine from the 1st Battalion the Queen's Regiment to which I belonged.

Well on Tuesday 19th October 1971, whilst in Mullhouse Street, Belfast, I had a dream that myself and another soldier in my section would be shot; I did not know when or where or how, but every time that we got a few hours sleep I somehow fell back into the same dream. When I got to the same part of the dream that we were being shot, I was woken up. This went on for three days and nights, but on Friday night, the 22nd, my dream went a bit further and I saw for the first time the outcome. I saw myself being injured and the other soldier whose face I could not see, get shot dead.

So I told 2 friends of mine, Dave Jennings and Robert Benner (who was killed a few weeks afterwards) about my dream, and you can guess what they said to me. However, it was so real, so I told a medic Martin Potter and he said that there was not much he could do about it as we all get those sorts of dreams, so I asked around and nobody had any of the dreams that I had so I left it at that.

(On November 29, 1971, Private Robert Benner (25) was abducted by the IRA as he headed for the border to cross into the Republic to visit his Irish fiancée. His body was found just outside the town of Crossmaglen where he had been shot and dumped. He was due to leave Northern Ireland the following month.)

On Saturday night I had the same dream again and it stopped at the same place, then on Sunday the 24th late afternoon bits of the dream started to fall into place, but who could I tell? Everybody was tired and a bit jumpy because we all sensed that something was up, with more people on the streets than normal. Then it all started; the crowds were getting bigger and the noise was getting louder and with the insults getting worse, and then I knew that this was it and I had to try to change it any way that I can.

So when we got near to Mullhouse Street, the order came over the radio to stop where we were and to take up a position to protect the street, and so all eight of us waited for the rest of 'C' Company to join us. My mucker, Ernie and I were sent to the intersection between Mullhouse and Grosvenor Road and told to be lookouts. We knelt down to make smaller targets, but our sergeant shouted to us to stand up; I argued, but he said: 'Get f---ing up!' The company still had not joined us and the crowd was forming across the street; mostly women and children banging dustbin lids and blowing whistles then, without any hint the crowed parted just enough to let two men in. As they did so, with children in front of them, they opened up on us with machine guns; I got a shot off and as I did I pushed hard against Ernie to cover him as he was in no position to return fire.

The next thing I knew, I was laying in the gutter, face up with my rifle underneath me and not being able to move. I remember hearing the sound of running feet; some other men in the company pulled Ernie away and said to him 'That's a lot of blood on the path mate.' Ernie said 'It ain't mine; it's Girdler's!' When they got Ernie away to safety, they came back for me; the medic saw me looking at him, he said to me 'Sorry John; we thought you had fainted.' But as they pulled me away, some more shooting came and I was dropped on the road; a PIG backed over me with its wheels either side of me, and as it drove forward I was grabbed and towed along the street towards safety. But, as the PIG drove forward, a sniper shot me in the chest and I was dropped again; the vehicle turned around and drove over me again and I was grabbed again and another vehicle backed away using itself for my protection.

After I had reached the Royal Victoria Hospital I was put into an unconscious state, and four days later I came to; in those four days, I was later told, that I had died three times and each time I was brought back to life. I was told that I had been very lucky as I had multiple gun shot wounds to the neck, chest, side, and right side with a deflated lung, and a dropped right foot with damage to the tendons, and will have to wear a leg calliper for the rest of my life. I also learned that Ernie had not died, but he had gun shot wounds to the right leg and no one else got hurt or died that day.

The doctors say that because of my dream I did not suffer from shock, but I was told that it would come out of me somehow and some time in the future and it does every time I get in a bad mood I can feel it. So, I try to calm down with the help of my wife Ann and in the last 34 years I have been very lucky to have her by my side. I have known Ann since before I got injured and she has stayed by me ever since; without her, I would have committed suicide by now. Through the flashbacks that I still get and the nightmares, she is always there for me; now that's love.

SPRINGFIELD ROAD

Brian Baskerville, R.A.O.C.

I can't remember the date or the full details of the incident but there was a shooting in the Springfield Road involving an RPG7 attack and shooting. The usual follow up in the aftermath ensued with Int being involved. The firing point was a terraced house from the upstairs front bedroom window and the gunmen made their escape through the back yard. For next hour or two, there were comings and goings of all kinds of agencies, all pretty routine stuff. All went quiet and the scene was reopened to normality. The following day a call was received from PIRA suggesting that SF return to the scene to deactivate the booby trap device left in the back yard. That was close.

It also begged the question: was it a 'come on' by the IRA to lure unsuspecting – and, certainly in the early days of the troubles, naive – soldiers to the scene. Alarmingly, for the EOD men, the IRA's bomb makers and tactics became increasingly professional as the troubles dragged on into a fourth decade.

RSM R.T. Saxby, Royal Army Medical Corps

I was posted to the military wing, Musgrave Park Hospital as WO2 (RQMS) in May 1988. At the time as has been reported earlier, the Provos were very busy .On my first day I was taken for a familiarisation drive around our part of Belfast, we drove to Lisburn, Belfast centre the Royal Victoria Hospital etc. On the way back we took a left instead of a right. Before we knew it, we were down the Falls Road, as my driver was black we were soon noticed. We drove into a disused garage forecourt to turn round. We were followed by a black cab; we drove off and returned to relative safety quickly with a sigh of relief. If I was a cat this would be life number one! (*N.B. It was known that the IRA 'ran' these black cabs for transporting weapons and explosives, and for occasional abductions.*)

It is easy to see how Corporals Wood and Howes could have made a similar mistake, with a much more catastrophic and sad ending!

The author stands at the site of the murder of three
Green Jackets in 1982 (Ken Wharton)

The British Army had been on the streets of Northern Ireland for almost two years, and if a survey had been drawn up amongst the soldiers on the ground at that time, then the Falls Road and surrounding areas would have been top of their hate list. Night after night, the mobs rioted, threw petrol bombs, rocks, almost anything on which they could lay their hands. As the second summer of deployment arrived, no soldiers had been killed on active service in this immediate area. However, that was soon to change, as already in the space of five months, in other parts of the province, six soldiers had been shot dead, two had been killed by bombs, and twenty others had been killed in 'non-battle related situations.' The Falls Road was merely biding its time.

For 21 months, it waited patiently, and then, on May 25, 1971, Sergeant Michael Willets (27) was on duty in the entrance hall at the RUC station at Springfield Road. A terrorist threw a blast bomb into the doorway which was packed with civilians; Sergeant Willets, with incredible bravery, and with absolutely no thought for his own safety, thrust two children out of the way and stood in front of the device. It detonated and he was killed instantly; for his bravery he was posthumously awarded the George Cross. As his lifeless body was being carried to the ambulance in Springfield Road, it was jeered and women in the crowd actually spat on the stretcher.

General Sir Peter Graham

A young soldier arrived in the 1st Battalion the Gordon Highlanders which I was commanding in 1977. He was welcomed and sent to a company. A few days later I was visiting patrols in the Lower Falls when I noticed him crouch down in a door way. It was a Saturday afternoon and it was raining heavily. I went across to him and spoke to him and asked how he was to which he replied he was all right. I then said 'Well it's not a very nice day and it's a Saturday afternoon and one could be doing better things. Indeed the Falls is not necessarily the healthiest of places to be and of course it's just bucketing with rain.' He looked me straight in the face and replied 'Well Sir, the rain only goes skin deep.'

He seemed to me to sum up all that was steady and sensible about the British Jock, a quiet, calm acceptance of life and you just get on with your job without fuss or bother.

In the very early hours of July 12, 1971, 1RGJ lost their second man of the tour, and their first on the Falls Road. Thirty year old Rifleman Dave Walker, a Welsh boy was manning an OP on Northumberland Street, just where the Falls road becomes Divis Street. He was shot by an IRA sniper, whilst he was on the roof of the Northumberland Street Mill and died shortly afterwards.

Two months later, on November 27, Guardsman Paul Nicholls of the Scots Guards was on a routine foot patrol in St James Crescent, when he was shot in the back by IRA gunmen who had taken over a nearby house. The 18 year old became the fifth Scots Guard to be killed in the space of just 7 weeks. As the Army's third Christmas in the Province approached, in the small hours of December 16, an

THE FALLS ROAD/SPRINGFIELD ROAD   133

Army patrol of the Glosters came under fire in the Alma Street area. In the fire fight, Anthony Aspinall (22) who was married and had three small children, was badly wounded and died of his wounds the following day.

The New year of 1972 was barely 5 days old, when one his comrades, Private Keith Bryan (18) was shot and killed on Ardmoulin Street in the Falls area. A Gloster soldier told me that, as the badly wounded soldier was being taken to hospital, several women from nearby houses came out and laughed and jeered. A week later, the RUC had their first fatality in the area, when one of their part-time officers, Raymond Denham (42) a married man with two children, was shot and killed whilst he was at work in a printing shop in the Falls area.

This year of 1972 would turn out to be the worst year for British Army casualties with 158 soldiers and UDR men killed in action. It would be the Spring before another soldier fell in this area. On May 11, Private John Ballard (18) of the Royal Anglian Regiment (RAR) was on a foot patrol when he was shot by the IRA as he walked along Sultan Street. The Lincolnshire boy died almost immediately. On May 30, Marcel Doglay, a native of the Seychelles and a respected member of the King's regiment was killed inside Springfield Road Police station. The IRA had penetrated security and planted an explosive device in the recreation area. He was 28 and was loyally serving his adopted country. [See Paddy Lenaghan's excellent account in A Long Long War by the same author]

Just two months later, the RAR or the 'Angle Irons' as they are known by other Regiments, lost two soldiers within 24 hours in the Falls area. On July 12, whilst in a mobile patrol convoy, Lance Corporal Martin Rooney (22) was shot and killed by an IRA gunman with the direct complicity of a group of men who covered him before, during, and after the fateful shot. The next day, Corporal Kenneth Mogg (29) father of a young child was shot and fatally wounded in a fire fight with the IRA at Dunville Park, in the Lower Falls area. Within four days, the Falls area had claimed another victim; it was another member of the King's Regiment, as West Belfast took its toll of this Merseyside/Manchester unit. Private James Jones (18)

The following month, in what one Light Infantry officer referred to as '...48 insane hours ...' three soldiers were shot and killed in the area. On July 17, Private Martin Boddy (24) from Peterborough was shot and fatally wounded whilst on foot patrol in Selby Street; he died of his wounds later in the Royal Victoria Hospital (RVH). He was the fifth RAR soldier to die in Belfast in the space of just three months; the Falls area would claim more victims from this famous Regiment within a short period of time. The next day, Private Ronald Layfield (24) from Burnley and a member of the King's Regiment was killed by an IRA sniper at Beechmount Avenue. Just hours later, whilst in a military vehicle, Light Infantryman Richard Jones (21) was shot and killed travelling along Roden Street.

Before this month of August was finished, two RGJ men would be dead, both shot in the Falls and a Kingsman would die of his wounds after a bomb attack. On August 28, Corporal Ian Morrill (29) of the Green Jackets, but attached to the Light Infantry was shot and killed at Beechmount Avenue; an Essex boy, he was killed instantly. Kingsman Roy Christopher (20) from the Lancashire area was horribly injured on the 18th of the month when an IED (improvised explosive device) detonated as he passed a shop in Cupar Street. Other soldiers were injured in the attack, but Roy Christopher lost both legs; he succumbed to his wounds, twelve days after the atrocity. On the same day, Rifleman David Griffiths, (RGJ) who was 20 and from Liverpool, was shot and killed by an IRA gunman on Clonard Street in the Falls area.

SPRINGFIELD ROAD

Pte Kev 'Errol' Flynn, 1st Light Infantry

I was out in Ulster with the Light Infantry on an Op banner tour 1982/1983, and was nearby when a civilian by the name of Thomas Reilly was shot and killed by one of the lads in 1LI. Reilly was also the road manager for a well known girl trio of the time.

A couple of days later, these lovely girls decided to have a stroll around Springfield road etc; unbeknownst to myself, as I would certainly have asked for their autographs. Whilst we were on the Springfield, they walked past my oppo' 'Spanner' Spence and poured out a whole load of foul-mouthed abuse at him etc., and finishing off with a projectile of phlegm right into his face. When he told us later in the patrol what had happened, we were in complete hysterics and full of mirth over the incident. Later that very same night, 'Spanner' was unluckily ordered out onto on the search team; he was called out in the very late hours, whilst the rest of the brick stayed in bed and had some well earned zzzzzs.

Three or four hours later, I heard the door to our room open and light cascaded in; all of a sudden, there was a rancid stench smothering us all. Poor 'Spanner' finished this hectic day off with having to climb down into a sewer manhole and was covered in shit, which again caused much merriment. If it wasn't for these little escapades and of course laughing at other people's misfortunes, the tour out there would have been woeful I'm sure.

On 9 August, 1983, Thomas O'Reilly, a civilian was shot dead by British soldier in West Belfast after an incident which ended in a scuffle. The altercation was between local people and an Army foot patrol, on Whiterock Road, near the Ballymurphy Estate.

BELFAST AGAIN

Tony Procter, REME

I was met by a few of my workmates who were expecting me. They drove me around to the barracks and filled me in on the latest situation. It did not take me long to get into the work routine, in fact almost immediately. I did wonder if they were saving all the work for me on my return. Before I had left on my leave we were experimenting on an electrification system for our armoured vehicles. The idea was to charge the hull of the vehicle with a very high voltage of electricity so that if anyone tried to climb onto it to disable it with a bomb, they would be thrown off with the shock. So on my return one of my jobs was fit this electrification modification to all our armoured vehicles and then to tour our many patrol locations and periodically test this equipment. The test involved switching on the charge and then connecting a metre between the vehicle and the ground and reading the voltage. This test was a little involved and on many occasions I did something I'm not proud of. Whenever we had a troop of our vehicles stationed in a housing estate there were always a crowd of kids mulling around along of course with a few nice mums. Well on these occasions when I was testing the electrification I would wait until a kid was touching the vehicle then I would throw the charge switch, if the kid was thrown off with the shock, the system worked. Using these live guinea pigs it didn't take us long to realise that this modification was a success. I am sure that this system eventually saved the lives of many soldiers. Earlier it was a big problem with rioters clambering on to our vehicles to disable them.

MARKETS AREA, BELFAST

Gunner John Swaine, Royal Artillery

As the hot summer of 1974 moved on, the days seemed endless, and it's strange how time moves so slowly when the weather's warm. Tiredness always was the key factor, even though we were all young kids in our 20s.

We had a young officer – a Lieutenant with us one night out on foot patrol; he let rip with a few rounds towards a street near the Markets after we had heard gun fire lower down. We heard an angry, urgent shout from the nearby street: 'Who the fuck are you c***s firing at?' It turned out to be a foot patrol from the Glosters and one of their Corporals – a real big lad – stormed up to our officer and gave us a right fucking over! It was their contact, although whether our officer was firing on the gunman or the Gloster patrol remains a mystery to this day; it could have been worse!!!!

This incident with the Glosters was scary but somewhat comical, because when we all first heard the gunfire from the Markets we all scattered for low ground and doorways. If holes in tarmac could have been dug with bare hands, they would have been that night, I can tell you!!! My thoughts were to stay put and not stand up, because knowing my luck, as I'm 6ft I would have caught a fucking round!!! But after the incident I did feel somewhat sick wondering about what would have happened if a soldier had had been killed by friendly fire!!!!

As the tour drew to an end we had an incident with Gunner Keith Bates who was badly injured in a mobile patrol accident and everyone was on a downer after this. Keith was on a routine mobile patrol at night he was in the rear of the Land Rover with a young Scouse kid called Ian Mitchell and the driver was a lad called 'Snowy' Miles. Anyhow, they were cruising around central Belfast late this night, when they approached a cross section junction with some lights, and their Land Rover was hit at full force at the rear end by an MP's mobile patrol. Sadly for Keith, they were driving a Makralon armoured vehicle. They were apparently involved in a hot pursuit before it hit Keith's landrover. Keith and Ian Mitchell were catapulted right out of the rear end by the impact and poor Keith's body was smashed at full force onto a set of iron railings surrounding a monument in a central island in the road

As our time to depart came, we left Belfast and 49 Field Regt RA took over from us. We were all hoping and praying that Keith would pull through ok. It wasn't to be, and a few days after returning to Germany we received the horrible news that Keith had died; we were gutted. The kid seemed so far away and we could do nothing to help him, but he was at peace.

Gunner Keith Bates was only 20 when he was killed in a tragic accident in Belfast's Markets area. He was from Shipley, in West Yorkshire and, although his name appears on the Wall at the AFM in Staffordshire, he does not appear in the 'official' roll of honour. I am pleased to rectify that oversight in this book's ROH.

A second view of the loss of Gunner Bates is recounted below:

MARKETS AREA, BELFAST

Ian 'Scouse' Mitchell, Royal Artillery

Let me begin by thanking you for my opportunity to express myself about some of the exploits I encountered in Northern Ireland. I have numerous memories, but will limit them to the most dangerous I'm 52, and served with 45 medium regiment (170 Imjin battery) from 1973/77. I did 2 tours in NI, both of which were in the summers of 1974 and 1976. We were posted to Belfast city centre and the adjoining areas, Ballymacarrat, the Markets, Unity flats and the outlying areas of the Pye rebro station and the BBC television mast at Divis Mountain.

My main story begins towards the back end of our first tour of '74, when, in the early hours of the 17th October, we were on a mobile patrol in the city centre in the pursuit of a suspected terrorist vehicle. As we approached a main set of lights which were on 'green', an RMP makralon Police vehicle jumped a set of red lights. In doing so it caught the back end of our Land Rover, and, in the process, catapulted all of us out of the vehicle. As the 4 of us were thrown out, Keith 'Basher' Bates was impaled onto nearby wrought iron railings. As the Land rover spun around and crushed him against them, I hit a metal traffic sign. The other two occupants shot along the road and pavement, sustaining minor injuries. Basher had fatal wounds, and died a number of weeks later; I had serious injuries, broken back in 5 places, closed head injury, multiply fractures to my pelvis and was casevaced to England.

I have to say that I received first class medical treatment for the length of time I convalesced, but it took a very long time, and I now suffer with a compressed fracture of my D6 vertebra. The RMPs were investigated over the incident but were acquitted and there were no charges. The incident resulted in one dead Gunner and another one was given the last rites by a Catholic priest, at the request of his mother. Funny, I don't remember this incident making the national news.

ALBERT STREET MILL

Bob Davies, RAOC

Talking of the RUC, in those days a member of their CID used to come to Albert Street Mill to take statements from the Operator if the task was likely to involve a court case in the future. On the same tour as the coffin incident I dealt with a crude incendiary device made up of Sodium Chlorate and a condom containing acid. The statement was taken in the Operators' communal area with all four of us present. The process began with a brief explanation of the task and how the device was intended to work. The RUC detective nodded sagely throughout this explanation asking the occasional question before beginning writing the statement down for my eventual signature. The whole process took about an hour before being ready for signature. It was as the detective was about to leave the room that he turned and said 'Just one more question sir, so I can tell my Sergeant, what is a condom?' As you can imagine we fell about in hysterical laughter when he'd left the room.

Another more serious incident took place at the start of my first tour. The guy I relieved, who must remain nameless, asked me to deliver some of his 'DIFS' evidence (Department of Industrial and Forensic Science) to the forensic laboratory. This evidence was left over from a Belfast 'D' Day (disruption day) that had occurred before I had arrived. For those not aware, a D Day involved multiple hijackings of vehicles by the IRA which were then left in strategic places causing massive disruption whilst awaiting the attendance of the frantic EOD teams – the '4 sprung-door technique' was much in evidence. It was usual if one of the vehicles contained an explosive device. This kept the teams on their toes and inevitably slowed the clearance process a little. In this case a device had been discovered early in the proceedings. What was not know however was that there were two devices involved in this 'D' Day, the other being contained in a small gas cylinder; my predecessor's DIFS. Obviously not knowing this I duly delivered the evidence, already sealed in an evidence bag, to the forensic laboratory where I had to sign, keeping to the 'chain of evidence' procedures. It was a couple of months later that I was asked to comment on why I had delivered a live device to the laboratory; I never did find out who had disarmed it.

On September 25, the toll of 'Angle irons' killed on the Falls continued to mount, when Corporal John Barry was shot as he rode inside a Saracen armoured vehicle as it passed Cyprus Street. He was 22, married and came, like so many men from his Regiment, from the Lincolnshire area. Four days later, Private Ian Burt (18) from Essex was shot and killed in a fierce fire fight with the IRA in Albert Street.

On the same day, the Army killed two IRA members in the Lower Falls area, one of whom was killed during the same fire fight in which Private Burt received his fatal injuries.

That September was a black stain in the history of Northern Ireland, as no less than 44 people were killed throughout the Province. During the thirty days of this month, 15 soldiers and 23 civilians died; additionally, SF shot and killed 4 IRA and 2 Loyalist terrorists. Two of the IRA dead were shot in the Falls area. A Royal Marine, Anthony David (27) from Wales was shot and badly wounded in the Falls area in mid-September and died of his wounds in hospital, on October 17.

In all, almost 500 people died through the euphemistically named 'political violence' throughout 1972. According to David McKittrick's *Lost Lives*, a staggering 280 of these deaths – well over half – were as a result of IRA activity.

1973 loomed large, with very little prospect of peace on the horizon; the 'real' peace was still almost 25 years into the future; a fact which would have depressed even the most pessimistic member of the SF. Four more soldiers would die on the streets of the Falls area that year, and, although the year as a whole would be bad in terms of the Army's death toll, the sickening heights of 1972 would never again be repeated. This year, on the Falls, at least, the 'Woodentop' regiments would bear the brunt of fatalities, with two Coldstream Guards and one Scots Guard sadly being added to the ever growing Roll of Honour.

The year was not even two months old, when, on February 6, Private Michael Murtagh (23) of the Queen's Lancashire Regiment (QLR) became the first soldier to be killed in Northern Ireland by the IRA's newest weapon; the rocket propelled grenade (RPG). His armoured vehicle was struck whilst on Servia Street. Just eight days later, a QLR comrade, Private Edwin Weston (21) was shot dead in an exchange of gunfire with several IRA gunmen in Cyprus Street.

Sergeant Kirkpatrick on escorts (Royal Regiment Wales Museum)

Only six more days had passed, when an IRA bomb killed two soldiers from the Coldstreamers on the Falls Road. On February 20, Guardsman Robert Pearson (19) from Leeds and Guardsman Malcolm Shaw (23) both died after a bomb and bullet attack by a large IRA contingent on the Falls Road. The following day, this famous Regiment would lose another man, Guardsman Michael Doyle shot by the IRA on the 'Murph. [*See section on the Ballymurphy Estate*].

The following month, 19 year old Private Gary Barlow of the Queen's Lancashire Regiment was murdered in cold blood by an IRA gunman in one of the most sickening incidents ever to take place during the troubles. Private Barlow was on a foot patrol in the Albert Street area and, as was not uncommon, he was separated from other members of the patrol. A group of women immediately converged on the frightened soldier and took his rifle from him. Eyewitnesses reported that he was crying for his mother and some of the women tried to help him, to no avail. He was then pushed into an empty building, and a gunman was summoned; when the gunman arrived – reportedly the same age as the soldier, he cold-bloodedly shot him in the head, allegedly to the cheers of the mob.

It would be New Year's Eve before the Falls claimed another victim; as 1974 approached, the IRA shot dead a Scots Guard after holding a family hostage in the Beechmount Avenue area. Twenty three year old Alan Daughtery, a married soldier from the North east was shot whilst on mobile patrol when his vehicle was hit by a hail of bullets. He died instantly.

Almost five years would pass before the Falls Road claimed another soldier's life, but sandwiched in between was the shooting of detective Constable Noel McCabe (26) a married RUC man. He was shot by an IRA gunman as he drove along the Falls Road on November 2, 1976.

Two and a half years later, on April 19, 1979, Captain Paul Rodgers, a 37 year old member of the Army Cadets, was murdered whilst visiting Belfast from England when he was fired upon by IRA gunmen in the Falls area. In August of that same year, RUC Constable, Derek Davidson, whilst responding to a call from a member of the public which turned out to be bogus, was shot and killed by gunmen in Clondara Street.

On October 28, 1979, Sergeant Major David Bellamy, of the Army Physical Training Corps (APTC) a 31 year old married soldier was killed during an IRA gun attack on the Springfield Road Police station. In the same attack, RUC Constable John Davidson (26) was badly wounded and he died of his wounds on November 18.

The death of any soldier or member of the Security Forces is indeed regrettable, and, for their loved ones, absolute tragedy, but it is a tribute to the SF, that almost two years would pass, before another would die. On September 29, 1981, a UDR soldier, Private Mark Stockman (20) was shot dead by an INLA gunman as he relaxed during his lunch break at a factory on Springfield Road. Almost a year later, on September 20. 1982, the Worcestershire & Sherwood Foresters (W&SF) lost a man Private Martin Jessop (19), a Derby man, was killed by the IRA after an RPG attack on the Springfield Road police station. He became the second of three members of his Regiment killed in the space of a week.

A further three years would pass before the next SF death in the Falls, but when that came, it would be a tragic day for the Royal Green Jackets and the second worst day for this great Regiment throughout the entire period of the troubles. On March 25, 1982, an RGJ vehicle was driving along Crocus Street which is very close to both Springfield Road and the Falls Road. IRA gunmen attacked the vehicle with an M60 machine gun. The weapon, acquired by the IRA through American sources, fires the standard 7.62mm round, but at a rate of 550 rounds per minute and with a muzzle velocity of 853 metres per second (2,800 feet).

Three RGJ were killed in that attack; Rifleman Anthony Rapley (22), Rifleman Nicholas Malakos (19) and Rifleman Daniel Holland, also 19. The first two Green Jackets died at the scene and Daniel Holland died a short time later in the RVH. The author, through his connections with the Regiment, knows the RGJ as a tightly knit bunch of soldiers, drawn predominantly from the London area; they are known by other Regiments of the British Army, as the 'Black Mafia.'

Only the earlier tragedy at Camlough (May 19, 1981) when four members of the Regiment were killed alongside an RCT driver surpassed Crocus Street.

Five days later, on March 30, an RUC Sergeant, David Brown who was 35 and married with children was shot and badly wounded in Springfield Crescent. The Falls area toll was added to, when, on April 16, Sergeant Brown died of his wounds. It was the turn of the Devon & Dorsets (D&D) twelve months later, when Corporal Gerald Jeffrey (28) died from the wounds he received from a bomb blast, a week earlier. His death on April 7, 1983 followed his serious injury after the IRA remote detonated an IED in a building on the Falls Road. He was married with children and came from the Plymouth area.

Nearly five years would elapse before there were further SF fatalities in the area, now known as the 'murder mile' and it would again involve a Policeman. On January 25, 1988, Constable Colin Gilmore of the RUC was killed in an IRA grenade attack whilst he was driving along the Falls Road very close to the Belfast Hospital for Sick Children. Later in that same year, in the early days of Summer, bomb disposal expert, Sergeant Major John Howard (29) of the Royal Army Ordnance Corps EOD (Explosives Ordnance Disposal) was called to an explosion. Earlier, two people had been killed when an IRA bomb had detonated and Sergeant Major Howard was examining the debris, when he stepped on a booby trapped device and was killed instantly.

The first soldier to die anywhere in the Province in 1989, was Royal Anglian Private, Nicholas Peacock (20) from Grantham, Lincolnshire; he would also be the last 'Angle iron' to die during the troubles. In the minutes between January 31 and February 1, he was terribly injured after the IRA remote detonated a bomb outside a pub in the Falls Road and died shortly afterwards. Private Peacock would be the last soldier to be killed in the Falls area.

The Falls, however, were not yet finished with members of the SF; the bloodletting was not yet complete. That fate was reserved for two Constables in the RUC. The two were patrolling along Chapel Lane and very close to a Police station when an IRA gunman shot them both in the back. The two officers were Harold Beckett (47) and Gary Meyer (35) and were well known and respected in the Falls area, showing an even-handed approach to, and respect for, members of the Catholic community. The murderer escaped through a nearby church.

Ten months later, the IRA used an RPG to kill an RUC officer on Beechmount Avenue whilst on mobile patrol.

This was May 2, 1991; a lasting peace was still six years into the future, but the killings of SF members had ceased, at least in the Falls area. The slaughter began on July 12, 1971 with the death of Rifleman David Walker and ended, almost twenty years later with the killing of RUC Sergeant Stephen Gillespie. In the intervening years, 45 soldiers and policemen would have been killed in the Falls and over 90 in four areas of west Belfast not much bigger, as stated previously, as the city of Wakefield in West Yorkshire.

Chapter 5

Divis Street/
North Howard Street Mill

O ne also needs to mention the notorious Divis Street and, of course, the flats which dominated it, a continuation of the Falls Road. It is a mixed area of post war Council multi-storey flats and areas like Leeson Street and Hastings Street which were – certainly back in the 70s – mirror images of the back-to-back terraced houses found on the Lower Falls. As one former squaddie said to the author, on seeing the flats for the first time: 'Jesus Christ! I didn't know that you could stack shit that high!'

DIVIS AND FALLS

Rifleman 'Mick', Royal Green Jackets

There were many incidents on this tour, too many to recount, and I don't wish to dwell on specific 'war stories' but tell you about life in general.

We were in North Howard Street Mill and in just under company strength and our tasked areas were around there. I should point out that the mill was strategically placed about half a click from the Loyalist Shankhill and the Nationalist Falls and Divis areas and we were stationed there in a 'buffer' role. Foot patrols were the order of the day and we spent a lot of time in and around the Falls and Springfield Road and on the Divis.

The Divis flats – how could stacked shit stand up like that – were all postwar council housing and all the Catholics were jammed in there, whether by choice or because they liked safety in numbers I don't know. There was the big 16 floor one where an off-duty lad had been killed earlier on and where several others were killed and a big, odd shaped complex which we called Zanussi for reasons I will explain later. These were 6 stories high and in zigzagged blocks of about 7 or 8 legs. The big block was a real bad arse building and we had a lot of trouble there with residents throwing things at us and spying on our movements and letting PIRA know what we were up to. Long, covered walkways with good sniper firing points and they were a real nuisance; gave us rice, I can tell you.

The Zanussi flats were so-called, because all manner of electrical goods products – TVs, fridges, washing machines etc – came flying out of the upper windows and the wreckage resembled an electrical goods showroom! A lot of shit was happening around then and we weren't liked and in turn we didn't like them. It was strange because a lot of us came from around the East End (*of London*) and some of us were from south of the river and there were Oxford geezers in with us too. The carrot crunchers from the home counties with their country mansions hadn't a clue about the poor housing we had come from and couldn't understand that the enemy and their supporters came from like backgrounds. We had black geezers and Cockney wide boys and we were proud to be the 'black mafia.' Alright, there was prejudice against the blacks and all but these were 'our' blacks and if we had heard any racialist shouts from other badges, they would have got grief.

Apart from the big tower and Zanussi, there were lots of old back-to-backs and old terraced houses and Albert Street, the Rosses, St Peters Church, Servia St, Milford street were all fun places and we had lots of crap from the natives. I came from near the Mile End Road and I knew what being poor was all about and I remember the rows of terraced housing – the ones what Herman Goring missed – and the people and the community spirit but these people had none of this. All they had was hatred, for us, for the Prods and for the RUC. Could you blame them? Perhaps not, but we were right in the middle. A major Rupert wrote a book called 'Pig in the Middle' and he was right; that's what we were. Around there was Leeson Street. Now there was a shithole. 3BN (*RGJ's 3rd Battalion*) had a real arsehole of a time there and one of their lance jacks from 'R' company won the DCM in a major league firefight with the PIRA. Dirty brick terracing which, after some of the trouble, looked like a scene from 'Band of Brothers' when they was street fighting in Normandy.

One day on one of the Rosses, we had gone firm and I was crouching down by a house and something wet and slimy and pongy was poured over me running down my beret and down my smock. Honest to Christ, it reeked and I realised that it was piss. I looked up and saw a bedroom window being hurriedly closed and I went over to the front door and I was going to kick it in and take some bastard's head off. The brick commander told me to forget it and I had to walk away. I stank all day because it was

RUC men in the Divis area (Royal Regiment Wales Museum)

several hours before we were back at the Mill and nobody would come anywhere near me, bastards!

They would spit at us and swear at us and tell us to fuck off home to England. They latched on to the fact that we was a London based regiment and called us cockney scum. One of the lads used to say that he'd heard worse from the Mrs.!

One memory I have took place near the Zanussi and, I'm not proud of it but it gave me a lot of satisfaction at the time. We were out on patrol on a cold day and we could see our breath in the air and we turned round a street and could see the zigzagged blocks. There was a bunch of youths, aged from about 14 to about 20 and they stood looking at us, looking daggers but they kept their traps shut and then one of them, about 16 years old started walking towards us where I was front man. I knew that trouble was looming because he kept looking back at his mates and smiling and they were like, egging him on. He got to within 2 feet of me and I could see his spots all red and shining. He just gobbed right in my bleeding face and stood there grinning. I was like, calm but he made the mistake of not running; just stood there and grinned, showing off to his mates. I had my SLR cradled in my right hand and just swung the butt upwards right under his jaw. You know the term 'went down like a sack of spuds' well he went down like that and didn't move. The next thing all his mates legged it and we walked on. Within 10 minutes the word had spread and the Micks were out in strength and we had a riot on our hands. No one ever asked me about it and none of the other geezers in the brick said a word. I was 21 at the time and couldn't really understand the hatred.

Kids in Divis (Royal Regiment Wales Museum)

NORTH HOWARD STREET MILL

Northumberland Street connects the Republican Falls Road with the Loyalist Shankhill Road and was viewed by senior Army officers as the ideal point at which to station soldiers. It was seen as an excellent place in which to provide a buffer between the two warring factions. An old Victorian flour mill was located about midway along North Howard Street and it was at once requisitioned for the troops. One soldier stationed there, had this to say:

NORTH HOWARD STREET: DAYS OF DISRUPTION

Malcolm Patinson, 3 Light Infantry

In 1991 whilst serving with The Third Battalion Light Infantry we where deployed on a six month Op Banner Tour of West Belfast, normally tours in Belfast would only four months due to the extreme pressure units were under on a daily. We were one of the first units to be tasked in this way; this would be a trial and a test of both physical and mental strength that would set new benchmarks in the durability of soldiers under extreme conditions putting more pressure on us in the fight in to combat urbanised terrorism. Belfast generated more incidents in one day than in probably a full tour in any of the rural areas of the province. At least in a rural setting you could withdraw into a defensive area and lay up to charge your batteries brew up and hide away in total stealth. Patrolling for two or three hours in the city

The author standing by the remains of North Howard St Mill (Ken Wharton)

was physically exhausting, and you are constantly being watched by all in sundry never able to withdraw until changeover.

It was my first tour in the City, and a totally different experience from anywhere else in the province I had been; the operational tempo was relentless, even people I still communicate with to this day still recall it was one of the hardest and most incident driven tours of all time. I was a full corporal in the Recce Platoon, attached to 'A' company based at the notorious North Howard Street Mill. I had heard so many stories about the Mill, I felt like that I'd already completed a tour there before i'd even set foot in the place. Our area of operation was all of the Lower Falls covering the fringes of the city and our northern areas where the Upper Falls, Beachmounts, Rockmounts, and the Ballymurphy, and Moyards all slung in just for good measure. Our areas linked up the Main police routes from Governor Road, Springfield Road, The Oaks, and New Barnsley Park in the Ballymurphy; although a relatively small area of operation it was without doubt the busiest area for incidents and terrorist activities and was home to some of the hardest and the most experienced ASU's (Active service Units) in the whole province. North Howard Street was an early Victorian Flax Mill and has been used as a patrol base since the start of the troubles, and through the years evolved becoming more of a huge fortress with a maze of blast walls intersecting the main court yards, and Sangars dotted all round the place.

North Howard Street Mill (NSM) was host to more closed-circuit television cameras than in the whole of Slough town centre; a vital asset to our base. Still despite the amount of protection it never deterred the terrorists from carrying out attacks on the Mill mounted on a regular basis. Our call sign was billeted on the third floor of the Mill the perks of this being it was the NAAFI floor, and the down side of it was, it just happened to be located just under the cookhouse, which meant we were totally infested with the biggest fucking Cockroaches I have ever seen in the united kingdom, millions of the little fuckers; we had to leave the lights on all day and night so the little bastards would not swarm over you as we slept, it was straight out of a Stephen King movie.

The IRA and associated factions certainly knew how to stretch us, using IED's (Improvised Explosive Devices) of all natures, but mainly the hand held types, such as IAAGS, (Improvised Anti Armour Grenades) and the very affective Mk 15 affectively known as the coffee jar bomb with a few sporadic shootings for good measure. They had some great ways of splitting up mobile support units luring them away from foot patrols and taking them on with RPG's and PRIGS (Projectile Rocket Improvised Grenades) a devastating home made weapon. You certainly had to give them credit in the way they operated masters of their own game, and we always seemed to be the pawns it was a bloody good thing that our CO was a top chess player or life would have been very hard indeed. One thing the IRA could not break down and that was the level of our determination and professionalism, we train better than any army in the world and that's what makes the difference between life and death in Belfast.

The most effective 'weapon' in the PIRA arsenal at the time was their days of disruption; these operations were carried out with the aim to cause massive disruption to the city bringing all traffic movements to halt tying up all emergency services, police army, EOD, fire service causing chaos in all locations. Their normal MO was to create multiple incidents and spring them at the same time. Kidnappings and car jacking would normally set the ball rolling; followed by some shooting and a bit of street violence directed at the patrols just to keep the troops busy, whilst the bigger plan got rolling. What was guaranteed, once the news filtered through of kidnappings and car jackings was that PROXY Bombs (Large Bombs left outside bases) were already on their way. What they would do is basically deny entry and exit from the bases and police stations by driving a bomb up to the gates, and, normally, just for good effect, leave some poor barstard chained to the steering wheel.

This would force the ATO (Ammunition and Technical Officer) to be deployed and go around and clear the devices as fast as humanely possible in order to let us deploy form the base and attend the incidents. The ATO's work was relentless. We would then be tasked to carry out VCPs in order to get the traffic moving and deal with the disruption and try to get back some normality so that people could get about their day. The incidents would vary in length they could last for a few hours or a couple of days, which meant that we would have to be relieved in place, and straight onto another task or patrol. Every man carried a day sack with a few essentials such as a bit of ket (chocolates and sweets), and some water, and copious amounts of cigs just on the off chance that we could pop into the cop shop for a piss .

Colin, Argyll & Sutherland Highlanders.

The sangars we used in North Howard Street Mill were basic to say the least. We spent two hours in each sangar, with about four sangars to rotate around, so things could become pretty boring at times. There was never any heating in the sangars which was a nightmare in winter and, in summer there was no air conditioning, which was also a nightmare. It wasn't as though we could open the windows.

The mill, home to many Regiments during their four months stints in Belfast, was eventually pulled down on October 10, 1995 under the city's urban regeneration plans. It had one huge chimney stack and a large flat roof, ideal to use as an OP. It would witness the deaths of three soldiers in a fourteen year period.

NEGLIGENT DISCHARGE, NORTH HOWARD STREET MILL

Rob Colley, Green Howards

The ND happened at the end of June 85 in the main guard room at the base at North Howard Street Mill at about 6 a.m. We had only been in

Belfast for about a week and this was our first guard duty. We went in to the guard room/sangar to do the handover and we only had combat jackets on with no flak jackets. Anyway the handover was uneventful as nothing had happened overnight and nothing unusual was due to happen during our stag; just the normal comings and goings. I was sitting with the boss sat at a little table looking at two 9mm pistols and ammo; me and my mate stood against the wall bored and trying to wake up properly. The boss then decided to play 'Dirty Harry' and picked up the pistols and did the old pointing them at us and quoting the old 'do I feel lucky?' Well, do ya, punk? Routine.

Quite a few unprintable words were said, at this point, to the effect of don't point those things at us. He just laughed and informed us that they were not cocked and then pointed them again and squeezed the trigger of the one in his left hand. A huge BANG was the next sound I heard and the world then seemed to move in slow motion for a few seconds; then the wall exploded in a cloud of dust and bits of breeze block went all over the place. I looked to my right and saw a hole in the wall at waist height about six inches away from me and the warhead on the floor next to my right foot. The room was full of smoke, and the boss was frozen to the spot, his face showing all the classic signs of sheer panic. After what seemed like an age but was in fact only a second or two, a few choice words were exchanged between us, basically calling him a few names and telling him what I thought about what he had just done.

His biggest concern was that we were ok and then his focus turned to the fact that the whole Mill would have heard the shot and the QRF (*Quick Reaction Force*) would be springing into action, and that his stripes were about to leave his arm at a fair rate of knots. His face reflected the fact that he was going to jail and he was facing a huge fine etc., etc. On the other hand, I was thinking '...you wanker! You could have killed me and I've only been here a week!' After a while he realised that no one had heard the shot and he then asked if we would say nothing and he would find a way of 'covering' the loss of the round and if push came to shove, he would take the crap for it. Because he was a mate, and we knew it was an accident even if he was being a total knob head, we decided to go along with it. So the great cover up began; we swept the floor, got rid of the warhead (in my pocket, although why I wanted a reminder, I haven't a clue!) and the boss stashed the brass. I got hold of some boot polish to cover up the hole in the wall, which fortunately, as you know, the walls were all matt black, and we then put on our turtles and carried on as if nothing had happened. Amazingly no one heard the shot and somehow the missing round wasn't noticed for 24 hours, by which time 4 handovers had taken place and no one could be found responsible for the missing round. This incident was never spoken about and the boss was never found out, I have never forgotten that morning and the sounds and the feelings, I know I was very lucky not to be shot and the memory still haunts me to this day.

NORTH HOWARD STREET MILL MYSTERY

Private, Royal Anglian Regiment

During the early part of 1979, whilst being stationed at Palace Barracks, Holywood with 3rd Royal Anglian Regiment, I had become interested in the mug photos of known/active members of terrorist groups, and being new to the battalion set about trying to learn all I could to remember the names to the faces. After a while not only was I remembering, the names but their addresses, date of births, etc.

During patrols, certain section commanders started asking me if I recognised a certain person that was stood in front of them, and of course being a keen 18 year old trying to impress I would more often than not give their name, address and DOB. This practice went on for a while, without any thought.

There came up a recognition competition within the battalion, which I entered with relish. Whoever won was to be given 3 days off, and they could do what they liked. Anyway, yours truly won the competition, and was given the next 3 days off. During the first day off, I was asked if I would escort two persons around Belfast, the next day's; naturally, I said yes, again trying to impress.

The Land Rover turned up outside my barrack block and inside were two persons, who I didn't have any idea were at that time, but found out as the morning progressed. Before setting off I was asked to face the rear of the Land Rover as we were going round the city, something I couldn't understand. As we started off, I found out the person sitting down without a weapon was a 19 year old army cadet, and the bloke facing the front was an army cadet officer, armed with an unloaded S.L.R. Then, for the first time, I questioned 'What the bloody hell was I doing here, when I could be relaxing in the NAAFI?'

After a while we started driving up the Falls Road, before going onto North Howard Street Mill, for a smoke break and a cuppa; when we arrived, the Land rover Commander went and did something or other, and me the other two and the driver had our cuppa and chat and I had a smoke or two. Just before leaving The Mill, it started spitting with rain and, as I had had the foresight to bring along my rain jacket, I quickly donned it. I said to the cadet officer that I would face the front as I had my jacket on and if he faced the rear he wouldn't get so wet.

As we proceeded onto the Falls Road, heading towards Andersonstown Police Station, I became aware of a known face stood on a corner, and then as we came up to the cemetrey on my right side, a car back fired, or so I thought. But then, as quick as that car backfired, the officer slumped against me and I realised that we had come under fire and shouted to the driver and commander that the officer had been hit.

Whilst this had been going on, another 2 or 3 shots had been fired and I had seen where I thought the shots had been fired from and quickly cocked my rifle. I returned fire with maybe 8-10 rounds; we then turned a corner and I grabbed the army cadet. My next thought was 'Oh, shit!', as we had driven into a cul de sac. As I said, I grabbed, the cadet, and my next thought was get him safe, as we probably had driven into a trap so I shoved him under a nearby car and knelt down beside the car to protect him.

Before I realised anything else, we were surrounded by a big crowd shouting, spitting and throwing objects. They started getting nearer so I fired 2 rounds into the air, then before I knew it, there were squaddies everywhere. It was at this point that I felt my left arm burning and warm fluid trickling down my face. I had 2 cut like injuries to my head and left arm, caused by 2 rounds grazing my skin.

Sadly, the officer had been killed, but one known gunman had been found dead in the grounds of the local hospital. I had 2 slight injuries, the cadet was safe, but what must have been going through his mind, God only knows. Everything from then just moved so fast, and I was questioned about how many rounds I had let off, why I had fired into the air, and everything that had happened and said from leaving Palace Barracks'; naturally, I told them everything.

It wasn't until later in life that I started asking questions, about that day; why was I asked to escort the two persons, when I was one of the least experienced in the battalion? Why was I asked to face the rear of the Land Rover before leaving Palace Barracks? Why did we drop into North Howard Street, when our first stop was supposed to be Andersonstown Police Station? What the hell was an Army Cadet doing there, along with the unarmed Cadet Officer?

The Cadet officer killed that day was Captain Paul Rodgers (37) who was on a brief liaison tour with the 'Angle Irons' and it remains a mystery to this day why he should have been taken into such a dangerous part of Belfast. An elderly woman was shot and wounded in that same incident but she recovered, helped to fitness no doubt by the IRA's *apology* [*author's use of italics*].

Another perspective on the killing of Captain Rodgers:

NORTH HOWARD STREET MILL

Sergeant John Black, Royal Army Medical Corps

Other strange and forgotten incidents which made the headlines after I had left the Army included a Combined Cadet Force Officer (CCF) for St Alban's School in Hertfordshire who, with some cadets were visiting their local Regiment (obviously a R Anglian Bn). They were taken out on mobile patrol on 19 April 1979 and the CCF officer was Captain Paul Rodgers aged 37 and a schoolteacher. The patrol was ambushed near the Falls Road where Captain Rodgers was shot and killed, and one of the CCF cadets suffered a hand injury.

This one came from a list of casualties attempted by the *Daily Telegraph* on March 15 2000. I know this one, because in 1979 I was a member of the

ACF, and remember almost instant directives coming out banning any visits to host battalions in the province. Who allowed this one I do not know, but I expect that both the local CCF contingent commandant and the CO of the Royal Anglians were invited to an interview without coffee somewhere! I am also sure that at least 2 Northern Ireland ACF officers were murdered by the IRA.

The Light Infantry were stationed at the mill in 1977 and on June 29 of that year, they lost two young soldiers. Private Richard Turnbull (18) from Yorkshire and his comrade Michael Harrison (19) from Sheffield were returning to the mill when they were ambushed. As their vehicle turned into North Howard Street, IRA gunmen opened fire and both men, who had only been in Northern Ireland for less than two days, died at the scene.

A succession of Regiments was based there, including the Argylls, RGJ to name but two. In the Spring of 1991, the RRF were in occupancy there and, whereas the killings had continued all around them, the mill had not witnessed any fatalities for some 14 years. Sadly, the IRA were not yet finished, and. On May 25, an IRA terrorist threw a hand grenade over the high security fence and when it exploded, Corporal Terrence O'Neil (44) was killed. Another soldier was horribly injured, losing both legs. Corporal O'Neil, a dog handler, was the last soldier to die at the mill. Four years later, it was no more and the demolition experts moved in and reduced it to dust and rubble.

Rifleman Darren Ware, Royal Green Jackets

The Mark 15 'coffee jar' grenade was a fairly new type of device at the time currently being used by PIRA. It was first introduced on 25 May 1991 when a soldier was killed in an explosion within North Howard Street Mill in Belfast when the device was thrown over a wall and detonated inside the security force base. The grenade was based on a design seen in the early 1980's. Up until the end of 1991 seven variants had been identified across Northern Ireland of which at least three had been seen in the Armagh area in a dozen incidents since July of 1991. The construction was very simple, consisting of a glass coffee jar which would have a tube inserted into it which would house the initiation device, on top of which was a bell push button. Surrounding the inner tube would be an amount of explosive and 'scrap yard shrapnel' – a collection of nuts and bolts designed to have the shrapnel effect when hit. The plastic lid would then be screwed on and at the same time pushing the bell push in to prime the device. When the coffee jar was thrown and smashed, the bell push would be released and detonate the device. There were slight variations to each device and mechanism.

March 25, 1982 would be a tragic day for the Royal Green Jackets and the second worst day for this great Regiment throughout the entire period of the troubles. On March 25, 1982, an RGJ vehicle was driving along Crocus Street which is very close to both Springfield Road and the Falls Road. IRA gunmen attacked the vehicle with an M60 machine gun.

Three RGJ were killed in that attack; Rifleman Anthony Rapley (22), Rifleman Nicholas Malakos (19) and Rifleman Daniel Holland, also 19. The first two Green Jackets died at the scene and Daniel Holland died very quickly afterwards. The author, through his connections with the Regiment, knows the RGJ as a tight knit bunch of soldiers, drawn predominantly from the London area; they are known by other Regiments of the British Army, as the 'Black Mafia.'

The attack took place in broad daylight, and was less than 40 yards away from the heavily fortified RUC station; five other people were injured in the attack. It was believed that an M-60 machine gun was used by the terrorists for the first time.

The three soldiers killed in that attack all belonged to the 2nd Battalion. It has gone down in the lore of the 'Jackets' and the killings still anger former members to this day.

I interviewed one of the first squaddies on the scene and he recalls: 'Two of the lads were already dead but a mate was attending to the third; I don't want to say who either one was. He cradled the lad in his arms and just said something like 'This is really going to fuck up your Mum's weekend.' The lad smiled and then became unconscious and died soon afterwards, but at least he died with a smile on his face. A lot of people have criticised this, but we were soldiers, comrades and we all had that wicked, squaddie sense of humour. With all the shit that was going on over there, we needed a bloody good sense of humour.' Alan Holborough of the Jackets told me: 'As I look back, the whole incident was a farce! We (the MO and Med Sgt's and attached RAMC personnel) were just not ready, emotionally or equipment wise to be thrown in at the deep end.'

NORTH HOWARD STREET MILL

Tim Marsh 2nd Royal Green Jackets

Our tour of duty in West Belfast was coming to an end. The Guards Regiment had their advance party in all our company locations.

On 25 March, 1982, I was Quick Reaction Force (QRF) Commander in North Howard Street Mill. On that day a loud burst of automatic fire could be heard in the distance. My team and I were sitting in the QRF room when the intercom rang and summoned me to the Ops Room. The duty Ops officer told me to go directly to Crocus Street and that we should go on foot, not in our vehicles. At this time there was a lot of noise from people in the corridor outside the Ops room. They must have all heard the automatic fire also. I sensed that something had happened in our company area. I rushed back downstairs to the QRF room and gave the lads a quick brief. We got all our kit together and left North Howard Street Mill at a very fast pace.

As we ran up the Falls Road, another of our teams on patrol duty was following up behind us in support. We ran towards the Clonards via Waterford Street and into Malcomson Street. As I ran up Malcomson Street,

I could see in front of me a Land Rover in the middle of the road. It was one from our other QRF team. As I got close to the vehicle there were 2 guys moving a Riflemen's body onto the road; he was severely wounded.

I then carried on up to the road junction which was mayhem. All the cars had been stopped by the RUC and a Saracen armoured ambulance was waiting to take on casualties. I ran to the front gates of Springfield Road Police Station to check on another member of the QRF team who was standing outside. I asked him where the QRF Commander was. He just looked at me; there were tears in his eyes. I ran into Crocus Street and it was carnage; this is when I saw the QRF Commander, he pointed down the road and said: 'Secure the Firing Point.' (FP).

My team and I legged it up the road to Cavendish Street, and my team began to seal off the front area and wait for the Specialist Agencies to arrive. I ran to the back of the FP through a back alley, but did not go right to the back of the house, as I saw that the ground by the rear gate had been disturbed. As I came back down the alley, an RUC Officer said to me that there could be a device down there. Corporals Jack Heron and Derek Randall stopped Corporal Bill Linfield entering the house in Cavendish Street; they had crashed out from Springfield Road Police Station and were first on the scene, Later on the ATO found a device by the back gate to the FP This was in a biscuit tin, buried under the ground. My team and I were relieved by other troops on the ground and returned to North Howard Street. The atmosphere in the Mill on our return was of shock and anger at those IRA murderers.

On that day, a Guards Corporal and a RAF Sergeant sustained wounds and three of our Riflemen lost their lives. The QRF Commander of the team we supported received the Military Medal for Gallantry.

IN THE DIVIS

Rob Colley, Green Howards

We were on a patrol of the Divis and I was in the control brick; things were quite normal, with the kids giving us the usual lip and chucking the odd brick and bottle. They also had their favourite BBQ on the go: 'roast family car' which they used as cover for throwing stones. After a few minutes standing near the BBQ, a young girl aged about 5/6 years appeared between me and the car; she just stood there, shouting to her friends and at us in the normal 'friendly' Divis way, when, all of a sudden, this metal bar was launched from the other side of the burning car towards me. Fortunately, I saw it coming and moved out of the way; unfortunately, for the little girl, the 'muppet' who threw it wasn't as strong as he thought he was, and the bar hit the girl on the head.

She just stood there, screaming for all she was worth, blood, tears and snot running down her face and onto her dress. I'll never forget her, she was so small, and she had blue eyes and blonde hair which by now had a very soggy red fringe. I made a move to go and help her but was stopped in my tracks by shouts from the R.U.C officer who was with us; he was shouting: 'Leave her alone; don't touch her. I've called for an ambulance and I'll get someone to get her mother to come and help her.' I don't know about you, but this made me sick; she was 5/6 years old and I had to stand there and watch her, as she was begging for help and I could do nothing for fear of the locals blaming us for doing it to her. They would have had a field day if they could have blamed us, and the worst part was that the kids didn't even help and they didn't give a toss about her. We left before the ambulance appeared and we never found out what happened to that little girl. A memory that hurts me more than when we were spat at, bricked, petrol bombed etc combined; what on earth was going on·in the place that meant we couldn't help an innocent child who was hurt?

Rob actually apologised to me if the tales were 'boring' and this is symptomatic of the lack of self esteem we were made to feel about our roles in Northern Ireland. A common thread was that we all felt that the public back home had no idea, no conception of what the British soldier faced on the streets of Belfast, Londonderry or a dozen other towns during the troubles. Rob served in the Green Howards,

Yoblets in the making, Divis flats (Royal Regiment Wales Museum)

The Divis complex (Royal Regiment Wales Museum)

cruelly dubbed the 'falling plates' from 1982-87; he was medically discharged just before Christmas, 1987.

Leeson Street was the scene of one of the RGJ's most epic battles, when their 'R' company fought a fierce gun battle with the IRA, killing two terrorists and where one of their Lance Corporals, Thompson, won the DCM. The major fire fight in Leeson Street on September 13, 1971, saw several hundred rounds expounded and was one of the first major exchanges between the Army and the IRA. It was also the scene of an IRA own goal, a year earlier in which four people, including three IRA members were killed. At about the same time, an IRA RPG attack on a Gloster PIG could have caused carnage but for the thin gossamer thread of fate.

LEESON STREET

Corporal Frank Jones, Royal Green Jackets

A short time after the company took on responsibility for the Lower Falls; I was involved in the action famously captured by Terence Cuneo in his painting 'The Leeson Street Patrol.' We had been briefed there would certainly be an attempt by gunmen to reassert their influence and demonstrate to the locals they could operate with impunity, well they certainly had something to prove having been kept quiet by 1RGJ and whilst our patrols had been shot at a couple of times since the departure of 1RGJ there was nothing to suggest gunmen had slunk back in numbers. This particular night a platoon strength patrol encountered groups of youths throwing stones with an obvious intent of enticing our riflemen to chase them down. Under normal circumstances the patrol would simply have 'bounced' them, however with the known threat from gunmen it wasn't a good idea to chase after yobs, even if the end result was usually quite satisfying.

My platoon was called out to deploy in Saracens with the aim of heading off and catching these youths as they ran from the platoon foot patrol. By now Company HQ was on the ground and had joined up with the foot patrol. If the War Lord our OC was on the ground then I knew things weren't going to go quietly that night.

Saracens provide small arms protection but are not that brilliant at night in the narrow streets of the Lower Falls. Furthermore if we drove to head off the youths they would simply dart through unlocked doorways and we would lose them through a honeycomb of backyards and alleys, or back to back housing. After a short time we were ordered to dismount to clear parallel to Leeson Street along Cyprus and Osman Streets and catch anyone trying to flee from Leeson Street. My section had one side of Cyprus with another section on the other. Our other two sections were to clear Osman; the third platoon was kept in reserve.

By this time the original patrol had been fired upon and although it hadn't been directed at me or even my section it concentrated the mind and suddenly I could no longer smell the acrid Falls Road air which is always heavy with the fumes of countless coal fires. Over the radio I picked up the contact report and listened as it was reported that shots had been fired down Leeson Street from the Raglan Street junction. I knew that much because I had heard the burst of automatic gunfire. There were no casualties and the junction had been quickly secured. I reminded myself the success of parallel patrolling is to always know where the other patrol is and not to cross its front without warning. I kept this in mind as we inched our way along Cyprus Street.

That night the company engaged a reported seven gunmen and fired in excess of fifty rounds and claimed two gunmen hit. Most of the action took place in Leeson Street, although there was some firing in Cyprus Street, and it was bloody frustrating hearing the major gun battle and listening to the radio, but having to stay firm in Cyprus Street. The IRA obviously felt for my platoon because just as the company was about to stand down a car drove through the company and as it reached my platoon a weapon was seen being aimed in our direction from where the rear window should have been. Only one rifleman was in a position for a clear shot and he took it, and whilst the car never stopped a man was later admitted to the RVH suffering from two gunshot wounds. A single round had obviously struck his gun hand, then his face as he aimed his weapon. If the operation mounted by the IRA had been to test our resolve and professionalism and to demonstrate to the locals the IRA ran the Falls they had chosen the wrong gunmen for the part and had certainly picked on the wrong company. After the operation every member of the company was in high spirits and despite the frustration I felt pretty good about it.

That night, on one of the Jackets' most celebrated firefights, a Lance Corporal of 'R' company was awarded the DCM, the second highest decoration a British or Commonwealth soldier can receive for his part in the action on Leeson Street.

SUMMER IN THE DIVIS

Corporal 'A', 1 The King's Own Scottish Borderers

The summer of 1983 for most was the year of Irene Cara and 'Flashdance'; Monty Pythons 'Meaning of Life' and generally enjoying oneself. For me and the other 3 lads in my call sign it was a summer of West Belfast; body armour, alertness and tension.

The journey to those Belfast streets was protracted. I'd first heard of the planned tour some months previously whilst in Sennelager carrying out field firing, during yet another bitterly cold German winter and there was a real buzz when we were briefed by the Company Commander. The Battalion was sending two composite platoons as reinforcements to 1LI, scheduled to take over as the Belfast Roulment Battalion (BRB) in May '83.

We flew by RAF VC 10 from Gutersloh and touched down in Aldergrove to the unwelcome news that information had been received of a potential threat to the convoy scheduled to convey us into Belfast. As a result this threat, we were flown by Wessex helicopter into Musgrave Park (MPH) and then moved onwards to our designated locations by PIG. Our journey to North Howard Street Mill was short; however I remember the look of stern concentration of everyone's face as we drove through some of the areas of West Belfast which were to become intimately familiar in the months ahead. The handover from the outgoing unit, The Black Watch, was intense and I spent the vast majority of my time embedded in a team, attempting to absorb every scrap of information from my counterpart. This involved taking part in numerous patrols around the key areas of our TAOR with my counterpart providing a running commentary of orientation, incident details and face to face introductions to known terrorist suspects and supporters. In due course, the remainder of the Battalion arrived and the Black Watch departed; it was now over to us.

Forget the media hype of shoot to kill policies and all that crap; the role of the British Army in Northern Ireland was simple: to support the RUC in the maintenance of Law and Order. In order to carry this out, we were integrated

Private Perry (RRW) at Divis flats (Royal Regiment Wales Museum)

Divis Tower sangar (Royal Regiment Wales Museum)

in a weekly cycle involving patrol East (Divis Flats Complex, Lower Falls and Distillery); patrol West (Clonard, Springfield, Shankhill), QRF and guard. The main aim of the patrolling program was to provide close armed support to RUC local beat personnel as they carried out their normal policing duties and to dominate the ground. Each of the areas had its own challenges and our tactics and methods had to be adapted as required. Probably the most difficult and challenging area to patrol was Divis. Named after the mountain overlooking West Belfast, Divis was a sprawling urban jungle it was home to a hostile population and was an area that had already claimed the lives of a number of soldiers and policemen. Safe entry and exit into Divis required skill, alertness and above all, team work. The blocks of flats consisted of various walkways and it was absolutely essential to have a foot on the ground at each level. Designated entry points would be assigned during pre–patrol briefings and teams would normally hard target into location. Thereafter, the patrol would move slowly and methodically throughout the route, dominating the ground and constantly on the alert. Each patrol was supported by the eyes of colleagues based in the fixed Observation situated on top of Divis tower, however there were a number of areas within the complex completely unsighted to the OP. These areas were classed extreme risk and moving through them was never an enjoyable experience. Some of these blind spots consisted of stairwells and patrolling though those, particularly at night, were certainly not for the faint hearted! Even today I can vividly recall the foul smells of rubbish decaying in the choked garbage slides; stale piss and burnt material.

All patrols into Divis were subjected to hostile surveillance and on occasion, the thought of multiple eyes observing our every move made the hairs on the back of the neck stand on end. There is no question that during the tour, our patrols were targeted for attack (the most favourable method being the IED) and only our alertness and aggressive patrolling skills deterred the terrorist from pressing them home. Many years later, whilst conducting an entirely different role in Province, it was sobering to read intelligence reports detailing some of the attacks planned against us, but thankfully, not carried out.

LUCKY ESCAPE AT NORTH HOWARD STREET

Malcolm Patinson, 3 Light Infantry

For reasons I won't dwell on, the company OC hated us but this story will actually thank him and in a way he was the man of the day because if he had not turned up at the right time when we were about to deploy from NSM one fine summer's day, I may have been mourning eight good soldiers and my mates.

That day we were back on QRF, preparing for another day of mass disruption, and it must have been around early afternoon when I heard over my radio that cars had been stolen in our area; then we got news of hostage taking, and then finally over the tannoy, suspect proxy bombs were at the back and side gates blocking all main exits out of camp all except the front gate. Luckily, the drivers of the proxy bombs were not chained to the steering wheels, so they headed for the sanctuary of NSM. Once inside the camp, they were taken to a secure de-briefing area where they were questioned by the police and our Int guys to try and get as much info on the bombs.

We were called in for a briefing and we found out that not only had NHSM been hit, but all locations in our area had been boxed in by suspect proxy bombs stopping all movements in one fell swoop. Reports from CCTV operators were reporting that the Falls Road was at a standstill and traffic was bumper to bumper. Me and Nick were on 15 minutes notice to move and the other call signs were already at the loading bay ready to deploy. The ops officer explained the situation, and he was intending to exploit the fact that the front gate was vacant, and he was intending to send out two call signs to man the ramps and try and control the traffic on the Falls Road. Whilst this was being discussed, ATO had arrived from the Shankhill end and was ready to clear the first Proxy bomb which would clear a safe route to the Shankhill and we could deploy troops.

My mind was in overdrive, running over the previous days events and through the countless contacts and attacks on NHSM over the years where exit from the side and back had been blocked and soldiers had been engaged whilst deploying form the front gate. I was very concerned that the ops officer was determined to follow the bigger picture and control the traffic on the Falls Road. My gut instincts were telling me this was a bad decision; a bad call. It might have been a moment of enlightenment or some divine intervention or call it instincts, but I just knew the big bad wolf was waiting for some fresh meat to deploy onto the Falls road from the front gates, and he was going to have it in full. I could not contain myself any longer and asked the Ops officer if it was a good idea, bearing in mind that the day before, we had been dicked by some big players and didn't he think something was wrong; we were being channelled into deploying from the Falls Road. The ops officer totally ignored me and said it was his decision and that was final. I then went on to say to him: 'Sir read the signs; hold on until ATO clears the back gate; play it safely. Don't risk sending two teams out into the unknown just for the sake of a few minutes.' That's when it all got heated and he reminded me that he was the ops officer, and it was he who was responsible. I answered back saying 'You send people out there, Sir, and they won't be coming back; how will you live with that, all for the sake of a few minutes wait.' It was then the OC appeared, he must have heard the Ops officer and me arguing, and just calmly told us that no one was to move without his authority.

At this point, we were told to remain in camp ready for immediate deployment. We retreated to the briefing room I walked out onto the fire escape balcony to get some air and I saw the remainder of N6UA ready to deploy out of the gates. We were listening in on the radio, when one almighty explosion shook the whole of NHSM and we could see a giant plume of acrid black smoke bellowing up from the area of the Falls Road/

North Howard Street Junction. From the front gate sangar, reports were coming in that a large explosion had gone off beyond the blast walls covering the mill and Falls Road ramp location.

The explosion was that powerful that the shockwave blew the front sangar man of his stool, and, as the smoke cleared, the CCTV revealed the aftermath of a large explosion which had gone off in the large paper mill which was adjacent to NHSM directly opposite the Ramp and in-between the two blast walls. It also revealed about fifty tons of masonry had fallen directly where the lads would have been standing if they had deployed out of the gate. Some of them would have surely been killed, and a cold chill ran down my back; it just did not bear thinking. I was just so fucking pleased that no one deployed from camp, and we were not pulling bodies out of that pile of rubble. The blast had made a hole about eight metres by eight metres in diametre in the paper Mill. My gut instincts were correct I felt justified to challenge the Ops officer's decision but more to the fact I was happy and slightly amazed that the OC intervened at such a critical moment. I was glad he did what he did; whether he did it intentionally or not he saved our guys, and for that he got a little respect which lasted about a millisecond then it was back to calling him a wanker and a tosspot.

I never mulled on this particular incident that came later; mind you, walking past the mountain of rubble was a very stiff reminder of what could have been, as for the PIRA, how did they know we had an officer who was determined to send out soldiers from the font entrance; they had played a blinder in the planning and execution of their operation.

Luck was clearly on our side that day, much to the disappointment of the PIRA, and all our lads lived to fight another day. For my part I was just glad I had the bottle to stand up and be counted and say what I felt at a critical time when things could have gone so horribly wrong and know that my own mind my gut instincts were justified and fitted in with the feelings and Moods of West Belfast. I was glad to be a part of such a great team of blokes like the Recce Platoon; as for my instincts and gift for reading a situation I knew I would need to rely on them again later in the tour. I think the last word should be for our OC; we never liked him one bit and he did not like us one bit either but he did come up trumps on a day that mattered most to me and my mates. For that I thank him for that as do lads of the Reconnaissance Platoon N60, N60B on that day of disruption way back in1991. This story is dedicated to all the lads who served with me in NHSM in 1991 strange but great days never forgotten.

Over the course of a 15 year period, beginning in February, 1972 and ending in March, 1987, seven soldiers lost their lives in or around the Divis Street flats. That figure should be certainly increased by one, even if only unofficially; this was the site of Trooper Hugh McCabe's death on August 15, 1969 which I shall deal with shortly.

The Glosters, as we shall see, fared badly in and around this part of Belfast. In addition, many times that number were injured in rioting and other forms of violence and, as one former Royal Regiment of Wales soldier said to me 'I've never seen so many soldiers crying before; they were in agony at being hit by objects thrown from the upper floors.' Squaddies joked that the insurance companies must have been left scratching their heads at the number of claims from the residents for televisions and fridges which had 'fallen' from their balconies.

The 16 storey flats were eventually put to good use by the Army and the large flat roof which was the residents' drying area, was sealed off, and used as an OP. The roof door to the steps and lifts were welded shut, and a sandbagged, armoured sangar was installed with listening and viewing equipment. Access for the soldiers was by helicopter only. The roof top OP was only removed in 2005 as the Army began to dismantle their bases on a Province-wide basis.

Unofficially, it was the scene of the death of the first British soldier in the troubles. Trooper Hugh McCabe (20) of the Queen's Royal Irish Hussars was home on leave from his unit in Germany, when he was killed. On August 15, 1969, the day after Harold Wilson sent troops into the Province, he was watching a riot from a balcony of the Divis Street flats. He was hit once by a large calibre round, probably fired by either the RUC or the out-of-control 'B' Specials. It must be stressed that Trooper McCabe was not taking part in the riots, merely watching. He received a full military funeral with all associated honours.

On February 1, 1972, Corporal Ian Bramley (25) of the Glosters was opening a security gate in Hastings Street, near Divis Street when he was shot and died soon afterwards. This was during a period of heightened tension and frequent rioting, in the wake of 'Bloody Sunday' which had happened just 48 hours earlier.

Almost a year later, UDR soldier Corporal David Bingham (22) was abducted and murdered by the IRA in Institution Place, close to the Divis. His car was hijacked and he was shot by a gunman. In the summer of that year, two more Glosters were killed, this time, actually inside the Divis Street flats. Privates Geoffrey Breakwell (20) and his 21 year old companion, Christopher Brady triggered an IRA booby trapped device placed by the IRA on the fifth floor. Another soldier was blinded and several residents of the flats were injured. It gave a further lie to the IRA's pious claim that they would avoid injuring civilians.

This incident, which took place on July 17, 1973, was a wake up call for the Army whose training techniques on booby trap devices had been somewhat amateur at the time. Nearly 250 soldiers had now died in Northern Ireland in just under four years, and now the toll had passed that of the Aden emergency in the 60s.

On September 16, 1982, over nine years and 300 military deaths later, the INLA placed a bomb on one of the landings of the Divis Street flats and detonated it as Lance Bombardier Kevin Waller (20) of the Royal Artillery walked past. The young soldier was terribly injured and died of his wounds on September 20.

On March 27, 1985, Lance Corporal Anthony Dacre (25) an Essex boy was killed in an explosion at the flats. The King's Own Border Regiment soldier was patrolling in an area which was normally thronged with school children. On that day, the Head Master of a nearby school kept all the children inside, ostensibly because of the cold. A senior soldier told me that it was a widely held view among military personnel, that the IRA had warned the school of the impending attack. No intelligence was fed back to the Army, and Anthony Dacre was murdered, once the IRA were handed a free run. Sources for both the school and the apologists for the IRA in Sinn Fein have always denied either collusion or intimidation; I invite the reader to draw their own conclusions. It is my strong belief that the IRA, seeking to avoid another disastrous 'crossfire death', warned the aforementioned headmaster. Some years earlier, a young boy, playing in his garden had triggered a bomb designed for an Army patrol and had staggered, horribly injured and dying into the arms of a soldier, crying out 'Help me, mister'. The squaddie tried desperately to save his life.

Two years and three days later, on March 30, 1987, Private Iain O'Connor (23) of the QLR was in a mobile patrol which passed under a pedestrian walkway in the flats. An IRA member dropped a grenade-like device onto the vehicle in which he was travelling, and the soldier, from the Preston area, was badly injured, dying shortly afterwards.

Private O'Connor was one of ten soldiers to be killed that year as a result of the troubles, compared with eleven the previous year. Only six soldiers lost their lives in 1985 and clearly, whilst even one death brings multiple grief to a soldier's family, the Army was winning the war with the IRA. As if to contradict this downward trend and, at the same time, demonstrate that they had lost none of their ruthlessness, Republicans killed 39 soldiers in 1988. This figure was swollen by two IRA 'spectaculars' when they killed 8 Light Infantry boys at Ballygawley and 6 soldiers returning from a fun run in Lisburn. The IRA added to this grim tally, when they murdered 3 off-duty RAF men in Holland and Germany in cold blood.

EUROPA BOMB BLAST

Ian Mitchell, Royal Artillery

When we were in Belfast, in 1976, with 45 Med Regt, bombs were the in thing as you might well imagine? The Europa Hotel was the most bombed hotel in Europe; apt name? We were detailed to the premises to evacuate personnel because a van bomb had been left in their main driveway. I ran down to the hotel with a full screw and he ran into the foyer, as I tried to get past the van, my flak jacket got caught on the barrier post and, as I struggled to get free from this, I started the van shaking in a vain attempt to get away.

Just then, a hotel employee ran out and ripped my flak jacket open and, together, we evacuated the hotel. About 20 minutes later I was 200/250 yards away with call sign 'Felix' (*bomb disposal*) and told him what had happened to me. He just looked at me and said:' You're lucky mate, that that van didn't have a mercury (*tilt switch*) on it, otherwise we would have been sweeping you off the pavement!' After our little chinwag, this ATO mush said: 'There's nothing in that van!' With that, he fired 5 rounds into it just make sure. Then, they sent in the wheelbarrow and put 2 ounces of gelignite under the back axle, once they had withdrawn this, they pressed the button. What happened next was a f*****g blur; the oxygen was sucked out of my lungs, and, in the Church where we were standing, a stained glass window exploded into a thousand splinters only for the lead in the glass to save me and this ATO guy.

In the vacuum that precedes the blast, all the windows were sucked out in sheets; cars were tossed 20/30ft into the air, not to mention the BOOM!!!! Flying roof tiles, strip lighting, and general debris come cascading down all over the place! The van had a 500lb bomb in the back of it; so much for our Int section????

NORTH BELFAST

North Belfast, for the purpose of this chapter is defined as follows: Shankhill Road, Crumlin Road, New Lodge, and the Ardoyne. The Ardoyne area which is above and to the west of the fiercely Loyalist Crumlin Road is a fanatically Republican territory and has, to its east, the New Lodge. Going south is the Shankhill Road, very much Loyalist land and to its south is the North Howard Street, where several generations of soldiers manned the Mill there. It will also look at the area of both Girdwood and the Antrim Road.

Although clearly defined – by virtue of the wall murals, slogans and preference of flags – as either Loyalist or Republican areas, much of this part of north Belfast is a political and logistical nightmare. Which is which was a question on the minds of many soldiers who served there during Operation Banner. A Loyalist street would back on to a Republican street and vice versa. Look at the nightmare which faced the Green Howards in the early 70s when, on one side of Crumlin Road was a Roman Catholic school and on the other, a Protestant one. Small wonder, that the 'XIX' as they are known, dreaded 'lollipop patrols.'

We will also look at the long, long Antrim Road, which leads from the north of the city well into the Centre and beyond, for soldiers and RUC men met their deaths there at the hands of the terrorists. Over the course of the troubles, a total of 43 soldiers would lose their lives in these politically diverse but physically similar areas.

Chapter 6

The Ardoyne/New Lodge/ Crumlin Road/Oldpark Area/Shankhill Road

Rows and rows of back-to-back late Victorian, possibly pre-Great War terraces, often ten to a row, some with no gardens and others with a tiny plot at the front and the occasional tenement type building; this was the Republican Ardoyne area in the 1970s. This area which merges into the equally Republican New Lodge was the scene of the first official British death in Northern Ireland. Gunner Robert Curtis (20) was shot and died very quickly following a gun battle with the IRA on February 6, 1971 at Lepper Street and the New Lodge Road. He was married and his pregnant widow gave birth to a baby girl, some 6 months later. His death had been anticipated, for, although some 21 other soldiers had died before him, in a mixture of accidents, RTAs and 'unnatural or violent causes, it was only a matter of time. In the same gun battle which left him dead, his comrade, Lance Bombardier John Lawrie was badly wounded, and he, sadly died of his wounds 9 days later.

On that night of February 6, 1971, a patrol of the Royal Artillery was engaged in a brief fire fight with members of the IRA in Lepper Street, near the interface between a fierce Loyalist area and the Republican New Lodge. Gunner Robert Curtis was hit several times and died very quickly after the shooting. One of his comrades, Lance Bombardier John Lawrie (22) was badly wounded and died from these wounds seven days later. Curtis was aged 20 and was due to become a father for the first time, later on in the year.

Curtis's death is seen as a tragic milestone in the history of the troubles, as it was the first officially admitted death of the Northern Ireland conflict. Readers should refer to the Roll of Honour in both this book and also in *A Long Long War: Voices of the British Army in Northern Ireland* where the evidence of 21 earlier deaths through the MOD's euphemistically termed expression 'violent or unnatural causes' is demonstrated. One of the killers was a local New Lodge IRA gunman, William 'Billy' Reid, killed in a shoot out with a soldier from a Scottish Regiment. With a supreme irony, Reid was shot and killed in Curtis Street after an ambush on an Army vehicle in Academy Street. The following is an account of his death by the soldier he tried to kill.

ACADEMY STREET, BELFAST

Sergeant, Scottish Infantry Regiment

My incident in Academy Street, Belfast on May 15, 1971 started when I saw a blue Ford Cortina, driving in a parallel road, watching me turn into another

164

street, mirroring my own manoeuvres. In my vehicle, I had two young Jocks, one of whom was just 18 and on one of his first patrols, designated the RT man.

The next time I saw the other car, it was sitting there, with three occupants, looking very suspicious. I was determined to find out what they were up to and after about 10 minutes or so, I turned into Academy Street. As I did so, I realised that so had they; so, with just one vehicle on this patrol, I blocked the road and went to investigate the other car. Just as I passed the end of my Land Rover, a long burst of machine gun fire passed just inches from my head and body, but my radio operator was hit in the stomach and fell to the ground. Then, my driver received the second burst, wounding him in the upper arm.

I was armed with a 9mm pistol and returned fire from about 10 metres, then took cover, waiting for the next chance to open fire. At that moment, one of them started to run away from the car, and I shot him. He fell and then got up and ran again and, as he did so, the other two – one of them wounded – also started to run, and I opened fire again and put the one who fell, just at the road junction. I had used up all 10 rounds and picked up the rifle of one of the wounded soldiers, although by this time, all was quiet.

I radioed the contact and went to the corner to find the body of the IRA man, I now know as Billy Reid. I had to drag the body closer to my Jocks as a crowd was starting to gather, shouting abuse and coming towards me, and I was forced to warn them to stay back, or I would open fire. I needed to look after my wounded, but the crowd kept coming, so I left the body, and just as I did so, soldiers started to arrive as did the civilian ambulance; both Jocks were taken to hospital. The dead IRA man remained for the usual SOCO (*scene of crimes officer*) who interviewed me on the spot. It was a short interview and soon I was allowed to return to the barracks, where the CO gave me a large whiskey.

After my debrief, I went back to the base, where my mess mates were waiting for me; needless to say, I had a few drinks. My driver, after a month's convalescence, returned to duty, but later that year, he left the Army. My radio operator was medically discharged, without any assistance or help from the Government!

The following morning, it was back to the daily routine: patrols, watch and more patrols. Two days after the incident, I was called to see the CO, who told me that the IRA had put out a 'contract' on me because of the importance of the dead man, Billy Reid. He was a killer and was responsible for the killing of Robert Curtis, considered, at the time, the first British soldier to die in the troubles, in an ambush. A further soldier died later of his wounds and the night that I killed him, Reid was out to kill more soldiers.

In the late summer of that same year, the Green Howards lost their first man of the troubles. On August 9, Private Malcolm Hatton who was only 19, was shot as he was keeping watch on rioters in part of the Ardoyne; a Middlesbrough boy, he died shortly afterwards. In three days, from August 9-11, no less than 24 people

Arfon Williams, Royal Regiment of Wales, at Boundary Street
Sangar, Ardoyne, Belfast 1971 (Arfon Williams)

died on the streets of Belfast. Three of the dead were soldiers, two were IRA and twenty were civilians; of these, the Army records state that, three were involved in petrol bombing.

A mere 20 days after Robert Curtis tragically passed into history, two RUC officers were shot during rioting. Inspector Cecil Patterson (46) and Constable Robert Buckley (32) were both killed when shots were fired during rioting in the Ardoyne area.

A THOUSAND DOORS AND WINDOWS IN THE NEW LODGE

Private Jim Ward, Parachute Regiment

My first tour of Northern Ireland was in the New Lodge, a strongly Republican area of North Belfast and we were based in an old camp, surrounded by 20 foot walls and barbed wire and we slept in cramped rooms, ten of us in there at once. Amongst the first things we did was to be briefed on the local players. We were given the rundown on just about every member of the community within our boundary; who they were, where they lived and what they did. We knew what their rank was within the IRA, past criminal records and what they were accused or suspected of doing.

As in most areas, we mainly had to deal with bottom rung of the ladder people, involved in rioting, assaults, thefts and other minor offences. However, we also had some hardcore members with offences related to firearms, bombings, armed robbery, even murder. The worst IRA terrorists were either serving time or had disappeared over the border. The only time they would return to Belfast would be to take part in operations against the Security Forces. Still, as I was to learn, it was incredibly frustrating to observe some of these villains going about business, knowing that they were terrorists, but unable to do much about it. I have always maintained that if the security forces in Northern Ireland had been given free rein and no political interference, the troubles would have ended years ago and many lives would have been saved. But, this is not the way of the world and civil rights and other issues had to be taken into account.

On the first morning, at 06:00 we were to take over from the unit which we were relieving; they had spent a week with our advance party, showing them the ground and sharing all the information they had. I did notice that they all looked tired and drawn and I knew that they'd had a rough time of it, losing two men to snipers and had injuries as a result of rioting and bomb blasts.

'You're on foot patrol tomorrow,' my section commander informed me and my first reaction was 'Great; you're getting out there.' We were issued with live ammo for our SLRs and it felt very strange as it was the first time that we'd been given these outside of a firing range and it brought home the reality of the situation. At the same time, we were issued with flak jackets and I must point out, that they were not designed to stop bullets, but were more for small explosions, nail bombs and so on. They weren't all that comfortable, but afforded a small amount of protection.

Anyway, the next morning at 05:50, there we were; 3 four man patrols (known as bricks), ready to deploy from the entrance; my heart was pumping; my first patrol. The IRA had made it a tradition to hit the battalions at the beginning of their tours to unsettle them, so who knew if, or when this would happen. (*Intelligence experts told the author that the IRA's network of spies and intelligence networks often knew which Regiments were being posted often before the squaddies themselves knew*).

'All right; let's go,' said Steve, my brick commander as we flew out of the camp; I followed, raced down through the barricades and out onto the street. We ran about 50 metres and took up positions in various doorways and front yards. I remember feeling excited and ready for anything; glaring at the few civilians who walked past. They didn't return my stares but walked stoically onward. I did notice one of two expressions on their faces that would become familiar to me on this tour; the first was of total indifference, the other, pure hatred or rage. But, at 06:00 on a Monday morning – did the IRA ever have that 'Monday morning' feeling? – their expressions were the former rather than the latter. The three bricks separated and went into patrol mode; no talking, just training taking over and manoeuvring through the streets.

We walked into the main road of our area, quietly and efficiently, slipping into a routine that would become so familiar that we could do it in our sleep. I was starting to calm down a bit and recall thinking that it wasn't too bad; nice and quiet; no welcoming committee from the locals; even the sun was shining. I had known what to expect from studying the geography of the area, the streets, waste ground, bombed out buildings and a large section of the Belfast docks. Even the look of the place seemed familiar; it should too; this was London, Manchester, Glasgow or any other large town and city in Britain. As we patrolled, more people came out onto the streets and I noticed that not a lot of them were going to work.

This was normal, apparently, as most of the hard areas were slums and unemployment was rife.

(*The author's own childhood, growing up in slums and one of the new sprawling 1950s council estates, mirrors exactly what many of us found in places like Belfast. Sidey Street in Hunslet, Leeds was the 'twin' of the New Lodge and the Swarcliffe Estate in many ways resembled the Ballymurphy and Turf Lodge Estates*).

We turned off the main road and onto waste ground and I noticed a strange and unfamiliar feeling; not sure of what it was, I tried to subdue it, but after a while, it came back and it struck me what it was; I was EXPOSED. I remember being briefed to be aware of our surroundings and one Sergeant had said: 'Stay alert.' I hadn't paid much attention to it at the time, but now it made sense. Those blocks of flats over there; sixteen stories; how many windows; three hundred, four hundred? Those derelict buildings; another hundred windows and doorways. Even the occupied houses, factories, churches or perhaps some other place unseen or unnoticed. I realised then; look, seek and don't switch off; this feeling stayed with me for the rest of the time I was in Northern Ireland.

Fortunately, the patrol finished as quietly as it started and we returned to base for a brief respite before heading back out again.

LEOPOLD STREET POLICE STATION

Terry Friend, Royal Artillery

Just a few yards from the Crumlin Road, when we moved here, it would be our fourth move in a matter of weeks, but this would be our final home until our tour of duty ended. We moved into an abandoned Police station

Royal Artillery getting ready
for a riot (Mark Campbell)

which, of all things was almost opposite the Flax Street Mill. However, this place was the exact opposite of the mill in that the rooms were small and cramped and we were stuffed into them like sardines! The situation was made no easier with the onset of warmer weather conditions and, what with the to-ing and fro-ing of kit-laden squaddies at all times of the day and night, proper sleep became a much needed and sought after luxury.

Thus it was that we began to patrol in earnest, both by foot and vehicle. The vehicles – mostly Land Rovers – went out in pairs, but we also had a couple of Saracens and one ton armoured PIGs as well. Foot patrols usually consisted of four or six men at most. Everywhere we went, it was the same old Victorian terraced houses; endless rows of identical streets with attached back alleys; a most depressing environment. The whole place looked like a city in decline; filthy, run down and demoralising. How on Earth, I wondered, did people live in such a state. The Protestant ghettoes were bad enough, but the Roman Catholic enclaves were fifty times worse; even when the sun came out, the place still looked bleak ! In many ways, it was like stepping back to the harsher times of the 40s or 50s.

Personally speaking, I was offended by the constant and ever present pervading atmosphere of animosity and hatred that each community had for its opposite number. The first time that I saw the red, white and blue painted kerb stones and Union Jack bunting in a Protestant enclave called 'The Village,' I was astounded. It seemed medieval and barbaric. There were long-haired and sullen faced youths hanging around the street corners in small gangs and they glared at us as we drove past. The hostility was so palpable; you could almost taste it in the very air itself.

As I said, the Roman Catholic ghettoes were even worse with their Republican tricolours flapping in the breeze on lampposts. It did offend me that these people dared to hoist a foreign flag on UK soil. Would anyone have had the effrontery to raise the Swastika over London during the Blitz. And, I bet that half of those bastards were gratefully holding out their hands to receive the weekly benefit payments, courtesy of the British taxpayer.

Alongside our role in Leopold Street, we also had a small permanent base in a house in Chief Street, which was just a few streets away to our west. In late 1969, when the rioting first erupted, the people in this street were forced out of their homes. In fact, everyone left, except for one family and we established a presence here purely for their protection. Behind this particular row of houses was a Catholic church and at the western end was a Protestant area; at the other was the Crumlin Road, beyond which, was the staunchly Nationalist Ardoyne. Once again, we adopted the role of 'Piggy in the Middle' and it always seemed to me that both sides resented our presence in the Province. It wasn't quite like that in the beginning, for without our protection, the Catholics would have been burned out all over the place. But, as soon as the IRA took a hand in things, we were tasked to go in and get them, thus alienating us from the Catholics. Add to that, the fact that the Prods hated us for keeping them away from the Catholics; a fairly simplistic view, but fairly accurate for all that.

FIRST DAY ON THE ARDOYNE

Private Eddie Atkinson, The Green Howards

Before I went to the Ardoyne in 1971, I didn't really know what to expect; the older sweats who had been to the Falls in the previous tour told me it was a bad area and it was where it all kicked off in Belfast in 1969. Our training seemed sufficient, riot control but it was the old system of box formation that had been use in the Far East. It was before NITAT (*Northern Ireland Training Centre*) times and the Army had a lot to learn and very quickly. I also had to learn very quickly because our first night on the streets turned out to be how it would be for the next 4 months unrelenting. The aggro would always be a small incident away it didn't take much to set them off.

The lollipop patrol in the morning and evening protecting the Protestant children to and from school was always going to be the opportunity the Catholic kids needed to start throwing bricks and it was bricks not small

Lollipop Patrol, Shankhill (Dave Bradwell)

stones. Half bricks were the norm, and then bottles, petrol bombs then later on nail bombs and then the shooting. Night after night, the riots went on. Internment definitely made the trouble worse although at the time I'm sure it seemed the right thing to do in an attempt to reduce the rioting and disorder. It doesn't seem that words alone can explain how bad it was. I don't know what the figures are for riots, shots at and shots returned, nail bombs and other IEDs. It was 4 months of sangar guards, foot and mobile patrols, mobile VCPs you couldn't stay in one place too long for fear of being shot at. Early morning lifts, it just went on and on. We lost 5 men that tour and on after one fatal shooting the Paras were brought in to ease the work, and we were taken off the streets for a while. However they went out in 30 man fighting patrols who in their right minds would take a chance at attacking that.

I do know I feel very proud that I served over there, but at the time, I can't remember feeling like that but I do know we did our best to allow normal people a chance to carry on as normal an existence as was possible. No one who has served there should feel anything but pride; we are members of a unique club, there have been some terrible conflicts since but, as in the past no other Army in the world would have done as disciplined a job as the British Army did.

COMING OF AGE IN THE NEW LODGE

Private Jim Ward, Parachute Regiment

I was just past my 18th birthday, and I had already been shot at; shot at somebody; fought hard in riots and seen what bombs can do. I had watched helplessly as a child had died right in front of me. I know that these events only intensified my feelings; mind you, I knew that a lot of the other lads felt the same way. We didn't sit around and talk about it, although many relieved comments were passed among us when we returned to the relative safety of the camp and the easing of the tension was plain to see; until the next time we went out.

If that wasn't bad enough, sometimes the locals would also know, or at least suspect that an attack on us was imminent and the streets would be deserted. It was made even worse when, on occasion, an anonymous phone call would be received telling us of suspicious activity in our area. More often than not, they were simply hoax calls made either to mess us around, or it could be the local IRA observing our response times or seeing how we reacted to these incidents. Occasionally they were a set-up, designed to lure us into an ambush and this happened and it gave the enemy the chance to have us exactly where they wanted us, to attack us on their terms.

Numerous casualties in the early part of the 70s were caused by these calls. The bombs were triggered by old-fashioned trip wire or, increasingly, the remote control. The 'beauty' of the latter was that the IRA team on the ground could watch our approach and time the explosion for when we were all within the killing zone. Besides, they would then see the carnage and it would be something to tell their grandchildren about as they grew old.

These types of ambushes were used to great effect over the years, and we, the soldiers on the ground, hated them, because, at least with a gun battle, you could fire back, defend yourself, but when a bomb went off, who did you fight ?

INJURY IN ARDILEA STREET

John Rafferty, 3rd Bn Light Infantry

During the same tour as the episode with the RPG7's – when they were being fired at us for the first time – we were on another foot patrol in the Ardoyne.

The section commander on the patrol was Cpl. Mel 'E' and we were patrolling on the main road, past several shops and near to Ardilea Street I think. We were passing some parked vehicles, which included a lorry, when a gunman opened up on us from the corner of that road with a sub-machine gun; a Thompson if my memory is correct.

The burst from his gun, only about 30 metres away from us, was sudden and startling. It was a short burst, only about six to ten rounds or so, but one of the bullets caught Mel in the top of his head. It turned out that it had cut a very deep furrow from his fore-head to the back of his head; he seemed to drop like a stone.

We had all reacted quickly and dropped to the ground to take up defensive positions. I lay behind a lamp post in a firing position, taking aim at the corner and just about to squeeze the trigger at the figure that I saw there for a few fleeting moments. Just then, the head of one of my patrol suddenly appeared in my sights. A lad called Martin had dived behind the parked lorry and was taking up a position behind the lorry's rear off-side wheel, and took a shot at the figure himself first. I cursed him for spoiling my shot, but was so relieved that I had seen him there, before I had pulled the trigger myself.

I don't believe that we managed to hit the gunman, as no trace was found of him. Certainly I don't recall seeing any blood there later. Our radio operator had meanwhile put in a 'crash call' for 'Mel who was still lying on the floor; blood all over his face, but thankfully, still alive.

A very short while later, a Saracen Armoured Personnel Carrier turned up to give us some support, and parked between us and the corner of Ardilea Street, in order to give us some direct cover from the gunman. One of the patrol jumped inside through the rear door, climbed into the top turret and fired a burst of .50 calibre from the mounted machine gun there into the Ardilea Street corner.

Shortly afterwards, we got back to the school that we called home, for our debrief and checked on Mel whom, we were told, was alive and well. He was in hospital for a while recovering from the wound, but eventually returned to us; though I do believe that he suffered with black-outs for some time afterwards.

One of the strangest events that I have ever seen in my life happened during this patrol when Mel 'E' was shot and wounded. When the gunman opened up on us from the corner of Ardilea Street with his sub-machine gun, he was hit in the head and dropped to the floor wounded; the rest of us followed him to the floor, almost instantly.

The weird thing for me during that event was that as I hit the floor, looking for cover, I can distinctly remember seeing the string of bullets coming from the gunman towards us. The scene seemed almost surreal in its appearance, in that the string of bullets seemed to be just suspended in thin air and moving towards us at such an incredibly slow-motion sort of pace. I felt that, if I had such a mind, I could just stand up, walk over towards the oncoming bullets, pick out any given one, pluck it from the sky to look at it, and then be able to place it back in line later, and allow it to continue on its merry way. I watched for what seemed to be a lifetime and I saw the bullets lazily make their way towards us; each one perfectly visible and seemingly harmless. It appears that I did not catch sight of the one that hit Mel.

The bullets carried on their way, towards and past us, mostly hitting the window of the shop that we were adjacent to at that time. Still in an incredible state of slow motion, I saw them strike the window of the shop, and then saw the window shatter and explode equally slowly. The glass bursting out and almost floating down to the floor like wedding confetti. Before the last round had hit the window, I found myself on the floor behind a lamp post, taking aim at the gunman behind the wall at the corner of Ardilea Street, now with the world moving at normal speed.

It was such a weird phenomenon and experience that was hardly believable even to me, let alone to my friends in the patrol, that I mentioned it to later. I saw the same thing once more in NI quite a while later during another patrol, but this time, just one bullet of many shot at the time; none of us were injured in that encounter.

I was the only witness to this strange phenomenon.

INCIDENT ON THE ARDOYNE

Sergeant Jim Parker, Light Infantry

The Services Investigation Branch (SIB) personnel are the Royal Military Police detectives. They are more often than not seen in civilian clothes. They investigate the somewhat serious crimes committed within the military community. When an officer and I fired three rounds between us one night, and claimed to have shot an IRA gun man we were both investigated at some length by the SIB. Did I give a clear verbal warning before firing? When did I last zero my rifle? When did I last clean my rifle, before and after the incident? Was I using anything other than iron sights at the time? And so on and so on. After that grilling I secretly thought I'd never claim to have killed anyone ever again.

Then one night in 1973 my section of about eight men was engaged in a gun battle that lasted eight hours. The Platoon Commander came to take over and he brought with him a GPMG team. We experienced incoming fire from the Protestant area behind us, but mostly from the Republican Catholic New Ardoyne area.

I had to place a sentry, outside to cover the back door in the 'safe' Proddy area, and during the action I changed the man at fairly regular intervals. There were observation or firing positions all around the Observation Post, and I had placed men at each. Some positions overlooked streets that were well lit. Others overlooked dark alleyways and so I ensured initially that the men who had an IWS or SUIT sights (both telescopic and with a form of night vision) in those places.

Not only did I change the back door sentry, but moved the men around the various observation posts. However the weapons with an IWS or SUIT sight remained where they were. Thus a lad taking over a position that

Grenadier Guards in Agnes Street, Belfast (Dave Bradwell)

covered a back alley handed his SLR over to the man who had covered that area for the last half hour.

On one occasion whilst I was manning a dark street, without a night sight I saw a gun flash and fired there immediately, and swore I must have hit the firer. (A couple of days later I observed the bullet hole in a metal door way exactly where I had aimed.) After eight hours another section came and relieved us. Luckily we had no casualties. One of their men had his flash eliminator smashed by an in coming bullet. That was the nearest we had to a casualty all night in that location.

After the elation of surviving unscathed and swapping war stories we were wheeled into an office to face the SIB. We sat around in a semi-circle in chairs with our weapons. The SIB gentleman introduced himself and taking out a document, which showed apparently the times when shots were fired by my blokes and in particular, when a hit was claimed. The reader will appreciate after 35 years I cannot remember the soldiers' names or the conversations in detail. But it went something like this.

'Okay, who fired a round at 7.30?'

'That was me,' said 'Alan' my Second in Command and raised his hand.

The SIB man took his name and asked him to read out the registration number stamped on his SLR.

Alan lifted up his SLR on which was attached the IWS, 'Um, 123987.'

Alan was quizzed as to whether he shouted out a challenge and when he last cleaned his rifle.

'Just a minute,' I butted in, 'Alan you were using Dan's SLR, because yours with the IWS was covering the back alley!'

'Oh, yes, that's true!' Admitted Alan, 'Dan give the copper your SLR's registration number.'

Dan read out, '456910!'

The SIB man was furiously rubbing out Alan's SLR number and replacing Dan's.

'Did you hit anything?'

'I don't think so.'

'A second shot was fired by someone at 8 pm. Who was that?'

'I fired that time,' claimed Barry, waking up.

The SIB man took Barry's name and asked for his SLR's registered number. He enquired when he had last zeroed his rifle.

'No, you fired just after me,' claimed Charlie.

'That's right', agreed Barry, 'You fired about five minutes before me!'

The SIB man did some more rubbing out, and took Charlie's name and asked for his weapon's registration number; when he had last zeroed it. This Barry gave willingly, but added, 'I was using Cpl Parkers SLR at that time!'

The SIB man rolled his eyes and took the number of my SLR.

'So Barry', he sighed, 'You fired at five past eight?'

The SIB took down Barry's details again, and then asked which rifle he was using. After a couple of minutes Barry remembered he was using the SLR with an IWS.

'Right the next shot was fired at twenty past eight and a hit was claimed.' He looked around expectantly.

'Oh, that was me!' I blurted out. 'I fired at the gun flash on the street corner!'

Having given my details he asked which SLR I had used. I thought it might have been mine, but Dan thought it was the one with the SUIT sight. But I pointed out I never used a SUIT sight all night.

The SIB man stood up, gathered up his coat and files and said, 'Fucking forget it!' and walked out.

NEW LODGE: A SOLDIER'S FEARS

Private Jim Ward, Parachute Regiment

The New Lodge became my whole world; although the tour was only halfway through, I had been shaken by what I had seen. I didn't expect it to be easy, but what I saw in such a short space of time did surprise me.

Before Ireland, I had not seen a dead body; now I had; more than one in fact. It wasn't like I was unable to take the sight of them, although some were grotesque and some brought out an emotional response in me, also it seemed so unreal. At first I found it hard to think of them as dead, and, strange as it sounds, expected them to wake up at any moment, even with the horrific injuries they often had. I think that it was because I couldn't really understand the horror of seeing what these people did to each other. They seemed like each other, they spoke the same language, lived in the same country, ate the same food, so what was it?

We had lectures on their history and all, but did I try and understand it? No, all I was bothered about was the safety of me and my colleagues and getting home in one piece.

At the start of the tour, patrolling was something to look forward to. But, after a while, the sheer, hard slog, long hours alternating between boredom and stress, seeing what we saw; knowing just how dangerous this place could be, patrols took on a whole different meaning. Nobody shirked their duty, but, as time progressed, most of us were not as keen to be out there as much as we had before, particularly the more high risk times. Times like when incidents were common or, worse still, when our Int section received information that we were about to be hit; not when or how, only that we were. These alerts happened frequently and, as a consequence, when we moved out onto the streets, our hearts would be in our mouths, the patrols would be extra vigilant as the observation posts in the area tried to cover us. They were not always able to as there were only five of them and we had such large areas to cover.

Our Quick Reaction Force (QRF) would be back at base, on permanent standby, geared up and ready to charge to the PIGs which were warmed up by the duty drivers. Other soldiers, scattered around the camp would feel the tension as they tried to sleep, eat, wash their clothes or any of a hundred other activities, all the while thinking: my turn out there next.

Wondering if someone else's team was the one taking the shots, the bomb blast, nail or petrol.

I need to explain just how I felt, walking those streets at times of heightened tension. It was fear, intense vigilance and heightened senses, vulnerable and, strangely enough, in a large city surrounded by all its inhabitants, a large Army presence with guys you could trust, alongside you, the feeling of being totally alone. (*The author can feel only a deep empathy here for the writer; having felt, on those same streets that you were the only person on the planet, whatever the surroundings, alone with your thoughts and fears*) Totally alone, no friends, no family, no home because it was just you; nobody could stop the fear, the bullet or the bomb blast that you expected, because the fear took over. Right at that moment, that patrol, that's all there was. Coldness would fall on me, also a kind of numbness that I used to give me some way of controlling the fear. It helped because I was able to turn some of that fear into aggression and force myself to think only of the task at hand. Now and again, one of the boys would have the attitude and accepted that they were going to get hurt at some stage in the tour, and by that, felt that it helped them just to get on with things. Whether or not they really believed this, I don't know, but I didn't feel better for it even though I strongly doubted my own survivability.

I'm not ashamed to say that I was afraid back then although we wouldn't talk too much about it; looking back, I think that we had a right to be.

RIOTS

Bill Callaghan, Royal Army Medical Corps

I was stood between two lines of troops one being beaten by Orangemen, demanding to be allowed to piss off the Catholics the other being beaten by the Catholics, who wanted to stop the Orangemen pissing them off. The irony wasn't lost to us, it was laid on too thick to be sad, it was funny and we laughed a lot. I got enough trade that day, cuts, grazes, dislocated fingers and some minor burns. One lad had a dart thrown into his neck and against years of training I removed it, I figured that if I left it in and tried to evacuate him it would probably tear an artery somewhere along the line.

A woman spat at me. I'd seen her earlier with her children; she'd seemed quite normal then, even pretty and her kids loved her, that was clear. When it got noisy I saw her close up she pushed her head over the shoulders of the troops and she coughed up a great big slimy one, the product of years of smoking and living in a damp house heated with a coal fire, she spat and her eyes were filled with a victorious rage as her phlegm splatted into my face. It slid from my eyes and hung off my cheek. She was so ugly at that moment but I wondered later what her children would see when she tucked them into bed that night. It wasn't me, it was just her shitty situation she was angry about, I became detached, I observed and this ignorant involvement was more comforting. How could one soul be so full of violent rage and still show love? It didn't look good for a future.

A NORMAL DAY ON THE ARDOYNE

Private Eddie Atkinson, The Green Howards

One dark evening, time unknown, 7 platoon were deployed to Brompton gap on the new Ardoyne side in a Saracen armored vehicle, due to rioting which happened every day. On arrival, we dismounted and I was standing 2 yards from the rear of the Saracen, when someone shouted a warning but I didn't hear it clearly. I turned slowly and saw all the lads crouched into the garden walls and, as I turned back towards the Saracen a nail bomb exploded a couple of yards away from me. How I wasn't hit by the nails I will never know but poor old Jed Morrison sat in the rear of the Saracen was riddled all down his side.

On another occasion, the full platoon was deployed onto Crumlin Road close to the junction with Butler Street at the bottom wall of the Holy Cross Church. We had 2 PIGs and a Saracen, and the platoon formed up behind the vehicles ready to advance towards the rioters at the Butler Street junction when 2 nail bombs exploded; one between the Saracen and the PIG. The second bomb went off under the other PIG and the majority of the platoon – me included – were blown off our feet; I ended up on my back with my ears ringing. The first thing I remember hearing was the vehicle revving like mad and I actually thought it was reversing and fearing I was going to be run over I jumped to my feet. Quite a number of the platoon received shrapnel wounds, but again I didn't receive even a

Car in which a prison officer was murdered, Crumlin Road (Mark Campbell)

scratch. I've thought, why I was so lucky; there lies the great debate, why is it some seem to be lucky and others just seemed to be in the wrong place at the wrong time? I'm sure many soldiers over the centuries have asked themselves the same question. No one can say it's just down to luck I reckon.

One evening my section commander put me on Ops room runner, whose job is to stay in the sleeping area just outside the ops room. It was actually just a mattress on the floor screened off with a blanket. The ops room runner's job is to go and wake any NCO or officer that was needed by the ops room. It was all quiet so I got my head down, unbeknown to me there was a 'lift' arranged for the early morning. I was oblivious to all this as I was in a deep sleep. The company turned out to carry out the 'lifts' and after the operation returned only to find me missing. I still hadn't woken up; anyone who has served over there won't be surprised by that because we were always tired. Anyway there was hell on and a right flap because my section commander had forgotten he had put me on the ops runner and as far as he was concerned I was missing.

The company turned back out en mass to search for me, and all these years later, I can imagine the flap and worry. Anyway I eventually woke up and wandered into the ops room just then it dawned on the OC and the company was recalled. The daft ending is when my section commander came back – Corporal Austin – I got a right bollocking off him; typical something for once wasn't my fault and I still got a flea in my ear. Nothing changes in the Army.

ON THE ARDOYNE

Terry Friend, Royal Artillery

We had only previously experienced the Ardoyne from the outside and we had spent many hours in a rooftop sangar overlooking the place from Chief Street. It was always dark, for they, the inhabitants had long since smashed all of the street lights. Often, when we were on stag, we were approached by Protestant women with tea and sarnies and, one night, one of them called up to us: 'Watch it boys; those houses on the edge are all empty, but there's a light on in one of them; be careful.' Such were the ways in which we would pick up the odd bit of intelligence here and there.

One night, my troop was tasked to take a foot patrol into the Ardoyne, and it would be the first time that we had actually gone into this Republican stronghold. We intended to go in under cover of darkness. A few weeks earlier, we had watched, somewhat bemused as the Royal Engineers had sealed off all the streets leading from the Crumlin Road into both the Protestant and catholic areas, with corrugated barricades the height of the houses. There was barbed wire on the top and a small pedestrian gate was put into each one, about the size of a normal household front door. If unrest was in the air, these small gateways would be manned by both police and soldiers.

Anyway, on this particular night, I was a member of the first foot patrol into the Ardoyne. Whilst I can't remember the names of the other guys, I know that it was led by a second Lieutenant – Charlie Crawford – and I recall that 'Janner' Dade was last man in the patrol and I was in front of him. It was almost surreal, for here we were in the middle of a rundown Catholic ghetto and the silence was eerie. The streets were deserted of either men or animals and it was pitch black everywhere with barely a chink of light from the curtained windows; it was like being in a ghost town? For the life of me, I cannot recall the hour that we had set off, but I do remember that we were all keyed up with our senses on very high alert.

What does come back to me, however, is just how seedy, rundown and rotten the place seemed to be; you could almost taste the damp and decay. They say that poverty has its own particular smell and I smelt it that night alright! As I mentioned, the silence was eerie, or at least it was until 'Janner' Dade dropped his tin helmet; it crashed onto the pavement and we all instantly dropped down, seeking cover in doorways and against the walls. Nothing happened and we spent a couple of hours in there and

Tea stop on the Shankhill (Dave Bradwell)

were much relieved to emerge from our experience unscathed. We were lucky that night, for many young soldiers lost their lives in that warren of rundown streets during the years of the troubles.

On another occasion, yet again, another of those periods of hectic activity and not too much sleep, I was stagging it out on the upper sangar of the Leopold Street location. Due to the three days of nonstop rioting that erupted, great palls of smoke drifted over the city, making it look very much like a backdrop to a World war Two film set. I was approached by a young officer leading a Royal Marines foot patrol and he shouted at me: 'Sentry! Forget the yellow card instructions; all looters are to be shot on sight!' 'What.' I gasped: 'No verbal warnings to be given?' 'No,' he stated 'Shoot on sight!' Then they tramped away, red eyed and stubble-faced, down the street. Meanwhile, I eyed the nearby shops with fresh interest; however, no looters came my way. Would I have shot one? You bet I would!

The Yellow Card

The following is from the yellow card which I still possess:
    'You may only open fire against a person:
    If he* is committing or about to commit an act LIKELY TO ENDANGER LIFE, AND THERE IS NO WAY TO PREVENT THE DANGER. The following are some examples of acts where life could be endangered, dependant always upon the circumstances:
    Firing or being about to fire a weapon
    Planting, detonating or throwing an explosive device including a petrol bomb).
    Deliberately driving a vehicle at a person and there is no other way of stopping him.*
    If you know that he* has just killed or injured any person by such means and he* does not surrender if challenged and THERE IS NO OTHER WAY TO MAKE AN ARREST.
    * 'She' can be read instead of 'he' if applicable.
    If you have to open fire you should:
    Fire only aimed shots
    Fire no more rounds than are necessary
    Take all reasonable precautions not to injure anyone other than your target.'

Small wonder that many squaddies thought along the lines of 'Sod this for a game of soldiers!'

MOBILE PATROLS AND SANGARS

Private Jim Ward, Parachute Regiment

We had two stripped-down Land Rovers; no doors, no windows, no covering. The regiment had learned in Aden that it was better to get out of the vehicle quickly whilst under fire, than to be in a covered vehicle that would not protect you anyway. Even so, it made you feel like a slow moving target as the Rovers moved at patrol pace which was 10-15 mph; still, driving was better than walking. On board the vehicles was riot equipment, tear gas, rubber bullets, riot shields and batons. I should also point out that these vehicles were also QRF to back up the foot patrols.

As part of the 8 day cycle, we also had a couple of days in Ops and we had a number of these in the area in different buildings and on top of high-rise flats. In the sangars of these Ops we had the latest in night vision equipment and telescopes and from these vantage points we could observe a large part of the area. Although the Ops afforded some respite from the exposure of the streets, we were still vulnerable whilst sitting in the outwards facing sangars, but, I must admit that these days in the Ops were considered rest days for us, because for the other 6 days, we always seemed to be working. We never seemed to have enough men or patrols and when incidents were happening, 17 or 18 hour days were not unusual; even 40 or 50 hours without rest depending on the situation were not uncommon. We were fighting fatigue and forcing ourselves to stay alert; stay alive.

A few days after we arrived, there was an explosion in one of the other Company's area and, though asleep, I was wakened instantly as the sound echoed around the city and felt a slight tremor under me. I froze for a moment and then sirens sounded and loud speakers crackled: 'Stand-By Personnel; stand-to; stand-to.' I grabbed my weapon. Flak jacket and webbing and raced to the stand-by room; the PIGs already warmed up and drivers waiting. Finally, information came through; a small shop had had a device thrown through its windows and, whilst there were no casualties, there were two very frightened shop-owners living upstairs.

We were stood down at 01:30, but, as I was back on at 04:00, I didn't go back to sleep that night. After this incident, I often heard the sound of gunfire or explosions in the distance, but I learned to tell the difference between sounds that were within our area or outside it. If it was ours, I was up and ready before the siren sounded; if not, I waited; they'd let us know if they needed us.

The next day, the drone of the motor could hardly be heard as we patrolled in the Rover above the noise of the shouting and screaming. Seeing as it was our first week in the area, the locals decided to welcome the Paras with a display of affection reserved only for the most 'respected' visitors. And, ever since 'Bloody Sunday' we Paras were certainly not on their Sunday Dinner guest lists and it was rumoured that the IRA had monetary rewards for killing British soldiers. £200 for a soldier, but £500 for a Para; nice to be popular, but after an hour or so, the abuse faded away.

Soon after, the patrol settled down to normal routine and I looked forward to mobiles as most infantry men enjoy a break from their normal mode of transport; their own two feet. I knew just how vulnerable we were, but I knew that it was no good charging through the streets because, even though I felt like a sitting duck, had we done so, we'd have seen nothing.

Although on foot, we could blend in more, speed up, slow down, mix with the shadows, lie down, use walls for cover and move along alleyways and gardens and take cover quickly. On a vehicle moving at snails' pace, it was nerve racking.

So there it was; our routine and our 'home' for the next four months.

FLAX STREET MILL

Corporal Keith Hazlewood, Royal Regiment of Wales

In 1972, I was based at the notorious Flax Street Mill with the Royal Regiment of Wales; I was a Private at the time in the field medical section. Our equipment was pretty rudimentary, and for ambulances, we had a PIG and a Land Rover.

The thing which shocked me the most when I arrived in Northern Ireland on my first tour in October 1971 was the language of the women; if indeed you could call them women; certainly they were no ladies. Even the mums and grannies were using words which you rarely heard in those days; awful it was. On one occasion, we were lined up and were being confronted by this howling mob and one woman tried to grab my SLR. Well, I went to stop her and ended up – accidentally, I assure you – whacking her in the face; I felt ashamed even though they were not normal women. They were completely hysterical and had such venom that it surprised me and, although I was 18, I wasn't used to such swearing. It was a period of growing up and you soon learned the ropes.

Inside Flax Street Mill (Dave Bradwell)

Anyway, back to the ambulances which we had to work with on our Ardoyne tour; we had to adopt as best we could and soon learned to cram in whatever we could with loads of medical packs, burns dressings, shell dressings and such like all crammed in behind the seats.

Our first casualty was a lad named Ralph Cooper who was one of our Privates and he was shot in what really was a silly, nonsensical situation. He had been ordered to go out and sweep the streets in front of his base because a senior officer was coming to make an inspection. He must have stepped out from behind a building and right into the sights of an IRA gunman. He was hit three times by a Thompson fired from the 'Bone area.

The 'senior officer' was in fact none other than Lord Carrington, the then Secretary of State for Defence who was making a top secret visit to the Ardoyne. It was, however, too high a price for the young Private to pay, even for such a notable politician.

Corporal Hazelwood:

We were unaware of the shooting at the time and he was treated by Pte Hopkins RAMC, 'A' Company medic and evacuated by a civvie ambulance to RVH. We wanted to be prepared the next time and so Capt Mackay our RMO instigated a crash call system and we monitored the RT traffic (*Radio*) and the words we listened for were 'Shots. Wait. Out.' If there was a casualty we would get a 'Crash Call' and immediately jump into whatever vehicle was available and, once we had learned the location, set off at break neck speed. In the team we had an RCT driver, a Doctor, an RAMC medic and me. We always had a crash crew ready and another to replace it when they were called out.

We would arrive at the scene of a shooting, generally after the incident was over and there were three main criteria; KIA, badly wounded or lightly wounded. The lightly wounded we could sort out ourselves back at Flax Street Mill; all others were taken to RVH.

One incident which I remember, clearly, took place on July 14, 1972 when we had a crash call for one of the 'A' Company lads. We were informed that he had been hit at the junction of Alliance Avenue and that the fire fight was still going on. On that day, the team was Sergeant Jenkins, Private 'Hoppy' Hopkins (RAMC), a real good lad, I might add, me and an RCT Driver.

I can't remember the RCT lad's name, but he was a smashing chap and always seemed to be with me and 'Hoppy' on all the really nasty jobs. I remember, after one fatality, we were back at the Mill and I saw him and he looked really down in the dumps and I asked him what was wrong. He just looked at me and told me that he just wanted to do some good and had volunteered to drive an ambulance, but of late, he just felt that he was driving a hearse; I can't remember what I said to him, but I do remember giving him a hug.

Unity Flats, Shankhill
Road (John Swaine)

Anyway, on this day, as I said, Sergeant Jenkins was in charge as our
MO had been wounded by shots a few days earlier. We got as close to the
incident as we could but the shooting was still going on and we stopped,
having driven through streets of burned out and ruined houses. We went
down a narrow back lane and we could see the casualty hanging out of
the window of the OP and we tried to get up the back to help him, but then
we came under fire. The Sergeant sized up the situation and sent me back
to the ambulance to get the driver to radio for assistance. He did so and I
set off back on my own to help Jenkins and 'Hoppy' who I thought would
be waiting, under cover.

Halfway down the back lane, I saw several of our lads from 'A' Company
with their officer and then everything seemed to speed up and take place
in fast motion. I started to clamber over piles and piles of rubble as they
began giving covering fire and the noise was deafening. Then, just as I got
to the bottom of the pile of rubble, I saw the Sergeant and 'Hoppy' with
the casualty already on the stretcher and shots continued to fly all around.
I reached down to grab the stretcher and we started back up the rubble
and we were really struggling. I seen one of our lads and shouted in an
angry voice for him to give me a hand. It was Sergeant-Major Gill (whom
I had not seen since Crickhowell) and I was shouting at a senior NCO not
realising, who it was, but he gave me a smile and this gave me a lot of
reassurance.

Anyway, we got the badly wounded lad – at that point, I knew it was
Private Tegwen Williams –into the ambulance and off we went. He had
been shot in the throat and me and 'Hoppy' fought like crazy to clear his
airway and dress the other wounds, as he was in such a bad way. There

was blood everywhere, and we fought desperately to save him and I still find myself crying to this day when I think of how we tried to do something for him. But we couldn't get fluids inside him and he had almost 'shut down' by the time we reached the Royal Victoria Hospital (*RVH*). At that time the Casualty department of the RVH was one of the most experienced in the world for treating battle casualties and if you got them there alive, they had a fighting chance. Sadly, the lad never regained consciousness and died shortly after we got him there.

Afterwards, back at the Mill, we got the stretcher and had to prop it against a wall and throw buckets of water over it just to get the blood off.

I just wanted to say that of all the Regimental medical staff, we were the real forgotten men. We had the dirtiest, most heartbreaking tasks in all

Gunner John Swaine, Shankhill Road (John Swaine)

the Army. We weren't trained paramedics, we were just good first-aiders. But in all the books and documentaries on Northern Ireland, I have never seen recognition for the job we did; we were just Regimental Medical Assistance; not RAMC. All the medics in the medical centre were really great lads and it was a privilege to serve with them.

I met Keith on a wet and windy day in South Wales and I was impressed by his honesty and his unashamed emotion as he recalled those difficult and tragic days for this famous regiment on the streets of Belfast's staunchly Republican Ardoyne. I am honoured to redress the imbalance which clearly angers and haunts this incredible former soldier; these men were unsung heroes.

Private John Tegwen Williams was aged just 22 and came from Lampeter in Cardiganshire, a fertile breeding ground for the famous South Wales Borderers, now the Royal Welsh. He was one of ten people, including four soldiers killed on a catastrophic day of violence as yet another IRA ceasefire broke down.

BRIAN SODEN

Sergeant John Black, Royal Army Medical Corps

You may consider one abiding memory that I have that conjures up my image of the 'Troubles'. On the Roll of Honour for the Royal Regiment of Wales is the name of Pte Brian Soden who was shot by the IRA whilst on mobile patrol in Belfast on 19 June 1972.

On a previous tour, Brian had married an Irish Catholic girl; imagine, a man from the Valleys, and Chapel, marrying a Catholic girl! Some three weeks prior to his death, Mrs. Soden gave birth to twin girls. Brian was shot by a sniper with an Armalite rifle, whilst in the back of a PIG in the Ardoyne. By this time the IRA were using Armalite rifles with armoured piercing bullets that could pierce the skin of a PIG. There was one shot fired which lodged in Brian's head; no other shot was fired. I have always considered that Brian was targeted by the IRA for marrying 'one of their girls'.

This was also the prevailing view at the time by some of his colleagues and the RUC; personally, I never knew Brian. His wife and twin daughters were housed in Military Wing Musgrave Park Hospital for some weeks and were looked after by our welfare staff. I met her a few times in the course of my duties, and she was a very attractive lady. I have often wondered what happened to Mrs. Soden and the twin girls. The twins would be in their mid 30s by now, and I have doubts whether Mrs. Soden could have ever returned to her own community! The Soden family is my haunting memory of Northern Ireland's 'Troubles'. Was it all worth it? This question is one which I still ask myself.

PAUL HAZELWOOD, ROYAL ARTILLERY

North Belfast, 1976

I joined the Army as a 17 year old, and was soon into training for Northern Ireland, as we were going out there for a tour in the summer of 1974. However, after completing training I was told 'You can't go Hazel; you're too young.' To say that I was absolutely gutted, is an understatement, as I wanted to be with the lads. Sadly, the powers – that – be wouldn't allow me to go.

Paul was a victim of the change in orders from the Government, following the terrible murders of three young soldiers from the Royal Highland Fusiliers, at Ligoniel in 1971. One of the dead soldiers was only 17 and it was therefore ordained that only the 18 plus personnel would be allowed to go on active service.

I bided my time, and then 1976 came and this time I was going, and I was able to put the disappointment of 1974 behind me. The incident which I would like to refer to, took place on a rainy Saturday afternoon; myself and three mates, in the brick, Ginge, Bronco and Scouse were on foot patrols for that day, with 2 on 2 off. We had just left Grand Central for our patrol, and it was drizzling with rain and we were heading towards uptown Belfast (in the Seamen's Mission, where we were based) for a brew. Bronco and Ginge were in front with me and Scouse at the rear. Bronco told me to go back round the corner, as dodgy looking couple had just clocked us and we did an about turn. Inwardly, I thought 'You're joking; it's raining; can't we just go for a brew?' Anyway, Scouse and I turned round and caught up with the couple; she had a plastic carrier bag, but he had nothing. I told Scouse to search the woman and the bag, whilst I started to search the bloke. As I was asking him to put his hands up so I could search him, he just looked at me with a completely blank expression. I can remember saying to him 'C'mon mate, it's pissing it down; I'm wet, you're wet; just let's get it over with!'

He still had a blank expression, but, at that moment, Scouse said to me 'Hazel, there are golf balls and a can of oil in the bag.' I was thinking: 'O.k., mate, what's going on,' but, at that moment, Bronco and Ginge had come round, when I heard someone shout: detonators.

I just shouted 'Put your fucking hands up!' He did as ordered and his coat came open, and there was a Smith and Wesson pistol in his pocket; my heart was pounding and I think my legs went a bit wobbly as well, but the training just kicked in. I kept my SLR trained on him and told him to use his opposite hand to get the weapon out half way then I got it the rest of the way. We had a closer look at the golf balls and we could see that it was semtex, and we got him to carry to the other side of the road cleared the area of civilians. I arrested both and took them back to Grand Central. I had never been so scared in my life and I thought that he could have just blown me away. But thanks to the training I didn't panic, although I did afterwards though. I know it might sound stupid, but as I am writing this, my hands are shaking.

ARDOYNE: 1991

Jason Benn 3rd Bn, Light Infantry

I've been out of the army now for 15 years and had always planned to write about my time in Belfast; however when I tried to speak to my civvie mates and family they just didn't understand. Time moved on and memories faded.

In 1991 I was a Lance Corporal and went to Northern Ireland on a six month tour. We were the first English unit in nearly two years after 3 Scots Regiments and word was that we were in for a hard time. We operated out of Girdwood with a TAOR of North Belfast and on the whole I enjoyed it. For once we were doing the job and not playing on exercise. Despite the extremely high number of bombings and disruption our platoon was fairly lucky and I had two contacts. The first was on a green patrol (mobile) just after leaving echelon at Musgrave Park Hospital. Just one round fired as we headed back up to the city centre. I was on top cover in the rear vehicle and we didn't even report it; the next time was on guard at the front gate of GWD, a lad in another team called Smudge and I had a testosterone-filled argument in the front sangar as a round went past the window. We were too busy fighting to know where it came from. There were also a couple of coffee jar bombings down in the New Lodge. One was the night before I went on R&R so usually I wouldn't be out but we were short so went out. After the bombing I was standing on a cordon at the New Lodge Road and Antrim Road junction. One of the players said to me 'Hope you have a good leave son'; I nearly shit myself.

The locals on the whole hated us, swearing, stoning and spitting became the norm. The first time I was spat on we were on a patrol in the Rosapennas and I smiled at a little girl of around 3, I said hello only to be spat on by her very good looking Mum and told to 'fuck off you murdering bastard' she then told the girl that we were the nasty men who had put Daddy in prison, the little girl said 'Youse c***s' and also spat toward me; you could already see the hatred which I found immensely sad; so much for the hearts and minds crap.

We had some good finds on the search team and quite often when there was no answer I had to use 'the key' showing the sledge hammer to the locals on the cordon before I smashed the door in. No wonder they hated us, but trying to be nice didn't work either. I never even thought that a house might be booby trapped; I guess if when I smashed in a door it exploded I wouldn't have known.

You quickly got used to the abuse and I remember a young lad telling me that a black man was at home fucking my girlfriend; I said more fool him because he'd have to pay her whilst I always got a shag for nothing. He didn't seem to get it and wandered off.

One of the 'A' Company lads was RPG-ed in the top sangar at the mill, he was one of my mates and luckily he was okay, but the day they coffee jarred the dog handlers was a different story. One lad was killed* and another lost his legs, as we were on mobiles at the time we went down to the mill and ended up taking the two dogs up to GWD to be choppered out. A very sad day. The next day all the locals were quiet, they knew what we'd do if they said anything. One old lady in the Ardoyne always stood at her gate and as you went past said 'God bless you son', she said to me 'I'm sorry about the soldier yesterday, take care'.

I was the youngest NCO in the platoon and as we were the only brick where none of us had kids or were married so we were the expendables. Every patrol or follow up we were always first out, last in. I didn't mind patrols; you were your own boss.

One evening we went by vehicle across to Tennant Street RUC station in the Shankhill. The patrol was up into the Ardoyne, across to Old Park and back down through the Rosapennas to GWD. As I've said I liked patrols but this evening I was scared to such an extent I went to the toilets and threw up. I knew that something was going to happen. We went up the Crumlin Road and down through the Elmfields and secured the Brompton Gap. From there down through the main area of Ardoyne and did some 'P' (*plate*) checks and couple of snap VCPs but on the whole it was very quiet. To move up to Old Park we had to secure the bottom of Ardoyne Avenue by the Flax centre. As a couple of the teams were still up at Berwick I decided to go behind Etna into the new housing behind the Highfields club. This was

Gunners hold back onlookers as a bomb is defused (John Swaine)

a series of newish brick built housing linked by alleys and courtyards. We entered Kingston Court and at once every one of us began to hard target; nobody said a word but we all covered each other out and strangely were all aiming at the same house. The rest of the patrol went off okay and we all said when we got back in that something was wrong.

The next day was a Thursday; each week the IRA hijacked cars and left them all over Belfast creating havoc as each one had to be cleared by ATO. We were in the Unity Flats and had been there for about an hour covering ATO down on North Street. I was patrolling backwards when I felt myself falling backwards and something hit me in the neck, I put my hand to my neck and pulled it away to see blood on it, I couldn't feel any pain but could hear a screaming. I put my hand back to my neck and pulled away a used sanitary towel and threw it back at the woman screaming at me. I'd tripped over a black bin bag and she'd thrown the towel at me, much to the amusement of the lads. When we got back in one of the INT cell lads pulled me. Apparently an ASU had taken over a house in Kingston Court the previous day, a patrol had turned up but the ASU binned the shoot because they were sure the soldiers knew they were there due to the way they had reacted.

In August we had a couple of riots in the Unity flats and New Lodge; one lad was petrol-bombing us from behind a wall when we were on Peters Hill, he kept popping his head up but didn't know we'd got up to the wall, as he looked over he was met with my truncheon in the head and the RUC lads snatched him. We went around the other side of the flats as more petrol bombers were on the roof and got bricked quite heavily from a ramp. As we were withdrawing, about 25 youths came down the ramp and

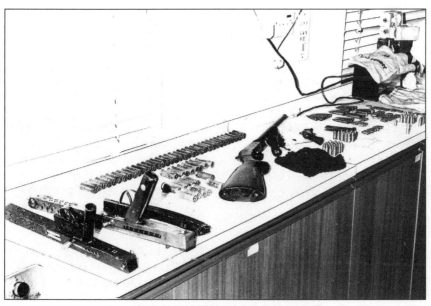

Arms find, Shankhill Road (Mark Campbell)

began pelting us. Suddenly, there was a loud crack, we cocked our 'gats' (*weapons*) and I turned to see an RUC lad on his back laughing. The crack had been his body armour hitting the floor as he fell over. For a couple of seconds we stood there laughing as did the youths, then it was back to stone throwing and baton rounds.

Towards the end of the tour our Boss went, he was a good bloke unlike the lad we got in return, straight out of Sandhurst and didn't like advice. He once told me that he knew more about Ulster because his girlfriend came from Bangor and he'd been across a couple of times. He must have seen advice as weakness. On mobiles one day we had to replenish the New Lodge OP on the flats, he said we'd park up under the flats take the fresh in and wait for the waste. I explained we should debus away from the OP, let the vehicles go mobile and have the OP override the lift and already have the waste on the way down, I said parking under the flats we'd most likely end up with a fridge thrown on top of us but he wouldn't listen, because we replenished when patrols were out on the ground. I knew it was safe to debus on the New Lodge Road. He didn't listen and Smudge ended up with a broken thumb when something was dropped on his wagon.

Many things happened back then and I was wired up for the next couple of years, checking lampposts, reading registration plates, looking down grates and up telegraph posts. I even once took cover behind a car after a firework exploded. My wife thought I was mad. My only regret is losing touch with the lads in my brick.

People should know what happened to us. It was great, but it was shit.

*The soldier to whom Jason refers was Corporal T.O' Neil of the Royal Army Veterinary Corps, who was killed by a home-made device in North Howard Street. He was killed on May 25, 1991; Corporal O'Neil was 44 and was due to leave the Army in just 6 months.

THE ARDOYNE

Glenbryn Resident

I lived in the Ardoyne until I was 16 leaving in 1975 and have many personal recollections of the 'Troubles.' Some good; some bad; some sad. Perhaps I could indulge in a few minutes of your time to allow me to recall to you one brief example that sticks in my mind to this day.

It was the summer of 1973, during the Ulster Workers Council Strike, when many areas of the city including ours and indeed the entire country were barricaded; preventing vehicular and security force access. Water, gas and electricity supplies were disrupted with drinking water having to be collected in buckets and pots from a standpipe at the top of the street. I remember my mother having to cook food over a coal-fuelled fire in the back yard. During this period, many of the local 'hoods' would parade within their own streets, as if they were totally untouchable. On one particular day a local well know hard man was walking down the street with a revolver strapped to his side like something out of a Wild West movie.

There was no effort on his behalf to conceal the weapon; in fact, quite the opposite. This man was making a visual statement to the local residents; they were safe; he was going to protect them from the other side.' I remember thinking at the time, even though I was only 14, how bad things were getting; however neither the sight I was witnessing, nor my thoughts at the time prepared me for what happened next. As this 'cowboy' proceeded to walk down the street, his 6 year old son saw him and ran towards him, from his friend's front garden where he had been playing. On reaching him the young boy exclaimed 'Whaoo, Daddy; are you going to shoot a Fenian?' The child's father simply laughed and carried on walking with even more strut in his step, no doubt satisfied and proud in his own mind, of his excellent nurturing and parenting skills.

The strange thing is although I witnessed many different events, for some strange reason this one always sticks in my mind. I think, because for me at the time it reflected the hopelessness of the whole general situation, how far bigotry and sectarianism had rooted itself in the upcoming generation, and the lack of value for human life; it seemed there would never be an end to it all.

I was lucky and my experiences were never really that life threatening compared to others but a compilation of such recollections does deserve to be recorded.

Whilst the book is strictly the voices of the squaddies and their loved ones, the gentleman here strikes a chord; living in and amongst the troubles, he should be accorded a voice in this book. I further understand that he is connected with the UDR and Royal Irish and I am honoured to have his unique perspective here.

A LETTER FROM THE ARDOYNE, 1971

Contemporary Newspaper report, July 1971

'Dear Mum...We kip with our boots on and sometimes they put razor blades in our tea.'

'Belfast, Tuesday. It has been pretty quiet where we are for the last few days, though of course it is a shock to see trucks with armed guards in them and sand-bagged observation posts and barricades in the streets. After all, it's all less than 90 minutes by air from Bristol.

I expect mum would be a bit shocked to see where we have to live. There's soldiers snatching sleep with their boots still on and we're crammed fairly full. Recently, a new alert has been brought in so that we can only have two pints of beer in 24 hours and can only go out in certain daylight hours in the city centre in groups of four –if we get any time off at all – and the number of vehicles going out on patrol together has been stepped up.

It's a kind of police job really – during marches (like the Orange Day Parade) the Army revs up heavy lorry engines so that the other side can't get worked up by hearing their opposite faction. Today we were in an area where they seem to like the soldiers and they gave us tea and played around a bit with the kids. Some of the lads say that you can sometimes find razor blades in the tea they give you but I haven't met anybody who's actually had this. But the people can be smiling one minute and throwing things next day.

You've probably read about the house searches we've been doing. They can be a bit alarming because the women in the houses shout a lot and bang dustbin lids and go round all the other houses trying to raise a crowd. I suppose in a way you can't blame them. We're foreign soldiers to them and nobody likes being woken up in the early hours of the morning for soldiers to search through the house. I think I ought to get some sleep now because I'm on patrol soon; I'll go on with this later.

Well, it's still quite peaceful although in some areas there has been some bomb-throwing and a football crowd beat up a policeman. I've met a few lads from Bath and roundabout. There's Pte Peter Flint who lives in, Whiteway. He married a Catholic Irish girl, and say's he's had threats on his life. Corporal Christopher Shaw of Bathwick Hill reckons the Army's hands are being tied and that we are being too gentlemanly with the thugs. Pte Walter Morse is the driver for the officer commanding 'B' company – he says that four months out there is quite long enough for him.

But Lance Cpl Geoffrey Moore says you can have a good time by doing a good job. He's from Hill Ground, Frome. Pte Roger Buswell from Eastmead, Welton was one of the lads who had to face a football crowd riot. I was worried about having to deal with one myself, but he said 'There were about 200 of them, yobbos and that. The bottles were flying. We fired rubber bullets and they went away.' Sounds easy, but still frightening. There's Pte Alan Smith of Whiteway, who looks after the ammunition for two of the companies and Phil Higgs of Paulton who's done 89 hours work in the last six days. And the Co, Lt-Col Robert Waight he has to go out in case there's trouble with a demonstration they're holding in the Ardoyne.

Wow, that was fairly nerve-wracking. There was a crowd of about 600 listening to speakers shouting about the Army's lies and brutality. Some of the crowd shouted at a nearby patrol to get out and they did – a little way. Then some of the crowd came down to Flax Street and we had to stand there, ready. They sat down and sang protest songs. The women and children were in front – they often do it that way – as some of the lads say that they can be a cover for someone shooting from the back, but nothing happened.

They did burn a Union Jack and tear one up and throw it over to us. Like Lance Cpl Tony McLaughlin says – he's from Frome – that sort of thing does get deep down, somehow. You do get absolutely cheesed off with the hours and the waiting and having to be alert and the constant pressure of feelings from one faction or the other.

The troops moved back to Ulster two years ago and there's still no sign of a solution. Everything you think of has dangerous disadvantages and all the lads expect to be back here next year. There must be a lot to understand about the situation – there's civil rights indignation against the discrimination against Catholics and it must be dreadful to have the Army cluttering up your town, though a Battalion is only as big as some of the crowds.

When you think about it, the passions and the plotting are all part of the historical background and might even be justified sometimes, but what I write to you shows you how the soldiers see it.

Your loving son, John'

SECTARIAN RIOTS IN THE ARDOYNE

Private Eddie Atkinson, The Green Howards

We were called out to the new Ardoyne due to rioting between the Protestants and Catholics in the area near to the bus depot. The Catholics were attacking the Proddies and they were moving out. To say it resembled a scene from World War II would not be far away. It was like refugees fleeing an enemy attack, with the Protestants taking what they could but, before they left they were damaging their gas pipes and setting fire to the gas. In some cases the gas trying to find a way out could be seen under the ground in the gardens like some huge snake.

This particular house was well alight and there was smoke covering the whole street; exploding roof tiles flying off the roofs. We were right by the wall of the bus depot behind our PIGs and Saracens. There was shooting coming from behind a barricade of cars down towards Etna Drive. Then out of the smoke came a figure with what appeared to be a red shirt on, when he got closer we could see it was blood and he had been shot in the shoulder. He told us there were people still in the houses further down the street. RSM Terry Latham came to us and organised a PIG and we were to advance down the street behind it and see if we could help. I remember

Private West (RRW) – looking for Sinn Fein's advice? (Royal Regiment Wales Museum)

there was the RSM, myself, Vic 'Fluff' Feather and a few more who I can't remember the names of. The RSM told 'Fluff': to give him his SLR rifle and he passed his Browning pistol in exchange. 'Fluff' looked at the pistol then at me and said: 'What the hell am I supposed to do with this if they open up?' Off we went down the road to the junction and then, half way down we were sent down the back alley, checking the houses. Most were empty but we checked a house out and sat in the smoke was an old lady in her living room; we couldn't believe it. We carried her out and back up the street to evacuate her. How could they do this to each other with no respect for life or property? A few days after I took some photos of the damage; there were whole streets like Farringdon Gardens, Velsheda all gutted; it really was like a scene from the blitz.

ON LEAVE AFTER NEW LODGE

Mick Pickford, Royal Artillery

I can remember getting to Gatwick to meet the family, doing five and twenty metre checks at the baggage reclaim and feeling bewildered at everyone going about their business in a normal way. I just couldn't get it; it was like I was looking in from a distance to another world. I was there, but not really. Talking at a thousand miles per hour all the way home in the car at everyone, and every other word was 'f*ck.' All the family was in the car, and I just talked and talked and talked; most of it rubbish, but I just wanted to talk, you know, just talk. I wanted them to ask me about me, not things that have happened, what I had seen; just me. Funny thing though, now that you have prompted me, I did notice how beautiful the world was and where I lived, the air was fresh and I could smell the grass; NOT f****g COAL! Still get memories of New Lodge when I smell coal burning.

My senses seemed to be going like a rocket ship, the birdsongs, and the serenity. What does stick out in my mind was the trees; the colour of the trees. And the nice sound of the wind going through them. And, noises, no sirens, thank God, no sirens. At this time, my niece was born and she was brought over to the house, and I remember saying to her on the quiet, 'you don't want to grow up and see what I am doing' but, I didn't feel anything, and I was starting to lose humility; empty words of wisdom I suppose.

I remember standing in a pub thinking to myself, and looking around, 'look at all you people, you don't know the half of it, and you just have not got a clue what I'm doing for you. Yes, you. With your flash car, nice wife, kids in private school, and its people like me that keep you safe at night, balance the economy, and keep you in the cosy life you lead.

Kicking down a pub's doors at closing time, because I thought someone had been looking at me in a threatening way (yes, I was well gone by then) and offering the whole pub out! After that night, my brother refused to go out with me at night saying to my Mum, 'I'm not going out with him anymore, and he's a different breed!' And I guess I was, I was angry and very frustrated, I wanted some thanks for what I was doing, that's all I wanted, someone to stand there and say, thanks, what a good job you are doing. All that you got was, yeah, well, blah blah. (F*ck off, stupid Civvie c**t)

Walking backwards down the high street, running past alleyways and checking windows on the way. The feeling of being constantly 'Dicked'. Total paranoid state. Visiting Lakeside shopping centre was a nightmare, and decided that staying away from crowds was a good thing.

Coping with the depression of people not really caring and hearing what I was saying, but not listening, and seeking comfort at the bottom of the Stella/Gin/Vodka bottles. I guess it was a greed and fear thing. I gotta do as much as I can because I don't know if I will ever see it again. And you know what? I cannot remember if I even hugged my Mum before I left to go back. I just wanted to get back to be honest; I felt like this world just wanted me back there, and that's the only place I had control in. Because I was 'the lean mean I can make a difference to all this shit' machine!

Oh, and another one The first question you got when you went out: 'When are you going back?' Mate, I've just got here, so just shut your grid, and let me enjoy myself. Nice!!

Mick's heartfelt words about the emotional turmoil which he faced once away from the relentless pressure of being on streets where you were the object of hatred are a common thread amongst contributors. From a purely personal perspective, I soon found out that no-one was interested, no one wanted to know; it was old news, it was 'boring' as one lady said to me. Was it ever thus.

SATURDAY AFTERNOON IN THE NEW LODGE

Private Jim Ward, Parachute Regiment

It was a relatively quiet period in the area and we were starting to relax a little as there had been no incidents for days. It was a Saturday afternoon and as usual on a sunny weekend, most of the locals were outside their front doors, or the Republican clubs or the shops. 'Gran' would be wheeled out to give her a bit of sun, kids would play and an almost carnival atmosphere would descend on the area. It almost made some of us feel like we were back home on similar summer Saturdays. In my mind, I would go back to Harrogate in summer, to a time just before I joined up, still at school, remembering the shopping trips with Mum and dad in the town centre. I remembered being with friends, trying to chat up girls, listen to music, eat ice cream and warm up under the sun. But, back in Ireland, we would be reminded of where we were as the odd insult would be flung our way and the animosity still remained; it wasn't always like this, and now and again, both sides tried to forget that the other was there.

However, this Saturday was to be different! I'd been on my two days of foot patrols, this being my second day and we had patrolled the area, twice in the morning and once in the afternoon. We'd gone back to the base for a bite to eat, when an anonymous call came in that two men had been seen in a derelict house in one of the many bombed-out and burned-out ones which were scattered throughout the New Lodge. In fact, there were many streets in which nobody lived.

The Company Commander and the Company Sergeant Major (CSM) came down to the gate as we were loading our weapons and one of them said: 'Now listen, lads; I don't like the feel of this one; I've got the two mobile patrols forming a cordon at both ends of the street and the QRF stood to, but I need you to sweep those buildings.' He paused and, ominously added: 'And, the mobiles and Ops are telling us that the street has just become deserted!' My heart sank, because I knew what that meant and a tight feeling bound my stomach into knots as the four of us moved out of the gates and headed towards the street in question.

The first thing I noticed was the difference from just an hour or two earlier. Gone were the crowds and the atmosphere had become very cold and edgy; in stark contrast to what it had been previously. There were still some of the men of the area gathered near the clubs, but they were quite some distance from us and they watched us closely as we moved forward. We got to the top of the street where one of the mobiles had taken up defensive positions and our patrol leader spoke quietly to his opposite number from the vehicles. I knelt in a doorway, tried to stay calm and take stock of the situation and the first thing I did was to check my equipment. We'd done this before leaving the base, but rechecking it seemed to reassure me a little; a small routine that I was developing each time that a situation seemed particularly dicey.

I made sure that I had no loose articles or flapping clothing that would create noise and give me away in an ambush, made sure that my flak jacket was as tight as I could bear it; the tighter, the better I felt. At this stage, and as we entered the building, my senses were on fire; myself and one of the others were to search the houses on this side of the street, whist the other two did the other side.

Now, since I'd been in Ireland, particularly with all that had happened, I knew that it was a risky business being out on the streets, but at least the incidents were sporadic. This though, was so different; we were expecting an attack, so it made it far worse. As we searched down the street, building to building, I concentrated hard on everything I had been taught, tried to stay as calm as possible and didn't really know what it was that we were searching for. Was it the two men who had been reported; if they were trapped, would they be prepared to fight; were they in the next room? We had to clear all the rooms at the same time expecting an explosion or a burst of gunfire.

We also had to look for the tell-tale signs of booby traps and we had to watch out for snipers as we went from house to house; all of this was made worse by the strange silence all around us. Three-quarters of the way down the street and still nothing and I was thinking that maybe that the bomb had to be in the final group of buildings. They were all clear and to call it an anti-climax would be an understatement! As we came out of that street, the relief I felt was immense; it was like being in a different world.

The Platoon Commander and Sergeant were there, along with a number of other people who wouldn't have been there normally but understood the seriousness of the situation. This reception committee included two medics and their red crossed painted Land Rover and served to underpin the catastrophic outcome that we had all expected.

The relief on everybody's faces was evident and it was clear that it wasn't just the four searchers who had expected a terrible outcome. Their relief mirrored ours and it was almost as if we had all held our collective breaths; but soon, order took over and we returned to normal levels of breathing and heartbeat. I don't think in these days of violent movies that it is easy to get over the message of how it feels to be a target, so easily recognised by your enemy and how vulnerable you feel. To confront the fact that there are people who want to kill you, who would take your life in a flash if they could is not easy; I felt it more on that day that I had previously, but, unfortunately, it wasn't to be the last time. Every soldier in that situation realises that he is not in a movie; that he cannot be the star who takes every adversity in his stride. Sure, nothing happened that day, but we were all sure that it would and that it was as bad, in some ways, as if it had happened. Later on, having spoken with some of the others, I realised that we had all been affected in the same way.

So, was it a set-up? No sign was found of anything untoward that day, but a week or so later, Int told us that an informer had reported that the IRA had intended to attack the area that day, but our quick response had scared them off. It was also revealed that the same IRA unit had previously attacked the company.

All the members of the patrol in that earlier ambushed had survived, but two were casevacced back to the Mainland; they were lucky that day; as indeed we had been.

CRUMLIN ROAD

Private Jim Parker, Light Infantry

Support Company moved into the Church Hall on Crumlin Road. My first duty was to stand on the street across the road from the Church Hall. Pte Meston an ex-Royal Marine and was somewhat older than the rest of us partnered me. The general public was very glad to see us, and came up to speak and shake hands. Jim Meston would have none of it! When our officer came around he asked if we might move onto the roof of the public toilet, which we did. Later, we moved onto the roof of the Fire Station, behind the toilet. Thus except for meals, and off duty sleeping I spent five days on the Fire Station roof. My combat trousers were ripped at the knees and backside from clambering about on the slate tiles.

One of the worst things a young soldier can do is 'fiddle' with his weapon. Jim Meston had to go down from the Fire Station roof for a meal or to the toilet. His personal weapon was a GPMG. It was a weapon I had had very little to do with, other than basic training at Shrewsbury over a year before. Jim borrowed my rifle and left me with an unfamiliar gun. However, I remembered one thing about the GPMG, the safety catch could only be applied if the gun was cocked (and ready to fire). I fiddled and pushed the safety catch, and was surprised that it clicked on and off. I opened the top cover and allowed the ammunition belt to drop free. I checked the breach to ensure it was empty, and pulled the trigger and the working parts flew forward with a clang. I reloaded the ammo belt. When Jim returned I told him he had left the GPMG cocked. For the next 50 years he and I have argued this point. He has always denied he left me with a cocked weapon and I'm convinced he did

The Green Howards lost a second soldier, when Private John Robinson (21) was killed on the Crumlin Road, an area which I shall deal with shortly. On August 23, Private George Crozier (23) was shot as he manned an OP on the top of the Flax Street mill. There are two excellent accounts of George Crozier, written by two of his comrades, in *A Long Long War* by the same author. The mill, home to almost every Regiment in the British Army at some time or other, is no longer there. It was one of the many Victorian mills producing linen and dated back almost to the birth of the Industrial Revolution in Britain. It was dirty, cold, and damp, and rust was forever peeling off its ancient pipes, but, soldiers being soldiers, made the best of a bad job.

FLAX STREET MILL

Terry Friend, Royal Artillery

This was an abandoned old mill, several stories high and on the corner of Flax Street and Crumlin Road and looked like something left over from a

St Peter's Church seen from Flax Street Mill (Royal Regiment Wales Museum)

Second World War bombing raid. The whole place was grey and appeared to be made out of concrete. It was damp, musty, dusty and freezing cold and stank of decay and neglect; even after all this time, I cannot recall if it had any windows. The only good thing that you could say about the place was that there was plenty of room to stretch out in.

I suppose that this was something which we didn't really appreciate at the time that we were there. By now, we were engaged in a constant round of foot and vehicle patrols or stagging out in sangars at our various bases. The worst thing of all would be the lack of proper sleep or adequate rest; it made us all very tetchy indeed.

FLAX STREET MILL

Major Peter Oakley, Kings Regiment

At this time, we had left Girdwood, with its memories of watching the UDR soldiers wending a boozy and unsteady path home in uniform after a parade night and we were attached to our 'A' Company. This was in the charred smell and noise of the Flax Street Mill, a building that had been badly burned up and cleaned enough to house some 140 soldiers.

I think what affected me most and stands out vividly in my memory was the time when houses were set on fire in neighbourhoods where the locals were being forced out because of their religion. It affected so many ordinary families who had lived in these streets for years and were friends and neighbours despite the differing religions. This was my first experience of 'ethnic cleansing' and I really did believe that the city had lost its soul and was being sent to purgatory. As we neared the end of that tour, the situation worsened. Rioters initially used bottles and bricks and anything else to batter us whilst we cowered behind our silly metal shields, which bent under the first brick, and a helmet that was more hindrance than help. You can plot the escalation of violence perhaps by the use of bottles. After first hurling them at you and not knocking you back, the next step was to fill them with urine. No good? Fill them with acid taken from car batteries; run out of acid? Fill them with petrol. Not effective enough? Fill them with sugar and petrol; the molten sugar melts and sticks to the skin causing extremely serious and deep burns. They became a much feared missile. I wonder to this day why we were not allowed to shoot petrol bombers!

We returned to Minden in Germany and, although we had had many long days with riots and a lot of injuries, it was nothing compared to what was to come later for all of us in Northern Ireland. The situation had continued to worsen; away went soft top Land Rovers and tea stops because the gun and bomb made their devastating appearances with the subsequent great loss of both military and civilian life and destruction of property.

At that stage, Peter's regiment, the Kings had lost none of its men to any form of death; that was all to change and seven of its soldiers would die in a three month period the following year.

General Sir Peter Graham

I was serving in Germany and was sent to Ulster on a reconnaissance for a staff job that I was to take up later that year. During my reconnaissance I was attached to the Belfast Reserve Battalion which was a Queen's Regiment Battalion. At some stage one evening, the Company I was attached to was called out to deal with a riot at the Artillery House in the New Lodge area of Belfast. I accompanied the Company Commander throughout and when we arrived we found a major riot taking place and all manner of articles were being thrown off the high rise Artillery House flats. Items included a javelin, beer crates, telephones, bricks, stone and all manner of odd items! The Company Commander de-bussed his soldiers from the armoured pigs in which we were travelling and tried to advance on foot to get into the flats to prevent the inmates throwing things down on us. We were beaten back. The Company Commander gave the order to get back in the pigs and then we drove at speed up the entrance so that we could de-bus in safety and get into the flats.

He sent soldiers to piquet each floor of the flats and then took the lift to the top. He and I then came down floor by floor checking that all was quiet.

On one particular floor the private soldier there stated that a lady in one of the flats on that floor was complaining because somebody had kicked her door down. The Company Commander questioned the soldier who denied that anybody had kicked the door down and indeed the door was standing closed! The Company Commander knocked on the door and a woman came out and asked what he wanted. He explained that he understood she had a complaint. She immediately said that her door had been kicked down by the soldiers. The Company Commander then asked if she had seen who had actually done this and she immediately said 'Yes, it was the Company Commander – Major X – I saw him myself 'and named him as the culprit. He drew himself up to his full height said to her 'Madam, I am Major X! I am the Company Commander and this Highland Officer has been with me all night and he will vouch for the fact that I have not been on this floor before and certainly did NOT kick your door down!' Quick as a flash she replied 'Then sure it's a man the spittin' livin' image of you!' I realised then that the Northern Irish problem was certainly going to be an interesting, unusual and difficult one!

When the British Army was deployed onto the streets of Northern Ireland on a very sunny Thursday on August 14, 1969, fixed bayonets were the order of the day. Indeed, many troops continued to patrol with fixed bayonets until later in the summer when the *Daily Mirror* ran a campaign to have them removed. During the research for this book, no bayonet charges were noted, certainly not ones of a mass nature; a young Light Infantryman named Smith has helped re-write the history of the troubles.

CRUMLIN ROAD BAYONET CHARGE

Private Jim Parker, Light Infantry

Private Smith was the Company Clerk; not only was he a pen pusher, but also looked like one. He was tall, but very thin with ginger hair and huge NHS spectacles. Furthermore, as there were so many Smiths, men with such names are called by their last two numbers. His service number was 00. He was known as Smith Blonk-Blonk.' 'Smith Blonk-blonk was on stag, on his own, on a street cornered in a rough area of Belfast armed with a Self Loading Rifle with fixed bayonet. Down the street came a noisy group of rioters. He was terrified, and knew he should not abandon his post. So, he brought up his rifle, pointing his bayonet at the rowdy crowd and charged

Dave Bradwell at Flax Street Mill (Dave Bradwell)

at them. And, they fled. Smith Blonk-blonk was utterly dismayed that whilst performing this most brave of deeds; no one was there to see him!

Less than a month later, the Green Howards lost another of their boys, when Lance Corporal Peter Herrington (26) the father of three young children was shot and killed by the IRA. He was guarding an ATO (Ammunition Technical Officer) as he examined an explosive device left in the street when he was shot. The incident happened where Flax Street meets Brompton Park in the Ardoyne and within sight of the mill.

A further month passed, and then the Green Howards lost Private Peter Sharp (22), shot whilst he patrolled Chatham Street on the Ardoyne. A Teessider, he was the fifth member of this famous Regiment to be killed over a period of just 8 weeks. The regiment – who also like to be known as XIX – were the only unit to win a Victoria Cross on 'D-Day' in 1944 when CSM Stan Hollis was the proud recipient of a bronze medal marked simply 'For Valour.'

Sixteen days later, on October 17, on Old Park Road, Sergeant Graham Cox (35) of the Queen's Dragoon Guards died of the wounds he had received two days earlier. On the 15th, he had been badly injured when he was shot whilst taking part in an armoured patrol of the area. He was married and had three children. The following month, two more RUC officers were killed, very close to where Sergeant Cox was shot. Sergeant Dermot Hurley (50) and a father of five children and his colleague Constable Thomas Moore (37) were both killed by IRA gunman whilst 'on enquiries' in the Oldpark area.

The same area witnessed the death of another RUC man when, on January 28, 1972, Constable Raymond Carroll (22) was shot and killed by the IRA on Oldpark Road, whilst off duty.

FLAX STREET MILL AND THE ARDOYNE

Sergeant 'W' Royal Highland Fusiliers

So we found ourselves back in Northern Ireland, Belfast again, and afterwards, a lovely tour to Singapore; but it was Belfast first.

I had I three mobile patrols, one of which I commanded and the other two were under a Corporal each. We arrived at the Flax Street Mill, a burnt out old flax mill which was the dirtiest place you could find; everything you touched was black and even laying on camp beds in a sleeping bag made you dirty.

(A common thread amongst squaddies who served there was that it was so filthy, one needed a shower just having been inside. One Welsh soldier recalled that every time someone walked on the floor above his bed, he was showered by rust from the rotting pipes)

Cooking was by number one burners in the archway to the entrance to the mill, and it was best to be out on a patrol rather in this filthy hole. Later on, I was moved to another factory, although this was even worse, with just one big floor and a flat roof with two hundred soldiers on camp beds. Patrols were ongoing throughout the Ardoyne; it was an area, other than being aware that it was a 'hot spot', of which we knew little; that was to change.

One night, whilst out on patrol, I came under fire from small arms – .22 and 45 calibre ammo – and took cover beside a brick wall and tried, without success, to find the shooter. As we moved back to our vehicles, an RUC special patrol, in an unmarked car stopped and the occupants asked where the shots had come from. I told them what had happened and off they went into the Ardoyne and into an ambush; all three were killed.

(As the troubles ground on, the IRA moved from ad hoc operations where everything appeared to be on the spur of the moment, to carefully planned, and sophisticated ambushes. In classic 'come on' situations, a deliberately aimed shot would fly over the heads of the SF personnel and they would be often lured into an ambush.)

'A' company arrived in a 4 ton vehicle and formed up in 'Box' formation in a large group, which was cheering. Just as they put up their shields, a gunman opened fire with a Thompson machine gun and, hard to believe, the shields stopped the .45 rounds! Immediately, a Sergeant – whom I shall just call 'Jake' – shot the gunman, although the body was never recovered.

Flax Street Mill, 1973 (Dave Bradwell)

During my time, working in the Ardoyne, we found out that the IRA was getting well organized with young boys watching and reporting all our moves.

During one patrol, we were told of a bank robbery and given the number plate of the getaway car. We gave chase and soon stopped it, after having blocked it in and arrested both the driver and the passenger. Shortly afterwards, the mob discovered the arrest and 'clocked' who had done the arresting and targeted us thereafter with rocks and stones every time we went out on patrol.

ARDOYNE OP

Private Eddie Atkinson, Green Howards

It was 1971 and we were stationed at the Flax Street Mill in the Ardoyne. I was with a lad by the name of Jack whom we called the Jezebel Kid (not his real name, which I can't tell you unless he agreed) and a Sergeant whose name I can't remember. We were told that we had to go on an O.P. in a derelict house off Herbert Street, in the old Ardoyne.

We left the Mill, as part of a normal foot patrol very quietly and made our way to a derelict house – entering from the rear – infiltrating in the small hours and spent 2 days in there with people living next door. You can imagine how dangerous this was this was and it was well before the days of COP (*Close Observation Platoon*) long before the time of the specialist close op groups with their sophisticated techniques. (*These were formed within each battalion.*)

I remember that our brief was to observe Butler Street covertly and, as a young 18 year old, I suppose it didn't register just how dangerous it was. Anyway the next day, a full riot started and more or less for the next 18 hours there were quite a few riots going on all over the old Ardoyne. My one overriding memory of it was about Jack (the Jezebel kid) he was always reading the J T Edson cowboy books and he fancied himself as this Indian called the Jezebel Kid. On patrols, he used to carry a big 'Bowie' type knife around with him and in the op we were chatting when he says to me 'Don't worry Eddie; if any IRA come up those stairs I will nail them with my knife !' And, after saying this he launched his knife at the wall just for us to see it hit the wall, handle first and drop with a clatter on to the floor. Well I was trying not to laugh out loud and but have you ever started laughing and tried to stifle it? It just made me worse. How we were never rumbled by either the rioters or any players who might have been about, is beyond me but anyway we finished the op without being compromised and returned to Flax Street Mill safely.

In May, 1972, during the Royal Regiment of Wales' tenure at the mill on Flax Street, another soldier died in the area. On the 15th of that month, whilst manning the top sangar at the mill, Lance Corporal John Hillman (29) was shot; he died three days later, leaving a pregnant widow and two young children. Two more RRW soldiers would die the following month at the hands of terrorists; Lance Corporal Alan Giles on the 12th and Private Bryan Soden on the 19th.

Alan Giles, a Cardiff boy, was shot and terribly wounded on June 11 in Alliance Avenue following a fire fight. He died in the hospital a few hours after his parents arrived from Wales. I was told by Aarfon Williams of the RRW Museum that he clung onto life just long enough for his distraught parents to be at his side. A week later in Brompton Park, his comrade Bryan Soden (21) [*dealt with earlier in this chapter*] was hit by an armour piercing (AP) round which went clean through the PIG in which he was travelling.

A month later, the toll of RRW soldiers continued when Private David Meeke (24) was shot by an IRA sniper on Hooker Street in the Ardoyne. A moving tribute to this soldier is to be found in the 1972 chapter of a 'Long Long War' by the same author. Royal Corps of Transport (RCT) soldier Peter Heppenstall, described as 'big, tall lad with blond hair' by his RRW comrades to whom he was attached was shot and killed on foot patrol on Alliance Avenue. Then, with a cruel twist of the knife, just hours later, in the same street, the IRA killed John Williams. Private Williams (22) a Cardigan, South Wales boy, was the fifth RRW soldier killed in the space of just 8 weeks.

The RRW were born out of the ashes of several Welsh regiments, but they feel that their roots lie in the 24th of Foot and trace their lineage back several hundred years. Whilst they are proud of all their Regiment's ancestors, I venture the opinion that the Welsh boys 'B' Company, South Wales Borderers, who

RCT soldier on the Ardoyne (Phil Morris)

withstood the might of the Zulu nation at Rorke's Drift, in 1879, would be their heroes.

ARDOYNE BUS DEPOT

Harry Knight, Royal Regiment of Wales

It was 1972, and I was already on my third tour of Northern Ireland. The first part of the tour had been quiet, with not an awful lot happening. My company – 'B' – was stationed in the bus depot up on the Ardoyne area of north Belfast, using it as a base. Whilst there, we were on a three day rota; guards, patrol and standby. When we were on a patrol rota, each shift lasted 12 hours and on this particular one, we were just coming to the end.

It was about 08:30, and we were doing one last sweep of the area on the Berwick Road just where two empty houses had been turned into drinking dens by the Prods. We were just passing, when someone ran out and shouted that a bomb had been left on the doorstep. I have to say, that I thought that it was a waste of time and yours truly walked over to check it out. There was a bag in the doorway and I could wires and batteries and as I bent to have a look, I could smell Marzipan which told me that it was P.E. (*Plastic explosive.*) We immediately pulled back to cover behind the Land Rover (I tip-toed, actually) and radioed the bomb disposal boys, keeping the area clear until they arrived. An officer checked it out and then pulled his Saracen across the road, took out a shotgun – a smashing, classy one it was – and put two rounds into the package. He then went over to check it out and found the timer device and said to me: 'Not to worry, Taff; you had eighteen minutes left!' So that was the end of that problem.

Then a couple of days later, there was a report of a parcel being left by the back gates of the bus park and I was sent to check it out. On getting to the parcel, I could see that it was wrapped and taped nicely, but there was no chance that I was going to open it. On the radio I went and called out the bomb disposal guys again and when they arrived, they had a good look and then came to the same decision as me. One of them said that there was no way he was going to open it and placed a small charge on the package and told us all to get behind cover. We got down behind a three-foot wall on the side of the road and counted off 'One, two, three' and then BANG! The next thing we knew, we were all showered in potato peelings; some funny bastard must have had a good laugh at us that day.

The IRA constantly disrupted the normal routine of both Army and civilians alike by constantly mixing hoax devices with the real thing as they stepped up their terror war aimed at the destruction of the province's economy and the withdrawal of the security forces. In the year that Harry refers to, there were a staggering 1,853 explosions and an unrecorded number of false alarms; no member of the SF could afford to ignore a single one.

THE ARDOYNE

Kevin Wright, RCT

It was a typical cold, wet, horrible January night in 1974 in Belfast when we rolled back into Flax Street Mill at about 2200 hours after a long tiring day patrolling the Ardoyne and Oldpark area. We had been given the runaround by the usual stone throwers and other bored kids. As we arrived, the patrol dived out of the Saracen into the unloading area as quick as they could to get indoors in the warm, in order to get a brew and egg banjo off the choggie wallah.

I pulled over to the fuelling area to fill up ready for my mate to take the next patrol out at 2300 hrs. Whilst I was refueling, I decided to clean all the broken glass from the bottles thrown at us, along with paint and bags of human and animal waste off the top and sides of the vehicle. BIG MISTAKE! Thinking that I was well protected by the walls of the compound I climbed on the roof of the Saracen with a broom and got busy sweeping off the debris. All I remember was slipping on a bag of shit and landing on my back on the driver's hatch; as I pulled myself up, I heard the dull thump of two shots hitting the building. I don't know to this day if the gunman had seen me from one of the surrounding buildings

Or was it just the boyos letting us know they had not yet gone to bed.

Well, the alarm sounded and the standby section came out and went roaring off into the Ardoyne to find the now well gone gunman. I remember walking into my room shared with 40 other guys as at least 12 to 15 rounds hit the wall above my mate's bed on the outside overlooking the Ardoyne; nobody even stirred and just turned over and went back to sleep. Just a normal night in the Ardoyne.

RPGS IN THE ARDOYNE

John Rafferty, 3rd Bn Light Infantry

I served with 3LI between 1970/73. I remember as though it were yesterday, that I was blown out of bed by the second RPG7 that was fired in Northern Ireland.

My memory for times and exact places has faded with time, but my Company (Support Company), were living in a commandeered school near Ardilea Street in Belfast. (*This street sits less than 300 yards from the Loyalist Crumlin Road and only 200 yards from the beleaguered Flax Street Mill*) I can remember that during the morning, I had been down in the rest room area, watching the news on the TV, when it was reported that an RPG7 had been fired near to the border. The comment was, I think, just how much longer before they manage to get some of those into the city to point at the rest of us, and thought little more of it.

Later that evening, several of us were upstairs in our bunks resting, after returning from a patrol. There was an almighty explosion on the wall about six feet from my bunk, which threw me off my bed, and onto the floor. I was in a daze. After getting to my feet, and looking to see what had happened, I saw a large hole in the wall, directly behind the heavy old cast iron school radiator that was now hanging awkwardly from the wall. Fortunately, no one was seriously injured in the blast, as it seems that the missile had initially struck a chicken wire screen that had been erected in the school playground, just before exploding on the wall next to the radiator.

This new devastating weapon had been only recently acquired by the IRA and it was thought that it was financed by the Irish-Americans in NORAID. Either deliberately or, naively, these people from four or five generations back assuaged their consciences by donating to 'the folks back home in Ireland.' It was used in the attack on a mobile patrol of the Parachute Regiment which killed one soldier and maimed another in the 90s.

The UDR lost one of their men on July 23, when Private Robert McComb (22) was shot and killed as he walked along Kerrera Street whilst off duty. Private McComb would be one of over one hundred and eighty UDR soldiers murdered whilst not on duty.

Then the Light Infantry became the new tenants and it was their turn to take part in the seemingly endless, seemingly inevitable blood-letting. The Ardoyne was an incredibly dangerous place to be and when 'own goals' or as the Army term it, 'blue on blue' occur, it became even more dangerous. On July 28, Private Tommy Stoker – Thomas to his loved ones in East Ardsley, a small village in the Wakefield area where the author grew up – was manning an OP in the Mill. A comrade in an adjoining room was in the process of fitting an IWS (individual weapon sight) to his rifle, when he accidentally fired a round. The 7.62mm bullet hit Tommy in the back and he was rushed by the 'crash' team to the RVH. He lingered for seven weeks, before dying of his wounds on September 19. He was afforded a full military funeral at St Michael's Parish church in his home village of East Ardsley.

When a soldier accidentally fires a round from his weapon, either accidentally or simply through carelessness or tomfoolery, it is termed a 'negligent discharge' or ND. These simple initials, this euphemism cannot adequately sum up the grief that was caused to the Stoker family and to the tragic lad who fired that ND.

On August 28, Private Ronald Rowe (21) was on routine patrol, when, tragically, a comrade mistook him for a terrorist and shot him dead. Just 6 days later, in another part of New Lodge, Gunner Robert Cutting, who was just 18 – the same age as Tommy Stoker – was shot by a comrade in what the Army delightfully and somewhat euphemistically term 'friendly fire.' Thus, his was the third such instance in such an incredibly short period of time, in just one area of north Belfast.

As September drew to an end, there was to be a double tragedy for the Light Infantry as they maintained their tenure of the Flax Street Mill. One year and sixteen days earlier, in Dungannon, Co Armagh, they lad lost Private John Rudman (21) from the second Battalion, shot as he travelled in an Army convoy towards Coalisland. On September 30, 1972, his brother Thomas (20) of the first Battalion, was shot and died shortly afterwards. He was on Ladbrook Drive, some three streets or so away from the mill when he was hit by an IRA gunman. The two soldiers lived in Hartlepool.

Two more soldiers would be lost in this part of north Belfast before the year was out. The Queens would lose 18 year old Private Richard Sinclair in the New Lodge to an IRA gunman's shot. The RCT would lose Driver Ronald Kitchen (20) who was shot whilst manning a VCP on the Oldpark Road on November 10, 1972.

The toll of LI soldiers continued as 1973 arrived and in late February, Lance Corporal Alan Kennington (20) was shot whilst on 'lollipop patrol.' At lunchtime the schools in Ardoyne were patrolled to protect the school-kids from sectarian clashes. As the children came out of school, the gunmen opened fire; he was from Lydeard, Somerset.

On April 29, whilst on a mobile patrol in the New Lodge, Marine Graham Cox (19) of 42 Commando was killed instantly when several gunmen opened fire on the patrol. He was the fifth Royal Marine to die in the Province and the second member of 42 Commando to die in the area in a month. His comrade, Marine Ivor Swain (26) was killed in a car crash in March.

With the old year of 1973 slipping away and a New Year – and new hope? – rapidly approaching, the Loyalist paramilitaries clearly had no thoughts of good will. On December 29, Constable Michael Logue of the RUC was shot at a robbery scene at Forthriver Road, just off the Crumlin Road by gunmen of the UVF (Ulster Volunteer Force).

Only six months would pass before another SF life was claimed in this part of north Belfast; two lives would be taken in fact. On June 22, 1974, Sergeant Daniel O'Connor of the RUC was shot and killed by the IRA. On the same day, another Leeds boy, Gunner Kim Macunn (18) of the Royal Artillery was shot and killed on Spamount Avenue. Another member of his Regiment died on July 30, when Sergeant Bernard Fearns (34) of the Royal Artillery was shot whilst on foot patrol near Hillman Street in the New Lodge. His death left three young children fatherless. Their deaths meant that, as a result of the troubles, no less than thirty three members of the RA had lost their lives in a period of just over 5 years.

NEW LODGE

Sergeant 'W' Royal Highland Fusiliers

After six weeks on patrol, the entire platoon was moved to a ship moored in Belfast harbour, HMS *Maidstone*. This was sheer luxury; a bath and a bed with clean sheets! That move changed our operational area to the New Lodge, which was close to the city centre. Soon after the move, we had our first riot which involved a mob of about 400 and 'B' Company were right in the thick of it, giving the 'baddies' a real hard time.

My platoon was covering the side streets, looking for possible ambush areas and any wounded 'baddies.' This lasted for about an hour before the crowds moved off, but not before the 'Jocks' had raided the local pub – the 'Starry Plough' and arrested the local MP who was part of the riot.

On another patrol, I had just turned a corner, when a huge explosion blew up a local pub and the blast lifted my vehicle; it was a real shock but we were all ok. We started our search inside the pub just as the local RUC arrived; the first thing they did, was to go for the cash. After that, all the unbroken bottles went straight into their vehicles. Funny as it may seem, a party was going strong in the back of the pub, and it continued with everyone ok and not in the least bit concerned!

There was a further incident a week or two later, when I spotted a parked car with four occupants and ordered my second vehicle to block the front and I hemmed the car in with mine. When I went to investigate, I heard a loud 'thump' and quickly searched the vehicle. We found two automatic pistols and one revolver; all four men were arrested once the RUC got there. A whole host of documents were also seized.

THE SHOOTING OF BERNIE FEARNS.

Gunner Stephen Corbett, Royal Artillery

The Parlour OP was situated on the Antrim road next to an old Presbyterian church; it offered good vision right down New Lodge Road and also left and right along Antrim Road. In large white lettering high on the wall was the name 'Wilton Funeral Service' and it was in front of this building that Kim Maccun had been shot dead on Saturday 22nd June – just ten days after our arrival.

On Tuesday 30th July I was on duty at the OP, and at around 4.15pm I made a report to G3 (base) that six to eight men had run out of the betting office across the road and had fled in various directions. They dispatched a mobile to the scene, but nothing was found of the men.

At 4.47pm two shots were heard in the area of Stratheden Street, and G3 came on the air and asked if I had heard anything. Sadly these shots had killed Bernie Fearns. The next thing I heard was someone from G11's patrol going on the radio; some poor lad had to go over to Sergeant Fearns to retrieve the pocket radio from his body. Even after all these years, I can hear him sobbing on the radio and asking for help.

The MO turned up at the scene with the ambulance, and a short time later he was busy describing the injuries over the radio – I could never understand why he had to do that. We found out later that Bernie had actually seen the gunman in the alleyway between Spamount Street and Stratheden Street and had knelt down to fire, but before he could – he was shot himself. I reported a man running away from the scene and into the Sheridan area, but he couldn't be found. In the follow up op an Armalite rifle was recovered.

Try and visualise that you are inside the building looking through the slit in the corrugated iron at the right hand window. That is where Dick Witts and Mick Krasnowski were, and on the other side of the street stood two gunmen arguing over who was going to carry the rifle. Dick Witts fired his rifle at the gunmen, but was unable to sight it properly because of the narrowness of the gap in the iron sheeting. The two IRA men didn't have a clue where the shots came from and scattered; the next morning the bullet marks were visible on the wall just over head height

When I first recounted the story to the author of this book I broke down in tears; it had never affected me like that before. I didn't know Bernie all that well, although we had done some training together before going to Ireland – but that was all. I was only attached to 97 Battery, as they were short of lads for the tour. I have never forgotten Bernie or Kim, and every year I put a cross on the cenotaph for them.

Over two years would pass before another SF member was killed here and it was, again, the Royal Artillery who suffered yet another loss. Gunner Maurice Murphy was shot and badly wounded near the Flax Street Mill on October 24, 1976 after a short fire fight with the IRA; he died of his wounds in the RVH on November 22.

The New Year of 1977 had barely been ushered in when, on January 11, the Royal Artillery suffered another loss and it was another son of Yorkshire who paid the price. Gunner Edward Muller (18) was shot whilst manning a VCP in the Oldpark area. On May 10, the IRA murdered UDR soldier Corporal Jack Geddis (26) whilst off duty on the Crumlin Road. In the August, the Gordon Highlanders, who had not lost a man for over 4 years, added Lance Corporal Jack Marshall (25) to their growing roll of honour.

In 1978, one soldier was killed in the area, when Gunner Paul Sheppard (20) of the Royal Artillery was shot in Clifton Park Avenue. It was the IRA's first use of the M60 machine gun and the young, married soldier was killed almost instantly.

Security Forces personnel would continue to die in neighbouring districts, as we shall examine in a moment, but for the Ardoyne/New Lodge area, it would be approaching four more years until death struck here again. On May 6, 1981, Constable Philip Ellis (33) was manning the security barrier between the Loyalist Tiger Bay area and the New Lodge when he was killed by an IRA gunman. A further nine and a half years would pass before the death of another RUC man in New Lodge and, having thwarted the gunmen and the bombers of the IRA/INLA, with supreme irony, the next slaying was a 'blue on blue.' Whilst on covert duties in Upper Meadow Street, on November 9, 1989, Constable Ian Johnston was shot in error by a colleague.

Earlier that year, in the June, the spectre of the 'blue on blue' emerged again, when Adam Gilbert (21) of the Royal Marines was killed accidentally. His comrades opened fire on a stolen car in New Lodge Road and Marine Gilbert was caught in the crossfire and died at the scene.

Then, on August 3, 1992, the Scots Guards were back in this part of north Belfast when one of their soldiers, Damian Shackleton was shot and died shortly afterwards. He was from the Blackburn area and was aged 24. He was on a routine patrol in the New Lodge area, and was the last Scots Guard to be killed in the Province during the troubles. The last SF member to die in the Ardoyne/Turf Lodge/Oldpark area was Constable Jackie Haggan of the RUC. On March 10, 1994, he was murdered by the IRA whilst off duty and watching a dog race in the Oldpark area; he was 33 and left a pregnant widow.

Mick Pickford, 4th Regiment, Royal Artillery

You know, I actually liked being in N.I; I thought, this is it; I'm at the top of my game. I'm bullet proof; untouchable. I'm a white knight sent to sort this place out. Until one night, on sangar duty at the Crumlin.

I cannot remember the sangar number, it was brand new. I heard the wind rushing through then I heard ziiiiip craaaack zip crack zip crack. I thought I was the target; I got my head down and my eyes open. Reported up the lines, turned out the other battery in the Ardoyne had a contact. I tell you: Mr 'bullet-proof' hit the ground hard.

On the 10 March, 1971, the IRA, an organization which had still, much evil and misery to inflict upon the people of Northern Ireland and the British Army, committed an atrocity which shocked the civilized world; although we could only suspect it, much worse was to follow.

Three young, unarmed, off-duty members of the Royal Highland Fusiliers (Regimental motto: Cuidich 'n Righ; Help the King) were picked up in the Markets area of Belfast and lured to their deaths on the pretext of a party. They were taken to Ligoniel, to the city's north west, where the car stopped and the soldiers got out, still clutching their beer glasses, so that they could take a 'pee break.' Two were cold-bloodedly shot in the back of the head and the third, turning around was shot in the chest.

Two of the three were brothers, Fusilier John Boreland McCaig; at 17 the youngest soldier to lose his life during the troubles; Fusilier Joseph McCaig (18) and their cousin, Fusilier Dougald Purdon McCaughey who was 23.

Two were shot in the head and the third, apparently as he had turned, shot in the chest, as they stood together on the lonely mountain road. Although it was widely assumed that the three were lured from a bar in the centre of Belfast, as I stated, an inquest was told in August 1971 that the full details of what happened were still not known. It was reported that they and many other soldiers had been drinking off-duty in a bar in Cornmarket in central Belfast during the day. Although soldiers later became much more careful in their movements, at that time such off-duty drinking was quite common occurrence.

A *Belfast Telegraph* editorial commented 'After all the horrors of recent weeks and months, Ulster people have almost lost the capacity for feeling shock. But the ruthless murder of three defenceless young soldiers has cut to the quick. These were cold-blooded executions for purely political reasons.'

It is a widely held view amongst those involved in Int work in Belfast, at the time, that one of those involved in the killings was an IRA member Patrick McAdorey who was shot dead in August 1971, in the Ardoyne; another of the killers was reputedly living in the Republic of Ireland

LIGONIEL; A SOLDIER'S VIEWPOINT

Sergeant 'W' Royal Highland Fusiliers

One night on patrol, I was ordered to the Co's office and informed of the murder of three of 'B' Company's soldiers. He told me that the battalion was to remain in barracks, but that my platoon was to cover all areas until the 'Jocks' had calmed down.

Up until that time, soldiers could walk into town for a night off. However, the three, two of whom were brothers and the third their cousin, were picked up by girls and taken by car to a lane in nearby Ligoniel. Three gunmen were waiting for them and all three were shot at point blank range; this was cold, bloody murder. Up to their funeral, a low profile was adopted because we knew who the killers were and we wanted revenge.

Dave Bradwell at Ligoniel, near the scene of the murder
of the three Jocks (Dave Bradwell)

The Aunt of Fusilier McCaughey said at the time:

I was sitting in the house watching television with a friend when the news given that three soldiers had been shot in Belfast. I never thought for one minute that one of them would be Dougald. Then only minutes afterwards the phone rang and it was one of the Fusiliers' officers speaking to me from Belfast. I could hardly take it in at first.

Chapter 7

Antrim Road

I deliberately isolated this stretch of north Belfast in order to focus solely on one road which was the scene of many killings. In doing so, chose to discuss incidents which happened to both east and west of it due to the significance of this one arterial route into the city.

It is the A6 which begins to the north of the city and emanates from the town of Antrim and starts as Belfast Road and then sweeps southwards towards the major city of the Province. It sweeps ever southwards through both Catholic and Protestant areas and eventually joins the Crumlin Road and then the modern day Westlink seems to swallow it all up. The area I have chosen to look at is above its merger with the Crumlin Road and northwards through the Oldpark area. It is an area which witnessed the deaths of 9 soldiers and 6 RUC men.

On December 4, 1971, Major Jeremy Snow (36) of the Royal Regiment of Fusiliers (RRF) was shot and wounded in a gun battle with the IRA in North Queen Street, to the east of the Antrim Road. He died of his wounds in the RVH four days later, leaving a widow and three children.

On July 15, 1972, RUC officer, Robert Laverty who, at 18, was the youngest Policeman killed during the troubles was shot by the IRA whilst on mobile patrol. On December 13, one of his colleagues, James Nixon, was murdered whilst off-duty by the IRA.

The following year, Antrim Road entered into the lexicon of the troubles in a moment of cold-blooded, sickening savagery by the IRA. On the night of Friday, March 23, 1973, four Sergeants of the British Army were lured to a party whilst off duty. Picked up by three women in the city centre, they were taken to a house on the Antrim Road. On the pretext of fetching another woman, three of them left and then IRA gunmen burst into the room and shot all four men. Three were killed, and the fourth badly wounded; those killed were Richard Muldoon (25) and the only member of the Royal Army Dental Corps to be killed in the Province; Barrington Foster (28) Duke of Edinburgh's Regiment and Tom Penrose (28) of the RCT.

The off duty murder of three Scottish soldiers at Ligoniel who were also lured to their deaths on the pretext of a party and the murder of Ranger Best in Londonderry, despite the assurances given to his family by Republican leaders must rank with these murders on the Antrim Road. The sickening depravity of the IRA in organising these killings gives one a valuable insight into their very psyche.

On October 16, a part-time RUC man, William Campbell (27) was shot outside a cinema on the Antrim Road whilst on a routine foot patrol

On March 22, 1974, Marine James Macklin (28) was badly wounded when his mobile patrol was fired upon near the Waterworks on the Antrim Road. He died of his wounds on March 28.

Just under two years later, the RUC lost two more of its officers when the IRA ambushed a two-man foot patrol at the bottom of the Antrim Road. On February 6, 1976, Sergeant James Blakely a 42 year old married man with children and Inspector William Murtagh (31) were shot as they patrolled the area. James Blakely died at the scene and his colleague died of his wounds the following day in hospital.

On August 31, the following year, as he returned to the Girdwood Army base, just off the lower part of Antrim Road, Corporal 'Billy' Smith of 1RGJ was shot by an IRA sniper and died shortly afterwards. There are two excellent accounts of this man by two former comrades (David Hallam and David Smith of the Green Jackets) in *A Long Long War*. Corporal Smith became the 15th member of this famous Regiment to be killed in the Province. The IRA member who killed the popular NCO was captured by another Regiment who told him that they were taking him to the Green Jackets at Girdwood Park. Mindful that he had just killed one of the RGJ, he begged them not to hand him over to the angry comrades of 'Billy' Smith.

Rifleman Kevin Stevens, 1st Bn The Royal Green Jackets

At the beginning of 1977 I was selected to join the company intelligence team for training up prior to a tour in Belfast; was to be my last tour of Northern Ireland. At this time we were unsure which area we would be going to although it was obviously going to take in both the catholic and protestant communities as teams were being trained up to cover both.

Unusually I was to part of a team led by my older and some might say wiser brother Keith, a Sgt at the time, better known as Steveo or Twiggy, who would command the Int team. Generally speaking the army quite rightly frowned upon brothers working in such close partnership for obvious reasons but we were both from the antitank platoon and perhaps they felt I might feel a little lost without my big brother to look up to! Whatever the reason I found myself part of a 9 man team, 4 working the catholic areas, 4 working the protestant areas and 'the boss.' Fully trained up and as prepared as we could be the team made their way to Belfast in the March of 77, we knew by now where we would be working and the battalion were due to arrive in the April so we had the best part of 4 weeks to settle in to our new location in Girdwood Park and get to know the local area and its inhabitants. Our general areas of responsibility were Little America, Cliftonville, Newington, a little bit of Tigers Bay and the stretch of the Antrim road running north out of the city. Our area started on the Duncairn Gardens which ran between our patch and the Ardoyne.

The outgoing regiment were the Devon and Dorsets; a decent bunch (for non Green Jackets of course) who spent the next few weeks showing us around. It was unfortunate, they said, that the whole of our patch was dead as far as intelligence and any chance of finding things was concerned and their tour had been a quite quiet one as a result. We as a regiment were to soon change that.

A couple of incidents before they left led us to wonder about their sense of humour. The first occurred about a week after we got there. A sports bag had been found in suspicious circumstances in a shop doorway. Of course the correct and immediate action or IA is to cordon off the area and call in ATO (ammunition Technical Officer) and for him to give it his professional treatment. However it would appear the other IA (*immediate action*) is to consider how long it will take ATO to arrive and if the time is a little on the long side then don't bother with ATO at all but send a senior Bn officer in to unzip the bag and look inside! In this case option 2 was applied; it is fortunate for the officer concerned that the bag only contained smelly sports kit.

The second occurred out of boredom, we were still working under the direct control of the D and D couldn't 'do our own thing' and so it occurred one night around about 11pm that the Int room was manned entirely by the Mafia whilst the D and Ds had sloped off for an early night. Just who suggested it I do not recall now but whispered into the airwaves went the following message to the ops room next door. 'Hello 4 this is 46 Bravo; P check over.' The conversation then went something like this '4 send over,' '46 Bravo, P check – Alpha, Michael Mouse, Bravo, Cuddly Crescent Belfast, Charlie, DOB 31/12/1930 (or something like that) Delta, believed to be an associate of a Mr. FNU (first name unknown) Bigheers of same address, over.' '4 wait out.'

We now sat back to wait for some vitriolic comments from the ops room, but when none came we wandered casually next door to see what was up to find the duty radio operator on the secure phone to one of the guards regiments elsewhere in Belfast trying to explain that he believed that 2 of their locals, a Mr. Michael Mouse and a Mr. Big Ears were in our area. The reply from the other end had to be heard to be believed and is certainly not printable. We made a sharp exit!!!! I am not sure if we were ever forgiven.

As 1978 drew to its bloody climax, with a mere six days before Christmas, James Burney (King's Own Scottish Borderers) was shot by an IRA sniper as his patrol finished a search in Baltic Avenue, immediately off the Antrim Road. He was 26 and from the Cumberland area.

A new decade – the third in which the Army had been involved – had been ushered in, but still the killings continued in this part of Belfast. On May 2, 1980, one of the most controversial killings of the troubles from the British perspective. The Special Air Service (SAS) or '22' as they are known in Army circles rarely admit to losing any of their troops. However, it was widely reported that Captain Herbert Westmacott (28) one of the most senior of their soldiers to die in Northern Ireland had been killed in an incident just off the Antrim Road. In an arrest which went tragically wrong, the Captain was severely wounded in a burst of M60 machine gun fire and died soon afterwards.

GIRDWOOD PARK, NORTH BELFAST

Major Peter Oakley, King's Regiment

I have to say that I felt a lot of sympathy for the Catholic population of Northern Ireland. The way in which they were treated with gerrymandering, housing and employment was a national disgrace. Subsequently it made no difference as to how we carried out our duties without any bias. A bottle hurts, no matter who throws it and a bullet kills no matter who aims it.

I was 2IC of Recce platoon in that first tour initially based in Girdwood Park. We tootled around our patch in pairs of Land Rovers with driver, commander and two in the back riding 'shotgun,' carrying out whatever recce and supportive tasks the CO thought necessary. I have distinct and shivering memories of endless cold and wet days and nights, particularly nights, but made easier by the routine tea stops. One of my men who was always in the back of the vehicle eventually married one of the young ladies from our favourite tea stop. He was always anxious to know from the start of our patrol if we were going there!

On one of those nights I was with a particularly dozy driver and on driving past the railway station, ordered him to turn right as I wanted to call into a local police station. Carrying out my order instantly and to the letter, he did so; swinging the wheel sharply, he took us up a few steps and came to a stop on platform 2 of Belfast Railway Station! He brewed tea from then on!

On another occasion, one of the Land Rovers was shot at by a gunman who opened up with a 'Thompson' sub machine gun. Three rounds went through the driver's door; one behind him, one under his knee, narrowly missing the petrol tank and one in front of his knee. On hearing this, the CO ordered us to stop patrolling that road. Being Recce platoon and good Kingsmen, we ignored that order and went on for some time, using a decoy Land Rover with a heavily 'tooled up' vehicle not too far away; sadly, the gunman never took the bait.

Eventually, we were issued with two new items of kit for riot control. CG gas – although we called it CS smoke so as to not frighten the local population – which we did hurl about with some success until they learned to throw them back. However it was gas/smoke so it went everywhere, depending on the wind, including into houses. We had to replace a budgie, belonging to a dear old lady, which had suffocated in his cage because of the gas! We also got the baton gun; very good piece of kit which came from America, in the original boxes and with a training manual. However, their baton gun was used to fire wooden bullets which had to be fired into the ground in front of the crowd and the resultant splinters caused much anguish and pain in the lower legs.

Our bullets were made of rubber; plastic was to come later. I leave it to the reader's imagination as to what happened when we fired rubber bullets onto the cobblestones of Belfast's streets. Suffice it to say, we got lots of bills for broken windows! I may have to stand corrected here, but I believe at this time we introduced two new 'weapon' into our arsenal later to be adopted and refined by the police. One was the 'Caltrop' a length of chain into which a series of very large nails were folded. The aim, literally, was to throw this in front of a vehicle to make it stop by destroying the tyres. It took some muscle to throw it but it did have its successes.

The other was to use a 'thumper; as a 'knocking your door down tool.' It was a cast iron tube, about three feet long, closed at one end and with handles on two sides of its length. It was used to drive six foot angle iron pickets into the ground to support barbed wire fences and goes back to World War One. Should a knock at the door not produce a timely answer, we used the 'thumper' as a battering ram and could enforce a very quick entry.

One of our tasks was to provide escort and cover for 'Felix' – the Ammunition Technical Officers (ATOs) – who went out to defuse bombs and other nasty parcels left by the opposition. We had two ATOs in Girdwood who worked day on, night off. The courage of these men is quite rightly well documented and I was, still am, in awe of how they coped with it all with such calmness and professionalism. As one of my men remarked '...they deserve a medal as big as a dustbin lid!' I later told one of our admiration for his skill and courage during our time together in Northern Ireland. 'Never mind that.' He remarked, 'I always felt safe when I looked around and saw your big boots and knew that you and your lads were looking out for me.' There is no answer to that.

Rifleman Kevin Stevens, Royal Green Jackets

Too much time sat looking at a map and trying to plot what the opposition are up is a bad thing. By way of a diversion, and to ease slightly the pressures on the platoons in Girdwood Park, 4 of us would undertake one of their late patrols a couple of times a week; usually going out about 11pm and returning 3 or 4 hours later. The timetable was never rigid and as we had roaming rights across our entire company area, would go wherever the whim took us. This of course meant that we were never predictable. Off we would toddle, each carrying a radio, now thankfully pocket sized, a starlight scope and infrared torch strapped to our rifles. This made signalling between us easy as the starlight scope could see infrared. It saved unnecessary talk on the radio as well.

One night the 4 of us ended up near York Road police station; this was a place we were told that was very anti army but no reason had been given. We had been out for a couple of hours so Keith, as I/C the patrol, decided to see if we could get a cup of tea out of them – nothing ventured nothing gained as it were. In to the station we went past their sangar to be greeted by the desk sergeant. Keith exchanged pleasantries and said we would just passing by and thought we would drop in and say hello. This seemed to surprise the policeman who suggested we might like a cup of tea or coffee. We hadn't even asked! It turned out that about a year previously someone somewhere had decided that police/army cooperation was not necessary and had refused to speak to the police in York Road. As each Bn had passed through on their 4 month tour so this message had been passed on until such time as we had arrived and the D and D had mentioned it to us. The police at York Road were really keen to re-establish a good working relationship with the army, and over the coming months this was to prove beneficial for both sides. It was that good, that we as an Int team even got our own desk in CID; what a great set of characters they were too.

We now knew the area was not intelligence dead because the police were keen to show us who was what and what was what etc. It was down to our CSM (Company Sergeant Major) Roy Trower to prove there was finds to be found in our area; he came up trumps time and time again. Was it luck, good intelligence from us or was he just 'super ferret' as he was soon dubbed by Brigade and Bn HQs? Whichever it was the inter-company finds contest soon became a no-contest when Support Company got so far in front that it was inconceivable that anyone would ever catch us up. Roy was awarded an MBE after this tour in the operational honours list for 1977 and rightly so.

Two finds stand out in my memory from this period. The first was the morning the search team, the Int team with myself doubling up as photographer were tasked to search a row of derelict houses. Normally a dicey job but as they sat beside the house of a staunch Republican, who we later lifted anyway for having a firearm in his loft, the likelihood of a booby trap was fairly remote however precautions were taken as normal. The search proved illuminating. First of all one of the derelict bedrooms had been turned into a classroom complete with blackboard with a diagram drawn on it obviously outlining a plan of some sort with all the streets named after various washing powders and secondly by carefully moving one of the blocks that boarded up the window slightly a clear view (and shot) could be had right down the street opposite. This in itself made for a good find but better was to come.

The search now complete, the team were making their way back towards the entrance, when one of them caught his crowbar on the railing at the top of the stairs. There was a rumbling noise and out of the bottom of the stairs popped a Remington Gamesmaster rifle. A most impressive weapon and find.

The second find was equally impressive and for an entirely different reason extremely interesting. The Company Commander, Major Nick Jenkins, had received a report from the police, not York Road I hasten to add, that there was a rifle hidden in the attic of a certain house in Newington. He therefore decided on a 3 pronged attack. It was decided that the Int team, with a member of the York Road CID on board would come in from one direction, the OC, and his team another while Roy Trower and his team of ferrets would approach from the rear! All this to be done using Land Rovers. We would patrol for an hour beforehand' before all swooping into Newington at the same from the aforesaid agreed entrances.

At the given time in we came and it was at this point the original plan went a little pear-shaped. As we approached in front of us was a row of lock up garages behind a high fence. Coming out of the gate was a woman carrying a plastic carrier bag who, spotting us, dropped the bag back behind the gate. This did not go unnoticed. 'We will just have a quick word with her,' says Keith, mindful of the primary task set for us. He approaches the woman who is still stood at the gate and asked what was in the carrier bag. 'What carrier bag?' she replied. To cut a long story short she was encouraged to retrieve her dropped bag and inside were 3 very new timer primer units or TPUs for short. We now called up the OC and told him of our find, he roared up in his Land Rover to join the party. Now unfortunately Roy Trower had not heard this on the radio and continued with plan A and steamed in through the back door of the suspect's house expecting to see other soldiers doing likewise through the front. Of course we were all now down the road 50 yards. Roy quickly established that the 80 year old woman who lived in the house was not hiding anything in her attic except spiders and stormed up to us a little miffed and made this fact known. He was a little mollified when we showed him our own find. A follow up operation now kicked in and Roy and his search team went in for a closer look around the garages and retreated twice as fast when they discovered the biggest bomb factory found in Belfast up to that time, and the explosives were not in the best of condition. ATO was called in at once. We like to preserve our officers!

There is a footnote to this story. Just a couple of weeks before the Int team had been tasked to keep an eye on a particular house in Newington which we had done for about a week working and sleeping in an old derelict which had a good view over the street. It was also directly above said biggest bomb factory! Unfortunately from our position we were unable to see into the yard of the garages otherwise we might well have caught the bomber at work. It was to be another 10 years before fingerprints found at the scene were matched up with someone arrested in the south.

On January 8, 1982, Private Stephen Carleton (24) a part-time soldier in the UDR was murdered by the IRA whilst working at a garage on the Antrim Road. It would be 1987, before the Antrim Road would witness a SF death, and it would be the last during the troubles. On June 23, Sergeant Robert Guthrie (41) was shot outside the RUC station on Antrim Road and he died from his wounds in hospital a short while later. The road or the A6 as the route planners call it had claimed its fifteenth and final SF victim.

NORTH BELFAST

Rifleman Dave Hallam, Royal Green Jackets

We left from Dover by troop train on our way to Liverpool. When we arrived it was off the train on to coaches down to the docks. Some time later bang Belfast it was happening one of the first things I saw was Harland and

Wolff where the *Titanic* was built. As the troop ship docked you could see some vehicles ready to take us to our new home for the next four months. It seemed very quiet and calm as we disembarked the ship. As a young soldier, and on your first tour, it's a lot to take in and for a lot of us it was our first time. When I look back now, I suddenly remember that we were all so young.

As we were driven to our base and looking around, you would think you were still in England. People just going about their normal business; how naive. Well, we finally arrived at base and found our bunks and were issued with flak jackets and baton guns. Down for a brief and within an hour, on the streets. I can tell you now that I was shitting myself. I remember this woman shouting out 'What regiment are ye so from?' Our section commander said: 'The 43rd and 52nd; now fuck off. 'The first patrol went well but there was a lot to take in; all that training we did paid off. I think the training we did was that good, it was like we had been there before.

As we got back through the gate, it was straight to unload our weapons, then a good cup of tea and a debrief. As time went on I don't know how but I got a cross. I had it just over my collar of my flak jacket and I would give it a kiss as I went out on patrol; it was my way of giving myself a bit of good luck, I think. The boys had their own way of dealing with their own luck; no one ever took the piss. As you get in to more patrols, you get to see the IRA we'd been studying for such a long time; there they are right in front of you. You think to yourself so you're the IRA ? They gave you the look and you look right back at them; right into their eyes; it was like saying: we're here now; ready to play.

It wasn't long before the riots started; they were pissed off over some arrest of one of their number . It didn't take much to give 'em a reason. It went on for hours on end; bricks, iron bars, golf balls with six inch nails through them, nail bombs. petrol bombs and stones. Cars set on fire, homes set ablaze. They even were throwing paint at the PIGs; no green though. Riot shields were breaking under the weight. It was full on; even hand to hand with some people; rifle butts and the odd Liverpool kiss with a steel helmet; sorry but this is the way it was.

So the next day, you're back out there again; walking the same streets; all the shit still all over the place from the day and night before. We never did see who cleaned it up. As we were coming back into base, I saw that there were three youths standing nearby. I looked back, as we turned the last corner, and saw that one had a handgun which he pointed at us. I shouted 'Gunman' and he turned and ran, so we ran after him; I got down on one knee and shouted 'Halt.' but he kept running. I cocked my weapon and shouted 'Stop or I will shoot', but he just kept going. I could have easily put a round into the back of his head, but the only thing that stopped me, was that he was running down a busy street and, knowing my luck, the round would have gone through him and into someone else, so I didn't fire. We ran after him but he got away; two weeks later, I ran into him again. Anyway, to cut a long story short, I asked him what weapon he had had. He said that it was a flying saucer gun; a toy gun?

Lots of things went on throughout the tour, but the day came to go home; same stuff' pack up, down to the airport, back to the UK. It took a long time to get back to normal because we were still in the same environment; cars, houses, people going about their every day stuff. I found myself in an odd mood, always waiting for some thing to happen. Once, I went round to see my Nan and granddad and found myself walking backwards and if I stopped to talk to someone, I was bobbing and weaving; not wanting to make myself an easy target for a hidden gunman. It's funny what four months can do.

Years have gone by since I was a young lad on patrol in Northern Ireland, but why can I still remember this, when I can't even tell you what happened last week and why I find myself getting upset. Mates we have lost, mates we will never forget. It was raining the other day I looked down at a puddle of water and I drifted off back to those times. I could see and smell, could even see the brick work as I knelt down on a corner of a street; funny, just getting on, I think. I say to myself: come on you silly old sod; get a grip.

I have to say, that I miss it in some sick way; miss the mates; miss what we had. I know it left a mark on me for the rest of my life.

Rifleman Kevin Stevens, 1st Bn The Royal Green Jackets

As the tour wore on so we got to know the local players better as we dropped in to the local public house called 'The Hole in the Wall' and contrary to popular belief they were not all thugs with no education. indeed one of them, with whom we played the old game of 'we know who you are and you know who we are but we will pretend to each other we don't,' with was in fact university educated. He was a very interesting person to speak to, as long as you stayed away from the politics of Northern Ireland. I often wonder what eventually became of him. His brother was perhaps a little bit lower down the evolutionary ladder and we had warned him right at the beginning that as long as he behaved himself we would leave him alone to get on with his life – he obviously took this warning to heart as only 2 weeks later was lifted by an alert policeman in Glengormley while trying to place a bomb on Mr. O'Plod's window sill. So exited Charlie from our tour.

In August another find grabbed the headlines. This time it was Cpl Brian Hesketh again of the Antitank Platoon (God we were good!) finding a large cache of rifles. To be absolutely honest he didn't actually 'find' them so much as they were presented to him by 'friendly' locals. During a quiet mobile patrol in the lower reaches of our area near Tiger Bay he had been 'directed to' a walled-up cavity below the stairs in which were concealed about 30 weapons, a combination of Steyr and Martini Henry rifles. They had been there probably since the early 1900s when the Protestants had smuggled them in. However a find is a find is a find.

The tour was drawing to a close and I was off on a course so leaving NI early but there was just time for one more find and this time it was mine. The Int section was out on patrol on foot. As we rounded a corner we literally bumped into a couple of young lads carrying a couple of tins of petrol. Maybe their car had run out of fuel but did they really need the additional bottles of petrol with wicks sticking out of them to get their car going? It was more likely they were to get someone else's car going ! The petrol was confiscated and I arrested them both for possessing bombs and bomb making equipment. It was not so much a case of me finding a find, more a case of the find finding me, really.

SHANKHILL ROAD

Fiercely Protestant, fiercely Loyalist, the Shankhill Road was viewed – by the Loyalists themselves – as the 'front line' against Republicanism. This 'front line' draws up their battle lines against the Republicans of the Turf Lodge and Ardoyne to the north of its other 'border', the Crumlin Road and to the Falls to the south. Many of the old back-to-back terracing has now vanished and newer homes and some modern industrial and commercial buildings have appeared, particularly where the Shankhill meets the Woodvale Road to its western extremity.

On this one road, three RUC officers and one soldier would die in the cause of peace keeping. On October 12, 1969, just a scant two months since British troops had deployed in the Province, the first RUC officer to be killed by political violence was shot on Shankhill Road. Constable Victor Arbuckle (29) was shot by Loyalist terrorists and the toll of SF personnel had grown to two.

Two years and three days later, two of his comrades were gunned down at Twaddell Avenue just off the Shankhill. The two men were Cecil Cunningham (46) and John Haslett (21) and they were ambushed as they guarded a post office. The one soldier to be killed was Sergeant David Taggart (33) of the UDR on August 4, 1986. He was gunned down without mercy as he returned home from his full time job.

Mick Pickford, 4th Regiment, Royal Artillery

To cut a long story short; I was 19 years of age in 1994. Just before deployment, the IRA blew up a house in Spamount Street, so it set the tone. My TAOR (*Tactical Area of Responsibility*) was North Belfast. Shankhill and the New Lodge; both areas have had their fair share of 'history' and I loved the opportunity of becoming part of it. As we all stood at the gates ready to bomb burst out, I can clearly remember the training and saying to myself 'If I make it to the garage, I'm f*cking lucky' (in Training at SOTAT you get hit every time). My heart was in my mouth; my arse was going like the clappers and my train of thought was like the Bullet in Japan especially after we had been told by INT that PIRA had flash detonators. I got to the Garage, relief. I was just waiting for the hit. It never came.

Some time into the patrol, we came across a 'player' of New Lodge, and we P-checked him, he gave the usual answer of either 'Brain Surgeon' or 'F*ck off.' I thought to myself, you ain't like the guy out of Harry's Game, then I thought, I ain't in f*cking Holywood either! Thankfully, it was a quiet night, no incidents apart from local abuse, stones, bottles dirty nappies etc.

The next day, it was time for the grand tour of the Carlisles; what a shithole. Plenty of rat runs, dickers on every corner. We got to know them, they got to know us. We would see them, and shout 'thanks for the info, fella.' They skulked away. One time, in the New Lodge, by the shops at the bottom of Spamount. I was passed by a mother pushing a child in a pushchair. Doing my bit for hearts and minds I said 'Hello' to the little 'un. The response was 'F*ck off, Brit bastard.' I thought he must have learned that before 'Mummy, Daddy'. That was the last time I said hello to toddlers. Four weeks later, we had a casualty in the other battery; he had the lower half of his leg blown off.

Chapter 8

Central & East Belfast

UNDERCOVER IN THE SHORT STRAND, BELFAST

Brian Baskerville, R.A.O.C.

One particular day, when I was living in a house on Knox Road within the perimetre fence, I had just picked up literally a boot full of guns and was taking them back to our 'hidey hole.' I stopped off at the house, which had double yellow lines outside to pick up my laundry. I parked there and ran in, taking a few minutes to gather things together. Unbeknown to me the guard patrol (with RSM accompanying) had spotted my car parked illegally and was in the process of reporting a suspicious vehicle. I came back out, got in and drove off. When they came back, of course it was gone. The RSM apparently had steam coming out of his ears and was frantically trying to track me down. Somehow he never did. I got away with it. Well I was hardly going to leave a car with an arsenal in the boot on the big main car park where I couldn't see, now was I?

A couple of co-workers at the 'hidey hole' were also in 9 UDR. No names, but one was an ex Para (really nice guy) and the other was a tall lanky streak of piss with an attitude as big as he was. At that time I

Gunners in Belfast city centre (Joe Jurkiewicz)

was very keen to be the lean mean fighting machine being in my early twenties, so I arranged to go out on patrol with them. I talked Jim also RAOC (storeman at 12 Coy) to go too. We got the necessary approvals from our bosses and duly reported to Castlereagh for our night patrol. Our patch was to be Central and East Belfast around the areas of the Ormeau Road, Short Strand, Victoria Bridge. At that time the Ormeau Road was known as tin can alley for the pot shots that regularly rung out around there. We exchanged our pistols for an SLR each and a mag of 20 rounds. Flak jacket with Kevlar plates donned, I had a problem with my webbing because I had only taken a 58 pattern belt and two ammo pouches. The flak jack was underneath the combat jacket and the bottom of it kept pushing my 58 belt down around my ankles. We resorted to dispensing with the webbing and using pockets.

Off we went patrolling in two Makralon Land Rovers with no back doors on. We were soon into the action on the Short Strand. Nearly crapped myself when a bottle hit the side of our vehicle as it sounded like a bullet. We would drive at speed up a very dark road along the river and my job was to train my rifle across the river and look for muzzle flashes. This is easier said than done when doing about 40mph, trying to stay in the back (not fall out), aim rifle, with both hands, keep cocking handle unfolded in readiness and jam yer boot against the tow hitch to steady everything.

Jim was in the other rover and the rotten sods put him up top with helmet and visor. We covered each other as we entered the bus depot on Short Strand and once inside patrolled around all the parked vehicles to ensure nobody about. Coming out was a different matter. A crowd had gathered and were throwing everything they had at us. Jim shot down inside and we hit the gas, both rovers flying out of the depot at speed. One local had a walking stick and he threw it like a dart at the front rover and it went right through the grill and windscreen as we left; no shots were fired. All safe; the toe rag lost his walking stick though.

OXFORD STREET, BELFAST

Kevin Wright, RCT

After speaking to the author, I have found the strength to put my view of the events on paper.

This day started the same as any other in Belfast, with people rushing off to work; loads of traffic crossing the Queen's Bridge into the city and traffic racing down from Holywood, passing us on the Sydenham bypass. I heard the radio crackle into life behind me as I was driving a Saracen towards the city; I could tell by the operator's reaction this was no ordinary shout. Little did I realise in a matter of an hour how many people would be not making the journey home from work.

As the section commander was shouting directions to me and to get my foot down, we came upon another unit at Oxford Street bus station, and we were told by them that there was a suspect car they were checking out.

I looked in the direction of the car, and I saw two guys talking and realised one of them was driver Steve Cooper from my unit in Germany. He was a member of 33 Sqn RCT but was attached to our sister Sqn for this tour. I gave him a shout and asked how he was and he replied giving me a thumbs up. I watched Steve and a Sgt walk in the direction of the suspect car. As I turned away with the rest of my patrol to get back in our vehicle, I felt a massive blast of hot air and pressure nearly knocking me over. In an instant two lives had been taken for no reason at all. I still thought for some hours after that maybe Steve and the Sgt had got away with it and survived the blast, but sadly they had not.

On this day there were 20 bombs planted in Belfast city centre with the sole aim to kill and maim; the 'I RanAway Army' issued a statement afterwards blaming the British army for the bombs and loss of life, stating they gave us ample warning, and we let this happen so a week later the government could justify operation motorman. They said the streets could have been cleared in time with loudhailers.

Bollocks they went out with the sole intention of killing innocent civilians. I was already in Belfast for 2 weeks before this event as part of the buildup of 'operation Motorman' so that blows their excuse out the water.

Every July 21st I remember these events and shed a tear inside not only for a friend lost but all the other innocents who never made it home from work that day. I just hope the guys responsible for these murders die screaming in pain.

Gunner Joe Jurkiewicz RA, Belfast city centre (Joe Jurkewicz)

A total of 22 bombs were planted and, in the resulting explosions, nine people were killed and a further 130 civilians injured. Warnings were allegedly given by the IRA via the local media to the security forces before the bombs exploded with 30 minutes' warning given for the first bombing and around 70 minutes' warning for the last bomb. The IRA leader, Sean MacStiofain, claimed that the warnings for the two bombs which claimed lives were deliberately disregarded by the British for strategic policy reasons. He also claimed that accurate warnings which were given by the IRA; however, they also called in two more hoax warnings which impeded the evacuation of the area. As a result, the Royal Ulster Constabulary and British Army only effectively cleared a relatively small number of areas before the bombs went off. In addition, because of the large number of bombs in the confined area of Belfast city centre, people evacuated from the site of one bomb were accidentally moved into the vicinity of other bombs.

The IRA claimed that the SF contrived to make maximum political capital out of the appalling attacks in order to ease the way for 'Motorman' – the clearing of the IRA 'no go' areas. One of the worst kept secrets at the time was the Army and RUC had planned to destroy the barricades and restore legitimate authority to the areas under nominal IRA control.

Thirty years after the killings the IRA issued a hollow statement of 'apology'.

Bloody Friday: A Chronology

14:10 The first bomb – in a car – explodes at Smithfield Bus station; extensive damage was caused.

14:16 A 50lb device explodes in a suitcase planted at the Brookvale Hotel, having been planted by three armed men. The Army had already cleared the area.

14:23 Another suitcase bomb explodes outside a Railway station on York Road causing extensive damage.

14:45 Two devices totaling 50 lbs explode at a garage on the Crumlin Road. Four devices have now detonated in the space of a little over half an hour, but thankfully no casualties; three minutes later, this is to change.

14:48 A car bomb explodes just outside the Ulsterbus depot in Oxford Street in a crowded street. Despite the Army's best attempts to evacuate civilians, 6 people are killed more or less instantly. Two soldiers and four civilians were killed in this blast.

Driver Stephen Cooper (19) of the RCT, from Leicester and Sergeant Phillip Price (27) a Glamorgan man from the Welsh Guards, were killed as they stood by one of the car bombs. Four employees of Ulsterbus were also killed; William Crothers at 15, and William Irvine at 19, are the youngest to die in this blast. Thomas Killops (39) and John Gibson (45) die alongside their two younger colleagues.

14:50 Another 50 lb device explodes outside a branch of the Ulster Bank in Limestone Road and whilst there were no fatalities, several people were injured in the blast. The site was only a few hundred yards from the first explosion, some 40 minutes earlier.

14:52 Another railway station, this time in Botanic Avenue is hit by a 50lb device and whilst massive damage was caused, there were only a few light injuries.

14:55 A massive device hidden in a car – estimated at over 160 lbs – explodes at the Queen Elizabeth Bridge; again, whilst damage was caused, there were no serious injuries.

15:02 A smaller device, hidden in a car, explodes at Agnes Street; no serious injuries are caused here.

15:02 Almost simultaneously, another 50 lb device explodes inside the 'Liverpool Bar' at Donegal Quay; several people are injured, some badly.

15:02 A bridge on the M2 motorway is hit and several people were injured.

Royal Artilleryman with civilian searcher, Belfast city centre, c 1973 (Joe Jurkewicz)

15:03 Another suitcase bomb explodes at York Street railway station and several people are injured.

15:04 A car bomb, packed with 50 lbs of explosives detonates in Ormeau Avenue and there are light casualties.

15:05 A massive car bomb, containing 150 lbs of explosives detonates outside a garage in Donegall Road and whilst there was much damage, there are no serious injuries.

15:05 Within seconds, another device explodes in Stewartstown Road and again, there are no serious injuries. It is now 55 minutes since the first bomb went off 17 minutes since the first fatalities and 15 bombs have exploded.

15:15 The number of fatalities increase, as a 50 lbs device in a car explodes outside a parade of shops in Cavehill Road, a mixed denomination area where Catholics and Protestants have co-existed despite the troubles. No warning is given and a mother of seven, Margaret O'Hare (37) is killed and her young daughter is badly injured. Brigid Murray, at 65, the oldest person to die on the day is killed and the youngest victim Stephen Parker who is only 14 is killed alongside her. There are many serious injuries in this blast; the IRA gave no warning of this device.

15:25 A device detonates harmlessly on a railway line at the Lisburn Road.

15:30 A landmine planted by the IRA at Nutts Corner is detonated as a bus packed with schoolchildren drives by; only the quick thinking and skills of the driver saved the lives of those on board as he swerved to avoid the blast.

15:30 Another device explodes outside a mail depot in Grosvenor Road but causes only slight injuries.

15:31 The Army bomb disposal unit safely defuses a device placed on the Sydenham bypass. It is the final bomb of the prolonged attack. It is the 20th such device in 81 minutes of mayhem and murder and nine people are dead.

CENTRAL BELFAST ON BLOODY FRIDAY

Ray Mitchell, REME, att: Scots Guards

I was home in Belfast from Windsor, where I was stationed with 1 Scots Guards, as a REME VM attached to aforementioned unit. My girlfriend and I decided to go into Belfast and do a bit of shopping; it was Friday July 21, 1972.

I don't recall buying anything other than a copy of the *Daily Mail*, which ironically showed in its centre pages, photos of the first 100 soldiers to die in Ulster. We finished our walk around the city centre and made our way to the top of Chichester Street to wait for the Bloomfield bus. I actually come from that area, although I now live in England. The Bloomfield bus service was notoriously slow and it always seemed that there were plenty of buses going everywhere else other than there! We had been waiting for what seemed like ages and this was before the bombs went off.

Although I never said this at the time to my girlfriend, I was thinking that, if the bus didn't come soon, we could go down to Oxford Street bus station and get a bus which would take us down the Newtownards Road. We could have gotten off there, near where my mother worked, pop in and say hello and make our way up Bloomfield Avenue and home. The only thing which stopped me going was that it was a hot, sunny day and I was too hot and couldn't be bothered to walk to Oxford Street. Thank God we stayed where we were!

Still no bus came and then, boom as the first bomb went off; boom then another. At that moment, our bus turned up and on we jumped; by the time we had travelled up Chichester Street and by the Law Courts, several others had exploded. Although I didn't know it at the time, the bomb which had exploded and rocked our, by now, stopped bus, was the one which went off in the bus station at Oxford Street where I had considered going. In fact, we were so close to the last blast, that an old chap on the bus shouted out: My God! If that had have been any closer, we would have all been blown to bits!

People then started to get really agitated and I stood up and hit the 'Emergency Door' button, and grabbed my girl and got off the bus. We

Gunner Joe Jurkiewicz RA, Belfast city centre (Joe Jurkewicz)

then made our way up Oxford Street and over the Queen's Bridge. There was slight damage to the road surface, but it was liberally covered in debris from a car bomb that went off shortly before we got there. As we crossed over the bridge and made our way towards the Newtownards Road, I was thinking: well, we've now got to make our way through the Short Strand, which was a pretty strong Republican area.

As I said earlier, it was a lovely sunny day and I was wearing a short-sleeved shirt; my arms were covered in tattoos, one of which was a Gurkha Kukri inscribed 'Borneo, Sarawak, Malaya, Singapore' and another one, depicting a soldier. These were real squaddie markings, and something you didn't need when traversing an area like the Short Strand. I was worried and lots of possibilities raced through my mind. Nothing happened, of course and I was pleased to see soldiers close at hand, blocking off the Sydenham Bypass. (*A huge device was defused there*) They certainly had green berets, though I'm not sure if there were Royal Marines in Belfast at that time, or if they were UDR. The reason I mention this fact, was they come into play later on in this account.

We walked down the Newtownards Road and called into the shoe shop where my Mum worked and told her about the bombs. At this juncture, we didn't realise just how bad things were; Jim, the shop manager was even more concerned, because, although he worked in east Belfast, he lived on the Antrim Road and wondered how he was going to be able to get home. He, too, now enters the story.

Gunners on the Loyalist Sandy Row, 1979 (Mark Campbell)

A day later, my phone rang and it was Jim; he asked me which unit had been stationed at the end of the Newtownards Road. I told him that, funnily enough, before I left Windsor, I was told to report to the nearest military so that they could check where I lived and keep an eye on me. I did so, and they were 16 Field Squadron, Royal Engineers, a unit I had been with in Germany. I said to Jim: 'Why do you ask?' and he told me that he was speaking from the 'Royal' (Royal Victoria Hospital) and that he had been injured.

He lived, as I mentioned earlier, on the Antrim Road and was registered disabled as a consequence of a back injury some years previously. He was picked up, regularly, by a taxi and driven home. Anyway, that night, his taxi was stopped by soldiers and the permit to travel pass which the driver showed was not recognised. Passes were issued in order to stop the local taxis from being stopped and harassed. Now, you must remember, that this was 'Bloody Friday' and everyone was pretty hyped up and the soldiers who stopped the taxi were in a state of heightened tension. Both Jim and the driver were dragged out of the car and put against a wall and Jim, who because he wore a support corset, was unable to spread his legs as ordered.

Allegedly, the squaddie shouted at him: 'I told you to open your fuckin' legs!' He then proceeded to kick his legs from under him; I think that you get the picture. His back was split and he ended up in hospital for five days, and we never did get to find out who did it, although I told him about the Royal Engineers. I did also mention the green berets and that I thought that a 'teeth' unit might have been more aggressive, but, anyway, we never did find out. May I just add that Jim never held a grudge and fully supported the Army in Ulster?

As a postscript to 'Bloody Friday', my wife's cousin – William Irvine – was killed there and he was badly torn apart by the blasts. They didn't find his head, I believe, for three days after they found his body. My girlfriend later became my wife and she still doesn't know to this day, the thoughts which whirled through my mind, when we were in the Short Strand.

As an author and former serving soldier, I have never sought to either condemn or condone some of the incidents in which soldiers behaved in a less than professional manner. In this instance, I do not seek to criticise the men in 'green berets' who roughed up Jim and the taxi driver; the incident does, however, put into some stark perspective, the reality of what 'Bloody Friday' meant to both the military and civil populace. Anyone who has not experienced that kind of prolonged and bloody terror can have little idea of what the soldiers in Belfast, during that time of mayhem and murder suffered as a consequence.

CENTRAL BELFAST

Soldier, RAOC, Attached to the 'Det'

I was on a night stint in the Int cell in Lurgan next to the Ops room, when one of the Radio men passed through a teleprinter message; it read: 'Volunteers wanted for operations out of Lisburn; must be a proven photographer with a background in Intelligence.' What the hell, I thought, beats going back to Germany, so I responded that night.

Three months later after training I arrived in Lisbon, went for familiarization training and was posted out to Belfast; calling officers (who you could only assume were officers) by their nickname or first name. It seemed strange to begin with, but when you considered the operators were putting their lives on the line, every time they left the safety of the compound within the camp, you could understand why. If you were abducted by the hardliners, you were not coming back and you would be put through it before they would put you out of your misery. Capt Robert Nairac was a prime example of the type of torture that they would put you through if they had the chance, hence the use of first names and nicknames only; that way, you could not identify colleagues. (*He was abducted, tortured and then murdered by the IRA whilst on undercover ops in South Armagh; see later in this book*)

Mind you, working in this environment was not all bad; we had an ACC duty cook on 24 x7, mainly for the operators. However if you were hungry you could go and order what you wanted; steak, egg and chips could be had at 2:00am and cooked fresh; a luxury in the province during the 70s. I remember the Queen's Silver Jubilee; the 'slop jockey' cooked a curry that day and served it up with red, white and blue rice; mmmm.

Life in the compound was never dull, the daily routines had to be done and the operators sent out on their ops but whilst they were away and if you were not on gate duty you could bounce a football around with some of the other support team lads. I remember once 'Stampy' had struck gate duty; as we were already inside a camp environment, we were guarding against our own getting in. The Jock guards who were on an 18month tour in our camp made it their mission to find out what went on inside the compound within their camp; they had seen civvie cars driving in and out but never knew for certain who these long haired yobs with ID cards were. They sent a junior Officer to knock on the corrugated iron gate; 'Stampy' slid the viewer back and asked: 'What do you want ?' The Jock officer responded: 'I want to see your CO.' 'Stampy' replied: 'We don't have one; piss off.' The officer looked stunned, and started to walk backwards and then turned to face 'Stampy' again and said in a very saddened voice: 'I only wanted to know if you chaps want to put a team together to play us at football this Wednesday at 2:00pm.' 'Stampy' being the diplomat replied: 'We would love to; thank you so much for the kind invitation; see you at 2:00pm; now be a good officer and piss off.'

To be honest the match was a blood bath as the Jocks tried to push us to the limits, but hey, they never found out who we were or what we did.

TEDIUM AND TRAGEDY IN ULSTER

Sergeant M.J. 'Benny' Hill, 3 Royal Anglians

At the time, I was stationed at Palace Barracks at Holywood and was now a Colour Sergeant. I suppose that I was, comparatively, getting long in the tooth, and no longer in a rifle company but involved in more mundane tasks.

To help me with a mountain of paperwork, a young lad by the name of Paul Wright from the Midlands was attached as a company clerk. He had ambitions to be an Officer and he used the time in the admin section to study and read up in order to achieve his ambition. He was a lovely bloke; very keen, intelligent and sensitive. Around the October of 1979, with the end of the tour in sight and the Royal Regiment of Fusiliers (our relief) were already getting their feet under the table. On that particular day, I entered Palace barracks and was told to report to the office ASAP. There I was told that Paul Wright, this lovely, sensitive soldier had been killed and that one of the other lads – Nobby – had been seriously wounded. It hit me like a blow to the head; so close to the end of the tour and we had our first fatality.

I was later ordered to 'bag and tag' Paul's personal effects and I found this an unpleasant task, as I was effectively 'wrapping up' a friend's life, especially when that friend had died such a violent death.

Gunner Joe Jurkiewicz RA, Belfast city centre (Joe Jurkewicz)

Paul Wright, a Leicestershire man, aged just 21, was out on plain clothes duty in an unmarked car. As he drove along the Whiterock road which separates the Turf Lodge from the Ballymurphy Estate, he was ambushed by several IRA gunmen. Fatally wounded, the car crashed and he died at the scene; another soldier was also shot and left for dead, but later recovered.

I have lost good friends before but was too tired to grieve properly and later, went to my room where I could cope with my own company and my own feelings. Later that night, I went to the bar and drank myself insensible. I was too drunk to care – or drive for that matter – and a good friend got me back safely. The next day was simply a matter of accepting that life – and work – had to go on. Sadly, I wasn't allowed to attend Paul's funeral.

The other lad who was injured in the ambush – Nobby – was rushed to the Royal Victoria Hospital (RVH) and his Mum was flown over from England to visit him. As I was a married man with teenaged kids, I must have been seen as a 'father figure' and I was asked to chauffeur her a couple of times. I found it difficult to make small talk with her, but I felt that to sit in silence would have been a lot worse. She was a very nice lady, very polite and caring, especially considering that my 'firm' had put her son close to death. I just hope that she got through it all ok; I know that Nobby did, but soldier's Mums are a special breed.

Gunner Joe Jurkiewicz RA, Belfast city centre (Joe Jurkiewicz)

As a former serving soldier who thankfully never had cause to visit either the RVH or the Musgrave Park Hospital, I cannot begin to comprehend the turmoil of emotions which must have whirled through the minds of these distressed parents. Quite how they felt as they saw their child, albeit a grown up, strapping soldier, lying there, swathed in bandages with tubes and pipes everywhere, mercifully, most of us will never know. As a civilian, I watched helplessly as my baby son, Robbie fought for his life in Great Ormond Street hospital in 1986 and was amazed by his recovery, so perhaps I have an inkling of their feelings.

Mick Hill continued:

I also served with another likeable lad by the name of Gary Meyer, who, after leaving the Army, joined the RUC. He was murdered by the IRA near North Queen Street police station, shot in the back by a craven coward. On the day that it happened, I was on holiday in Wales and I heard the news on the TV. It is difficult to grieve when you are on holiday with your kids; you just have to bottle it up and get on with things.

Every year when I go to Duxford, I go into the Royal Anglian Museum, read the names in the 'Book of Remembrance' and put faces to the names of those I know – especially Paul Wright – listed there. Each year the list grows longer and I then go and find somewhere quiet and sit on my own for a few minutes, alone with my thoughts and memories.

As a father, I watched my son go off on tours to Northern Ireland, and I saw the changes in him after each of them and wondered if I had changed that much after 9 tours, but who would I ask ? My kids were too young at the time and my ex-wife found it too difficult to discuss; all she said was: 'You were different.' Now that it is, supposedly, all over, I feel that the people who did all the dangerous, difficult and demanding work which made the peace possible, the 'Toms', the 'Crabs', the RUC and the UDR have all been given a 'shit sandwich' whilst the undeserving feast at the banquet of fame, renown and acclaim. But then, after every war, it has always been so.

Mick speaks about Gary Meyer, an RUC Constable who was 35 and married with two children. He and his colleague, Harold Beckett (47) were both gunned down in Chapel Lane near the Falls Road. The gunmen shot the two officers in the back and then made their escape through a nearby Catholic church. One comment made throughout my interview process was of the alleged collusion between Catholic Priests and the IRA. Even senior Army Officers felt that the terrorists, often practicing Roman Catholics, were often able to 'assuage' their guilt by going to Confession and simply admitting their complicity in murders to their confessor priests.

UNITY FLATS, CENTRAL BELFAST

Mick Pickford, Royal Artillery

In the Unity's, we had the usual, 'Gaaht any pens, got any sweets?', and so I said sure. I got a bundle of them out of my pocket and threw them down an alley; put it this way, if they went to get them, we would follow. Sugar Bribery was the thing. I was even asked by a young child to remove my helmet as she thought we had horns under them, so I showed her; we ain't devils, love. Look. One night, we took out packets of salt, got any pens, any sweets, no, got some salt though; and they took it, ate it, and we got the abuse, but I tell you, it lightened the mood.

I went home on leave from NI, once and drank too much, got banned from every pub, and walked backwards through parts of the High Street, looking through the windows before passing shops. And bitter because nobody cared or spared a thought for what we were doing. Also, during leave I had a tumble with an off duty copper, he was slating us for doing a glorified cop job and he couldn't care a f*ck that one of our guys had his leg blown off. I put him straight, straight on his arse. I found out, 5 years later, he got run over outside a pub and lost his leg. I can't say I'm sorry hearing about that, if I did, I would be a liar. But, what goes around comes around.

Gunner at Belfast city centre security gates (Mark Campbell)

NEAR DIPLOMATIC INCIDENT IN BELFAST

Bob Davies, RAOC

On my first tour in the winter of 74/75, I was in Albert Street Mill, Belfast, not far from the Republican Falls Road. During most of the time on this tour there was an IRA 'ceasefire' in operation; despite this I managed over 120 tasks. The suggested MO for dealing with suspect cars at the time, especially those illegally parked in the city centre exclusion area was to drop a charge inside the vehicle and open it up for inspection (four sprung door technique). In this way you could be tasked, do the job, and be writing the report within the space of 45 minutes. The justification was that it kept disruption down to a minimum. Of note is that usually we used 'captured' Frangex as the charge as it did not set the vehicle on fire as PE4 often did (no maxi-candle then).

Anyway my team was called to a task involving a car parked close to some Government offices in the exclusion zone. The Incident Commander reported a large box like object covered by a blanket on the back seat. The well practiced routine went into action and the wheelbarrow was on its way to the target within a couple of minutes of arriving. The robot was just approaching the vehicle when a large RUC man came running towards us shouting for us to stop. His explanation came out at 100mph indicating his relief that he had prevented us doing our thing. The box like object turned

Belfast city centre security gates (Mark Campbell)

out to be a small coffin containing the body of a child. The Government office was the Registry for Births, Deaths and Marriages. The IRA ceasefire carried on for a couple of months more but there is no way of knowing what might have happened if we had done our normal thing.

BELFAST CITY CENTRE

Sergeant M.J. 'Benny' Hill, 3 Royal Anglians

In 1972, we were based in the Hastings Street Police station, just off the city centre and I was with the Recce platoon. In those pre-COP (*close observation platoon*) and specialized task days, the Recce platoon did a lot of escorts, Ops, search team protection and various other ad hoc duties. When it was decided that Belfast city centre would be closed off to traffic sometime in 1972, it was decided to put troops on the ground, in numbers, 24 hours a day.

Until specialist soldiers could be drafted in for this, battalions nearby were given the role; this on top of their already full workload. For us, this involved taking over from the UDR at 06:00 hours, patrolling the centre with only two short breaks for a snatched meal. To do this, reveille was at the un-Godly hour of 04:30 and food was grabbed back at Hastings Street; this continued until 01:00 the following morning, when, utterly exhausted, we were relieved by the UDR. If we were lucky, we might grab a couple of hour's kip and then it was start all over again. I think that we did that routine for about four days at a stretch, but by the third day, we were reduced to

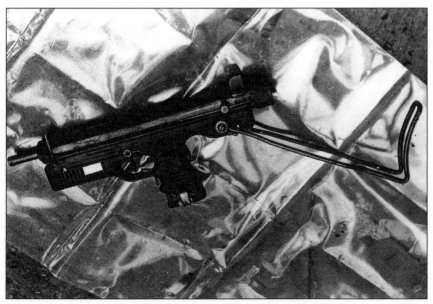

Arms find, Markets area (Mark Campbell)

having cat-naps in cinema doorways; at that time, all the cinemas were closed as they were too obvious a target for the IRA.

I can honestly say that in all my life, I have never been so tired and even now, I love to smirk when I hear sweet young things in the town say: 'I'm exhausted; I had a really late night and a stressful day in the office!' Exhausted? They don't know the meaning!

THE SHORT STRAND, EAST BELFAST: 1973

Driver Lawrence Jagger, RCT

I was in the RCT and on one of the worst tours I can recall. We were deployed in the Grand Central hotel along with various other units – I was attached to the Welsh Guards – and my duties included ambulance driving, ferrying around the EOD (bomb disposal) boys and then undercover driving with the Special ops people.

We spent a lot of time in the Short Strand area, a Catholic enclave just over the Albert Bridge in east Belfast, which, frankly was just one big hell-hole. We had lots of contacts from the Markets area and in addition to these live rounds; we had plenty of petrol bombs and nail bombs. The riots seemed to be daily and I can remember as though it were yesterday, burned out buses, lorries, cars and just about anything the bastards could get their hands on and burn. On one occasion, whilst on foot patrol, we got cornered as we went out by mobs and we only just managed to get out of that situation by the skin of our teeth.

East Belfast is a shit-hole it really is and I don't recommend that anyone takes a holiday there. In fact, I have a photograph of me in there and I am still wearing a shiny cap badge which made a nice target for an IRA sniper to aim at. I was proud to be a member of the RCT although lots of the 'glamour' regiments such as the Paras and SAS grab all the glory, where would they have been without the 'tail' troops like us who drove them, who supplied them with ammo and food etc?

When I was the ambulances, a lot of the time was boring, nothing to do and we were just waiting around, but later on, it was all go and you just hoped that you could grab a bit of sleep because when you are on constant casevac, there is just no let-up at all. We used armoured ambulances, because the bastards would not think twice about attacking one; though can you imagine if a Provo casualty was being taken to hospital and our lads had attacked it? There would have hell to play and public sympathy for the IRA.

On one occasion, as we raced to the scene of a shooting, the bastards threw bricks, bottles, petrol bombs, tins of paint; whatever they could lay their hands on. We got there and the wounded soldier was screaming in agony – sometimes they have already had morphine and a big 'M' is marked on his forehead and they are on 'cloud nine' – and the medics had to work quickly in order to keep the poor bastard alive. Sometimes, they are just deathly pale and very, very quiet, but we still had to get them as quickly as possible to the RVH which had a secure military wing. Once that was over and the wounded soldier was safely delivered to the doctors and nursing staff it would be just a matter of waiting until the next inevitable casualty.

Later on, I was driving around the EOD guys and whilst it was almost constant, when you would be called out or where you would be called out to you would never know; it was all over the place and the pressure was relentless. When the calls came in, some would be just hoaxes, designed so that the IRA could stretch our resources or just watch our operating methods. (*As the IRA terrorist was dressed like all the other citizens of Northern Ireland they could stand with impunity among the crowds of watchers. Unless they were known players, they would blend in and carefully observe EOD procedures and then use this information about the SOPs in order to plan more intricate and unexpected devices.*) We had to take every single call seriously and that stretched us to the limit and beyond. I watched these bomb disposal guys and their methods varied; sometimes they would use the little robots and other times they would use the controlled explosion method.

We had several booby traps and a number of the guys were killed and maimed before we began to suss out some of the IRA bomb-makers' methods. When we were searching and using sniffer dogs, we found the armoured Saracen a good place to watch from! I remember when we received a warning that the IRA had planted a bomb in the big Woolworths in Belfast and we got there pretty quickly to check it out. I was standing by the Saracen and the EOD guys were inside the building and then, without warning: Bang! Up it went and I just thought inwardly 'Oh, no.' But then, through the dust and smoke, staggering almost drunkenly came a figure covered from head to toe in dust; he looked comical at the time, but thank God, he was alive.

FAREWELL TO BELFAST

Tony Procter, REME

Our unit was to travel back to England on the public car ferry, 'The Ulster Queen,' which took us to Liverpool. I can't tell you how relieved we all were to board that ferry. Our time in Belfast was difficult and at times very scary, in fact I had even started smoking again, and I had given up the weed about a year hence in Germany. In retrospect though, that experience I had in Northern Ireland was extremely interesting and rewarding, one I'm glad I took part in. I think though everyone involved in the peacekeeping in Ulster were saddened at the futility of the whole situation and of the bigotry and the hatred of the Irish who are normally so affable. If there were no more violence from tomorrow it would take at least thirty years, a generation in fact, for people to forget and erase their hatred. For those who have had loved ones killed or maimed, they will never forget.

Thus, a semi-circular section of north Belfast, comprising the New Lodge, the Ardoyne, Oldpark, Antrim Road, Shankhill and Crumlin Roads and the mill at North Howard Street had claimed scores of SF lives. Including all those aforementioned areas, no less than 45 soldiers and 19 RUC officers had died in the war against terrorism. Countless others were injured, some terribly and still, today, bear those scars inflicted on them by both Loyalist and Republican terrorists.

Part Two

Londonderry

Derry or Londonderry; Irish: Doire or Doire Cholm Chille, meaning Oak wood of Colm Cille, often called the Maiden City. It is a city in Northern Ireland. The old walled city of Londonderry lies on the west bank of the River Foyle with the location of old Derry on the east bank; the present city now covers both banks The City side to the west and Waterside to the east; the river is spanned by two bridges.

We will look at the old walled city, the hilly slums of the Bogside, the new slums of the Creggan Estate and walk the Buncranna Road to the V2 VCP near Coshquin where the IRA killed five members of the King's Regiment, cynically using poor Patsie Gillespie to drive a proxy bomb. We will walk in the area known by separate generations of British soldiers as the 'city with two names.'

Chapter 9

Londonderry

L ondonderry, or, as the squaddies being sent there called it, the 'city with two names', is to the north west of Belfast and, like Crossmaglen and the aforementioned Belfast, is one of the three most recognised places in Northern Ireland. Divided by the River Foyle, it nestles close to the border with the Irish Republic and, if one left Bligh's Lane (pronounced by the locals as B-l-e-e-s) and drove to the centre of Belfast, is a short journey of just 73 miles or 117 km.

If one is a resident of the Bogside or the Creggan or Gobnascale and a Republican, it is Derry. If, on the other hand, one is a resident of the Fountain, or a Loyalist, it is Londonderry. It was the site where, on Bloody Sunday (January 30, 1972) innocent civilians were tragically shot dead by the Parachute Regiment and where the IRA were no innocent bystanders. It was also a city in which many members of the Security Forces were cruelly cut down.

It is, or certainly was during the 70s and 80s, a place with strict sectarian and, synonymously, political boundaries. On the west side of the Foyle sits the Bogside, an uninviting and fiercely Republican estate, sited just outside the ancient city walls. Directly opposite on the other side of the river is Gobnascale, or the 'Gob' to successive generations of squaddies. Go slightly north west from the Bogside and there is the equally uninviting Creggan estate. Isolated away from these is the Loyalist Fountain area which still boasts the famous, or perhaps, infamous, slogan 'No Surrender'.

STRAND ROAD, LONDONDERRY

Tim Francis, Royal Artillery

My second tour of NI was as part of the deployment of my new unit, 94 Locating Regiment, RA for deployment in Londonderry in November of that year when we were due to be divided between the Bogside, the City area and the main RUC station on Strand Road. We arrived in November on the same day as the wedding of Princess Anne to Capt. Mark Phillips; there was a suggestion of a whip round for a fellow soldier which received a fairly predictable response!

We had known for some time that my battery would be based at the Strand Road RUC station where our principal duties were to man checkpoints, sealing off the city shopping centre from bomb attacks there, with all pedestrians being searched. We also had to stop and search the few vehicles allowed into the area and also checks on all vehicles passing along the quayside. On the day of our arrival, 3 guys from the unit we were relieving were hit in a shooting incident in the nearby City area. As it happened, I knew one of them; he had been 'best recruit' of my intake

5 years previously. It seemed a very small dangerous world indeed but fortunately the injuries were not life threatening.

From the start we entered a strange new world of hundreds of body searches every day, investigating the contents of women's handbags and daily abuse from the inhabitants of the Bogside which adjoined our area. It was clear after a while that checkpoints F1, P9 and the Shipquay Place checkpoint were the busy checkpoints. F1 in particular being a regular flashpoint as it formed the main access to the Bogside via William Street. This checkpoint had an armour plated sangar looking down William Street; this was commonly known as the 'coffin' as there was a rumour that a previous occupant had been hit by a sniper there.

In fact, it was just outside F1 on a busy Saturday afternoon when I was hit by a flying bottle, but fortunately I saw it coming and got my rifle butt in front of my head in time to take the impact. My initial reaction was utter rage and I saw the lad who threw the bottle and pursued him down William Street until I lost him in crowds; probably not the wisest hot pursuit and one which did not amuse our Battery Commander who just happened to be in the vicinity. By pure chance, the same evening, I was working on another checkpoint in Shipquay Place just around the corner from F1 and the same

Royal Artillerymen at Fort George, Londonderry, 1973 (Joe Jurkewicz)

guy appeared as I was on searching duty. I think it clicked in his head who I was just as he accidentally collided with the wall nearby!

FATIGUE

Pat Moir, Royal Artillery

1st September 72 having only finished a 4 month roulment tour of Belfast, in May, the Regiment found itself in Derry on an emergency tour, our fifth in 24 months. This NI lark was getting irksome; in fact N I was like a splinter in the backside. We had taken over from a tank Regiment, who had been withdrawn early, for failing to get to grips with the bombers. Like most regiments at the time we were understrength, and with year-long guard commitments we were going to be stretched. My Battery were lodged in though old armoury in fountain street, all the junior ranks squashed into one large room on the first floor, in two tier bunks. Our domain was the old walled city, our task to man check points on the four city gates, two road blocks and a mobile foot patrol, plus a guard on the armoury itself. A complicated rota was drawn up involving 4, 6 and 8 hour shifts, on a six duty basis.

The seventh day was bliss, we could get a shower in an outside portacabin, go to bed undressed, get a full eight hours kip, and wake up to freshly laundered clothing. Then it was back to six days of sleeping fully clothed boots and all. Eating and cleaning our kit ate into our kip time so we never got a full eight hours in the sack. On top of that we had to contend with other sections coming on and off duty, and the clanking of helmets and riffles. Boredom was another problem especially during the night stags, and all done on foot in a very small area. Frisking everybody entering the city was the dirtiest job; my hands were always left feeling sticky after a stint on the gates. The only thing to look forward to was nosh, and didn't the slop jockeys do us proud. Gone were the old BAOR days of 'who called the cook a bastard?' 'Who called the bastard a cook?' These unsung heroes spent weeks on end in cramped conditions dishing up the grub day and night. 'Fried egg mate; how many; two or three?' All with a huge grin, not bad for 3am. My hat will always be raised to these guys churning out quality food and always with a smile.

Our biggest fear was the threat of bombs getting through our ring of steel. One tactic that still appalls me to this day, is young mothers putting a fifty pound bomb in a pram then adding the baby, and pushing the pram into a city centre, parking the pram outside a shop, lifting baby and enter the shop but leaving the pram behind when exiting the shop. We had a WRMP attached to each section, just so women could be searched. At the time the favored bomb maker tactic to get a bomb inside a secured area, was to use women, as they had one more orifice than men. Women would bring in the bombs in little bits at a time. When all the bits were inside the area the bomb maker would enter the area and make the bomb. Only two bombs got through in our ten week stint, with no injuries or deaths.

They did break the boredom, as did a little rumble between rival tartan gangs.Yobs dressed like the 'Bay City Rollers', with tartan scarves tied around their wrists, were in two gangs of about fifty each; one wore the green tartans the other the red tartans. Woolworths on a corner opposite the war memorial suffered what today is called steaming, as a gang stormed through the Ship Quay Street door through the tool department, grabbing hammers and choppers, and out through the Ferry quay door. We were tasked to evict these morons from the city, it was welcome break from the boredom, and we got to play with our rubber bullet guns. It was about the eighth week when acute tiredness set in, I felt dead on my feet all the time. Even being woken for the next shift made me irritable, and my eyes were always sore. Looking at the other bods, you could see the tiredness in their eyes. In this day and age it could give the impression that we were all on dope, we certainly were not, and it was pure fatigue. At last after ten weeks the powers that be decided, that they could spare us, and I said goodbye to that fair city for the last time.

Guardsman Lawrence Bowman, Grenadier Guards

As a teenager growing up in the early 70s all I had on my mind was the latest fashion, Top of the Pops, chasing girls and most importantly of all a footballing career with Chelsea or Manchester United. Every night I would sit in front of the TV and watch the latest news footage of the murder and

Gunner Joe Jurkiewicz RA, Londonderry, 1973 (Joe Jurkiewicz)

mayhem in a place called Northern Ireland. What did I care, and, after all it wasn't on my door step and tomorrow the new top 30 would be published.

As I sat across the desk only feet away from the recruiting Sergeant, he looked me in the eye and said: 'You do realise son that within a year you will be serving in Northern Ireland?' What did I care; after all, anything was going to be better than the two years i had just spent after leaving school down the local coal mine.

Then it was announced that we were being deployed to Northern Ireland and, following the customary NI training, we were sent on leave. After the customary weeks leave, which I spent with my grand mother, who commented that it was disgusting to send 'boys' of my age to fight. She had lost most of her men folk of an older generation on the Somme battlefield. I found myself billeted along with the rest of Support Company at Bridge camp, so named as it was positioned right at the foot of the river Foyle. And so would begin the cycle of platoon duties; 2 days camp guard, 2 days patrolling the city centre and the Brandywell, our 2 main areas of operational responsibility. One day quick reaction force and 2 days manning the city centre checkpoints.

On the second night in country I had just left the cookhouse, when the most almighty bomb exploded in the city. I was just so taken aback by the sheer noise and turmoil, and stood rooted to the ground, thinking to myself 'What the hell am I doing here?' I was just 19 years old; 3 years out of school.

Royal Artillery vehicles at Fort George, Londonderry, 1973 (Joe Jurkewicz)

Private D.C. Queens Regiment

We used to go to the interrogation centre in Londonderry weekly and pick up pictures of the latest arrests. When up there you could see the vehicles from Loughall, from the SAS shooting outside Omagh and various other vehicles from covert contacts in the province. Some friends and I drove over an 80lb semtex culvert device in Antrim that resulted in the arrest of 11 suspects by the SAS. They had been followed from Belfast and the young lad, who lived amongst the soldiers in the married quarters, was arrested packing the culvert. We drove over it because the cordon had been set, so the RUC and UDR didn't think it wise to let those that were within know what was happening.

When on my 4 month tour on the way to a patrol our Lynx was diverted to a fresh incident in Tyrone. An off duty soldier had been blown up by a car bomb outside his house. The funny thing was that we set up a cordon and a man started to walk up the rod, from the direction of the incident and when he arrived with us, he said he just wanted to have a cup of tea at his mate's house, next to us. His hair was on end, his face was covered in soot and his clothes looked a bit torn!! Looked like something out of a Laurel and Hardy film! He had been the victim but luckily for him the terrorists didn't have the balls to put the device under the driver side because it was lit up with street lighting. When the device initiated it blew the passenger seat out of the roof and he got blown out of the driver side. There wasn't a scratch on him!

SEARCHES AND BOMBS

Tim Marsh, Royal Artillery

I had a mate called 'Jock' who was a bit of a ladies' man, and one day we were carrying out a 2 man bomb patrol of the shopping area. These patrols consisted of random stop and searches of people, handbags, and packages at busy periods. Suddenly we found ourselves being given some very strange angry looks from a relatively young mother and her daughter aged about 18 or 19 who were very familiar to us from a different atmosphere and we beat a very hasty retreat indeed to equal any of the other great retreats of history ! One of Jock's other great moments came later in the tour when having struck up an acquaintance with another young lady and actually sneaking out to the local cinema with her he found himself at a security briefing where a photo of a young lady was shown and she was described as being extremely dangerous with various contacts at high level within the local Provos. The gathering was asked if anybody had seen her and Jock uttered the immortal words in my ear: 'I shagged her last night!' Yes, it was his latest conquest and needless to say she was not seen again.

The 2 man bomb patrols could be quite boring but they did give the opportunity to stop girls at random and check their bags or ask them to open their coats for anything suspicious! One of the streets covered also bordered one of the few remaining shirt factories of Londonderry; this being formerly a major industry there and this also gave the chance to chat up girls through the window there. But, where there is a will there is a way and one of the Troop actually married one of the girls from the factory which was some achievement in the circumstances.

Amongst these activities there were of course very serious moments; a lot of unpleasantness and, occasionally the experience of real fear including quite a large number of bombs finding their way into our area despite our ring of checkpoints. We were always aware that we were a deterrent rather than a totally effective preventive measure. The bombs generally caused material damage but not usually casualties, apart from a serious injury to an ATO over the Christmas period. I happened to be on leave at the time as I had actually won the draw for Christmas leave which was much sought after; somebody did suggest I should give it one of the married guys but my response was fairly blunt. My own personal potentially bad moment occurred late one afternoon as a suspect car was reported and the area was cordoned off as normal procedure.

Gunner Joe Jurkiewicz RA, makes canine friends, Londonderry (Joe Jurkewicz)

My section of 4 was around a corner from the suspect car and a disturbance then broke out in another nearby street and our assistance was required. The only route to get there quickly was running past the car. We did query this as we were not keen on the idea but the order was confirmed and we made our sprints past the suspect car to the corner of the street with me as the last man, and, as I took off out of my blocks like some Olympic sprinter and passed the car, there was a huge yellow flash. There was a wall of flame, and, as with my previous experience of close explosion on my first tour, I don't remember a bang; just a sort of roaring noise and being hurled against a doorway. I was thinking, this is a waste; I am only 21 and this is it, the end. Although it could only have been a matter of seconds, I then realised I seemed to be in one piece and thought I had better get out of there as there was a lot of flames and debris falling. I picked myself up and ran around the corner, much to the surprise of the guys already there who were certainly not expecting to see me, other than to be scraping up various body parts off adjacent streets. I did seriously lose it at this stage and told the Battery Commander who had ordered us down the route precisely what I thought of him in many words of 4 letters!

It transpired that it had already been radioed back to base that I was down, which in military language meant probably dead, as I then discovered on return to base. I walked into the canteen to be greeted with great surprise and the query from our battery clerk 'What are you doing here; you are supposed to be dead!' It was certainly a turning point for me as I decided this was probably where my army career should be curtailed; to put the explosion in perspective the front bumper of the car landed about 200 metres away.

As a regiment we suffered 3 fatalities on that tour; two together in the lobby of what was then the Rossville flats in the Bogside in an ambush. Although I did not know the guys personally I will remember until the day I die hearing the 2 bursts of gunfire on a cold evening as a colleague, John Gale and myself were entering the back gate of the RUC station. Ominously, hearing the shots, knowing it was not good as it was clearly not an army weapon and there was no answering fire.

The two soldiers killed were Gunner Joseph Brookes (20) a single man from Staffordshire and Bombardier Heinz Pisarek (30) from Celle in Germany. Both were shot and fatally wounded by the IRA, whilst a Royal Artillery patrol were inside the Rossville Flats; the two men died on their way to hospital.

Billy Fitzgerald, King's Own Royal Border Regiment

I did some work with the Green Jackets in Northern Ireland; 2 RGJ had a Company in Derry on Bloody Sunday; they were based in Ballykelly. I was also attached to, I think, 3 RGJ in the Ballymurphy in the Summer of '72. I remember that one very well; they had two lads killed from a burst of gunfire into the back of a Saracen, and I think an NCO died later from the same attack. There was romance when I was there I had a girlfriend. We were called out to Portadown and the coverage was all over the TV. When I got back to camp, I was in full battle order so to speak – 'cammed up', and had bands of GPMG ammo around me, 3 rubber bullets in each of the pockets of my flak jacket, together with rifle and rubber bullet gun. As I got out of the vehicle, she shouted my name and came running down to me and threw her arms around me. She cried that she thought I was going to be killed as she had been watching the events in Portadown on the TV. It was the most romantic thing that has ever happened to me; sadly she ran off with my best mate!

I had the unlucky experience of having a two year tour in N Ireland in 72/73. During those two years I was involved in every major incident which happened. We arrived on January 7, 1972 and went straight into action which did not stop until we left in 73! I was involved in Bloody Sunday, Bloody Friday, and Operation Motorman to mention just a few. Bloody Friday started haunting me again after 9/11. Those pictures of people running away from the towers brought back the memories of us going towards the bombings on the day. Our Role was province stand by at Ballykinler and I hit every town in Northern Ireland. I saw much action during that tour; in fact to be honest, I suffer from PTSD and I am haunted by my experiences there.

I could write some hair-raising stuff of my 72/73 tour; the worse thing which happened to me, to be honest, was being attacked by a gang of Irish men in Liverpool – my home town – for being involved with Bloody Sunday. I fought for my life, as they were like a pack of wolves on me. The attack was by some houses which were being knocked down. I grabbed a broken window frame and hit one of my attackers with it , it skidded across his skull lifting his scalp like a trap door; I went berserk and battered them; in fact the police saved them from me killing them. I was never the same after that. The troubles had been brought right to my Liverpool doorstep. Bloody Sunday. Well it is history; we were told we would be back in camp for 10 pm! We had covered a Civil rights march everyday that week and the climax was Derry. The brief was the same: 'There will be a march, a speech and riot afterwards.' – The Paras got pulled out and we were left in Derry to get the full impact of the locals, and I experienced hatred there like as if it was physical pain. The hatred from the locals; the spitting in our faces and the after riots left me with no respect for the Paras. I was also back in Derry for the 1st anniversary! This was not a pleasant experience either!

I served with the King's Own Royal Border Regiment – I left in 1976 due to being mentally downgraded – and I am still fighting the Irish trouble 35 years later ! I reflect on the madness I have experienced since my two year of N Ireland: alcoholism, tranquiliser addiction and PTSD and nearly 30 entries into nut houses! Would you believe they are still saying to me 'Your problem is so severe that we do not have the staff to treat you.' 'Combat Stress' said the same to me only 3 months ago when I went there for the first time. But they did say if I went private that I could receive help ! No help at all in all this time – just a few days in the nut house and then 'on your way.'

Chapter 10

The Bogside

The Bogside was built up in the 1800s and the 1900s, and in recent years its architecture has suffered from poor funding. It has cheap constructed blocks of flats; one notorious high-rise was the Rossville Flats, featured in most film shots of the city. It was a hot bed of trouble. Much of the old terraced houses of the Victorian era are now all gone; one of which, was Nailer's Row. It was a terrace of houses that ran along the bottom of the city wall, of the old two up and two down with the old tin bath hanging on the back wall. Today, seen in its modern context, there are newer houses, some council some private and the gable end murals are almost respectable, certainly artistic. The 'blackness' of Bogside in the 70s and 80s is still there though and it lurks just below the surface.

The Bogside is a fiercely nationalist neighbourhood outside the city walls of Londonderry, and is an area has been a focus point for many of the events of the Troubles, from the Battle of the Bogside and Bloody Sunday in the 1960s and 1970s.

The first soldier to be killed in Londonderry, as a direct consequence of 'political violence' was 18 year old, Wiltshire boy, William Jolliffe (18) of the Royal Military Police who died of his wounds on March 1, 1971, several days after he was badly injured in a petrol bomb attack. Later that year, in the August, the Royal Artillery lost Bombardier Paul Challenor who was 22 when he was shot by the IRA near the Army base in Bligh's Lane and died from those wounds less than 2 hours later. Just a month later, in the same location this famous regiment lost Sergeant Martin Carroll, who was 24 – from Wales – and who was also shot; his two brothers were heartbreakingly close to where he was killed.

The grim toll continued, as the 'Jackets' (RGJ) lost 24 year old Rifleman Joseph Hill, shot in the Bogside; he was from Kent and, despicably, his shattered body was jeered at, by youths from the nearby Rossville flats as it was taken away. In the space of 10 months, the Army had suffered nine deaths in the 'city with two names.'

In 1972, the Bogside's desperate yearning to become the most dangerous part of the world for a British soldier to tread resulted in the deaths of 3 soldiers in that fiercely Republican area in less than two weeks. Lance Corporal John Davies (22) died of his wounds having earlier been badly wounded there and then just 3 days later, the Scots Guards lost Guardsman John Van-Beck (26), shot whilst patrolling in the Bogside. The IRA's propaganda department no doubt went into overdrive as it claimed that the Army was using German 'mercenaries' once it had learned the name of the latest soldier that they had killed. The IRA unit based outside the city walls then claimed another victim from the same proud Regiment when Guardsman George Lockhart (24) was shot and killed, just a week later. Lance Sergeant Thomas McKay became the third member of the Scots Guards (29) to be killed in a period of a month when he was killed in the city centre, close to the entrance to the Bogside.

Days later, the Bogside claimed the life of RGJ Rifleman, James Meridith who was 19 years old. Londonderry killed its last Gunner in the October, when Leeds boy, Paul Jackson (21) was killed in a bomb blast on the Strand Road, whilst filming a suspect device. The year drew to an end when, with a poignantly cruel sense of timing, having been wounded earlier in the Bogside, REME Lance Corporal Colin Harker died of his wounds; it was Christmas Eve, 1972 and he was 28 years old.

On April 11, 1973 Gunner Idwal Evans (20) was killed in the Bogside. The gunmen on the Creggan continued also, this time to match their murderous comrades from the Bogside and in the space of a week, they killed Royal Anglian Anthony Goodfellow (26) and another Artillery soldier, Sergeant Thomas Crump who was 27.

On June 21, on the day that the author celebrated his first birthday in 'Civvy Street' Captain Barry Griffin (29) was killed defusing a bomb in Lecky Road, Bogside; the officer was the ninth bomb disposal to lose his life in the troubles. The Bogside's IRA killers were not yet finished for the year and, on October 3, in what was seen as an unprecedented lapse in security, a hand-delivered letter, whilst being opened exploded and killed Second Lieutenant Lindsay Bobbie of the RAOC and terribly wounded two other soldiers. To this day, no one has been able to explain why should an entirely avoidable tragedy was allowed to take place. The blast took place at Bligh's Lane in the Bogside.

The Rossville flats, situated in the Bogside was the scene of a double shooting when the IRA ambushed a four man Royal Artillery brick on patrol there. Bombardier Heinz Pisarek (30) and Gunner Joseph Brookes (20) were hit on one of the upper floors of the flats by machine gun fire; Pisarek died almost immediately and Brookes died in the ambulance on the way to hospital.

1974 was only three weeks old, when the Gunners lost another soldier as a bomb explosion claimed the life of Sergeant John Haughey (32). The soldier who was the father of two young children was killed by a booby-trapped device whilst patrolling the Bogside. Less than two months later, the 'Duke of Boots' lost a Leeds boy, Corporal Michael Ryan (23) who was shot by the IRA whilst on mobile patrol in Bogside's Foyle Road area.

There is an element of mystery surrounding the next killing in the IRA stronghold of the Bogside. A Coldstream Guards officer, Anthony Pollen (27) and allegedly attached to 14th Int, an Army undercover intelligence unit, was attacked by a mob and shot dead. He and a comrade were taking photos of an IRA funeral when they were attacked; one soldier escaped, but Captain Pollen was killed. [*See later in this chapter*]

On May 10, 1975, Constable Paul Gray (20) was killed by an IRA gunman whilst on foot patrol in the Bogside. It would be 12 more years before another policeman was to die in this place the soldiers simply called the 'Bog.'

BOGSIDE DAYS AND NIGHTS

Corporal Mick Copp, 2nd Bn Royal Green Jackets

In March, 1971, when with 2 RGJ, we arrived at Shackleton Barracks in Co Londonderry for an 18 month unaccompanied tour; thank goodness I was not married then. The troubles were in their infancy and Derry was relatively quiet, but Belfast on the other hand had already had the Springfield Road bomb which had killed Sergeant Willets of the Parachute Regiment. Trouble in Derry began with some stone throwing and although guns were few and far between, it was known that there were a few Thompsons about. These were used by the 'spray and pray' brigade who didn't cause us too many problems. Soon enough, however, these were replaced with M1 carbines and soon the dreaded Armalite.

Those early days were 'Groundhog Days' and after lunch every day rioters appeared at the end of William Street (a name known to every soldier who served in Derry). They would start throwing stones and anything else that they could lay their hands n and this would then see the Army coming out and replying with rubber bullets and later, as the riots grew worse, CS gas. Initially the rioters were of varying ages and numbering 100/150 but later on in the coming months, when things really deteriorated, the crowds on the edge of the Bogside could number as many as 500. It was a pretty scary scenario especially as their 'armoury' now included nail bombs and petrol bombs; it wasn't unusual on a Saturday to see a comrade being dragged away with several nails protruding from a limb.

At this particular time, in 1971, I was in the Recce Platoon and our duties consisted of patrolling the County in sections consisting of a Ferret scout car and a Land Rover; this meant, of course, that we didn't have the intense exposure to rioters as the rifle platoons. However, one day whilst we were based in Strand Road RUC station, a young officer came up to me and explained that the company commander wanted to try out a new tactic. I was wary straight away, because any idea an officer has doesn't usually include the welfare of the troops! He walked us round to the rear yard, where sat a short wheelbase, open top Land Rover on top of which was the largest searchlight I had ever seen; it was like something from a Second World War film.

The plan was to wait until the Bogsiders turned up for the evening's entertainment and, at a given signal, drive around to the top of William Street and stop in line with the platoon stretched across the road. I cannot remember who the driver was but he didn't look too happy and the only protection we had were the flak jackets, helmets and a couple of Makralon shields. Our communication was the good old 'Storno' radio. Anyway, as it got dark and the locals' entertainment got under way, the two of us got ready for our task; it was fair to say that we were both crapping ourselves! My job was to operate the light whilst standing in the back of the vehicle and I emphasised to the driver that he must not, on pain of death, stall the rover. After an hour or so, the trouble had reached its peak and I received the order over the radio to proceed and, shaking like a leaf, we drove off into the unknown. Then, as we drove into the Bogside, via William Street, the full horror unfolded.

A rifle platoon was taking a real hammering, crouched behind their shields and everything including the odd kitchen sink, was being thrown at them; manhole covers were a particular favourite. There must have been upwards of 400 people massed in the street as we pulled up, level with the platoon. I then switched the light on, not really knowing what to expect and this huge beam covered the whole of the Bogside and beyond. The whole crowd stopped what they were doing and stared, but only for a couple of seconds. Then the roar of the crowd got louder and missiles began to rain down, but the only difference was, that everything was now aimed at this latest 'secret weapon.' It was horrendous and we were being battered; the driver, thank God, kept the engine running and was underneath the dashboard and I was trying to protect myself with the shield but it was hard work. The brick dust filled my mouth and, what with the smell of cordite as the platoon fired volleys of rubber bullets and CS gas, I thought that the end of the world was nigh ! The Land Rover was slowly but surely disintegrating and, although it had mesh all over it, it wasn't doing much good.

Also, the platoon was now taking a harder bashing than before we had arrived and one bloke shouted up: 'Are you fucking off or what ?' It was obvious that it wasn't working and thank God, over the radio came the call to return to the police station. We took what was left of the Land Rover and drove back to the rear yard. The officer who had sent us out was there to greet us and his face, when he saw the state of the vehicle, was a sight to behold, partly because I'm sure that he would have had to explain the state of said vehicle to the QM; suffice to say, neither the vehicle nor the light were ever seen again !

As posterity was to record, however, for all the 'funny' stories from the Bogside, there were a score of tragedies to counter them. Mick Copp's sobering after words show that quite starkly.

Up until October, 1971, we had received no fatal casualties, although several of the lads had been wounded as the IRA received more training and better weapons, notably the Armalite rifle. Every day out on patrol we were taking our lives in our hands; if mobile, from culvert bombs; if on foot patrol, from the more proficient sniper. These people had been able to zero in their weapons over the border in Donegal.

Things were to change and we lost Rifleman Joe Hill, shot dead in the Bogside during a riot. Then Major Robin Alers-Hankey was hit in the stomach by a high velocity round whilst protecting firemen in William Street. When the news reached us, it was quite shattering as most of the other guys had only received relatively minor wounds; this was serious. In fact, Robin died of his wounds several months later. After the events of 'Bloody Sunday' I felt that I needed a change and returned to my old platoon – anti-tank – who were operating in a rifle company. I decided that I wanted to see what it was like at the 'sharp end'. I was a section commander and my new colleagues were much younger than the previous 'old sweats' I had been with.

Soon we were out on foot patrol in Derry city and on the fringes of the Bogside and Creggan. The vehicles we had – like the 6-wheeled Saracen – were not ideal for urban areas but safer than the ubiquitous PIGs. They were still in still in their yellow desert paint, although this didn't really matter, as on most patrols tins of paint were dropped or thrown at the vehicles and they returned looking like objects of modern art. The snipers were now very proficient and would spend hours waiting for a patrol to appear and removing a brick in a wall to make a firing slot was a favourite move.

The next to die was Rifleman Taylor who was shot dead on March 20, 1972, not far from where Major Alers-Hankey was fatally wounded. Then on June 26, we had our last fatality when 'Ginger' Meredith was shot, just four hours prior to yet another ceasefire. We were gutted as he was in our company and he was a great mate to all. None of these deaths made us any less determined to carry on and see our task through. During this time, Rifleman Harry Hatton from the Ant-Tanks was hit in the neck by a high velocity round whilst on the city walls. Poor Harry was left paralysed from the neck down and this really shook us up as he was the life and soul of the party and an old sweat. I then realised that the other lads had mates and they would have been feeling like us; sadly, Harry was just another statistic and was to die some years later, still a paraplegic.

This was a busy time and soldiers were being shot dead all around us, and the other resident battalion – the Royal Anglians – lost men as did numerous other Regiments. The people we felt sorry for were the Gunners for, at least we were doing what we had been trained for, and whilst they had to do the best that they could. We lost four men dead with 30 or 40 wounded by various means, although, for an 18 month tour at the height of the troubles, these statistics in purely military terms were not bad. However, the families of those boys rightly would never see it like that; that that they did not die in vain I am sure, because Northern Ireland is now a different place which I visit on a regular basis and it is good to see.

Mick refers to the four losses suffered during his tour. These were Rifleman Joseph Hill (24) from Kent, Major Robin Alers-Hankey (35) from Winchester who died on Bloody Sunday, a full four months after being wounded, Rifleman John Taylor (19) from Wanstead and Rifleman James Meredith (19) who was from Nottinghamshire. It was a bad period for the Jackets who lost a total of 49 soldiers from various causes during the course of the troubles.

BOGSIDE

WO2 Roy Banwell, Cheshire Regiment

Our Platoon was on duty in the Rosemount RUC station on the 14 April 78, and I was in the operations room at the time monitoring the Company's radio net. One of Rosemount's sangars overlooked a road that led downhill to the Bogside. Two thirds of the way down this road it dips out of sight of the sangar, and one of our patrols was heading down this road; as it disappeared from the view a shot rang out. Corporal Joey Somerville, who was commanding the patrol, gave a contact report over the radio, stating that Private Duffy had been shot. Luckily the gunshot wound was not fatal and the 'alert' platoon was scrambled to seal off and search the area, (while trying to preserve any evidence), also to try and locate then destroy the enemy if possible. It was never very easy to carry out all the things that needed doing. To seal off an area, search it, evacuate the wounded and preserve evidence all at the same time was problematical. All the while you were as mad as hell trying to catch the sniper. It was normally the evidence that got lost due to the fact that so many people were swamping the area in such a small space of time. It was not just our platoon's 'alert' sections that were called out; it would be part of a city wide plan that was designed to close down vehicle and pedestrian activity preventing movement of IRA weapons and personnel. If you could keep the sniper, bomber or weapon in the area of the incident, there would be more chance of getting him or it.

Private Copper (B Company) was shot in the Brandywell area of the city on the 30 March, whilst out patrolling; again not fatally. I nearly said luckily, but there is nothing lucky about being shot. On this occasion the weapon and the spot from where it was fired were both found. The weapon was taken away for forensic tests then destroyed, and the firing point examined for clues. A couple of weeks later a Captain Huntress was over visiting the Battalion, (he and Sgt Bob Brimson who was showing him around the area), went to view the firing point from where Pte Cooper had been shot, probably out of morbid curiosity than anything else. There lying in the firing position was a Mauser K98 rifle, and you can just imagine the stunned silence at this discovery. It transpired that the rifle had been placed there ready for another shoot that very afternoon; talk about luck. Everyone who was due to go out that day on patrol counted their blessings, as it could have been any one of them on the receiving end. It just shows you even with the best of planning that luck plays its part as well.

ANOTHER DEATH IN THE BOGSIDE

Tim Francis, Royal Artillery

I will also never forget January 21st 1974 as long as I live; my section was on a temporary week's deployment in the Bogside. We were based in what was commonly known as the Saracen factory where we were attached to another battery of the regiment for the period.

Our time there was spent under the command of Sgt John Haughey whom I knew pretty well as I was a Regimental cross country runner and he managed that team. On the day in question we were due to go out on a foot patrol straight after lunch under the command of John. It was a mixed patrol, including some lads from another battery who were more familiar with the area and, as we assembled, we realised we were one too many. John said to me 'You may as well stay back and have a rest.' I didn't need much encouragement to accept the offer and was just getting back to my bed space when there was the most almighty bang obviously very close to hand. Instant reaction set in, with bodies very quickly on the spot to see what had happened. Just down the road at the junction with Stanley's Walk, John had paused momentarily to take cover at an electricity junction box. Tragically, it had been set up with an explosive device which was then detonated by remote control. It hit John hard at very close range and also wounded 'Chalky' from my own section behind him.

We then went into action over the next few hours to attempt to trace where the detonation had been carried out from particularly in houses nearby. There were numerous incidents particularly with the local female population, some bottle throwing, and myself forcibly removing a local councillor from a house being searched. It was during this period that we heard that John had not made it which certainly did not improve anybody's mood. I will never forget the sickening gloating of the locals as the news spread, particularly the women and I will also not easily forget that it could have been me; this was quite easily the lowest point of my time in the army.

Generally a lot of the checkpoints were fairly mind numbing although the occasional incidents did enliven things. We stopped the brother of Martin McGuiness (then the most wanted man in Londonderry as commander of the local Provos) at a VCP. We recognised his name and address, and, on checking it with base we were told he was not wanted but to make his life difficult. This involved stripping his car and generally

Tim Francis (Gunners) in prone position, the Bogside (Tim Francis)

having a chat about the recent whereabouts of his brother about which he was unsurprisingly not very forthcoming. Another incident was whilst manning a 3 person checkpoint one evening with 2 mates: Ginge and Dave; guys I knew very well. This worked on the basis of one unarmed guy searching, guarded by another armed, whilst the third had a sit down in the sangar keeping an eye down a side street whilst having a smoke or a coffee.

I was searching with my best mate Ginge guarding me when a local girl, Claire, well known to several of our unit, approached with the biggest Scandinavian looking merchant sailor that I had ever seen; in fact the biggest man I have ever seen to this day. The golden rule was that all males entering Strand Road were body searched with no exceptions but unfortunately this guy said no and he was huge and an argument broke out. This also involved Claire who I managed to upset when searching her handbag and seeing her collection of army cap badges said 'You have been a busy girl!' This seemed to upset her for some reason! We were in a stand off position when Ginge decided the next step was to cock his rifle; at which point our colleague Dave in the sangar helpfully called out 'Go on Ginge, shoot him.' Fortunately, commonsense prevailed and the guy accepted the search and he and Claire departed with Claire giving me a few choice verbals as she went on her way.

Despite the various distractions the overall memory of the tour is of mind numbing hours and hours being spent either manning checkpoints or on guard in sangars in 6 hour stags. Three in a row on some occasions; not fun particularly if you only then had 6 hours to carry out the general acts of living such as eating, washing' laundry, letters, phone calls, cleaning kit and weapons. As well as getting some sleep, potentially interrupted by any incidents. I can remember having to spend 6 or 12 hours with guys that you did not necessarily like or have anything in common with but had to talk to in order to remain awake. I have a particularly painful memory of spending 6 hours on stag with one of our UDR friends whose only response to anything I said was: 'Ar, to be sure, to be sure, to be sure.' I gave up after a while and occupied my time thinking of ways to accidentally kill him and get away with it! Our deployment in Strand Road RUC station was a relatively soft option compared to the Bogside but, soft option or not, it was still an exhausting tour with its never ending cycle of stags and checkpoints.

My army career came to an end about 4 months later as I decided the car incident was as close to death as I wanted to be at this stage of my life. However, within another 4 years I found myself heavily involved in the Iranian Revolution which is another story altogether although my army training certainly got me out of trouble a couple of times there.

Tim refers to Sergeant John Haughey (32) a father of three children from the Manchester area. He was terribly wounded by the explosion at the corner of Stanley's Walk and Lone Moor Road on January 21, 1974 and died of his wounds in hospital.

INCIDENT IN A BOGSIDE FISH AND CHIP SHOP

WO2 Haydn Davies RRW attached DERR

A late summer night; the pubs were closing. People were making their way home. We were patrolling with a group of eight in two separate groups about a hundred metres apart. We were moving down Cable Street and were confronted by a very hostile middle aged man, quite a huge man. I thought to 'P' check him but thought it not worth the trouble, He was drunk and I had seen him quite often before, he was normally quite law abiding. He had stood and berated me for some minutes, and moved off only when he saw I was not 'biting'. We started to move along the street when the Radio from the Ops room told me to 'P'check the abusive man.' The patrol behind had passed the details of the 'Verbal abuse incident' to the Ops room. I silently cursed them for it, but went after the man.

I made my way with my half of the patrol down Cable Street to where I saw our man entering a well lighted Fish and Chip shop. I followed him in, and stood in front of him and asked his details. He must have been a well known man to the remainder of the people in the queue; they all quite silently made themselves very scarce indeed. I was left alone with the large man and the white coated purveyor of chips who stood behind the counter and looked worried. The big man stared with hatred and venom into my face. He became quite speechless with rage. He started to scream and shout and threw off his donkey jacket for a fight. He then walked to the counter, raised the flap and come running back towards me with a sizzling hot saucepan of boiling fat which he had scooped out of a boiling vat.

He held it in the 'Throw position' in front of me and called me all the vile stuff that he could muster. I did only what I could to protect myself. I pointed my rifle to his face and positively cocked the action. His two handed hold went back in preparation to throw the sizzling fat at my face. I stood and stared into his drunken eyes and his spitting venom and pointed the weapon centrally on his face. If he moved first, I had to beat him to it! That was all that I could do!

There was silence for a half a minute. The white coated man said 'Don't do it Duffy! He'll pull the trigger.' I said nothing then I heard myself saying: 'I have no option.' We stood like that for about a minute. Then he slowly put down the pan of boiling fat on the floor between us and walked out of the door. I watched him go with great relief. I cleared the round from the chamber of my rifle. The fish shop man said 'Bugger off and let people have their fish and chips in peace.'

I thought to myself; at least I have his name but what a bloody awful way to get it!

There was a road which more or less divided the Bogside from the Creggan, called Lecky Road; I was standing on that particular road one day when an RMP vehicle pulled up. The driver said to me from under his peaked cap! 'Watch yourself on the way down; we had a lot of stoning on the way up.' I looked at his vehicle and commented on the holes in his

Makralon protection on the back of the vehicle. He said 'Jesus Christ.' He only then realised that they had been fired on. It was about six Thompson rounds the size of your thumb.

BOGSIDE ON 'THAT' DAY.

Soldier, Royal Signals

In 1972 I was a member of the Royal Signals serving with 216 Signal Sqn; I was attached to 1 Para when they were sent from Belfast to Londonderry because the authorities were expecting trouble. This turned out to be Bloody Sunday; the 31st of January, 1972. We were told not to go past the Free Derry Wall, not to get involved in a running battle and not to enter McFadden Park. We were the ones who came under fire, not as the media reported at the time, that we fired first; we did do everything that we were told not to do, so I suppose we did disobey orders, but as I stated, WE WERE THE ONES WHO CAME UNDER FIRE FROM THE IRISH, NOT THE OTHER WAY ROUND.

Another time when I was there, I fired a gas canister into a crowd, we had to fire them so that they arched over into the crowd, everyone bar one man dispersed, he stood there watching it head straight for him, it hit him smack in the face, breaking his nose & knocking him unconscious, we all wondered why the hell he didn't move out of the way, we just put it down to him being a 'Thick Mick.'

In 1974, I was in another area of Derry attached to 20 Medium Regt Royal Artillery when we were sent to search a house that had a gas leak, the Captain in charge of us told us not to smoke as there was a gas leak (like we had lost our sense of smell or something, we all noticed that), he said that he would keep an eye open outside to make sure that no-one tried to blow us up, whilst we were inside searching, he stood in the doorway and, probably not thinking, lit a cigarette, immediately blowing up the house with us still in it. The CO immediately had him posted and RA Records in their wise wisdom gave him a mention in dispatches oak leaf for being mentioned. Albeit something like: '... get this stupid bastard out of my regiment now, if not sooner...' and promoted him to Major on posting. With people like that watching your back, who the f-- - needs the IRA?

I.E.D.S IN LONDONDERRY, 1973

Bob Gallagher, 26 Squadron, R.A.F. Regiment

We were out on patrol one day – in brick strength – in the walled city of Londonderry, assisting the Royal Artillery, and as we passed a particular house, we were invited in for a cuppa. We had no sooner settled in, when the section commander received a call over the radio that 3 bombs were placed at various locations within the area we had just patrolled. In short, we had been followed by the bastards who had actually been planting the IEDs.

After a quick exchange over the radio, we had to go back over the area and clear it of all the planted devices, assisted by the RUC; suffice to say, nobody was hurt in that area on that particular day.

The one thing that stuck out in my mind as a 19 year old squaddie at that time was this: an old man at the time had arrived back after a visit to his local pub, only to be confronted by a cordon around the area which included his actual dwelling place. The old man aged about 70 at the time was absolutely frantic at the thought that his wife may be in the house which was directly above the shop where one of the devices was laid. The policeman who was with us at the time had to firmly restrain him and this poor man was crying and screaming that his wife was in danger, even though his house had been cleared, he was physically fighting with the police and trying to get past them to get to his wife. The terror in his eyes at the thought that in his mind his wife may be killed was a sight I'll never forget.

Bob later pointed out to me that IED did, indeed, detonate but that, thankfully, there were no casualties.

The IRA, supposedly the defenders of the Catholic community had, yet again, risked the lives of their own people on the off chance of killing or maiming a member of the security forces. No matter how much, in the days since the 'Good Friday' agreement, the IRA/Sinn Fein have apologised, there can be little doubt that, certainly viewed through an historian's eyes, that they caused much terror and panic even in the very communities that they professed to defend.

An excellent example was the Shankhill Road bomb, Belfast in 1993. On October 23, of that year a meeting between senior loyalist faction leaders, including several senior members of the Ulster Defence Association and Johnny Adair, one of the leaders of the UFF, had been scheduled to take place in a flat above Frizzell's Fish Shop on the Shankhill Road in the afternoon. The meeting time was rearranged for later the same day.

However, the IRA's remarkable intelligence network had heard about the original time, location and date of the meeting, and saw an opportunity to remove several of their most senior enemies in one blow. To this end, Thomas Begley and Sean Kelly, two IRA members, entered the fish shop dressed as deliverymen with a large bomb hidden under a cover on a plastic tray. They intended to leave the time bomb in the shop, where it would detonate once they had made their getaway. It was late afternoon on a Saturday so the shop was crowded and, as the two men made their way through the people inside, the bomb detonated prematurely. The device only had an 11 second fuse; Thomas Begley and nine other people, including two children and the owner John Frizzell and his daughter were killed in the subsequent explosion.

The building collapsed, crushing many of the survivors under the rubble, where they remained until rescued some hours later by volunteers and emergency services. Many people were seriously injured in the explosion.

In addition to the terrorist, the following people were killed: Leanne Murray (13), Michelle Baird (7), and her parents Michael Morrison (27) and Evelyn Baird

(27). John Frizzell (63), his daughter Sharon McBride (29), George Williamson (63), his wife Gillian (49). Wilma McKee (38) died of her terrible injuries the following day.

At Begley's funeral – a full IRA funeral with a volley of shots fired over the graveside – Gerry Adams was there, clearly proud to be associated with terrorists and killers.

The Bogside had been quiet for some time, then, as Christmas, 1976 approached, the IRA shot and killed Sapper Howard Edwards, a 24 year old Royal Engineer from Rotherham.

It would be the following spring before the IRA would kill another soldier and again, mystery surrounds the abduction of RCT Sergeant William Edgar (34). He lived in the south of England where he was based with his RCT regiment and was known to visit Londonderry from time to time. On April 15, 1977, whilst on a family visit, he was abducted by the IRA whilst drinking and his body was dumped at a graveyard near the Bogside. The IRA claimed that he was an undercover soldier and, although this was palpable nonsense, they stuck to their outrageous story in order to excuse yet another cold-blooded killing of an unarmed man.

The Republican area was the scene of the ambush of a Scots Guardsman, Lance Corporal Alan Swift (25) who was dressed in plain clothes and was sitting in a car on Letterkenny Road. The IRA alleged that he was a member of the Army's undercover Intelligence unit, 14th Int. He was the only soldier killed anywhere in Londonderry during 1978.

The Bogside, over the course of the next few years would provide a fertile breeding ground for the 'Derry Youth' who continued to take their toll of injured soldiers, but it would be 1981 before another soldier would die. On January 20 of that year, an IRA sniper shot 21 year old Private Christopher Shenton of the Staffs Regiment whilst he was closing a security gate just outside the notorious estate. Three weeks later, the IRA, having observed UDR soldier David Montgomery (27) at his place of work in a timber yard in Strand Road, callously shot him dead in front of work mates.

In 1982, the Bogside's killers raised their ugly heads again. Just before lunchtime, on 'April Fool's Day' an IRA gang opened fire on an unmarked Army car which had just left Rosemount RUC station. The gang had held civilians hostage whilst they prepared their attack. As Corporal Michael Ward (29) of the Signals and his REME comrade, Michael Burbridge (31) drove past, they opened up with several automatic weapons and killed both the soldiers.

Later that same year, on October 15, Private Alan Stock (22) of the Queen's Regiment was killed and a comrade badly wounded by an IRA bomb which exploded near a cemetrey on the southern edge of the Bogside. In the spring of the following year, a mobile patrol of the same regiment was attacked by petrol bombers on the south-eastern side of the estate. As the soldiers jumped clear, an IRA sniper shot and killed Private Neil Clark who was 20 years old. Private Clark who was due to marry the following month was from Margate in Kent; he was the last soldier to be killed by terrorist action on the Bogside.

On March 23, 1987, two police officers were killed at Magee College by an IRA bomb whilst they were investigating a crime scene. They were two

Detectives; Sergeant John Bennison (41) and Inspector George Wilson who was 31. They were the last two RUC officers to be killed in the Bogside.

CORPORAL 'B' ROYAL SIGNALS

Bogside

One time, whilst on mobile patrol we had a young 18 year old squaddie with us, on his first tour. He was in the back of the PIG. Not long afterwards, we arrested a man and kept throwing him into the back of the PIG. However, he kept coming straight back out, and we kept battering him and throwing him back in. Anyway, after about 3 or 4 goes at throwing him back in, we noticed that the young squaddie simply kept kicking him straight back out! Another time, I once saw another squaddie from my platoon fire a rubber bullet at a rioter, but got the angle wrong and instead of it bouncing away from him it bounced back at him, knocking out 3 of the poor sod's teeth. Once, we were driving past the Free Derry Wall, and, as usual, the kids were stoning us when we noticed a small boy at the back crying; we stopped to ask him why, and he replied that he had no stones to throw at us. Naturally, we being idiots, actually got out to collect some for him, and, on our way back out, he was also stoning us, waving to us with a beaming smile on his face. Talk about mad squaddies!

Major Pat Moir, Royal Artillery

Whilst manning the permanent check point at the old city wall gateway opposite the Rossville flats, a dear little old lady discreetly slipped me a flask of tea, for myself and the boys. In previous tours in Protestant areas we were always well fed and watered by the local populace, but here in the heart of Catholic Derry, this had to be a first. Being artillery men we were less robust than most infantry Regiments and we had won the 'Wilkinson sword of peace' for 'With Hearts and Mind' projects, on a previous tour. All my bods were decent young men that any parent would be proud of. Obviously living in the Rossville flats, this lady had daily contact with the Regiment, and must have been impressed with the way we conducted ourselves, but her kind gesture left me in a quandary. Not wishing to offend her I waited till she had gone then treated the flask as booby trap. Behind a sand bag wall, I gingerly opened the flask; all was normal, but I still could not be sure that there was no ground glass or some other lethal additive in the tea, so I committed the contents to a drain. As the dear little lady returned to leave the city, I returned the flask with great gratitude. 'Was there enough sugar, dear' she asked, 'Just perfect', I replied. As the years pass, I often think of that kind soul, and if the lads and I had supped that tea it would probably have been the best cuppa we had ever tasted.

Ted Edwards, 12 (Minden) Battery, Royal Artillery

Now a month in the maiden city of Northern Ireland – Londonderry, patrolling the infamous Bogside, made famous by the Paras and a, now well known Minister for Education within the Sinn Fein party; Martin 'I never fired a shot on that day' McGuinness, MP! Also on the West side to patrol, were the Creggan, Galliagh, Shantallow, plus other Republican/Nationalist estates. Then there was the solitary Loyalist 'Fountain' area, just outside the citadel and boasting 'West Bank Loyalists: Still Under Siege, No Surrender.' Well, they had to give the Bogside's 'You Are Now Entering Free Derry' a run for its laundering money!

September came along with my 22nd birthday and a two day belated present. 'CONTACT, WAIT OUT.' Top cover (on an armoured Land Rover) and six feet of me stood up exposing around two feet, to whoever felt it necessary to take a shot at me. My 'oppo was on detachment from 'Billy Smart's Circus' of performing midgets, so he didn't have a lot to expose! Either way, he was a Lance Jack, and led the way through the front gardens, as we merrily hard targeted down the street in the direction of the RUC's later confirmed shoot, with whom we had been patrolling with, on mobiles. The 'Howards' QRF was with us in no time, followed by our Brick Commander and our other member; our pissed off driver, who had stalled the Land Rover on an incline as me and my 2IC bailed out the back of it, was not a happy chappie. Nonetheless, it was a pleasure to be reacquainted. Throughout the night we sat and chatted about our adventure and like squaddies do during times like this – dismissed it and got on with the job and tour.

One memory which stays with me; is that of 'Snoopy' the dog, our adopted Jack Russell from a nearby house, close to the checkpoint on Buncrana Road. He took a bullet from a Military Policeman. 'Make my day – punk;' as he popped a 9mm into the, now squealing dog, which tried to make its way back home. Amazing, a talking murdering monkey!

Shit happens and we were now into October and becoming hardened veterans of Ulster. We house searched with the curtains closed in the front room, with the occupier watching the Teleprinter giving the days footy scores – 'Oh bejasus, Derry City lost again' – 'Yeah, but the Gunners didn't'! Earlier that day after prising a few floorboards up and then vacating the premises with no result; I swiftly returned, knocked on the door; I now remembered something very important – 'Can I have my tools back – please?' with a face like a tomato.

After a full days searching and finding sod all, we returned to the Fort.

Not all days were like this; we had finds in Rosemount and ended up on the BBC 9 o'clock news followed by News at Ten. One of the largest arms finds at the time and credited to the RUC.

MINI RIOT IN LONDONDERRY

Bob Gallagher, 26 Squadron, R.A.F. Regiment

My mate and I were on bomb squad patrol within the walled city of Derry. One of us was armed with an S.L.R. and I with the baton. Whilst we were patrolling the streets, just along from the 'Diamond' we became aware of 2 girls of about 16, fighting in the street. There were 2 R.U.C. officers, one male and one female who proceeded to intervene, and, as they seemed to have it covered my mate and I didn't get involved. It was about 3pm and quite busy, as we turned to see how the R.U.C. were getting on and then, all of a sudden, the situation had changed.

The two R.U.C. officers were now being attacked by both the girls who were fighting, along with a few others. My mate and I decided to give them a hand as they were trying to arrest the girls and get them into their Land Rover. In short, by the time we had escorted them along the street to the 'Diamond' the Land Rover was crawling along, due to the sheer weight of people now around it. Eventually, we got down to the bottom by the wall and it had now developed into an extremely ugly scene. It was claustrophobic as the crowd were all around us and we had no way out as my mate and I were at the rear of the Land Rover and the crowd were all around doing their usual, kicking, spitting, and punching. Our only defence at that precise moment was to use the baton and butt of the rifle. Fortunately, a nearby VCP alerted the ops room who then turned out the standby section to reinforce us and eventually subdue the mob.

That scene was happening all over the province and being endured by soldier and civilian alike. I had never seen such venom by such a hostile crowd and at that age or indeed any age; it was very scary.

ON THE BOGSIDE

Private Simon Richardson, Royal Hampshire Regt.

My experience of Northern Ireland was from 1989 – 1991; a 2½ yr tour of Londonderry. As most Infantry soldiers are, I was keen to put my training to the test. At the age of 19 I remember my first foot patrol. The week before, I had seen the news; two Royal Artillery soldiers had been killed in the city, when their vehicle was attacked by an I.E.D on the Buncrana Road. Reality hit home when I found out that one of the guys killed had been a pupil at my school.

The two RA soldiers were Gunner Miles Amos (18) from Bristol and Lance-Bombardier Stephen Cummings (24) from Hampshire, who were killed in an IRA landmine attack on the Buncrana Road, Londonderry on 8 March, 1989.

After loading up, we shot out of Rosemount SF base, one by one and hard targeted along the Marlboroughs and before long I found myself in a fire position whilst we conducted or first VCP. The team commander was stopping cars, and I noticed that passers-by were crossing themselves as they walked by. I started to feel seriously concerned and called to the team commander that I thought we were about to 'get it.' As a veteran of many tours, he pointed to the church we were standing outside of, and reassured me that it was normal for Roman Catholics to cross themselves when passing.

The stagging on was hard going at first, until you got used to it; guard at Ebrington barracks was a killer. It was two hours on, two hours off, for twenty four hours, and I can remember being so tired one day, that after half hour in a sangar, I realised I'd been staring into camp through the wrong window. If you were unlucky and the oncoming team were short that was you on again for further twenty hours with no shower or relief from the body armour or a good sleep.

Unlike in the U.K on the precious time we did have off, we were left alone to do whatever we wanted. Getting pissed was a good pastime to relieve pressure, and we soon worked out that if anyone was going to get picked for a short notice patrol or guard duty, it wouldn't be us as we would be unfit due to being pissed.

I remember our first contact clearly as if it were yesterday. We were in Masonic SF base, and I was sorting my kit. I then heard a succession of crack's followed by the thumps and I knew from NI training it was an AK47 (*delightfully known amongst the IRA as the 'Widow maker'*). I ran to the ops room and saw Roy, the guard commander trying to raise Woody in 'kilo' Sangar via the intercom. There was no answer and we all looked very concerned; as I was a team medic I told them I was going to check on him. Anyone who knows Masonic would know there is a 50 metre dash from the back gate to 'Kilo' sangar. I got to the back gate and looked right along the city wall; it looked clear, so I dashed along left to 'Kilo', zig – zagging like fuck and ducking at the same time. I arrived and banged on the locked door shouting for him to open up. He did and I asked him if he was ok; he said that he was and looked a bit shaken but he thought he might have the details of a vehicle.

I then legged it to 'P5A' sangar and saw Nath' who looked very calm and said he was ready to shoot if needed, and, as they were both o.k., I shot back to the ops room and met my team commander. It wasn't long before we were out on a cordon in the Bogside. There were players everywhere and some were openly writing down our cordon position's and counting up how many of us were on the ground; you had to watch your back as they would sneak up behind you and try to listen to what you were saying on the radios.

NEAR MISS IN LONDONDERRY

Soldier, Royal Corps of Signals

I was born and bred just outside Belfast. For as long as I can remember all I ever wanted to be when I 'grew up' was a soldier. As a kid during the 70's and 80's I used to love seeing the soldiers on the streets. I knew every vehicle, could identify the choppers by the sound of their engines. I had relatives serving in the UDR, but that never appealed to me. I wanted to see the world, have my adventure so at the age of 17 I joined the Royal Signals.

For the first few years of my service the troubles, whilst never causing me much concern never quite left my thoughts. I had leave cancelled a couple of times due to security clearance not being granted. When I did get home I was conscious of where I went. I turned up the volume when news of another incident came on the radio. I was in touch with school friends who had since joined the UDR or RUC and told me of how things were for them. While not wanting to join them I had a hankering to soldier at home. I requested a posting to N. Ireland which was granted within a few months. A two year tour in Londonderry. In fairness it wasn't the most taxing tour. I spent most of the time in the Ops room, grew my hair longer than average (didn't all of us?!) and even was allowed out on the occasional patrol. The hours were long and the occasional incident brightened the weeks up, but none of it was happening to me directly so I didn't bother too much. I looked forward to a few beers at the bar in Clooney or an overnight pass to Thiepval and the occasional night out in Portrush.

A fairly regular duty for me however was driving about the province, in plain clothes with one of my mates. Think along the lines of glorified delivery men. One advantage of this was if the run took us near my folks, we would park the CMV in the driveway, tuck our Brownings into the car bag and pop in for lunch/tea. While they lived close to a hard area, it didn't phase me. This was great while it lasted, which was about 8 months. The first I was aware of something wrong was when the SSM asked to speak with me. Not demanded, not requested, but actually asked if I would call into his office and speak with him urgently. I went upstairs, and was marched in to my O.C.s office. He spoke and told me to think very carefully before I answered. 'Have you been visiting your parent's house while on duty?' I figured out straightaway that he knew so I didn't lie. When asked how many times I again figured there was no point bluffing so I admitted that once/twice a month at least. He then told me to go to my room and pack. I did so that evening. The next morning I was on a flight to England. A week after arriving in my new unit I found myself on a plane out of the U.K. I didn't get leave approved for another year and a half. In retrospect I was very fortunate. I was also bloody stupid. Somebody somewhere got this information to the relevant people. I'm eternally grateful to whoever it was.

EVEN PARAS HAVE A SENSE OF HUMOUR

Soldier, Parachute Regiment

Patrolling the streets in Northern Ireland wasn't for the faint hearted, especially not in Londonderry. Everyone had to be on their toes from the moment they left their 'little fortresses' of safety until the heavy gates closed behind them when they got back. Once on patrol you had to maintain a wide space between yourself and the man in front of you while at the same time scanning a wide arc in all directions. The last man in a patrol not only had to do that but he had to turn around constantly to check for anything at the rear which meant walking two or three steps backwards. For the duration of the patrol the stress levels would be off the 'Richter scale', and by the time you got 'home' you felt as if a giant hand had reached down from above and played table tennis with you. Yet day after day, week after week you were expected you walk the streets where everyone hated you and death was waiting patiently to make you yet another military statistic.

'Henry' had just joined the battalion and it was his first day out on the streets. The battalion was stretched to the limits because it simply didn't have enough men to fulfill the tasks it had been allotted, but it was no use complaining as every other unit was in the same boat, and the government didn't give a shit anyway, in fact it constantly tried to play politics with your life whenever it suited it. Having been introduced to his section the night before and spent an uncomfortable night worrying how he would perform on his first patrol, Henry was already emotionally drained. But if the lads could go out on the streets, then he could.

First out the big gate was the armoured PIG that was going along with them in case they needed to be transported quickly to somewhere where there was trouble. Once it was sitting like a giant bullfrog on the opposite side of the road, in ones and two's they all sprinted out after it; lodging themselves in doorways, behind walls and anything else that would protect them. When everyone was out they all stood up and began to patrol slowly, the ugly Humber PIG rumbling along somewhere in the middle. 'Henry' had been given the task of bringing up the rear. Psychologically he was on a knife edge. Every step he took he expected to get shot at and by the time he'd walked the length of the road he was sweating profusely even though it was a cold day. He could literally feel the animosity, even from the young children. Some people even spat at his feet after letting out a string of foul abuse. The rest of the lads ignored it, or made caustic comments about the individuals' sexuality or lack thereof. They were used to this kind of treatment.

Half an hour into the patrol and they came to a busy intersection. He turned to check the rear when he heard the high pitched whiney of the PIG as it revved up and took off. He turned around and saw everyone sprinting like rockets, disappearing around the corner in a flash, following the vanishing vehicle. He was at a total loss as to why nobody had called out to him; he was also left flat-footed. The whole patrol had gone and his ears were telling him that they hadn't stopped either as the sound of the engine was fading into the background noise. Suddenly he felt totally alone and all around him he could see people watching him like a nest of spiders study a lone fly trapped in a web. A good ten seconds passed before he reacted, and then he bolted, from zero to top speed in no time at all. He never realised how much absolute fear could motivate you. He took the corner like Charlie Chaplin in one of his comedy movies, bouncing off a parked car and falling flat on his face as he did so. He must have skidded five feet along the path and in the process collided with a woman and her shopping. The contents of her shopping bags dropped all around him like falling confetti, but he didn't give a flying fuck, and was up in a millisecond only to find that the crowded street was empty except for civilians looking in the general direction that the patrol would have gone.

This couldn't be happening to him; not on his first day. With his brain churning over in a thousand scenarios now was not the time to worry about being a gentleman and he barged his way through the crowd swearing and screaming for them to get out the way. Forty or so yards further on he zoomed past an alleyway and was about to keep on running to the ferry and Liverpool when he heard a loud 'Fooled you !' combined with a roar of the PIG's engine kicking in. He skidded to a halt and turned around. There crowded in the entranced to the alleyway was the rest of the patrol grinning like Cheshire cats and slowly emerging back end first was the PIG. It was their 'Welcome to Northern Ireland gift' and it wasn't even his birthday.

LONDONDERRY

Brian Baskerville, R.A.O.C.

Some of the largest arms finds in the province were loyalist doomsday caches. (*So called, as the Loyalists had long prepared for a massive 'backlash' against the IRA and for the day when the conflict became a civil war and a British Army withdrawal.*) Generally old 7.92 Vetterlis or Martin Henry or Lee Enfield No1 and found, usually in chests in lofts. These weapons were in pristine condition and had been brought into the province very early in the 20th century by a certain ex army officer whose name escapes me but he was famous, or rather, infamous for it. He was reputed to have brought around 3 million of such weapons. These weapons and their ammunition were all stamped on the butt with the UDA 'Hand of Ulster.' Normally the find would be as a result of the elderly occupant of the house dying and his or her family would come to clear out the house and find the arms and hand them in. Although these were not treated as terrorist weapons due to the time lapse since their import and never having been used, they were usually sent for cutting up.

However the family were given the opportunity of retaining one and having it deactivated and unbelievably turned into a very unusual standard lamp. The Vetterlis were really good for this because they were extremely long rifles.

One night after a usual session in the 'Greenfly' bar, which was on the ground floor of the block, I was woken by the guard at about 1am. 'You're wanted up at your office in HQNI – NOW!' I quickly staggered out of bed, dressed and made my way up to the HQ., where we had a portacabin under the control of 12 Int at the back of HQNI. When I got there, a very sober looking boss was standing in his office. He simply said: 'There's been a bombing at Ballykelly. Some of our lads were in there and I need to get across there now. You're driving; get a couple of guns and meet me at the gate in 5 minutes.' On this occasion my own gun was in my desk drawer at work (under lock and key) so I got a couple more out of the filing cabinet in Colin's office. I gave one to the boss and stuffed the other down my trousers. Still intoxicated, I went and got a car and we were off. It was a bit of a horrible night and we drove out in the Londonderry direction over Glenshane. It was an out of bounds route but the quickest and most direct. We were in a covert car and armed so we went that way; always risking the possibility of a VCP by either side.

About half way there, I can't just remember how but suddenly I was wide awake with a huge tree right in my headlights coming towards me very fast. I swerved and somehow managed to miss it. The boss in the passenger seat never said a word. When we arrived we had to do the usual things that we did which that night involved a lot of standing around and looking and getting very cold. There was nothing we could do for any of the victims because they were dead and the way the bomb had gone off it had taken out the roof support pillars and the large flat concrete roof literally came down flat. Thankfully, the bomb didn't kill many. Fortunately, there were only such things as broken legs and perforated ear drums for our lads but nobody was fit for work. I had sobered up by the time we set off home. The tree was never ever mentioned.

LONDONDERRY: RECOVERY UNDER FIRE.

Bill 'Spanner' Jones, R.E.M.E.

We were in Fort George, an old Navy base on the 'wrong' side of the river. It was late Autumn and the sun was going down as we finished work and went back to our billet to clean up for dinner, followed by a quiet evening with any luck. We were just getting into our lockers, looking for something clean to change into from the dirty coveralls we were wearing when the door opened and AQMS (Q) Simms came in with a posse of Gunners in his wake.

'Ah, Cpl Hinds,' he called out to Mat, our recovery mechanic, 'Just the man; we have a PIG broken down in a bad place and the locals want to burn it. Half the regiment are out to stop them but we need it out of there quickly. Who do you want to take with you?' Better take Jonesy I suppose, he's the PIG man. I had been known since Belfast the year before as the

'PIG man' not something I sought but just had to put up with it. 'Take young Staffs as well,' Q added 'It will be good experience for him, the gunners will provide an escort, and they know where it is.'

So it was set, Matt, Mick and I, we put on our flak jackets, grabbed our weapons, SMGs and followed the gunners out of the door. Mick and I walked with the Gunners and I asked what they knew about it; one told me he had been the driver, and that they had been driving along on a regular patrol when car sped past them and fired shots which bounced off the armour of the PIG. The Lt in command told him to chase after the car. 'In the PIG?' I asked, surprised, because they were not high speed pursuit vehicles.

'We were keeping close,' the driver added 'until we went over a speed bump and then everything locked up and we couldn't move at all.'

Matt came around with the wrecker, a Bedford RL fitted with a heavy jib and winch gear, a good old workhorse. I climbed into the cab and told Matt what the driver had told me. Mick stowed his toolbox in a side bin and joined us in the cab which had only two seats so I crouched on the engine cowling in the middle, the gunners, eight of them, had mounted their open Land Rover and we followed them out of the front gate at which point I stood so that my head and shoulders were through the cupola in the cab roof, my SMG at the ready. The gunners had plenty of fire power but we had to show willing.

As we left Fort George, we turned right taking a road unfamiliar to me but they knew where they were going and it took about fifteen minutes until we could see the glow of small fires and the sound of constant shouting, a sure sign that we were close to a riot, and there we were. It looked to me like all of the regiment were out not just half.

I looked at the surrounding houses, I had been told that one of the complaints of the locals was discrimination in housing but these were better than anything I had grown up in back in Birmingham. There was a large square of grass, about half a football field, to our right with a road running around it and the houses set back behind their own gardens around that. The PIG was to our right, facing us with the right side close to the grass so it was on the wrong side of the road, the speed bump just behind it. We turned to pass the PIG as we needed the back of the wrecker at the back of the vehicle, a loud howling came from the crowd of onlookers, they could see what we had come for and did not like it, they wanted to burn it.

Matt drove past it, put the left wheels close to the curb by the grass, reversed up to it and stopped, leaving the motor running as we would need that to power the lifting gear. Now we had a decision to make, the SMGs would be more of a hazard than a help as we climbed under and around the stricken PIG so we agreed that the best course of action would be to unload the weapons, put the mags in our pouches, we each wore one, and stow the weapons behind the seats, out of sight. This done, we left the cab, locking the doors behind us and got on with what we hoped would be a routine task.

Suddenly, 'Thunk thunk' came from the jib, followed by 'Ping ping 'from the PIG's armour, a more familiar sound. 'I think some one is shooting at us.' Matt stated. 'Tell them we're REME,' I said, 'they're not supposed to shoot at us.' It was an old joke but it made Matt smile, 'You go tell 'em; I'm busy.' The shots had come from the direction of the nearest houses; the Bedford had lift controls between the cab and the work bed on both sides so Matt went to the grass, keeping the wrecker between him and the houses.

'Pang pang,' two rounds bounced off the tread plate that formed the work bed, Mat was a big man and had to keep his head down but was not deterred. There were no sparks or whining sound that you get in films or TV, just the sound of the rounds hitting the different metals, the armour of the pig, the tread plate, the thick, heavy steel of the jib. We worked out later that the gunman was coming between the houses, firing off two shots and moving quickly before the Gunners could line up on him, he seemed to have freedom of movement behind those houses. Matt vaulted up onto the work bed, he was very agile for such a heavily built man, and he clambered in through the cupola with a 'Thunk Thunk,' to speed him on his way.

We were making good progress, but a couple more pings encouraged us to keep on the move; the PIG was between us and the gunman but he was not giving up.

'Scrrrk, Scrrrk; ping ping,' a new tactic; the shooter was trying to deflect shots off the road and under the PIG bolt ends. Mick looked at me. 'I think someone's shooting at us Bill.' I grinned. 'Don't worry; Matt's going to tell him not too soon.' Ping, ping. It was under this type of constant pressure, that we managed to get the job done. This true story is dedicated to all 'attached ' personnel , tradesmen, engineers, signallers, medics, and all who due to the nature of their jobs cannot do as S.O.P.s dictate, when coming under fire, take cover, set up defensive positions with covering arcs of fire. Some just had to be there and take it because that is what we do,

RSM Haydn Davies, Royal Regiment of Wales

It always amazed me how we found some really decent people living among all the baddies. Some retired folk, some ex-army WW2 just letting their lives drift along and not communicating with anyone. They would talk to us quietly as they passed, often just to say very quietly 'God bless you son.' When we used to change the men in the OP on the top of the Rothville flats it took a whole platoon to do so. When men were detailed for the task of this OP they did not know if it was for two days or a ten day stretch. As a unit we were keen on the change over being very tightly controlled. Two days after we left and handed over to an Artillery unit, they lost either two or three soldiers shot to death. They were casually taking extra stores up the stairs for the OP on top, rumours said, extra rations and blankets. One of the soldiers killed had a German name; The IRA made much of this by saying we were employing mercenaries from our base towns in Germany. We got our fair share of trouble from there; it was demolished eventually.

The soldier is thought to be Guardsman John Van-Beck who, far from being German was a Scot from East Lothian. He was 26 and died of his wound on September 18, 1972, having been shot the previous day.

BEAUTY IN THE BOGSIDE

Corporal Mick Copp, 2nd Bn Royal Green Jackets

Every day was a riot day, especially on Saturdays, and the programme went something like this:

12:00 Out of bed after a late night stoning the Army.

13:00 All meet up at William Street; smash a few shop windows, hijack some cars.

13:30 Stone the soldiers as they respond to the trouble.

17:30 Home for tea.

19:00 Back to the streets for more stone throwing.

22:00 Home for a drink then bed to prepare for tomorrow.

Occasionally, something would happen to lighten the mood. One day whilst firing rubber bullets at the yobs that were lobbing milk bottles and throwing stones, something did happen. A tall, beautiful girl came walking from the Bogside; she walked down the road and then proceeded to cross it between the two warring factions. She was dressed in a trouser suit and held her head up high and the mob stopped throwing stones and we stopped doing anything and just stared; she was really worth looking at. Once she was safely across the road, both sides resumed the fight. Someone in the Saracen said: 'Do you know who that was?' It was a rhetorical question because straight away he answered his own question: 'That was Sean Keenan's daughter.'

Sean Keenan was an IRA Godfather at the time and no yob was going to risk a kneecapping by hitting his daughter with a stone. I think that her name was Bridget and little did she, or we, know that within weeks, we the Green Jackets, were going to bring grief to her family.

On March 14, 1974, Colm Keenan (19) described at his funeral as a member of the IRA's Londonderry Brigade was shot by soldiers after a fire fight in Dove Street. The Jackets had penetrated one of the 'no go' areas and had three soldiers wounded in the incident.

Chapter 11

The Creggan

The Creggan is a huge council estate which was as huge as the Ballymurphy estate in Belfast; it also bred as much trouble. It was built onto a large bank that faced the entire city. It had its own IRA unit and bordered onto the Bogside, and it started life as an army camp to house the Americans in WW2 prior to D day.

The name 'Creggan' originates from the Gaelic word 'Creagann' meaning 'rocky ground.' The estate is a large housing complex situated about two miles from the centre of Londonderry. It occupies a picturesque but exposed landscape, overlooking the River Foyle and the city centre. The estate is one of the oldest in Northern Ireland, with the first houses being completed in 1946 and in common with other working class areas, the Creggan has suffered an excess of violence over the three decades and more of the troubles.

When Creggan camp was vacated in 1944 the locals from the North and the South moved in, and, bit by bit it became the estate it is now. It had its own factories which employed mostly women. Different Regiments of the Army lived there in 1972 in the Knicker Factory. This was a focal point for local hatred and many shots were fired into the walls, almost as a pastime for the gunmen. There was an entire infantry battalion dedicated to the Creggan; it had a host of safe houses; with small blocks of flats and groups of shopping areas. The Army and RUC suffered in almost the same way which the English police have in Moss side Manchester today! The one difference is, even on a bad day in Moss Side, the Creggan was always much worse.

In 1971, the 'Angle irons' (Royal Anglians) suffered two fatalities as first, in October Private Roger Wilkins (31), was shot in Bishop Street and then, a month later, Lance Corporal Ian Curtis (23) who was shot, close to the River Foyle.

The heartbreak for the Gunners wasn't over, and on July 11, Bombardier Terence Jones (23) was shot by an IRA gunman as he walked along Great James Street; worse would follow. Another month would pass, before the CVO (Casualty Visiting Officer) had to make another call as a direct result of events in Londonderry. The Coldstream Guards lost Sergeant Anthony Metcalfe (28) in the Creggan to a gunman's bullet on August 27.

Before the year was out, the Royal Artillery would lose three more of its soldiers as the 'drop shorts' or 'long range snipers' as they are known – affectionately, it is claimed – would mourn the deaths of Gunner Angus Stevens (18) and Lance Bombardier David Tilbury (29) both killed in a firefight at Lewis lane on October 27. They would then lose Gunner Richard Ham, shot, in the Creggan, just as that terrible year of 1971 drew to a close.

The following year, the worst in the troubles, in terms of SF fatalities, would witness 4 killings in the space of a week, as the Creggan grew in tragic notoriety, claiming 3 of them. On January 27, the estate claimed the lives of RUC Sergeant Peter Gilgunn (26) and Constable David Montgomery (20) shot in an IRA

282 BULLETS, BOMBS AND CUPS OF TEA

ambush on the Creggan Estate; a week later, on February 6, the IRA abducted and murdered UDR Private Thomas Callaghan in the Creggan.

In early March, the IRA displayed its ruthlessness and abducted and murdered an off-duty UDR officer, Captain Marcus McCausland who was 47. Before the month was out, another young Rifleman from the 'Jackets', John Taylor (19), would be dead, shot at the corner of Lower Road and William Street. In mid-April, the Gunners lost two young Bombardiers killed in a bomb blast in Brooke Park; Eric Blackburn (24) and Brian Thomasson (21) were added to the 'drop shorts' grim tally.

The very same month, the Royal Welsh Fusiliers lost Corporal Gerald Bristow (26) and the Worcesters lost Private Martin Robinson (21) both shot by the IRA on the same day, less than half a mile away from each other. In late May, the Official IRA abducted Ranger William Best from on the Creggan Estate and took him to waste ground and then cold-bloodedly shot him in the head. What left a particularly nasty taste in the mouth about this deplorable murder was that the IRA had promised his parents a safe homecoming for the soldier. Ranger Best, who was 18, wanted to come home on leave from his unit – the Royal Irish Rangers – in Germany. His parents, apparently, approached the local IRA commanders who promised him safe passage to return to the Creggan as long as he was in civvies. The very same night of his return, he was abducted and murdered. The Official IRA – known to their Provie enemies as 'Stickies' – admitted murdering the young soldier.

He had returned home to the Creggan Estate and, wisely, took the conditions to heart and did not wear his uniform. On the evening of May 21, he left his parents' home and went to make a telephone call. The next morning, his body was found on waste ground by a nurse returning home from the night shift; his face was bruised and the wound – a single shot to the back of the head – bore the hallmark of an IRA-style execution. This murder led to an outcry amongst the locals and his funeral was attended by almost 5,000 people and was led by many Catholic priests.

One finds it impossible to get into the mind of the local Official IRA commander who claimed that Best was seen in suspicious circumstances and was abducted and 'tried' and found guilty. I have italicised the words tried as it was by one of the notorious kangaroo courts so cherished by the IRA. Quite what went through the spokesman's mind when he said the following, is quite beyond my limited comprehension: 'Once we had him, there was nothing we could do but execute him.' It is widely believed that the revulsion felt by their supporters led to a permanent ceasefire by the Official IRA.

The author spoke to one of his sources in the Belfast area and he indirectly confirmed that a leading Creggan Provisional and now prominent Sinn Fein official 'had a hand' in it, to a degree.

'It appears that the Stickies [*Official IRA*] had come under sustained propaganda from the Provos in the area for being 'soft', in that they had detained – and then released without harm – a British military intelligence officer/soldier they had detained in the district a week earlier.

Apparently this chap gave evidence to the Saville Inquiry that the Stickies had decided to release him but a leading Provo – now a top Sinn Fein man –

THE CREGGAN 283

popped up and was hovering outside the Derry house angling for him to be killed but the Sticks ignored him. This was turned on them by the aforementioned Provie. So, the group that detained Best felt under pressure to show they were as hard as the Provies and when they had Best, opted to kill him, to illustrate their credentials. It would appear too that Best, like other local Catholics in the forces home on leave, were known to indulge in the rioting that was going on. Then, the Provies played their part in manipulating the genuine anger and disgust at Best's murder, as it offered them the added bonus of removing the Sticks as a rival 'force' and cleared the field for them to present themselves as 'the genuine and only' resistance available; cynical as hell.

In the June, the UDR lost Private Ted Megahey(45) and a couple of days later, the Royal Artillery continued to suffer, losing Gunner William Raistrick who was only 18 and Bombardier Terrence Jones (23), both shot by the IRA on the Creggan. The RUC station, at Strand Road was the scene of the next SF death in the city when a young Fusilier – Kerry McCarthy (19) – was shot by the IRA; he was the last soldier to die on the Creggan for almost 3 years.

As the Autumn of 1975 began, the Yorkies lost their second man of the troubles, when another son of Leeds, Private David Wray of the Prince of Wales Own Regiment of Yorkshire was shot and wounded on the Creggan estate. Despite his brave fight for life, he died of those wounds in the Altnagelvin Hospital on October 10.

The Creggan would claim no further soldiers' lives for several years, but when that tragedy did occur, the IRA showed that there were no depths of depravity to which they wouldn't stoop. Rifleman Christopher Watson who was 20 was allowed leave from the 'Jackets' to visit the Creggan and comfort his wife who had just delivered a stillborn baby. Whilst in an Inn at Rosemount, two IRA gunmen walked up to where the unarmed soldier was chatting to his wife and cold-bloodedly shot him in the head and killed him. He was the 18th Royal Green Jacket to die in the troubles; tragically, there were 31 more members of this famous Regiment to die before Operation Banner had run its long and tortuous course. He was, however, thankfully, the last soldier to die on the bloody Creggan.

The Security Forces suffered many deaths and injuries on those streets during the full period of the troubles. On 27 January, 1972, two RUC officers were shot dead whilst on mobile patrol. Sergeant Peter Gilgunn (26) and Constable David Montgomery (20) were ambushed and killed on the Creggan Road. Officer Montgomery had been due to marry less than 2 weeks later.

On 21 March, 1988, Constable Clive Graham (25) was shot and fatally wounded whilst manning a VCP at Lislane Drive on the estate. A male bystander carrying a small child was also wounded, as the IRA demonstrated, yet again, that, despite their pious post-incident apologies, they had no regard for any human life at all. Clive Graham was the last RUC officer to die on this 'rocky ground.'

BLOODY CREGGAN

Lance Corporal, 2 Royal Green Jackets

I was in Londonderry in 1971/2 with the 'Black Mafia' and I seen a lot of stuff from both sides which will be eternally with me. I don't want to go into the gun battles and the explosions; there are others more articulate than me who can tell you all about that kind of stuff. I want to tell you about some of the people that we had to contend with, the locals, the mobs, what some would call the flotsam and jetsam of a poor community.

We would do foot patrols into the Bogside and we done lots of night stuff in there especially when the no-go areas were up and running. The IRA ran IVCPs (*illegal vehicle checkpoints*) and they done it with swagger and they thumbed their noses at us and the RUC lads refused to go in there anyway. It was only after Motorman that they went in and only with us for protection. Hey, don't get me wrong; they was brave lads and it was their country; they couldn't nip off back to the smoke (*London*) and the Home Counties after a tour like what we done. If there is an arsehole in this beautiful world of ours it is located somewhere in the Bogside or the Creggan; it even smelled like one.

Lots of terraced housing like them northern monkeys lived in (just joshing) (*a jocular reference, one trusts, to the author's northern background*) and outside lavvies and no gardens and Friday night tin baths and one of which – I forget the name – which was on a steep hill. Mind you, they all seemed to be on hills; sod of a run up there. We'd go out in bricks of 4 blokes, usually a brick in front, one in the centre and one following up in the rear. We'd alternate between walking forwards and walking backwards; always watching your back and knowing another geezer was watching your back as well.

As soon as we were through the City walls and patrolling the street, out would come a woman and she'd scream 'Brit bastards!' and honestly, you'd feel like twatting her with your rifle butt. She'd then run in and get the dustbin lid and start banging it on the street making a real din; fair gave me a headache I can tell you. Then another would come out and she'd do the same and then they all started to gather and shout insults at us. The young ones must have been a bit under nourished because none of them had any tits at all; they were all flat-chested ! The older hags had big droopy ones and I smile to myself even today and wonder if they grew them when they got fat ! They were skinny bints with long greasy hair but skinny they might have been but what gobs they had on them. I was called a nigger (my Ma' will tell you that I'm as white as a sheet) a c**t, a f**k pig and thems were the nice ones !!! They threw shit at us, jam rags, piss and even food slops from their dustbins; anything they could lay their grimy mitts on. One of them got some dog shit on a piece of wood and tried to smear me in the face but missed and it went down my arm; I nearly retched and moved on and tried to wipe it off against a wall. I stank of dog-shit all day.

Once the hen patrol had called out the reinforcements, they gathered and began pelting us with anything they could lay their hands on and we had a lot of injuries and a good mate had his ankle broken and another geezer from the Company got a nasty bit of cobblestone in his mush. The kids would join in and I do mean kids; sprogs they were, of 6 or 7 and they would lob whatever they could find or were given. They used swearwords which at that age, they had no chance of knowing what they meant. It was shit, I can tell you and then we'd finish and go back through the City Walls and some other poor bastards would follow us in. Northern Ireland was a shit sandwich and we all had to take a bite. God bless you, mate for telling our side of the story; it needed it.

2 RGJ were involved in several 'beat the no go areas' patrols and sustained some awful injuries which included the shooting of an attached Officer who subsequently lost his leg following an ambush in the Bogside.

THE CREGGAN OR 'PIGGERY RIDGE.'

WO2 Roy Banwell, Cheshire Regiment

The Battalion flew to Belfast and was taken under escort, in coaches to Londonderry. We arrived at Creggan camp or 'Piggery Ridge' as the locals called it (funny, pigs seem to always turn up somewhere!). The camp was much the same as all camps in NI, the layout stayed, in the main, the same, and it was only the size that changed. The camp as I said sat on top of a ridge overlooking the Creggan estate hence the name.

It must have been depressing for the local people to have an army camp prickly with surveillance devices looking down on them. I was, in my spare time, part of the company search team, ably lead by Corporal Phil Lydon. This meant many an early morning start to cordon off an area and search it for terrorists or arms and explosives. On one particular search, we had to go to a flat in the Creggan; occupied by a man and his sister. It was filthy, and in the bathroom, the toilet was blocked, so they had used the bath as a toilet. The stench was vile; in the kitchen, cans of food had been opened and left everywhere. Black bin bags with their rotting contents lying were everywhere; cockroaches swarmed around and fleas seemed to make the piles of clothing come alive. I am scratching myself again just thinking about it. The search had to be as thorough as any normal search; it would have been a sin to miss something just because it was filthy. Every bag was opened and searched, every cupboard, all the cloths thoroughly checked. The CSM WO2 'Skiddy' Allmark, was the Company's search team advisor and he appeared on the scene, quickly assessing the situation and declared that he could see we had everything under control and would see us back at camp for a debrief.

Can you imagine the reception we would receive after banging on a house door at five in the morning ? Imagine waking a family of the hard line persuasion, with a view of searching for a wanted member of their family or to be looking for arms and ammunition after a tip off? All manner of people would burst into the house as soon as the door was open, with us leading the way, rounding every member of the household into the living room for a head count and identification. People would then be arrested, if required, and taken away. Any specialist agencies would then leave if they were no longer required; leaving us to the full bile of the remaining family. The full fury of what was happening to them would pour out and wash over us like a tidal wave. The abuse we received had to be heard to be believed; all mainly coming from the females. The men folk would just let the situation develop and leave it to the girls, who are much better equipped at foul mouthed abuse.

Getting bricked and bottled was a constant threat; especially for the back man, who had to walk backwards all the time covering the rear of the patrol. The local kids – whom never seemed to go to school – would follow us around in packs. As soon as they were able to walk they would be out on the streets bricking and bottling the troops. The older kids would be out directing the campaign of attack. They would also use their Hurling sticks (this is like a curved and flat baseball stick) to great effect, to get the extra range they needed to avoid getting caught. We didn't mind the kids being about, (yes they were a nuisance) but it meant that we were reasonably safe from other dangers, like snipers and small explosive devices. We would stick as close to the public as possible, even at the risk of being spat at or verbally abused. They knew what we were up to and they didn't like it one bit. The chances of being shot or blown up when standing so close to a civilian was slim, but as we have seen in the past; not impossible.

On one occasion, the Land rover that I was commanding was moving to a location to cut off a car, and we rounded a corner to find the car minus the driver coming towards us. Luckily the car mounted the curb and hit a garden wall before us. We gave chase to the driver on foot but his head start allowed him to escape. On returning to the car, the remainder of the multiple had secured the area and we were the proud owners of an American Armalite rifle that had been stuffed between the front seats. A good day's work and another lethal weapon removed from the terrorists' hands.

I had to admire the expertise of the rioters in Londonderry; their accuracy with stones and petrol bombs was excellent. They could follow your patrol along a road throwing bricks, bottles and petrol bombs over the top of houses with such accuracy that it was beyond belief. Their co-ordination of the riots was excellent and must have taken years to perfect and organise. I must admit, that at times I was scared for my safety, but this made it all the more enjoyable. The thought that your life hung in the balance and the outcome was as much to do with luck as it did with our cunning, made for thrilling times. I am not a glory or danger hunter by any means; people would have to experience what it was like to be caught up in a riot situation, to appreciate what I mean. I am sure, that the feeling was the same for the rioters as it was for us; why else were they so popular with the locals?

IN THE CREGGAN

Private Simon Richardson, Royal Hampshire Regt

About two weeks later our team was on patrol in the Creggan, and a small boy had walked beside me, and said that his Granny had said he couldn't play in the reservoir area as there was a bomb there. I remembered a day or two before as I walked into the same area a local had said: 'Hey, soldier, don't go down there.' And, as I turned to ask why a door was shut firmly in my face and I'd thought nothing of it. I'd now put 2 and 2 together and told my team commander. A full scale clearance was instigated and a 1000 lb bomb was found. Whilst on the cordon I stumbled upon the firing point; it was two wires sticking out the ground and the distinct imprint of two bodies that had been lying on the grass ready to detonate the I.E.D some 400m away. When I look back, the shooting was clearly done to draw us into one side of the city whilst the bomb was setup the other.

I soon became very confident, as I was 'volunteered' to be the one who stopped and chatted to drivers on VCPs. Although you shouldn't set patterns, someone in the ops room was still putting us on the Craigavon Bridge at set times and I became very good at remembering names faces and addresses, which seemed to impress some of the locals. A mate of mine went one step further and for some reason was remembering vehicle VIN numbers.

We started to get paranoid that any intelligence that was given on the patrol briefings had already been compromised. An example being when we did a two night lurk on a store in a retail park. We had been told it was going to be blown up and there was a chance of us arresting or killing terrorists. The night after the lurk finished, it was indeed firebombed by a very crude device, yet we were not on the scene to stop it.

I was also search-trained and found myself on many house searches, whilst the ones who weren't would have to stand out on cordons for up to 5 hours at a time.

We would look out the windows at them and rub our hands and make gestures as to how warm we were inside; just for a bit of fun and a wind up. I never really liked doing the searches, especially when there were young children. Most of the houses in the Creggan area weren't very well furnished and most didn't have a penny to their names. Apart that is the players, I remember in one player's house, his drawers were full of nice clothes from a well known High Street shop; the tops were £40 – £50 each. I pointed this out to the RUC man and he asked him how he could afford such items as he was on the dole, I still remember the cheeky grin and shrug that was given as if to say: 'Why ask what you already know?' However, the RUC man was soon distracted when my mate Baz let out a scream from the kitchen. He had been searching under the sink and had found a mouse trap that had been laid; naturally, we all fell about crying with laughter at Baz's expense. The only thing that was found was a rifle barrel cleaning rod, and the player said he had bought it from a junk shop and didn't know what it was and used it to prop up his fire guard.

That same player had walked past me in the Bogside once and said: 'Hey, soldier; watch out for lampposts,' but, as he kept on walking there was nothing to go on. However, not long after that I was on mobile patrol on the waterside and we heard several small explosions close by the Foyle Bridge. The OC came up on the net and said we were to stand off at a safe distance as it could be a 'come on' as a civvie had called it in as being on the railway line behind their house under the bridge. We waited at the roundabout a few hundred metres away, resisting temptation to investigate. As we suspected, a secondary device in a lamppost litter bin went off; it was in a lay by on the bridge approach road and an I.C.P (*incident control point*) position. The OC was switched on that evening and probably saved our skins. After 18 months continuous hard work, I was considering leaving, but, after a chat with the OC, I was persuaded to go for Close observation platoon selection. I completed the selection and came second, and my mate Gaz, who was in our platoon came first .

I spent the remaining year in the province working in COP. I then felt I was doing a real job and felt I had made the right decision. We all enjoyed the fact that we were allowed to grow our hair and we would look like hippies when we came off an OP and hadn't shaved for a week or so.

As you can imagine there were lots of incidents on our tour, but I just like to remember the good times. But sometimes I'm taken back and can remember things as clearly as if it happened yesterday. I could be laying in bed awake for hours at night going over and over things in my head or just sitting watching TV and something triggers me to drift back and start remembering. I feel a bit embarrassed about the whole thing sometimes. I have been to combat stress in Surrey and they gave me some help which I use when this happens; I'd just like to thank them for their help.

THE CREGGAN

Corporal Mick Copp, 2nd Bn Royal Green Jackets

The Creggan was a large housing estate situated just above the Bogside and overlooking the River Foyle and, in another time, the views could have been described as scenic. The place was as dangerous as the Bogside for us soldiers. There was an Army post situated between both these estates and every soldier who ever served in this city would have heard of it; it was called Bligh's Lane. It was an old factory complex and stood next door to a shirt factory producing Ben Sherman shirts and was one of the largest employers in the city.

It was, essentially, a platoon position, but the rioting got so bad that it was reinforced by several platoons. Most days the base was stoned and petrol-bombed with occasional nail and blast bomb thrown in for good measure. With the crowd numbering several hundred on a good day, we would force them back with PIGs, CS gas and rubber bullets.

One Saturday, it was apparent from very early on that this day was going to be different and my platoon was sent to assist and even the CO was there. Colonel Mostyn was known to us as 'Eggs on legs' as he was rather rotund. Hundreds of them began to gather on the green above the base which was, unfortunately several feet and seventy yards or so below. We could see a dumper truck driving backwards and forwards to the local dairy and dumping milk bottles for use by the crowd, who in turn, filled them with petrol, urine or anything else they could think of.

After several volleys of milk bottles, a large flatbed truck appeared at the top of the green and it was obvious what their next move would be. Two scrawny 'volunteers' climbed into the cab and it began rolling down the slope towards the rolls of barbed wire surrounding the base. The crowd cheered as it rolled forwards and it was then that their plan went pear-shaped. Just before the truck rolled into the barbed wire, the driver jumped out and was promptly run over by the rear wheels; now it was our turn to cheer. Fuelled by adrenaline, the driver jumped up and rejoined his comrades, but the passenger was frantically tugging at the driver's door before realising that it was stuck. As the truck hit the wire, he managed to throw himself out of the cab and promptly landed in amongst the coils of barbed and razor wire and we cheered even louder. Several of his mates managed to drag him clear back into the crowd minus most of his clothes !

The Colonel had had enough and, with his helmet on back-to-front, and minus his gas mask (we carried ours everywhere) he stepped forward carrying a megaphone to address the crowd. He informed them in his English upper class accent that if they did not disperse, '...something most unpleasant will happen.' The crowd responded with a roar of laughter and abuse and it was obvious by their replies that we were not the only ones who thought that he resembled an egg. He summoned two riflemen and ordered them to fire CS gas into the crowd and it was painfully obvious to us what was about to happen. We got our gasmasks handy and, sure enough, as the gas landed amongst the crowd, it slowly rose in a spiral and drifted back towards the bases. The Colonel who had no gas mask began slowly walking backwards, until on reaching his vehicle, he began fumbling for his mask, as we were all enveloped in the gas; it was now the crowd's turn to cheer.

ON THE FOYLE

Hugh Heap, Army Bomb Disposal

The Craigavon Bridge crossing the River Foyle in Londonderry was essential to military and civilian movement from the Waterside area on the east bank and the main part of the city lying west of the river. All traffic was controlled by military check points established on both levels. I was serving as an EOD (Bomb Disposal) Section Commander in Londonderry in October

1972 when the intelligence boys came up with a tip-off that the IRA were experimenting with a floating bomb that could be detonated by a radio signal to a receiver attached to the bomb. The information suggested that this would be used to attack the bridge – those who know this bridge will realise this to be the product of rather fanciful thinking; not just by the IRA, either! Nevertheless, the threat had to be taken seriously, especially as even a minor explosion on the water under the bridge would be seen as spectacular success among IRA supporters.

The Brigade Commander gave his short orders to the, then, guardians of the bridge, the Royal Horse Artillery, and the EOD Team.

'It must be stopped from reaching the bridge,' he said. Easier said than done,' said the Gunner's CO. 'The bomb will have to be detonated via a radio controlled signal to an aerial on the bomb' said I, without too much confidence about how to stop it.

At that time, there was evidence that radio-controlled bombs were likely somewhere in the Province and the boffins were coming up with detection equipment which could, theoretically, detect a receiver and then jam any radio signal transmitted to it. My problem was that, to date, nobody had managed to detect one and, even if we did manage this unlikely feat, how was I going to stop it reaching the bridge? My solution; rely on my Royal Signals colleagues for the first part and then employ a marksman from the Gunners to attack it with small arms fire when the bomb the bomb was in range. The Gunners' CO took some convincing, but, not having any better ideas, he accepted my plan and made his own to support it. No-one stopped to ask me how I intended to recover the bomb from the river after we had successfully completed the tasks set in my plan!!

My other big worry was that, even if the threat was real, there was no indication of when it would be, and I had very limited resources within my section which had also to go about its operational duties across the 8 Bde area. I set up a roster to have an EOD team on watch alongside an RHA search squad and marksman. Shortly before midnight, some 60 hours, and several false alarms, after the operation commenced, I was the ATO on watch when clandestine movement was spotted at Waterside by an infantry patrol. My Royal Signals colleague identified a trace from a radio receiver which, he said was 'different' to the false alarms, and then a sharp-eyed member of the search squad pointed out a tea-chest at some 200 yards distance floating towards the bridge. With little delay, the marksman fired about 15 rounds during which the lid and aerial came off and the trace disappeared, but the tea-chest was still afloat, by then, less than 50 yards from the bridge. It was at that moment that I realised that I had made no plan for recovery!! A vain attempt was made to catch the tea-chest with a grappling hook but, of course, this was all far too late and the tea-chest and its contents were gone. On the positive side, I did see it was filled with bags of apparent home-made explosive, therefore I was ready to claim it as the first radio-controlled bomb detected in the troubled Province. But how could I prove this??

My only idea was a visual search of the mud banks after first light so, via the Brigade Major, I arranged that I would be taken on the river in a light boat or 'tinny' crewed by an efficient and determined sailor. Of course, one couldn't simply go cruising down the river in those days. An armed escort was needed to watch our backs and, as always, this task fell to the ubiquitous squaddie. The morning happened to coincide with the last few hours of a 4 month tour of duty in the Fort by the Light Infantry. My quickly nominated escort was a young Lance Corporal who, an hour or so earlier, had got out of bed in the knowledge that he had only to complete a few minor handover duties then pack his kitbag and head for Blighty at the end of the day. He will have felt secure in the knowledge that, while his battalion had suffered several casualties during its time in Londonderry, he was one of the lucky ones. When I met him at the boat, he was not a happy bunny, his assumed security having been turned on its head. I knew we would be exposed and vulnerable out on the river, but here was just the man I needed to keep an eye out for enemy on the banks; his own security being his priority, so meaning that I had nothing to fear for my own!! Almost inevitably, the search proved fruitless, but I still claimed the 'bomb' to be radio controlled. My escort was back at the Fort to move to Aldergrove and his flight home to his family. I did not keep a record of his name but, to that Lance Corporal, I owe my thanks for watching out for me and my apologies for raising his blood pressure on his last day in the Province.

'Felix' was the radio name given to EOD Operators, hence the well-used term 'Fetch Felix.' It was a dangerous job, some would argue far more dangerous than the squaddie in a brick, section or platoon, patrolling places such as the 'Murph or Andersonstown. A glance at the roll of honour for the RAOC will show the deaths of 23 such 'Felixs'. For these incredibly brave men, the 'longest walk' would prove to be their final one.

LONDONDERRY CONTACT

Rifleman Tim Marsh 'C' Company 2 Royal Green Jackets

It was a lovely sunny day in Londonderry. Our section was on the junction of Strand Road and Great James Street. Senior Riflemen Tony Moore and 'Chalkie' White were standing by a pub in Great James Street carrying out searches on the public. I was carrying out searches on the other side of the road, facing down Great James Street. Suddenly shots rang out down the street; the rounds impacted the wall just above my head. This was time for me to take cover, so I ran over to the pub doorway. There was a lot of screaming coming from the locals. Very frightening for me, as I was a young rifleman and had not been in Northern Ireland that long. Tony and 'Chalkie' took cover behind the large concrete blocks that made up the barrier; the Royal Engineers called them dragons' teeth.

Platoon Sergeant Mick Mander came running over from Waterloo car park to support our section. Mick, Tony and 'Chalkie' skirmished down Great James Street towards the gunman's location. Halfway down the Street they made contact with the gunman and he dropped to the ground. An ambulance from the Knights of Malta (who were a Catholic ambulance corps) pulled up at the top of the road, saw to him and then he was whisked away to a hospital.

As a measure of how forensics improved, later on in the troubles after incidents like this a follow up would be carried out to find any empty bullet cases. My section 2 I/C said a handgun had been fired at our section and the next day, the local paper which one of our section acquired said that Mr. 'F' had been murdered by the British Army.

I think it must have been a few days later; we were still based in the Waterloo car park. For all of us it was a very tiring time, catching up on sleep when we could. I was with 9 platoon 'C' Company and it was our rest period, in some dilapidated portacabins. We had all been asleep for a couple of hours, when, suddenly there was a huge explosion outside the location, which of course woke everyone. We found ourselves covered in broken glass from the windows. We all rushed outside to see what was going on, only to be greeted by a rain of pigeon shit! The birds must have had the same shock as us!

The car park floor was covered with small red and white metal fragments which had come from a 'Mothers Pride' van that had exploded outside our location. A section corporal Ted Case had been checking on the sentry's by the front Police post and had been blown down the stairs by the force of the explosion; he was rescued quickly by members of the company from the debris.

Ebrington Barracks

In the troubles this housed a resident Infantry Bn, before that it was the old 'Sea Eagle', a naval shore base for the Royal Navy in World War II. Derry was a Submarine base, but I cannot vouch for that. The Barracks faced the River Foyle and the square was open to the view of the city from over the river. It was dodgy to hang about in the open, although the distance was about 800 metres. The Barracks were very well built of stone and brick and was as good as any barracks that I have stayed in. The married quarters; these were occupied by married soldiers, but this surprised me, because they were outside the barracks and were quite vulnerable.

OPERATION MOTORMAN IN LONDONDERRY

Rifleman Tim Marsh, 2 Royal Green Jackets

I was a young 20 year old Rifleman in 1972. Our company was based in the county locations, in towns with names like Kilrea, Maghera, Dungiven, and Magharafelt. There was talk in our location that we were being relieved by the Royal Artillery and told that an operation was about to happen; we returned to Ballykelly Camp.

We had only been there for a short while and I remember the early morning move from Ballykelly Camp to Ebrington Barracks. Our Convoy joined other companies forming up on the main square. One of my memories of this Operation was up behind the Creggan, in a farm area. We had been joined by 'B' Squadron of the Blues and Royals detachment and it was the first time I had seen a Saladin Armoured Car. The Officer in charge was carrying a Mauser pistol, which he had bought it in Germany in a holster strapped to his leg. The task we had been set was to man an OP overlooking the Creggan, to catch any IRA men moving out of Derry into our area.

I can remember being in a college above the City walls overlooking the Bogside and Brandywell, and, through the night, Corporal Pete Watts, myself and Bernie Udall manned the OP overlooking Lecky and Lonemoor Road. That night, there was an explosion from a BT junction box, which scared the crap out of us all, and we radioed the explosion report through to our ops room. None of the other Platoons were near this area at the time. Others in the company had been doing patrols in the Bogside and graveyard, and we were informed by our section Commander that we were to escort the Royal Engineers by Land rover to various barricades in order that they could rip them down with huge diggers. This happened in the early hours of the morning, when it was very dark.

Well there was just me, my SLR and a driver and his huge Scooby doo! (wicked name for a digger!) . Our barrier location was on the junction of Lecky Road and Anne Street. The noise was horrendous at that time of the morning. How people slept through that and we didn't draw attention to ourselves was amazing; also that no one came to investigate. After the huge barriers had been ripped down, we escorted other Engineers, brushes and paint in hand, to cover over anti-British Slogans on the City Walls.

To conclude; 'C 'Company had one of the more difficult tasks; entering the Brandywell area of the Bogside to carry out searches. A significant amount of bomb making materials was found during this time by members of the Company; this of course was a huge morale boost for us all.

Chapter 12

Rural Londonderry and other areas of the City

SHANTALLOW

Shantallow was a mixed area which crossed the sectarian divide slightly and Catholics – however uneasily – shared the ground with Protestants. It was in the very north of the city, sitting on the west bank of the Foyle, above the Creggan. It first came to notoriety, in 1990, when Patsy Gillespie became the IRA's first 'human bomb' and he was killed, along with 5 soldiers from the King's Regiment at nearby Coshquin.

It was on Moyola Walk, in the Shantallow, that the Light Infantry lost Sergeant James Whiterock (24) as he was shot by the IRA whilst on foot patrol; he was on the final part of his third tour. Just five days before the Christmas, UDR soldier Private George Hamilton (28) was shot dead by the IRA as he worked as an electrician at the Croppy Hill reservoir. That same night, the UVF demonstrated that they could be as bloody as their Republican counterparts and murdered five innocent civilians at the 'Top of the Hill Bar' in the city.

1973 arrived, and an off duty UDR soldier, Staff Sergeant David Deacon was abducted by the IRA and murdered; his body was dumped at the side of the Letterkenny Road, a few miles outside of Londonderry.

Shantallow, Londonderry, near where Patsie Gillespie was living
when used as an IRA proxy bomb (Joe Jurkiewicz)

294

RURAL IRELAND

Bob Davies, RAOC

And finally on my second tour in 1979 as SAT Belfast Section an amusing incident involving a traffic accident. Corporal Dave Major, a number two at the time, was returning from an admin run to Lisburn when his vehicle crashed and overturned. He reported the accident to the Belfast Section ops room, where I was plotting tasks on a map, with the immortal words 'I've just turned the Rover over, over.' I've heard people use these words since in jest but this IS a true story.

On January 25, the following year, whilst conducting a follow-up investigation after an IRA attack, the previous evening, the Duke of Wellington's lost a young officer, Lieutenant Howard Fawley (19). He was killed instantly whilst examining an explosive device at Ballymaguigan, Co Londonderry. Later that same year, the Staffordshire Regiment lost Second Lieutenant Michael Shaw (21) when he was shot by the IRA on the corner of Racecourse Road and Greenshaw Crescent in the northern part of the city.

With just a week before the Christmas festivities began for 1975, the IRA struck twice in Bank Place in the city centre. Gunner Cyril MacDonald (43) and Craftsman Colin McInnes (20) were killed by an IRA bomb. They were killed together while manning an OP/Sangar on the Derry Wall next to the entrance into the city on Strand Road.

Four weeks later, Gunner Mark Ashford aged 19 was shot dead while manning a busy pedestrian checkpoint in Great James Street in Londonderry on January 17. Later that year, as the Summer warmed up, another young Gunner, 19 year old William Miller was shot and killed by an IRA sniper whilst manning a pedestrian checkpoint in Butchers Gate in the city.

Just two more weeks had passed, as the rest of the UK basked in record-breaking Summer temperatures, before the IRA had moved just 26 kms east and killed Private Alan Watkins (20) of the Royal Hampshires in Dungiven.

On February 23 of the following year, UDR Major, John Hill (45) was shot by an IRA gunman at his place of work in Daphne Gardens in the city. This tactic of targeting off-duty UDR personnel by the IRA continued and five weeks later, at Maydown in the city, Corporal Gerald Cloete (46) was shot and killed as he drove to work.

On October 30, 1993, several UFF members entered the Rising Sun Bar in Greysteel, near Limavady in Co Londonderry. Inside was a Halloween party in full swing, and so the masked men were not noticed until they produced an AK-47 and an automatic pistol, and started shooting into the packed crowd; one of the men yelled out: 'Trick or treat !' as he opened fire.

The bar was targeted because it was in a Catholic area, and thus represented a 'Nationalist electorate', according to the UFF statement which followed the atrocity. Ironically, two of the eight people killed in this attack were Protestants, and none of the victims had any known political role or affiliation within the Troubles. The UFF sickeningly claimed that they conducted the attack as a revenge killing, following the Provisional Irish Republican Army's killing of nine people in the Shankhill Road bombing seven days before, in a failed attempt on the life of Johnny Adair and other senior loyalists.

The following contributor has asked me to dedicate the following piece to his father Jozef (1925-2008). It is my honour to do so.

LONDONDERRY

Gunner Joe Jurkiewicz 137 Java Battery 40 Field Regt RA

When we arrived in Londonderry, I was 18 years and 3 days and the next 4 months were to be a rollercoaster of a ride, with bombs, bullets and stone throwers. We were billeted near the edges of Londonderry and part of the Regiment was on a ship and the rumour was that they got good food. Amongst the lows of the tour was that one of my friends, Gunner Kerry Venn was shot dead by a sniper.

It was late afternoon and we were between 2 housing estates; we were leap frogging each section, covering ourselves as we were going up the slope. Suddenly a shot rang and we thought they had missed, but unfortunately not; at that moment if any trouble had come about all hell would have erupted we were in no mood for games. But this is where our training kicked in and we acted professionally.

(Gunner Venn who was 23 and married was killed by a single shot as his patrol was on waste ground on the outskirts of the city.)

Our section was shot at three times altogether; a friend was shot in the leg and on this particular patrol, two of us were told to stand down and

Shantallow, Londonderry (Joe Jurkiewicz)

go on the next one. As a consequence, we were playing pool when it was announced over the speakers that there had been a shooting. The third time the whole squad nearly got hit in the same Shantallow area; a single crack flew overhead, and within a heartbeat, the squad had dropped to the ground except for one Gunner who was known to be slow. Then, as he stood there, rooted to the spot, a burst of machine gun fire just feet in front went from one end to the other of the patrol; just like you see in the movies with the dirt getting kicked up. If the gunman had aimed higher, a lot of soldiers would have been shot that day; as always, nothing was found of the sniper.

On a lighter side, if you can call it that. On our notice board they would list all the hits and misses of the day; there was one where they were on the lookout for a gunman who had had his arm shot off by a burst of a GPMG (*General Purpose Machine Gun*). I wonder if they ever found him!

There was a picture of our squad leader talking to a known terrorist without knowing it and, in true squaddie fashion, someone had written in a funny caption below it. This same squad leader must be one of the luckiest men alive because we were out looking for a landmine, when his squad got out of their vehicle right on top of it ! The Bomb Disposal guys blew it up and lot of house windows in the immediate vicinity were broken that day and I bet a lot of squaddies were cheering; did our government pay for new windows? A rioter was shot in the head and we were told that, sadly, he was brain damaged so a representative from our group went to apologise; we gave cover because all we needed then was the IRA to come out.

VCP, Co Londonderry (Joe Jurkiewicz)

At our base, I was coming back from the showers – just a short walk from our sleeping quarters – when suddenly the earth shook and it started raining steel. Just a short distance away, a car bomb went off without warning, as far as I know no soldiers were hurt, except for those in the sangars who were blown off their feet. Finally there was a black American living in the Shantallow area; of all the places to live in Ireland he picked that area and of course he was the only non white person there. We believed that he was one of the gunmen but we had no physical proof only that we gave him a good search every time he came to a check point. This tour was very intensive and now I can understand how our fighting men and women can relive the past as if it was yesterday.

THE MARINE HOTEL, BALLYCASTLE

Jimmy Mac, Ulster Defence Regiment CGC

The passage of time has erased the exact dates from my mind, but I'm almost certain it was 1978. For some reason or other I think it was a Saturday, because when we arrived, there was a large number of people gathered around the cordon of Land rovers, barriers and tape. The day had started as any other day and, as always, we were going to be busy. At that time we were working up to 120 hours per week; one minute everything would be quiet, and then out of the blue we'd be whisked off to wherever we were needed. Often we would be told to get our kit together and prepare for being away for a few days; sometimes this wasn't needed and was purely precautionary, but more often than not we would find ourselves out for 3-4 days at a time.

Our immediate area itself was pretty quiet and low-key compared to some other areas, but we had our moments with a number of bomb explosions and shootings in our town. As I said, this particular day started like many others. We were briefed, and my section was tasked with 'Eagle' VCPs. This is where you fly out by helicopter, land in a field somewhere, then make your way to the roads to perform Vehicle Check Points for a period of time before moving to another location. On this particular day we were already on the heli-pad awaiting the approach of the Wessex when we got a message from the Ops Room telling us to wait, and to disregard the previous Orders. A few seconds later the Intelligence Officer came running out of Bn. HQ to tell us that a bomb had just exploded inside the Marine Hotel in Ballycastle causing extensive damage, and that we were being tasked to the area immediately. Both the helicopter and the pilot that day were from the Royal Navy, and anyone who served in the province and who is familiar with the helicopter pilots will know what I mean when I say that the Royal Navy helicopter pilots were renowned for being more than a little 'hairy', and they didn't disappoint us that day. The whole way to Ballycastle we could have reached out and touched the trees or the roof tops. He was trying everything to make us puke and he made no bones about it, but we loved it, with the exception of one lad who hated flying. When we flew he was always sitting beside or opposite the door, for obvious reasons).

We arrived in Ballycastle after about 20 minutes in the air; the pilot hovered near the Hotel for a few seconds, just long enough to allow us to get a view of the area and to get our bearings, before moving to a green area just inside the cordon and hovered about 10 feet off the ground, and then the Load Master shouted 'JUMP'. There were a few anxious looks, but when we realised he was serious and that the pilot had no intention of landing this chopper, out went our packs, closely followed by us. When flying in helicopters you didn't wear your beret. Today was no different, and the people gathered to watch had no idea who we were, although I remember seeing a face in the crowd I knew. I hoped that she hadn't recognised me, and was pretty sure that that was the case. One of the biggest problems for soldiers of the Ulster Defence Regiment was being recognised, particularly by Republicans, and no matter how you tried this was almost impossible because somewhere, sometime, it was inevitable that you would be recognised, and therefore compromised; as well as your family.

We had a quick brief of the situation before going about our business. The getaway car used by the bombers had been located and was abandoned on a road just outside the town and I and another L/Cpl were tasked to make our way there, observe the vehicle, and wait for Felix (Bomb Disposal) who were on their way. We checked our maps before being ordered to approach the vehicle through a densely wooded area, which we did. After what seemed like an eternity fighting our way through thick branches and pine needles, we emerged out of the forest/wooded area full of cuts and scrapes. There on the road in front of us was the suspected getaway car, with the engine still running and the doors wide open; the typical scenario. We radioed through our position, then watched and waited, and a short time later saw the distinctive shape of two Bomb Disposal vehicles approaching. They stood and talked for a few moments before deciding to let the abandoned vehicle 'soak'. Our task now was to accompany them wherever they went and act as their cover. They informed us that they were going to do a recce of the hotel and asked us to follow them. When hearing that we had made our way on foot, they invited us to go with them, which we did. I have to say that this was our first time in a Bomb Disposal vehicle, and I was on cloud nine. These guys were the heroes of all British Soldiers, and here I was working with them. But any thoughts of grandeur were soon dismissed as we arrived back at the Hotel and you could sense the seriousness and apprehension.

They planned to do a sweep of the Hotel perimetre first of all and asked us if we were OK with that, and we acknowledged that we were more than happy to do whatever they needed done. One operator then donned his protective suit, and before we moved off he told us to follow him at a distance; which we did. He made his way round the perimetre of the Hotel, with Andy (the other L/Cpl) with me about 15 yards behind. At one point he stopped to try to move some rubble out of his way. The cumbersome weight of his protective suit was obviously hampering his movements, so we closed in on him and cleared a path for him through the bricks and rubble. He thanked us and we joked with him, and I said that he could buy us both a beer later. He moved on along the side of the hotel, but a few seconds later, all hell seemed to be let loose as the side wall of the Hotel was blown out in front of us.

Those responsible had placed a secondary device inside in the hope of murdering soldiers and policemen in any follow-up search. This was a ploy the IRA and other Republican terrorists had used successfully in the past and would, unfortunately, use many more times in the future. Thankfully this time they had not succeeded, and we were very lucky boys. The blast blew out the side wall of the Hotel only a few yards in front of the ATO, and we were only a few feet behind him. Andy and I were blown off our feet by the blast, as was the Felix operator. None of us were badly hurt, although I banged my tail-bone on a pile of rubble and it still gives me pain today. All three of us were covered in dust, and as we looked up we could see that Felix was struggling a bit to get up because of his heavy armour-plated suit, so we each grabbed a hand and helped him to his feet, then proceeded to dust ourselves down. I realised that we were alright and hadn't suffered any injuries, but for me the scariest thing at that time was the ringing in my ears. I could see people talking to us, but I couldn't hear a thing, and the deep, penetrating ringing inside my head was frightening because I feared that might be deaf. A few minutes later, although it seemed like a lifetime, the ringing subsided and it everything was fine. If I remember correctly this all happened around midday, but what we found really surprising was that we were back in Camp that same evening. The Felix guys came to our camp and stayed there that night, and they did buy us a beer. It was the closest I've ever been to an actual explosion, and I can clearly remember thinking that these guys (Bomb Disposal) put themselves in that position on a regular basis.

We worked closely with the Bomb Disposal on many occasions, but that was my very first time 'up close and personal', and I will never forget it. I can't remember if anyone was killed or injured in the initial explosion at the Hotel earlier that day, but what I do remember very clearly is walking back through that cordon covered in dust and dirt, full of cuts and scrapes, and being stared at by the hundreds of onlookers. Looking back, they must have thought we were a couple of untidy scruffs, but little did they know; welcome to the world of Northern Ireland terrorism.

In late 1977, Magharafelt, some 50 kms south west of Londonderry and only 6 kms from picturesque Lough Neagh was the scene of another soldier's death in the county. 34 year old Lieutenant Walter Kerr of the UDR was killed when a bomb, planted underneath his car exploded as he set off to drive to work. The following February, 11 kms north of the scene of Kerr's murder, another UDR soldier, Corporal William Gordon (41) was killed along with his daughter when an IRA bomb detonated as he too, drove to work. Lesley Gordon was just 10 years old when she died alongside her soldier father at Maghera.

In May of the same year, the IRA shot another UDR soldier, Private Thomas Ritchie (28) whilst he was on mobile patrol on the Gulladuff Road. The scene of his murder was very close to where the Gordons had been killed by an UVBT several years earlier. The following September, the tactic continued and off-duty UDR man, Private Alan Clarke (20) was murdered as he walked down Hall Street in Maghera.

On November 17, 1983, the IRA targeted an off-duty UDR soldier Brown McKeown at his place of work at a shop in Maghera. Whilst the 40 year old man sat with his 13 year old son in a car on Coleraine Road, he was approached and shot. The gunman could see quite plainly that the young passenger was almost within the line of fire, but shot anyway.

On March 8, 1989, the Royal Artillery's roll of fallen continued to rise when the IRA detonated a landmine on the Buncrana Road just outside of the city. Gunner Miles Amos (18) and Lance Bombardier Stephen Cummings (24) were both killed instantly by the blast; several other soldiers were injured. In October, the IRA killed a TA soldier, whilst off duty; Thomas Gibson (27) was waiting for a lift to work, in Bank Square, Kilrea, County Derry.

On May 31, 1993, whilst driving – off duty – along the Carrydarragh Road, Moneymore a UVBT exploded under the car of Christopher Wren of the Royal Irish Regiment. Private Wren was 32 and his death was to prove a milestone in the long period of violence in Co Londonderry. Although the trouble had not yet run their vindictive course, as far as soldiers were concerned, this was the last fatality through terrorist actions in Co Londonderry.

BALLYKELLY

WO2 Roy Banwell, Cheshire Regiment

The darkest day for the Battalion in Ballykelly was the 'Droppin' Well' pub bombing. The Battalion had been in NI for nearly a year, and my unit had just been extracted from an operation in South Armagh. As we were driving back to Ballykelly, I was told that I had been promoted to Sergeant that very day, so I was in a tired but happy mood. We arrived on the outskirts of Ballykelly just as dawn was breaking. It was with a due sense of dread that we saw the cloud of smoke hanging over the town. Thinking the camp had been attacked, we radioed in to find out if it was safe to approach the area. We were allowed into camp and were informed it was the Droppin' Well pub that had been blown up the night before. A small bomb had been placed next to a structural support in the main dancing area, and when this support was blown away the roof came down and crushed the people below it. The bodies of the dead were laid out in neat rows in the Guardroom; so many bodies, and so many young people; their lives cut short.

11 soldiers had died that night, eight Cheshire's, two from the Army Catering Corps attached to the Battalion and one Light Infantryman. The Droppin' Well had been out of bounds so many times as a security risk but in the interests of normality the place was opened up again for use. I myself

had been in there with my father the week before, when my parents had visited us. When I arrived home after our debriefing session, I found Bridie sitting on the stairs crying. Our two little boys lay in bed asleep, when the angel of death had visited Ballykelly, and she was convinced that I was dead and would not be coming home again. She had spent the whole night crying on the stairs. That night we lost some very close personal friends and we will always hold their memories with great affection.

On one very exciting mission my patrol, along with Corporal Doug Holmes, were tasked to cover a 'wedding' between two very prominent IRA families. Doug was on the high ground a couple of hundred yards from the church grounds, and I was in the graveyard between a tree stump and a square gravestone. There was only room for me so the remainder of my four-man patrol were on the outside of the graveyard but in close support, in case I needed to extract myself quickly.

Doug was using long lenses on his cameras and I had a small hand held camera; between us, we took just over a thousand pictures. The Platoon's photo developer, L/Cpl (Joanna) Jones had his work cut out producing three copies of each photo all by hand. The mission went beautifully and the photographs, could have taken pride of place in the bride's photo album. A lot of intelligence was gathered in that small space of time, and it was one of the few times that we ever got feedback from the tasking agents. It was normal to do the task, hand over the information and hear no more about it.

AFTER 'DROPPIN' WELL

Dave Langston, Army Catering Corps

I was serving at a Junior Leaders Regiment in the Midlands when I was called into the SQMS (Q's) office to be told. 'You're off to Northern Ireland next week as part of the Pool.'

The ACC held a 'pool' of cooks that basically went wherever they were needed in the province, mainly to units who were short on 'Cabbage-Mechanics.' After three days leave I flew to Aldergrove and on arrival I made my way to the transit office to await my transport. After a wait a driver from the RAOC arrived and we made our way to a non-descript van. As I got in the driver said 'That's yours,' and pointed to an SMG in the passenger foot well. I spent my first night across the water at Moscow Camp and the following day went down to Ballykinlar where I underwent N.I. Training.

Having completed that I was driven to Ballykelly where the Cheshire Regiment were based. It was only on arrival that I found out that I was there as a temporary replacement for one of the ACC lads killed when the IRA bombed the 'Droppin' Well' Pub late the previous year. I should point out, that amongst the 18 people killed there, 11 were soldiers and two of them, Private Terence Adam and Private Paul Delaney, were Army Catering Corps. Although I was only there for a couple of weeks it was a strange experience, knowing that not far from where I slept members of my own corps had lost their lives.

I moved around the province quite a bit ending up in Armagh, West Belfast and Kinnegar, just along the road from Palace Barracks. Whilst I was in the Province, with other units, I did half a dozen patrols whilst I was there but to be honest not a thing happened. The ACC wasn't the most prestigious of regiments but some 20 odd years later when I was compiling a Roll of Honour for NIVA that I saw that six ACC lads lost their lives in the province, it sort of brought it home that although we didn't do the time on the ground many did that the threat was still there. Those lads who patrolled the streets, fields and glens 24/7, day in day out, put their lives on the line every minute for months at a time. I guess that shows the mettle of the British soldier.

One of the things that struck me was seeing the lads come in from their patrols; they were knackered and as young men, some looked aged beyond their years. All they wanted was some scoff and a brew. They were tired, sometimes dirty, sometimes they had been out for long lengths of time, and sometimes they had seen friends injured or possibly killed. I guess that the conflict took its toll in more ways than one. My abiding memory of the conflict ? I had left the army and was on a weekend break on the south coast with my wife and daughter. I heard on the news that a young soldier had been shot dead whilst at Lichfield train station. William Davies was 19 and a member of the Royal Regiment of Wales. He had just completed his 12 weeks basic training and was on his way home on leave. His callous murder shows the length to which the terrorists would go and that no serviceman or woman was ever really safe.

Since NIVA started I have like many, become more and more aware of the sacrifices made, the number of those who suffer physically and/or mentally and of those who are homeless who once served in the military and police in Northern Ireland. That's why it was formed to try to help and to provide an online meeting place for those who served in the province.

Dave, known personally to the author does himself an injustice and, although often the butt of many squaddie jokes, the 'Aldershot Concrete Company' was invaluable to the lads on the ground. The question was often asked amongst serving soldiers: 'What's the hardest course in the Army ? Chefs, because no bastard ever passed it !' But the ACC lost 6 men whilst in Northern Ireland. These were Private Leonard Thompson (1971), Sergeant Peter Girvan (1977), Private Terence Adam, Private Paul Delaney (both in 1982), Private John Mayer and Private Richard Biddle who were both killed in 1983. These 'slop jocks' were frontline soldiers like the rest of us.

ON THE LONDONDERRY BORDER

Corporal Mick Copp, 2nd Bn Royal Green Jackets

In late '71, I was on Border patrols with Recce Platoon. It was dodgy, because even in those early days, 'the boys' were getting their act together and culvert bombs were a real threat. But, at the end of the day, patrols had to be done and you just hoped that it wouldn't happen to you. One day, the normal section patrol, consisting of the Ferret and Land Rover was approaching what I believe were the ruins of the customs post at Buncrana. The post had been partly demolished. We came up a dirt track to what was left of the post and as we drove up onto the main road, two men ran from the bushes and stood next to the Irish Customs Post, about 50 yards up the road. One of them was carrying a large parcel and the other a handgun. It was obviously a bomb team who we had disturbed in the act of finishing off the job of demolishing the post on the northern side.

The southern customs man was not a happy bunny and we could hear him shouting at the men to 'Bugger off and play somewhere else!' These were very early days and we, even if so inclined, could not have shot them as they were over the border; notwithstanding that the man with the revolver was not so stupid as to point it at us, let alone fire it. We last saw them running down the road. In a postscript to this incident, I recently read a book by Liam Clark and Kathryn Johnston, two Irish journalists. The book was an unofficial biography on Martin McGuiness and in chapter three, a man known as John Joe McCann describes this very incident. Who knows; perhaps if things had have turned out differently, we could have changed the face of Irish politics!

TOOMEBRIDGE

Jimmy Mac, Ulster Defence Regiment CGC

Again, the exact date eludes me with the passage of time, but it was about 1980. We were on our way into Toomebridge In County Londonderry. More often than not this would be a hot-bed for trouble, as it was a predominantly Republican area, and staunch at that. Trea Gardens was a cauldron of hatred, as was the local hotel at the corner just as you entered Toomebridge itself. A typical patrol into Toome (as it's referred to) would be to exit the Land Rovers just outside the area and patrol in on foot behind the vehicles, with the driver and top cover man the only two men in the vehicles. As you entered the corner of the main street you would be jeered by those gathered outside the hotel, then the jeering would give way to bottles and bricks, and it wasn't unknown for the occasional battle to break out between them and us as they attempted to snatch our rifles from us.

It wasn't unusual for some of the full time guys to go out on patrol with one of the part time Companies and we had a permanent base in Toomebridge RUC Station. Two men would be based there in a fortified room upstairs and their job was to monitor every vehicle passing through the area and check their details against those stored on military file at HQNI (*Head Quarters Northern Ireland, based at Lisburn*). Basically the two full time lads would be in there for anything from two days to a week at a time, depending on what was happening, etc. The RUC had no dealings with us, and we had no dealings with them as far as this particular job was concerned. We took in our own food and cooked it ourselves; it could be boring and monotonous. When the guys inside Toomebridge RUC Station were being relieved it was usually our own full time lads that went in to perform the change-over, but not always.

One particular day I was going in with one of our part time patrols, and we had already dismounted from the vehicles and were just turning the corner when the sound of smashing glass broke the silence, closely followed by the thuds of bricks and stones against the Land Rovers. One of the perpetrators must have been feeling particularly brave this day because he ran towards big 'Dessie', one of the part time Corporals and proceeded to try to pull the SLR from his grasp. For his troubles, he got to see the butt of Dessie's SLR up close as Dessie let him have it in the face. Dessie was a big cub, and there was no holding back. I remember that incident with much happiness; it really was a picture to behold.

We made our way into Trea Gardens; this was a Republican den, filled with hatred for all things British; particularly the British soldier. The saddest thing of all was that this vile hatred was in-bred, and as was the case in the majority of Republican areas such as this, they taught their children (and other peoples) to hate from the minute they were able to walk. It was common for the adults to hold a picture of an IRA man/woman looking as ugly as always in their illustrious black beret and dark glasses up to the window as you walked past and at the same time taunting you as they made a gesture with their hand to represent a gun, or to shout at you to let you know that they knew who you were, and where you lived. The stress of that in itself was worse than anything else because while most of it was simply a means of trying to scare you and wind you up, there was always the doubt that perhaps they did know where you lived. And if that was the case then it just wasn't you who was in danger, but your family, your wife; and even your children.

Returning to the subject of children, and in particular those who lived in Trea Gardens, I saw children not old enough to say their own name, yet they could say 'Fuck Off', 'You're dead' and 'British Bastard' with the greatest of ease. I often wondered how any parent could teach their children such things, let alone allow them to say such things without so much as a word of chastisement. In fact, the opposite is true, because instead of rebuking them and telling them not to do that, they would blatantly stand there and teach them more choice phrases. That both saddened and angered me, and even more so when I became a parent myself. The local Roman Catholic Chapel was directly adjacent to this estate, and even that was used to attack the soldiers and then hide.

Getting back to that 'scuffle' earlier on; it was obvious to us that they would have regrouped and called in the heavies and reinforcements for our return. We were aware of this and could have chosen to go via another route, but we weren't for running from anyone. Sure enough there they were, five or six deep across the road outside the hotel (at least that's what they said it was). This was our route out of Toomebridge and back to base, and we weren't getting through without a fight, and a big one at that. There were twelve of us – two Land Rovers with six in each one, and there must have been at least 120 of them, standing with their Hurley sticks, and anything else they could get their hands on. We were severely outnumbered, but we weren't going to run. We were scared, but we weren't going to show it, at least not to them. We had no helmets with us, so we decided that it would be best to radio the RUC Station and ask for assistance. The local' Cop shop' was, literally, only 75 – 100 yards behind us, but they refused to come out and help. This wasn't the first time they had done this, and it wasn't to be the last. I, personally, was locked out of Toomebridge RUC Station on three separate occasions as we battled against a barrage of stones, brick and bottles.

So what were we going to do this time; did we lock ourselves in the Land Rover and try to ram our way through them, knowing that if we injure any of them then we'll be hauled over the coals for it while they get huge sums of British money for their injuries? No, we'll stand our ground and do what we always do; we'll de-bus, and we'll walk behind the wagons, the only difference this time is that we'll need a couple of bicycle clips for our ankles because we were now just about crapping ourselves, and at the same time the adrenalin was making us laugh. There was a bit of a scuffle and a lot of shouting; theirs were shouts of hatred, while our shouts were that of controlled aggression. Perhaps they didn't think that so few of us would even consider trying to walk through them, and perhaps (just perhaps) this took them by surprise, or maybe they thought we were mad as we all had silly grins on our faces and were laughing, but that was the nerves. Either way, we got through and lived to fight another day.

AROUND LONDONDERRY

James Henderson, UDR

The Ulster Defence Regiment was very much a family. I was starkly reminded of this on more than one occasion. I was briefing a patrol, which was a multiple from B Coy of 5th (Londonderry) Bn. Our TAOR was rural Co Londonderry (Dungiven/Claudy etc.).

The assembled soldiers were very aware of course that we had, the night before, taken casualties within another Company of the Bn. The last Land Rover of a mobile had been fired on, resulting in the death of the young driver and serious injuries to others including his father who had been rear cover sentry. This particular evening, as I stepped up to the lectern to give my pre-patrol company brief my Admin WO handed me a signal from Bn HQ, suggesting I read it before I begin.

The signal informed me that I must avoid detailing close relatives to the same patrol, and certainly not in the same vehicle. I read it again and looked down the room. Directly in front of me was a husband and wife and nearby their two sons! Around the room were brothers and sisters, uncles and nephews, nieces, aunts, cousins, couples 'walking out' together; an entire extended family almost.

(*In the author's youth, long ago though that was, 'walking out' and 'courting' were two oft used expressions to describe a couple in a 'steady' relationship.*)

These people had just spent the day at their various civilian occupations, rushed home to change and eat, and with less than two hours between, presented themselves for a dangerous task which would occupy them until at least the following dawn! What must I tell them? That half of them should go home! Or stay in Base while some of their number carried out under-manned duties? I reminded myself that they did not join for that; they were always aware of the worst that could happen. And they were volunteers doing exactly what their forebears had done for hundreds of years, standing up for themselves and their kinsfolk. I read the signal aloud to them and invited them to think of what it meant, and to deploy themselves around the vehicles in conformation of the instruction from Bn HQ.

When we left Base soon after I could see little difference from the usual, wives were sitting behind their driver husbands while busily establishing communications by radio, a sergeant was berating his private soldier brother for holding them up by going for a 'buttie', and nowhere was there an indication that they felt intimidated or concerned. These people were aware that the grim reality was that they were in as much danger of attack while off duty as when on duty. An even grimmer scenario was of course that while off duty they could be taken alive by the terrorist and tortured to death. Sticking together in little family groups who might die together while on duty was preferable.

All the Companies within the Bn received the same instruction. All the Companies were made up of close family groups. I have no idea whether it was a general order to the entire Regiment or whether the Commanding Officer of the 5th had initiated it. I do not think it was even an order; it was probably more of a general guideline.

There was little opportunity to make photographic records back then as it was difficult to find a safe developer. There were times when soldiers innocently sent or took photos to developers such as the local (*censored*) only to have them sent on to Republican sympathisers. Even sending them to English companies was not considered safe. We did eventually have the use of Army facilities in Ballykelly but I never made much use of this. Think of the photos we might have had if we had the use of digital then!

James makes a fair point about the depth of Republican sympathisers in this context; whether they were actual members of the IRA or simply wannabees trying to gain the support or patronage of the local unit is a moot point. The bombing at Springfield Road RUC station where a device was smuggled in and killed Marcus Doglay of the King's regiment in 1972 is a fine example. The civilian worker who smuggled a time bomb into the military wing of the Musgrave Park Hospital in 1991 is another and there were many more. The tentacles of the IRA were longer than most civilians could ever imagine.

Ted Edwards 12 (Minden) Battery, Royal Artillery

Welcome to Fort George, west of the River Foyle and nicknamed by some 'sweaty sock' regiment, but officially known as RUC Shantallow, this was home to our four troops; 1 ('Ard as Fuck), 2 (Alligator), 3 (Bad Brick) and finally; BHQ (Harry's Troop). We shared this 4 star shithole with both the RUC and City Company of 1 Battalion, the Green Howards, who had been in Ulster for some time and based on the other side of the river in Ebrington Bks.

The Fort was a line of Portacabins entombed in concrete walls. The facilities were like some throwback to Victorian times. The ablutions were a disgrace and you were lucky to get a hot shower after your patrolling, but you made do – after all, we weren't in a holiday camp. We had a NAAFI, a canteen that never closed for us, sangars and a gate to man.

THAT WALL AT MONEYGLASS

Jimmy Mac, Ulster Defence Regiment CGC

A few miles outside Toomebridge was the hamlet of Moneyglass, another predominantly staunch Republican area, and a close neighbour and ally to the boys from Toome. I think it was 1980 (or maybe 1981) and we had had a couple of weapon and ammunition finds in the area and there was hardly a day or night that passed without us showing our presence. It's possible to say now that perhaps it was then only a matter of time before we would be hit.

The local Chapel was suspected of harbouring some IRA and Republican elements, as was the adjoining parochial house that was occupied by the priest. The road between Moneyglass and Toomebridge was open, and just past the Chapel and parochial house on the left hand side was/is a dry stone wall. This wall stood/stands about six-feet high and runs for a few hundred yards, at least. There was/is a number of holes in the wall where some of the stones had collapsed over the years, and we would often comment when passing that if ever they (the IRA) were going to ambush us along this route, this would be the ideal place to do it, if only from a distance and using the wall for cover of movement; that's exactly what they did.

I was always the 'stop man'; the one who would stop the vehicles and question and observe the driver and the passengers. I always joked that I was the ideal person for this because of my natural charm, but that was just the usual bit of banter between us. I was always at the door of the rear Land Rover, but on this particular evening I was in the front Land Rover, and my usual place was taken by Ian who was on his very first patrol. In fact, Ian had just completed his basic training and this was his first time 'out the gate' on an operational task. As we passed that wall at Moneyglass the crack of gunshots rang out, followed by the groans of pain. Ian had been hit; he'd been gut-shot, and he was in agony. He was sitting where I would normally have been. We eventually got him to the hospital in our own home town where he underwent emergency surgery, but I have to pay tribute to the Greenfinch in our patrol that terrible night, as I have absolutely no doubt that she saved his life due to her quick thinking and skill while we soldiers spread out in search for the gunmen. Another Soldier was also injured slightly as a bullet clipped his ear and lodged itself in the top of the Land Rover just by the sun visor. It was a topic of laughter some time later because, believe it or not, after being patched up for a graze to the ear at the local hospital, his main concern wasn't that he had nearly died, but 'what will the wife say'?

As for Ian; I can remember that just before he was rushed into theatre he was visited by the Colonel, just as they were cutting his uniform off in preparation for surgery. I can remember the Colonel saying, 'Don't worry son, we'll get you a new pair', to which Ian replied, 'I'll not need them.' And he didn't. We were debriefed, but the next morning we were back at the hospital to guard him. The only people who were allowed in were the medical staff, his family, and his minister. Ian had been extremely lucky to escape with his life and it could so easily have been me. When he was able to be moved he was transferred to Musgrave Military Hospital in Belfast. Ian survived, and he returned to uniform after a period of time, but not to the Ulster Defence Regiment. Instead he joined the Royal Ulster Constabulary; maybe he thought it would be safer there!

DEATH OF AN RUC MAN

Soldier, Ulster Defence Regiment

A policeman friend waved goodbye to his wife and wee children as they stood at the door, but little did he know that within seconds he'd no longer be playing a part in their lives. He wouldn't get to grow old with the wife he loved, he wouldn't get to see his children grow up and have families of their own, and they wouldn't get to see him again, ever. What they would get to witness though, because of the actions of evil men, would be their father's gruesome death. As they waved him goodbye he turned the ignition in the car, and immediately there was an explosion.

The IRA had planted an Under Car Booby Trap (UCBT) underneath the driver's side of the family car. He had, as he had always done, checked his vehicle, but somehow this one had gone undetected. He was, quite literally, blown to pieces. His torso was flung across the passenger seat, his head was lying in the rear passenger seat, and there were bits missing. A man, who only seconds ago was a human being, had now been murdered and mutilated by other so-called 'human beings.' His remains were taken to hospital and the Coroner attempted to put his body together again; he lifted body parts out of plastic bags and placed them where they should be; a piece of an arm, a hand, a bit of his leg; but there were still bits missing. The torso had been lacerated to such a degree that the inner organs were visible. This was supposed to be a human being I was looking at, and those responsible for this evil act were supposed to be human beings.

The policeman who accompanied the remains to the morgue was a friend of the deceased. He's now a Presbyterian minister, and he told me that as he accompanied the remains of his friend to the morgue the undertaker had to stop the vehicle because the smell of the body and the smell of the explosives were almost overpowering. I'll never forget that sight. I realise that this is a gruesome story, but I feel it needs to be told if only to let the world know what the soldiers and the security forces in Northern Ireland had to contend with, and the evil of the IRA that knew no bounds, and had no thought or consideration for anyone, not even the children who would watch their father die in such a terrible, evil way. Maybe God can forgive them, but I can't, and I will never forget.

Footnote: I could never mention the man's name because to do so could identify the family and cause undue and unnecessary pain.

COSHQUIN POSTSCRIPT

James Henderson, UDR

I passed through the area where the Coshquin checkpoint used to be when I was there last year. I was on a visit to relatives in the Irish Republic – relatives I did not dare visit during my time with the UDR. It was against regulations then for UDR and RUC personnel to cross the border except for extreme situations such as funerals etc – when they would be given a Garda escort.

There is nothing to see now but an untidy area of broken concrete and rubbish by the roadside, surrounded by new houses. There are new developments in the immediate area on both sides of the border. The crossing point here is barely noticeable but for the different style of road signs.

Patsy Gillespie was an ordinary man holding down a job like any other. His job was in a civilian organisation providing catering facilities for the Security Forces in the area. He was at the time working in Fort George, the old Navy base at the end of the Buncrana Road. This was a short drive from the Border and Victor Two. Living nearby he was an easy and soft target for the local IRA. The despicable act which caused the death of Patsy Gillespie and the young soldiers here and which the IRA termed 'war' must never be forgotten.

When I think of the years of cold wet nights spent around the 'Enclave' (as it was called then), and at this place I wonder if anyone now (outside the Security Forces) knows or cares of the death and injury caused for nothing here and in the surrounding district. The deaths were unnecessary and in vain. The Border still exists. There is no memorial here of course, it would not be left intact, and it is not the place for a memorial. It still has an aura of inhospitality and unpleasantness; I did not stop long.

Photo essay

'Helicopters over Ulster'

by K.A. Boyd

Introduction

Two years' Ulster Defence Regiment service in the mid-1970s enabled me to quote my service number to a search patrol commander on 5th November 1988. This undoubtedly helped when I then asked him if the reason for his unit's presence, hidden along a Co Tyrone hedgerow beside the former Dromore Road railway station site, had anything to do with the Wessex helicopter bimbling around Dromore village, ten miles south of Omagh and, if so, would it be OK to photograph the cab when it arrived to extract them? After he'd established my ID and that I definitely wasn't a dicker, merely a photographer recording railway architecture abandoned some thirty years previously, a few words with the 72 Squadron aircrew via his signaller gained me a, "Rightoh. They're happy. Stand here. That's the HLS" (pointing to the next field). "No faces".

Thus I recorded XR517'N' with the last four frames in the camera that afternoon, little realising what that first chance encounter would lead to. My subsequent request for signatures on two framed prints resulted in an invitation to visit 72 Squadron and clearance to record less-sensitive SH/JHFNI ops at various FOBs, initially with 72's Wessex, but eventually the Lynx and Gazelles of their 5 Regiment Army Air Corps colleagues, 230 Squadron's Pumas and the various RN detachments who pitched up as well. The following views give some idea of the extent of heliops in the province, with the 'then & now' images demonstrating the impermanence of many military facilities. I can never adequately thank everyone who I encountered during those years, including that patrol commander, for their unfailing courtesy and help and for permitting my unusual hobby. Some of you reading this might recall the camera-carrying civvie round the helipads at Dungannon, Drumadd, Bessbrook and Omagh during the 1990s through to the end of Op BANNER. If you wondered "Who he?", now you know.

Brilliant memories and a privilege for me to have met so many dedicated, unselfish members of H.M. Forces.

Alex Boyd.

All images in this section © K.A. Boyd

Bessbrook, 09.00 hrs 3rd May 1996 and a patrol from 1Bn Coldstream Guards prepares to board 72 Squadron Wessex 1, XR499'W' on spot 5 while two others wait at spots 2 & 3 for 655 Sqn Lynx ZE381 and XZ205. 665 Squadron Gazelle ZB674 and 655 Lynx XZ655 occupy spots 9 & 10 in the 'Well' section of the helipad.

Eleven years later and only the background identifies the scene. The main helipad facility closed on 7th September 2006, with subsequent heliops from the two mill 'garden' pads and the last troops - a platoon from 2nd Bn Princess of Wales's Royal Regiment - left Bessbrook Mill on 25th June 2007, two weeks after this shot was taken.

11th August 1997. View from the east fence as 1st Bn Welsh Guards' patrols depart from spots 6 & 7 on Lynx 8, XZ174 and Lynx 9, XZ665.

XZ174, with the door gunner calling the height as Lynx 8 returns to spot 6.

Again, only the Mill confirms the location with the Buzzard Cell, tower, accommodation, terraced helipads, departure lounge and fence all demolished.

72 Squadron Wessex XR525 'G' overflies Millvale Road, Bessbrook, with the village, Mill and south Armagh as the backdrop. This was the final month of Wessex ops in the ARB, with the type's withdrawal from UK RAF service at the end of March 2002.

Sugarloaf Hill OP (Romeo 12) from 655 Sqn Lynx 5, XZ176. Looking south, with Slieve Gullion, Croslieve and Mullaghbane Mountain beyond.

Landing on. Inside the fence of Crossmaglen joint RUC/Military base. At that time (July 2005) 1 Para were the Armagh Roulement Battalion, the last Parachute Regiment battalion to serve in south Armagh.

Says it all, really. The famous greeting for new arrivals to XMG.
230 Squadron XW211 departs for Golf 10, 7th July 2005.

Two weeks later, in much improved weather with Slieve Gullion and Crossmaglen visible
beneath the Puma's tailboom, XW229 lands on the pad at Golf 10 (Creevekeeran) OP.

And departs seconds later.

The loadmaster's view as XW229 begins the return flight
from G10 to Bessbrook, 22nd July 2005.

Beginning of the end. 9th February 2006 and 230 Squadron Puma XW199 lifts from spot 2 at Bessbrook while 18 Squadron Chinook ZH894 is shut down on 6 before commencing that day's tasking - the early stages of the demolition of the OP towers.

The same view in September 2008. The "1k tree" stands on the horizon at mid-frame in both shots. Rule-of-thumb for AAC and RAF aircrew - if they could see the tree, they could fly. And you all thought it was scientific?

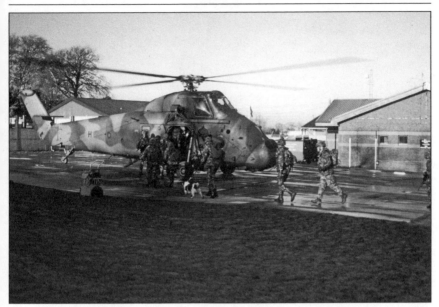

On to Co Tyrone (the ETB). Temporary AM2 helipad, Killymeal House, Dungannon – Yellow 453 for the initiated – where a search patrol from 2nd Bn Light Infantry board 72 Sqn Wessex XV721'H' to discover that,

Either Rufus has had too many Bonios – or his handler too many Mars Bars. At any rate the cab was overloaded and they had to wait for the next lift, 26th November 1993.

A month later and the CO of 2LI leaves Killymeal in Gazelle XZ 321 at the end of his battalion's six-month ETB tour while...

In the secured field outside the fence, 2LI soldiers file on to 7 Squadron Chinook ZA 711'ET' for their flight to Aldergrove, 28th December 1993.

2LI handed over to 1st Bn Royal Anglian Regiment in December 1993 and this 20th April 1994 view records their patrols boarding XR529'E' on Killymeal's main helipad. Today 'Echo' is one of the few Wessex to remain in RAF service - as Gate Guardian at RAF Aldergrove.

In June 1994 1st Bn Scots Guards took over the ETB duties from the Royal Anglians and one of their platoons waits beside the Buzzard Cell as XV728'A' lands on the AM2 pad, 24th October 1994.

The next East Tyrone roulement battalion was 1 Green Howards (December 1994 - June 1995) and this 19th April 1995 view has one of their patrols with Wessex XV725'C', again on the main pad's centre spot.

Joint Army/RUC tasking as well that same day required heavylift assistance – a 7 Squadron Chinook ZA712'ER'. The main pad could accommodate three Wessex, but when a Chinook arrived, everything else was diverted to the AM2.

All gone, apart from the concrete.

ZA712 returns for the next load.

The scene on 7th May 2007. In 2005, after the buildings had been cleared, press reports stated that this 13 acre site was sold to a private developer for £13.2 million. Present post-slump value? Who knows, but it remains derelict today.

These two shots were taken on 20th October 1995 during 1Bn Irish Guards' tour. A quarry-lift with XV728'A' again and the dispatchers look anxious as Argonaut struggles to lift the load.

Another 7th May 2007 comparison with the previous view.

The concrete-filled barrel for underslung load practice stands outside the Buzzard Cell. This was the first of four lifts to various quarries in the Cappagh area that day.

The short telecoms mast in mid-frame and the growth of what were shrubs
along the retaining wall in the previous view link the two scenes. Surreal.
Apart from those who served here, who could imagine all that ever existed?

Taken from the fuel replen pump house on the east side of the main pad,
XT688'S' departs for Aldergrove from the south spot on 26th November 1996.

The first of two post-closure visits to Killymeal, albeit only a month apart. Cloudy and dull on 7th April 2007 with no foliage on those trees - fairly similar conditions to that day more than a decade earlier.

21st January 1999; just over ten years ago and Wessex 5 still tasked from Yellow 010 - Lisanelly Barracks in Omagh. Here the 48 hour line cab, In this instance XT676 'I' lifts from the FOB to return to Aldergrove. On my first visit there, in mid-1976, a detachment of AAC Sioux and Scout helicopters occupied the MT sheds on the right. Can anyone recall the unit?

5th June 2007 and the demolition contractors are on site, starting
to dig up the helipad. The end of Omagh's military history.

Compare this with "The boys of bomb disposal" photograph on
pg 301 of *A Long Long War*. Lisanelly, 5th June 2007.

They would recognise this one as well.

5th November 1988 (see Introduction)

Part Three

Ulster Countryside

U lster's border with the Irish Republic or 'Free State' as romanticists are wont to call it, runs for approximately 330 kms and is as porous as wet tissue paper. There are few defined crossing points, manned spasmodically by the Customs officers of the Republic and, back during the days of the troubles, only marginally more so by their counterparts in the 'North.' In those days, the IRA successfully, using the proximity of the seemingly arbitrary frontier, and the tacit compliance of Republic officials, could blow up the customs posts, and then melt away across the fields, knowing that the SF would not follow them.

In those days, the undefined, higgledy-piggledy border could be recognised by the piles of white rubble which denoted where a Customs post had been blown up, courtesy of an IRA bomb. From Cullaville, Co Armagh at its most southerly, Belleek, Fermanagh at its most westerly and Culmore, Co Londonderry at its most northern point, the British Army and RUC had to try and prevent the transportation of arms, explosives and paramilitaries across that border. Geographically and logistically, it was a waking nightmare for the SF with the crossing points in the middle of woods, across streams, and through hamlets; many years of cross border smuggling had honed the IRA's skills in this context. It must also be remembered, that in parts, much of the 'North' was further south than the Republic with Co Donegal in the Republic being some 140 kms further north of Ulster.

Army engineers did their level best to prevent motorised incursions of the border by blowing huge craters in the roads, but compliant and supportive – or merely intimidated – farmers would use their tractors and fill in the craters with rubble and thus nullify the work of the Sappers. Against this background, the British fought their border war in rural Ulster

NIGHT TIME VIGIL IN THE NORTH ANTRIM COUNTRYSIDE

Stevie, Ulster Defence Regiment

One week in late 1979, at a time when the Provos had recently killed or wounded four prison officers, I was on guard (which also provided a QRF for our area) one Thursday night. We were tasked to the home of a local prison officer, as information had been received that he had been positively threatened so we went to his house, a bungalow out in the country. It stood on a hill, approached by a single-vehicle tractor track that passed close to tho house. There was no cover around the outside other than a short wooden picket fence.

My section commander and I went into the kitchen of the house, just as the family were preparing for bed. The man himself came and went around the house, clearly in a state of anxiety but trying not to pass this on to his young children. At one point as he passed me, I noticed he had a nickel-plated .38 revolver stuck in his pajama trousers waistband; looking around the kitchen and in other parts of the house, we could see that he had boxes of ammunition on every windowsill.

I think the family were sleeping in the living-room, fearing that the Provos may simply fire blindly into the bedrooms; anyway my boss and myself settled down in the kitchen, taking one hour on 'stag' in a chair facing the slightly open back door, and one hour in a similar chair bent over the table trying to catch some 'kip' (bit like you did at infants school). I was roused from my sleep by my boss shaking my elbow (for many years afterward I would wake and sit up instantly if disturbed) – glancing at him he put his finger to his lips, 'don't say anything', and, listening, I could hear the quiet rumble of tyres and a car engine, slowly getting louder as it got closer.

We opened the back door fully – not daring to look out – and took turns making 'ready' (i.e. putting a round in the breech). We both knelt, in the shadows of the kitchen table, facing out the door toward the back gate, about twenty plus metres away, and waited for the car to come into view. The bonnet of a Mark 3 Cortina came into view and stopped at the back gate; the rear window wound down; I was yawning, couldn't stop. (I'm told this is a nervous reaction). Seconds – that felt like hours – passed, the safety was off and we had both taken up 'first pressure' (well I effing had!); you could almost feel the thoughts of those in the car, what did the open door mean, should we go and see, and do the job? After hour-long seconds the driver let out the clutch and slowly drove off. All this time my boss had been frantically trying to get in touch with our 'back-up' who were slowly trawling the local area in a single rover, but they had stopped a car which was a 'Stop 3' from a Republican area and possibly traced PIRA. They were dealing with this at the same time as we were badly in need of their services.

Anyway – the car disappeared, and after a few minutes our back-up arrived. Clearly we needed to maintain a presence for the rest of the night so two others stayed while we raced back to base to get a quick meal and to tool up with more resources, that is more ammunition (in LMG mags) and an IWS (*individual weapons sight*), and then returned to the house.

For my mate and I the rest of the night was a dreary anti-climax; at first light I went outside and did a clearance around the outside of the house, using the IWS to check for any activity.

We were relieved by another patrol at 0800 after a long draining night. The RUC took over for the weekend, until the Sunday, when the man and his family, with minimal belongings, took the next flight out to the USA leaving the house and details to his solicitor.

To my best knowledge they never returned.

Between September 1974 and December 1986, a total of 29 prison officers were killed, mostly off duty by the IRA, INLA and UVF. The deaths included two women officers and, on February 3, 1979, an officer was killed at home and in the same attack which killed Officer Patrick Mackin, his wife, Violet was also murdered; the IRA admitted responsibility. A thirtieth officer was killed by the IRA in 1993.

LARNE: DANGER SIGNS

Tony Yarwood, Parachute Regiment

This particular tour of Belfast was with 3 Para as I had moved across from the Parachute Regiment Depot (as 2 Para) to gain promotion in a new battalion. I decided to take my family across to Northern Ireland with me so we headed off in my car to catch a ferry across.

I made a route map out to follow, once we got off the ferry; however I was shocked to find that all the motoring signs that direct people around the Province were missing, once I got off the ferry. It was pitch dark outside the kids were asleep and I was cursing every roundabout because I did not have a clue which way to turn. They say that the terrorists did this on purpose to catch soldiers out. Not a bad tactic actually because if anyone saw me driving around at about midnight with English number plates and looking lost would certainly know that they had snared a soldier.

I did not let my wife know that I was now in panic mode as I drove on in the darkness into the unknown. It did not help that my wife and I saw the shocking news footage on TV about the two signallers who were brutally murdered by a pack of locals whilst they were driving covertly in their car, having took a wrong turn in the wrong place at the wrong time.

The inevitable happened eventually and I drove into an estate that was covered in IRA paintings displayed proudly on the sides of houses, with IRA flags draped from the windows row upon row. The wife knew the score and gave me a slap telling me to quickly turn the car around and get out of there. Before the stinging of the slap faded, I was driving back down the road away from another potentially lethal scenario unfolding. I could see the morning newspapers – 'off duty soldier killed in front of his family after driving through an IRA hotspot.'

Thank God the kids were asleep I thought as I eventually got to Holywood barracks and safety.

MORTAR ATTACK AT ROSSLEA

Trooper (later Sergeant Major) Gary Smith, 5th Royal Inniskilling Dragoon Guards

I was a 20 year old Trooper and had been in the Regiment – 5th Royal Inniskilling Dragoon Guards – for 2 years. The Regiment was on their first tour in Northern Ireland and we were trained in, but no, obviously equipped with, Chieftain Tanks; recruited from several areas in England but also from Northern Ireland. In my estimation, at that time that we had about 25-30% of Irishmen in our Regiment. I don't think a Regiment (other than the UDR) had ever been on an operational tour to Northern Ireland with so many men that were from there.

Our troop was based in Rosslea, County Fermanagh; I remember being surprised at how small it was when I first arrived. Most civvies think of an Army base as a sprawling camp with a guard room and red and white barrier but this was just a three story house and some portacabins surrounded by wriggly tin! We did a rotation of 'in camp' and VCPs. 'In camp' consisted of sangar duty, QRF, patrols and sleep. The VCPs, which we built ourselves from sandbags, were manned normally I think by three four man teams.

On Saturday 9th May 1981 I was at a VCP about a mile or so away from camp and we had been on high alert as the hunger striker Bobby Sands had died four days before and I think everyone in Northern Ireland was expecting it to kick off big style. At about 11.00 pm it did. I can't remember what I was doing at the VCP but I heard what I thought were fireworks going off and immediately looked in the direction of the sound which was the direction of the base. I still didn't register what was happening because the sounds really were like firework rockets going off then all of a sudden I heard the crump of explosions. We all knew then what had happened; a mortar attack on the base. We all stood to, doubled up in the sangars and had perimetre patrols and static cover out very quickly. The VCP commander Cpl Baz Port was calm and professional and kept us all informed what was going on. This is where our training was really kicking in because no one had ever served on an operational tour in Northern Ireland before.

We heard all the radio traffic and it was very calm from the commanders at the base and the QRF wanting more information before flying out to support us. Before long the helicopters were dropping off the QRF near the base and it was a mass of noise, fire and light from the night sun. During all this time the commander at Rosslea had said there were two casualties and described them by the codes we had for each person; Corporal 'Thommo' Thompson had been slightly hurt but Trooper Dennis Edwards had been more severely wounded. We found out later that 'Thommo' had a slight head injury but Dennis had been caught in a blast and had a large hole ripped in his cheek and his back and legs were badly lacerated. 'Thommo' made a full recovery but I only saw Dennis once more when we returned to Osnabruck and he had terrible physical scars; he left the army soon after that.

We stayed out at the VCP for a few extra days and then returned to Rosslea. I was amazed at the destruction and that not more had been injured or even killed. All the portacabins had been hit but the one with the least damage was the one that housed the TV and video. As luck would have it, nearly all of the lads in camp had been in that portacabin watching the replay of the FA Cup final played earlier that day. Our team room/portacabin had taken a battering and we gathered all our stuff up as best we could. I wasn't angry at losing some kit and civvies, or even at the IRA for the attack, I was just very grateful that no mates had been killed although we were all concerned for Dennis. Within a short time I was on sangar duty and I could see the damage to the base from above. I still can't believe that no one was killed. I could also see that the farm next door to the base had taken a couple of 'drop-shorts' and was told quite a few pigs had been killed.

When one reads the roll of honour which details the enormous, unexpected and, in the public's eye, unknown amount of fatalities suffered by the British Army, we forget those who were wounded. With over 40,000 injuries, we should never forget those like 'Thommo', 'Tiny' Rose and David Dews all badly injured during the troubles who lost their careers and had to fight for their futures with no help from the MOD or the Governments which sent them there.

LISNASKEA

Private D.C. Queen's Regiment

I was one of 7 RINCOs (Regimental Intelligence NCO), posted to HQNI in Lisburn under the newly formed FIU (Force Intelligence Unit). It was a 2 year posting and when we arrived, not knowing each other and being from different units, we were asked, on the spot, who wanted which location. The choices were Bessbrook Mill, Crossmaglen, Lisnaskea, among others. We were mortified as we had taken the 2 year posting with no knowledge of where we were going. 3 of us were married and had brought our wives with us but opting for Crossmaglen or Bessbrook Mill would have meant being confined to camp and helicopter extraction only, as CPVs were not used in those areas. The single guys opted for the awkward locations and I took Lisnaskea, housed in Enniskillen and then Omagh.

I was no stranger to Northern Ireland as I had already completed 2 tours. 4 months in Omagh on Operation Triple Crown and one and a half, years based in Aldergrove doing a month – on – month – off cycle at Aughnacloy PVCP (*Permanent Vehicle Checkpoint*) and patrolling in some of the worst Tyrone areas including Carrickmore. Therefore, of my 11 year career in the army, 5 of those years were spent in Northern Ireland, on operations.

Our job was to become familiar with the local 'suspected members of a well known terrorist organization' (political correctness!!) as since the Loughall incident, where allegedly 100s of copies of the incident photos, showing the bodies in situ, had been sent to the press and as a result, the press discovered we were carrying 'montages' of the local faces, which contravened the Data Protection Act (political correctness!!). Therefore, there was a necessity for troops 'on the ground', who were there long term, to pass continuity information to the incoming unit (every 6 months). In order to achieve this we had to work closely with Special Branch (SB) and the local UDR Company. My relationship with SB was very good and we spent a lot of time drinking together but I always had the impression that within the intelligence community, at that time, there was a 'log jam' in the information process between the police and the army. SB seemed to know a lot that they weren't going to pass to the army because they either didn't trust them or they were jealous. Either way, for 3 years, because I took a one year extension, I tried to bond with them to achieve snippets and to be fair to them, they did, but not by extraction, purely because they wanted to, which gave me Kudos with my superiors, or was a deliberate attempt at misinformation.

I considered my position to be very dangerous as the incoming units were only there for 6 months and they were not allowed out of the barracks, so their life was contained within the base for 6 months. I had to live and work in the community, primarily in Enniskillen and Omagh. An easy task if you are UDR or RUC and have a local accent; but you stick out like a sore thumb with a southern English accent. Because of the risk, we were armed with Browning 9mm pistols which were in our possession 24 hours a day, which is quite a strange feeling and it takes a lot of self discipline, bearing in mind that my day to day routine continues. Drinking in a bar and being intertwined in a normal, alcohol fueled environment, knowing that you have a loaded pistol, holstered on your hip, takes a lot of self discipline and is the ultimate buzz and demonstration of trust. This is quite a unique scenario for a British soldier but not unique for the boys of the RUC and UDR who's life revolved around this type of situation. They deserve credit and respect for their persistence during that dark phase of Northern Ireland's history.

Chapter 13

Lurgan/Dungannon/Banbridge

Dungannon – from the Irish: Dún Geanainn meaning Geanann's fort – is a town in County Tyrone in Northern Ireland. It is the third largest town in the County (next to Omagh and Strabane) and has a population of 11,139 people.

The area under review includes Lurgan, Portadown, Cookstown, Cappagh and Craigavon. This was a deadly area for the SF, as during the course of the troubles, 72 members were killed. 37 RUC officers and 35 British soldiers were killed in this picturesque part of Ulster. The three worst atrocities in this area took place over a seven year period. On June 18, 1972, whilst investigating a house near Lurgan, three soldiers from the Gordon Highlanders were killed by an IRA bomb. The men were: Sergeant Major Arthur Macmillan (37), Lance Corporal Colin Leslie (26) and Sergeant Ian Mutch (31); Arthur MacMillan was from Hull and the other two from the Orkneys and Nairn, respectively.

Less than 3 months later, in Dungannon, the Jocks were made to pay the price of the Government's decision to end internment as both the innocent and the paramilitary were released back on to the streets of the Province. On September 10, an IRA mine exploded under an armoured car carrying Duncan McPhee (21), Private Douglas Richmond (21) and Private William Mcintyre (23) were inside the vehicle. Two of the men were killed instantly and Private Mcintyre terribly wounded; sadly, he died of his wounds the following day.

On 20 March, 1974, there was a tragic 'blue on blue' incident at Mowhan near Glenann, in which two Corporals from the 14/20 King's Hussars were shot dead by the RUC's SPG [*Special Patrol Group*]. The soldiers were called Michael Herbert from Prestwick, Scotland and Michael J Cotton, who was from Nottingham.

On December 16, 1979, four members of the 16th Air Defence Regiment, Royal Artillery were killed at Glenadush near Dungannon by a 1000lb IRA culvert bomb. The four men were: Gunner William Beck (23), Gunner Keith Richards (22), Gunner Alan Ayrton (21) and Gunner Simon Evans who was 19; such was the power of the blast, that all four men were killed absolutely instantly.

[*Author's note: strictly speaking, the IRA ambush at Ballygawley roundabout should be included as it is close to the area under review; however, as that was dealt with extensively in* A Long Long War *it will not looked at again in this book. It will, however, be the subject of further analysis in the next book by the author.*]

Corporal Frank Jones, Royal Green Jackets

Despite being flown out from several different airfields, each flight landed at Aldergrove Airfield and from there we were transported by road to Long Kesh; at this time still an old disused and windswept airfield. On arrival I was pleasantly surprised to find tents had already been erected, toilets dug and washrooms made usable. Obviously someone had been keeping abreast of the deteriorating situation and was expecting us.

The first couple of days were spent settling in, drawing riot gear, practicing box formation IS drills, and being briefed that our role was to be that of Province Reserve and as such we would be unlikely to be used in Belfast or Londonderry. This was greeted with some disappointment, certainly by me. I had been denied an opportunity to see my wife before flying out and I so badly wanted to exact revenge on some rioter's skull.

Our protective riot gear was initially slow to appear and therefore to compensate for a lack of leg protection we slit our combat trousers at the knee and inserted rolled newspaper and other cushioning material; handy enough against stones and bricks, but a problem if petrol bombs were thrown. We joked the officers had better protection because they could utilise the *Telegraph* and *Times* colour supplements stolen from their mess. A similar Heath Robinson affair became the employed solution for making all Land rover and four tonner windscreens seem brick-proof, although here a local bakery was relieved of dozens of bread trays. Initially short metal shields were issued for personal protection and whilst they were light they did leave a vulnerable gap between our newspaper reinforced knees and the lower torso. In the event of wanting to protect that particular part of my anatomy a movement with the shield would only serve to expose my chest and head. Later and to everyone's relief, and possibly inspired by the Jock battalion sharing Long Kesh, an answer was found by simply wearing our respirator cases at the front as sporrans.

At Long Kesh we had practiced platoon debussing drills from a 4 tonner, which entailed doubling round to the front of the vehicle to form-up in classic box formation; with every rifleman taking up his allocated position in the box, then advancing toward the 'enemy' striking our shields with our batons as the left foot hit the ground. At Lurgan and after a period of waiting 'C' Company platoons were ordered to deploy to prevent tribal mobs getting to within stone throwing distance of each other. Inside the packed confine of our platoon vehicle there was a buzz of expectation and excitement, and when we finally came to a jerking halt we debussed with enthusiasm on command from our platoon commander who was sitting up front with the driver. The secret to success is to de-buss in a speedy, but orderly fashion; the aim being to Shock and Awe protestors with our steadfast determination and professionalism. Of course the other secret to success is to ensure the vehicle arrives at the correct location.

Whether the difficulty of navigating narrow unfamiliar streets placed us facing the wrong way, or whether it had been a brilliant tactic will never really be known. I suppose what must have impressed and led to the eventual outcome had been our ability to successfully counter-march to face the crowd, for instead of the expected violent tribal confrontation there was a period of tense stand-off before the crowd grudgingly dispersed after a smattering of applause for our efforts and without either side joining forces to target us. This was both satisfying and frustrating. Although, had it come to a proper encounter my role as a roaming 'sniper' within the constrained area of the box meant I could probably have dodged incoming missiles.

Over the days 'C' Company kept pretty busy searching great swaths of wet, windy countryside and isolated farmhouses, or setting up road blocks, or sitting in our vehicles in support of other units and hoping to be called in to action. B Coy experienced our only real, full blooded riot when it very successfully supported The Queens Lancashire Regiment at Coalisland. Even so, we were duly alarmed to receive news that a Battalion boxer and certainly the hardest man in the 3rd Battalion had been downed by a ball-bearing probably fired from a catapult. When this filtered down to all platoons I remember we reinforced our respirator-cases with any pieces of wood we could lay our hands on.

As the days passed we received vast quantities of improved protection including the first issue of the transparent plastic shield. Some of the equipment was pretty decent but some items were only of use if you wanted to stay transfixed and receive everything that could be thrown. Even the OC's Land rover eventually sported a made-to-measure steel mesh screen to replace the not too unsuccessful paracord and bread tray shield. In addition the council Sludge Gulper serviced our field toilets twice a week and as a thought to improving our ability to render an unruly mob passive my suggestion that it could be used against rioters in the blow' rather than 'suck' mode was never taken seriously.

LURGAN

Mike Davies, Royal Anglians

The following story concerns my first tour of Northern Ireland. This was back in 1974 and, at that time, was a keen, if not green, young 18 year old soldier stationed in Lurgan.

Now in those days, the Army had many expressions of how to do this and how to do that, but it was up to the soldier on the ground as to what stance they adopted for whatever operation they were designated and a safe way of going about their duties. Well, our night patrols, of which there were many, were called Lurk Patrols, which basically speaks for itself. You lurk in the shadows, then grab any unsuspecting passer-by and drag them in for a check, and on many occasions they were so frightened, they'd peed themselves before we could check them over the radio.

Anyway, the night in question we were lurking about on our way to a Republican club to apprehend an undesirable and were told there were Dickers front and back of this club. However, on our way I found I suddenly needed the toilet and after a while this rapidly became a matter life or death. I informed our Platoon Sergeant, who went absolutely ballistic, albeit in a silent way, because of the nature of our patrol. Once he'd calmed down, he approached and whispered in my cammed up ear, 'See that house over there? Well it belongs to a terrorist'. 'So go and have a shit in his garden, and make it a big one.' So off I went as ordered.

Now, I don't want to give away too much information at this point, but I crept in and eventually found the guy's compost heap at the bottom of his garden and deposited a 'babies arm' in a fashion that 'Mr. Whippy,' the Ice Cream man would have been proud of and couldn't help laughing under my breath at the thought of what was about to greet his wife in the morning, when she went to deposit the tea leaves from her pot! After I'd sorted myself out, I rejoined the patrol and we approached the club from an easterly direction to the rear. But, there was still one last obstacle to cross, the dreaded river!

Because there was no moon that night, all instructions were passed by ear and, as I was the new boy on the patrol, I was tail end, backward walking, Charlie. Anyway, what should have been passed down the line was, left foot on the first strand of barbed wire, then right foot on the top strand, then last but not least, hold the tree branch with your right hand and jump across. What was actually passed down was, put your foot on the lower strand of barbed wire, grab the branch and jump, which I did, but unfortunately my combat trousers got caught on the top strand, which catapulted me backwards before being thrown spread-eagled into the river, which as you can guess, woke even the dead! When I finally surfaced, the reminder of the patrol were on their knees crying with laughter and by then, the Dickers had passed on their warning, so whoever we were after, had long got away. Having dragged myself out of the river, I thought 'fuck it! I'll have a piss' and would you 'Adam and Eve' it? If bad luck comes in two's, it was certainly my turn that night as I pissed straight on an electric

Eddie Atkinson (Green Howards), Lurgan (Eddie Atkinson)

cattle fence, resulting in more hysterical laughter from my so called mates. They said my hair shot up and out and lit up like a Christmas tree, Bastards! But, bad luck number three was approaching fast!

Two weeks later, while making my way to breakfast at Lurgan camp, I was approached by this rather small aggressive looking long haired Scotsman, who proceeded to punch me in the face and knock me to the ground. He then went on to stand over and inform me that the next time I wanted a shit, to kindly do it somewhere else! Apparently an O.P. had been placed under the compost heap and for the last two months, had two men secreted in it! Unfortunately the little Scotsman and his mate had to endure my 'Mr. Whippy' handiwork until relieved two days later!

UNEXPLAINED DEATH AT LURGAN

Sergeant John Black, Royal Army Medical Corps

A Pte in the Royal Pioneer Corps stationed at 3 Infantry Bde HQ, Lurgan was killed in a training accident. His unit did not carry out any notification procedures but brought the body all the way from Lurgan to Musgrave Park Hospital with an RCT driver and an irate Captain from the Royal Signals.

I was day orderly Sergeant and had overall remit of casualty and reception, and I refused to accept the body as it had been taken without permission out of the jurisdiction area of the Lurgan coroner. I suggested to the Captain that he take it back before the coroner and the RUC commander for Lurgan found out (it was still an unexplained death!). He was arrogant and rude; however, unknown to me, my CO who was also Assistant Director of Medical Services Northern Ireland was listening in the wings, in his role as duty medical officer. He was a big strapping Highlander and intervened. It was the first time I had heard Gaelic being spoken, or had ever seen the 'old man' in such a rage. Neither have I ever seen a full Colonel pin another officer by the scruff of his neck with his feet off the floor before! It was sheer joy to watch and boosted the morale of waiting casualties and staff alike.

The outcome was, that the body was returned from whence it came, and the staff at 3 Infantry Brigaded had to undertake all the notifications, and the Captain was officially reprimanded by the GOC and I got my substantive sergeant. All I can tell you about Pte Pioneer is that he came from Leeds.

Would you believe this though; on returning home to Lurgan, this same Captain phoned up and requested help in sending NOTICAS signals! Some two months prior to his death Pte 'Pioneer' had been a patient at the military wing, Musgrave Hospital for appendix removal.

Despite my best efforts, I have been unable to identify the name of the Royal Pioneer Corps Private killed at Lurgan. I trust that I will be able to do this in the fullness of time and add his name to the Royal of Honour.

CULVERT BOMB

David Henley, RTR

In the summer of 1974 an observation post (OP) had been set up at a border crossing near Clogher in County Tyrone the night before the border was due to be sealed. The patrol was led by Sergeant Roger Lichfield and one of the patrol members was my friend Trooper Tommy Macmanaman. The next morning I was to drive my section to the border in order to clear the area and to provide cover for the sniffer dog and its handler and also to search culverts each side of the road leading up to the bridge which represented the border crossing. Before we left the Deanery, Tommy, who had returned at first light, told me that he had detected a smell of diesel in the area leading up to the crossing; he told me that he had reported the smell but nothing apparently was done about it.

We arrived in the border area shortly before an Engineer Search Team arrived so that we could conduct a liaison briefing. It was established that my section would deploy three men either side of road to search the immediate area and to cover the dog handler who would operate about 10 metres ahead. I was to drive the empty Saracen at tick-over speed just behind the dog handler. There was about half a mile of road to search and everything went off quite routinely for the first quarter mile or so. Geoff Lumsden and Loz Lockey, who were in the field to my left, decided that as things were quiet they would share a brew. A flask was produced and they poured a cup each while the dog handler took his dog to sniff around an old lorry chassis which had been dumped approximately 3 metres into the field on the right side of the road. I brought the APC to a halt so I could watch the dog carry out its investigation to the wreck. The handler let the dog out on a long lead and it seemed to disappear into a hole under the rear wheel. All of a sudden I heard a muffled thump rather than a loud bang; the dog was blown high into the air and the dog handler fell onto his back. Geordie and Loz simultaneously threw their flask cups into the air and dived to the ground; the front of the Saracen seemed to lift up in the air then fell back to the road and everything went deathly quiet for a few seconds after.

After a moment or two I quickly jumped from the driver's seat into the Commander's cupola to man the .30 Browning machine gun. I quickly realised that the bomb must have been detonated by terrorists using a command wire (an electrical detonation via a wire hundreds of metres long) so I trained the gun in the general area of where the terrorists would be hidden (which was just over the border about half a mile away). Predictably, there was no obvious movement in the area which did not surprise me as the terrorists would have cleared the area as soon as they heard, or saw, the explosion. The dog was blown about 5 metres and landed on the road; we all thought it must be dead but all of a sudden it staggered to its feet and ran towards the border. Geordie ran and caught the dog before it reached the bridge, he brought it back and placed it gently in the back of the Saracen. Loz went to the aid of the dog handler and immediately realised how lucky the handler was. His visor, which covered the whole of his face and neck, was peppered with shrapnel marks and his flak jacket was torn in places. His legs, which had only been covered with his combat trousers, were also torn and he had shrapnel wounds in his thighs and shins. Although injured, his main thoughts were for the well being of his dog but shock soon set in and the poor man started to cry when he saw the condition his dog was in. It had shrapnel wounds down whole of the left side of its body and blood was pouring out of every wound.

Dave Whalley, my section corporal, told Geoff and Loz to help the dog handler and his dog into the rear of the vehicle and ordered me to drive back to the Deanery "as fast as you can" which was something any driver relishes! I had to reverse back down the road with the aid of Loz commanding me until I could find a spot to turn the vehicle round then set off at full speed. The roads were extremely narrow but I kept the Saracen nearly flat out; at one point there was a sharp left bend which led onto a bridge and I came close to knocking the side of the bridge into the water, but I managed to keep it on the road. The trip, under normal circumstances, would take about an hour but I covered it in about 40 minutes. When we arrived at the Deanery a helicopter was waiting to take the handler and his dog to hospital; the handler thanked me for getting them back safe and quickly and disappeared into the chopper.

Happily, the handler and his dog both made full recoveries and the dog was actually deployed back on operations within two months of the incident. The dog would have been deployed earlier but for the handler

Steve Corbett, Portadown (Steve Corbett)

taking longer to recover – whilst in hospital recovering he tried to move his bed, slipped and broke his wrist! – now there's irony for you!

NEWTOWNARDS CHRISTMAS

Tony Yarwood, Parachute Regiment

Whilst on this two year tour of Belfast with 3 Para in 1989, I was working in the Close Observation Platoon (COP) who had a different role to play during these troubled times in Northern Ireland than that of the rifle companies. Although it was very interesting and challenging it meant that I would be away from my family a lot of the time therefore when I was home in my married quarter, I made the most of it.

One day we decided to go to an area that was classed as safe, in order to do a bit of shopping for Christmas. We took the two kids and headed for a bike shop as we were going to buy them bikes for Christmas. At this stage I had changed my number plates to Northern Ireland plates so that I would not stand out whilst driving around the province. I always checked under my car whenever I had parked it up to ensure that there were never any unsuspecting parcels containing explosives left for me. Again these checks had to be done without any of the locals seeing me as this would give away the fact that I was in the Army.

My young kids would always ask why I had to check under the car so I explained that I was simply checking everything was ok underneath. I couldn't tell them that there might be a bomb there to blow me and my family to smithereens. The only problem I had whenever I was walking around Belfast with the kids was if they saw a soldier on the streets or in green vehicles driving about they would shout out: 'Look soldiers like you daddy.' Other times they would run back to the car to see who could look underneath it first – to check that everything was ok!

As we entered the bike shop, my wife went to the counter and asked the lady if we could order two bikes for our kids. The lady went through to the rear of the shop out of sight for a while whilst my wife and I stood by the counter. She informed us that the bikes that we wanted would have to be ordered as the one in the shop was a display model only. She told us to come back in three week and they would be ready for pick up. Three weeks later, we headed back to the shop to collect them. My wife went to the counter whilst I walked around the shop having a nosey about at all the other bikes.

I noticed that we were hanging around again and did become slightly concerned. I was just about to head to the counter when suddenly I saw two guys were standing by the main entrance. Because of the job I was now doing I thought I recognised them and had visions of me being shot in a shop; off duty. I actually said to myself that I could not believe that I had fought in the Falklands War from day one with 2 Para and served a two year tour of Northern Ireland previously and now I was going to die in a shop of all places. I did not say anything to my wife as she stood at the counter completely oblivious to what was occurring in front of her. I had to think quickly and pulled off the biggest bluff ever to get out of the situation unscathed.

I was wearing a thick waist length jacket that had a zip running from top to bottom. I turned towards the two guys who did not flinch as they stood there looking menacingly at me. I began pulling the zip of my jacket down with my left hand and slowly placed my right hand into the jacket as if going for a pistol. As soldier sometimes carry pistols on certain duties, the two guys did not know whether I had a pistol or not and fled from the main entrance. I grabbed the wife and left the shop immediately. The funny thing was this all occurred within minutes and she did not have a clue until I told here later. Needless to say I never went near that particular safe zone (not) again.

DUNGANNON BOMB

Dave Maltby, Queen's Dragoon Guards

Having done a previous tour in 1974 in Londonderry, 1976 saw the Queens Dragoon Guards in Co Tyrone and Co Armagh. I was a member of 'C' and we were located in Dungannon at Castlehill Camp; located just above the Market Square. I was Troop Corporal under S/Sgt 'Dinger' B-- – and Troop Sgt 'Taff' E---. Both were great lads and they really knew their stuff. My section of 8 men consisted 'Manny' B, 'Dia the Dog' who could smell a find yards away; 'Ginge' C, 'Pud' Walker, 'Batley W, 'Teatime' Jones (so called because his last three Army numbers were 430) and 'Akidoo' T.

This tour would prove to be both a challenging and eventful tour over the next four months. As a section we were responsible for patrolling our TAOR (*Tactical Area of Responsibility*) consisting of Dungannon, its outlying areas; South to Moy and north to Coalisland. Our second task was to operate as Squadron Search Team as and when required. Our tour started on 4th January 1976, and I think we took over from the 13/18 Hussars.

The first month started off quite peacefully, with us getting to know the town and the rural area. There were some nice people in the area mixed with a few players mainly located on the 'Ponderosa' estate. In fact, over the next few months I was to search one player's home at least 5 times.

Our first successful find was in mid-February, we had been tasked to search a one mile square area south of the 'Ponderosa'; after a few hours into the search there was not much to talk about and I could see boredom was starting to set in, so I halted the search for a tea break and a rethink. So looking at a few likely spots re-deployed the team and within five minutes Dia 'the dog' came up with a find. A small hole in the bank revealed some black plastic wrapping; the hide was constructed of a wooden chute. Being the team commander, it was my responsibility to 'pull' the suspect wrapping with a long cord and hook. This was in case the hide was booby trapped. Anyway, after the pull, it was revealed that Dia had found an M1 Carbine and ammo. Being our first find we were dead chuffed and over the next few months Dia was on heat because there was no stopping him after that, and we had quite a few finds.

On one occasion, his nose nearly got him into deep trouble. We had been tasked to search a wood for some suspected explosives; I found the easiest way to do this was to form an extended line and do a sweep. After about 20 minutes we heard this cry of 'Oh Shit; Help!' from someone in the line. After a good look around we found Dia in a pit surrounded by bags of unstable ANFO Explosive. The stuff was seeping, and the job was now how to extract him from the pit without incident. After some thought we came up with the idea of placing an SLR (unloaded) under each armpit and extract upwards and sideways. In the meantime we had summoned ATO who came along and blew the ANFO up on spot as it was unstable.

We had now had a few highs but the lows were yet to come. The section was working extremely well and being such good characters, everybody was looking out for each other and there was some great camaraderie amongst not only the section but the Troop as well.

On Wednesday, March 17th, we were tasked to patrol the town at 1930 hours that night, and having previously been told not to set a pattern and stagger times, I had the section assemble in the 'Choggie' shop for a quick cuppa and kit check. We hung around for a further 10 minutes just to see the beginning of 'The Magnificent Seven' on the telly. Whether or not this 10 minutes played a part in what was about to happen will never be known, but is something I often ponder on still after all these years.

We headed out and made our way through the Market Square, proceeding towards Anne Street in the Catholic part of Dungannon; the street boasted of a grocery shop and a pub called 'The Hillcrest.' At this time our means of communication were PYE radios, which I found as much use as a chocolate fireguard. They were unreliable and prone to black spots and here I had one at the top of Anne Street.

We split into 3 men on either side of the street; there were a few cars parked on my side and unable to do any car checks due to having no comms, I told the lads to check cautiously in the cars. Moving further on, I saw that were two young boys sitting on milk crates outside the shop. I called 'Evening' but received no reply so moved on. We got down to the bottom of Anne Street without incident and turned the corner. With that, a car came past at a fast speed, but I didn't think much of it at that time. Next minute, there was brilliant flash of light into the night sky and a vacuum which knocked my last man off his feet. Just for a micro second I became disorientated and thought 'What the F*** was that?' Realising it was an explosion, we all turned around and legged it back up Anne Street. The front of the 'Hillcrest' had been blown out and the carnage was unbelievable. There were at least four dead, with two of them being the two young boys I had briefly spoken to earlier.

The ambulances turned up out of the blue; they were very quick. The problem I had was how to call it in, having no comms, I quickly got the section to cordon off the area, instantly regretting giving two of the lads the night off, and quickly looked for a house with a telephone. A dear old lady let me in and allowed me to use the phone. I called Castlehill Ops Room, and my troop leader happened to be the watch keeper. I told him what had happened and requested QRF and ATO assistance.

I quickly got back to the section who were now starting to get aggro off the locals and we found it quite hard to keep the cordon whilst waiting for the QRF which was taking a long time. The QRF eventually turned up led by the Squadron Leader accompanied by the SSM (very high powered QRF, thought me), later followed by ATO. The OC took over control from me, which allowed me to go and bring the ATO up to speed telling what we had seen prior to the explosion etc.

The OC then instructed me to make my way back to camp and do a debrief, write my patrol report and then stand down. It turned into a very long and eventful evening. Getting into my pit later that night, a lot of 'what if' thoughts went through my mind, such as what if we had have been 10 minutes earlier, would we have caught the bomber or if ten minutes later would we have been caught in the blast ?

The speeding car I had seen was later found burnt out and it was established that the bombing was done by the UVF.

On that night, 17 March, 1976, four Catholic civilians were murdered in this outrage by the UVF. The dead included Andrew Small (62) and Joseph Kelly (57). Tragically, two 13 year old schoolboys – the two children seen outside playing when the soldiers walked by – were killed in the blast. James McCaughey (13) and his friend Patrick Barnard also 13 perished, with Patrick dying of his terrible wounds the following day.

MY CLUMSINESS IN DUNGANNON

Bill Callaghan, Royal Army Medical Corps, Att: UDR

I scabbed a lift into the centre of Dungannon, the driver dropped me off and I went into Woolworth's, I needed toiletries and most importantly 'Comfiebum' – bog paper – the issued stuff was an irritation. I reached up to get a six-pack of this from the top shelf when I felt my pistol slide out of my clip holster and it clattered to the floor. (*The author can attest to this fact; there is little worse in Army life than using the 'sandpaper' which the MOD provided and any soldier going home on leave looked forward to soft toilet paper.*) I must explain I was not, nor ever was, an undercover operative, but I was in plain clothes. There's no way I'd have survived walking through Dungannon in uniform and it would have been a bit costly on time and resources to mount a full patrol to get my toiletries.

So there I was, in the middle of Woolworth's; short hair, trademark jeans and desert boots; looking down at my pistol which had clattered onto the floor; I wasn't alone. The shop that had seemed empty was suddenly very full and everyone was staring at the weapon on the floor. 'Oops!' was all I could manage; it wasn't very professional. I noted that some youth had gone running out of the shop and assumed he was away to tell the boyos about an easy target in Woolworth's.

'KNOB!' I screamed at myself inwardly. Regaining my composure, I picked it up, slowly inspected it for damage, and returned it to the clip holster that I now clipped. I took the goods to the till and paid, resisting the urge to wave the pistol and ask 'Browning Express?' I was too scared for that. I actually bolted out of the shop, I believed I'd compromised myself and I didn't want to hang around. That produced two problems; firstly I'd not got any toothpaste and secondly I was early for the RV with the driver.

Gareth Dyer, Royal Irish Regiment

I was serving in the general Belfast area as a platoon commander with the Royal Irish Regiment (Home Service). One evening when reporting for duty we were briefed on an incident earlier that day where a homemade Claymore mine had been discovered by a Royal Irish call sign just outside Banbridge. We were briefed that the guy who had found the device was the platoon commander of the patrol and had practically fallen over it.

Having done so he had calmly walked down the road, informing the rest of the patrol of the need to take hard cover. I remember turning to my platoon sergeant and remarking, 'That was pretty cool of him.' His reply was along the lines of, 'Tell you what sir; if you ever fall over a landmine while the rest of us are in the area, fuck being cool. I'll expect you to come running down the road screaming like a wee girl, giving us all plenty of notice of your discovery!'

Steve Corbett, Portadown (Steve Corbett)

A few months later I was chatting to said mate, and I mentioned the incident, knowing it was on his patch. I also mentioned the reaction of my platoon sergeant. He replied that, funnily enough, him being the fellow involved, the corporal with him that night had told him he would have fully expected his platoon commander to do the screaming girly bit the next time he discovered a Claymore!

IRA MAN IN CAPPAGH

Bill Callaghan, Royal Army Medical Corps, Att: UDR

I was helping out two of the operators, Tom and Dave, they were busy trying to locate the site of a recently published photograph of a group of players, there was no really imperative reason, it just placed people in space and time, this would implicate or clear them of involvement in some other activity. I was going through *An Phoblacht* (Irish Republican News) looking for anything that might mention people in our patch and I noticed a similar photograph; it was of a hooded Gunman with an M16 Armalite Rifle and another with an M60 Machine Gun. There was no building in this picture but there were people looking on I looked again at the picture Tom and Dave had; it was the same people, in the same place and judging by the shadows it was the same time of day but it was from a different angle. They were pleased with this; it was an additional piece to the jigsaw.

Tom thought he recognised one of the kids and said that it might be in Cappagh, he wanted to locate the site to be sure so they decided they'd drive out to the village. The asked me if I'd like to go with them, they sweetened the Ops room with the logic that they were in radio contact and I'd be on the ground in the most likely location should I be needed. I was strangely delighted and troubled at the same time. Both of these boys had lived with the war for sixteen years, they went home to their regular families, in their regular houses, in their regular estates where the ding dong of the door bell could just as easily herald a balaclava'd assassin as a perfectly coiffured Avon Lady. I didn't and still don't know how they could live like that; I felt sick with nerves every time I left the security of the base.

I'd heard of Cappagh, there were serious Republicans in that village not quite the fabled bandit country of south Armagh but just as deadly. The car was a red Ford Cortina and I sat in the back with my Bergen hidden in the boot. I was not reassured by the array of weapons. I had my own 9mm pistol as did they and in addition under my seat was a Sterling SMG. If anything happened I wasn't sure how I'd react.

Something happened and I reacted badly, we had driven through the village slowly and Tom identified what he thought was the place of the picture. As we left the village a blue Hyundai Pony overtook us and in the driving seat was a guy whose face I knew, so I waved. He looked at me as if I was a loony. I then realised I didn't know him but had recognised him from my sighting list: he was a known terrorist, and he saw that I saw him. It took me a moment to register but Dave knew him straight away.

'Hello, what're yer up to here yer bugger?' he muttered to Tom and himself. 'Bill? Dis, is probably nottin' burrit may be a deal or summat, check yer weapon.' Tom commanded and I heard him but my brain needed time to catch up. 'That's 'X'!' I said brightly as the name sprang into my head. 'Yeah, we know, Bill; check yer guns will yer?' Tom was smiling but he looked cold, I suddenly felt it. 'Fuck me, are we going to fight?' My voice seemed higher to my own ears. 'Fekkin' hope not, we're miles from any help,' Dave replied as he climbed through the gears. The Pony was about 200 yards ahead and our car was in a lazy pursuit, trailing not racing.

I slipped the magazine out of my pistol, checked it, re-inserted it and pulled back the slide to chamber a round. I applied the safety and stowed it in my jacket pocket. I then took out the SMG from under the seat. I figured to start my fighting with this as it had the most rounds and a fully automatic capability. It might scare them off if I got lucky or so I thought. I checked the mag on the SMG and slotted it home, shook it and ensured it wouldn't fall out. I cocked the weapon and applied the safety catch. I kept the stock folded to make it easier to use from the car and rested the gun across my lap, mag up, finger on the trigger guard with the muzzle toward the door. You have to understand this; I'd never done these drills in anything other than the clinical area of a range firing point. To do them now in a rolling car whipping along country lanes was a step beyond my comfort zone. Tom and Dave were laughing at me; I'd been muttering orders to myself.

'Load! Safety Catch! Magazine! Ready! Check Safety Catch!' I caught myself doing this and in spite of the tension I had inside I actually laughed with them, I finished off the sequence, for their amusement 'Watch and Shoot! Watch and Shoot!' 'Oh, I fekkin' hope not!' Dave repeated, but he was driving, I was settled into my drills now and though scared I felt ready for it. I could see that Tom looked up for a scrap too.

The terrorist was slowing, he approached a large yellow vehicle parked where the road crested a hill, there were a group of men there and our visibility beyond was denied by the crest. Dave pulled up 200 yards short and we observed him chatting with these men through the binocs. They were linesmen, working on the telephone lines along the lane. 'X' pulled an unhurried three-point turn and came back toward us. As he closed on us Dave and Tom began waving at him, he waved back and smiled but as he passed us I realised I was trying to make myself as small as possible. The linesmen were taking an interest in us by now and we drove toward them.

This was it, they weren't linesmen at all and they were going to slot us. I barely had time to register that they were tooled up before the windows shattered and the doors were ripped apart by automatic fire, my right thigh exploded with the impact of an unbelievably large bullet, I had time to notice this but couldn't shout out because my jaw was hanging off and my right lung had just been ripped to pieces by the same burst. I saw Tom's head explode and Dave's hands stayed on the wheel as the stumps of his arms flew up to protect what was left of his face; the stumps were jetting blood everywhere, red, red, red.

Happily in the real world, as all this swam through my head, we did a slow drive by and looked them over, it seemed they really were linesmen. I felt exhausted, I had been primed and ready to go I now had to calm down. I told Tom and Dave I was going to clear the weapons and they agreed that that would be a good thing.

'Detail! Unload!' I began. They laughed but I could have cried.

FURTHER GRIEF FOR DUNGANNON

David Maltby, Queen's Dragoon Guards

We were later involved in another bombing incident, this time Dungannon Market Square, which was also the town centre. We were on our way back to Dungannon after doing a mobile pickup of an OP from an Infantry unit. As we got to the Thomas Street barrier, we were instructed by Ops not to go any further and wait out on further instructions. When I received the further instructions, I was told that a car bomb had been reported in the market square and I was told to cautiously go forward and have a look. So, getting down on all fours, I had a look through my binocs at a suspect car parked outside the bank. It was a 'Mini' with two dustbins in the back with cortex coming out. I informed Ops Room and was then instructed to get a cordon into and around the town square. This was going to prove a bit of a headache as I had to think carefully how to get the lads in position without getting in line of sight with the bomb. It is said if you are out of line of sight and a good distance away, you're pretty safe! Fortunately, I had the infantry guys to assist, so pairing one up with each of my lads, I got them into positions using the backstreets.

With the cordon in place, it was just a matter of waiting for ATO to turn up, but the bomb had different ideas. 30 minutes later it blew. There was this almighty flash and an immense vacuum and then silence. Later came the sound of falling debris. I observed to my left an RUC guy and two of the Troop who had come out of Castlehill, all hiding behind this one lamp post; crazy bastards I thought ! At THAT moment in time, car's engine was still in orbit and came crashing down between the three of them. Happily, not one of them was injured, although one slight casualty was 'Pud' who had somehow got caught in the blast and was a blown through the window of a fruit shop; so he stayed to have a little fruit cocktail.

After things cleared, I was then tasked to set up an ICP (*Incident Control Point*) to control the key holders coming back in to the badly damaged town centre; you had to see it to believe the damage. It also fell to me to brief ATO on his arrival. During all this, I had a young infantry lad near me when the bomb exploded, as well as the smell of the bomb there was this distinctive and familiar smell, I realised it was shit and it was very close. The lad looked at me and said 'Corp'; I think I have shit myself !' He had, literally!

Next morning we were out on a morning patrol through the town, and I was amazed to see business as usual; some shops had had their windows repaired, others were boarded up but still open. The resilience and resolve of the Dungannon residents was amazing.

Chapter 14

South Armagh 'Bandit Country'

SOUTH ARMAGH

Dave, Royal Tank Regiment

So, what do you know about South Armagh? Well, let's go through it; it's big, very green, pretty flat, has lots of water knocking around; scenic winding lanes and hedgerows; some really ugly villages, plenty of long abandoned farm houses and outbuildings; in fact, it's a tourists' treat.

Unless, of course, your 'tour' lasts for four or six months, and you're wearing a uniform. Then, South Armagh is a killer; literally. Like many other British soldiers, I spent time in South Armagh. It was during the early days, when we were not organised, and at a time when the so called 'freedom fighters' had pretty much a free rein. This was a time when the RUC stations at both Crossmaglen, and Forkhill were just that; stations ! 1920s built brick buildings painted grey, with no protection, no fencing, no sangars, no fields of fire; in fact, no nothing.

South Armagh border (Mark Campbell)

355

On my first visit to Crossmaglen, we drove through the silent village, where you could taste the unseen hostility. Past the abandoned cinema, which sported a tattered tricolour from its empty and mocking open window; a flag rumoured to be booby trapped, in case a passing Brit soldier happened to take a flying snatch at it. (*As was the case when Rifleman Nicholas Smith of the Royal Green Jackets was killed by a booby trap there on March 4, 1978.*)

We were met at the door of the grey building by an ancient policeman, holding an even older Webley Mk6 revolver. The gun had been manufactured in 1916; the ammunition for it, we later found out, was obsolete, and had itself been made in the 1920s. The chances of the gun ever firing were very slim indeed. It just got handed over, shift to shift, as it had been for many years. Being an inquisitive soul, I enquired from this old worthy, how many were on duty with him that day. His answer was a bit of a stunner; it was the same as every day, he replied; just him. He took us into the tiny back yard, where, sitting in a bit of upturned pipe, was a huge rocket, of the type you might expect to see at a coastguard station. It transpired that in the event of an attack, he was to run into the yard, light the blue touch paper, and then hopefully the rocket would signal the RUC station at Forkhill that all was not well; IF anyone there was watching or listening.

My first trip to South Armagh, (or just SA, as we called the place), was on an 'emergency' tour, which lasted just six weeks. We had arrived in the small town of Bessbrook, as the first British troops ever to be stationed there. Later, the local mill would be commandeered, but for now, we had to make do with the primary school, chosen because it had a cinema type projection room overlooking the school hall, which was deemed to be secure for use as an arms store. We were there for just about a week, but must have stirred the locals into some sort of offensive action, because during that time we had a drive-by shooting, and the unwelcome attentions of a sniper, whose location we never did pin down.

In a flurry of movement, we were sent packing to the nearby town of Markethill, and, more specifically, to the 19th century folly castle of Gosford. Long unlived in, with a badly leaking roof, this Victorian country residence had been constructed to replicate a Norman castle of about 1200 AD. It looked like one, smelt like one, and had the draughty stone corridors of one. However, it was placed in many acres of its own grounds, and had a massive tarmac area outside for our many and varied vehicles; mostly it could be easily guarded, and was right slap dab in the middle of our patrol area. The hum-drum routine of twenty four hour border patrols now started; but not for long.

The IRA were becoming very adept at positioning culvert and roadside bombs, which became very clear soon after, when a Land Rover patrol outside Newry one night was blown up. A young soldier called John Warnock was killed, adding once more to the total number of slain soldiers, which was rapidly growing in Ulster. (*The soldier mentioned here was John Warnock of the Royal Tank Regiment, killed at Derrybeg Park by an IRA* *landmine on 4 September, 1971.*) A week later we lost another of our own men, when Cpl Ian Armstrong* was tragically shot following a border incident. His death lay at the feet, and at the fault, of a senior officer, later to be knighted, and receive staff rank. Mysteriously the MOD contact report has been altered to not include this fact. In a hundred years time, when the last surviving ex soldier 'in the know', is long dead, then the official history will be taken as the honest truth; clever guys, these historians.

And so it went on, and our next casualty was a Sergeant friend of mine; once again wounded in a hidden roadside attack. He was hit in the face by a six inch coach bolt, but managed to return fire, and drive the ambush party back over the border. His driver did a marvellous job of getting him to medical attention before he lost all his blood. The plastic surgery and bone reconstruction took many years to complete. A few weeks later all Army patrols and transport were suspended in the SA region indefinitely. From that time on, it was either transport in and out by helicopter, or patrols on foot.

The conditions we were living in were at best, pathetic, and at the worst, a serious health hazard. In the 'great hall', the fantastic cooks had set up their cookhouse, and I remember with gratitude returning from patrol in the wee small hours, to be greeted by a cheery smile, a thick steak 'banjo', cup of steaming tea, and a couple of 'Mars Bars' slipped into my flak jacket top pocket. Then, up to the troop room, under a blanket, boots still on, munching that hot dribbling steak 'butty', swigging the tea down to the last drop, then curling up and sleeping into oblivion. There was no heating, and the damp Irish air was taking its toll on us. Water was at a premium, (with no hot stuff), which meant shaving in the cold stuff, which soon ripped our faces to bloody shreds. No beards allowed on active service in those days; the only thing about the modern British Army I would have welcomed. We all soon were scratching; lice had 'set in', and so had the dreaded crabs; cockroaches were getting to be a problem.

Early one morning, I remember awakening to the strange sound of steam blowing off; puzzled, and rubbing sleep from my eyes, I peered outside. Wonder of wonders; a mobile shower unit had arrived!!! Stripped off to our birthday suits, and stood in long lines on the car park, then trooped into the canvas showers, carrying as many pairs of socks and 'shreddies' that we could manage, soaking up the delicious hot water and steam, whilst scrubbing our smalls. This was definitely the high point of the tour; full marks to those guys with the shower unit. Much has been said over the years about the 'fighting' men in Northern Ireland, but without our support services, cooks, store men and logistics, then we would have been beaten from day one. And so our tour ground on, until once again we were on our way home.

(*The author would like to wholeheartedly associate himself with these remarks from Dave.*)

Three years ago, I returned to Gosford, now once again abandoned and asleep. Nothing has changed; the place is now boarded up, but still casts its brooding countenance over the surrounding parkland. The old car park is unchanged, and I was captivated with the place, somehow unable to drag myself away. We left as night was falling, and as we walked to the car, I heard the strange, unmistakable sound, of a Saracen APC starting up; a sound unforgettable. I turned around quickly, in surprise, expecting once again to see the Regimental 'Sarry, standing on its once familiar spot. The sound ceased; there was nothing there. Just the ghosts of my youth; or was it?

* Ian Armstrong's death is dealt with separately in this book

LAURENCE JUBB

Geoff Moore, Royal Engineers

I found the reference to Laurence Jubb, killed in I believe April 1972. In 1972 I was a member of 36 Engineer Regiment based at Maidstone, we had four squadrons 61 Field support (that I was a member of) and three Field squadrons 20, 50 and 60 all three of these squadrons were doing regular emergency tours, I believe in primarily Engineer roles.

Laurie Jubb to my best recollection was attached to 50 Field Squadron; he was an RCT driver as has been referred to elsewhere and was certainly not in the 'Long Range Snipers'. While our Regiment did have Catering Corps, Medical Corps and REME attachments I can only recall one RCT cap badge (this does not make me in viable but is my best recollection). At some stage I worked in the Regimental workshops and I was aware of Laurie driving AEC 10 tonners and other plant; however he was not a regular acquaintance of mine. As to the circumstances of his death we were given to understand back in 1972 that he was driving a Scammell Constructer with its trailer when he was stoned by youths, as was their want at the time. Whether he lost control or tried to avoid those in the road was a moot point, however the vehicle turned over and he was severely injured, not sufficiently to discourage the youths from continuing to stone him. I believe some of the public went to his aid but he soon succumbed to his injuries.

A short time after this two other members of 50 squadron were shot by a sniper while fortifying XMG, one of those Sapper Hurst was killed and an NCO injured. As a result of these and other incidents 50 squadron earned the nickname of 'Fighting 50 squadron'.

Driver Jubb (22) from the Doncaster area of South Yorkshire was killed on the Killylea Road just outside Armagh City. He left a young widow who gave birth to twin daughters within days of the tragic death of their father.

UNDERCOVER IN SOUTH ARMAGH

WO2 Roy Banwell, Cheshire Regiment

We undertook a large operation in a town in South Armagh, as a movement of IRA weapons was thought to be about to happen. It involved us spending several days in 'hide' areas. Sergeant Dennis Farrell came on the radio; in those days those radios had scrambling devices fitted to them to enable secure speech. He had seen four men carrying large holdalls entering a suspect's house. Our operations room contacted our tasking agents in Armagh, and it was decided that another unit who were on standby to support us on the operation, would be called in. A lull of a few hours passed whilst the operation gathered momentum. The radio came to life again with, 'Hello 'Six One' this is John, radio check over' (call sign 'Six One' was my call sign). I said nothing, without some form of identifying code word or number this could have been anyone and there was no way that I was going to answer him. He tried a couple of more times, until our operations controller Kenny Wallwork asked me to respond to 'John'. John explained that he was approaching my position and would pass us within a few minutes; he asked us to keep our weapons 'tight' (meaning: don't shoot us).

The other unit passed just below and to our left, and they surrounded the house. At this stage a young Policeman was dragged to the front door; he looked very pale and not too happy with his lot. He was forcibly held at the front door, whilst the other unit's commander knocked on the door from behind him. I could hear the Policemen saying something, and, then the door opened; the other unit were in the house in a flash. Unfortunately, over the intervening hours the weapons had been spirited away. The people in the house were taken away for forensic tests and the house searched in great detail. Even though the operation was now over it was a good few hours before we could extract ourselves without being seen. As I have said before, it was vitally important that we entered and left the area without leaving a trace; one day that position might be needed again. If the position was compromised, there might be something nasty waiting for the next people who go there, plus it would be the first place the IRA would look prior to carrying out an operation to ensure there were no troops in the area.

THE PLAYERS

Bill Callaghan, Royal Army Medical Corps: Att: UDR

Sometimes I'd manage to get out on to regular foot patrols myself. To be brutally honest I was something of a liability, no experience, no tactical awareness, no appreciation of ground and far too active an imagination, I kept myself scared for most of the time. The boys knew it too. We drove out one night and set up a VCP I was always the one to do 'the chat' while the boys covered me, and ran a computer check on the vehicle and driver. It was good fun sometimes and humbling at others.

I was always aware that I was impinging on their privacy while searching a vehicle and apologised for doing so. I never had any trouble, even with the players, we stopped one chap, I searched his car and we spoke amicably for a good while as I did so. He asked me how long I'd been in Ireland I told him, he asked me where I was from I told him, He asked if I was really UDR and I told him, he wished me well and hoped I'd get home safe, I thanked him. He had interrogated me! I really felt he meant that about getting home safe but then as he drove away I was informed he was a killer. He was shot dead at Loughgall by the SAS the following year, I felt saddened but he deserved it.

Intelligence reports now made public showed that the IRA planned to murder an off duty SF member and the job of 'containing' this was placed in the hands of the SAS. They had placed a soldier inside the station, and deployed a squad of 24 soldiers split into six groups around the station building. Just after 7 p.m. on 8 May 1987, IRA member Declan Arthurs drove a stolen JCB carrying the bomb through the perimetre fence of the RUC station. The van carrying the rest of the IRA unit pulled up and they jumped out and opened fire on the station. The IRA just managed to detonate its 200 lb bomb, heavily damaging the police station, before the SAS opened fire.

The SAS riddled the JCB and the van with bullets. In addition, the car of passer-by Anthony Hughes was fired on by the SAS. Hughes, 36, was killed and his brother badly wounded. Subsequent security forces statements said with

UDR in South Armagh (Mark Campbell)

regret that they had been innocent passers-by caught in crossfire. All eight IRA men were killed and the soldiers fired more than 600 rounds; the IRA men fired 70 rounds but did not hit any of the soldiers. The British recovered eight IRA weapons, including three Heckler & Koch G3 rifles, three FN rifles, a Ruger revolver and a Spas-12 shotgun. The RUC linked the guns to 7 murders and 12 attempted murders in the Province. One of the guns had been taken from a reserve RUC constable killed two years earlier.

The innocent civilian, Anthony Hughes, who was shot dead by the SAS, had been travelling in a car with his brother, Oliver, unaware of the ambush. Unfortunately, both brothers were wearing blue overalls similar to those sometimes worn by IRA members on operations and so were mistaken for IRA men engaged in the attack. As they attempted to reverse out of the gunfire, SAS troopers positioned nearby assumed that they were an IRA back-up unit and opened fire. Mr Hughes' widow later received compensation from the British Government for the death of her husband.

SOUTH ARMAGH 1971/72

Tim Francis, Royal Artillery

My first tour from September 1971 to January 1972 was on secondment to a missile battery from our Regiment. I am not sure how deployments were within the regiment as a whole were decided but we certainly eventually found ourselves to be one of the first units to have the pleasure of serving in what became known as 'bandit country' in South Armagh.

We were deployed for the first month or so of the tour, initially on what was then known as Province Reserve, based at Ballykinlar and then Magilligan carrying out a variety of duties including helping out with arrests in Londonderry and a lot of VCPs in the surrounding countryside. We also had the dubious pleasure of manning checkpoints controlling and searching traffic into rallies from both sides of the sectarian divide; events including Bernadette Devlin speaking in Enniskillen and an Ian Paisley rally in Newtownards. This latter incident was where our inimitable Troop Sergeant Major chastised the man himself for jumping the queue , with the words 'I don't give a f-- – who you are; get back in line.' Those of us in the vicinity found it hard to recall this approach in the various lectures we had received on how to address members of the public, particularly those wearing dog collars.

A number of us also spent a memorable night in a convent which had received threats of an imminent attack which fortunately did not materialise, the highlight of this night was when our troop commander, having just lectured us about language and behaviour, tripped in the chapel and inadvertently used the 'F' word ! We were also 'volunteered' to be part of the studio audience for a live Cilla Black show at Aldergrove airport one Saturday night; Cilla was great but all the guests were elsewhere and linked up.

My troop was the first to move into what was then the Newtownhamilton RUC station in the autumn of 1971. Other troops in the battery went to Crossmaglen and Forkhill RUC stations. When we first arrived in the town the locals were generally friendly but gradually as the days went by you could feel the pressure being put on all around by the local boyos and the friendliness fell away and we knew it was better not to pursue this to avoid good people getting into trouble.

Whilst at Newtownhamilton we were regularly accused of having the cushy option and it probably was in some ways, but we did have our moments sometimes humorous sometimes not nice at all. Accommodation was pretty basic; 30 of us slept on double bunks in an old shooting range at the back of the police station with one bath and 2 toilets between us and also the fact that our cook was not a 'master chef' to put it mildly. Our TSM certainly had this view as at one stage early in the tour at Magilligan he locked him in a cell as a punishment for the latest burnt offering. At the end of the tour when we were carrying out an inventory of kit and ammunition we discovered that we had a couple of spare rubber baton rounds, the question of what we do with them was asked and as we were thinking about it, our intrepid cook came into view and there was an instant flash of inspiration from all including Pvt. Price of the ACC who was out of the door and back in his kitchen before anyone could move!

'CONTACT' IN SOUTH ARMAGH

Haydn Davies, Royal Regiment of Wales

The word 'contact' was banned from the telephone or radio traffic unless the caller was actively engaged or had contact with the IRA.

A sleepy Ops officer in South Armagh was drowsing in his Ops room chair in the small hours, in his drowsiness he heard the word 'Contact' being used on his Radio. He grabbed the handset and screamed into it. 'Hello all stations; this is Zero; do not use, I repeat do not use the word 'contact' on this net. Use the alternative words 'get in touch' over!' There was silence for about half a minute when a broad Scots accent replied: 'Hello Zero this is 13 Alfa; the IRA are trying to get in touch me with an RPG and a 20mm cannon. Over.'

AUCHNACLOY

Dave Maltby, Queen's Dragoon Guards

At the end of March, the Squadron was re-deployed to Aughnacloy, with orders to carry out rural Patrolling and manning of the VCP. Not sure of the date, but I think it was 6th April 76; my section was manning the VCP. Two men were located on the barrier and one in a sangar with a GPMG, commonly referred to as a 'Jimpy' and a Saracen equipped with

.30 Browning on a fixed firing line to an area known as the 'Butts,' a well established firing point by the IRA.

In the middle of the VCP was a further Saracen, again on a fixed firing line to the 'butts.' Finally, there were two men on the northern barriers accompanied by an RUC officer. Although the Saracens were unmanned, they were part of our IA drill should we come under fire, with certain individuals delegated to man the Browning. All this was controlled by our Troop Leader or Sgt from a Portacabin located in the centre of the VCP.

It was a warm evening coming into April and things had been going pretty smoothly. It was starting to get dark and it was pretty quiet with not much traffic coming through. Suddenly two shots rang out from the southern barrier. I turned around and saw 'Pud' sitting on the ground with his rifle to his shoulder and returning fire at a gunman on the road who had opened fire on him. The next minute, a machine gun and single shots were fired at us from the, butts,' and Sgt 'Taff' who was in the control room, quickly extinguished all lights and the lads took up their IA (*Immediate Action*) positions. Both Saracens opened up on the 'butts' and I dashed up to the southern sangar, to assist 'Ginge' with the Jimpy. Rounds were bouncing off the front of the sangar coming from the butts. There was sporadic fire over the next 90 minutes from both sides and we had now been joined by the QRF who were also laying down fire. What we really could have done with was illuminating flares and tracer for the .30s.

Eventually, things quietened down and the IRA obviously legged it. There were no reports of any hits from the follow up next day. This did surprise me due to the amount of fire laid down. As the 'butts' were the other side of the border, they could not be checked by our own people for obvious reasons. On the upside, a local farmer came out to congratulate us saying 'I have lived here over 30 years, heard and seen a few cross border gun battles – but that is the best one yet. All my teacups fell off the shelves yah bastards!'

One other point of amusement was that located in the north overlooking the VCP was a house with the gable window facing the VCP. Whilst all this was going on, the inhabitants had their faces to the window watching while the rounds from the 'butts' bounced off the wall; crazy people. Sadly, the same night a Greenfinch was killed on our Regimental TAOR in Middletown, so this episode took second place.

That concluded a very eventful tour, some successful finds and incidents, with everybody returning home with their thoughts either good or bad. I have good and bad memories after 32 years, in particular, the Hillcrest bombing, something that I live with after all these years.

The 'Greenfinch' – a female UDR soldier – to whom Dave refers was Gillian Liggett (33) who was shot whilst on patrol on the Armagh-Middletown Road that same night as the QDG's fire fight. A moving account by Haydn Davies who was close family friend can be found in the author's *A Long Long War*.

Colour Sergeant Ken Ambrose, Royal Green Jackets

In the latter part of 1974 I was contemplating my fifth tour in the Province. The previous four tours had all been in Belfast but this one was going to be in South Armagh, known to most as `Indian country` and not without just cause.

The skills the Recce platoon had developed in its manning of covert OPs in an urban area were honed to a high standard by the end of our previous tour. However, our knowledge of rural close observation was limited and as a result the Boss nominated me and one of the section sergeants to attend a 10 day course being run by one of the covert units in Northern Ireland. The course brief read well with a large proportion of the first week being taken up with classroom and theory work, equipment requirements, photography and weapons, planning and reconnaissance. The culminating point was to be a 72 hour insertion on to an actual target in South Armagh. Having completed the course we could then pass on our knowledge to the remainder of the platoon.

The theory part of the course passed without incident and Pete and I were given the target for our final x. After carrying out the laid down procedures for Recce, equipment checks, routes, radio and emergency passwords we were dropped off by heli about 3 miles from the target. The trek into the target area and insertion into a very large bramble bush about 5 metres from the target's front door were all completed by about 3.30am. Pete agreed to take the first watch and woke me up at around 6.30am. The camera equipment was already set up and as I moved into position Pete crawled into our only sleeping bag and was asleep in no time at all.

It was about 7.15am that the first activity occurred at the farmhouse and by around 9am I was already on my second roll of film. There were a lot of visitors and I was busy snapping away and logging the frames as they were taken.

At about 9.30 the male occupant at the farm came out of his front door and leaned against the door frame smoking and talking to someone in the house over his shoulder as he stood at the door. I took a couple more pictures of him for good measure and it was at that point that Pete let out a very loud snore. The guy at the front door did a double take and looked directly us. He was only yards away so I could not make any sudden moves towards Pete for fear of shaking the bush we were in. The guy at the door shrugged and shook his head and carried on talking to whoever was behind him. I had just started breathing again when Pete let out another loud snore. This time the guy began walking towards us and at that moment I made my decision.

As the fast moving man got within two yards of our position I leaned back, shook Pete hard, and pulled the hammer back on my Browning pistol, pushed the camera back behind me and at the same time I stood up. The man stopped with a totally surprised look on his face. There was no more than a yard between us. 'Hello mate,' I said. 'Sorry if we startled you. We got separated from our patrol last night and lost our way in the dark.

Our radio was on the blink so we decided to rest up until it got light I hope you didn't mind us using your bush to grab a few winks.'

He looked me up and down, clocked the Browning and responded with 'You British bastard,' and turned on his heel towards the front door. I turned to Pete who had already finished packing his rucksack. He said 'What was that all about?' I responded with 'Later' and shoved the Pentax camera into my sack, finished tying it and swung it on my back and grabbed my SLR. 'Let's go.' I said and headed off across the field towards our emergency pick up point. As we walked Pete was talking on the radio calling in our ride home. We knew that the farm had a phone and the fact that the nearest populated area was about 8 miles away but there were other farms in between and we did not know how close `the boys` were and how long it would take them to get to us. Judging by the not over friendly greeting at the target farm we needed to be extracted quickly.

Some cover was provided by the rolling countryside but apart from that and the odd makeshift farm wall we were completely exposed and in some directions for up to five or six hundred metres. By the time we had travelled another half mile I could already hear distant helicopter activity and hoped that this was our taxi. As luck would have, it was. When we got to the PUP (*pick up point*), we were there no more than a couple of minutes when the Scout appeared.

Several weeks later and back in Dover Pete and I started the platoon training programme for the forthcoming NI Tour and when we came to the OP layout we both of us, not surprisingly, insisted that every member of an OP party must be no further away than arms length when resting. We also thought about the provision of anti-snoring devices as well!

SOUTH ARMAGH

Private Richard Smith, Duke of Wellingtons

It was 25 April, 1987, and we were tasked to help refurb the border crossing O.P.s near the Sugarloaf Mountain. We were choppered in by Chinook and dumped on farm land. We Immediately set about digging up this poor Farmer's land in order to make earthwork support for the tents. The Farmer was, understandably furious, but we were doing as we had been told and just ignored his rantings. Basically, our job was to show a high profile SF presence on the border, which is basically what we did!

On one of the days, were on foot patrol and carrying out roving VCPs on the road, when, suddenly, the whole ground shook and threw the four of us off our feet. We immediately dragged ourselves up and, although we knew that we had been in an explosion, had no idea where it had happened or what injuries had been caused.

It was only later that we found out the PIRA had planted a landmine and detonated it under the car in which a senior Judge, Maurice Gibson and his wife, Cecily were travelling and killed them both.

(The judge (73) was one of the most senior of the Northern Ireland Judiciary and he and his wife (67) were targeted by the IRA for presiding over the case of an IRA terrorist. The landmine exploded at Killeen close to where the Duke of Wellingtons were patrolling and killed them both instantly. The car was being protected by Garda Sichona up to the border and from there by the RUC; the massive security lapse led to strained relations between the police forces of both countries.)

It was on this same op, that we heard on the RT, the words 'SAS 9, IRA 0) and the news broke about the Loughall shooting, where the SAS had ambushed and wiped out an IRA ASU. I do remember that the weather was so lovely, that we had taken off our NIBAs and just patrolled in combats; then one morning, we woke up, covered in snow! The Army had to fly 1950s style Parkas in for us.

NEWTOWNHAMILTON

Tim Francis, Royal Artillery

We had 2 incidents of accidental discharges; one guy, much later a senior NCO, forgot his unloading drills in Ballykinlar, cocking his SLR with the magazine still on, not looking in the breech and pulling the trigger. He then said: 'Who was that?' the result was 28 days in the Paras' nick. The second incident was on a foot patrol at night on the County Armagh

IRA van after the SAS ambush at Loughall (Richard Smith)

border where the guy in question was carrying the radio for the evening; meaning he carried an SMG instead of an SLR. He fell down a ditch in the dark, accidentally fired a single round and again 28 days resulted. This guy later had a distinguished career in the police including being decorated for gallantry.

We spent a lot of time hanging around on standby, much of which was spent by some of us in playing poker; becoming quite the experts by the time the advance party of our relieving unit, the Devon and Dorsets arrived. One of them, a Corporal, made the fatal statement of 'I have brought £100 with me to last the tour as I am not going to draw any pay during the whole time.' He did rather fancy himself as a card player but by about the 5th night of his tour, we had relieved him of it all. We also had an incident with our troop commander at Newtownhamilton towards the end of the tour; he obviously had some issues with life and got drunk one night and threatened to shoot an RUC officer resident there. The officer came looking for him at a later date and there had to be a forced separation of them with cells having to be used .Troop Commanders were not often confined to a cell in my experience, not a word of this left the troop as far as I am aware but it was certainly a potential disaster with pistols being waved around.

On our last night in Newtownhamilton we were due to go on our last mobile VCP patrol; not something we were massively enthusiastic about on a cold wet January night. As we were getting ready we noticed the Saracen had a puncture and started to change the wheel and, being men of initiative, we then realised that if the jack was to slip we would have no means of getting it jacked up again and what a disaster that would be as we would be unable to patrol ! We looked at each other and then a comrade who was not renowned for doing such things applied a size 11 DMS boot very hard to the jack which did the trick; no last patrol !

What I do vividly remember is the different relationship between the guys who had been on the tour and those who had not gone; a sort of unspoken trust that was a result of the fact that you had, on occasion, relied on others to watch your back; literally. There was also a different relationship with senior ranks as they came to realise that they also had to rely on junior ranks in a way they probably had not previously believed was necessary.

Newtownhamilton takes its name from Alexander Hamilton, a descendant of a John Hamilton from Scotland who founded Hamiltonsbawn in 1619. The parish was created in 1773 out of the neighbouring parish of Creggan. Back in May 1920, IRA man, Frank Aiken led nearly 200 volunteers in an attack on the RUC barracks there, forcing the police to surrender and then burning the building and seizing the arms contained within.

THE IRA AND NORAID

Bill Callaghan, Royal Army Medical Corps

In July, the IRA launched a spectacular for NORAID, the fundraising organisation for Americans who supported Irish terrorism. The Birches was an unmanned police station at night, which was something of a propaganda coup for the IRA as it implied that we, the evil oppressors were scared of the dark and in a part time retreat. Conversely, if it had been a manned station it wouldn't have been the target for such a ridiculous assault. The destruction of the Birches police station involved the theft of a bulldozer, a low-loader to transport it; several cars and a speedboat for a dramatic if silly and unrealistic get away.

Explosives were placed in beer kegs these were held in the bulldozer's bucket scoop and the lot was driven on the low-loader to the target. One cell placed a cordon around the deserted location and once 'secure' another cell arrived with the goods. The bulldozer was driven off the low-loader and through the surrounding fence. The bucket was then driven through the wall of the station and the bomb's timer began running. The cells made their way to the getaway cars and some of the crew were driven to a stolen speedboat on Loch Neagh.

The bomb went off and the community's police station was destroyed. This attack didn't kill anyone but it terrorised the people who'd had their vehicles hijacked and then stolen to make the attack possible. The timing and execution of this raid, during a visit of NORAID's chief operator, was perfect. So much so that we believed at the time it had been staged for

UDR in South Armagh (Mark Campbell)

a film to show the valued contributors just what they were getting for their 'terror dollars.'

PLAIN CLOTHES IN ARMAGH

Bill Callaghan, Royal Army Medical Corps, Att: UDR

We were driven to Dungannon by the MT comedian and on the way we stopped for a drink in Newry. He pointed out a few places of recent terrorist activity. I was aware how obvious I looked, I'd had my hair cropped for a course and I was wearing jeans and desert boots; it was a little unsettling being in a place where your clothes could get you killed.

We arrived at our base, Killymeal House, the HQ of 8th Battalion Ulster Defence Regiment or 8 UDR in 'armyspeak.' I was introduced to a few key personnel of the Regiment; they'd been celebrating something and seemed pretty happy but were largely disinterested and unhelpful. I was told that I'd be accommodated elsewhere for the evening. I was then issued a Browning 9mm pistol, a full clip and a spare. I was taken to the MT pool, given the keys to a red van and some directions to Drummad Barracks in Armagh.

I set off; apart from some hastily and largely incomprehensible shouted directions, I was totally unprepared and was soon lost. I didn't dare ask directions. It was early summer, and there were crowds about. It was difficult to drive through the throng and I had to come to a halt by the green in Armagh. Men in immaculate whites were playing cricket. It was all so traditional and normal like any village in England. I knew it wasn't and I was nervous; my pistol was loaded and cocked with the safety on, in the map pocket of the door, on the other side. Through the few millimetres of steel that made the door, brushing right by, were children, old dears; the general populace of Armagh. They were all possible enemies, killers, targets, and I felt fraught. At any moment, I imagined they'd notice that, despite the heat of the evening, my windows were all wound up, just as I was. They'd see my fear, they'd know I was alone, they'd rip me from the car and they'd slot me. (A little less than two years later, from the comfort of their armchairs, through the box in the corner, the nation watched with horror as two Royal Signals NCOs suffered exactly that fate. As I watched I then remembered these moments of my own and wept uncontrollably.)

I stared out of the window; a wicket shattered and the cry of 'Owzat?' was answered with cheers. The hapless batsman walked off the crease, head down, not wanting to be seen or talked too. I knew how he felt. The crowd eased and I drove on, I made it to the Barrack gates and was bathed in sweat.

Chapter 15

Crossmaglen

Crossmaglen; In Irish: *Crois Mhic Lionnáin* or Lennon's Cross. It is a village in south County Armagh. It had a population of 1,459 people in the 2001 Census and is the largest village in South Armagh. The village centre is the site of a large Police Service of Northern Ireland (PSNI, formerly the Royal Ulster Constabulary) base and formerly of an observation tower.

The town's name means Lennon's Cross, a reference to the two roads which intersect at the town square, linking Dundalk with Keady and Carrickmacross with Newry. Lennon is believed to be Owen Lennon, a local resident in the 18th century, who was famed as the owner of a shebeen, an illegal ale house.

The square's name commemorates Cardinal Tomás Ó Fiaich, a local man who became Primate of All Ireland. Locals claim the square is the largest in Western Europe, after Saint Peter's Square in Rome. Crossmaglen has been described by Belfast journalist Malachi O'Doherty as 'a southern town that had the border laid down on the wrong side of it.'

During the Troubles, at least 58 police officers and 124 soldiers were killed by the IRA in South Armagh, many actually in Crossmaglen itself. South Armagh is known locally as the 'Orchard County' but to the security forces it will be forever known as 'Bandit Country' a term coined by the late Merlyn Rees, MP, when he was Northern Ireland Secretary during the Wilson/Callaghan Labour government. It is the subject of an excellent book by Toby Harnden, bearing its eponymous title.

On 11 August 1970, Samuel Donaldson (23) and Robert Millar (26), of the Royal Ulster Constabulary, were killed by an IRA booby trap bomb attached to an abandoned car, near Crossmaglen. They were the first RUC officers killed at Crossmaglen during the troubles; they would not be the last. The tragic toll of British soldiers is thought to have been started when Irish-born Private Robert Brenner (25) of the Queen's Regiment was abducted by the Official IRA, either in, or en-route to visit his fiancé in Dundalk on the Republic side of the border. He had been shot and his body dumped at Teer, just outside Crossmaglen itself on November 28, 1971. On May 17, the following year, whilst working outside of the RUC station in Crossmaglen itself, Sapper Ronald Lewis (25) of the Royal Engineers was shot and killed and a comrade wounded. Just three miles and two months later, Captain John Young (22) was killed whilst defusing an IRA bomb at Silverbridge. The following day, two soldiers of the Duke of Wellington's Regiment, Corporal Terence Graham (24) and Private James Lee (25) were killed by an IRA landmine just outside Crossmaglen.

A month later, whilst in a mobile patrol, the Royal Scots Dragoon Guards lost Trooper Ian Caie (19) to a similar IRA device. On October 25, 10 days after being wounded by an IRA bomb, 32 year old Staff Sergeant John Morrell of the South Staffs died of his wounds after a brave struggle for life; he had been airlifted to a hospital in England. 1972 and 'bandit country' proved again that it had not finished its toll of the SF and in late November the Argylls lost two of its men to another IRA bomb attack at Cullyhanna, just three miles away from Crossmaglen village. On the 20th of that month, Captain William Watson (28) and Sergeant James Strothers (31) were killed by an IRA booby trap device in an abandoned farmhouse; the toll was mounting.

1973 arrived – the second worst year of the troubles in terms of SF deaths – and on March 8, Corporal Joseph Leahy of the Duke of Edinburghs died of his wounds, several days after being very badly wounded near Forkhill by an IRA booby trap. The Corporal, attached at the time to the Royal Hampshires was 31 and came from Swindon. Five days after his death, one of his Hampshire colleagues, Private John King was killed by a similar device at Cooldferry Bridge near Crossmaglen whilst on patrol. It would be the May and the approach of another Ulster summer before the IRA struck again in the Crossmaglen area. At Mowybane on the fifth, two soldiers from the famous 17/21st Lancers, motto 'Death or Glory' and with battle honours dating back to the Charge of the Light Brigade were killed. Trooper John Gibbons (22) and Corporal Terence Williams (35) were killed by an IRA landmine whilst on foot patrol; killed alongside them was a Sergeant Major from the Parachute Regiment, William Vines who was 36.

Later the same month, Sergeant John Wallace (31) of the Parachute Regiment and Royal Engineer Sergeant Major Ian Donald (35) were killed by an IRA bomb at Cullaville near Crossmaglen. In late October, just hours after the clocks had 'gone back' and British wintertime was just starting, Private Stephen Hall (21) of the Light Infantry was shot by the IRA. He was killed in the square in the village during a brief fire fight.

The new year of 1974 came and with it all the hopes that one traditionally associates with the birth of a new year but died very quickly. On Monday, February 18 when RAOC soldier Sergeant Alan Brammah (31) was killed defusing a bomb at Moybane. A month later, two Paratroopers were killed in a burst of automatic gunfire just outside Crossmaglen. Forkhill, close to Crossmaglen despite being a tiny village in South Armagh did its best to live up to the title of 'Bandit Country' and it was never far from the headlines during the ugly course of the troubles. On March 10 1974 Michael McCreesh (15) and Michael Gallagher (18), both Catholic civilians, were killed by an IRA booby trap bomb hidden in an abandoned car and intended for a British Army foot patrol, at Drumintee, near Forkhill; the older boy died on 14 March 1974. Roy Bedford and Phillip James (both 22) were hit by IRA gunmen who were firing from across the border with the Republic.

On August 13, as Ulster basked in the late summer sunshine, two Royal Marines were killed at Drumuckaval, some two miles from Crossmaglen in a tragic incident which belied the professionalism of their senior officers. An observation post had been unmanned for over a week and the IRA, ever vigilant, ever desperate to kill British soldiers were unable to resist this opportunity, and booby-trapped the post. Michael John (20) from St Albans, and Dennis Leach (20) from Leeds were killed when the IRA detonated the device planted during the period between occupations of the OP.

The morning after Bonfire Night, six IRA gunmen took over a house in the village centre and when a 6-man patrol of the Duke of Edinburgh's Regiment

(DERR) walked past, they opened fire and killed Private Brian Allen (20) and Corporal Stephen Windsor (26). Corporal Windsor was from the Devon & Dorsets on attachment to the DERRs; one of the men died at the scene and the other whilst being airlifted to hospital. A third soldier was wounded and he reported that villagers had walked by after the shooting, smirking and making sarcastic comments.

As the tragic year of 1974 drew to a close, the area had not finished with the SF and with only two days of the year remaining, Green Jacket Michael Gibson (20) an East Ender, died of his wounds received at Forkhill 15 days earlier. He died while attending the scene of a burglary near Forkhill along with 2 members of the RUC. When their car arrived at the scene, one of the Police Officers went to the house leaving the other and Michael in the car; a number of gunmen then approached the rear of the car and fired in through the rear screen. Most of the shots were fired towards the Police Officer as he was in uniform; 2 rounds hit Michael at the base of the spine. He was first flown to Daisy Hill Hospital in Newry but concerns over security prompted a move to Musgrave Hospital in Belfast. Constable David McNeice (19) of the RUC died at the scene of the shooting; Rifleman Gibson died of his wounds 30 days later on December 29.

The Grim Reaper worked all over Northern Ireland during those days; in the Crossmaglen area, he worked overtime.

The following summer, four soldiers were killed by an IRA landmine in the worst single incident in the Crossmaglen area. On July 17 at Cortreasla Bridge, Fords Crossing near Forkhill, an Army helicopter had landed a four man team to investigate an abandoned milk churn – a popular method of IRA bomb makers – in a field as it was thought that it may contain a device. As the four

Forkhill Base, 1980 (Tony Yarwood)

man team approached, hidden bombers detonated a landmine in a nearby hedge; the explosion killed all four men. Major Peter Willis (37) Green Howards; ATO Edward Garside, RAOC; ATO Calvert Brown (34), RAOC and Sergeant Samuel McCarter of the Royal Engineers all died at the scene and a badly injured soldier was airlifted to hospital. On October 10, Corporal David Gleeson (29) of the Royal Regiment of Fusiliers (RRF) whilst travelling in an armoured car was killed by an IRA bomb at Lurgancullenboy, near Crossmaglen. Six weeks later, Crossmaglen claimed 4 more RRF lives; on November 21, Sergeant John Francis (29) from Kent was killed by an IRA booby trap and then in a scene tragically reminiscent of a World War II 'last stand' three more members of the Regiment were killed and a fourth badly wounded. At Drumuckvall, scene of the earlier tragedy which claimed the lives of two Royal Marines, a four man team from the RRF was dug in, in a hidden OP near the border. It came under heavy and sustained attack from a large party of IRA gunmen from over the nearby border. Bizarrely, an IRA gunman called upon the soldiers to surrender; the soldiers refused and three were killed and a fourth, badly wounded, managed to crawl away for help. An IRA spokesman the following day made a series of statements – bizarre in the extreme – confirming that they had wanted the men to surrender. The fate of their 'POWs' does not bear thinking about. The three to die were: Fusilier James Duncan (19) from Oldham; Fusilier Peter McDonald (19) from Manchester and Fusilier Michael Sampson (20) from the Isle of Man.

The following summer, Paratrooper Private William Snowdon (18) was very badly injured by an IRA bomb just outside the village; 6 days later, he died of his injuries. Two months later, in an incident covered in both this book and *A Long Long War* by the same author, James Borucki (19) also of the Parachute Regiment was killed by a booby trapped device in the centre of Crossmaglen.

1977 arrived and with the celebrations barely a day old, the Royal Highland Fusiliers lost 23 year old David Hind, a Kilmarnock man, in a firefight inside the village with IRA gunmen. He was not the first IRA victim of the New Year, as the terrorists had killed a 15 month old baby in North Belfast with the New Year barely hours old. No further British soldiers were killed in the area for the remainder of the year, although on or about May 10, 1977, Robert Nairac (29), an undercover soldier, was abducted by the IRA outside the Three Step Inn, Drumintee, near Forkhill. He was killed there after torture and his body was never recovered. Nairac was posthumously awarded the George Cross.

On March 4, 1978, in an incident again covered later in this chapter the Green Jackets lost Rifleman Nicholas (Nicky to his friends) Smith when an IRA booby trap exploded as he attempted to pull down an Irish tricolour in the centre of the village. What the previous year had given in better news, this year was to snatch back and a further 6 soldiers would be returned to their families in Union Jack-draped coffins. On July 12, the Parachute Regiment lost another of its soldiers when Private Jack Fisher (19) was killed by an IRA bomb. On August 17, 1978, Royal Marine Corporal Robert Miller (22) was killed by a car bomb in nearby Forkhill. On November12, another Royal Marine Gareth Wheddon (19) from Sussex died of the wounds he had sustained in an explosion.

The year's final tragedy – for this part of 'bandit country' at least – took place a bare four days before Christmas. A four man brick of the Grenadier

Guards was on routine foot patrol in the centre of Crossmaglen when a stolen GPO van raced into the village and gunmen sprayed them with automatic fire. Three of the Grenadiers were very badly wounded and all three died in the helicopter evacuating them to hospital; the IRA had sickeningly delivered an early 'Christmas present' to families in Sussex, Cheshire and the Blackpool area of Lancashire. The three dead soldiers were Glen Ling (18), Andrew Duggan (20) and Kevin Johnson who was 20. Merlyn Rees' dubbing of the area as 'Bandit Country' was proving to be grimly accurate.

1979, and the approach of the tenth anniversary of the troubles, arrived, but for once, Crossmaglen was not centre stage; that 'title' would belong to a beautiful part of the border area over to the East; to Warrenpoint in Co Down. On a sunny day in August, the IRA would have its single biggest 'success' in its war against the SF, when 17 members of the Parachute Regiment and two soldiers of the Queens Own Highlanders (QOH) were killed by two IRA bombs.

In that year, the QOH lost Private Alan McMillan (19) who died of his wounds following a terrorist bomb attack on July 8 in the village square in Crossmaglen. He had only been in the Province for two days and died with his grieving parents at his bedside. Close to Christmas, Private Peter Grundy (21) of the Parachute Regiment was killed by an IRA bomb at Forkhill; with a tragic irony, it was noted that he had survived the slaughter at Warrenpoint, four months earlier.

New Year's Day, 1980 saw two more Paratroopers killed but in desperately tragic circumstances; that oxymoron 'friendly fire' was the cause of the deaths of Lieutenant Simon Bates (23) and Private Gerald Hardy (18). Both were shot by members of their own Regiment at Tullydonnell, near Forkhill in the Crossmaglen area. Mistaken in the darkness for terrorists, they were both accidentally shot and died at the scene. The younger of the two had only turned 18 on the 30th of the previous month. In the March of that same year, 1 King's Own Border were in occupation and lost three of their young soldiers – two of whom were only 18 – in the space of a mere 10 days. On March 15, Private John Bateman was shot and killed by an IRA sniper from a firing position in a graveyard in Newry Road, Crossmaglen. Morale was still high among the Battalion whose HQ was Carlisle despite the fact that, 8 days earlier, another Borderer, Sean Walker had been terribly injured in a car bomb attack. The author has personally seen the correspondence between Major Andrew MacDonald and the boy's family and can attest to the poignancy of the incident; sadly, after a long fight for life, Private Walker died of his wounds on March 21. In addition to these tragedies, the Battalion had already lost Private Owen Pavey (19), killed in an accidental shooting in the area on March 11.

On August 9, the Parachute Regiment lost 29 year old Sergeant Brian Brown killed by an IRA bomb at Forkhill and he was the 40th soldier from the Parachute Regiment to die in, or as a result of the troubles; he was the 50th soldier to be killed in the Crossmaglen area.

Almost a year was to pass before there was another soldier killed in the area, partly as a result of improved tactics, a rapid growth in experience, and the discontinuance of mobile patrols, with air transportation being the favoured and safest form of deployment. However, the IRA in that part of South Armagh was patient and bided their time. That time arrived on July 16, 1981 when senior officers decided to set up an ill-conceived ambush in a scrap yard at Glassdrummond, close to Crossmaglen and within sight of the border with Co Monaghan in the Republic. Three members of the Royal Green Jackets, including John Moore and Lance Corporal Gavin Dean [*see John Moore's excellent piece in* A Long Long War *by the same author*] were inside two scrapped vehicles in the OP attempting to set up an ambush of an IRA gang. Suddenly heavy and sustained automatic fire was directed into their position from the direction of the Republic. At the end of a brief fire fight, both John Moore and Gavin Dean were badly wounded and the third Jacket unable to help them. Both wounded men were eventually airlifted from the scene, but sadly, Lance Corporal Dean (21) from Kent died of his wounds in hospital. John Moore was shot in the spine and is now confined to a wheelchair.

A further 28 months would pass before the IRA struck again in the Crossmaglen area and, on November 6, 1983, having wounded by a bomb, some 10 days earlier, Stephen Taverner (24) of the Devon & Dorsets, died of his wounds. It would be not until the following May that the IRA struck again in the area. On May 29, Lance Corporal Steven Anderson (23) of the Staffordshire Regiment was killed by an IRA landmine whilst on a joint Army-RUC patrol.

On July 9, 1986, almost 5 years to the day of an earlier Green Jackets tragedy, Glassdrummond was again the scene of Army fatalities. On that day, Private Carl Davis (24) and Private Mitchell Bertram (23) of the Royal Anglians were both killed when an IRA booby trap exploded as they examined a suspect vehicle. By this stage of the troubles, mercifully, Army deaths in that part of 'Bandit Country' were few and far between and it was almost 2 years later before another soldier was killed. On May 21, 1988, an Army dog-handler, Corporal Derek Hayes from the Royal Pioneer Corps and his dog 'Ben' were killed at Castleblaney Road, Crossmaglen. They were investigating a suspect box in a ditch when he trod on a pressure pad which detonated the device; both were killed instantly. *Lost Lives* notes, poignantly, that the ashes of 'Ben' were buried alongside Corporal Hayes.

On July 27, a joint RUC-Parachute Regiment was patrolling at Cullyhanna when a landmine detonated; several were wounded, but Sergeant Michael Matthews of 1 Para was dreadfully injured. He died of his wounds two days later. 1988 came and went without the 'Reaper' appearing in the Crossmaglen area but the following May, the Worcester & Sherwood Foresters lost Corporal Stephen McGonigle (31) to an IRA bomb at Silverbridge. He was the father of two young children and came from the Newark area.

On May 5, 1990, the Scots Guards were based in the Crossmaglen area and were patrolling near Cullyhanna village when they came under heavy fire from an abandoned village. Lance Sergeant Graham Stewart (24) of the Scots Guards was hit and died almost immediately; Army sources claimed that the IRA gunmen were members of the notorious 'Cullyhanna gun crew' who killed DERR men, John Randall and Lance Corporal Kevin Pullin and wounded Lance Corporal Mark Overson. 1990 was a difficult time for the Scots Guards, losing Guardsman Alex Ireland, a victim of the euphemistic term 'death by violent or unnatural causes' and Guardsman Paul Brown killed in an accident.

The following year, Lance Corporal Simon Ware was killed in an area between Newtownhamilton and Crossmaglen. He was 22 years old and was from the 2nd Battalion, Coldstream Guards; he had been in the army for 5 years and was on his second tour of Northern Ireland. On Saturday 17th August 1991 he formed part of a 12 man patrol forming three four man teams and was the third man in his team when they were approaching a helicopter pick point north of Carrickovaddy Woods near to Newtownhamilton. They were returning from a three day operation and were 20 minutes from being picked up when they entered a track through the wood. As Simon exited a left hand bend, a device functioned in an embankment to his right killing him instantly. The device was approximately 250lb and so large was the explosion, that it was heard and felt up to 6 miles away. Simon left a widow who he had married only two days before he deployed to Northern Ireland.

Three months later, on November 27, the IRA continued their sickening policy of targeting part-time members of the UDR at either home or work and murdering them. Only 25 days after they had appallingly attacked the military wing of Musgrave Park Hospital and despite the revulsion of the civilized world, they abducted lorry driver Kenneth Newell (31) as he delivered soft drinks in Cullaville. He was then allegedly tortured, before being shot and dumped at the roadside.

In the summer of 1992, using the .50 Barrett – an American weapon – the IRA shot and killed Light Infantryman Paul Turner (18) as he stood in the centre of Crossmaglen. Eyewitnesses told that the force of the impact was so great, that Private Turner was killed absolutely instantly.

1993 was, after the slowdown of soldiers' deaths in the area, a year of tragic disappointment for the Army, as four were killed. Before the toll of soldiers continued, RUC officer Jonathan Reid (30) was shot and killed by the IRA on Castleblaney Road, Crossmaglen; he was the last RUC officer to die in that part of 'Bandit Country.' On March, 17, the Royal Scots lost Lance Corporal Lawrence Dickson (26) shot in Forkhill. He was hit by a single shot and, although wearing NIBA (Northern Ireland Body Armour) due to a design fault, there was no side protection and he died within an hour of the shot. In June and July in incidents described movingly by Mark Overson in *A Long Long War* the Duke of Edinburgh's Regiment lost John Randall (19) and Kevin Pullin (28) in the Crossmaglen area.

The Regiment's Casualty Visiting Officer (CVO) was spared a further trip to an unsuspecting family in England by sheer luck on April 3. On that day – a Saturday – Lance Corporal Mark Overson was on a roving VCP on the Creggan Road, near Crossmaglen. Having just checked a car which then drove off, he was shot in the back as he turned to get back under cover. The round penetrated his back but didn't kill him as his change in body position meant that it impacted in a less than deadly manner. The year ended in further tragedy on December 30, with the killing of a Grenadier Guardsman in Newry Street, Crossmaglen. Daniel Blinco (22) from Derbyshire was shot and killed whilst on foot patrol in the centre of Crossmaglen.

The 'Grim Reaper' made his final call to Crossmaglen on June 22, 1998, a full year after the 'final' ceasefire. Gary Fenton of the RGBW was on a VCP near

Crossmaglen when he was run down and killed by a lorry which refused to stop. Although his comrades shot and wounded the driver, he escaped over the border into the Republic; Private Fenton was posthumously mentioned in dispatches.

In the intervening years between November 28, 1971 and June 22, 1998, 70 soldiers had been killed in the Crossmaglen area alone. Additionally a total of 13 RUC officers were also killed; 83 members of the SF had perished in such a small, rural area of the Province. Although Merlyn Rees' prophetic labeling of the area as 'Bandit Country' extended to other areas of South Armagh, Crossmaglen did its level best to 'earn' the epithet all on its own.

CROSSMAGLEN BAPTISM

Jim, Argyll and Sutherland Highlanders

On 29th July 1972, I left Scotland bound for Ireland. Around the same time the army, in N.I. began 'Operation Motorman' which began in the summer of '72. Motorman was as a result of the increased activities of the Para-militaries – which was, in turn, as a result of 'Bloody Sunday' in Londonderry.

We crossed by ship, overnight, from Campbeltown to Belfast where we transferred to army 3-tonners. Two people per truck were given ammunition. The rest of us could only sit tensely watching out of the truck. We drove in convoy to Bessbrook where we were split up into platoons of thirty men. This was as far as we could go using the roads. Working the border meant moving on foot or by helicopter. We were then flown by helicopter to our base at the police station in Crossmaglen. I still break out in a sweat thinking about arriving in Crossmaglen and the landing on the playing field behind the police station. We jumped out with all our gear to the screams of our sergeant telling us to hit the deck. I thought we were under attack or something as he threw ammunition at us and we frantically tried to load our magazines. Nothing was actually happening; this was simply a way of introducing us to the next four months. We had to realise, quickly, that it was no longer an exercise or a game – but the real thing. Within a couple of hours we were out on patrol.

That first patrol was to Cullaville, a village a few miles to the west of us, on the main Dundalk road. Since we were at platoon strength we were split into three groups of eight men, covering three areas; guard section, patrol section and standby section. Within a year XMG was to become a company area. Patrols now consisting of around thirty heavily armed men. We were there during the worst year of the 'Troubles' and only eight of us on a patrol. Although we wouldn't generally use transport, a daily routine was to clear the road north to make a link between bases. The theory was that if you checked the road for bombs the IRA couldn't plant a bomb to catch us out that day.

The IRA gave us about ten days to settle in. We were on a patrol a few miles from base (at Cullaville) when we were approached by a woman telling us about a burning lorry down the road to Dundalk. Our sergeant (Jimmy Kilcullan) had us running down the road towards this incident –

Christ that got the adrenalin going. As we got near to where the incident was we left the road and went up the hillside to get a look. We could see the smoke but no sign of activity so we made our way slowly down to the lorry. It had been a butter lorry and the stink was hellish. We could have been walking into an ambush or booby-trap, but we were hyped up, our training taking over. Luckily there was nothing but a burning lorry.

We tried radioing – using A41 radios – weighing in at 18 lb 8 oz with the battery with a 1.5 to 3 mile range, in but couldn't get through. Looking at the map there was a single track road nearby which was a quicker way back to the base so we headed for it. We found a burnt out car blocking this road. We still couldn't get through on the radio, so we decided to head back to base along this road anyway. It was a very warm afternoon and we were hot and tired. Almost at the other end of this road we found a 45 gallon oil drum and when someone shouted that it was a bomb – we scattered, getting maybe 120 feet from it when there was an almighty explosion.

Everything stood still; we were on the deck watching this cloud of dirt and rubble slowly rising – it was quite a sight. Then it all came back down a lot faster. A falling rock snapped the pistol grip of one rifle and one man had been knocked unconscious. We got up and stood around shocked and confused. Then the ground started kicking up around us and the sergeant shouted that we were under fire. At one point someone (Alec) shouted for me to follow him and I did so automatically. We went down a wall towards the general direction of the firing, but couldn't see anything so came back. The shooting stopped as quickly as it had begun and for some reason the radio worked and we got the standby section down to help us reorganize but the gunmen had already disappeared over the border. What we understood was that we were supposed to find the lorry and car, call in and vehicles would come down and along the road with the bomb and the bombers waiting. So, we couldn't contact base and walked towards a bomb from a direction the bombers weren't expecting – by the time they realised we were there we were already scattering.

CROSSMAGLEN AND STEVE TAVERNER

Brian Smith, 1st Devon & Dorsets

In the October of 1983, seven platoons arrived in Drumadd Barracks Armagh city for a 6 week tour of duty. We had arrived in a blue Army 4 ton Bedford truck which some pillock of an officer thought looked like a civilian truck. No doubt it was the same officer who bought 98 out of the 100 Bedford vans in the province.

9 Platoon were sent straight from Armagh to outside Crossmaglen to provide a cordon for a couple of local South Armagh farmers oil Lorries that had been hi-jacked and booby trapped blocking two roads into the village of Crossmaglen. Later on, a company of the Grenadier Guard requested an extra platoon to go into the S.F base to help with extra patrols.

7 Platoon was the only platoon left in 'C' Company so we were sent down to Crossmaglen. My team consisted of team commander Steve Taverner, Gunner Jeremy 'Nigs' Richards, Dave North who had just joined us fresh from NITAT and me. We arrived in XMG Late on the 27th October 1983; had a full brief on the local players' history and general lay out of the town.

At the time XMG was the most dangerous area to be a British Squaddie in the world. We went out at 12:00hrs for a night patrol to get familiar with the village. It was very quiet and the patrol took about an hour; we were all quite nervous but it went well and as soon as we knew it we were back in the base. It had been Dave North's first patrol in the Province and he had lost the top of one of the shamullys he had been carrying and we were ribbing him that he would have to go back out by himself to look for it.

Our next patrol was 13:00, so we all went and got a bit of shut eye. The Guards had kindly put us up in the roof area of the S.F base. We were all shaken from our slumber to get our meal at the 24hr cook house before going in for our briefing. The briefing room had a full scale model of XMG in the centre of the room. Cpl Reid the resident Int for XMG gave us the Int brief. We all knew 'Reidie' from the D & Ds; he was later hurt with the Staffords near the end of our tour and these days, does a sterling job at the regimental museum in Dorchester. We were told all about the local players in the area and about the oil Tankers which 9 platoon were looking after; all the usual stuff. The only difference with this patrol was we were going out as a four team multiple. Captain Watson's team; Sergeant Tony Mace's Team; Corporal Brian Harvey's team and L/Cpl Steve Taverner's team.

We all went out to the loading area and loaded up. The worst time I found in Ireland was the hour before the patrol. Every one used to go into their own private world of thoughts. I always used to get a knot in the gut. As soon as the S.F Base doors opened, all this nervous energy used to release as you rushed out of the base running and pepper potting. Covering each other until you were at least a 100 yards from the base. The patrol went very smoothly, and I even had an old guy come up, as friendly as anything and told us to be careful. Steve stopped the local IRA Int Officer who was chatty as anything even commenting how short the Guardsmen were becoming now days. We were all wearing Guards Berets and our average height must have been 5ft 8' and I am only 5ft 6' same as Dave North. As we were finishing the patrol, we were the first team to reach the Square near the IRA Phoenix Memorial.

Steve told us we were going firm to let the other three teams to go through to cover us across the square. Steve and 'Nigs' covered forwards while myself and Dave covered rear. The three teams went through us and Steve prepared us to move. The next thing I knew was a large explosion. I had the feeling of floating and landing. After the dust had settled I looked down at my feet and saw them smoking. I had this strange thought that I must have run fast because my boots had caught fire. After getting my thoughts together I realised my Puttees had caught fire. I looked and saw Dave North who I later found out had tried to pull me out of the way when a large lump of the car that had just exploded took the wall down where I had been kneeling.

I grabbed Dave and we ran around the corner into the Square to find 'Nigs' and Steve. We found 'Nigs' first between a car and a wall; he had broken the golden rule of going between a car and a wall which saved his life. His legs were peppered with shrapnel from the car. We shouted 'Where's Tav?' He pointed at what we thought was part of the car's burning under-chassis near the butchers shop. It wasn't until we saw the boots attached that we realised it was Tav. All the Northern Ireland training came to the fore and for a while it just seemed like another exercise at Lydde and Hyde. I went to Steve while 'Nigs' Hobbled. Dave covered us until Tony Mace's team arrived. Everything was going like slow motion. I got to Tav' and started putting the flames out with 'Nigs' helping; he was still conscious and trying to tell us what to do. He was a mess and had suffered 75% burns. All this gunge was coming out of his mouth blocking his airway; I tried to use a plastic airway which was no use so I don't know what happened next.

I know some Guardsmen who had been on patrol the other side of XMG had come across to assist, and I looked up and saw a Guardsman, Kelvin Daye who was my Nan's next door neighbour who I had grown up with in Manor Road, East Ham. We both opened an air way in the throat to by pass his mouth. The Guards Ambulance Saracen seemed to take ages to arrive; when it did arrive the Medical Sergeant promptly threw up all over us and Tav'. While this was going on one of our platoon threatened the Bank Manager with his rifle because he refused us water. The other memory I have is the local Priest would not help us or give Tav' his last rites; I lost faith in the Catholic Church that day.

Steve and 'Nigs' were heli-lifted by Lynx to Musgrave park hospital, and it burnt its engine out getting there. The whole experience was unreal and didn't hit me until I got in to the mess room for a cup of tea. I didn't even notice my own injuries. Even now, a day does not go by when I don't think of this incident. I re-live it in my own private world at night time. It wasn't too bad when I was still in the Army, but when I left, I was away from people who could understand my mood swings or knew when I needed somebody to talk to or when to leave me alone. Yes I admit I had problems and still have problems. I eventually, sought help, following an incident with the police. That help was Combat Stress, a charity run for servicemen who suffer from P.T.S.D.

Mark Hale asked me to write this; if it was anyone else I would have told them to get f****d. Mark was one of the guys who helped me, and I hold him in great respect .Believe it or not just writing about Steve has helped. I didn't know I could write about it. We take the Queen's Shilling and we take our chance. Somebody had to be there, and unfortunately it was me, Dave, 'Nigs' and Steve Taverner.

Steve Taverner later died at Woolwich Military Hospital on November 5th 1983. Later, the Queen's Gallantry Medal was awarded to one of the team which I believe was awarded not to that one Person but everyone who was there, including Steve, who, though badly injured still acted as if he was our team Commander.

Lance Corporal Steve Taverner, who was 24 and from Whipton, near Exeter was badly injured in the terrorist attack in Crossmaglen on October; sadly he died of those wounds, 10 days later. He was the second D&D to be killed in Northern Ireland during that year; in the April, Corporal Gerald Jefferey died of the wounds he received after an IRA bomb attack on the Falls Road in Belfast.

BOMBS (AND GOATS) IN CROSSMAGLEN

Tim Francis, Royal Artillery

We visited Crossmaglen fairly regularly as it was our BHQ and although it was then, nothing like as bad as later, it was still not a pleasant place to be. I remember seeing my first dead body there; an Irish born soldier who had been shot whilst on leave and I remember having to step over him to get into the makeshift canteen in the police station there. Forkhill was probably worse than Crossmaglen at that time and our troop deployed there certainly had more than their share of shoot outs; usually across the border therefore unable to pursue. We were probably one of the last units to patrol South Armagh in vehicles; the end of this mode of transport being speeded up by the fact that our vehicles on patrol were hit by three mines during our stay there.

I was in the first PIG to be hit; a weird sensation, a big flash and then suddenly a very heavy armoured vehicle was airborne until hitting the road again on its wheels with a heck of a thump. I don't remember a bang or being scared, just the flash and being off the ground. There was total confusion then, as Geoff our driver at the time got it under control and to a halt and we piled out in disarray; fortunately without a follow up attack being staged. A second attack took place a few weeks later. I was in the PIG in front this time as the second was hit; very similar big flash and the following PIG again brought under control on the road, as good fortune would have it the driver was probably the strongest member of the troop.

We were a bit more organised this time as we deployed a little more professionally than previously. The third attack took place on one of our last patrols of the tour when we had changed vehicles to Saracens and our response was suitably robust as we all wanted to get home in one piece and a few bursts from the turret machine gun into the surrounding countryside deterred any follow up. Amongst these attacks we had the usual round of VCPs, stake outs of border crossings, and an emergency 36 hours in Newry. This followed 3 unarmed young tearaways being shot by security forces from an OP, in the act of robbing a shop. Serious rioting then ensued. I was the opening shot of the BBC News that night; a Sunday evening much to the horror of my watching mother and the huge jealousy of our intrepid PIG driver, Geoff who was on leave at the time. He did like seeing his own image whenever possible!!! I also have a vivid memory of grabbing riot helmets with visors from the back of a PIG to discover that somebody else had obviously forgotten theirs and nicked mine in true army tradition.

I also remember searching a car during the early hours of a very cold, very late night totally in auto pilot mode; looking under the drivers seat and seeing the usual stuff: torch, pliers, spanner, pistol, screwdriver, first aid kit ,etc and thinking something is out of place here. But not being quite sure what, until I thought perhaps the pistol may not be quite the norm! I grabbed it and quizzed the guy about it, to which he replied: 'Oh yes, I forgot; that is my pistol.' It actually turned out to be legally licensed' although it took about an hour of radio debate to confirm.

We also carried out a lot of rural foot patrols including a memorable one where we came across a sign saying 'Welcome to Northern Ireland' but unfortunately we were approaching from the wrong side! I remember a stakeout of a border customs post that Int had warned may be attacked where we lay all night behind a hedge on a little hill under the command of our TSM when we were discovered by an evil smelling stray goat that took a liking to me. It just would not go away, despite not so gentle persuasion. The TSM could hear me moving and asked the reason why and when I responded said 'It's only a goat; shoo it away.' Having failed to do this, he came closer to se the problem for himself, recoiled in horror at the smell and ordered me to kill the f------ thing. We then had a difference of opinion as I responded 'How does that help; we have then got a dead evil smelling goat that is not going to go anywhere or improve in smell!' Fortunately at this point the goat obviously realised its future was in serious danger and moved off.

XMG; DEATH OF A MATE

Rifleman Lee Wilkins, 2 RGJ

We started our tour at Crossmaglen in December 1977; the base was an old police station close to the market square. At the time we were at XMG, a detachment from the Royal Engineers were making the base mortar-proof; parts of the place looked like a building site with cement mixers lying around, wooden shuttering for concrete and steel props around the place. The Engineers remained in the base for most of their tour; this must have been boring for them as they would occasionally ask to go out on foot patrol with us. The sleeping accommodation was a small narrow room holding about five or six triple bunks for the riflemen, which was always very cramped. We spent four hours on and six hours off; when we were on duty it was either guarding the base in the sangars or urban or rural foot patrols. These were usually longer than the street patrols as we were flown out by helicopter for specific operations in the surrounding area, referred to as the 'Cuds.' On one such occasion we came under fire from a machine gun, probably an M60; we were out in platoon strength and we all managed to get into the cover of a ditch by the road. I was the G.P.M.G gunner and returned fire towards a hedgerow from where the shots were thought to have come from, but the players were probably gone. I had heard that there was a large bomb further back from where the shots came and the reasoning for me to stitch machine gun fire across the hedgerow was that it was a possible detonation point; in hindsight, it seems we were lucky to get away without any casualties.

At the time I was there, about five stray dogs lived on the base; these dogs used to follow us out on patrol and sometimes would be encouraged to go ahead of the patrol through waste ground as a form of bomb detector. The reasoning was that they would trigger a tripwire device rather than a soldier. There was one in particular and it stayed in the area for years and ended up receiving an award for its efforts, and bravery as it was blown up several times, I think it was called 'Rats' and it ended its days in retirement somewhere on the mainland. However other dogs didn't fare as well, as it was decided by the higher-ups that they were in the way and maybe even a hygiene risk, as they ate and slept on the base. So a vet was sent in by chopper one day and put the dogs down. I think only 'Rats' and one other was spared and when the other – a collie cross – injured its foot, someone shot it in the pipe range: an underground pipe converted into a range used to zero in weapons.

Whilst I was there, the IRA was flying tricolours from telegraph poles around the town. The order came that these were to be removed, and initially it didn't seem much of a risk; usually a rifleman was able to climb up on to a PIG armoured carrier and take them down Indeed, some of the men used to take turns doing this and the flags became valued items back at the barracks, trophies; I remember one guy using one as a counterpane on his bed. One day in March 1978, I was coming off a foot patrol when I noticed my friend Nick's section loading their weapons at the loading bay ready to go out on patrol; not thinking too much about it at the time. I just thought that we would probably meet up later on. About a half an hour after that there was an explosion that was heard from the base; it was quite loud. A medic returned, covered in blood and said that Nick had been killed by a bomb; a tricolour flag had been booby trapped and Nick had tried to take it down. The IRA had sewn explosives in the seam of the flag.

As a consequence, my section were deployed back out again, as the company photographer – Dick Lettington – was with us, and whilst we provided cover, he was to photograph the scene of the bombing. I remember seeing forensic officers casually walking round picking through the crime scene and being quite casual about it, to the point of laughing and joking with one another. I was shocked and angry at the time, but looking back on it I suppose they were hardened to a very tough job and had seen the consequences of IRA bombs many times.

Nick Smith was a good friend of mine and we'd had some great times on our previous posting to Gibraltar; I'd stayed at his parents flat on leave prior our N.I. posting. Over the years I have gotten to know his family really well and was always made welcome when visiting. I was aware of the pain they were all suffering due to the loss of a much loved family member. I still sometimes feel sad that I never said anything to him that time I saw him loading his rifle ready to go out on patrol at Crossmaglen.

Another fatality on that tour was our C.O Lt Col Ian Cordon-Lloyd who died in a helicopter crash after a contact on the ground; I'm not sure but had heard it had been shot down. The C.O was someone who would always get involved in whatever was happening on the ground, despite his rank, he led by personal example, and I suppose he could have delegated more, but didn't.

Some time prior to the chopper going down, he went out with a patrol out to investigate a flat bed truck used by the IRA to place mortar tubes to launch an attack; I can't remember the base it may have been Forkhill. The truck was booby trapped and the Colonel was caught up in the explosion but came out relatively unhurt then. That was about a month before the helicopter incident. The chopper pilot also died in the crash, but I think the co-pilot survived and another passenger, Captain Schofield survived, but with terrible head injuries. Towards the end of the tour we had our company photo taken, the entire company assembled in front of Borucki sangar, and after the picture was taken, the O.C Major Robertson and C.S.M Dougie Curl led us around the X.M.G square as we marched at the double. At the time this was risky, but I think it was meant as a show of defiance just to let them know we weren't being intimidated, and it was a boost for our morale because it was a very hard tour; we had a few weeks till we went home, but still needed to be very cautious.

I can reach Nick Smith's brother but haven't spoken to him for years, his mother lives in the Home Counties somewhere, but am not sure of the exact location. I did manage to read your recent book and found it informative and really true of that era, and it was sad that the war went on for so long and there were still casualties in XMG till the mid – late 90s.

Rifleman Nicholas Smith was from the Battersea area of London and was aged just 20 and unmarried. His death, close on the heels of the tragic loss of the Battalion's CO was a desperate blow to the morale of the Jackets.

PLATOON COMMANDER KILLED IN CROSSMAGLEN

Jim, Argyll and Sutherland Highlanders

Possibly the worst incident was a shooting which killed our platoon commander (2nd Lt Stewart Gardiner.) Information came in that a bomb had been planted on a border road and we had to check it out. We were helicoptered in two groups of four. As we made our way downhill to the road I found a length of wire. I told the Colour Sergeant to come down and have a look and we followed it along the side of the road. I thought we would walk into a bomb but there was nothing attached to the end of the wire. We then retraced our steps in the opposite direction. At one point the wire crossed the road in a cleverly concealed groove. The other side of the road was over the border so we had to call up the Garda. When they had checked it out – no bomb or control point – we stood at the side of the road talking. I said I'd go and start rolling up the wire and walked maybe fifty yards when there was a burst of gunfire. Bullets pinged past me as I dived for the ground. I thought it was me that was the target, but it was the other group. I shouted to check if they were OK and began crawling back down. Even being so close to the others I felt totally isolated.

When I got back our platoon commander was lying on his back with blood spurting out of a hole in his side. We put a bandage pack on the hole and the blood came through, another bandage and it still came through. We used about four although we knew that more than two and it was pointless. He was in deep shock, not registering anything. His face was draining of colour and it was as if he was clenching his teeth, breathing hard through them, so we gave him morphine which didn't really help. I called in a report as the radio operator had been shot as well. We were told to get out of the ambush area before help could come. We moved up the road a bit and called for help again. We were told no again by the company commander. It was too dangerous for vehicles to come down. We decided to get our own transport and stopped the first car that came along and dragged the driver out. I got in the back with the platoon commander on my lap and we sped off for the base, two miles away. The others stopped another car and followed us shortly after. The platoon commander was all but dead. I had his head in my lap, totally freaked out and in shock to the point of thinking the rear heated window was actually bomb wire and we'd be blown up.

There was nothing we could do when we got back other than wait for a helicopter to take the injured men away. We were confused, upset and angry that we had actually had someone killed. We had done a rifle check and discovered we'd lost a rifle during this incident. We wanted to go back down to look for it but weren't allowed. Two plain clothes cops offered and were allowed. They went off in a wee green sports car, and within an hour we heard shooting. The cops came screaming back and into the base where we discovered both had been shot. How the driver made it back with his injuries was beyond us.

It seemed that we had to listen to the screams of agony for hours – obviously not though. One of the tankies, a big guy from Aberdeen, got the company commander by the throat against a wall and threatened to kill him because they had wanted to come down to help us. Our CSM (Danny the Chin), who was a hard man, grabbed this guy and led him off, talking quietly to him. I don't remember talking much about what had happened and life continued for us. Because I was the last one to see him alive I was sent to Stirlingshire to represent the platoon at his funeral.

The IRA on the border were supposed to be the most experienced and together group in the whole of Ireland and we were put up against them, young and inexperienced. It was decided to bring others in to support us. A heavily armed platoon was sent out to live on the border. We were then set up as a sort of duck-shooting gallery in an area where everything happened. We spent a few hours walking up and down a road wanting something to happen but hoping it wouldn't. We had just given up when there was shooting over where our ambush group were. We headed off as fast as we could, listening to this heavy fire all the way. It turned out that some gunmen had sneaked or stumbled into the middle of two groups of soldiers and opened fire, wounding one soldier. The two groups were confused and for a while were shooting at each other. We heard later that a van had been stopped on the border and bodies and guns were found inside.

Part of my training had included a search course, looking for weapons and so on. We had been called out to a farmhouse north of our base. One of the other platoons had discovered what they thought was a rifle but felt it was booby trapped. A dog handler had confirmed this and advised that no one should enter the building. We were on call in case it was a hoax and the building needed to be searched. When we arrived our search commander and another officer wanted to go into the building. Such is rank, we couldn't tell them although they should have known. After they went in there was an explosion and the farmhouse disappeared. Soldiers quickly began digging in the rubble but it was a waste of time. I had been on the radio getting other support. As I said before, the similarity between the pig's body in training and the bodies in that rubble was unreal. One body seemed to be intact apart from the combat jacket being torn, with nothing but dust on it. I still don't know what happened; whether one of them picked up the rifle butt or whether something else triggered a bomb. What was clear was how quickly life could be lost.

Second Lieutenant Stewart Gardiner was aged 23 and was killed by a burst of automatic fire from IRA gunmen hiding over the border with the Republic. An RUC officer was also badly wounded in this attack and was rushed to hospital. One further tragedy was added when his mother collapsed and died at his bedside caused by the shock of seeing her terribly wounded son. On that day, the IRA claimed two lives.

YANKEE REPORTERS IN BANDIT COUNTRY

Tim Francis, Royal Artillery

Our BHQ at Crossmaglen were lumbered with an American reporter for a while who went on and on about Vietnam and his time reporting there and how NI was a little sideshow and not really dangerous and what was all the fuss about, etc, etc. Whilst accompanying a patrol, the Land Rover in which he was sitting in the passenger seat was then hit by a burst of about 10/12 rounds of automatic fire which passed through the Land Rover diagonally between him and the driver without touching either of them. He underwent a strange change of colour and was not heard to mention 'Nam again during his visit or ask to accompany another patrol!

TONY YARWOOD, PARACHUTE REGIMENT

Forkhill: So Close yet so Far

Many months after the Warrenpoint incident, 2 Para and my platoon had a chance to even the score when we were deployed to Forkhill in South Armagh. Our platoon sergeant was away at the time so the senior corporal was acting Sgt for the duration of this particular op.

We had a new platoon commander who was very green behind the ears and inexperienced. He gave us our orders before leaving Forkhill base, which was to ambush a certain railway bridge that the terrorists always tried to blow the tracks on. The platoon commander decided to patrol through the country side in the pitch darkness towards the bridge, which was a good idea as the locals could not tip the terrorists off that troops were in a certain area.

Once we had carefully and quietly made our way to the ambush area, something which we had done on many occasion before, the platoon commander decided to do the ambush his way and his way only. He did not place the two cutoff groups out which were meant to kill anyone that may have got away from the main ambush killing area. He also failed to have the complete manning in the killer group and instead decided to have himself and the GPMG gunner on the position whilst the remainder of the platoon were getting their heads down at the rear. The acting sergeant was a great guy but the platoon commander took advantage

Members of 2 Para at Forkhill, c 1980 (Tony Yarwood)

of the platoon sergeant being away and listened to no one but himself on this occasion.

The gunner was lying down with his GPMG facing the bridge which contained a full belt of 200 rounds of ammunition. His finger was running along the trigger guard and the gun was cocked and ready. After a while the gunner noticed through his night viewing sight that there were people under the bridge and that they were armed. In those days he was not allowed to open fire unless his life was directly threatened (the rules of the yellow card). He quietly released the safety catch and grabbed the platoon commander to inform him what he saw. The platoon commander ordered him to place his safety catch on and not to do anything. The gunner was infuriated as he clearly saw people and weapons moving around under the bridge up to no good. Suddenly and without warning the platoon commander jumped over the small hedgerow and shouted, 'Stop; Army, or I'll fire,' to the annoyance of the gunner. In seconds the people under the bridge dispersed in all directions on foot and in vehicles. At this stage we were woken up to the chaos that ensued. I witnessed one vehicle heading towards what would have been a cut off position before disappearing in the distance probably laughing his cock off. Once the commotion calmed down the scene under the bridge spoke volumes and only demoralised the remainder of the platoon once they found out.

They were terrorists, about 6 of them and they had dropped their weapons on the floor when the platoon commander challenged them – a clever maneuver which meant we could not shoot them because there

Members of 2 Para at Forkhill, c 1980 (Tony Yarwood)

was no danger of us being shot. They had also dropped their radios and placed explosives on the track and in a culvert under the road next to the bridge. Not a bad night's work for the terrorists, but a total disaster for us which could have been icing on the cake, if the ambush had been set correctly in the first place.

FORKHILL, 1985

Fusilier David Dews, Royal Regiment of Fusiliers

We were based in Forkhill RUC station for this tour but it was our second visit to the area. Back in '81, we were sent down to provide defensive cover for the Royal Engineers and the Chunkies (*Royal Pioneer Corps*) who were changing the location of the station and building fortifications. It was felt that the proximity of some of the Ops to ladies' bedroom windows was not conducive to good security.

(*The IRA, aware of the legendary nature of the sex-starved British soldier would get women to undress by their bedroom windows knowing that this would distract the squaddies whilst IRA sympathisers could move arms and ammunition under the very noses of the observers.*)

Our brief was to rely on mobile armour for patrols but as it was so boring there, just to liven things up we would go out on foot and stir the natives up a bit; so little was happening, that we tried to make it happen. It was, as I said, very quiet and I had this thought that it was so, for two possible reasons. 1) We were so good that the IRA was frightened of us, or 2) our Battalion knew that we were so shit that they stuck us in a place where nothing ever happened. Personally, I think that it was the latter reason.

On October 25, we were just finishing a 7 day OP on Foxhill, observing movement in and out of Forkhill village on a 24/7 basis, with night vision and telescopic glasses; nothing had happened. On that night, a Wessex helicopter was sent with our relief and to collect us; I should point out, that the only safe way in or out was by chopper. In it came, dropping off our four man relief and their kit and we quickly jumped on without ceremony, for our two minute flight. As the RAF lads kept stressing, the longer we stayed on the ground, the longer the chopper was a sitting duck target and we never bothered strapping ourselves in until we were airborne and safer from attack.

At 19:55 it landed, disgorged and embarked and lifted off all in the space of a few seconds and immediately swung to the left, climbing quickly. The last thing I can remember is a huge crack like a whip and falling towards the door. This was Friday night, and, I woke up in Musgrave Park Hospital (MPH) on Monday morning; some 60 hours later. I opened my eyes and could see my parents and my then wife, standing around my bed, looking very concerned; I simply burst into tears. On looking down, I noticed that both of my legs were hanging in mid-air with metal pins through both knees and ankles and attached to ropes and weights. My left arm and chest were encased in plaster and pinned to wood in order to keep my arm at an angle. My right arm was studded with needles and intravenous drips; the full works. The pain was so excruciating that I can't even begin to describe it; even the slightest movement was simply too much to bear.

My memories are hazy but I do remember going for the third re-break of my legs and the RAMC Major in charge of Surgery told me that I was the worst behaved patient he had ever had. I replied to the effect that I hadn't even 'fucking' started. He threatened to charge me but, whilst I couldn't have cared less, nothing came of it.

I was in MPH for a month or so, before being transferred to Woolwich and during that time, I found out what had happened to the rest of the lads and the RAF crew. Sadly, Sergeant David Rigby had been crushed by the impact and had been killed almost instantly. Lance Corporal Peter Brookes had fractured his skull and was in a coma for quite some time; Fusilier Dave Cox had fractured his femur and left arm and Fusilier Jimmy Mitcham also broke his femur and was in traction for quite some time; poor lad. I had lost 6 inches of bone from my right femur and am still in pain today.

(*The author, having met with Dave in his home in North Yorkshire and having seen some of his injuries can attest to the extent of the physical damage and the pain he will carry with him as a legacy of his service to his country and a grossly ungrateful Government.*)

Sometime after the crash, I found out exactly what had happened from eyewitnesses. As the pilot took off and climbed, he clipped the top of a 105' high Radio mast and crashed immediately. The other two crewmen had cuts and bruises, but sadly David Rigby, as I said, was killed.

I was in hospital for almost two years and at the end of which, I was medically discharged from the Army and had to undergo the rigmarole of going to Catterick for de-kitting, whilst still on crutches. I finally left Catterick in February, 1987; for my service to my country, the Government and the MOD treated me like shit and refused to help me in anyway. They offered me the pittance of a pension and then washed their hands of me.

Today, I am still suffering from the effects of the crash but neither my Regiment nor the have the MOD ever asked about my welfare. Bitter? You bet I fucking am.

CROSSMAGLEN

Andy Wood, Coldstream Guards

In March, 1991, I was dropped by Lynx helicopter at Crossmaglen which was to be my home for the next seven months. I was designated light support weapon (LSW).

The accommodation in the 'Cross' was like being in a submarine or a sardine can (no offence to the sardines). it came down to doing a few town patrols to orientate ourselves to the area, and on the first patrol I was crapping myself my heart was thumping as if it was going to stop or jump out of my chest and then I zig – zagged out of that base so fast, that not even a lion would catch me. On that first patrol, I met a local girl who was walking home from school and I said hello and she just spat in my face and snarled 'Fuck off home, ye Brit bastard.' I felt mixed emotions ranging from wanting to kick the shit out of her and confusion of you don't know me why are you being so nasty?

After a few of those patrols we settled down a bit until one day I was patrolling in the town square when my 'Antler' radio headset crackled into life; 'They are crossing the square now,' in an Irish accent; the hidden beauty of the 'Antler' was that it picked up radio messages too, so I knew we were being dicked by PIRA. I was slightly bricking it, and was looking at all possible firing points; curtains moving, anything. I ran up to my brick commander, Captain Chris and blurted it out loud and started getting very scared and excited at the same time! I thought this is it; my heart started racing and my body was tingling; this is it, this is what we have trained for!

We made a bee-line to the outskirts of the town and went a few kms out and returned from a different direction but something was wrong; very wrong. We went firm and even the two RUC officers with us knew that something wasn't right. Borucki sangar then sent a message saying that several cars were flashing lights at each other going through the square. I looked round and everyone was looking scared as if something was definitely about to happen; it was as if time had stood still. It went very quiet and we just stayed put for about fifteen minutes. After what seemed like an eternity, we saw a white van scream down the road and away towards the border which was only a few hundred metres away.

It turned out that this same van was used a few weeks later to mortar another base in the province; a white transit with a false polystyrene roof. We had accidently stopped 'Cross' from getting mortared; well possibly! Then it was our turn to go and man an OP up on a big hill overlooking the border. We were pretty safe up on G40 (*'Golf' Tower 40*) because, if the PIRA contacted us it would be too hard for them to get away in time, so it felt safe.

I even used to go and sit outside the razor wire and lay in the grass looking up to the sky and wonder how people can fight such a dirty war in their own land when it's beautiful.

We were patrolling back and came across a farm, so we went firm and checked the area and, as I knelt against a boulder, got an electric shock off it. On closer inspection, we could see that there was an electric fence touching the other side of it, and it was humming as there was so much power going through it. The farmer had wired it up to the mains because he was sick of squaddies wrecking his hedge; touching that fence could have been fatal.

In mid-tour we went up north for a bit of training, in Ballykelly I think, and it was time to get a few spare rounds in case you needed them (nudge, nudge; wink, wink). You got hefty fines for losing rounds, and, on one occasion I did lose a few when the bottom of my magazine popped off and scattered the contents into the middle of a field in pitch – darkness! I had some red nail varnish to make normal rounds look like tracer; don't ask about the nail varnish I just found it honest!

As the tour went on, we had various tasks and patrols and I was the team 'chatter.' For example, I would do all the questions at VCPs etc., and it was quite bizarre coming face to face with the players and asking them for i.d. when you knew exactly who they were and they wanted to kill you and you were praying to catch them in the act so you could shoot the shit out of them. I had one of them on his own in front of me and I wanted to hurt him. I told him that I knew who he was and it was a matter of time until we got him off the face of the earth; he was a coward and I tried to entice him to kick off so I could shoot him. I have to admit that my anger was getting the better of me and I had to back down when he laughed and said he might do a bit of shooting at the weekend. I wanted to take my knife out and dig it in his chest and kill another human being because he was being so smug about the fact we couldn't do anything unless he was caught in the act.

I sometimes got my own back by telling them I had seen their wife with somebody else and they were getting quite intimate in his car; just to put that seed of doubt into their heads.

On a lighter note, our brick accidently strayed into the south; only by 50 metres for God's sake. We spotted a well known player who was gobbing off at another of our bricks in his barn saying that this was the border and they couldn't cross it!! The trouble for him was, we were stood behind him and to see a player nearly crap himself is worth its weight in gold.

XMG: LUCK WAS ON OUR SIDE

Private Stuart Corns, Duke of Edinburgh's

In 1983 I was serving with the Duke of Edinburgh's Royal Regiment (DERR) at Crossmaglen joint SF base as a young private soldier on my first tour of duty in the Province.

On June 22, my platoon – 3 platoon – were assigned to carry out a rural patrol of the border area; south of Crossmaglen. The RAF 'taxi' was booked (Wessex helicopter) for 11.45 hrs approximately and after the normal patrol brief, the section assembled on the heli pad opposite the pipe range. After a short period of time, we received the signal from the buzzer room that the Wessex was due in minutes and that it would be dropping supplies off first, and then proceed to pick up each of the sections.

I could hear the distinctive sound of the Wessex approaching from the direction of the football pitch which was to my right, and, by this time we were lined up and ready to go. I was watching the approaching Wessex negotiate the perimetre wall, in preparation to release the under slung cargo net of supplies. Then, suddenly, what looked like dust, debris and shit being blown around by the down draft from the Wessex helicopter blades appeared. It wasn't; it was in fact, smoke and debris from the mortar base plate that had just been triggered.

Debris, dust and white smoke appeared just above the perimetre wall with tube like objects tumbling from within it towards us, and getting bigger and bigger. Within seconds the MK10 mortars hit the heli pad, 10 metres to our left; splitting open and oozing a yellow green mush (dock yard confetti). Subsequently a third one fell on the left and the fourth to my front; exploding and part destroying the Sangar and injuring a colleague. The approaching Wessex promptly aborted the landing and took off at speed toward the town square.

We all stood in amazement and looked at each other, then realising what was happening, we promptly hit the ground making our way into the cover of the accommodation block. The initial reaction was for the section to go out of the back gate towards the Lismore estate and secure the mortar base plate firing point. However, we were all told to remain under cover until further notice; meanwhile the Wessex had dropped its cargo net of combats, a couple of tea urns onto a house roof to the annoyance of the owner. (Tough shit).

It later transpired that gunmen had been warning residents on the estate to vacate their properties and the rumour on the block was that if anyone had attempted to secure the area of the base plate a reception of armed men lay in wait for anyone exiting the back gate.

To this day I can still see the Mk 10 mortar tumbling through the air towards me, as if it was yesterday.

Under the banner headline 'Provo Raid Terrifies a Village,' the *Daily Mirror* of June 23, 1986 reported: 'A massive cross-border hunt was on last night for a Provo mortar bomb gang who attacked an Army base. A soldier was injured by shrapnel as 10 mortars were launched from a lorry parked in the middle of Crossmaglen's Lismore Estate. Minutes earlier, masked IRA men ran from door to door telling people to flee their homes. The injured soldier was hit as the bombs blasted through the perimetre wall of this heavily fortified base.

An Army Wessex helicopter, about to land with a load of supplies slung underneath it, swung away at the last moment. The pilot jettisoned the load which then smashed into a roof. After gaining height, the helicopter flew on to Bessbrook, 12 miles away. Said the owner of a local shop, 'It was terrible. A lot of people were badly shocked. The sound of the exploding bombs was terrifying – and we thought the helicopter was going to crash on top of us.'

An RUC spokesman said the station – the most attacked in South Armagh – was not touched.'

This again was a fine example of the ruthless and callous determination of the IRA to launch a 'spectacular' against the SF with little thought of the carnage which could have been wreaked had their actions succeeded in bringing down the helicopter. No doubt their 'mouthpiece' – Sinn Fein – and their Irish-American backers in NORAID would have found a way in which to find the SF responsible for any consequent deaths.

CROSSMAGLEN: A BOIL ON THE BUM

Tom Clarke, Royal Corps of Transport

Having spent two months in preparation in our home base in B.A.O.R involving P.T. every day, five and ten mile marches with full kit and weapons, weekly range details and night and day driving of Saracen and Humber PIG armoured cars, we were ready to crush all before us.

We flew to Belfast's Aldergrove airport and, once there, there the Squadron was as gathered together in a large hanger to collect our belongings and to be broken down into our various detachments. My 'oppo, 'Chink' Joiner and I joined the detachment for Bessbrook Mill, to be flown there by Wessex helicopter. Once at the mill, Chink and I transferred onto a Gazelle helicopter for an eye popping, gut churning ride across open hills, dales and lochs; low and fast was the order of approach to this beleaguered base which ended in ended in a 'Khe Sanh' style landing, This involved a very steep climb and turn, followed by a very steep dive, pulling up level across a small sports field, landing, with rotors and engines on maximum revs, off-loading, up and away. This left a short dash from the heli-zone to the back gate, once inside, gate slammed and bolted, unload weapons, breath; you've made it.

To the un-enlightened, the base at X.M.G. as it was affectionately known was like a cowboy wagon train, cut-off and surrounded by hostile Indians. It was in fact a very old brick police station with the once exercise yard now crammed with four large old army Nissan huts. These were used as housing and stores, and the brick police station was used as the base H.Q. officer's quarters, cook house and the two permanent police officers had a tiny little down stairs room. The Choggy Wallah had a garden shed to live in.

The base had two large sangars; one at the front of the base that could see down into the market square and covered the front gates and main road, and the other was at the rear of the base. This covered the playing field at the back and the Heli-Pad and was always double manned when Helos landed. There were two Saracen armoured cars, but because of the lack of space, one was permanently parked under the rear sangar outside the base so it could be kept an eye on.

The whole complex was covered with scaffolding and wire mesh to prevent rocket propelled mortar attacks, (it didn't work). When the base was attacked by mortars, as it was twice in my four month tour, I knew what it was like to be frightened, nowhere were to run, nowhere to hide is the phrase of the song that springs to mind and to top all the base was dry; this meant no alcohol whatsoever was allowed, so no Disco's or girls, no popping out to the shops, one T.V. set in the Choggies, and about seventy other guys to spend the next four months with.

Crossmaglen itself, was a little market town right on the border of South Armagh, otherwise known as Bandit Country. The houses in the town at that time consisted of mainly stone cottages and brick houses, although there were some new houses being built around the edges of the town, but the hub of the area was the market square and all roads led to it. Once outside the village the land just opened out into sprawling countryside, with hedges, ditches, copses, woodland, brick walls, barbed wire, brambles, nettles, just like a walk on the Yorkshire moors really and it always rained and now and then there was the odd culvert mine or two to deal with and the odd ambush or sniper. It beat playing golf to spoil a good walk.

The local people were something else; it was like living in the 'Village of the Dammed.' Hostile was a polite phrase to describe their feelings towards us and they would actually celebrate openly if they learnt of any security force injuries or deaths. They would antagonise patrols to try and get a reaction in order to escalate a situation; they very nearly got their wish when they openly applauded the death of young Borucki

(Private James Borucki (19) of the Parachute Regiment was killed by an IRA booby-trap in the centre of Crossmaglen. On August 8, 1976, he was killed when a package placed on a bicycle exploded as he walked by.)

The Paras were about to take that village apart and I will not put into words what my orders were at the time and to this day, I don't know if I would have been able to carry them out. The people there, needless to say, didn't like or want us there and the feeling was mutual. There were things they did and got away with, but we had our own way of getting our revenge, as could only be dreamed up by squaddies.

I spent every year from 1971 to 1977 at some point in some god forsaken dump in N. Ireland. Some were good, some were bad; some were happy, some were sad. X.M.G. finished me. It was like taking on George Foreman with both hands tied behind your back. And what for when you look back on it all; mates lost and injured, mothers, wives and children left without husbands and fathers. To add insult to injury, the perpetrators are now wined and dined by the British Government and living on fat cat wages.

But would I do it all again? You Bet Your Bottom Dollar I Would. As I slide down the banister of life, I will always remember Crossmaglen as the splinter.

THE MURDER OF PTE TURNER XMG 1992

Lance Corporal 'Bugle' Light Infantry

We had been out on a border operation and were flying back into XMG at about 0400hrs when I saw torch lights coming from the graveyard. After I had landed and unloaded my team I reported the sighting to the ops room and thought no more about it.

After sorting out my 'shit' (admin) I got my fat head down for a couple of hours before taking over guard commander. The stag was mainly uneventful apart from an Int message stating that a sniper or machinegun shoot was expected in Crossmaglen (XMG) and all patrols had been cancelled by the RUC until further notice. As I handed over, the QRF were outside the sangar getting ready to go out to do some house calls, which, had been done many times, but the Ops officer, Captain 'S' wanted them done that day. It is not rocket science to work out that the powers that be in 'D' company at that time knew how dangerous it was to send out a patrol that day knowing the likely outcome would be a contact. They were medal hunting, hoping they could get a kill.

Just as I got to the accommodation, a high velocity shot rang out. I was immediately grabbed by 'Kell' Kelland, Sergeant in the Bugle Platoon, and along with anyone we could get our hands on went straight out on the ground and set up the cordon. Sean Carmody, a good mate of mine and a member of my team got to 'Tommy' Turner – who had been hit – first, with the medic; they did what they could for him but death was instant. He had been hit by a .50 from a sniper only 130 yards away. The firing point was the graveyard, and the contact point was the junction of XMG square and Newry road. To say that the Company was pissed off and angry would be an understatement. To really send our emotions even higher was the callous way that the OC sent a message over the net: 'Don't bother with the ambulance; just bring a body bag.' I always thought he was a tit, but that confirmed it. Tommy was from my neck of the woods and I had given him a lift home a few times from Tidworth; 18 years old; what a fucking waste of a young man's life all because certain officers were medal hunting.

There were some serious mistakes leading up to Tommy's murder such as why wasn't the graveyard checked out when I reported suspicious sightings of torch lights? Why was the QRF sent out when all patrols had been cancelled? To this day, it still winds me up when I think about it. I blew 'Last Post' and 'Reveille' at 'Tommy's' funeral. I had done many before that, but to play at a friend's funeral is a harrowing experience; one that thankfully, I did not have to repeat again during my 25yrs service.

Tommy's multiple and myself dossed down at his father's place out in the cuds of Herefordshire, near Bromyard. He had his own bar so we all got shit-faced the night before Tommy's funeral; well, it was the thing to do and it was a form of release for most of us. We gave him a fucking good send off.

'Cede Nullis', Tommy Lad.

Private Paul 'Tommy' Turner of the Light Infantry was hit once whilst in the main square in Crossmaglen on the evening of August 28, 1992. He was just 18 years old and came from Herefordshire. Sources claim that it was the first time that a .50 calibre round had been used to kill a British soldier.

INCIDENT AT XMG

Andy Wood, Coldstream Guards

On June 4, a nice summer's evening, as I recall, and we were sent out on foot patrol to satellite around Crossmaglen, in order to give cover to a convoy of vehicles bringing in supplies and equipment, to refurbish the observation towers dotted along the border with the Republic.

After patrolling through fields for about four hours, the four of us in our brick were getting bored hot and bothered; that's when I came up with the bright idea of having a quick sit down and rest in the hedgerow so I pointed to a nice shaded part of the field we were in. As I went over to said corner, I cradled the LSW (*Light Support Weapon*) in my arms and looked at my watch; 21:54 hours, still light when can we go back into base I thought, and I could really eat an egg butty.

Just at that moment, as I got a hold of my weapon properly, the whole corner of the field suddenly bubbled and erupted in slow motion as a blast of warm soggy mud and crap hit me. Then everything went into fast forward as Tye Elliot and I were hurled backwards and I landed on my back with a thud, knocking the air out of my lungs. Tye muttered or shouted something and I said: 'Yes; shit!' As I looked upwards, a big chunk of mud was airborne and heading straight at me, so I rolled over gasping and with a sickening pain, it caught me square between the shoulder blades giving me my second winding in as many seconds. As strange as it sounds, the song 'Paint it Black' by the 'Stones' started playing in my head.

It was then that the horror struck me; where were Tony and Steve who were in the corner of the field to my front and they weren't there now! I thought shit; I need to send a contact report and Steve had the radio and he has been blown to bits! I was going to be sick as I would have to get the radio off his body; I now started to panic. Suddenly Tony and Steve came scrambling out of the huge crater, splattered with mud and fighting for breath; the terror and shock etched on their faces. That look is still imprinted in my mind and even today, I can still see it.

At that moment, the sense of overwhelming relief of seeing them still alive and in one piece was unbelievable and I just started laughing even though nothing was funny. The mud and debris were still raining out of the sky and the first thing Steve did was light a cigarette or try to! He was shaking so much, that he couldn't hold the lighter and his eyes were still wide with the shock of what had just happened and blood was starting to trickle out of his ears. However, he managed to compose himself somewhat and between gulping in air sent a contact report: 'Explosion 150 metres south-west of the church; wait, out.' He then shouted at us: 'Stay down; there might be a secondary bomb, followed by a shoot.'

I didn't need telling twice and just lay there laughing and then shaking and felt a bit weird as the shock had set in and I didn't know what to do. I tried cocking my weapon, but there was no chance as it was splattered with mud and the working parts didn't want to oblige! All four of us lay there, wondering what the hell had just happened and trying to get as low to the ground without digging in. When the device had gone off, my weapon had smacked into my shoulder and it was a bit sore but the adrenalin had taken care of that and I didn't know if I was alive or dreaming.

We must have lain there for about ten minutes until another call sign came to our location which was being led by the CSM; I've never been so pleased to see a friendly face before in my life. He asked if we were ok and

I replied I wanted a bottle of whisky which is very strange as I can't stand the stuff but I would have quite happily gulped a pint of it.

As there were no green (*i.e. Army*) vehicles in XMG, we had to walk back to the police station; it was so quiet, almost surreal as all the locals were hiding. It was like a ghost town it was either very quiet or my hearing had gone; I couldn't even hear birds singing or footsteps it was a blur.

Once we were back at the station, we went straight in to the Scots Guard medic for a once over and after that, I went back to my bunk and just lay there not believing what happened; people were coming in and patting us and saying how good it was to see us alive.

The next day, the RUC came to take statements as it was attempted murder and it was then that it started to hit home what we had survived. I thought I should phone home and say that everything was alright only for them to ask what the hell I was talking about as they didn't see it or hear it on the news. I was gutted because nobody even had a clue what we were going through over here and I started to feel a bit teary and wondered why I was really there.

A cordon was set up and ATO moved in to do his stuff and it turned out our own ECM had set the device off; bloody typical. It was about 350lb of homemade explosive dug in between two trees and was an obvious crossing point; luckily for us it was designed to go off on the other side for maximum effect and on seeing one of the trees embedded in somebody's roof a hundred metres away made us feel very lucky.

The crater was 25ft across and 7ft deep. I didn't know it at the time, but I had shattered my shoulder and fractured my neck that day and was medically discharged sometime later. The IRA ruined my life but I was alive at least. There were many men before and after that weren't so lucky and that guilt still haunts me to this day.

Overall, as the tour went on, we as a battalion had more incidents and more patrols and unfortunately our Regiment had a fatality! Simon Ware who was lost to a similar land mine in the last few weeks of the tour. Simon you will not be forgotten and will always be a Coldstreamer; nulli secundus!

I went to Ulster a boy and came home a man!

Tragically, on that same tour which led to Andy's discharge on medical grounds, the Coldstreamers lost a popular Lance Corporal. Simon Ware (22), a married man from London, was killed instantly when an IRA landmine detonated in a forest at Carrickovaddy, just outside Crossmaglen. A poignant account of Simon's death is written by his Green Jacket brother, Darren in the author's *A Long Long War*.

Major Pat Moir, Royal Artillery

In order to stop the illegal passage of arms from the Irish Republic, the Army tried to close the unauthorised roads crossing the border. Some were blown up and others blocked with concrete spikes. At Crossmaglen, the locals were determined to keep their road open. By day the Sappers installed the spikes; by night the locals removed them. It was decided the only solution was a permanent one. A Vapid was a large set of sand bag sangars clad in corrugated steel, with accommodation for a number of men, and another OP was furnished with a mind-boggling array of electronic sensor devices plus a radar set. 'J' battery, 3 RHA, based at Gough barracks, Armagh were tasked to man it for about eight weeks.

One day, an exited radio op reported they had intercepted a load of Nitro Glycerine. A local milk float would cross over to the South in the mornings, full of milk and return in the afternoons full of empty bottles, only this time the bottles were not empty, but full of a clear liquid smelling of marzipan. After closer examination the liquid turned out to be none other than the famous potent Southern Irish home brew. I don't know what happened to the milkman or the booze for that matter, but at least the incident did break the boredom of VCP duty for a little while.

INCIDENT AT CLONOE

Gareth Dyer, Royal Corps of Signals

Londonderry 1992 – (Incident occurred however at Clonoe, County Tyrone) I can tell you that it was the first time I was happy hearing of the death of another human being. I remember it clearly. It was 16 February 1992. Was I ashamed at this? Am I ashamed now? No. I was a young squaddie serving in Londonderry at the time, and on that date was working in the commcen (*Command Centre*) on night shift.

Earlier that evening, I had been up with the Brigade watch keeper, passing on signals etc. Normally he would have been there on his tod, however that night there were several other bods knocking about, listening in to a couple of radio sets that had been installed in the corner of the room earlier the day before. I'd no idea who they were, but could probably have made an educated guess. There was a real buzz about the room; an almost palpable excitement amongst them and I could hear a fair bit of radio traffic from the sets they were gathered round. I asked the watch keeper what was going on (in all honesty expecting him to reply it was none of my business!). He replied: 'Word coming through of a good job, just outside Coalisland.' As he did, one of the guys in the corner turned and looked at me, a big grin all over his face. He went over to the big ops map on the wall (those huge ones that took up most of a whole wall and outlined OOB, TAOR and had lots of little magnetic pieces showing all sorts of info such as call signs etc). He reached into his pocket and took out three green, white and orange coffin-shaped magnetic pieces and placed them side by side near to where Coalisland was designated on the map.

I looked at these magnetic coffins, and knew instinctively what they referred to. I said to the guy: 'Three? Really?' Still smiling he just looked at me and said, 'So far, maybe one more. Just been ambushed after shooting up the police station down there.' I let out a very audible whoop and thought to myself, 'Happy days.' The watch keeper then told me to get on back to the commcen and not let slip of what I knew to anyone else on duty. 'They'll find out soon enough,' he told me. After going back downstairs, and within a short time, several signals came through of the incident, confirming the basic details. I was still smiling while reading them. I smiled even more when the press reports gave a version of what had happened and showed footage and pictures. It never occurred to me that these people were somebody's son, brother, husband. They may have been all of these, but at that time, and still today, to me they were terrorists before they were any of those other things. They weren't soldiers, they weren't brave guerilla fighters. They were criminals who hid in the shadows and murdered somebody's son, brother or husband while they were unarmed and defenceless.

I wasn't happy at their death per se. What I was happy with was that four less of these scumbags were walking the streets. They didn't come out into the open and try and take us on very often at all. I was happy that as was proved on this occasion and many before and after is that when they did, they came off second best. I was happy that at least some of their mates were bound to be thinking they weren't as good as they thought they were. I was happy that the next time they were told to go on a job, it would be in the back of their mind that somebody better than them might be waiting for them.

On 16 February 1992 , Kevin O'Donnell (21), Sean O'Farrell (23), Peter Clancy (19) and Daniel Vincent (20), all members of the Provisional IRA, were shot dead by undercover British Army members, in the car park of St Patrick's Roman Catholic Church, Dernagh, near Coalisland, shortly after they had been involved in a gun attack using a Soviet heavy machine gun, a Dushka, on Coalisland British Army/Royal Ulster Constabulary base.

The Dushka is a Soviet heavy anti-aircraft machine gun firing 12.7x108mm Soviet cartridges. The weapon was also used as a heavy infantry machine gun, in which case it was frequently deployed with a two-wheeled mounting and a single-sheet armour-plated shield. One can only imagine what those rounds would have done to the frail body of a human being.

THE FUNNY SIDE OF XMG

Andy Wood, Coldstream Guards

G40, the highest of the observation towers had its moments, and sometimes, whilst on duty on the rear sangar I used to get very bored and emptied some of the powder out of my cartridges so the noise of the discharge wasn't so loud. I used to shoot at the sheep on the hillside; I wonder; can I still get done for that?

The shower block was across a series of walkways so one day walking across them wrapped in just a towel, helmet on and weapon in one hand shower gel in the other, a Lynx helicopter decided to drop in on the helipad blowing my towel off; oh yes I looked good. Then one day, an officer who had to go down to the helicopters, when they landed, to sign for new encryption codes, decided that he couldn't be bothered and sent me instead. He told me to put on his smock, complete with Captain's pips and sign for it. Off I scuttled down to the pad, trying for the entire world to look like an officer. I looked into the back of the heli and was greeted by, shall we say, very special looking soldiers and I could tell they knew I wasn't a Captain! The fact that I was a baby-faced, 20 year-old, nine stone dripping wet was maybe a bit of a giveaway!

Chapter 16

Belleek

B elleek is famous for its pottery. The Belleek pottery factory, producing the world renowned fine glazed Belleek porcelain, was established in 1857 and is Ireland's oldest pottery factory. This picturesque village sits in a beautiful rural valley; it is just the image which is now used by the Northern Ireland tourist people in order to encourage visitors. During the troubles however, it represented something far less colourful and idyllic.

Belleek sits on the most westerly extremity of Ulster's border with the Irish Republic. It straddles the River Erne which feeds into the beautiful Lough Erne and is less than six miles away from the Atlantic Ocean. Because of its geographical location, it made a perfect point for IRA gunmen to smuggle arms and ammunition into the Province. It was also a place where they could easily scuttle back into the safety of the Republic as Security Forces tried to arrest them.

Aftermath of IRA attack at Belleek (Dave Henley)

Sergeant David Henley, RTR

Belleek is the furthest western British town in the UK and situated in the county of Fermanagh. The population was very Republican and during our time there, (Apr 73-Nov 74), only one shop would serve us. The town itself was typically Irish – one long main street with one or two side streets. At the bottom of the main street you would turn right to the RUC station. At the very bottom of the main street stood the Hotel Carlton, which was bombed a couple of times and just past the hotel was a bridge which marked the border (the world famous Belleek Pottery is next to the bridge). Halfway over the bridge marked the border and once over you were in the Republic for about a quarter of a mile until you reached the north again.

The bridge and road were obviously out of bounds to us, but on occasions when there was a crash-out or if we were chasing suspicious vehicles, we would take the chance to drive over the bridge and into the South (a southern fort overlooked the bridge which housed southern Irish troops) otherwise it was a 20-odd mile trip to reach the same point by staying in the north. The RUC station was on the River Erne, which marked the border. A railway bridge next door to the police station connecting the two sides had been blown up, I believe in the 50s during the IRA's brief foray.

'SPLAT CORNER' AT BELLEEK

Lance Sergeant Kevin Gorman, Scots Guards

My tour of Belleek came in the middle of my tour round about August –Sept 1989; I can't remember exactly what month it was but I remember that it was constantly raining. So, for anybody who has served in Fermanagh, they will know that it was during the 'rainy season.'

I was part of L20A and we were dropped off by a Puma, a few kms away from the town. The plan was to patrol into the town making it look like a normal patrol rather than a changeover. There was nothing unusual about our load as we always patrolled with Bergens so the local civpop (*civilian population*) probably just thought it was a routine patrol heading back to the station. On reaching the outskirts of the town I thought it looked like a right typical border town; lots of traffic coming in and out of the only main road leading to Ballyshannon across the border. We had been well briefed on the fact that Belleek was close to the border on three sides and also one of the IRA's favourite spots to hit us. The Battlements across the border were on high ground and they had made good of use of it in the past; this was evident when you ran across 'splat corner.' The many splash marks on the corner of this one house from previous cross border shoots told me that I should never become complacent when patrolling this area; especially with me being 'tail end Charlie.'

The RUC station itself was nothing special; it was a fairly new building with old sangars at the back looking across the river into the South. I remember being shown around and seeing the old RPG marks on the walls; again it was a stark reminder that Belleek had seen its fair share of attacks. Our accommodation was the usual portacabin within a blast proof shell, and the only two good things I remember about the station were the food and being able to use the phone without standing in a 2 hour queue. As a patrol base it was good because the patrols were not boring; we went out on different tasks each time. I remember one of the funniest ones. It was a Friday night and we went out about midnight and headed for the main street, and, as we ran across 'splat corner' and round the back of a house we went firm up an alley waiting for the pub across the road to start kicking out its customers.

However, as time went on, we realised they were having a lock in. Anyhow, as each customer came out, one of us in turn would 'p-check' him. We had a guy called 'Crooky' who had to 'p-check' the next guy to come out. As he came out, it was evident he was well oiled but 'Crooky' went right up to him as I was covering him with my LSW. I wasn't listening to the conversation as I was too busy keeping my eye on the Bridge area and the Battlements. After a few minutes we returned to the alley and 'Crooky' gave the Platoon Sergeant the man's details, and to this day I will never

On patrol in Belleek, 1974 (Dave Henley)

forget what he reported. The Platoon Sgt said: 'Right; what's his name?' Crooky replied: 'Billy Shannon', and the Sergeant, writing it down, asked: 'Right where is he from?' 'Bally Shannon', was the reply, and the whole brick burst out laughing. 'Crooky' never lived it down after that, but like most of us he was on his first tour and was only aged 18. We managed to 'p-check' the same guy again when he was sober and got his right name.

As Belleek was famous for its Crystal, we saw a lot of Yank tourists during our patrols and we must have scared the shit out of them when we were hard targeting it back to base; the look on some of their faces said it all!

Towards the end of my time in Belleek, the Devon & Dorset Close Observation Platoon arrived and took up residency in the old sangar block. As far as we were concerned, something was going down if a COP platoon was in town. The COP always thinks they are 'special forces' and liked to keep everything secret. One night one of our guys took a peek at their log book in the Ops room. The next day on patrol he told us the good news. When we had been out on a foot patrol of the town in the early hours of the morning of the same day, it was recorded in the COP log book that an IRA

Belleek, c1974 (Dave Henley)

unit had been compromised on the Battlements by a Garda patrol. They were waiting for us at their favourite site; it was a lucky escape. As my tour ended I found out they were going to hit us with a Dushka! Ironically, on my R&R I got a local Taxi in my hometown and the driver who knew my family got a bit chatty, he told me he had just come back from holiday, so I asked where he went, he told me 'It's a place you have probably never heard of; BALLYSHANNON', I just remained quiet and laughed within; if only he knew.

Sergeant David Henley, Royal Tank Regiment

On Sunday 25 November 1973, I was coming towards the end of a night guard duty at the RUC Police station in Belleek, County Fermanagh. It was a small and scenic, but immensely Republican, town. I was on stag with Trooper 'Pidge' Brooks from 3 Troop; 'Pidge' was with me in the Courtyard enjoying a cigarette, but should have been on the ramparts at the rear of the building that overlooked the river and marked the border between the North and South of Ireland.

Belleek RUC Station (Dave Henley)

Over the previous few years, there had been quite a few shooting incidents from terrorists having a go from over the river as there was a lot of natural foliage cover on the hill overlooking the station. It was about 07.30 hrs and as we were due to be relieved at 08.00; I told 'Pidge' that he should return to the ramparts before anyone in authority appeared. He climbed the steps and disappeared into one of the two GPMG posts situated at each end of the ramparts while I turned to walk towards the bunker at the station's main entrance. All of a sudden, I heard a long burst of machine gun fire and my immediate thought was that he had been messing about with the GPMG and caused an accidental discharge (later to become a negligent discharge). Before I had chance to call him a pillock, I heard an almighty crash at the rear of the building and saw debris falling into the Courtyard. Situated about half way up on the rear wall of the building overlooking the border, we had placed a sign measuring approximately 6 x 3 feet which was painted brown, red and green (the regimental colours) with the words '1 RTR – BELLEEK' in the centre of the sign. We later realised that the PIRA had used the sign as an aiming point for the rockets so, needless to say, the sign came down in a hurry after the attack. At that point everything seemed to happen all at once so I shouted 'Stand to. Stand to,' and, almost immediately troops started appearing from the building. Rockets were either hitting the building or flying straight over the roof (and subsequently landing in a Catholic housing estate situated beyond the Police station).

3 Troop Sergeant, Don Crassweller, manned the .30 calibre Browning machine gun which was mounted on the top floor of the building and had a commanding view of the border. He later claimed at least 3 unconfirmed hits, one of which was an unfortunate cow who had strayed into the area being used by the terrorists. Most of the lads headed for the ramparts so they could return the fire. They appeared in all different modes of dress; Barry Winrow had jumped out of bed as the first rocket hit, pulled on his boots without tying the laces, put his protective helmet (bone dome) on his head, grabbed his rifle and ran outside. He made such a comical sight as he stood on the ramparts in boots, underpants and bone dome trying to push the other lads out of the way as he vied for a better firing position. For a moment I stood mesmerised watching the rockets hit the building but then turned and made my way to the main entrance. A Police Land Rover was already on its way out and a couple of foot patrols were being dispatched into the town, just in case the attack was diversionary and another attack was being set up from the front.

The attack lasted for about 20 minutes, and somehow we had avoided any casualties, probably more by luck than anything else, but the building had taken quite a battering. In the stories that emerged in the aftermath of the attack, it transpired that when the first rocket hit the wall, a Policeman walking down the stairs had to duck as the centre piece of the rocket drilled its way through the wall and went out through the other side. One of the troop leaders (possibly 2Lt Stephen Evans of 3 Troop), whose room was in the attic of the police station, was just about to leap out of bed when a rocket shot through his door, went under his bed and out of the wall at the other side of the room. I was later asked to produce a sketch showing the locations and firing points of the terrorists. The sketch formed part of a written operational report from the Station Commander which I presume was forwarded to the brigade headquarters for operational analysis.

SERGEANT DAVID HENLEY, ROYAL TANK REGIMENT

Defuse your own bomb

On 15 July 1973 we attended a briefing from the troop leader who informed us that we would be taking part in stake-out which should lead to the arrest one or more terrorists. A culvert bomb had been found on the Ballynaghra-Tirigannon road east of Belleek and was used frequently by troops but the bomb had not been primed. We deployed in Land Rovers (being quieter than Saracens) after dark to the location of the culvert bomb, we were

Foot patrol in Belleek, c 1974 (Dave Henley)

shown our arcs of fire and settled down to wait for something to happen. After about two hours we were aware of two figures moving down the hedgerow towards the bomb; the two men obviously thought they were alone as they were talking quite normally but had they known that about 20 pairs of eyes were on them they may have preferred to have been elsewhere.

The ATO, SSgt Ron Beckett RAOC (who was later killed when defusing a bomb in a post office) allowed them to prime the bomb before making our presence known; it became apparent later on that they had only been instructed how to prime and not defuse the device. We all took great pleasure in seeing the terrorists' expressions when they realised that they were surrounded by troops and had been caught red handed. They ran away but were chased by the troop leader, Lt Roddy Hine, Cpl Rod Hepworth and my mate, LCpl Dave Taylor and caught them hiding under bushes; they were arrested and brought back to the area of the bomb. The ATO decided that he was not going to attempt to defuse it and instead ordered one of the terrorists to defuse it. The terrorist started crying and

Dave Henley RTR in Belleek (Dave Henley)

shouting that they had only been told how to prime the bomb, not how to defuse it. The ATO made it clear to him in no uncertain terms that he would have to carry out the task. By this time the terrorist was crying and shaking and had actually pissed his pants with shock and fear but everyone retreated to a safe distance while he attempted to defuse the bomb.

After what seemed an eternity the terrorist announced that he had managed to defuse it by reversing the priming action. When the ATO was satisfied that it had been made safe the Police Inspector formally arrested them and ordered a joint Police/Army escort to take them to Enniskillen RUC Headquarters via the main hospital in Enniskillen as the terrorists were complaining that they had contracted injuries. Geordie Lumsden and me were detailed, along with two RUC constables, to escort the terrorists. The Police handcuffed them and ordered them to lay face down in the back of the Police Land Rover.

On arrival at the Hospital, well after midnight, we took them one at a time to be examined by the Duty House doctor. It was obvious what the doctor thought of terrorists and their activities. He was prodding and poking without any remorse and when one of them complained that he thought his leg was broken the doctor grabbed the leg and shook it – the terrorist gave out one almighty scream and nearly fainted with the shock. The doctor told him not to be such a baby as it was only a bruise (it later transpired that the injury was worse than the doctor had diagnosed). When the doctor had declared them both fit to be apprehended in Police custody, we took them straight to the Police barracks in Enniskillen where they were both whisked away. I personally never saw them again but they both received 12 year jail sentences.

Chapter 17

Omagh/Lisburn

Lisburn (Irish: *Lios na gCearrbhach*; meaning fort of the gamblers) is a predominantly unionist city in Northern Ireland, south-west of and adjoining Belfast. The Head Quarters of the British Army is based there and it lies just a few miles from 'Bloody' Belfast.

Omagh is situated 70 miles from Belfast and 34 miles from Londonderry and, prior to the slaughter of innocents in a Real IRA bomb attack, it was a town largely untroubled by the troubles, although the surrounding areas witnessed their 'share.' A market town, it was visited by both locals for the quaint and varied shops there and by tourists alike. Like Clady before it, it had been lulled into a false sense of security when, on August 15, 1998, the 'Real' IRA committed the worst atrocit°°y of the troubles, somewhat ironically, after the 'final' ceasefire.

On the day of the bombing, terrorists parked a stolen car filled with 500lbs of explosives outside a clothes shop on Omagh's Market Street. They could not find a parking space near the intended target, the Omagh courthouse. The car bomb detonated at about 3pm, in the crowded shopping area. That morning, three phone calls had been placed warning of an attack in Omagh, and, with only 28 minutes to the deadline, a further warning was telephoned to Ulster Television.

Twenty nine people including a pregnant woman were killed in the worst atrocity to hit Northern Ireland throughout the long years of the troubles.

During the course of the troubles, 70 members of the Security Forces were killed in the Omagh area, including 42 soldiers and 28 RUC men. The three single worst incidents, all involving the IRA took place over a tragic 10 year period. On May 18, 1973, the IRA planted a bomb underneath the car of a soldier, outside the Knock Na Moe Castle Hotel in Omagh; four soldiers died at the scene and the fifth died of his wounds 16 days later. The soldiers killed were: Barry Cox (28) Blues and Royals; Arthur Place (29) Prince of Wales Own Regiment; Derek Reed (28) Royal Marines and Sheridan Young (26) of the Military Police. On June 3, the wounded man, Frederick Drake (25) of the 'Skins' (5th Inniskilling Dragoon Guards) died in hospital. On June 2, 1977, an RUC patrol was ambushed at Stewartstown, near Lough Neagh by IRA gunmen firing automatic weapons. In the carnage, RUC Officers Samuel Davison (24), Kenneth Lynch (22) and Hugh Martin (58), a father of seven children were all killed. On July 13, 1983, 4 UDR soldiers were killed by an IRA landmine at Drumquin, just 6 miles from Omagh; they were: Oswell Neely (20), Thomas Harron (24), Ronald Alexander (19) and John Roxborough who was also 19.

In the Lisburn area, the worst single atrocity took place on June 15, 1988. Six soldiers who had been on a 'fun run' Lisburn in order to raise funds for the local YMCA – an organisation that cared for both Catholic and Protestants – were killed when an IRA bomb planted underneath their lorry exploded. In what many view as an alarming lapse of security, the six men were allowed to climb on board their lorry which had been left unattended and was therefore an opportunistic target for the IRA bombers. Many have felt that since Lisburn was such a major garrison town, full of military personnel, attacks were highly unlikely. On that terrible day, the following soldiers were killed: Sergeant Michael Winkler (31); Lance Corporal William Patterson (22); Mark Clavey (24) and Lance Corporal Graham Lambie (22) all from the Royal Corps of Signals; Lance Corporal Derek Green (24), RAOC and Corporal Ian Metcalfe (36) of the Green Howards. Whether the Army and RUC had become complacent in the area or the six men were tired and distracted after their exertions will never be known.

OMAGH, SOUTH FERMANAGH. 1985

Corporal Ian Jones, 3 Light Infantry

Omagh had never been what you would call the centre of the IRA's attention. Over the years there had not really been that much terrorist activity to talk about. That appeared to be changing through 1985 and 1986 when there was a noticeable increase in hoax bomb threats and actual terrorist attacks.

UDR soldier, Co Fermanagh (Mark Campbell)

In early 1985 a car bomb was discovered on Campsie Road, Omagh. This was successfully defused by those men from the 'loony farm', the Bomb Disposal Unit. Hats off to them; mind you I'm sure most of them must have been on something to do that job. I stood at their command vehicle watching this Captain walk up to the boot of the car which was packed with explosives after it had been opened by the wheel barrow and as calm as you like start pulling wires as though he was pulling Christmas crackers; then just as calmly walking away as if it were just a stroll in the park.

19:00, Friday 13th September, another wet, cold miserable day in Omagh. I was QRF commander with my 2IC being Colin Lambert. We had already been called out twice that day; mind you we should have guessed it was going to be busy with the date being what it was. Colin's lot had recovered an old weapons stash, a couple of old shotguns and some cartridges, from a hedgerow just outside Omagh and the always reliable, suspicious car. Oh, and there was always the joy of running the gauntlet of the local Catholic youths on the Lisanelly Heights Estate when we were doing the daily outer perimetre checks of the barracks.

They used to fly a tricolour from the roof of one of the blocks of flats to see if they could tempt us into going and taking it down then attack us with whatever they had to hand, probably the odd petrol bomb thrown in for good measure. We would even go as far as pulling up outside the flats at speed and 'star bursting' from the Land Rovers as if we were going to go for it. You should have seen them, getting all excited, shouting as loud as they could that we were going to try and get their flag, only for us to jump straight back in the vehicles and speed off. That really used to piss them off. It was all part of the game. Looking back I sometimes wonder how close we might have come to getting into some real trouble. Anyone of us could have got seriously injured or even killed. The problem is you don't think about it like that at the time; it all seemed like a game.

We were just tucking into our well earned meal when the call went out that there was another suspect vehicle in Omagh Town Centre. Everyone, including me, was having a damn good bitch about it; three call outs in one day and it was only 19:00. It certainly was Friday the 13th. I got the information that the suspect car was on Market Street in the town and that the RUC were already on their way. It is a strange feeling to think that 13 years later the IRA would deploy another car bomb in nearly the same location that would cause so much death and devastation.

I was to take my lads to cordon off the junction of Drunragh Avenue, Dublin Road, Campsie Road and Market Street at the bottom end of town. When we got there, I got my mate Rob Wyatt to take his Land Rover and block off Campsie Road on top of the bridge over the Drumragh River; strangely enough only 10 metres from where the car bomb had been left earlier in the year, and I sent the other vehicle down Dublin Road.

Colin and I were then met by the RUC commander at the junction. Omagh town centre has a dip in it, sloping down from the Courthouse then up to the top of the rise on Market Street before dipping down to the crossroads. The car bomb itself was in the dip on Market Street near to Scarffe's Entry. We were standing in the middle of the crossroads, out of sight of the device discussing the evacuation of the town. It was late night shopping and there were a good number of people still about. We were also talking about possible 'come on' situations as we called them. It was not uncommon, in fact it was an IRA tactic, to place a device, be it a real explosive device or a hoax in a location with the intention of luring the Security Forces to that area. Then placing a bigger explosive devise where they thought we would place our cordons. This tactic had been used successfully, from their point of view, on many an occasion. Our biggest problem was that, in a built up area like Omagh, there were only a certain number of places you could set your troops to provide an effective cordon, and there were cars parked everywhere. Anyone of them could have been packed with explosives taking out a number of my lads, or the RUC. You just had to hope for the best.

I was standing looking at a shop which had large windows, when, suddenly there was a loud explosion. Then as I looked at the shops I could see cracks in the windows starting to appear, stretching out like tentacles from the start points in slow motion. I heard Colin shout 'Cover,' and the three of us just darted for the nearest doorway that we could find. As I turned to run, I remember briefly seeing Rob at the front of his Land Rover looking back towards us, and then I leapt for the doorway in front of me. Colin and I had gone for the same small entrance and we both landed on the floor trying to escape the blast which suddenly rushed past us. I could feel the force of the explosion pulling at my legs as if trying to drag me back out into the street.

A cloud of dust then came rushing down the street, enveloping the junction. I could not see more than a few feet. I then thought about the RUC guy and hoped he had managed to find cover. As the dust settled, Colin and I emerged from the doorway to a sight which made us look at each other wide eyed. There, right where we had been standing not a few seconds before was the twisted remains of the cars chassis. We were then joined, thankfully, by the RUC bloke who was covered in dust. He took one look at the wreckage, looked at us cursed the IRA and then ran off to check on his own men.

I looked down Campsie Road towards Rob's Land Rover to see him emerging from behind the bonnet. I went to check on him and the other lads. When I got to his vehicle he was examining the front wing. There, embedded in the Kevlar wing, exactly where he had been standing was a piece of metal from the car. That cockney voice of his, bursting into a volley of obscenities. I know he kept that piece of metal as a souvenir for many years after.

Despite the fact that the bomb had exploded earlier than we had been told in the telephone warning, another likeness to the bomb in 1998, there had only been two minor casualties. An RUC Officer had slight injuries to an eye and a female member of the public was treated for shock.

The one thing that still irritates me to this day is the seeming total disregard some of the locals had for their own safety. Like I said before it was not uncommon for the terrorists to use the 'come on' or even to use two explosive devices at the same time in an attempt to cause as much death and devastation as they could. Yet once the dust had settled, rather than dealing with matters at hand I found myself constantly being called to the cordons to deal with members of the public demanding to be let through so that they could recover their vehicles or visit their premises to check on the damage. Don't get me wrong; it wasn't everyone, but there were enough of them to get my blood boiling. I had to shout them down to get my point over that it was for their safety that they could not go back into the area until we had made everywhere safe.

Fortunately there were no more concerns or devices found. We were all glad when Friday the 13th came to an end. This was the second time I had escaped an IRA bomb without injury; the third time I would not be so lucky.

On May 20, the following year, as Ian rightly states, he was not so lucky. He was badly injured near the village of Donagh in Co Fermanagh when the IRA detonated a bomb in a building which he was passing. His excellent account of the incident can be found on pages 343-346 of *A Long Long War*. He was unconscious for three weeks after the incident. At the time of writing Ian could not remember the name of the person who gave him first aid and saved his life, referring to him only as 'the Company Clerk'. That can now be corrected; below is the story of Simon Hodges, aka 'the Company Clerk' who gives an account of the incident.

Pte Simon Hodges 3LI

May 20, 1986 was a memorable day for many reasons, I had been in the army for 3 years and 1 day; it was the day I first doubted God existed and it was the second time during my 2 year residence in Northern Ireland that I was to be on the business end of an IRA bomb.

I wasn't meant to be on patrol that day, but I volunteered to go out with a section from 8 Platoon. I had been the Company Clerk for 3 months, but to be honest, I missed the open countryside; being cooped up a lot in the patrol base at Lisnaskea unless I was an escort on a ration run. The reason for the patrol was to conduct a route check of the main Rosslea-Lisnaskea road commonly known as 'the Dash' in South East Fermanagh; this would be the route the ballot boxes would take for the upcoming elections. We were out early, and I don't remember the mode of transport out but we were on foot all the way back to Lisnaskea. At some point during the patrol we met up with an RUC foot patrol on the road prior to a village called Donagh.

Donagh is a staunchly Republican area; it straddles a small river; on one side is the pub called the Donagh Arms, a shop and some houses around a crossroads. A single stone bridge crosses the river leading to a housing estate on the other side. This estate dominates the high ground and is dwarfed by a prominent tree flying the Irish tricolour at the top. On this day we were approaching Donagh from the East; from that direction of travel the shop was the first building on the right immediately followed by the adjacent Donagh Arms, the river bridge being the other side of the tiny car park with fields beyond the bridge. The cemetrey and church is on the left behind a stone derelict with a couple of white houses the other side of the crossroads.

Myself and Ray Ewart were on the right flank out in front of the main road party; I believe Dave Wilson was the hedge man. A couple of blokes walked out of Donagh toward Rosslea laughing and joking on the road as we walked forward, and we were then both funnelled behind the Donagh Arms by the river. Ray and I went and checked under the bridge crossing the river (I remember a shopping trolley in the water). We shared a joke about something and then proceeded up the bank where I crossed the fence onto the road leading on to the bridge where Dave Wilson was standing.

I had only been on the road a matter of seconds when there was this almighty bang to my left at the crossroads; Dave and I looked at each other and our survival instinct kicked in; we both ran for our lives over the bridge cocking our weapons as we went. I took up a fire position on the right side of the road and Dave on the left. Looking back at the crossroads, the scene was blotted out by a large brown dust cloud and I could see all sorts of shit falling from the sky. Within seconds, we were both back on our feet and crossing the bridge at a trot, weapons at the ready. I was

UDR in South Armagh (Mark Campbell)

immediately aware of a profound silence save for 3 sounds, someone was laughing, someone was screaming hysterically and someone else was screaming like nothing I had ever heard before. As we crossed the bridge I identified the source of the hysterical screaming; it was a female sitting in a blue car on the bridge; the car was missing all of its windows. A male presumably from the car was exiting a public callbox; I shouted something (I don't remember what) at the male and pointed at the car. I never located the source of the laughing and I presume the other was the soon to be discovered casualty.

Dave and I were now entering the crossroads which was littered with rubble from what was once the stone derelict. Looking at me, he pointed to the far side and said: 'Go and see who that is.' I looked to where he was pointing and saw a pile of combats lying amongst the largest part of the rubble;' shit,' I thought; 'it's one of us.' I remember worrying about a secondary device. I got to the casualty and started throwing rubble off his body as fast as I could; he was lying face down in a pool of blood, and I honestly thought he was dead. I knelt and gingerly turned him on his side, I then recognised the body of the patrol commander Ian Jones; as I lifted his head he let out a moan and his face started to fall away like a peeled banana exposing his jaw and what was left of his teeth. I shouted out: 'Half his fucking face is missing!' I wasn't to know, but Ian told me much later that he heard me say that.

Dave was by now frantically trying to raise the Ops Room at Lisnaskea but getting nothing; eventually, he ran to the first white house on the crossroads and without ceremony kicked in the front door, to use the telephone to call for help. In the meantime my attention turned to Ian; I put his face back together as best I could and was trying to take Ian's First Field Dressing (FFD) out of his jacket pocket. Gary Dawson arrived and at the same time started to remove his own FFD; I now already had the first one open and Gary helped me apply it to Ian's face. I took out my knife and cut off the radio on his back; I was now left worrying that Ian might drown in his own blood because I wasn't going to leave him face down, and I was also aware that his arm was possibly broken due to the moaning I received when I moved it but I didn't have the means to do anything about it. Gary left me his FFD and went to join our very thin cordon. The occupants of the white houses were by now standing watching along with a small crowd near the derelict. The occupants of the shop were stood looking out through shattered windows at us and a very large crowd with perfect line of sight of the incident were gathered at the housing estate. Not surprisingly no-one stirred from the pub, the occupants having already left just prior to the IED going off, due no doubt to a warning from the IRA.

A couple drove into the village but we turned them away and then an armoured RUC Cortina turned up coming over the bridge from the side of the housing estate with two officers on board; they proceeded to block the road. A young woman pushing a pram then tried to enter the incident from the road between the now demolished derelict and the white house that Dave visited earlier, I told her that she couldn't come through, to which she replied: Fuck you!' 'Well fuck you too, missus,' was my response, and she walked away. I then saw a man in blue overalls and he looked vaguely familiar but he turned and walked away.

Ian by now was obviously in great pain but not making a fuss and he was trying to talk to me. Instead I talked and Ian listened, and where needed, squeezed my hand; once for yes; twice for no. I talked about football, about the possibility of him being discharged, about his family and his daughter (Heidi I think her name is, (apologies if that's wrong Ian). Every time I heard the distant noise of an engine I falsely got his hopes up thinking it was a helicopter, only for it to turn out to be a tractor or another RUC vehicle arriving. I can't swear to it because I had no idea of the passage of time but it took something like 2 hours for the first helicopter to arrive.

The Lynx landed in the field beyond the bridge on our side of the river and disgorged its passengers, including the MO Captain Morton and a stretcher. The stretcher was formed and Ian lifted onto it, he again cried out in pain from the arm, (it wasn't broken but his whole side had been peppered with tiny bits of shrapnel from the explosion). A group of us then lifted him, carried him across a barbed wire fence into the field and onto the helicopter. The immediate area was well cordoned by now and Dave Wilson got us to collect our weapons and then the remainder of the patrol walked a short distance to the grass bank opposite the white houses. Ian's kit along with his boomerang shaped SLR stayed in the rubble. He stood us in a line and we made our weapons safe, and then sat down in the grass. It was at this point that I couldn't contain myself and the stress took over, tears started to flow freely and I sobbed for a short while until Dave took a grip of me and I stopped.

We later found out that the device used to send the signal to detonate the IED was located under paving slabs in an ice cream container where the large crowd had stood watching on the housing estate. We made it back to Lisnaskea and went into an extensive debrief by the Int cell, at which I pointed out the male in the blue overalls from a picture on the extensive photo board in the briefing room, he was a known local player. I later phoned my mum but didn't say anything about the day; I didn't want her to worry. It was a long time before I told anyone about the events that had taken place, years later in fact.

LISBURN

Brian Baskerville, R.A.O.C.

We used to go into a pub just down the Saintfield Road from Lisburn near to Sprucefield where I worked; it was called the 'Perseverance.' Where you would normally expect to see plates, bottles, Toby jugs etc., around the place on shelves, he had rubber bullets, Red Hand stuff, and any and all things UVF. The landlord was as you can expect a staunch loyalist. During my tour, relations with Dublin were at an all time low; however we still had monthly visits from the Garda boys. We took them in to the 'Perseverance' for a quick pint; on one particular visit, in we went with the strict instructions of keeping mouths firmly shut in earshot of the proprietor. He sussed them immediately that they came in the door and ordered them out. It was as if he was expecting them; how did he know?

I used to visit my current wife in Scotland quite regularly which involved a train journey to and from the ferry port at Larne. However Sunday night the boat train got into Victoria Road station about 10pm but there were no trains back to Lisburn. Over a period of months, I got to know a taxi driver who worked for Red Star taxis opposite the Europa Hotel. He would pick me up and run me back to Lisburn and drop me about a half mile down from the main gate at HQNI. I would walk the rest. He was quite trustworthy and a nice bloke. One night he said he had another job to do and did I mind. I told him that was fine, although, worryingly, he told me to keep my mouth shut. We drove into West Belfast and picked up a fare (a man with a small carrier bag in his hand) from one of the infamous flats. We then drove back into the city and dropped him off. I was kacking myself thinking they were going to do me, although I needn't have worried but at the time I did.

He also once told me of the imminent release of 'Butcher' Murphy (the Shankhill Butcher) from jail and that there was a contract on him. Two weeks later he was out and a week later his car was sprayed with automatic fire and that was the end of him. I think he was done by his own side to keep the peace

THE FIRST PIRA ATTACK ON WIVES AND CHILDREN OF SERVICEMEN IN NI

David Henley, RTR

The Regiment's married quarters were situated behind the camp and could be accessed either through camp via a guard-controlled gate, or by taking a slip road north of the camp which was for public access. At the time no PIRA attack had ever been made on wives and children and no one ever expected them to carry out such a cowardly action. On the morning of 9 August 1973 I recall having just walked out of the accommodation block just after 9 o'clock intending to go down into Omagh town as we had just started a stand down from operations for a short time. I can't remember if there was a loud bang or just a muffled roar, but as I looked at the windows they seemed to go from concave to convex before some of them broke (our block was not far from the MQs). No one seemed to know where the explosion had come from and chaos reigned until it was established what had been bombed.

It transpired that the terrorists hijacked a Post Office van and placed 500lb of fertiliser mix complete with a timer device inside the vehicle. They then forced the driver to deliver the van into the estate (his family were being held hostage and warned that they would be killed if he did not carry out the delivery). The bomb detonated shortly after the driver had managed to shout a warning to those in the immediate area. About 20 or 30 houses were damaged, some badly, but luckily many of the families who lived in those houses had returned to England on block leave. A few women and children received cuts from flying glass and many children suffered from shock and nightmares for weeks afterwards.

I heard of an amusing incident which occurred in the aftermath of the bombing. One of the lads who lived in a house affected by the bomb decided he would try to get a new TV set out of his insurance company. Because of the seriousness of the situation and the fact that wives and children had been involved, the insurers pulled out all the stops to get assessors in very quickly. The soldier in question retrieved a house-brick from outside and threw it through his TV set. He told the assessor that he had been on leave in England when the bomb had gone off and everything in the room was just how he had found it on his return. The insurance assessor immediately smelled a rat and questioned how the rest of the room, including the windows, remained undamaged, but a brick had seemingly appeared from nowhere and placed itself inside the TV screen? Needless to say he did not receive anything from the insurers and ended up having to buy a new TV to replace the one he'd damaged – he was well out of pocket!

As a result of the bombing the married quarters were fenced in as part of the barracks with a sentry post provided to control access to the patch from the public access road – another duty for us to perform but a totally necessary one.

Private D.C., Queen's Regiment

On the map of your area of responsibility, it was not unusual for 'Out of Bounds' areas to suddenly appear, for no reason. The main reasons could be that there had been a weapons find or a device had been found and had been watched, or that other units would be operating in the area and didn't want to be shot by their own troops.

As I worked in Lisnaskea daily, I needed to ensure that I changed my route on a daily basis. I had my own map where I had marked different coloured routes from Lisnaskea to Omagh, trying to ensure that I used a different route each day. I also made sure that my colleagues were aware of the route I was taking, for my own protection. The IRA were very good at identifying patterns in routine and carelessly getting into a routine was guaranteed to cost you your life because they will suss you out and they will ambush you at the first opportunity. Identification of my car was easy as it had to exit the barracks every day and no doubt, they could recognize me too.

One evening, I left Lisnaskea to head for Omagh. As far as I was aware, I had picked a different route from the night before but perhaps not. All of the roads between these two locations were B roads and very winding and it was dark. I must have been half way through the trip when I came across white Vauxhall Cavalier in front of me. At first sight, nothing seemed unusual until it started to slow down, as though to let me pass, which was very odd, as the road was so narrow. In my own mind, there was no way that I was going to pass this vehicle and end up broad side to it, so I also slowed down and fortunately, we soon arrived at a T junction. This junction was the type where it was Y shaped, so if you were going left, you would have split off that way and also if you were going right. I gave the vehicle in front no idea of which direction I was going, which would always have been the opposite direction to him. I peeled off right, he peeled off left and I maneuvered into the road. As I moved away, I caught a glimpse of the Cavalier appearing to go left but then it sharply turned right and seemed to pick up speed. By this time I was shitting myself so I put my foot down and belted up this B road, at great risk to myself and any oncoming traffic but as far as I was concerned, at this stage, my life was definitely at risk. The pursuing vehicle was making an effort to keep up but I had managed to gain an advantage and as soon as I came over the brown of the next hill, in dead ground, I threw my car into a small farmers track, with the lights off, threw myself out of the car and into some nearby bushes and cocked my pistol.

I had never been in a fire fight or a close contact before, but to me, at this point, this was going to get messy and the adrenaline was pumping. One of two things was going to happen. The car was going to drive past or it had seen me and was going to drive into the lane and hit my car with its engine running and the door open, me in a bush!! As it happened, the vehicle had driven past, slowed down, obviously realizing that I had diverted somewhere and eventually drove off.

I got home and reported the incident immediately. I changed vehicles the next day and when I arrived at Lisnaskea I was de-briefed by SB and I noticed that an Out of Bounds Area had been put in place where I had been and I was told, in no uncertain terms that what had potentially happened to me had matched vehicle and intentions wise, information that they had received. One of the few lucky occasions of my life!

OFF Duty UDR Protection: Soldier, COP, 1 GLOSTERS

Due to the increased threat to off duty UDR personnel, our platoon was tasked to provide close protection at the home of a UDR soldier. I thought it was a bit of a lame tasking, as we were never going to be that lucky to be waiting on terrorists, to have them actually turn up, but I lived and hoped it would happen.

We were deployed one night, with a team as cut off/early warning on the only track up to the house; our team was tasked to find a suitable position in the barn near the main house of the UDR soldier. We had to make sure we had a good view of the main door to the house and were able to get out quickly to engage any terrorists who might want to crash our party. The family knew we would be in the area but not the exact place.

That night when we got into the barn, their dog just kept on yapping, and yapping, it got to the stage where we were going to withdraw from the barn, but just before we moved out the wife of the UDR guy popped her head into the barn. We all froze not really knowing what reaction we were going to get. Our team commander spoke to her and just told her who we were, then she disappeared, and the dog stopped yapping. We waited for what seemed like an age before the old lass popped back into the barn again, this time she had a flask of coffee and some biscuits for us. Wow I thought; I was not expecting that. We all had a good chuckle, and wondered if we would be pushing our luck if we asked for a few bacon rolls. After we had our fill we then pulled back to the cut off position due to the noise from the dog. The evening went by°° quietly and we were picked up just before dawn. Once back all the usual happened, de-brief, food, shower and sleep.

We were sent back out again, to do the same task, but this time we were staying put in the barn for a longer duration, this was to cut down unnecessary movement around the area, so not to try and compromise what we were doing. We still had a team along the track acting as cut off/ early warning and we had a team in the barn, thankfully I was in the barn.

Once in the barn, we got ourselves sorted then waited; that was all we could do. We had 2 of us on, doing 3 on, 3 off, for the duration of the task.

During the task I never really thought about much except, to make sure I was doing what needed to be done, cover your arcs, radio checks, just all the stuff we had been trained to do. In the back of my mind was: what if; what if we got compromised; what if the shit did hit the fan; what if we got contacted. I never let it worry me, just trusted the guys I was with and just hoped the training would kick in if things did go pear shaped. We were never cock sure of ourselves, we were just a bunch of young guys doing what had to be done.

RURAL ULSTER

Brian Baskerville, R.A.O.C.

The story is recorded on the daily briefings of the time I was courting the present Mrs. Baskerville and had a routine after work of telephoning her from the welfare phone outside 39 Brigade HQ. This phone was usually very handy because it took 5p coins which regularly got stuck and enabled you to stay on the phone literally until you got fed up of talking. However, being that way, it was regularly in use and a long wait was the result if somebody else beat you to it.

During my tour I was one of the very few who had a permanently issued Browning (*Author's note: many off-duty soldiers illegally took out 'shorts' as they called revolvers; 'just in case'.*) which was literally entrusted to my care along with 20 rounds and 2 mags which only had to be checked by the 39 Brigade armourer once a year. Ammo was exchanged every six months for new batch of operational ammo.

On this particular evening I had finished work and put my gun in my locker with the intention of going down the Brigade to make my phone call. It was busy so I decided to drive down to Finaghy just beyond Dunmurry, and combine a phone call there with a fish supper from the chippy there. Being a relatively safe area I didn't even consider that the gun may be was required so off I went.

On my return from Finaghy I drove along the Lisburn Road and it rises up over a slight brow of a hill and as I came down the other side I saw what I immediately recognised as an automatic pistol lying in the road. Moments like that are quite surreal as you drive past in slow motion thinking: 'there's a gun in the road – that's unusual.' Senses clicked in and I hit the brakes and pulled in. Once out of the car I was running back and, about 10 yards away from the boot of the car, I suddenly was aware of a truck which had stopped on the opposite side. Then, a guy was also heading for the gun and had at least 15 yards on me. He got there first and picked it up, at which point I had stopped out in the open with no cover. At this point he pulled the slide back to put one up the spout, and I raised my hands and smiled. Fortunately for me, either the mag was empty or the slide jammed to the rear. He smiled at me, pointed it at me then ran back to his truck and took off. At this point the blood had drained from my face and I went into auto pilot. I was back in the car, doing, not quite a handbrake turn but something similar and off we went towards Belfast. I followed him off the main road into Twinbrook and stayed with him for as long as I felt safe, being careful to keep my distance. Having no radio or mobile phone all I could do was follow and eventually find a phone box to call 999 for help.

I called my OC, and we made the report for the RUC and all was recorded. They were quite surprised that I could even identify the gun type until Rod explained what job I was doing in the province. The upshot of the incident was that we identified the guy from the truck and where he lived (happened to be a traveller) but he was never found nor arrested. We deduced that he must have been covertly moving the gun perhaps strapped or taped under his vehicle.

A bit of a dull story perhaps until you start to think. What if he had succeeded in loading the gun? More to the point, what if I had taken my Browning with me on that night? Would I have drawn it? Would I have fired? If not, would I have arrested him? Having no backup, how would I have detained him and how would I have summoned help? For me personally I think I had a lucky escape from all the possible outcomes that night. That was one of my most memorable 'What ifs?'

Chapter 18

Newry

N ewry is taken from the Irish: *Iúr Cinn Trá* meaning 'The Yew Tree at the Head of the Strand', short form An tIúr, 'The Yew.' is the fourth largest city in Northern Ireland and eighth on the island of Ireland. The River Clanrye, which runs through the city, forms the historic border between County Armagh and County Down.

There were a number of SF deaths in the Newry area. The Newry area covers both Warrenpoint and Bessbrook.

The area was a dangerous place to be for the SF, with 36 soldiers being killed between September 4, 1971 and February 12, 1997. The first soldier to be killed was RTR Lance Corporal John Warnock (18) by an IRA bomb on the fiercely Republican Derrybeg Estate in Newry. Almost 26 years later, Lance Bombardier Stephen Restorick (23) of the Royal Artillery was shot and died of his wounds whilst manning a VCP at Bessbrook Mill. Symbolically, his death is regarded as being the final military fatality, but in the course of the author's research, there were several more fatalities among British Army personnel. Additionally, the RUC suffered grievous losses, with 34 Officers killed in terrorist incidents in the Newry area.

The single worst incident involving the RUC took place on February 28, 1985, when 9 Officers were killed in an IRA mortar attack on their station. This is covered in this chapter. On April 17, 1979, 4 RUC men were killed in an IRA landmine explosion on the Bessbrook-Newry Road and on July 26, 1986, three officers were gunned down in the Market Square in Newry itself. The men were: Karl Blackbourne (19), Peter Kilpatrick (27) and Charles Allen (37), all Officers of the Royal Ulster Constabulary. They were shot and killed from close range by the Provisional IRA while sitting in their stationary armoured patrol car at Market Street, Newry.

The worst three incidents involving Military multi-casualties took place, chronologically on August 27, 1979 at Warrenpoint, Co Down when 19 soldiers were killed by two IRA bombs; on January 6, 1981 when 3 UDR soldiers were killed by an IRA landmine and at Camlough on May 19, 1981, when four Royal Green Jackets and their RCT Driver were also killed by a landmine.

Civilian fatalities included, on 31 July 1975 – Fran O'Toole (27), Brian McCoy (33) and Tony Geraghty (23), all civilian members of the Miami Showband, were shot and killed by the Ulster Volunteer Force shortly after their minibus was stopped at a bogus vehicle check point at Buskhill, near Newry.

DISASTER AND HEARTACHE AT WARRENPOINT

James Yarwood, Parachute Regiment

This was my first tour of Northern Ireland and I was very anxious about serving in the province at that time as the troubles were not only confined to Northern Ireland but in mainland England too. When the IRA began shooting soldiers who worked in Army Careers Offices or placing explosives under vehicles belonging to anyone who was involved with the services on our home soil, the general public were also very concerned.

In 1979, 2 Para were to carry out a two year tour of Ballykinlar situated on the South Eastern side of Northern Ireland in County Down about 12 Km South West of Downpatrick. When I first arrived there I remember how picturesque the rural countryside was with the Mourne Mountains set in the background and the smell of the clean country air as it flowed from the open bus windows. Farmers drove their tractors ploughing slowly through the wide open fields with young children playing happily with one another, innocently in the background, oblivious to the hidden perils that lay around the countryside. I saw no locals waving or cheering as we drove from the docks to County Down in an unmarked bus that was clearly full of squaddies in civilian clothing. What I did see was hatred in the eyes of some people as we passed through some villages which only highlighted my nervousness in the bus.

I was trained to fight for my country and the people of Northern Ireland that wanted us there so I fully understood the dangers of travelling through bandit country in unmarked vehicles. That is why my heart was in my mouth every time we drove round a sharp corner and especially when we drove over any culverts that were piped in under the roads. I remember thinking to myself that I didn't want to be blown to pieces before the tour began.

I was a private in 'D' Company and had only been in the battalion for about 10 months when the tour began. Once we settled in to life in Abercorn Barracks we were quickly ready for action and set about a routine that we basically stuck with for the duration. One company would be on duty with another on fatigues or training whilst one would be in bandit country South Armagh. After about 5 months, my anxiety began to subside slightly as the weather was good with the sea and beach only a stone's throw away at the rear of our camp. We had not had any casualties, but things were about to take a change for the worst.

During the back end of August 1979 I was in the camp at Ballykinlar talking away to some of my mates in the small shop that was on camp which sold egg banjos and other goodies. The smell alone was enough to drag soldiers towards the shop as the eggs sizzled away in the frying pans. That day 'A' Company was getting ready to deploy to 'bandit country' for their six week stint patrolling the countryside and they all appeared to be in a positive mood.

I noticed that there was some 4 ton trucks lined up and naturally assumed that they were going to be used to ferry equipment for the 'A' company lads. I was wrong; they were there to ferry the lads across to their destination. Once the trucks left the camp I watched in apprehension as they disappeared into the distance with the grey smoke from the exhausts bellowing into the air and into the rear of the trucks.

That afternoon I was in my room with my mates when a news flash appeared on the TV stating that a convoy of trucks had been blown up at Warrenpoint and that there were casualties. We initially thought that the trucks belonged to the Royal Marines who were operating in that area at the time and were shocked at what we heard.

The trucks were driving along the shores of Corlingford Lough a sea inlet which forms the boundary between Northern Ireland and the Republic of Ireland. As they passed a parked trailer stacked with bales of hay concealing a huge amount of explosives the terrorists set off the bomb that devastated the convey causing massive loss of life and severe injuries. As reinforcements arrived the terrorists had callously placed a secondary device in a position where they knew the quick reaction force would park their vehicles to help the injured. This device was detonated killing those going to assist the casualties as well as a soldier who was at the scene in a helicopter believed to be the CO of the QOHs.

16 brave young men from the 2nd Battalion the Parachute Regiment died that day and before this particular tour was over a further 5 soldiers lost their lives totaling 21. We were called to the cookhouse by the hierarchy as the names of those killed or wounded were read out. This is the first time that I saw experienced grown men – battle hardened paratroopers openly cry. I personally felt empty, annoyed and sickened at what had occurred and the reality and dangers of serving in Northern Ireland hit me like a sledge hammer.

On August 27, 16 men of 2 Para and 2 men from the Queen's Own Highlanders were killed there; it would be the worst single day for loss of soldiers' lives during the troubles. It would also be the worst day's loss of soldiers' lives for the British Army since the Aden mutiny in June, 1967.

Driver 'W', Royal Corps of Transport

I was based at Newry in 1981 and I was unprepared for what went on, not only in that area, but all around Northern Ireland. When I was younger, I watched a lot of war pictures at the flicks and on telly and I loved seeing Germans blown up and shot and having their throats cut by Resistance men. One of my favourites was 'Where Eagles Dare' with Clint Eastwood; in one of the scenes, the good guys blow up a bridge and a German vehicle full of Nazis gets blown up.

The vehicle comes down in pieces and in flames, and presumably all the Germans are killed. I thought that this was great and never paused to consider the reality behind it. Then a mate in my Regiment, (*Paul Bulman*) on attachment to the Green Jackets was killed in, I think, May of that year, along with four of their soldiers. I saw the wreckage at Camlough and the first thing that struck me, the flashback was that film, except, it was real. This was the reality; there were no stuntmen and that; these were dead soldiers.

I've been out of the Army now for nearly 20 years and I've not watched a war film since. If one comes on and the wife or the kids want to watch it, I go upstairs and read or I take the dog out for a long walk. Whenever I see explosions, I think of those 5 lads at Camlough and I feel sick.

ON THE DERRYBEG

Soldier, Parachute Regiment

Towards the end of our 1974 tour and we were driving through Newry and its Derrybeg estate. There were two open topped Land Rovers with GPMGs mounted on roll bars manned by the lads in the back. The light was starting to fade and as we pulled around a corner at the end of the street it appeared, at first that the pavement was on fire. With the warning about the strange sight up ahead from the guys in the front, the two of us in the back checked our sights were up and braced for action. What kind action at that moment nobody was exactly sure.

As we get closer it becomes apparent that someone's set up an impromptu shrine on the corner where one of the poor locals (tomorrow he'll be one of the valiant fallen and a much mourned loving father etc) had been shot as he had tried to take a pot shot at one of our patrols, the previous week. Anyway there were pictures of him propped up and surrounded by candles. We're just coming level with all of this and becoming a bit wary as there was not another soul on the streets and there were no lights showing in the houses.

Green Howards at Newry (Joe Harris)

When suddenly Tich screams out for us to stop and he's up and jumping off the back of the rover, and I'm off with him. Before I know it I'm right up his arse because he'd stopped in front of the candles. I scurried off into a doorway and Tich, the mad bastard bent down in front of the candles and photos.

Squatting Tich placed his weapon across his knees and starts to sing 'Happy Birthday' then blows all the candles out. Within 10 seconds of our arses hitting the seats in the back of the wagon, the streets were full of brick-throwing locals, eating our dust as we disappeared into the darkening night. 4 days of rioting followed. But we had to have left something for the Royal Marines advance party to experience. It was getting a bit boring and we only had 14 days to the end of the tour.

NEWRY RUC STATION

Brian Smith, Devon & Dorsets

Th-waank Th-waank Th-waank.; this noise and the vibrations rattled through the A.R.F. (Air Reaction Force) hut at Bessbrook. We knew the explosions were close and instantly got off our pits and ran to the helipad of Europe's busiest helicopter base. We were on the Lynx helicopter before the pilots ready to go and see what had happened.

On the flight to Newry we were told that the R.U.C. station there had been hit by a series of I.R.A mark IX mortars. When we got there and landed, there was complete chaos which could only be expected. We quickly de-bussed and set up the inner cordon. This was almost second nature after being in the Province for 18 months. Sgt Bill Kelsall came up to me and said 'Smudge boy; you have just come back from your medics course at Aldershot; I think its time you put it into action.' I just thought: cheers, Sarge!

I went into the R.U.C station to what can only be described as a butcher's shop. The station was being, ironically, mortar-proofed so they were using a portacabin as a makeshift canteen. The mortars had landed right on shift handover, so there was double the amount of policemen and women in the canteen. I got in there to give first aid, but where do you start? Luckily a few of the senior policemen started to take control. All I can say is I soon learnt my 'Bleeding Breathing Breaks and Burns.' I don't really want to write too much about that butcher's yard because I still get a lump in the throat thinking about it. Let's say nine brave R.U.C men and women died that day and many were injured who still bear the scars.

I was picked up off the ground at 07:00hrs with Richard 'Bomber' Brown and Clive Bridgeman. We had been granted leave to go back to the U.K for Philip Marland's wedding. 'Bomber' and Clive were ushers; I was Best man. Back in the UK, the thing I remember most is sitting on the underground looking at the headlines in the papers and noticing 'Bomber' Brown's ugly mug on the front page with a caption: 'A member of 2 Para at the Newry Mortar attack.' It seemed surreal that here we were, 3 hours afterwards, sitting on a train in another world. It's amazing how you quickly adjust from carnage but it still, over time, creeps up and gnaws at you.

The attack was jointly planned by members of the South Armagh Brigade and an IRA unit in Newry. In the early evening of 28 February 1985, nine shells were launched from a Mark 10 mortar bolted onto the back of a lorry that had been hijacked in Crossmaglen. Eight shells overshot the station, but one 50-lb shell landed directly on a Portacabin containing a temporary canteen. Nine police officers were killed, and 37 people were injured including 25 civilian police employees; the death toll was the highest inflicted on the RUC in its history.

In that dreadful attack, the following officers were killed: Chief Inspector Alexander Donaldson (41), Sergeant John Dowd (31), Woman Constables Ivy Kelly (29) and Rosemary McGookin (27), Reservists Geoffrey Campbell (24), Denis Price (22), Sean McHenry (19), Paul McFerran (23) and Constable David Topping who was 22.

After the murderous attack on Newry, the IRA carried out a further nine mortar attacks in 1985. On 4 September an RUC training centre at Enniskillen, County Fermanagh was attacked. Purely by luck and poor intelligence by the IRA, 30 cadets narrowly escaped death. The cadets were expected to be still asleep, but were instead eating breakfast when the bombs landed. In November 1986 the IRA launched a second attack at the RUC station in Newry, but the bombs fell short of their target and landed on residential houses. A four-year-old Catholic girl was seriously wounded and another 38 people injured, prompting an IRA spokesman to admit: 'This incident left us open to justified criticism.'

RURAL INCIDENT

Bombardier 'Taff' Fitzgerald, Royal Artillery

My platoon was tasked with putting in VCPs around the town of Belleeks (*also known as Belleek in Co Armagh and not to be confused with the other Belleek in the far west of Ulster*) as part of the cordon for a Republican march. When I hit my allocated position with my brick and an RUC constable, I noticed something odd about the road surface. We were right on the edge of the marching route and the road was pock marked and scraped. I turned to the RUC bod and said, 'I wonder what the fuck did this.' He explained that two of their lads had been hit there a couple of years before. He said that as they left the village a transit type van was parked in the road. When the two PCs pulled up behind it in their armoured Sierra, the back doors of the van opened and they and their car were laced with a 50 cal.

I was standing on the strike marks of bullets that had travelled through them, the engine block and the armour of their car. That's some power. I assumed that both men were dead. I know now that 25 year old Constable, Michael Marshall had been killed instantly, but miraculously his 21 year old colleague survived with serious wounds to his legs and a shoulder.

When the march came in towards us it was being lead by the most infamous player in the area. We had been told by Int that he had eighteen confirmed kills to his name but always got off on technicalities. He saw me standing on the strike marks, made eye contact and smiled; I nodded and smiled back.

Constable Marshall (25) and married with two young children was killed when they were ambushed by the IRA at Belleeks, between Bessbrook and Camlough on October 20, 1989. His comrade, as Taff rightly says, survived by what can only be described as a miracle, their car being hit by 66 armour-piercing rounds in the savage attack. The probable weapon was found by the Garda Siochana in Donegal some days later.

NEWRY INCIDENT

Soldier 'S' Att: Royal Military Police

It was a cold wet Saturday Autumn evening in 1992 and I had been in Province for around one year I had served with HQNI (*Head Quarters, Northern Ireland*) and with the 'witness protection' guys. I had now moved on to 175 Military Police Unit, Lisburn Garrison to train with the Close Protection Units (CPU) and to join another specialised unit.

I had pulled a weekend duty with my new section, the Unit Investigation Element mainly due to my Special Investigation Branch (SIB) background and was busy counting down the hours whilst listening to the radio. I could hear the mad goings on in the nearby RMP Corporals' Mess who were having an all ranks function and the comings and goings of the notorious night life of the Strip in HQNI. A hotbed of booze, drugs, girls and drunken troops from Lisburn Garrison or visiting soldiers fresh back from border ops.

I had operated in civvies and in unmarked vehicles since arriving in the Province and was confident moving around relatively unnoticed. On the occasions when we used helicopters or green vehicles to move around in I used to feel like I had a target pinned to my back; I actually preferred being a covert operator. The office phone rang around 2130 hrs from the HQNI Watch keeper with some information from the police who wanted to speak over the secure 'red 4' telecommunication system. Our phone lines were subject to IRA monitoring, so no sensitive information could be discussed on normal land lines; everything was said in 'squaddie code.' A typical conversation on the normal phone would go 'Hi' John; will you be in the obvious at the obvious time?"' 'Yes, but I am going to be late due to the obvious so I will be one zero past orange at the obvious.' There were no mobile phones, only bleepers, so cock ups were plenty; obviously.

Therefore the pain in the arse 'red 4' was the only way and the system would suddenly cut out and sometimes take so long you would revert to the normal system. After speaking with the police it soon became apparent that a soldier had been set up in a Honey Trap (a term used to describe a local girl befriending a soldier then getting him back to her place for sex and assassination) and he was due to be killed by the IRA that night somewhere in South Armagh. Things started to then move fast, as it became apparent that a Soldier from a Scottish Regiment, who had just finished a tour in South Armagh had gone AWOL from his Unit in Germany and was now back at a house south west of Newry. He had met her on routine VCPs and had become familiar whilst he was doing 'chat up.' At some stage they had arranged for him to go AWOL and stay with her knowing the Military had enough to do without looking for some stupid Jock AWOL somewhere in Europe, let alone in 'bandit country.'

The Private was now in his love nest, in South Armagh where he was to be killed. I had been involved with some dodgy things up until that time, so it really didn't put me up or down listening to this message from the police, as usually these things didn't come to much. The phone rang again, 'Listen,' said the police guy, 'We have no time for your secure phone lines shit; this guy is going to be killed soon. We will confirm the address with our informer ASAP. We haven't got time to go through the usual channels so what do you suggest?'

Now this was getting tasty and I was really fired up, so I called my oppo, Corporal 'A' and we made a plan to get on the road into South Armagh and to the RUC Station in Newry to see how things developed. We bombed up at the Armoury, grabbed the car bag then booked out of camp through the Ops room and headed off. I had travelled all over the Province in unmarked vehicles and knew the territory we were heading to reasonably well, usually moving freely between places like Bessbrook, Keady, XMG and Middletown. However, late at night in an unmarked vehicle with only two of you and no back up could get a little scary. Sure, in essence the Ops room were supposed to know where you were but that often wasn't the case and from flash to bang you could forget any QRF getting to you and even then you risked a 'blue on blue.' (*Being shot by 'friendly' fire; surely the greatest oxymoron of all time.*)

We knew that, if the shit hit the fan we were on our own so our 'actions on' had to be rehearsed and carried out with aggression if we were compromised or ran into an IVCP. Now the adrenalin was pumping; what if this, what if that, what if the 'greens' (*Uniformed British soldiers*) opened up on us and so we psyched ourselves up and we were an invincible two man, fucking army by the time we left the outskirts of Lisburn. Driving along in the dark, looking at everything other that what was on the road, getting more intense towards South Armagh, 'bandit Country.' The in-car commentary was non stop: 'Man left, parked car right, car approaching right, car turning ahead, car slowing down, slowing down; stopping people, getting out; stand by. Stay away; o.k. go! he's moving again; move on; VCP Army ahead, stopping now, weapons away. OK, 'chat up' is coming.' Engage with small talk, show 'get out of jail free card', and move on without getting any interest from the other stationary vehicle occupants, and so the road commentary would go on until safe arrival at a secure SF base.

When we arrived at the RUC Station an hour or so later, I called the police guy who now had the address and some more information. An IRA ASU was being put together as we spoke, to take the squaddie out, so we had little time to waste and now was the time to report to the HQNI watch keeper for authorisation to go in. Information passed to and fro, and it soon became apparent that target house was in a real dodgy area about 20 minutes drive from the base in Newry, IRA Central. The local Army commander had stirred up a hornets nest in the previous weeks, with clampdowns on arms and ammo movements which had resulted in his men being blown up, shot at and generally not being treated very nicely. When I made him aware of the situation, he point blank refused to let his men go back into the area during the hours of darkness, 'You must be mad; no way am I committing my men to any op in that area to save some stupid soldier who could be dead anyway. I will get ready to go at first light.'

Well that was that then! We were screwed as the RUC commander obviously needed Army protection to get his men in. Could we do it without them? The commander's look was sufficient; we were not going in until first light when the shifts had changed. Both myself and the police guy were really disappointed, and I was thinking: ' Jock bastard; I will kill you if we get you out alive. Early the next morning, the shift commanders changed and so did the situation; rapidly. The oncoming Commander was really up for a scrap, after I briefed him he said: 'What are we waiting for; let's do it.' Wow! As simple as that; I was well impressed, and minutes later, four armoured cars, lots of wired up RUC men and us two RMP were on the road and moving fast along the country lanes. It was now snowing and it looked really nice and like a Christmas card. On we went, silence in the car as we all knew this could be tasty if we arrived at the same time as the IRA ASU.

Joe Harris (Green Howards) at
Newry, 1975 (Joe Harris)

Funny thing, the thought of being killed at night in the snow really upset me. I always thought it would be nicer to get it on a sunny day, perhaps in nice fields or something like that. At times like these men reflect on certain things which are dear to them, then are catapulted into reality.

Suddenly, the radio spat it out 'Standby, figures three to target:...2....1.... Standby...go.' We had discussed our roles at the station and so we all knew roughly who was doing what; I was in the rear car and we were the snatch team. The house was in darkness and seemed nice and quiet in the snowy picturesque scene; this was about to change. The first three cars deployed the occupants into a perimetre, with men standing, kneeling and lying in whatever cover they could find; we ran straight to the front door. Were they there to meet us; were they on their way; no time to think; now just go in hard and fast and get the fuck out.

The sounds of guns, men and equipment, radios, car engines and loud tactical shouts during any live op can never be forgotten. Its just pure aggression at its best, or worst if you are on the receiving end, if you see what I mean. Lots of shouting, punching, hitting, kicking, door splintering, smashing of ornaments and furniture, crying, screaming , pleading, then seconds later silence, utter silence. The group drove away at speed, with silence in the car except for the radio. 'Leaving the target, no casualties; we have the soldier; now clear, on our way back to your location, Bravo route over'

This silence in the car was broken by the Jock who had regained consciousness; he was pinned in the rear foot well, 'Who the fuck are you, what's going on ?' Suffice to say, he regained consciousness back in the cells of the RUC station; payback for risking our lives.

Sunday morning and the best thing was waiting for us as usual and is still one of my fondest memories of Northern Ireland: the good old Ulster fry-up for breakfast, which always tasted better after a busy night's work.

SOUTH ARMAGH

Sergeant-Major 'W' Royal Highland Fusiliers

My final tour of Northern Ireland took place in 1976, where I was 'Buzzard' at Bessbrook Mill Helipad. The job, South Armagh, for me, was an extremely demanding one, controlling all flights of troops and supplies to XMG and Forkhill, as well as the movement of all patrols.

During this tour, Bessbrook Mill came under mortar attack and two landed just short of the base and exploded, although one mis-fired. Sadly, on January 2nd, I heard a contact on the battalion net (*radio*) and the ARF was scrambled. An hour later, I dispatched a second helicopter, together with a body bag; that was when I realised that it was for one of our 'Jocks', Lance-Corporal David Hind who had been shot and killed. Two other 'Jocks' were wounded and Fusilier Reid, the remaining uninjured man returned the fire and assisted his colleagues until medical aid and reinforcements arrived. For this action, he was awarded the Military Medal.

David Hind, a married man from the Kilmarnock area was aged just 23 when he was killed on the first Sunday of a New Year; by the time that month was out, five more SF members would have died at the hands of the IRA.

NEWRY: RETURNED TO UNIT

Steve Burke, Argyll & Sutherland Highlanders

My unit was stationed in and around Newry which, not exactly 'bandit country' was still a very dangerous place to be if you were a British soldier. This is when we were introduced to the Humber PIG!

I was barely 19 and one of only two in my section with a driving licence, so I was often nominated as PIG driver but was not given any familiarization training at all. It was expected of me that I should just jump straight in and drive it! Of course, I had to endure all the unhelpful comments from the backseat drivers when I crunched the gears etc as I learned to drive it on the job. I remember that the view of the road ahead was very poor because of the tiny window and huge bonnet; the steering was heavy and lacked power steering! The actual wheel was huge and when you turned a corner, to you had to turn the wheel back because of its tendency to over steer.

About half way through the tour, they sent us a new 'toy' from England to play with; this was a 'Saracen' complete with its newly qualified RCT Driver. Properly called the FV603, Alvis Saracen Armoured Personnel Carrier, ours was a sandy-pink colour no doubt camouflaged for the Ulster desert! I must confess that it looked the 'business' with its big gun turret and six big road wheels, but the boyos could hear it coming from miles away due to the distinctive whine from the engine. I need at this stage, to tell you that in the middle of each wheel was a large, studded hub, sort of reminded me of the spikes sticking out of Boudicca's chariot! On our first patrol, we had only travelled about half a mile, when we came to an abrupt halt. I found out why, when we were ordered out and into all round defence. It was then that I saw a saloon car opposite, with the whole of its outer skin wrapped neatly around the hub of the 'Sarra' as if it were paper tissue. That was the last we saw of the Saracen, because after just one day, both it and the RCT Driver were RTU-ed to England in disgrace; the Driver to face a charge of negligence.

Clogher – *Clochar* in Irish – is a village in County Tyrone, Northern Ireland, situated on the River Blackwater, 18 miles south of Omagh.

FIRST UDR FEMALE TO BE KILLED IN ULSTER

Sergeant David Henley, Royal Tank Regiment

On 2 May 1974 whilst still on operations but based in camp we were crashed-out and told to head for the Deanery at Clogher as the troops based there had been attacked by a large terrorist group using mortars and rockets. I drove the Saracen flat out all the way and when we arrived we were directed to the road behind the grounds to where the main thrust of the attack had taken place. As I approached I could see a group of UDR soldiers in the immediate area, some were looking at something on the ground next to the boundary fence. The lads dismounted and set up a VCP while I wandered over to the UDR men to see what had caught their interest. On the ground was a home made mortar, a couple of rockets and a pile of mortar bombs. It appeared that the main attack had taken place from this position but after firing for about 5 or 10 minutes the terrorists had decided to leave their munitions behind to facilitate a quick escape.

Later that day the ATO arrived and decided that the terrorists' rockets and mortars were in an unstable condition and could therefore not be moved, so he announced that he would be making a controlled explosion in order to destroy them. After he had prepared the explosives he ran a command wire and asked me to drive the Saracen a little further away to a safe distance. As he was connecting the wire to the control box I asked if I could carry out the detonation; 'Why not?' he replied, so I closed the rear doors, pressed the button and watched through the rear observation hatch as the ammunition exploded. It was such a good feeling knowing that the terrorists would not be using any of those mortars or rockets in attacks against the security forces at any time in the future.

It was only later when I had the chance to speak to Trooper Barry Winrow of 3 Troop that I found out exactly what had happened. The attack started with a mortar exploding close to the building and small arms fire being directed from a couple of firing points around the perimetre fence. Barry ran round to his FSC and started firing the 3.0 Browning in the direction of the gunfire. More mortar fire was being directed onto the building and at least one RPG7 rocket hit an upstairs wall. Sadly, just at the time when the rocket hit the building, Private Eva Martin (28), a part-time UDR 'Greenfinch' who was a school teacher in civilian life, was running down the stairs from the operations room to take shelter on the ground floor. Her husband, also a part-time UDR soldier who was a civil servant in civilian life, was descending the stairs just behind Eva. As the rocket struck, the blast knocked him onto his back and Eva took the full brunt of the impact from the debris and shrapnel. Eva became the first female member of the UDR to be murdered whilst on duty and everyone who knew her, including me, was extremely saddened that such a vivacious and bubbly young woman should have had to die so tragically and needlessly.

CLOGHER; IRREVERENT SWEEPSTAKE

Dave Maltby 1st Queen's Dragoon Guards

The early 1980s saw us stationed for two years at Lisanelly Barracks in Omagh, on a 2 year tour. At this time I was Troop Sergeant; leader of 1st Troop 'C' Squadron. One of the Squadron's tasks was to carry out operations from

The Deanery in Clogher, a small market town not far from the Fermanagh border.

In the May of 1981, we were operating as an OP Troop, meaning that my troop got all of the covert OP jobs on the border. One of the longest we did was 12 days which proved to be quite a worthwhile operation. It was at this Bobby Sands was about to peg it, so as a bit of an inspiration I organised a 'sweepstake' as to when he was finally going to snuff it. It cost a quid a go and I spread it out amongst the Squadron and our UDR colleagues whom we were sharing the Deanery with. Whoever got closest to the time won the pot of £300. Everybody thought it be a good laugh; our well justified contempt for the IRA had no bounds.

As the time drew closer we were given a radio codeword so that when Sands met his maker, the codeword would come over the radio and we would know when it – the inevitable rioting – would all kick off. The night Sands died we were on a covert OP somewhere on the border. The codeword duly came over that Sands had died. Nobody in the troop was that bothered except my Troop corporal whose sweepstake time was quite close to when Sands went. He dashed across to the radio, snatched the 'mike' off the operator and came up with the message 'Hello Zero; what time did it happen?' Needless to say the watch keeper came back with a few choice words. Poor sod; he was out by 2 minutes and the pot went to a UDR lad; how we laughed.

I have often told the story to a few civvy work colleagues, who respond with absolute horror and cannot believe we did such a thing. Squaddie humour is so raw they would never understand it; and do I care? Do I hell.

Robert Gerard Sands, commonly known as Bobby Sands, was an IRA volunteer and, incredibly enough an MP in Parliament. He died on May 5, 1981 after a long hunger strike whilst in HM Prison Maze for the possession of firearms. His death sparked off days of violent rioting and resulted in deaths of both the security forces and civilians alike.

UP TO OUR NECKS AT BESSBROOK MILL

Bombardier 'Taff' Fitzgerald, Royal Artillery

In 1991 I served in South Armagh where my battery was attached to 45 Cdo, based at Bessbrook Mill. Patrols in the area lasted anything from eight hours to 5 days. Blackthorn hedges, barbed wire and electric fences – most of which were on top an earth bank paralleled by deep ditches – had to be crossed every fifty yards or so, making the going heavy.

On one of these patrols we had been given the task of photographing a culvert. This photograph would have been compared to older photos to see if there had been any changes to its shape or construction; culverts were favoured places for hiding bombs used to take out vehicles. All morning we had noticed a yellow light aircraft repeatedly flying over us and we started to feel that we were being dicked.

When the time came to do the culvert check, I had been nominated to take the photograph and a lad whom I shall call 'Ed', from another section within the platoon, was tasked to come with me as ECM cover carrying the 'bomb stopper.' This was effectively a jammer that would give off either a one, two or three tone alarm depending on what band width was 'attacking' it.

Before we left the rest of the patrol, my best mate, Paul Dewhurst, winked at me and said, 'Bags your boots!' (*A lot of soldiers had this fatalistic sense of humour, rather like the RAF pilots of both Fighter and Bomber Command who had 'bags' on the equipment of a comrade who didn't return*) Anyway, we set off down the hill to get on task and, as soon as we hit the flat ground that surrounded the culvert, we realised that it wasn't as green and lush as it looked at a distance. It was what we called wobbly grass; big clods of grass that basically floated on a bog. We tried to balance on these clods but within ten metres we were sunk past our waists. It was difficult to move because we were wading through the bog which was thick with the long grass roots, reaching for the surface, and soft, stinking mud. Every time we moved, this rotten smell would bubble up right under our noses. It became comical and we were soon giggling like a pair of school girls.

We got to within twenty-five metres of the culvert and were just about to get into line of sight to be able to look through it and take the photo, when Ed stopped me and told me he was getting an alarm. I thought he was joking at first but his face told me that he was deadly serious. I looked up at the sky and saw the little yellow plane flying above us, looked at Ed and started laughing again. Somebody was trying to kill us, we couldn't run away and the first thought that went through my head was that if the battery goes down on the bomb stopper, and this bomb goes off, my boots were on the safest part of me. 'Ed' started to flap a bit just in case his battery did go down, so I made my way over to him and recorded the alarm for the Int section. Discretion being the better part of valour, we beat a slow, soggy, stinking retreat.

That was just about Ed's last patrol. Within a couple of days, he put his weapon down and told the powers that be that he was not playing anymore. It spelt the beginning of the end of his time in the army. I still laugh at the ridiculousness of the situation but I still think about 'Ed' and wonder how he's getting on. I don't think anyone told him not to worry about it; I'd like to tell him it was ok.

Taff explained to me that 'Ed' wasn't his real name, but that Paul Dewhurst's name was real. Tragically, Paul was killed in an accident on exercise in Canada two years later. Whilst I cannot add his name to the Roll of Honour for Northern Ireland, Taff wanted to pay tribute to him here.

NEWRY

Mark 'C', Royal Artillery and UDR

Although our own TAOR was in Belfast, we were deployed as a platoon down to the border RUC stations in Keady, Newtownhamilton and Middletown about 3 times a year. During one of these 2 week deployments an officer in the Royal Anglians had been killed by a booby-trap bomb in Crossmaglen. Part of his unit had been deployed at the border crossing on Cloughe Mountain just outside Newry. Of course they needed to bury their comrade with full military honours back on the mainland , so they needed to be relieved ASP.

We had only just got back home, when the word got round to return to camp, this was done mostly by word of mouth by the first one the brass could phone and so on; remember there were no mobiles and very few had land lines.

Yes, our platoon was going back down to the border, and I didn't even have time to do my kit. Eventually and by some miracle' we were able to assemble the whole platoon, even though a few had already been on the drink. Of course we were not happy, as we were supposed to have a few days off after the border op; there were a few swear words etc directed at the 'brass.' But then our Sgt Major who had the nickname the 'Skull', and one of the best I had every served under shut us up and put everything in perspective.

UDR on patrol in Newtownhamilton (Mark Campbell)

He said 'Remember another soldier has died, and if you think you lot have got it rough, my Da' was called up by the TA in 1939 and my Ma' did not see him again to 1945; get on with it.' Again it was the army way of injecting humour to a serious situation that would see us through. In reality the fun – if that is the right word to use – was only just beginning as we flew by chopper down to Newry to relieve the Anglians.

We landed and in half an hour we were in control of one of the border forts; eventually, by the 90's they would become watch towers and have permanent presence on the road. But now to be honest I had never seen a place like it; all there was there, were a few glorified garden sheds with blast walls built round them, a heli pad, with sangars in each corner, and the whole lot was surrounded by barbed wire. There was even an open air urinal, which I never could fathom as PIRA had snipers operating all along the border, with the wooden duck boards running from the huts to the sangars etc; it looked like something out of a Vietnam war film set, but this was 1986 and very much part of the UK.

As I said in the days before the PVCP were established on the road, you had to patrol down from the base on the top of the mountain to the road to do the VCP with the RUC. The only way down was to follow a barbed wire route that had claymore type mines running along it in case of attack. These were supposed to be able to be set of from the sangars, but we UDR men had never had this technology in the sangars in Belfast or even the Border RUC stations, so everyone was a bit wary. It was quickly decided to push the button, only if, at least half the Provisional IRA was attempting

UDR, Newtownhamilton (Mark Campbell)

to get over the wire. So it was a bit unnerving having to patrol past the mines usually in the dark knowing that a young UDR soldier in a sangar had control over them.

Our problems did not stop there. The Anglians had been due for ration replenishment as they had almost run out; so in fact, all what was left were tinned pilchards and stale bread. Unfortunately the clouds and rain drew in, and all chopper flights were cancelled, and there was no military road movement by vehicle along the border in case of landmines. The cook, sorry, Chef did his best, and, apparently, pilchards and bread was one of his specialties.

So we had to patrol up and down the mountain, try to avoid being blown up by our own side whilst on an empty stomach, and even the RUC took pity on us and brought up fish suppers in their armoured patrol cars from Newry. Sadly, I missed out on that.

When I do look back on this time it is hard to believe this was the UK not somewhere in the middle of Afghanistan or something, I don't think the public would believe now never mind then.

Incidentally a couple of years later when it had become a PVCP and Watchtower on the road, it was attacked several times and in one incident a soldier from the Royal Irish Rangers won the Queen's Gallantry Medal for saving his comrades by shouting a warning about a bomb sadly, losing his own life in the process. Ingeniously, the PIRA had rigged up a bomb onto a railway chassis and pushed it down the line towards the VCP, to be then set off by remote control.

OP TIGER

Bombardier 'Taff' Fitzgerald, Royal Artillery

My brick was volunteered to take part in a new initiative. Because of the nature of the area of South Armagh that we were in, the RUC didn't normally get the chance to do 'ordinary policing'. On one occasion we'd stopped a car in a checkpoint that had probably not seen an MOT in ten years and the RUC just let the driver go. When I asked why he didn't charge the bloke he said it wasn't worth it, the bloke would still drive it. Anyway, the idea of Op Tiger was that four squaddies would go out with four RUC in two armoured Sierras and act as cover for the coppers to do their thing.

They picked us up on a Saturday night from Bessbrook Mill and briefed us that we were going looking for drunk drivers. So off we went. RUC in the fronts, squaddies in the backs. I thought this was going to be fun but it's not fun hacking it down country lanes in the back of an armoured saloon car. You can't open the windows, they had the heating on full blast and the armour made it fucking bouncy in the back. I felt sick as a dog within ten minutes. And the reason why he and a colleague were going so fast? To beat the bombs; God help us.

So, we're looking for drunk drivers while hammering it around country lanes like a Gary Boy (boy racer) on crack. They didn't tell us that we were going to be targeting the drunk drivers as they actually leave the pub. The first thing I thought was, `These fuckers are actively looking for a riot!'

As it turned out, it worked. The most memorable success of the evening was a bloke coming out of a pub in Whitecross. He had parked his car with the drivers' door about a metre away from the entrance, so he'd planned ahead. We were waiting in the shadows as he came staggering out, mumbling and belching, and immediately rested his head on the roof of his car and started poking and scratching the driver's door with his car key. He was absolutely bladdered; it was like a sketch in some comedy show. The look on his face, when he saw two RUC come out of the shadows was priceless; I reckon he thought there was something wrong with his beer. It was worth it, just for that.

They did about six drunk drivers that night, more than they had done in the months previous and afterwards. For all its success, that was the only `Op Tiger' of the tour. For that matter, I don't know if any more were done after that.

Part Four

Mainland and European Attacks

1971 31 October: A bomb explodes in the Post Office Tower in London causing extensive damage but no injuries. The 'Kilburn Battalion' of the IRA claimed responsibility for the explosion.

1972 22 February: The Official Irish Republican Army kills six civilians and a Parachute Regiment Padre in the Aldershot bombing.

1973 March 8: The IRA detonated two bombs outside the Old Bailey in London; one man is killed.

1973 10 September: The Provisional IRA set off bombs at London's King's Cross Station and Euston Station injuring 21 people.

1974 4 February: Eight Soldiers and 4 civilians are killed by the Provisional IRA in the M62 Coach Bombing.

1974 17 June: The Provisional IRA plant a bomb which explodes at the Houses of Parliament, causing extensive damage and injuring 11 people.

1974 17 July: a bomb explosion in the Mortar Room in the White tower leaving one person dead and 41 injured.

1974 5 October: Guildford pub bombing by the Provisional IRA leaves 4 off duty soldiers and a civilian dead and 44 injured.

1974 22 October: A bomb planted by the Provisional IRA explodes in central London, injuring 3 people.

1974 21 November: The Birmingham pub bombings, 21 killed and 182 injured by Provisional IRA bombs.

1976 15 March: An IRA bomber shot a train driver dead after the man chased him following an explosion on a train.

1979 30 March: Airey Neave killed when a car bomb exploded under his car as he drove out of the Palace of Westminster car park. The Irish National Liberation Army (INLA) claimed responsibility for the killing.

1981: On 10 October, a bomb at Chelsea Barracks killed two people and injured 40 others. On 26 October, a bomb in Oxford Street killed the bomb disposal officer who was trying to defuse it.

1982 20 July: The Hyde Park and Regents Park bombings in London by the IRA kill eleven members of the Household Cavalry and the Royal Green Jackets.

1983 17 December: Harrods was bombed by the IRA. Six are killed (including three police officers) and 90 wounded during Christmas shopping at the West London department store. (See 17 December 1983 Harrods bombing)

1984 12 October: Brighton hotel bombing, 5 killed and several injured in an attempt by the IRA to kill Margaret Thatcher.

1989 22 September: Deal barracks bombing: Eleven Royal Marines bandsmen are killed and 22 injured when base in Deal, Kent, is bombed by the IRA.

1990 May 16: Wembley IRA detonate a bomb underneath a minibus killing Sgt Charles Chapman (The Queen's Regiment) and injuring another soldier.

1990 June 1: Lichfield City railway station 1 solder is killed and 2 are injured in a shooting by the Provisional Irish Republican Army

1990 20 July: The IRA detonated a bomb at the London Stock Exchange causing damage to the building. Nobody was injured in the blast.

1990 30 July: Ian Gow MP killed by a car bomb planted by the IRA while at his home in Sussex.

1991 7 February: The IRA launched three mortar shells into the back garden of 10 Downing Street.

1991 February 18: A bomb explodes at Victoria Station. One man is killed and 38 people injured.

1992 February 28, 1992: A bomb explodes at London Bridge station injuring 29 people.

1992 April 10: A large bomb explodes in St Mary Axe in the City of London. The bomb was contained in a large white truck and consisted of a fertilizer device wrapped with a detonation cord made from Semtex. It killed three people: Paul Butt, 29, Baltic Exchange employee Thomas Casey, 49, and 15-year old Danielle Carter. The bomb also caused damage to surrounding buildings, many of which were also badly damaged by the Bishopsgate bombing the following year. The bomb caused £800 million worth of damage, £200 million more than the total damaged caused by the 10,000 explosions that had occurred during the Troubles in Northern Ireland up to that point.

1992 25 August: The IRA plant three fire bombs in Shrewsbury, Shropshire. Bombs were placed in Shoplatch, The Charles Darwin Centre and Shrewsbury Castle. The latter causing the most damage as the castle housed the Shropshire

Regimental Museum and many priceless historical artifacts were lost and damaged by fire and smoke. No fatalities or injuries were recorded.

1992 October 12: A device explodes in the gents' toilet of the Sussex Arms public house in Covent Garden killing one person and injuring four others.

1992 16 November: IRA plants a bomb at the Canary Wharf, but is spotted by security guards. The bomb is deactivated safely.

1992 3 December: The IRA exploded two bombs in central Manchester, injuring 65 people.

1993 20 March: Warrington bomb attacks. The first attack, on a gasworks, created a huge fireball but no casualties, but the second attack on Bridge Street killed two children and injured many other people. The attacks were conducted by the IRA.

1993 April 24: IRA detonate a huge truck bomb in the City of London at Bishopsgate, It killed journalist Ed Henty, injured over 40 people, and causing approximately £1 billion worth of damage,[12] including the destruction of St Ethelburga's church, and serious damage to Liverpool St. Tube Station. Police had received a coded warning, but were still evacuating the area at the time of the explosion. The insurance payments required were so enormous, that Lloyd's of London almost went bankrupt under the strain, and there was a crisis in the London insurance market. The area had already suffered damage from the Baltic Exchange bombing the year before.

1994: March saw three unsuccessful mortar attacks on Heathrow Airport over a five-day period.

1996 9 February 1996: The IRA bombs the South Quay area of London, killing two people.

1996 15 June: The Manchester bombing when the IRA detonated a 1500 kg bomb which destroyed the Arndale shopping centre and injured 206 people.

1996 February 15: A 5 lb bomb placed in a telephone box is disarmed by Police on the Charing Cross Road.

1996 February 18: An improvised high explosive device detonates prematurely on a bus travelling along Aldwych in central London, killing Edward O'Brien, the IRA operative transporting the device and injuring eight others.

THE M62 COACH BOMB

Mo Norton, Sister of Terence Griffin (Royal Artillery)

February 3 1974 was the last time I saw my brother Terence. It was a Sunday and he had been home on leave from Catterick that weekend and had brought to the family home in Bolton with him a friend Len (Jezz as he was known to his mates). Terence nearly always brought colleagues home at the weekend and it was not unusual for me and my sisters to get up on a Saturday morning and find several soldiers sleeping in our living room.

Terence and Jezz had spent a happy last weekend with us all. They left on the Sunday evening to catch the bus from Chorlton Street Bus Station in Manchester which took forces personnel and their families to Catterick.

The following morning I was driving to work unaware of the bombing that had occurred during the night as I had not listened to the news. I felt very uneasy as I drove through the town centre as though I knew something was wrong. I felt as though something terrible had happened or was about to happen but I did not know what. I had to concentrate very hard so as not to have an accident. I arrived at work and one of my colleagues happened to say that there had been a coach bombed during the night. I froze as she told me about it. I then rang my father at the family home to ask if Terence was OK. He replied in a broken voice that he did not know and that he was waiting for news. I just put the phoned down and burst into tears.

I hurriedly left work and went to my mother and father's home, where along with my two sisters they were all anxiously waiting for news. The television was on and news flashes were regularly shown with a telephone number for families to ring for any news. A bomb had exploded in a coach on the M62 near Hartshead Moor in Huddersfield, Yorkshire. My mother and father repeatedly rang this number only to be told that there was no news and for us not to ring again and that they would ring us as soon as they could give us any firm information.

Throughout the afternoon we carried on watching the news and as the TV cameras scanned the M62 they zoomed into what we recognised as Terence's personal belongings and could see some of his album sleeves; one of the songs on this particularly album was a song about little children, which would later seem poignant.

By around 5pm my mother could take no more waiting. It was complete agony, to wait and wait for a telephone call, to keep watching the news and seeing the terrible carnage strewn over the motorway and not know whether Terence was safe or not. Some 17 hours had passed from my father hearing the first news flash just after midnight. My mother made yet another call to the number that was given out. This time Terence's battery commander came on the line and informed my mother that Terence had been positively identified and was dead. Within 10 minutes of being told that Terence had been killed, his name and that of his friend Jezz was given out on the news. To say we were all devastated would be a complete understatement. The pain was indescribable, the most heartbreaking trauma I have ever experienced in my life. An hour or so later Terence's Commander, along with an Army Padre knocked at the door.

In the following days funeral arrangements were made. My father had been in the RAF for 28 years and had been in the Army during WW2 and he wanted Terence to have a military funeral. My mother wanted Terence buried as her son, but my father persuaded my mother to agree to a military funeral as he said that Terence's grave would always be looked after by the MOD. So a military funeral was arranged. A few days before the funeral we received a telephone call from somebody with an Irish accent saying that they were the IRA and that the funeral would not reach the cemetrey gates as we would be blown sky high.

Terrorists had killed a wonderful man, a true gentleman; he was kind, considerate, funny, and crazy at times but above all he was mine and my sister's only brother. He was the only son my parents had. We were devastated beyond belief.

12 people died in the M62 Coach Bomb Blast, two of these were little children. Many more were injured and maimed. My father never ever got over Terence's death; he blamed himself as he had to sign for Terence to go into the Army aged 15. My father would not eat and became ill. He died 2 years later aged 55.

The coach had been specially commissioned to carry both Army and RAF personnel on leave with their families to and from the bases at Catterick and Darlington. This was during what the press labelled the 'winter of discontent' and industrial action, strikes and go-slows were rife. The vehicle left Manchester, and was making good progress on the M62 motorway between Chain Bar, near Bradford, and Gildersome, Leeds, Yorkshire. Then shortly before midnight, a large explosion tore through it whilst most of those aboard were sleeping. The blast, which could be heard several miles away, reduced the coach to what the 'Yorkshire Evening Post' described as a 'tangle of twisted metal' and threw bodies out of the wreckage.

The explosion killed eleven people outright and wounded over fifty others, one of whom died four days later. Amongst the dead were two soldiers from the Royal Artillery, three from the Royal Corps of Signals and three from the 2nd battalion Royal Regiment of Fusiliers. One of the latter was Corporal Clifford Houghton, whose entire family consisting of his wife Linda and his sons Lee (5) and Robert (2) also died. Numerous others suffered severe injuries, including a six year old boy who was badly burned. There is a memorial to those who were killed, situated in the entrance hall of the westbound section of the Hartshead Moor Motorway service area, which was used as a first aid station for those wounded in the blast.

Those killed were Signalman Paul Reid (17), Signalman Leslie Walsh (19), and Michael Waugh (22), all Royal Corps of Signals, Gunner Leonard Godden (22), Bombardier Terence Griffin (24), both Royal Artillery, Fusilier John Hynes (20), Lance Corporal James McShane (29) both Royal Regiment of Fusiliers. Three days later, Fusilier Stephen Whalley (19) died of the terrible injuries he suffered in the outrage. Even more poignantly, an entire family was killed; Corporal Clifford Houghton (23) of the Royal Regiment of Fusiliers was murdered alongside his wife, Linda (23) and their two young children, Lee (5) and Robert (2).

In the same year, Judith Ward, a former woman soldier was sentenced to 30 years in jail for her part in the outrage; 18 years later, her innocence was proven and she was released. None of the real murderers have ever been apprehended.

THE MURDER OF WILLIAM DAVIES. LICHFIELD RAILWAY STATION: 1990

Private Neil Evans, 1 RRW

It was a Friday afternoon – 1st June 1990. I had just joined the Army 12 weeks previously and I was going home for the weekend from Whittington Barracks Lichfield. It would have been my fourth or fifth time leaving camp to go and visit my family in Wales. I left with two other men whom I had met when I first joined the Army.

They were: William 'Robert' Davies, also from Wales, who lived about 6 miles from my home town, so we became best mates; and Robert Parkin who was from Cheltenham Spa. We all became good friends whilst in training, as we had all joined at the same time (in March 1990) and our training was a 21 week basic training. Myself and Robert Davies were in the 1st Battalion the Royal Regiment of Wales, whilst Robert Parkin was cap – badged The Gloucestershire Regiment.

We left camp at 17.15hrs in a taxi to go to the train station in Lichfield. We arrived at 17:45hrs and got our tickets. We asked the lady behind the counter what time our train was to Birmingham, and she informed us that it was the next train in. As she said this, the train was pulling in so we all made a dash for it under the subway, but we realised that it was the train going to Lichfield Trent Valley, the opposite way.

We were waiting for our train, when I noticed two young men walking down our platform towards us, having just got off the train going to Lichfield Trent Valley. When they got about 6-7 feet away from us, they pulled out two pistols and started firing at us; I noticed that the guns were 9mm revolvers. 'Robert' Davies took the first round in the back of his head because he had his back turned towards them and I took the next in my right forearm. I then ran onto the other platform and as I was running, the station guard, who was on duty, ran out of his office – which was on the platform that I was heading for – to see what was happening. One of the men aimed at him which led to him to take cover, and, as I continued to run, the man fired another round at me which I heard whistling past my left ear, just missing my head by millimetres.

Robert Parkin took two rounds, one in his right shoulder which stayed in his back, and the second was meant to kill but crossed the back of his neck and the top of his left shoulder. 'Robert' Davies was lying on his back on the platform after the head shot and the gunmen then shot him twice in the chest as he lay helpless. In total, 7 rounds were fired but I was the lucky one because I only got hit once.

We were all taken to Good Hope Hospital in Sutton Coldfield which was about 5 miles from Lichfield and there we were stabilised before being transferred to Queen Elizabeth Military Hospital in Woolwich just outside London. Unfortunately 'Robert' Davies died in Good Hope Hospital.

I was back in training on August 16th 1990 then finally left the Army August 2003. R.I.P Robert.

Private William Davies who was from Pontarddulais in Wales was only 19 years old and was returning home on leave after basic training. He and two other soldiers were gunned down in cold blood in a cowardly attack by the IRA on unarmed men. The killers were never caught.

On February 18, 1991, an IRA bomb exploded in a litter bin at Victoria Station, killing one man, David Corner, and injuring 38. The warning given by the terrorists was insufficient to evacuate the station. This is the story of one of the survivors

VICTORIA TRAIN STATION

Sue Hanisch

The last morning of my life that I jumped out of bed and headed into the shower to wash and dress quickly, prior to my early departure was Monday Feb 18th 1991. My alarm had gone off at quarter to six and I was eager to be on my way as I was heading back to Holland to join my husband, having been in London for the weekend. If only I had washed and dressed more consciously and more slowly that morning, zipping my feet carefully into my boots with all the love, gratitude and respect they deserved. I would not ever have that opportunity again. How much we take for granted. So, farewell, my darling right foot, I have missed you SO much.

There were two options that morning; either to catch the coach to Sheerness from the Tower Hotel, or a quarter of an hour earlier on Wilton Road outside Victoria Station. If only I'd been sure of the location of the Tower Hotel and where to catch the connection I'd have gone straight there; but as it was I didn't. I headed off earlier to Victoria and consequently ended up with 15 minutes to play with on the concourse. I decided to make a quick phone call to my Mum and Dad just to say 'Good Morning' to them before they headed off to their working days in Lancashire; where did the expression 'killing time' originate?

I hadn't quite finished dialling when the explosion happened. The ceiling came down on my head and I was in the filth on the floor with both legs badly blown apart and my right foot hanging off. There were wires and blood everywhere, people screaming and legs running to and fro as travellers desperately sought a place of safety. My right hand was covered in blood and I could see exposed flesh. My hair was burned and the acrid smell which filled the air was nauseating. Several times I tried to get up, but onto what I ask myself now? Despite seeing the devastating damage to my legs I couldn't quite work out why I couldn't stand on them. Strange survival instincts kicked in without me even realising what I was doing, or that I even had such resources residing silently in my body for such an occasion as this.

The guy next to me, David Corner, took the main blow and died there and he probably saved my life. Even now I can sense the urgency as the paramedics tried to breathe life back into his body; but he was no longer there. I begged him to return to life out loud, but he probably didn't hear me. Goodbye David; you didn't know me in life, but I have certainly known you in your death and am sorry I never had the chance to meet you alive. I hope you had a good life.

There had been three bomb warnings earlier that morning, so as I lay on the floor of Victoria Station there was a sense of urgency among some people to get away, and yet others stayed with me; holding my hand; speaking words of comfort and refusing to leave my side. Angels; but not in disguise at all.

By the time it was my turn to be escorted off the premises to go to Accident and Emergency at Westminster Hospital most of the other injured had left and the station was almost deserted. My legs had tourniquets around them and I was wrapped in silver foil. I had remained conscious throughout the hour I had been lying there, and even managed a laugh and a joke with those around me to make this perverse situation a little more bearable. When the paramedics finally arrived, I realised it was my turn at last. But when you see retching paramedics standing over you and you realise that it is the sight of your legs which has caused their reaction, it's a bit of a worry. So be it; they took me on my own in the ambulance. Funny what is important in those silly minutes of altered reality, so long ago now; whatever was I thinking at the time? I insisted that my luggage stayed with me, as it contained my diary, personal effects and the few clothes I had brought for the weekend. Another bizarre detail was that I was wearing some very expensive Swiss lace knickers and I would not allow them to cut them off my body; even though I'd just lost my foot! When in future your Mum tells you to put your best knickers on because you never know what might happen; DON'T!!

I have been told that because I lost my right leg in an IRA bomb at Victoria Station in London in February 1991 that I am part of the conflict and the IRA have made me a part of their troubles; maybe, maybe not. By the same token, I suppose I am equally part of the agreement regarding the Balfour Declaration and how we have abandoned the Palestinians; partition in India and all the resulting atrocities; divide and rule in Africa and so it goes on. But wait a minute, how much blood can I get to cover my hands? I don't need to jump for every ball, and this is certainly one I will allow to come crashing to the ground on its own.

My government has never had my permission to oppose or violate anyone on my behalf. I have been a conscientious objector all my life and yet been caught up in two bombings as a civilian. The first bomb was on Christmas Eve in Bethlehem December 1976 and the second at London Victoria Station, 18 February 1991. I was only in England for the weekend and that morning I was on my way back to Holland where I was living at the time; And no-one gets away with it, do they? Both my grandfathers were also conscientious objectors, and yet both died in England during the Second World War, one in Coventry; also in Feb; also on the 18th, but in 1941 and the other Grandfather died while fire-watching in Hull the same year. Having discovered that my bombing was on the 50th anniversary – to the day – of my paternal grandfather dying in Coventry I am left knowing beyond knowing that that is no coincidence.

But I refuse to remain in pieces; I refuse to stay broken like 'Humpty Dumpty' in the ruins of the chaos which I faced as a direct consequence of my bomb. I am now at peace with myself and after ten years rehabilitation and ten years Post Traumatic Stress Disorder I have finally found a way of forgiving myself for being imperfectly part of the Human Race; with all that entails. I have faced my brokenness; I have experienced shame and felt fiercely self-conscious of my difference and my vulnerability. I am at last PERFECTLY HUMAN and can accept that fact, love that fact and be completely comfortable about it, without having to resist it, hide it or fight it. What a blessed relief. At last I can love myself in my imperfection, and I can also love you in yours. The rendezvous I avoided with myself for years and years cost me so much time that I could barely spare and when I finally had to face myself, there was nothing I couldn't deal with after all. The fear of the fear is a terribly crippling illusion; your body continues to be on red alert even when the danger has long passed.

It's a complicated business, you know, being blamed and shamed for being human and for holding a different opinion. Why would anyone want to try to make me feel guilty for holding and voicing an opinion which is different from the one they hold? I am beyond such overt manipulation, I used to be a people pleaser and say yes just to keep other people happy, what sacrilege, and what abuse of a free-thinking, freedom-loving mind which is happy to sing, dance, and play. Maybe I would have been burned at the stake in years gone by for my determination in speaking my truth. Having been to an all girls' grammar school in the Ribble Valley in Lancashire obedience and conformity were definitely the order of the day, hence for 7 years from 11 to 18 I was not allowed to have my own opinion, because it just wasn't kosher within such a repressed environment. No wonder that I later rebelled in the way I did.

But I can stand up and be counted:-
Counted for never having raised a fist to anyone.
Counted for never having joined the services.
Counted for never having voted in my life.
Counted for being a conscientious objector.
Counted for being born on British soil.
Counted for never wanting or seeking revenge.

I refuse to be lost in bitterness and hatred. My life has been spared and there is nothing more precious to me than that; although I have no fear of dying either. So maybe some people can't handle me not wanting to blame and shame and join them in their anger. Maybe they need to accuse me of something in order to project their own guilt away from themselves for whatever reason, so that they feel better about themselves. Who knows, it's their emotional baggage handling, not mine. So I suppose I can allow people to try to project their stuff onto me, it's worth a try, but it won't stick, I'm beyond being tempted to catch that ball now. They will still have to find their own answers and their own resolution to their own conflicts. I wish I could help them in that, but ultimately it is a personal choice which only we can make individually for ourselves; or not, as the case may be.

I see guys on a weekly basis, for counselling, returning from Iraq and Afghanistan, shattered and broken, splintered and fragmented into a million little pieces, still no evidence that war works. They are living but really dead on the inside, frozen into the horror of war and what it has done to violate their soul. What tragic loss; our souls are not built for conflict; haven't we noticed that yet? And so it goes on.

How happy I am to step out of the blame game, I have my life to get on with; what's left of it, I lost 10 yrs to trauma, so I can't spare anymore time in fighting the events that have overtaken my plans, my hopes and dreams. Life is good while you're alive, so let's wake up and live a real life, free from shame, blame, guilt and hatred. It's time to release the shackles that we so unwittingly climbed into.

And so, here I sit in a room in Enniskillen, September 2008, with 16 complete strangers, members of Sinn Fein, UDLA, IRA, PSNI, Catholics, Protestants, plus those completely disillusioned with the label 'religion', but with enough men with LOVE tattooed on their knuckles to convince me the yearning is still intense and very much alive and maybe there's just enough love still to make the world go round ... yet ... and we will survive the agony and the ecstasy of dancing and engaging with life.

But as we all rise from the ashes of our individual bombs, whatever they may be, there is a quality to the ash, which leaves a mark in our soul, and warmth in our heart and a taste on our lips which leaves us changed and with the knowledge that we are intensely human, intensely divine and intensely precious and loved. Surviving is hard, dying would have been easier, but we don't always get that choice. In many ways I feel that I have already died and come back, so now I can live 'with nothing else to fear,' because there really isn't! I can be hurt by nothing but my thoughts and I will not hurt myself today now that I have got my soul back. At last it has returned to dwell in my body again after so many years of being absent. My body is now once again a safe vessel for my soul to reside in and the world around me serves me well.

May you find this sanctuary too.

TUESDAY 20 JULY 1982

Hyde Park and Regent's Park Bombs

The IRA exploded two bombs in London, one at Rotten Row, on Hyde Park's southern carriageway and the other at the Bandstand in Regent's Park, resulting in the deaths of 11 British soldiers.

The first bomb exploded shortly before 11.00am when soldiers of the Blues and Royals were travelling on horseback for the changing of the Guard duty at Horseguards Parade. Three soldiers were killed instantly and a fourth died of his injuries on 23 July 1982. A number of civilians who had been watching the parade were also injured. One horse was killed in the explosion but a further six had to be shot due to their injuries. The bomb had been left in a car parked along the side of the road and is believed to have been detonated by a member of the IRA who was watching from within Hyde Park.

But it was the sudden shock of death that affected Britons most profoundly. Bystanders who rushed to help victims of the first blast in Hyde Park were repelled by the senseless attack on ceremonial guards. 'I saw one trooper with his head blown off and two others lying on the ground covered with blood,' said a businessman. Wounded troopers staggered in the road muttering, 'Bastards, bastards.' Of the 27 people who were injured by the nail bomb in Hyde Park, 17 were civilian bystanders. Said a worker in nearby Knightsbridge: 'The first thing I saw was a middle-aged lady on her hands and knees screaming, with part of her foot blown away. Soldiers were lying on the ground partly hidden by the dead horses.' In addition to the four soldiers who were killed, seven horses either died immediately or were so badly wounded that police had to humanely kill them.

The soldiers, all from the Blues & Royals, were Trooper Simon Tipping (19), Lance Corporal Vernon Young (19), and Lieutenant Anthony Daly (23). Three days after the outrage, a fourth member of the Regiment, Corporal-Major Raymond Bright (36) died of his wounds in hospital.

In 1987, an Irishman, Danny McNamee was sentenced to 25 years for the Hyde Park bomb despite McNamee insisting that he was innocent. In 1998, shortly after his release under the Good Friday Agreement, a judge overturned his conviction, deeming it 'unsafe' because of withheld fingerprint evidence that implicated other bomb-makers.

The second device, which exploded less than two hours later, had been planted under the bandstand in Regent's Park. The explosion killed 7 bandsmen of the Royal Green Jackets as they were performing a concert at the open-air bandstand; performance of the music from Oliver! Over two dozen civilians who had been watching the regular performance were injured in the explosion. It is thought that the bomb had been triggered by a timing device and may have been planted some time in advance of the concert. The crowd was peppered by shrapnel from the iron bandstand, causing dozens of injuries amongst the audience, as well as killing or wounding the entire band. The blast was so powerful that one of the bodies was thrown onto an iron fence thirty yards away, and seven bandsmen were killed outright.

At Regent's Park the devastation was, if anything, worse. One concert-goer described the scene: 'I counted 16 soldiers lying on the ground. One was groaning, with his hands on his stomach and blood pouring through them. Another's head was a mass of blood.' Others spoke of bodies, and of a single leg, literally flying through the air. A kettledrum and French horn came to rest 30 yards from the blast. An injured civilian told the police: 'It was a massacre without warning. Children were splattered with bits of the bandsmen's bodies.' Seven musicians died. The other 24 were wounded, twelve seriously.

The 'Jackets' killed were Sergeant-Major Graham Barker (36), Corporal John McKnight (30) and Bandsmen John Heritage (29), Robert Livingstone (31), Keith Powell (24), George Measure (19), and Laurence Smith who was also 19.

Public opinion, the whole world over, with the possible exception of the Irish-American communities in the USA, was outraged by these attacks. The consensus at the time was that the IRA and INLA were trying to sicken the British public by the continued slaughter of soldiers, as well as ordinary civilians. They attempted to do this to the extent that they – the public – would put pressure on their elected representatives for a withdrawal from Ulster.

The Attack at Deal

On September 22, 1989, at precisely 8.27am a 15lb time bomb placed in the recreational centre changing room at the School of Music by members of the Provisional IRA detonated. The blast destroyed the recreational centre and reduced the three storey accommodation building next to it to a pile of rubble. It also caused extensive damage to other structures and nearby civilian homes. The blast was heard several miles away, shaking windows in the centre of Deal, and creating a large pall of smoke over the town. The majority of the personnel who used the building as a barracks had been awake for several hours and were in different locations within the camp. Some of the bandsmen were practicing marching on the barracks parade ground when the explosion occurred. The marines therefore witnessed the buildings collapse, and many of the teenaged personnel were in a state of shock for days afterwards.

Some Marines had remained behind in the building for a variety of reasons, and thus received the full force of the explosion, many being trapped in the rubble for hours, despite desperate rescue efforts. Kent ambulance services voluntarily agreed to end industrial strike action to aid those wounded by the blast and firemen and military heavy lifting equipment were needed to clear much of the rubble to rescue those trapped beneath it. In all, ten marines died at the scene, most trapped in the collapsed structure, although one body was later found on the roof of a nearby house. Another 23 were seriously injured and received treatment at hospitals in Deal and Canterbury. One of these men, 21-year old Christopher Nolan, died of his wounds on 18 October 1989.

One week after the bombing, the staff and students of the School of Music marched through the town of Deal watched and applauded by thousands of spectators. They maintained gaps in their ranks marking the positions of those unable to march through death or serious injury.

The Marines killed were: Band Corporals Dean Pavey (31), Dave McMillan (26) and Trevor Davis (39) and Musicians Richard Fice (22), Bob Simmonds (34), Mick Ball (24), Richard Jones (27), Tim Reeves (24), Mark Petch (24) and Andy Cleatheroe (25); as stated, Christopher Nolan died of his wounds.

Major Paul Weston, Royal Marines

I am a retired Royal Marines Major (Director of Music) and although I wasn't in Deal on Sept 22, 1989, did my training there from 1979. I served in the Staff Band from 1982-1987, and began a course there the following week. My two best mates: Dave McMillan and Taff Jones were amongst the casualties, and I of course knew everyone affected.

My personal thoughts, other than those associated with grief and how we had been let down by a Defence Budget which left R.M. Deal woefully neglected with regard to base security, revolve around the use of the word 'murder'. For many this action was seen as political, and the plaque at the garden of rest I believe stills refers to the dead as being 'killed'. There are some of the Band Service who still hold a former senior officer following the bombing, responsible for allowing this to happen.

Even though events in NI have moved to a level I don't think any of us imagined possible 20 years ago, I cannot look at or listen to any member of the IRA or Sinn Fein, past or present, without a burning feeling of hatred. Ironically, in 1985, Dave and I were in the States touring with the Deal Band and went to an Irish bar in Boston. We were stunned by the hostility felt towards us as 'Brit Squaddies' and astonished by the mis-representation of Catholic rights in Ulster. Everyone there believed Catholics were not allowed any number of privileges, including the right to vote, and that the British Government were dictators, with a mindset to oppress Catholics into submission through a regime of brutality and force.

Indeed, it was astonishing how openly NORAID was allowed to gather funds on US soil under the notion of 'Freedom Fighters' struggling for survival. They even went so far as to hand out leaflets to the audience prior to our performance claiming 'members of the Marine Band playing here this evening are responsible for the murder of several Catholic children in their beds in front of their parents'. This was never restricted by US officials, and so I find it quite ironic that they have their own 'terrorist' issues to deal with now.

THE BRITISH SOLDIER WHO WAS IRISH

Gareth Dyer, Royal Corps of Signals

This didn't take place in Northern Ireland, but does relate to events that occurred during the time of Op Banner. I think about this incident often, and it's only in recent couple of years that I've been able to reconcile myself with my actions/inaction and feelings about the incident. I suppose I always had a fairly insular view of the military involvement during Op

Banner, being a 'local.' This really brought home what it possibly meant to those who weren't from the province and had limited dealings with in it. The incident took place over the Easter weekend in 1993 (April of that year I think and was in Stafford)

During the Easter weekend in 1993 I was a serving British soldier; born and bred in Northern Ireland. At this time I was attached to a unit in the south of England and had not long returned from an Op tour in the Middle East. The previous year my two year tour in the province had been cut short after 11 months. This was due to an imminent threat on me. Anyway, at this time I was seeing a girl, also from Northern Ireland but who was at university in Manchester. I'd gone up to visit her that weekend and as a treat, took us both to Alton Towers for the day. The trip back was by train, from Stafford railway station and whilst waiting, there I got chatting to the bloke in the ticket office. It turned out he was an ex squaddie himself. I'd literally only exchanged a few sentences, but as I stood at the counter chatting with him I became aware of another guy standing just beside me.

He reeked of drink and was practically standing right up against me. I turned to him and asked if he was alright. 'Fucking murdering paddy bastards; you need to fuck off back where you came from.' I was completely stunned for a second or two, and took a step back from him and asked him what he meant. In retrospect I know full well where he was coming from. A couple of weeks previously, two young kids had been murdered in Warrington by a PIRA bomb left in the town centre there. My girlfriend who was standing beside me then spoke. I can't remember exactly her words but I do recall she made some comment about how what was going on was nothing to do with us, but hardly got a couple of words out before the drunk guy lurched towards her, shouting in a loud voice about: 'Fucking child-killing Irish bastards !'

I got between him and my girlfriend and we grabbed at each other. It wasn't exactly a punch-up, more just a bit of grappling before the railway bloke I had been chatting to earlier, got between us both. He pushed me towards his office; telling us both to get inside, whilst at the same time, shoving the drunken guy towards the exit. I was by this time aware of several other people in the waiting area; about a dozen or so. I will never forget the way those people looked at the pair of us; my girlfriend and me. Although none of them spoke, it was obvious from their expressions that, whilst they might not have agreed with the drunk's actions, they did so with his sentiment. I announced to none of them in particular that I was a British soldier and then turned and ushered my girlfriend to a seat.

After we sat down, I looked around but not one of those people would then look at us. No one spoke. We waited in complete silence until the train to Manchester arrived. Up to that point I had always been proud to be an Irishman, a British citizen and a serving British soldier. In that waiting room though I have never felt so Irish in my life, and never been as ashamed to be so either. Often I think about that incident. In the days and months afterwards, I thought how I should have made my background known. Perhaps made some loud and grand announcement to all there, at how I was a British citizen, a British soldier, and how I had been forced out of my own country by the same scum who had taken the lives of those two young boys not far from that railway station waiting room.

But I didn't and today I think I did the right thing in the circumstances at that time. What would I have resolved? Given what had happened in Warrington, would me gobbing off about how it had nothing to do with 'Ordinary decent Irish folk' have convinced these people? I doubt it. I think I did what British soldiers did throughout Op Banner. Take it on the chin; say nowt. Let people think you are the bogey man if that's what they want to think. I knew better. That day, because of the actions of scum supposedly acting on behalf of the Irish people, I was never before or since so ashamed to be an Irishman. In contrast however I've never been ashamed to have been a British soldier.

The IRA made two attacks on the town of Warrington during the late winter and early spring of 1993. The first attack took place on 26 February, when three devices exploded at the town's gasworks causing extensive damage. A police officer, PC Mark Toker, was shot and injured after stopping a van connected to the attacks.

At 11:58am on March 20, less than a month after the first attack, the telephone help counsellors, the 'Samaritans' received a coded message that a bomb was going to be detonated outside the Boots shop in Liverpool, fifteen miles away from Warrington. Merseyside Police investigated, and also warned the Cheshire Constabulary of the threat, but it was too late to evacuate. At 12:12pm two bombs exploded, one outside Boots on Bridge Street and one outside the Argos catalogue store. It later turned out that the bombs had been placed inside cast-iron litter bins, causing large amounts of shrapnel.

Buses were organised to ferry people away from the scene and 20 paramedics and crews from 17 ambulances were sent to deal with the aftermath. Eyewitnesses of the time reported that the first explosion had driven panicking shoppers into the path of the next blast, just seconds later.

There were two fatalities from the blast. Three-year-old Jonathan Ball died at the scene, accompanied by his babysitter, who survived. The second victim, 12-year-old Tim Parry, died in hospital from his injuries five days later. 54 more people were injured, four of them seriously.

ALDERSHOT

Corporal, Royal Military Police

22nd February 1972 was a chilly but sunny winter's day. The Garrison town of Aldershot was being redeveloped into a modern home of the British Army. Many of the old style barracks had been or were being demolished and the new ones being built were of the 'open plan' type, with no walls or fences. Buller Barracks home of the RCT training camp had just been finished and many new recruits had been moved into it from the old Beaumont Barracks. Among the new style barracking were the camps of the Paras, RCT, ACC,

WRACs and RMPs; all within a short walking distance of each other, these surrounded the church on the corner. Open plan meant there was no real security other than the main entrances and access was an easy walk on to camp. As you can imagine this caused lots of shouting seeing the odd stranger walking across the RSM's hallowed square.

Around about lunch time we had all sat down to eat when the room shook, tables moved across the room and some fell on the floor. Within seconds the Duty Sergeant burst into the dining hall and shouted 'Para Barracks NOW!' we all piled out to witness some incredible devastation. The new building being of pre-cast concrete panels had collapsed like a pack of cards, a huge dust cloud was swirling high above and beginning to settle as a grey film over the devastation, police, fire and ambulance sirens in the distance were fast approaching, the whole place was in chaos.

The police and fire brigade arrived almost together and quickly assessed the situation, trying to preserve the area as it was a crime scene whilst at the same time assessing casualties and building safety an impossible task, at the same time keeping onlookers and pressmen from walking all over the area.

RMP-SIB spent the next few weeks interviewing every soldier on camps at the time and eventually the bomber was caught and jailed, he later died whilst in prison of a heart attack, it was understood the attack was a retaliation bombing for the events of 'Bloody Sunday' which had happened a few weeks earlier.

6 members of staff died during the attack and a Priest also died, the effects of the blast were felt in Aldershot town centre more than a mile from the scene. I will never forget the scene or the incident or the after effects.

On the morning of February 22, 1972 a Ford Cortina with a large bomb hidden inside was left in the base car park, of the Parachute Regiment in Aldershot; deliberately positioned outside the officers' mess.

The time-release bomb exploded suddenly and the blast destroyed the officers' mess and wrecked several nearby army office buildings in an explosion which could be heard over a mile away. The soldiers who were the intended targets of the bomb were not present, as the regiment itself was stationed abroad and most staff officers were in their offices, not in the mess. Nonetheless, seven people were killed, including an elderly gardener, five kitchen staff who were just leaving the premises and Father Gerard Weston, a Roman Catholic army chaplain who had just parked behind the car bomb. Nineteen people were also wounded by the explosion.

In addition to Father Weston, the following civilian staff were also killed; Thelma Bosley (44), Cheri Munton (20), Joan Lunn (39), Jill Mansfield (34), Margaret Grant (32) and John Haslar who was 58.

Authorities were shocked and concerned by this first major attack in Britain, and lax security at many bases was tightened up in an effort to prevent a repeat of the attack.

MURDER IN GERMANY

Corporal Ray Mitchell, REME

I was a Corporal in REME and was with the Scots Guards at Bielefeld in Germany; they had graciously granted me the appointment of Lance Sergeant and was thus able to enjoy the comforts of the Sergeants Mess. The downtown was Corporal's pay with Sergeant's fees!

I had arrived in late January, 1980 and on the night of 16 February, I drew the duty of Orderly Officer; it seemed like just another ordinary day, but the events which unfolded were to prove otherwise. I was in the Orderly Officer's bunk just relaxing when the phone rang and I answered it. It was the CO, Lt-Colonel Macintosh and the words he used will stay with me until the end of my life: 'Macintosh here; give me a sitrep on the shooting of Colonel Coe.' I was gob smacked and just gasped: 'I'm sorry, sir; what?' This time his response came back, more urgently: 'Give me a sitrep on the shooting of Colonel Coe!'

Incidentally, Lt-Col Macintosh was CO of HQ Company, 1 British Corps in BAOR. My reply was along the lines of: 'I'm sorry, sir; this is the first I've heard of it.' Down went the phone, and I rapidly made my way to the Guardroom. The defence of the HQ was the responsibility of a Royal Pioneer Corps company and by this stage of the incident; they were already well organized by their own senior NCOs. Now, you must remember that this was my first duty and I really didn't have a clue. I entered the guardroom and just 'went through the motions' and noticed that all the personnel who were not on stag, were otherwise engaged, watching videos of, let's be delicate here, an adult nature!

Later on, I made my way to the HQ block and I quickly realised that this situation was way above my responsibility, as a full Colonel had been murdered. The adjutant was in his office, as was the RSM and then, when a Brigadier called in, I decided that I was surplus to requirements and went off to bed; yes, in all that drama, in all that seriousness of an IRA attack in Germany, all I could do was to go to bed !

I was, of course, shocked to hear of Colonel Coe's death as I had only just spoken to him that morning when he called into the LAD (*Light Aid Detachment*) to book in his car for a service. He was a very pleasant man and chatted to me about my new posting and wished me luck. He was very observant, quite befitting his role of Chief of Staff.

Later on, we got his bullet-riddled car back and we had the unpleasant task of repairing it; not a pleasant experience.

On 16 Feb. 1980, Colonel Mark Coe, OBE, Royal Engineers was shot at his home, in Bielefeld, Germany; aged 44. He was off duty and about to put his car away, at his home in Married Quarters when he was approached by a man and woman and murdered; he left a widow and 6 children. The IRA admitted that they had killed him. Colleagues of Colonel Coe described as a '... very well liked guy.'

The author is well known in the Tadcaster area and it would be remiss, probably even disrespectful not to mention the murder of Special Constable Glen Goodman. On June 7, 1992, whilst on a routine patrol in the Tadcaster area of North Yorkshire, PC Goodman (37) from Sherburn-in-Elmet, and another constable stopped a Ford Sierra and whilst he made routine enquiries he was shot and killed by a member of a two man IRA ASU. The other policeman, though wounded, survived and managed to alert colleagues and the two men were later caught and sentenced to life terms. A monument to Goodman can be found by one of the three major breweries in the town of Tadcaster.

Part Five

Soldiers' Loved Ones

For every one of the estimated 100,000 squaddies who served in the Province during the course of the troubles and beyond, based on 300,000 tours of active service, between 1969 and 1998, there was a group of loved ones at home, waiting anxiously for news.

For every Dave Hallam, George Prosser, Paddy Lenaghan and Darren Ware, there was a parent, a wife or a girlfriend who would see the nightly news from across the water, that is, until the media decided that it was unfashionable, and worry for their safety. It has been a common theme amongst both the contributors to this book and amongst soldier acquaintances that they were perhaps oblivious to the sufferings of those left at home. Soldiers have argued that, given a riot situation on the Falls, a frightening night time op around XMG or a foot patrol on the Turf Lodge, thoughts of home were far from their minds. Only in moments of quiet reflection, perhaps in some crowded room in an old Mill or Mission Hall, stinking of B.O., sweaty socks or the omnipresent blue fog of cigarette smoke, did we think of our families and partners.

Wasn't it ever thus, that the soldier goes away to fight and his family spends every conscious moment, concerned for their safety? What was different about Northern Ireland? That it was different is not open to debate; it was not as far away as the jungles of Burma, the desert of El Alamein, from the mud and mountains of Italy or even the plains of the Rhineland during the last conflict. It was, arguably a similar distance to Belfast as it was to the waterlogged trenches of Ypres, Verdun and the Somme, but the difference was that it was on British soil. It was close to home and the environment in which British soldiers fought was the same as that of their homes, whatever social class they belonged to.

It was not a jungle, or a desert and it wasn't a mud-filled trench in which their soldier loved ones fought; it was in streets and cities and towns and villages and in the green fields of Northern Ireland that they tried to emulate their fathers and grandfathers and even their great grandfathers of several earlier wars. But, whether they fought in a desert or a jungle or on the streets of Belfast, the loved ones' lot was to wait and worry.

WEDNESDAY 15 MARCH 1972

Gerry Butcher

The day was just like any other day in the lives of the Butcher family. My father Will had left for work as a printor at 7.00am as usual, my mother Vi' was getting some sort of breakfast ready for me and my older sister Christine. The other members of the family had moved away from home and were getting on with their lives; all apart from my brother Tony. He was on his second tour of duty as a bomb disposal officer in Northern Ireland.

We all got on with our lives, but in the back lived the fear that something would happen. The day was coming to an end for me but I still wanted to watch a programme on the television so had the nod of approval from dad to stay up a little longer. Then, a news flash.

'Two bomb disposal officers were killed in Belfast.' The screen was filled with a picture of two men in big protective gear moving towards a car; then a flash and lots of smoke. I watched the footage like an outsider; numb. I was watching my brother being murdered and I could do nothing. My father said: 'That was Tony.'

That's when the stream of phone calls began to Pat, Tony's wife, who was in the married housing in Wilton near Salisbury. She was there with their nine month old daughter Tracy Anne. Then came the confirmation; it was Tony. My father and my eldest brother Bernie got in their car and went straight to Wilton, to be with Pat and Tracey. Both my sister and I were ushered to bed by our mum. I can't remember sleeping but I can remember that all I heard was the sound of crying coming from downstairs.

The morning brought its own new problems. My mum was in the house on her own and the family started to arrive; the pain was visible on her face as she met them at the door. The tea making and smoking of cigarettes was in constant flow. The reporters having already been down to Wilton, thought they would try and get a story from the family. My mum gave them short shrift and nothing was said; if anyone was to give a statement it would be my dad.

The time between the first news and the funeral was a complete blur. It was a constant stream of people coming to the house and either trying to console us or do things for us. My mum and dad had very old school values, and the outside world would see a very composed Butcher family, whereas what was said and done inside the house was a different matter.

The day of the funeral came round and it was to leave from our house in Woodford Green. We had to get ready and somehow we all got into the clothes and prepared ourselves for what was to come. We were inside the house when the word came through that the hearse had arrived. It was a very surreal; my brother had come home only to leave without coming in; he was in that box and we could not say goodbye.

The cars arrived and we got in. I now understand the phrase 'in a goldfish bowl.' As we drove through the streets to the church, they were lined with people gawping. They could never understand what was going on and to them it was a spectacle they just had to see. We arrived at the church and we were met with the honour guard from Tony's barracks. There was also a Colonel who was there to oversee the proceedings. As they lifted his coffin from the hearse it all became so real. They marched with such reverence, so precise. They carried their precious load with tears in their eyes, and deposited the coffin on the trestles and retreated to the back of the church. The service started and finished in a flash. The honour guard came back to recover the coffin and with the same reverence returned Tony to his last ride.

The drive to the graveyard was as before; people lined the streets and we were back in the goldfish bowl. My mum, dad and Bernie were in the first car with Pat, the rest of us were in the following cortège. I can remember so well the silence that was deafening in our car; nobody spoke on that long journey.

As we arrived at the graveyard, there was a small crowd who probably knew and wanted to show their support, but again they were just a blur. We followed the honour guard as they slowly made their way to the graveside. When we arrived the priest directed us around the plot. A few short prayers were said and from just behind us a lone bugler played the last post; his emotions got the better of him at the start, but he pulled himself together and played beautifully. As he played, the coffin was lowered down and it was at this point that Pat's emotions just gave way and she needed to be supported by Bernie. I stayed for a moment to look at my brother's coffin, turned and joined the others.

We had a wake at my brother's pub, 'The Flower Pot' in Walthamstow, east London. The honour guard were invited back and graced us with their presence. These young guys were not much older than me and they had to go through all of this and then go back to work, back to NI and the possibility of not coming home. The Colonel stood with dad (a WW2 RSM) and chatted. He said that this was his first funeral. My Dad just looked him straight in the eye and said: 'It will not be your last.' This would be the last time we ever saw him or any Army officials.

The changes that the loss of Tony had on our family were different for each one of us. My mum and dad had lost their son and became very protective of us all including Pat and Tracy. The family holidays were never the same as there was a major part missing. Birthdays never were the same again as there was always someone missing. The rest of the family were affected in different ways. Some had the hatred of all things Irish and others had the view that retaliation was the way to go. But, to all of us it was the anger that was to change our lives for ever. Every 15th of March the whole family feels the same pain as they did on that terrible day.

The family that was, would never be the same. It would be stronger and more supportive; we would look after our own.

On the day that forever changed the lives of the Butcher family, Sergeant Anthony Stephen Butcher (24) and Staff Sergeant Christopher Robin Cracknell (29) had been called to a suspect car in Willow Street, just off Grosvenor Road, Belfast. After a controlled explosion, they were returning to the car when a device exploded; both were killed instantly. Staff Sergeant Cracknell was from the Leamington Spa area and was the father of a young son.

I had the honour to meet Sergeant Butcher's brother, Gerry at the Guildhall in London along with his niece, Sergeant Butcher's daughter, Tracey; there are times in life when the word 'honour' is over used. In this instance it was both an honour and a privilege to meet and talk with this dignified, brave and courteous couple. I listened to their story and later wrote it down; on both occasions, with tears in my eyes. Sergeant Butcher had been in the Army for around 9 years when he was killed and that year, 1972 was the worst year for the men of the bomb disposal unit, as the RAOC lost seven men.

A DAUGHTER'S STORY

Tracy Abraham

On the 15th March 1972, my Dad, Sgt Anthony Butcher was called along with his Staff Sergeant to an abandoned car on the junction of Willow Street and the main road. A policeman had told the patrol that a man had jumped out and been picked up by another car. The soldiers quickly cordoned off the area and my dad and his Staff Sergeant were called from nearby Albert Street Mill, but when they arrived they decided to let the car soak and went off to another suspect car in the Whiterock area. Then, having successfully carried out a controlled explosion they headed back to Willow Street.

At around 7.30pm, the Staff Sergeant walked to the car and noted a cardboard package on the back seat and fitted a cortex charge to blow open the boot, in which there was an empty box. Now convinced there was a bomb in the other box on the back seat, they decided to try and radio-detonate the bomb with their own equipment but were unsuccessful. They then decided, along with another Sergeant, to use the hook and line to pull open the rear door of the car. This operation was completed by my Dad and the next move was to attach a line and pull the box free of the car. As my Dad and his Staff Sergeant reached the car my Dad leant in to the back window and almost immediately there was a whirlwind of fire and shrapnel as the bomb went off killing them instantly, even before the smoke and debris had settled, gunmen in positions overlooking the scene fired several shots at the remaining police and soldiers but no others were injured.

Little did I know that this incident would have such an impact on my life; I remember being around 10 years old, when I found out about how he had died. I came across the military funeral photos at my Nan's house, but they were hastily taken away and Mum then had to explain. She told me that she was waiting for the right time to tell me, so we went home and got Dad's old army case out and Mum went through the photos and letters explaining things in careful detail. I always knew who Dad was as there were pictures of him in nearly all the family homes, but didn't really know who he was. Everyone told me tales about him and told me I was very special to them; now I understand why. I spent a lot of my teenage years being paranoid, wondering would the IRA come for me, was he really on a secret mission, and the name calling at school when you tell kids how your Dad was killed, they would sometimes sing 'I'm forever blowing up daddies; ugly daddies everywhere.' That is something I try to forget. And as mum had remarried again it was hard sometimes to ask questions because I knew it was painful for her, so I used to go to my Nan Butcher for things to do with him and would sit for hours listening to her talk about him.

Then one day, out of the blue, my uncle received a letter to say that the historical enquiries team was to re-investigate my Dad's death. So he in turn contacted my mum, and mum rang me to explain; I knew in my heart that this was something that I needed to do although this wasn't an easy decision to make for either my mum or myself. But I knew this was my time to find out what had truly gone on and answer some of the questions that had been running around in my head for years. So after talking things over with my mum and my husband, I decided that I would go through the process. I was assigned a liaison officer who kept me up to date and helped me make arrangements and, at the first meeting, the family gathered and gave their recollection of events. I had little to contribute at this point as I felt it was more about finding out more information for me, having being protected by the family for years. I was somewhat protected from the effect it had on them; my Dad was one of a family of eight so as you can imagine the Butcher clan are very tight knit bunch. After that meeting I began to realise that I lived my life as if my Dad's story was just that; a story. What I hadn't done was deal with the feelings and emotions that went with it.

I returned home and that's when I started to feel like part of my life was missing; what had happened to Dad's friends in the army? I knew very little about him as the friend, the sportsman and that's when I started to join different forums in search of his old friends, I did eventually find my Dad's friends; his best friends in fact, and they told me tales about going out getting drunk; the usual squaddie behaviour. How he played rugby and hockey and liked to run cross country, but one thing stood out; there was not one who had a bad thing to tell me, they all said the same thing: 'he really was a true gent.' I never thought about how much my Dad's death had an effect on his friends; I am still in contact with all his friends that I found and one has even been to see me and my mum; finally my jigsaw pieces are coming together.

We again returned for the final report from the HET (Historical Enquiries Team) and this meeting was somewhat difficult as we went through the report and the finer details began to emerge. Some of them were quite distressing, and at that time it's all too much to take in and your head begins to swirl and the anger and hurt begins to rear its ugly head; it's so hard to deal with, but you feel you must contain these, for now at least, so that you get to know everything.

I came away from the meeting with all the answers to my questions, but disappointed in the justice system. I have names of suspects and the findings of the initial investigation, but what I didn't have is justice for my Dad. He was a young man of 24, a new father, a loving husband, brother and son; cruelly taken away from us all. I still carry all those feelings from that day; I just contain them very well, but my pain will never go away. I will still long to be held in his arms, I will still wish he could tell me how proud he is of me (even though I know he is). The sad thing is I have out lived my Dad instead of growing up with him; every day I see his photo: a young man eternally 24; he would have been 60 this year.

I can honestly say what a roller coaster ride that was; the whole process unleashed emotions and pain that I'd not addressed before and for the first time I was able to grieve for him. I've found people are like me in so many ways, and that it is ok to grieve for someone you never met but who is ultimately a part of you. I miss my Dad and always will, but my heart bursts with pride when I speak about him because he saved many lives.

My Dad; my Hero.

Annaliese Bowman

Dad was 29 when he was killed; I was 2 ¾, my brother was nearly 5 and my little brother was 15 months old. I can't remember him at all, so I can't tell you what he was like; I can only tell you what I have heard about him. Friends, family and his former colleagues have told me that he loved life, playing practical jokes, playing hockey, reading boys' comics and just generally seizing the moment and enjoying it to its maximum. He lived life to the full, sometimes as if he knew he didn't have much time to fit it all in. He loved his job and he loved the army life. He had many friends and was a great team player.

Dad was the eldest of 5, and was cheerful and dedicated to his family and friends, and, after finishing school, he went to Welbeck College, and then on to Sandhurst. He decided to join the RAOC and worked on bomb disposal, maybe partly because it was interesting, and not so dependent on him having been educated at a public school, or being part of a team who spent a deal of their free time drinking alcohol. Dad was pretty unusual for an officer, as he was teetotal and chose to follow his father's footsteps by becoming a Christian Scientist. Before being posted to N. Ireland, he had the good fortune to travel to many parts of the world, including African countries, Middle and Far Eastern countries, Australia, besides Europe. He came back full of what seemed exotic tales and gifts to his younger siblings. He was posted to N Ireland in 1973 whilst we were based in Catterick. The night of 20th June 1973 was a busy one and there had been 6 explosions and 9 mortar attacks between 9:30pm and midnight; Dad's team was heavily committed so he answered this call.

At about 11pm, 2 youths were seen leaving a Nissen hut being used as a garage at the rear of some houses on Lecky Road. The patrol could smell explosives from outside the hut and found explosives inside; the lads were apprehended but escaped during subsequent rioting. The patrol secured the area as a crowd was gathering and becoming hostile, throwing stones and bottles and the occasional blast bomb. Because of the proximity of the houses and the people it was decided to start clearing the hut immediately as it seemed to be a straight forward bomb-making factory. Dad needed one of the soldiers to hold a torch for him as it was so dark in the hut. A Saracen was called for loading up the explosives and he was nearly finished, very pleased at the large haul that they had found, when at about 12:15am on June 21st dad picked up what looked like a partly made bomb. It exploded killing him instantly and injuring 3 others; after the explosion, the crowd cheered and sang rebel songs.

All these years later, I still feel very sad that he's been missing from my life. People tell me to get over it and move on, but it's as if losing him has left a hole in my heart that no-one else has the right to fill. All the small events and all the big events in my life that he wasn't there for; celebrating the good times and helping each other through the bad times.

I have been over to the bomb disposal HQ in Northern Ireland and now have a copy of some of the notes which were in his file; witness statements, police reports, etc. I have found comfort talking to men who were soldiers in NI and trying to picture what it was like for them and understand the context. I have also found comfort talking to the people of NI who have shown me the way they understood the politics and above all the kindness and warmth of their communities.

I have been told by various people that many techniques were learned from the knowledge gained in the first few years of the troubles in N Ireland, that have saved many lives since. The kit they used in the early days was not highly technical, such as the wheelbarrows which were only starting to be developed at that time, but were in fact just basic tools from the DIY store.

My dad must have been so brave.

Barry S. Gritten who was 29 and came from the Liverpool/Southport area was killed by an IRA bomb in a derelict spot just off Lecky Road in Londonderry. He was a Captain in the RAOC and was the father of 3 young children. Several others of his comrades were injured in the same attack, one of whom lost an eye. I had the honour to meet Annie on a beautiful, sunny, early autumn day in N.W. England during the research for this book. I was struck by her sincerity and open, friendly manner and her poignant telling of her Dad's death; she has written in the same poignant way and I am doubly honoured to include her account in this section of the book.

The Son of a Soldier

As the son of a soldier killed early on in the Northern Ireland conflict, I have always had mixed feelings about this conflict. In some ways I am grateful that people have finally started working together towards peace in Northern Ireland. However, I still find it difficult knowing what they did, to see people like Martin McGuiness and other former terrorists talking on television, as I imagine others do. The roots of the conflict go back a long way but one of the truest things that could be said about the Northern Ireland conflict was that it was fought by young men on behalf of old men who kept the hatred going. Hopefully now we have peace the future will be built by young people together in friendship. I guess one of the hardest things that, as children, my family had to put up with, was the misapprehension that people had about the role that the army had in Northern Ireland. It was a peacekeeping role and in fact our father died carrying out bomb disposal duties but people could sometimes prefer (and still do) to characterise the role of soldiers in Northern Ireland as one of non-stop slaughter. Our father died a hero in a conflict that the majority of British people have preferred to forget or ignore. When it was mentioned people would frequently seek to change the subject or avoid talking about in order to cover perceived embarrassment about the subject mainly on their part although I am proud of his role.

I guess the generation of children that are now losing fathers in places like Afghanistan and Iraq will face similar prejudices as they grow up. I hope they won't and that people will start to appreciate the role of the armed services instead of hearing comments like 'You wouldn't find me putting my life on the line for my country', as if it is something stupid to be done instead of the last bastion between freedom and tyranny. Nor do people ever appreciate the fact that soldiers fight the wars that politicians get them into and that the person who votes for that politician is responsible for sending that soldier to war and the least that the country can do, is thank them for it and acknowledge the sacrifice they made.

I started writing this post with the main aim of writing something positive about the impact that my father's sacrifice had on my family and so far I have failed so in my final paragraph I will try and put that right.

It is true that over the years we faced hardships but it has also meant that we have learnt from our hardships and we have benefitted from it. We probably appreciate our mother for the way she managed to raise us far more than others do. I continue to be impressed by the work that my sister carries out in her work with people on all sides of the conflict to heal the scars. I also think that both my brother and sister put their families first because of what happened and that this will help with the future. I look forward to seeing what will happen with the next generation.

Although this contribution is anonymous, I know the identity of the writer and can vouch for the authenticity of this account.

Rob Colley, Green Howards

I read your first Northern Ireland book, and have passed it to my mum now; she never really knew what me and my brother did when we were in NI. We did one tour together in 1985; I was attached to C Coy and my brother was attached to B Coy.

My mum told me that one day she was in the front room she looked out the back window and to her horror she saw two RMP (NCOs) and an Officer wandering around 'looking for someone' as she put it. She told me that she froze saying to her self 'Don't come here. Please don't come here.' She watched them until they left the square; I think she was relieved a little when they had gone. A little while later, the lemonade man came to the house and knocked rather loudly on the back door (a policeman's knock as she called it). She was terrified and when she opened the door and saw who it was, she ripped him to pieces for knocking like that. He just looked stunned and asked her what she meant, and she explained to him that she had 2 sons in Belfast and the way he knocked, she thought it was the police to tell her that one of us had been killed or Injured. He apologised and never knocked like that again; poor lad!

My mother is from Glasgow and can be a feisty wee thing when she gets going. She told me that when either of us was in NI she never watched the news and worried like hell the whole time, bless her she never said.

Felicity Townend, wife of Lance Corporal Pete Townend

Pete was due home to Middlesbrough on leave in a couple of weeks and we were going to finalise our wedding arrangements. It was just going to be a small affair in the local Registry Office as all my family was home in Australia, so we would have just a few friends and Pete's family to come along. But it didn't quite work out the way we planned.

That day I was sitting in the staff room at my place of work, a hairdressing salon in Middlesbrough, having a cuppa in between clients. The radio was on and my attention was quickly focused when the newsreader said that another British soldier had been killed in Northern Ireland and 2 more had been seriously wounded. There were no further details and as I sat there I couldn't explain the cold shivery feeling that had overcome me; it was an awful sort of numbness. I truly had the feeling that if it wasn't Pete then he was so close to death and that nothing mattered anymore.

It was very soon after that I was called out by a workmate, only to see the head of my soon to be brother-in-law coming up the stairs. I knew it was bad; he would never have come into a salon otherwise. He told me the news that Pete had been badly wounded by a sniper and that there wasn't much hope. I was shattered; I didn't know what to do.

I left work and went to my bank and withdrew money, then I can't remember how, but I ended up with a ticket on a flight to Belfast via Heathrow. Such a long way round but it may have been the only way to get there; anyway it was the first available flight. It was agonising waiting at Heathrow for the connecting flight, and it seemed to be taking forever and anything could be happening in the meantime. Pete's mum and younger brother were travelling on the same flight, as the Army had taken care of them, but as Pete and I weren't married, I had to make all my own arrangements. Fortunately I had some friends living in Belfast; he a terrific Irish fellow and she was a fellow Aussie, both of whom I had worked with a few years earlier.

We arrived in Belfast very late that night and my friends were there to meet me. An armed escort met Pete's mum and brother, big burly soldiers all kitted out in their combat gear and flak jackets and carrying their guns at the ready. It was all so surreal. There were people everywhere and it seemed as though they were all looking at us. My friends and I quickly joined the group as it was ushered out and into waiting vehicles, which then set off to take Pete's family to a hotel. There were barricades all over the place, boarded up shops and buildings. It was like being in a war zone; so hard to comprehend that it was a war zone!

We peeled off the convoy and went to my friends' home. The next day I went with my friends to their place of work, (they ran a business in Belfast) and as soon as I could I took a taxi to the hospital, meeting up with Pete's mum and brother. I had been told not to tell anyone why I was there and certainly not to mention anything to do with the army. As I had a different accent to locals the taxi drivers were always asking me questions so I could easily say I was in Belfast visiting friends.

It was terrible seeing Pete for the first time after he was shot; he was in the intensive care unit and the Sister had told us not to get upset because he had a few tubes sticking out of him and so on. Sadly, the warning didn't quite prepare me for what he looked like. He had an oxygen mask on and was lying on his side, tubes coming out of everywhere! Three bullets had hit him, his lung was punctured, his spleen had been removed, and the third bullet had gone through his shoulder from the back, coming out the front and skipped the side of his neck. It looked like he had been cut in half. He'd had a total blood transfusion.

I was afraid to touch him and started to blubber. Pete indicated to the nurse that he wanted the mask off, and in his gruff Yorkshire accent all I could hear were the words: 'What are you crying for?' I knew then that he would be ok, his voice was strong and his cheekiness was still evident. I visited him every day for the week that I was in Belfast, and each of those days had me sharing the waiting room with the wives of three Irish fellows who had blown themselves up making bombs. Oddly enough, each time they would ask me 'Och how's your man?' I can remember on one of those days, a nurse being very upset and crying, it seems her house had been bombed and her wedding dress was gone.

There was another very young lad, a squaddie, in the next intensive care room, I could see him through the glass; I don't think he made it home. How lucky we were, Pete would survive and come home.

So many other families would not have that.

Pete and I were married 3 months later, at the Registry Office in Middlesbrough. It was the same day that the Green Howards marched through town after being given the Freedom of the Town. One of the lads was our Best Man and another couple of lads were able to join our little celebration. There was so much emotion that day. Here in Australia in the years since then, when summer arrives and Pete gets his shirt off, there is always someone asking him where he got his scars from; he tells them that a shark bit him; it makes more sense to people here than the truth.

Lance Corporal Pete Townend, of the Green Howards, was shot three times at the corner of Flax Street and Brompton Street in the Ardoyne on September 16, 1971 (see pp 80/1 in *A Long Long War* by the same author). His comrade, Peter Herrington was shot and killed in the same attack.

Mo Norton

After my brother Terence was killed on the M62 Coach Bomb Blast on 4 February 1974 each of us in the family had to deal with our grief in our own way. It was an incredibly hard time for us all. Terence was a very much loved and wanted son and brother. I found the months afterwards particularly harrowing. I suffered from really frightening nightmares where I would dream terrible dreams of the M62 and the carnage that was shown on the television and in the newspapers, these dreams would repeat over and over again during the night time. I started to lose patches of hair and the doctor confirmed that it was alopecia and brought on by the trauma of what had happened. I thought I was coping and I was not. I tried to hold it all within me and it had to show in some form and physically was how it came out. I often think of the other people who lost loved ones in the M62 Bomb and wonder how they have coped. I especially think of the relatives of the Houghton family whereby a whole family was killed, a young soldier, his wife and two lovely little children. How did their families cope in the aftermath?

After Terence's funeral everything seemed to go quiet. There were no weekends where our family home was full of soldiers, cracking jokes, having a drink. The Army made no contact afterwards to check if my parents were coping OK. There was no support whatsoever. A couple of weeks after the funeral a crate arrived from Catterick which contained Terence's personal belongings. This was a particularly painful time for my parents, having to deal with all Terence's personal possessions.

Several weeks after the bombing Judith Ward was arrested for her involvement in the M62 bomb. The court case later that year only brought us more pain. There were more photographs of the carnage, more details and more information in the press. Ward was convicted for her involvement and jailed for 30 years. Approximately 18 years later the conviction was deemed unsafe and Ward was released.

Time moves on and life goes forward and for the other people you love within your family you just have to cope. You hide from your family and friends just how terrible and traumatised you feel about what happened. Nobody could possibly prepare you for such a horrific event. In life we lose friends and relatives maybe through illness, or even accidents, but losing somebody you love because somebody chose to plant a bomb; to purposely take your loved one's life without them even being able to defend themselves is unbelievably painful. We were offered no support, no counselling, nothing.

A year after the M62 Coach Bomb we attended a memorial service at Hartshead Moor Service Station on the M62 (Westbound). A plaque is in place bearing the names of the 12 lives lost, two of those are little children.

My father prematurely died, his illness being brought on by losing his only son. My mother seemed to be the strong one in the family. I did so admire her strength and courage, although I know she too was devastated and heartbroken, but she put herself last and made sure we were all OK.

She pushed herself into joining associations and taking courses at college and maybe that was her way of coping. We have all had to deal with our grief differently.

In 2003 I was approached by Jo Dover who works at the Peace Centre in Warrington and asked to take part in a Needs Analysis to establish what needs I and others had in relation to the Northern Ireland War. I soon became involved with programmes that the Peace Centre run such as Storytelling and Peace and Reconciliation courses. I also, for the first time, travelled to Ireland both the North and the South and met with others whose lives had been devastated through the war. It is so very humbling to hear somebody talk about what their life has been like, living amongst the bombings, shootings and terrible conflict that was only a 30 minute flight away from where we live.

Through the Peace Centre at Warrington I have become involved in a group called STEPS (Steps Towards Empowerment and Positive Survival). We have come together as a result of our shared experiences of being caught up in many different incidents in the 'Troubles'. Members of the groups have been affected by bombings, deaths of family members, the trauma for soldiers and emergency services personnel, and the sufferings of physical injuries and psychological traumas. We met initially and talked

Gunner Terence Griffin, who was killed in the M62 bomb outrage (Mo Norton)

about our experiences and started to realise we had a lot of common experiences, such as finding that some support services are not easily accessible, statutory services often have little understanding of how people are affected at these times, which made it difficult for us to seek out the support, help and understanding we should have been entitled to. We found that because we have been affected by this war, others around us never understood and we often felt isolated and alone! But even through these painful experiences, we now believe there is life after trauma and we are learning to be survivors, coming through a learning journey on our own, and together as a group. The STEPS group has been a really important group for me because as it has helped me to focus on helping others who have been affected by violent conflict. I feel working together with others to try to change things for those that come after us is a real motivation for me as sadly terrorism continues to blight many peoples lives.

In 2004, Jo Dover at the Peace Centre surprised me by informing me that my brother had a tree at the National Arboretum near Lichfield in Staffordshire. I was amazed and very touched that Terence had a tree planted for him with his name on and I was not aware of this. Jo took me to see the tree and it was an emotional time for me. The Arboretum has over 700 ash trees planted in the Ulster Ash Grove, one for each soldier (with his/her name on) who was killed due to the Northern Ireland War. I found the Arboretum a beautiful and tranquil place and get comfort from visiting Terence's tree, it is as though there is something living borne out of something terrible it is a living memorial.

In October 2007 I was asked to represent those families who lost loved ones during the 1970's at the Dedication Ceremony at the Armed Forces Memorial at the National Arboretum. I introduced the Queen, Prince Philip, Prince Charles and the Duchess of Cornwall to my two sisters. Whilst it was a very proud moment, it was also profoundly sad for my sisters and me. The memorial has over 15000 names on it. These are servicemen and servicewomen who have lost their lives in various campaigns since WW2. The sad aspect is that there is room for 15000 more names.

There is a sort of peace now in Northern Ireland and who would have thought that Ian Paisley would sit on the same platform as Martin McGuiness. If only they could have done this earlier, so many lives might not have been lost; so many lives might not have been ruined. The war might be over, but the suffering of those that I have met whose lives have been torn apart goes on.

If anyone is interested in getting involved, they can contact Jo Dover at the Peace Centre on 01925 581240 or look at their website: www.foundation4peace.org.

Liz Burns, Sister of Linda Haughton who was murdered in the M62 Coach Attack

We all feel emotions of love, pain, heartache, loss, bereavement and so forth, and when death strikes it is tragic and a sense of hopelessness. The loss of a loved one through age, illness, accidents etc is hard to come to terms with, but on the whole, it is a way of life and will continue to be so.

To lose someone by another person's actions, through terrorism, bombings, or murder is a tragedy that is hard to come to terms with; it is hard to accept, comprehend and totally unreal. My younger sister Linda, along with her husband Clifford and their two small sons Lee and Robert were taken from our lives by an IRA terrorist bomb on the 4th February 1974. They were travelling on a coach carrying service men and their families back to Catterick Camp. Twelve people were to be murdered that day and therefore changed the lives of their families forever, and for those of us who were left; my mum, dad, four sisters and three brothers it was a time of turmoil, heartbreak. Anger, bitterness and tragedy; how do you come to terms with such evil deeds and the destruction of one's family when the circumstances of their deaths is implanted in your brain? The pain you physically bare is stored in your heart and the memories of their lives are your very being.

We were a very close knit family and provided support for each other. We did not receive any outside help from any authority and were left alone to deal with the aftermath. We understood what each other was feeling without even having to speak, and our eyes that once glistened and danced were now dull and empty and nearly always full of tears. My Mum suffered a series of strokes and my dad just existed to care for her. Their lives were changed from ordinary life to one of constant pain, heartache, nightmares and loss. It is hard to grasp that someone has been taken from your life through an evil deed and takes years to come some sort of sense.

We always keep our precious family alive through our chats, discussions, memories and tears and they live on through us; they will never grow old or be forgotten. The tragedy that took them from us will also live on through our thoughts, memories and discussion and again will not grow old or be forgotten; we will not let it. It was an evil deed on someone's part that continues to rob us of the loss of someone dear and precious to us all; Linda, Cliff, Lee and Robert.

I had the honour of speaking with Liz and she gave me permission to use the following which is on the headstone of the Haughton family grave:

'Too precious to lose.
Too young to die
Forgive us, God
For asking why.'

Rifleman, Royal Green Jackets

I came from a relatively poor, certainly working class, background and, in common with many people in the 1970s, we didn't have a 'phone.

Before we left for Northern Ireland, we were told that those of us who didn't have a phone should inform NOK (*Next of Kin*) that a CVO would visit, generally in the company of a local Bobby and inform loved ones personally of any bad injuries, or, in the worst case scenario, death. Back in those days, News at Ten on the ITV, always began with the death of a squaddie over the water; that is, until it became unfashionable, not-newsworthy, or because the f*****g Government was too embarrassed. Every time the unseen newsreader, between the bongs of Big Ben, announced that 'In Belfast, another British soldier has been killed' my mother refused to watch more and sat by the window, all night. She stayed there until the dawn came, as though the CVO and his police escort wouldn't deliver bad news whilst the sun shone, and, only once she was convinced that some other poor family was now grieving the loss of a son, husband, father or brother, did she sleep. No doubt, she would have said a prayer for that poor lad's loved ones.

I will always hate the IRA and the others for what they did, not just to my comrades, but also to the ones waiting anxiously at home.

I rightly paid tribute in the first book, to the men and women of the UDR, a brave, underrated – in my opinion – organisation whose chance of death or injury was far greater than ours, the British soldier in Ulster. Of the 223 deaths of serving UDR personnel during the troubles, around 180 were killed by the IRA or INLA at home or at work or driving between the two. Put another way, approximately 80% of the fatalities suffered from this Regiment were whilst off-duty.

These men and women of the UDR did not get the recognition they deserved and I will always, through my writings, pay full tribute to them.

Laura Speers, Daughter of a 'Greenfinch'

I was two years old when mum joined the UDR and 22 years old when she left. I was aware from a young age that I was never to reveal my mum's occupation. I was to say that she was a civil servant or a secretary. I have carried this right through until today.

I remember wondering why mum was always dropping her car keys when she went out to get into the car. She would drop her keys and then pick them up and say, 'Silly me!' and then off we would go. Of course I know now that she was checking under the car for bombs. I also remember taking different routes when we went on car journeys and mum explaining it was just another adventure. I was told never to answer the door to strangers and I was always aware if there were unfamiliar cars around the area. To this day I still remember number plates.

I knew that I must never disclose a name on the telephone until I knew the identity of the caller and that is still with me when I respond to a telephone call today. My father was in the police so we had to be security conscious at all times. It's amazing that I have carried some of these practices through to my adulthood. We were brought up not to differentiate between Protestants and Catholics in our home in terms of attitudes or friends. There was no hatred for Catholics in our home – no stereotyping or derogatory comments, and that has shaped my attitudes today, particularly with my Catholic friends. I also have positive memories. I remember the great craic at the Christmas parties at the Camp and Santa flying in on a helicopter (although I figured out that it was really the Sergeant Major dressed up!) and we were getting an extra present from this Santa. It was like a subculture of people when we were together. Everyone was able to have fun and relax with families and colleagues at those parties in the big hall. It wasn't like an office party – it was like a family within a bigger family. I remember helping mum to make sandwiches for family days out – we had great outings. I made friends with children of other soldiers.

Now that I am older I understand the risks and dangers my mum had in her job. Not like my friends' mums who worked in the dentists or whatever. But it wasn't just a job. There was a sense of selflessness of doing her duty for the country. When I grew up I realised that she must be thinking, 'What will happen tonight?' or 'Will I be coming home?' When I think about this I get an overwhelming realisation of what she must have faced. I have a great sense of pride in my parents. I don't think their service got the full recognition it deserved.

Mrs. Marie Hale, mother of Kingsman Vincent Scott

My son Vincent was killed by an IRA bomb at Coshquin in Co. Londonderry on 24 October, 1990, with four of his friends. We are from Walton on Merseyside and he was due to leave the Army a month later.

What can I say about Vinny? He was a lovely lad but no saint, and I came down on him like a ton of bricks if I thought he needed it. As a teenager, he played football for the Liverpool boy's team and visited Northern Ireland to play against one of their teams. When he came home, he told me about the soldiers walking the streets with rifles, and going around in their armoured cars, but little did I think that by the time he was 17 that he would become a soldier. When the family went to his passing out parade, I was absolutely bursting with pride. He was 21 on October 14 and was killed 10 days later on the 24th.

The Army sent all his birthday cards home to me and they are still in his bedroom. Thank you for your time and for keeping the memory alive for me and all the families of our brave soldiers. I am crying now so will leave my words in your capable hands.

The author had the pleasure and honour to met with Marie Hale at the 18th anniversary of the attack at Coshquin; the only comment I can make is, that if Vincent Scott was just half the personality of his fantastic family, then he must have been a superb person. His relatives treated me like a member of their family; I remain, deeply honoured.

There are dozens and dozens of different roles a soldier can be asked – or ordered – to fulfill, within each Regiment and Corps of the British Army. Arguably, the role which is the worst of all, the least sought after is that of the Casualty Visiting Officer or CVO. During the long, long course of Operation Banner, for a variety of different causes – battle deaths, accidental shootings, road traffic accidents, suicides or other deaths from what the MOD somewhat euphemistically call 'violent or unnatural causes' – CVOs made c. 1300 visits. The following account which continues the story of Kingsman Scott is just one of them.

RSM Peter Oakley, CVO of the King's Regiment

My last and perhaps my most sad and difficult duty for 1 Kings was to act as CVO to a family of a Kingsman who lost his life at the PVCP known as V2 at Buncrana near Londonderry. A CVO is appointed to support the family and act as a focal point and conduit to deal with all military matters; a system we also now see performed by Police Families Liaison Officers.

I got the telephone call, early on the morning of October 24, 1990 and was briefed on the incident and instructed to act as CVO for Kingsman Vincent Scott's family who lived in Walton, Liverpool. Vincent – known as Vinnie – had been killed by an explosion at the PVCP. Killed with him was Stephen Beacham, Stephen Burrows, David Sweeney and Paul Worrall; all had individual CVOs appointed to him.

(*See Chapter 23 of A* Long Long War; Voices of the British Army in Northern Ireland, 1969-98.)

In full uniform and with my wife, we met up at the local Police station with the family's Parish Priest and a Policewoman who would accompany us. Her radio was a valuable asset if we needed to contact anyone quickly which she explained when we met.

We arrived at the address of Vinnie's mother, Marie, and met her in the street but she already knew what had happened; I introduced myself and asked her if we could go indoors. As gently as I could, I then told her formally the very sad news that Vinnie had been killed, with four other Kingsmen, and a civilian who had been forced to drive the van containing the bomb, in an explosion at V2; the driver's family had been held hostage.

Having given Marie that devastating and distressing news, I thought it best to leave consolation and pastoral care to her priest. I am so grateful that he immediately took over. Vinnie's brother, sisters and nephew came quite quickly, so I explained as briefly and as simply as possible what my role was and left, with the Police Officer. I left my contact details with the assurance that I would be available to the family at any time, but in any event, would come back the following day.

I explained to Marie and her family about the options for the interment of Vinnie. They could have a private funeral or a full military funeral, and that the MOD would fund whatever they decided. They decided that they wanted a funeral with full military honours; this we did.

Sometime later, the five Kingsmen were flown from Northern Ireland to Liverpool airport where the families waited in a large hangar to be reunited with them. There was a considerable distance for the uniformed pallbearers from the aircraft to the hangar, bearing the five coffins, each draped in the Union Flag. After a short and moving service, the Kingsmen were moved to the assembled hearses and the families went across to gently lay their hands on their respective coffins, and spend as much time as they wanted with their private thoughts and prayers.

On the day, the journey from Marie's house to the church, the cortege passed by many people who lined the streets bare headed and bowed in respect, an act which I am sure, gave the family a feeling of support and appreciation to help them through the day. The church was full to overflowing with family, friends, neighbours and a great many soldiers, not just from 1 Kings. After the service and burial, we went to 5/8 Kings barracks in Townsend Avenue, Liverpool, where so many had gathered to give them their condolence and what comfort they could. Soldiers have a natural empathy in these circumstances which is borne out of the Regimental family spirit. Marie and family mingled with the very many soldiers who had come across for the funeral or who were on leave.

There were, of course, four other Kingsmen who died that night, so there were five of us acting as CVOs. Until all of the funerals were completed, we would meet each evening at Peninsula Barracks, Warrington to report back to the CO on the day's events. These meetings were very helpful and supportive as we discussed what we were doing and got advice and help from each other in the planning and co-ordination of the funerals. They were all completed successfully with each man being fittingly honoured.

Each year on a Saturday closest to the actual date of this atrocity, there is a gathering of Kingsmen, ex-Kingsmen, family and friends in St John's Gardens in Liverpool. Known as the annual V2 reunion, it is to lay wreaths and flowers and have quiet moments of remembrance around a plaque that was bought by individual donations. It is placed there with the names of all the Kingsmen who lost their lives in Northern Ireland inscribed upon it.

This was started by Kingsmen Mike Ashcroft and Steve Miller who were friends of the soldiers who lost their lives at Buncrana. Mike attended a memorial service at the site of the bombed PVCP to which family members had been invited. The distressing and harrowing scene of people gathered about on the windswept location of the tragedy had a profound and lasting effect on Mike who, with Steve, had been going to Vinnie's grave each year. Eventually they met Marie and decided to mark the anniversary in a more special way. So from a few friends and one family meeting to remember V2 it has now grown to be an important date in many calendars.

The reunion is now extended to recall all of 1 Kings who lost their lives on Op Banner and their names are read out on the day. On leaving to go home, Marie and her family are always given a noisy and good-natured farewell as everyone gathers outside the pub to give a rousing rendering of the Regimental song: 'The Kings are coming up the Hill,' much to the amazement of the good people of Liverpool.

Marie wrote to me 'Our Vinnie spent the last four years of his life in the Army and he once said to me: "Mum, you never have friends anywhere like the friends you have in the Army" and he died with four of them.'

I am still deeply moved by these memories. There was no bitterness from the family and no recriminations, just a wish to remember Vinnie as a shining example of the young men we are so proud to have served with.

Until it is experienced it is impossible to imagine how you could cope with the violent death of a loved one so far away. A member of the family passing away is hard enough to bear but when it happens in such circumstances and in the full glare of publicity it is a very burden indeed.

I so very much hope that the family and friends of all the service personnel who lost their lives as a consequence of 'the Long Long War' will find solace and comfort knowing that their loved ones contributed greatly to the peace in Northern Ireland. And, although the loss of so many brave, proud, dedicated and loyal men and women will forever be painful, it might help to know that their ultimate sacrifice was not in vain. And, that they truly did make the difference that eventually brought peace to the good people of Northern Ireland who should never forget and will forever be in their debt. We who remain and mourn them should never forget that we are honour bound, and have an obligation and duty always to remember them and their families.

Finally, my thoughts are always with the families and the CVOs who will support them when I hear those chilling and heart stopping words: '....and the family has been informed......' and will remain so in the desperately bleak and sad days to come.

Peter Oakley's incredibly poignant and articulate words merely serve to reinforce the assertion this author made earlier. That behind the tragically but simple words '....another British soldier has been killed...' lies layer after layer after layer of grief and sorrow and emotion as the families come to terms with the loss of their son, or brother or father or, as demonstrated recently, their sister or daughter. From the explosion at V2 on the Buncrana road, Coshquin to this very day, almost 18 years later as I write, the layers of grief and sorrow and regret continue, unabated, beyond the public view; long after our memories have erased the words, '..... another British soldier has ...'

I would like to 'dedicate' the following contribution to the members of NORAID and to every American or other citizen who ever donated money to the perverted cause of the IRA. Innocence, wide-eyed naivety or a blind prejudice against the British is no excuse for the actions of those who donated money to NORAID.

Mrs Kathleen Gillespie, Shantallow, Derry

On the 24th of October, 1990, the IRA finally murdered my husband, Patsy. I say finally, because four years previously, they had held us hostage and forced him to drive our car, loaded with 200 lbs of explosive, into Fort George, the local barracks where he worked. He was a civilian worker in the kitchens there in Derry. In our climate of unemployment, my husband had two choices: the job offered by the MOD or the dole. He chose to work and feed his family and mercifully, on that occasion, the only casualty was our car.

Patsy was offered a change of job and location but he was adamant that he would not be dictated to. We remained and convinced ourselves that lightning wouldn't strike twice. We reasoned without the cruel and devious mindset of the IRA!

I will not go into minute detail of the night of my husband's murder, but suffice to say that our house was taken over whilst myself and our family was held hostage and Patsy was driven away in our car at midnight. Four hours later he was chained to a van containing 2000lbs of explosive and forced to drive to the Army checkpoint at Coshquin; five soldiers from the King's regiment and Patsy lost their lives that night. Several soldiers who survived have testified that their lives were saved by Patsy shouting a warning, even though he had no chance of escape himself.

The author in the company of George Prosser, ex-King's Regiment, visited the site of the atrocity on a lonely, windswept road outside of Londonderry, with the Irish border only a few hundred yards away. There, embedded in the wall, is a plaque which reads: 'In memory of Patsy Gillespie. Civilian, Husband and Father. 24th October, 1990. Presented by the soldiers.' It speaks far more eloquently than I can.

The immediate period after Patsy's murder has gone by in a blur of hatred, pain and anger; all caused by the IRA. Patsy and I had been married for 20 years and he was killed on our eldest son's 18th birthday; happy birthday, Patrick!!

The compassion and goodwill of people all over the world seemed to be directed at my family at that time and for a long time afterwards. I have suitcases full of heartrending correspondence which poured into my house in the days and weeks following Patsy's funeral which was broadcast worldwide. Many of these cards and letters didn't even have a proper address on them, but nonetheless, they arrived without fail. One letter from Canada had the address 'Mrs Gillespie, Ireland' and another, from Australia was addressed to: 'The woman whose husband was murdered by the IRA, N. Ireland.' One man from England, who had recently lost his wife, put £5 in a letter and instructed me to buy a bottle of Vodka. If you are reading this, 18 years on; 'Cheers; I'm still fighting'.

The concept of the human bomb rocked the world and it seemed as though the IRA had sunk to the lowest depths of depravity. Six men were arrested and taken into custody at dawn on that day, one of whom was William, the brother of Martin McGuiness. Unfortunately they were released because of insufficient evidence and I have had to learn to live with the fact that Patsy's murderers are walking free. But I have great faith. There are many ways of punishment; maybe not all in this life, but I can hope.

My means of survival over the years has to become involved with peace groups and programmes and I have two sons and a daughter who I am so very proud of. One of the worst days in the past 18 years was my daughter Jennifer's wedding day. Her father would have been so very proud of that day; she looks so much like him. I now have two little grandsons who are my lifeblood but they should not have been deprived of their grandfather. They are still too young to understand, but who can; certainly not ordinary, decent people.

One of the most significant differences to my life over recent years was to become involved in a programme some 9 years ago in Wicklow. I have met and spoken to at length, many people from many walks of life who have been affected by the past 35 years. This has culminated after many years of running away from it, in a dialogue with ex-paramilitaries. I have developed a reputation among my groups of not being afraid to speak out and I challenged ex-paramilitaries to meet with the people they have injured. I have faced up to politicians seeking answers to my questions, but I have not yet faced up to Martin McGuiness who has said: 'Patsy Gillespie was a legitimate target of war.' I would like him to look me in the eye and explain to me who gave him the right to make that statement.

Meanwhile I continue my life as best I can without Patsy; I have my children and my grandchildren and I have wonderful friends. I should have had my husband to accompany me through these later years of our lives.

On a cold November Saturday, in 2008, on the outskirts of Derry – to respect her name for the city – I met with Kathleen and her sister to talk through her story and what she was prepared to do for my book. The word honour is often overused and overstated; in this instance, I can only say that the choice of the word honour in meeting this brave woman is neither overstated nor misused. I consider it a privilege that she has written for me

IRIS WRIGHT

Mother of a soldier in the R.C.T.

I felt really concerned when I was told that Kevin was going to Belfast, because, at that particular time, soldiers were being killed on most days. As a consequence, mothers were listening for each news bulletin, dreading the thought that it might be their son.

Kevin was doing three month stretches in Belfast and, at 18, he wasn't really a man; like a lot of the others, he was just a boy really. Serving in Belfast made him a man. Anyway, after this stretch, he went back to West Germany where I knew that he would be at least safer. Then, there was a whole series of incidents in Northern Ireland which meant a lot of soldiers were being sent out. This would be 1972, when he was about 20, and he was sent back for the emergency but he didn't tell me.

On this particular night, as usual, I was watching the BBC News and it showed a lot of kitted-up soldiers boarding a plane for Northern Ireland. I spotted Kevin and told all the family, but they thought that I was raving mad and didn't believe me. A few hours later, the phone rang and it was Kevin. He said 'Alright, Mom?' and I just said: 'You're in Belfast, aren't you?' I told him that I had seen him on the television and asked him why he was there. He never did tell me, to this day, in fact.

The next day was 'Operation Motorman' and then I suddenly realised why they had all been sent back out there. It wasn't a very nice thought for me, knowing that he was in a war, even though he was a soldier. It was a dreadful time for mothers, not only in England but in Northern Ireland as well.

All mums worry about their sons and I was no different; when peace came, I was so happy.

Operation Motorman took place on July 31, 1972; it was the largest 'peacetime' operation in which the British Army took part. Until the series of well planned and synchronized raids, the IRA – as well as some loyalist copycats – had barricaded off large Republican areas of Belfast and Londonderry. These 'no go' areas were patrolled and controlled by them and the Security Forces kept away and the situation was tolerated only long enough for a concerted operation to take place.

On that date, the Heath Government gave the go-ahead and the Army attacked the IRA strongholds and with troops and armoured earth moving equipment, seized control again of the no go areas.

A WIFE'S PERSPECTIVE

Hilary Reynolds, Wife of a UDR Soldier

My husband joined the UDR in 1974 and I am very proud of him for that. But as the years went by I always felt so lonely. It wasn't that I didn't have friends, but I always had to be on my guard, always afraid of letting something slip that would put my husband's life at risk –it was a dangerous time. I originally came from the country so I did not know many of people in the town. The only people I knew well were my in-laws. Of course my immediate friends and neighbours knew that my husband was part-time in the UDR but even at the school gates I couldn't let anything slip. Because of the personal security risks I didn't join clubs or get involved in school parents activities.

Patrol Preparation
When my husband was on dayshift from 8am-4pm I would make his dinner for 4.30pm. After dinner he would have a wash and then sleep for a few hours. I would have his uniform laid out on the bed so that he could get ready for duty at 7pm. That would be the last I saw of my husband until 4am or sometimes 6am the next morning.

Daily Routine
I just got on with my daily schedule; I had to keep the house running and look after the children as well. The gardening and the electrical work around the house became my responsibility as well because my husband was away from home so much. He just worked and slept and never attended school interviews or sports days. It was the same for all the other UDR men in the area.

Phoning Home
There were no mobile phones in the early days so if my husband was later than usual I just walked the floor hoping that everything was OK. One morning he did not return home until 7.10am. I feared the worst when two of his mates called at the house. But they were only calling to let me know that he had been delayed clearing up a road accident.

At the height of the terrorist campaign there were many emergency call-ups from one up to six weeks in duration. On one occasion I didn't see my husband for three weeks and to make matters worse for the family phoning home was banned for security reasons.

Personal Security

The letterbox was sealed up with metal so that nothing obnoxious could be posted into our home. I was always wary of answering the door. That was a chore when you were alone with a couple of curious toddlers following behind. I never answered the door without carrying a security device that would dissuade any potential threat to my family or me. I was an independent countrywoman and I just had to get on with running the family home and constantly checking everything. For example, I could not go out and open the garden shed without first checking for terrorist devices. The stress eventually took its toll and I lost a lot of weight. Then at the age of 28 I took a stroke and ended up in hospital.

Health and Welfare

The UDR was a new Regiment and they didn't have a coping mechanism for dealing with families and family problems. I had a friend whose husband was in the fire service and they had counselling from the beginning but the Regiment was primitive in that respect. After I suffered from a stroke my husband decided to resign from the UDR, as there was no one to look after the children. The whole situation had an adverse effect on his health. Before he was a highly independent person but now his confidence had gone. He is now suffering from the effects of long-term exposure to stress. He has horrendous flashbacks, night terrors and problems sleeping. Today he just gets up and gets on with it but sometimes the fear and depression gets to him.

Personal Feelings

I feel cheated by the British government. I was brought up in the country and my parents were of a mixed marriage. They talked about poverty and explained that all of us, Protestants and Catholics had poverty in common. We were all equal; we had no running water and no electricity and that was only fifty years ago. I do realize that I am in a more fortunate position than many other women in Northern Ireland. Many wives suffered the terrible loss of their husbands and children at the hands of the terrorists. I can recall a soldier's widow being given £2000 compensation after her husband was murdered by terrorists. The judge told her she was young enough to go out and get married again!

I don't like it when people run the Regiment down without knowing the real facts. I remember saying to one person visiting us, 'While you are in my house don't run down the UDR.' I am very proud of everyone who served in the UDR. The country was deliberately thrown into turmoil by murdering terrorists and it was people like my husband who stood up for everyone. If it happened again I would make the same commitment.

There appears to be no real understanding in the wider community of our experiences. I've never discussed how I felt like this before. I'm not even sure if people would be interested.

THOSE LEFT BEHIND

Mick 'Benny' Hill, 3 Royal Anglians

One of the things which came as a real surprise to me during the tour was the television and newsreel coverage. After a tour of Aden, we came back and found that the general public were unaware of what we had been doing and were mostly unsure of exactly where Aden was; they just thought that we had been on a 'Swan' because of the suntans !

Belfast was different; every one had an opinion; everyone knew how to sort out the troubles. After all, they had all seen it on 'News at Ten.' For us, it was somewhat bizarre, as we could spend the day playing 'dodge the brick' and then go back and watch the 'action replay' on the late news. A lot of the reporters were even handed, but some weren't and I suppose that the problem in those days was that the Army was not good at PR and handling the press. The IRA on the other hand, was very good.

It must have been difficult for the wives back in the UK as they would see absolute mayhem on their TV screens, night after night and then get a hurried phone call from their husband, assuring them that everything was quiet. We all had a standard line: 'All the problems are in someone else's sector. Luckily, in those days, reporters were not good at recognising Regiments; all soldiers looked alike to them and the practice of blackening cap badges didn't help!

The wives left behind in BAOR were spared all that uncertainty as over in West Germany, there was no BFBS (*British Forces Broadcasting Service*) in those days. However, in a lot of cases, 'R&R' was a complete disaster. She had plans for the three or four days; he wanted a long, hot bath, the chance to get his feet into dry socks and no boots, and just sleep. One wife explained to me that shopping was a complete disaster; she was looking in shop windows, he was looking at roof tops on the other side of the road.

The rest was nice but in some ways it was a relief to get back to Belfast and finish the tour; from normality to a civil war zone in just 45 minutes and vice-versa; surreal or what ?

Soldiers' wives put up with an awful lot and it is amazing how many marriages lasted and no surprise at all that so many fell apart. I heard one wife say to her friend:' I loved the man who went, but I didn't really like the one who came back!'

Some wives found it nearly impossible to understand that you had two 'families.' Her and the kids; very important but sometimes in the back of your mind; and the other 'family' of Dave, 'Titch' George, Stan, the other Stan, Browning et al. The latter ones were always in the front of your mind and in some ways; I knew them better than I knew my own kids. You see, with the best will in the world, you aren't with your kids 24 hours a day for four months.

Soldiers' families are the unseen and unrecorded casualties of any war. No one really understands what they have to go through and in many cases, their husbands won't tell them what they went through. Yeah, it was ok; a bit hairy sometimes' doesn't really explain a lot and as for talking to opinionated civvies: in your dreams; no chance !

Even though Mick was technically not a 'loved one' there could be no more appropriate place in this book for this heartfelt and anguished account of the 'other' casualties of the troubles. Of course, there were casualties on the 'other side', the loved ones of those killed by, or as a result of terrorism, it is not my remit to write of other than soldiers and their families.

Felicity Townend, Wife of Green Howard, Pete Townend

The newspapers and TV were full of it, reports of Bernadette Devlin's slapping the Home Secretary's face and calling him a '... murdering hypocrite'. It came on the heels of the 'Bloody Sunday march in Londonderry; a terrible day for all.

I can remember feeling so bloody angry with her; after all, my husband had been seriously wounded and many other British and Irish people had lost their lives in this war that I didn't really understand. How dare she blame others when she also was responsible for so much ? Anyway, in my naiveté, I sat down and wrote a letter of protest to the local paper, nothing too fancy, just saying I'd like to slap her back.

I think it was on a Friday that the letter was published, along with another in the same vein, and there it was, bold as brass, my name and address, there for all to see! I hadn't thought to ask for anonymity at all. I was a bit nervous after that, I was alone in our flat as my husband was with the Btn in Germany. He had been to Northern Ireland a couple of times at that point and we were aware that strange things could happen.

Monday was my day off and when the mail was delivered there was a copy of the 'Irish News' slipped through the letterbox in the door; it was musty smelling and old, but sure enough had my name and address on the wrapper. I just sat there in a state of shock, as I didn't quite know what to make of it. So, after thinking about it for a while, I took it to the Major at the Recruiting Office, who knew my husband, as I thought he would tell me what to do. He phoned the local CID and I had to go to see them. They had me go through the paper, page by page, to see if there were any direct references to anything familiar, but I couldn't find anything relevant at all. They told me to take precautions at home, like keeping the door locked at all times etc.

I went home and then decided to see my sister-in-law who lived further up the same street. I told her about the paper that had been delivered, and we had a cup of tea and talked some more, but I was getting edgy, as it was coming on dark and I needed to get home. I ran all the way, and unlocked my flat door, went in and locked the door behind me. The flat was situated above a shop on a corner; the stairs went up in the middle, with 2 rooms either side of the stairwell. I had put the light on to go up and thought I had better put the milk bottle out on the step. Before I could pick up the bottle there was a noise coming from the front door, I stopped in my tracks and listened and realised that someone was pushing on the door; it was unmistakable! I hit the floor in the kitchen, with the light on I could be seen from the other side of the road, and I had to get the stair light off before I could cross to the other rooms to look out of the window to the street below. I honestly don't know how long this took; I was scared stiff.

Eventually I slid my hand up the wall and switched off the light, ducked into the bedroom to the window, but by then there was nothing to see. I stayed awake all night, and was just too afraid to sleep. For the next couple of days one of the girls from work stayed with me, at least I felt better for the company. Nothing else happened, fortunately, and later in the week, at work, a lady I knew congratulated me about the letter in the paper. I told her I wish I had kept my mouth shut and told her what happened. I didn't know it at the time but she was married to a policeman and I found out later that they had put surveillance on my flat for a period of time.

That was without doubt the most frightening experience of my life!

Whilst not an everyday occurrence, undoubtedly, the IRA or their supporters were not loathe to playing mind games with relatives of the dead soldiers. On at least one other occasion, the author recalls a grieving Yorkshire family receiving a letter, purporting to be from the IRA, blaming the dead soldier's parents for his death as they had 'allowed' him to join the Army. I understand that there were other instances of this occurring, as the IRA showed that they were beneath contempt.

FAMILY HAVE YET TO BE INFORMED

Mr & Mrs Peter Briscoe, Parents of an Artillery Soldier

Those are the chilling words you dread to hear when you are a parent of a soldier. I tried to dissuade my 19 year old son (*Mick Pickford Royal Artillery*) from joining the Army back in the 90s, mainly due to the troubles in Ireland – to no avail; he still went ahead and did it. Whilst on his tour of duty in NI we had gone to Norfolk for a week's holiday and my husband and I were sitting in a cafe having a cup of tea and half listening to the radio in the background. Then we heard the words: 'Soldier from the Royal Artillery has been shot dead in Northern Ireland – family have yet to be informed'.

Our eyes met across the table – how could we be informed if we weren't at home – no mobile phones then. We enlisted the help of the local policeman who made many a phone call for us. We were lucky – but some other parent wasn't. We were so proud of him and it must have taken a lot of guts knowing he would have to go to NI. We believe they did not then and do not now get the recognition they all deserve for doing something they believed in. A mother must believe in and support what her son/daughter wants to do – even if it means their children putting their lives in danger for a one-sided conflict – although that is much easier to say than do. It seems to me that the general public was not aware or did not care what went on over the water.

The author is aware of the probable identity of the soldier killed that day that the Briscoes must have thought that their worst nightmares had come true; it is not appropriate that I reveal it.

ANOTHER CASUALTY OF THE TROUBLES

Ruby Hill, Former Wife of a Royal Anglian

The battalion was going on its first N. I. tour, and for most of us this was the worst we had encountered. Like a great many of the wives, I was worried sick for the safety of my husband. We didn't have a T.V. but knew how bad it was from the papers and radio. Not having a television was good as far as I was concerned, because it meant the children were protected from the awful scenes shown; at that time they were 9, 8, 6, and 4 years old. I had been an army wife for 9 years by then, so separations were not new to me, and long before this I had been doing the finances. We thought it best as we never knew what would happen and, of course it did make sense. Before the men left, a pep talk was given to the wives, as to what we could expect; it was all wrapped up though, so not to scare the life out of us, I guess. One thing was made quite plain, in a roundabout way; do not worry the men with family issues. Yes, it made sense but meant I had to take everything on my shoulders; adding to the stress that I was under. My father had died in the January and I was still grieving for him, and my mother was on a visit. Looking back this was the wrong time for it, as she never did understand what I was going through or why the children were behaving differently. She made my life very difficult at a time when my father's death and the NI tour should have brought us closer; it didn't.

Our nine year old son took to running away at night, sometimes being gone for hours, and it was his way of dealing with things I guess. Who was there to turn to; no one, and I couldn't tell Mick; family were too far away. My best friend's husband who had stayed behind tried to talk to him to see if he could help, but at nine, knowing how you feel about things is difficult. Looking back, maybe SSAFA. (*Soldiers, Sailors, Air Force Association*) could have helped but that was admitting I couldn't cope. I did cope because I had to and this made me a very strong person; too strong sometimes.

Most days, life went on as normal, except you were on your own and very much a single mum. Nights were the worst; this was when I wrote my letters; cried for hours some nights and would read all night for 3 or 4 nights at a time. My friend's husband used to bring my mail, even turning up at 5 am one day with a pile of 6 letters, as he knew I was worried as I hadn't had any for ages. He also knew I would be awake, listening for the door or any sound. I hated being on my own at night; I still do. I returned to the UK from Germany on a visit and Mick came on leave, and this was the first time my children had seen the television news. What do you say to a 6 year old when they ask if that's their daddy; that people are throwing things at and: 'They won't kill my daddy, will they?' You can't say no, as it could happen. This was also the first time I had seen just what they were going through;

those pictures would come back into my head most nights and also when I heard his Battalion mentioned on the news.

Mick had changed and was of course very tired and jumpy; trips to town were hard for him. A loud noise or bang would have him jumping into a doorway or crouching down; even an Irish accent would have him looking around.

During that tour my 6 foot 3 inch husband was knocked out by a 'lovely' lady with a heavy galvanised dustbin lid and that incident was the beginning of the end of our marriage. Mick suffered headaches for a very long time and withdrew into himself. Post traumatic stress wasn't heard of then and it was very much a case of 'get over it.' Tests were done but no injury was found, well, not a physical one anyway, but the mental ones don't show up do they? We were posted to Ipswich soon after that tour and at the time I was over the moon; he wouldn't be going back to N. I. for a while. How I wish we hadn't gone on that posting because if we had stayed with the battalion I would have had people to talk to and confide in and maybe get help. Life was hell, and it got that I was glad when he left for work, because the stress in the house was awful, I tried to keep things as normal as possible for the children.

Typical day; Mick went to work; he worked irregular hours with the cadet training team, and when he came home I was lucky if I got 2 words out of him; if he did, it was about work and never the family. His head was always in a book; it was the first thing he did on getting home. Hours would go by without a word between us, and, at first, I would try to get a conversation going but gave up as most times I got nowhere. If he wasn't reading he was playing war games on the dining table sometimes well into the night. But most of the time, I may as well not have been there. Even the children were ignored. I remember to this day the look on our son's face when he refused to play football with him along with all the boys and dads in our close. His head was in a book.

A male friend of ours came to see us one night and took one look at us and realised how bad things were. He said to Mick: 'I'm taking Ruby out for while.' 'O.k., if you like,' was the reply. This was the friend who used to bring my mail and knew us very well. We walked into town and I poured everything out; it was the first time I had been able to do this. Mick hadn't even realised I had gone. Not every day was that bad but there were more bad days than good; I even got as far as thinking of leaving him. Two friends talked me out of this and both have said they did the wrong thing.

Over the years things did not get better; that Irish lady did not kill my husband but she may as well have done. I loved the man that I sent to Belfast; I didn't much care for the man I got back.

Epilogue

Aftermath: Northern Ireland

Arfon Williams, (Will71) Royal Regiment of Wales

The biggest problem I have on N.I. is the fact that the same people in the same streets in the same area for years started a fruitless conflict that ended in the death of over 1300 troops of the British Army; why?

The mindless morons led these groups and called themselves protectors of the people, the 'Freedom Army' of the Catholics, and the 'Freedom Army' of the Protestants. But why, when, like the rest us they live in a country that has more freedom than the rest of the world.

We, the members of the British Army did not want to be a part of this conflict but as members of the Army we have no say in where we went and what we did. Ours is not to reason why, ours is to do or die. Over 1300 British troops died; why?

I, like the rest of my Regiment, was sent to N.I. and at the time did not know what the conflict was about; all we were told to do was to protect the people. This we did but who were we protecting the people from? We were 'pigges in the middle' protecting neighbours from neighbours living next to each other; madness; why?

I lost some very good friends in this conflict, and still, after all these years, cannot fathom out why, the British Government put us on the streets in N.I. in August, 1969 and we stayed until the end of OP Banner in 2008. This Government which sent the troops into N.I. has today betrayed all the troops by the use of the Good Friday agreement; murder is still murder! For them to release these murderers back into the community after only a couple of years is a betrayal of the highest order; why ?

The Government today are still spending millions upon millions with enquires upon enquires about 'Bloody Sunday.' Can you please tell me how many enquiries have been held into the deaths of my friends and other troops who were killed in the line of duty by these murderous thugs? Not one!

These thugs that led these outlawed organisations from the very start are now members of the N.I. Government. How many have sworn allegiance to Her Majesty the Queen? Not many, if any, but they still Govern in her name and pass legislation; why?

I cannot and will not forgive the members of these organisations or the people that knew who the members were on both sides. And I will not forgive tho so called British Government that betrayed the good people of N.I. and the troops that were sent there in their name and died for what?

To this day I cannot go back to Ireland (north or south) to think these are people of the U.K.; only fifty minutes travelling time from Cardiff, and

489

some still live and praise the murder of British Troops; the very same troops that were sent there to protect them; why ?

Hatred is a human reaction to someone or something that as happened, and with time you forgive or forget, but time has not let me forget and defiantly not let me forgive. The only question I can ask about N.I. is why; who won??

Today I sit and listen to the news about the Gulf and Afghan and think will someone in 30 years be doing the same as me today, writing about their war?

AFTERMATH

John Girdler, 3rd Bn, The Queen's Regiment

John was shot and badly wounded in Mullhouse Street, Belfast on October 24, 1971

My parents were sent a telegram saying the following:

MRS L. E. MEARS REGRET TO INFORM YOU YOUR SON NUMBER 24128958 PRIVATE JOHN ALFRED GIRDLER OF 3 QUEENS IS VERY ILL IN ROYAL VICTORIA HOSPITAL BELFAST SUFFERING FROM A GUN SHOT WOUND IN THE NECK STOP NO FURTHER DETAILS AVAILABLE NOW STOP REPORT RECEIVED FROM HOSPITAL WILL BE SENT TO YOU IMMEDIATELY STOP ENQUIRIES TO MINISTRY OF DEFENCE +01-499 8040 STOP LETTER FOLLOWS = MINISTRY OF DEFENCE +

When the police got to my mother's house, they found no one at home as earlier that afternoon she had sensed that something in the family was wrong, and went round to my sister June's house to tell her. When the police turned up to tell her about me, she said to them: 'It's John isn't it? They said yes and gave her the telegram.

They flew to Belfast the next day and stayed for a week, and when I was out of danger my parents went home to England with a promise that I would be looked after. Later, I was interviewed by the S I D and then I was allowed to see the other 6 members of my search team section for a few hours, and they knew how I felt about the way I got injured and asked if I blamed the sergeant for his mistake. Yes I do! I am not saying that if we had been allowed to have knelt down that we would not have got shot, what I am saying is that we would have stood more of a chance being a smaller target.

After the lads left that day it was the last I saw or heard from them; I did not get a visit from my Company Commander, Major P. Hiscock or the C S M W O 11 D. J. Bailey, until Aug 1973 when I was posted back to 3rd Bn for a medical discharge. To make matters worse, nobody knew who I was, and when I told them they said that I had died, and true to their word when I went into the CSM's office there on the placement board on the wall right hand side under DEAD it read Benner R, Girdler J, Gilliam E, so I pointed out that the last two names were still living, and I was one of the names. CSM Bailey simply said: 'Oh, right; I will get that fixed.'

All the time I was in hospital and in rehabilitation – and that's nearly 2 years – I never saw or heard from my Commanding Officer, Company Commander, RSM, or CSM. We in the Queen's Regiment were left to sink or swim on our own; we did not get a letter or a telephone call asking how we were or did we need anything. Or even, thank you for all the weapons you found and lives that you helped save, and thank you for your time with us.

I asked Ernie if he had asked for the Military Cross or the Military Medal that we were told we were getting. He replied that he hadn't and that what we had caught was that old Army disease: 'out of sight out of mind,' and that other one called 'you're just a number.' I shall never forget the way we were left to fend for our selves with no help and no advice from any one in the Regiment; it was and is, an unforgivable act of neglect and one that has never been put right. To add insult to injury, our Northern Ireland medals were sent to us by post, and given to us by the post NCO; now that was insulting!

Back in November 1971, I was sent from the Royal Victoria Hospital to the Military Hospital in Musgrave Park Hospital Belfast for a couple of weeks and then I was put on a military plane to England. I ended up at the Royal Herbert Hospital at Woolwich and from there I went to the Rehabilitation unit at RAF Chessington, Surrey for nearly two years. In all that time, I did not have a visit from anyone in the Queen's Regiment, unlike those from the other Regiments who got welfare visits all the time; we were really left out in the cold like orphans. With us was another Queen's man called Colin Wattern who had been shot in the head; he is now at this time in the 'Star and Garter' home in Richmond Surrey, and with my help he did get the odd visit and presents from RHQ, as he will have to be looked after for the rest of his life. Whilst I was in Rehabilitation in Chessington, I tried to help him as much as I could and even told the Battalion on my return. I would liked to have said more about the way we were treated, but that would not be fair to any one, as they were getting ready to go to Gibraltar.

I have and do help other disabled ex soldiers, as much as I can and put them in contact with other organisations that have helped them; certainly much more than the help I got from any one in the Queen's Regiment.

Jim, Argyll and Sutherland Highlanders

As a footnote, I worked in a computer shop and was introduced to a young woman. She was concerned about her brother coming out of Sandhurst and going to Afghanistan (2008) with the Argylls. She said she had an uncle, a 2nd Lieutenant whom she'd never seen, as he was killed in Crossmaglen. Immediately I knew it was Stewart Gardiner and asked if it was him; she said 'Yes.' I said that I was there when he died; neither of us spoke and eventually she left. 30 odd years on and I still choke; his face, and that incident as clear today as it was in September 1972.

Major Peter Oakley, King's Regiment

I have seen through many years of service both men and women on operations and have a deep respect for their professionalism, dedication and devotion to duty. Going on, despite the odds, displaying so many acts of unrewarded bravery, never giving in and always with a good dose of humour, even if sometimes black. Truly the best Army in the world and I was so very proud to serve with them and to serve for them.

My final thoughts? Men and women die serving their Queen and Country; why therefore are the returning servicemen and women killed in action not met, if not by the Queen, then by a senior member of the Royal Family? A member of the Government, no matter who or how well intentioned is just not sufficient. And at long last for those who lose their lives on operations there is to be some formal recognition for their families; why did that take so long?

EPILOGUE

Terry Friend, Royal Artillery

I lived in Belfast, both in and out of uniform, for 12 months. In early January, 1972, Jeanette and I were walking down a street in Cheltenham, job hunting, for we had just left Northern Ireland a few days previously. The morning was crisp, bright and very sunny. As we walked along, hand in hand, a passing car backfired several times and, without a moment's hesitation, we both dived into a nearby shop doorway. During my flight, I distinctly remember being shocked that no one else had reacted to the sudden noise! And then it dawned on me, just as quickly, that this was not a street in Belfast and there was no reason for the passers-by to react at all. We both felt rather foolish as we recovered our composure and resumed our job-hunting chore. It occurred to me that, after all that time in the midst of the hatred and violence that passed for daily life in Belfast, a certain amount of adjustment would be required on our part in order to fit back into normal life again.

Would, indeed, anything ever be normal again?

Gareth Dyer, Royal Irish Regiment

The night Op Banner officially ceased I was a serving police officer, on night shift. I was also an ex squaddie with two turns at Op Banner. At about ten minutes to midnight I excused myself and went into the station yard with a brew in hand. I found a quiet spot, sat down and reflected. A hundred and one thoughts, feelings and images from my own past whirled about my head. I tried to nail a couple that I thought were significant and concentrate on them, but my head was swimming. I looked around the station yard and thought of the sights, the conversations the feelings and emotions this one single station had seen, heard and felt over the last few decades.

I'm not a religious man but as the church bell in the town centre struck midnight I said a small prayer of thanks. And then I stood up, finished my brew, gave my eyes a rub and went back to work.

THE DEATH OF AN ARTILLERYMAN

'Onion' NIVA and Royal Artillery

I left the army in 1977 shortly after my second tour of NI which had been based at the Ormeau Road gasworks bordering on the Republican Markets area just south of Belfast city centre. I was just 21 years old having joined as a boy soldier aged 15. Like many before and since, I struggled to adjust and settle down in 'Civvie Street' being briefly homeless. With the help of family, friends and the love of a good woman, I eventually came good and am now in a well paid job I enjoy helping others.

At first, I was constantly reminded through press and TV of the continuing 'Troubles'. I sought to box off my memories of NI and keep them tucked away somewhere at the back of my mind whilst getting on with the rest of my life. But, over the last few years, something had been nagging away at the back of my mind. With age comes a sense of looking back so I suppose what happened was that bit by bit the string around the box I'd stored away started to unravel bringing back the memories. One memory in particular – that of my friend George Muncaster.

I wasn't there, I didn't witness it. George Muncaster wasn't in our section or troop; he was based at the Mission Hall on Cromac Square maybe half a mile away. But we were fellow junior leaders, both worked on the command post, lived in the same barrack block in Germany, ate and drank together but he died and I didn't. So why did I feel guilty after all these years? Why was he robbed of his life and I wasn't? Why did I go on to make a relative success of my life? Why so many whys? Nowadays it's recognised as survivor's guilt, PTSD, and then it wasn't. You just got on with things, or didn't. Many a single soldier failed to readjust to 'normal' life after returning to BAOR and either went AWOL or bought themselves out; I did.

At the time things were beginning to bother me again I discovered the internet and the Northern Ireland Veterans Association. They helped me come to terms with myself and recognise what was bothering me. Most days I'm OK but on others feel like crap for no apparent reason except now I know why. What can I do? Well, if nothing else, I can make sure George's life is not forgotten along with all the others left behind, not just names in a long list of names of those that gave their all for a nation that all too soon forgets.

When you visit the National Memorial Arboretum at Alrewas in Staffordshire, make the long walk down to the Ulster Ash Grove and visit George who is commemorated by tree number 183 planted in honour of his life lost. Look around and behold the forest of young trees planted to remember other fallen young comrades and say hello. Tell him and the others they are missed by family and friends alike. Tell him to rest quietly with his new friends and let your eyes fill up and the tears fall, as mine do now writing this, then stand proud and remember, remember the sacrifice of giving his life in war so others can enjoy the peace, never to be forgotten, not while we live on and the trees grow.

Obituary from the Regimental Journal of 49 Field Regiment, Royal Artillery:

'Gunner George Muncaster – It was just past 10 o'clock on Sunday night 23rd January that one of our best known and best liked friends was callously murdered whilst patrolling with his section on the hard line Republican streets of the Markets. Scouse was a man who smiled well and whose contribution to the happiness and welfare of our community was always large. His discos were a regular success, generally noisy and always jolly. Our Battery dances will never be the same again. Coming from the Junior Leader's Regiment in 1974 he immediately became one of the Regiment. Football was his great love and on a number of occasions he played for the Regiment as goalkeeper. During his Northern Ireland tour he was a rifleman in 1 Troop based on the Mission Hall. To his parents, brother, sisters and friends, we join in deep sympathy and sorrow. We are proud to have served alongside him.'

George Mitchell Muncaster, 55 (The Residency) Field Battery Royal Artillery, died 23/1/77 aged 19 years.

As a footnote, I have since visited his grave in Bootle, walked past a mural on Friendly Street, Belfast, commemorating the 3 bombers and stood at the spot, (more or less, due to redevelopment), where George fell and paid silent tribute 30 years later. Job done.

So, it's all over; peace is here; entrepreneurs sell tickets for tours around the 'murder mile' uncaring of the tragedy which resulted from the collective madness, just so long as they put bums on seats. British young men from the same streets of England from whence came Tommy Stoker, Vincent Scott, Dave Walker, Keith Bates, Derek Reed and Ian Harris, now choose Belfast as a cheap and prime location for a 'stag weekend.' They would be the same ages as many of those who served and fell; they would, for instance be the same age as Stephen Beacham, killed at Coshquin in 1990 or Bob Bankier killed in Belfast's Markets area in 1971. They will walk the streets of central Belfast and pour lager and vodka down their throats on the same streets that British soldiers like James Nowastad were gunned down by cowards; and they will walk along past shops in Donegal Street where the blood of those killed in the Abercorn restaurant stained the pavements.

But is it all over? I have never believed for a second that the IRA or INLA or the other paramilitaries have decommissioned their weapons and explosives and that all it will take is one spark to ignite the simmering sectarian hatred which still exists; under the surface sometimes, on the surface at other times but it still exists.

I am in my late 50s and I pray that it does not happen again in my lifetime or my children's lifetimes or my grand children's lifetimes. Perhaps if someone reads this in a hundred years time, in say 2109, they will know if my words are prophetic or not.

Northern Ireland Roll of Honour

(1,188 Military Names)

9/12 Lancers

LT JOHN GARNER-RICHARDS	4/04/75:	RTA in Co Armagh in suspicious circumstances

13/18 Hussars

TROOPER ROBERT BARRACLOUGH	28/09/75:	RTA
TROOPER PAUL SHEPHERDSON	16/07/78:	RTA
TROOPER PHILIP SMITH	27/07/78:	RTA

14/20 King's Hussars and 15/19 King's Royal Hussars

SGT JOHN PLATT	3/02/71:	Killed in RTA following IRA ambush at Aldergrove
CPL IAN ARMSTRONG	29/08/71:	Ambushed at Crossmaglen
2ND LT ROBERT WILLIAMS-WYNN	13/08/72:	Shot by sniper in West Belfast
TROOPER JOHN TYSON	28/02/74:	RTA
CPL MICHAEL COTTON	20/03/74:	Killed in friendly fire Co Armagh
CPL MICHAEL HERBERT	20/03/74:	Killed in same incident
SGT WILLIAM ROBERTSON	8/02/75:	Shot by sniper Mullan, Co Fermanagh
TROOPER GARY LINES	28/05/79:	RTA

15/19 Hussars

TPR DAVID JOHNSON	18/10/71:	Accidental shooting
TPR JOHN MAJOR	29/11/74:	Death by violent or unnatural causes
SGT WILLIAM ROBSON	7/02/75:	DoW after being shot by IRA at Mullan, Fermanagh

17/ 21st Lancers

CPL TERENCE WILLIAMS	5/05/73:	Booby Trap bomb Crossmaglen
TROOPER JOHN GIBBONS	5/05/73:	Killed in same incident
TROOPER KENEALY	14/09/73:	Killed in training accident Gosford Castle

16/5th Lancers

CPL DAVID POWELL	28/10/71:	Bomb attack Kinawley, Co Fermanagh
2/LT ANDREW SOMERVILLE	27/03/73:	IRA landmine near Omagh

1st Regiment Royal Horse Artillery

GUNNER TIMOTHY UTTERIDGE	19/10/84:	Shot on the Turf Lodge, Belfast

5 Regiment Army Air Corps

SGT I C REID	24/06/72:	IRA landmine, Glenshane Pass, Co Antrim
L/CPL D MOON	24/06/72:	Killed in same incident
PTE C STEVENSON	24/06/72:	Killed in the same incident
C/SGT A PLACE	18/05/73:	Booby trap bomb, Knock-na-Moe Hotel, Omagh
C.O.FH. BR COX	18/05/73:	Killed in the same incident
SGT DB READ	18/05/73:	Killed in the same incident
SGT S YOUNG	18/05/73:	Killed in the same incident

WO. D C ROWAT	12/04/74:	Killed by IRA landmine, location unknown
MAJOR. J D HICKS	18/12/75:	Aircraft accident
WO. B A JACKSON	7/01/76:	Aircraft accident
CAPTAIN MJ KETT	10/04/78:	Killed in helicopter accident
CAPTAIN. A J STIRLING	2/12/78:	Killed in helicopter accident
CPL RD ADCOCK	2/12/78:	Killed in helicopter accident
CPL. R JACKSON	5/07/80:	RTA
CPL B McKENNA	6/04/82:	Died of natural causes on duty
L/CPL. S J ROBERTS	28/11/83:	RTA
L/CPL. T ORANGE	20/10/87:	RTA
S/SGT. J N P CROFT	14/08/89:	Violent or unnatural causes
CAPTAIN ANDREW NICOLL	22/12/03:	Helicopter crash Londonderry
SERGEANT SIMON BENNETT.	22/12/03:	Killed in same incident

5th Royal Inniskilling Dragoon Guards

SGT FREDERICK WILLIAM DRAKE	3/06/73:	Died of wounds: bomb, Knock-na-Moe Hotel Omagh

Adjutant General's Corps

CPL GLEN A. SLAINE	3/11/95:	RTA
L/CPL PAUL MELLING	3/09/97:	Natural causes

Argyll and Sutherland Highlanders

L/CPL DUNCAN MCPHEE	10/09/72:	IRA landmine Dungannon
PTE DOUGLAS RICHMOND	10/09/72:	Killed in same incident
2nd LT STEWART GARDINER	22/10/72:	Shot by IRA sniper Drumuckavall, Armagh
PTE D. HARPER	12/11/72:	Killed in train accident
CAPT WILLIAM WATSON	20/11/72:	IRA booby trap Cullyhanna
C/SGT JAMES STRUTHERS	20/11/72:	Killed in the same incident
PTE JOHN McGARRY	28/11/72:	Friendly fire
PTE DOUGLAS MCKELVIE	20/08/79:	RTA
CPL OWEN MCQUADE	11/11/80:	Shot outside Altnagelvin hospital, Londonderry
CPL STEWART MARSHALL	20/08/98:	RTA
PTE WILLIAM BROWN	20/08/98:	RTA
PTE STEVEN CRAW.	20/08/98:	RTA

Army Catering Corps

PTE LEONARD THOMPSON	31/12/71:	RTA
SGT PETER GIRVAN	12/02/77:	RTA
PTE TERENCE M. ADAM	6/12/82:	INLA bomb attack: Droppin' Well, Ballykelly
PTE PAUL JOSEPH DELANEY	6/12/82:	Killed in same incident
PTE JOHN MAYER	19/03/83:	RTA
PTE RICHARD R. BIDDLE	9/04/83:	IRA booby trapped car, Omagh

Army Cadet Force

CAPTAIN PAUL RODGERS	19/04/79:	Shot by IRA sniper near the Falls Road, Belfast

Army Intelligence Corps

CORPORAL JOHN ROESER	31/08/78:	RTA

| CORPORAL MICHAEL BLOOR | 31/08/78: | Killed in same RTA |
| CORPORAL PAUL HARMAN | 14/12/77: | Killed on covert op by IRA Monagh road, Belfast |

Army Physical Training Corps

| WO2 DAVID BELLAMY | 19/11/79: | IRA ambush, Springfield Road, Belfast |

Black Watch

| L/CPL EDWIN CHARNLEY | 18/11/71: | Shot by sniper in East Belfast |
| PTE MARK D. CARNIE | 19/07/78: | IRA bomb Dungannon |

Blues & Royals

TROOPER EDWARD MAGGS	25/02/79:	Death by violent or unnatural causes
STAFF CPL JOHN TUCKER	25/02/79:	Death by violent or unnatural causes
TROOPER ANTHONY DYKES	5/04/79:	Shot by IRA snipers, Andersonstown RUC station
TROOPER ANTHONY THORNETT	5/04/79:	Killed in same incident
LT DENIS DALY	20/07/82:	Killed in Hyde Park bomb outrage
SQMC R BRIGHT	23/07/82:	DoW from same incident
TROOPER SIMON TIPPER	23/07/82:	Killed in same incident
L/CPL JEFFERY YOUNG	23/07/82:	Killed in same incident

Cheshire Regiment

PTE D.A. SMITH	4/07/74:	DoW after being shot, Ballymurphy Estate, Belfast
PTE NEIL WILLIAMS	6/12/82:	IRA bomb Droppin' Well pub, Ballykelly
PTE ANTHONY WILLIAMSON	6/12/82:	Killed in same incident
L/CPL DAVID WILSON-STITT	6/12/82:	Killed in same incident
L/CPL STEVEN BAGSHAW	6/12/82:	Killed in same incident
L/CPL CLINTON COLLINS	6/12/82:	Killed in same incident
L/CPL PHILIP MCDONOUGH	6/12/82:	Killed in same incident
PTE DAVID MURREY	6/12/82:	Killed in same incident

Coldstream Guards

SGT ANTHONY METCALF	27/08/72:	IRA sniper Creggan Heights, Londonderry
GUARDSMAN ROBERT PEARSON	20/02/73:	Killed by IRA snipers, Lower Falls, Belfast
GUARDSMAN MICHAEL SHAW	20/02/73:	Killed in same incident
GUARDSMAN MICHAEL DOYLE	21/02/73:	Killed by sniper, Fort Whiterock, Belfast
GUARDSMAN ANTON BROWN	6/03/74:	Killed by sniper, Ballymurphy Estate, Belfast
CAPTAIN ANTHONY POLLEN	14/04/74:	Shot on a mission, Bogside, Londonderry
L/CPL SIMON WARE	17/08/91:	IRA landmine explosion, Cullyhanna, Armagh
CPL JOHN SPENSLEY		RTA

Devon & Dorset Regiment

PTE CHARLES STENTIFORD	21/01/72:	IRA landmine, Keady, Co Armagh
PTE DAVID CHAMP	10/02/72:	IRA landmine, Cullyhanna, Co Armagh
SGT IAN HARRIS	10/02/72:	Killed in same incident
CPL STEVEN WINDSOR	6/11/74:	Killed by sniper, Crossmaglen
CPL GERALD JEFFERY	7/04/83:	DoW, IRA bomb, Falls Road, Belfast
L/CPL STEPHEN TAVERNER	5/11/83:	Dow, IRA bomb, Crossmaglen

Duke of Edinburgh's Royal Regiment

CPL JOSEPH LEAHY	8/03/73:	DoW, booby trap, Forkhill, Co Armagh
S/SGT BARRINGTON FOSTER	23/03/73:	Murdered off-duty by the IRA
CAPTAIN NIGEL SUTTON	14/08/73:	Died in vehicle accident, Ballykinler
PTE MICHAEL SWANICK	28/10/74:	IRA van bomb attack, Ballykinler
PTE BRIAN ALLEN	6/11/74:	Killed by sniper, Crossmaglen
PTE JOHN RANDALL	26/06/93:	Killed by sniper, Newtownhamilton, Co Armagh
L/CPL KEVIN PULLIN	17/07/93:	Killed by sniper, Crossmaglen
MAJOR RICHARD ALLEN	2/06/94:	Helicopter crash, Mull of Kintyre

Duke Of Wellington's Regiment

PTE GEORGE LEE	6/06/72:	IRA sniper, Ballymurphy Estate, Belfast
CPL TERRENCE GRAHAM	16/07/72:	Landmine attack, Crossmaglen
PTE JAMES LEE	16/07/72:	Killed in same incident
PTE BRIAN ORAM	7/04/73:	RTA
CPL DAVID TIMSON	7/04/73:	Killed in same incident
PTE JOSEPH MCGREGOR	24/05/73:	RTA
2ND LT HOWARD FAWLEY	25/01/74:	Landmine attack, Ballyronan Co Londonderry
CPL MICHAEL RYAN	17/03/74:	IRA sniper at Brandywell, Londonderry
CPL ERROL PRYCE	26/01/80:	IRA sniper, Ballymurphy Estate, Belfast
PTE JAMES RIGG	25/11/88:	RTA

Gloucestershire Regiment

PTE ANTHONY ASPINWALL	16/12/71:	DoW after gun battle in Lower falls area, Belfast
PTE KEITH BRYAN	5/01/72:	IRA sniper, Lower Falls area, Belfast
CPL IAN BRAMLEY	2/02/72:	IRA sniper Hastings Street RUC station, Belfast
PTE GEOFFREY BREAKWELL	17/07/73:	IRA booby trap, Divis St Flats, Belfast
PTE CHRISTOPHER PATRICK	17/07/73:	Killed in same incident
PTE D.J. McCHILL	17/08/78:	Died during the tour – not as a result of terrorist actions
L/CPL A P. BENNETT	4/06/80:	Killed in vehicle accident, Limavady

Gordon Highlanders

WO2 ARTHUR MCMILLAN	18/06/72:	Booby-trapped house in Lurgan, Co Down
SGT IAN MARK MUTCH	18/06/72:	Killed in same incident
L/CPL COLIN LESLIE	18/06/72:	Killed in same incident
L/CPL A.C. HARPER	8/08/72:	RTA
PTE MICHAEL GEORGE MARR	29/03/73:	Shot by sniper, Andersonstown, Belfast
CAPT RICHARD LAMB	17/05/77:	RTA
L/CPL JACK MARSHALL	28/08/77:	Shot in gun battle Ardoyne, Belfast

Green Howards

PTE MALCOLM HATTON	9/08/71:	Shot by sniper, Brompton Park, Ardoyne
PTE JOHN ROBINSON	14/08/71:	Shot by sniper in Ardoyne, Belfast
PTE GEORGE CROZIER	23/08/71:	Shot by sniper Flax St Mill, Ardoyne
L/CPL PETER HERRINGTON	17/09/71:	Shot by sniper, Brompton Park, Ardoyne
PTE PETER SHARP	1/10/71:	Shot on Kerrara Street, Ardoyne
PTE RAYMOND HALL	5/03/73:	DoW: Sniper attack, Belfast
PTE FREDERICK DICKS	5/06/74:	IRA sniper, Dungannon
MAJOR PETER WILLIS	17/07/75:	IRA bomb, Ford's Cross, Armagh

CPL IAN METCALF	15/06/88:	IRA booby trapped lorry, Lisburn

Grenadier Guards

CAPTAIN ROBERT NAIRAC G.C.	14/05/77:	Murdered by IRA on undercover mission
GUARDSMAN GRAHAM DUGGAN	21/12/78:	Killed in attack on Army patrol, Crossmaglen
GUARDSMAN KEVIN JOHNSON	21/12/78:	Killed in same incident
GUARDSMAN GLEN LING	21/12/78:	Killed in same incident
CAPTAIN HERBERT WESTMACOTT	2/05/80:	Killed on undercover mission in Belfast
GUARDSMAN PAUL MACDONALD	5/03/86:	RTA on duty at Ballkelly
GUARDSMAN BRIAN HUGHES	11/03/86:	Killed in same RTA
GUARDSMAN DANIEL BLINCO	30/12/93:	IRA sniper in South Armagh

The Highlanders

HIGHLANDER S. HARRINGTON	9/07/95:	Accidentally shot

Intelligence Corps

CPL PAUL HARMAN	14/12/77:	Killed after his vehicle was hijacked, Turf Lodge, Belfast
SGT JOHN ROESER	31/08/78:	RTA
CPL MICHAEL BLOOR	31/08/78:	Killed in same incident
CPT HENRIETTA STEEL-MORTIMER	11/06/98:	RTA

Irish Guards

SGT PHILLIP PRICE	21/07/72:	Killed by car bomb, 'Bloody Friday' Belfast
GUARDSMAN DAVID ROBERTSON	24/11/73:	IRA landmine, Crossmaglen
GUARDSMAN SAMUEL MURPHY	14/11/77:	Murdered in front of his mother whilst on leave, Andersonstown, Belfast

King's Own Royal Border Regiment

C/SERGEANT WILLIAM BOARDLEY	10/05/72:	Shot in Strabane by IRA gunman
PRIVATE RODING	72:	Died of natural causes after being taken ill.
CORPORAL JAMES BURNEY	19/12/78:	IRA sniper, Newington, Belfast
PTE OC PAVEY	11/03/80:	Accidental shooting, Crossmaglen
PTE JOHN B. BATEMAN	15/03/80:	IRA sniper, Crossmaglen
PTE SEAN G. WALKER	21/03/80:	DoW, car bomb, Crossmaglen
L/CORPORAL ANTHONY DACRE	27/03/85:	Bomb attack, Divis street flats, Belfast
PTE HATFIELD	24/02/92:	Vehicle accident, Londonderry
PTE MK THOMAS	17/05/95:	Vehicle accident, Belfast
PTE DR MILRAY	21/02/95:	Road accident
WOII MC WHITE	13/12/01:	Training accident, Ballykinler

King's Own Scottish Borderers

S/SGT PETER SINTON	28/07/70:	Violent or unnatural causes
L/CPL PETER DEACON SIME	7/04/72:	IRA sniper, Ballymurphy Est. Belfast
L/CPL BARRY GOLD	24/04/72:	DoW after gun battle at VCP in Belfast
C/SGT HENRY S. MIDDLEMASS	10/12/72:	IRA booby trap, Turf Lodge, Belfast
S/SGT H. SHINGLESTON MM.	25/11/76:	Cause of death unknown
PTE P. B. SCOTT	10/10/79:	RTA
PTE JAMES HOUSTON	13/12/89:	Killed at VCP in gun and grenade attack, Fermanagh
L/CPL MICHAEL JOHN PATERSON	13/12/89:	Killed in same incident

King's Regiment

CPL ALAN BUCKLEY	13/05/72:	Shot on Turf Lodge, Belfast
PTE EUSTACE HANLEY	23/05/72:	IRA sniper Ballymurphy Estate
PTE MARCEL DOGLAY	30/05/72:	IRA bomb, Springfield Road, Belfast
PTE JAMES JONES	18/07/72:	IRA sniper, New Barnsley, Belfast
PTE BRIAN THOMAS	24/07/72:	IRA sniper, New Barnsley, Belfast
PTE RENNIE LAYFIELD	18/08/72:	IRA sniper, Falls Road, Belfast
PTE ROY CHRISTOPHER	30/08/72:	DoW after bomb attack, Cupar St, Belfast
SGT DENNIS DOOLEY	15/03/75:	RTA Outside of Londonderry; died in hospital
PTE DAVID OWEN	14/10/75:	Died of natural causes
PTE PETER KAVANAGH	14/11/75:	Death by violent or unnatural causes
PTE CHRISTOPHER SHANLEY	11/04/79:	Ambushed and shot Ballymurphy Estate, Belfast
L/CPL STEPHEN RUMBLE	19/04/79:	DoW from same incident
L/CPL ANDREW WEBSTER	19/05/79:	Bomb attack, Turf Lodge, Belfast
PTE STEPHEN BEACHAM	24/10/90:	Killed by IRA 'proxy bomb' Coshquin, nr Londonderry. 5 soldiers killed
L/CPL STEPHEN BURROWS	24/10/90:	Killed in same incident
PTE VINCENT SCOTT	24/10/90:	Killed in same incident
PTE DAVID SWEENEY	24/10/90:	Killed in same incident
PTE PAUL WORRALL	24/10/90:	Killed in same incident

Life Guards

CPL of HORSE LEONARD DUBER	21/02/73:	DoW after riot in Belfast

Light Infantry
1st Battalion

PTE. R V JONES	18/08/72:	Shot by sniper in West Belfast
PTE. R ROWE	28/08/72:	Shot accidentally in Ardoyne, Belfast
PTE. TA STOKER	19/09/72:	DoW after accidental shooting in Flex St Mill, Ardoyne
PTE. T RUDMAN	30/09/72:	Shot in Ardoyne, Belfast (Brother killed in 1971 in Northern Ireland)
PTE. S R HALL	28/10/73:	Shot in Crossmaglen
PTE. G M CURTIS	10/06/83:	IRA bomb, Ballymurphy Estate, Belfast
PTE. N I BLYTHE	12/11/87:	Killed in accident
PTE. J J WILLBY	6/02/88:	Violent or unnatural causes
PTE. B BISHOP	20/08/88:	Killed in Ballygawley coach bombing; one of 8 soldiers killed
PTE. P L BULLOCK	20/08/88:	Killed in same incident
PTE. J BURFITT	20/08/88:	Killed in same incident
PTE. R GREENER	20/08/88:	Killed in same incident
PTE. A S LEWIS	20/08/88:	Killed in same incident
PTE. M A NORWORTHY	20/08/88	Killed in same incident
PTE. S J WILKINSON	20/08/88:	Killed in same incident
PTE. J WINTER	20/08/88:	Killed in same incident
PTE. G SMITH	3/12/88:	Violent or unnatural causes
PTE. A J RICHARDSON	12/03/97:	Killed in attempted ambush by IRA after ceasefire.

2nd Battalion

PTE. J R RUDMAN	14/10/71:	Shot in Coalisland area
SGT. A W WHITELOCK	24/08/72:	IRA sniper in Londonderry

CPL. T P TAYLOR	13/05/73:	Killed in bomb attack, Donegall Road
PTE. J GASKELL	14/05/73:	DoW from same incident
PTE. R B ROBERTS	1/07/73:	Shot by sniper in Ballymurphy Estate, Belfast
PTE. R STAFFORD	20/07/79:	Killed in car accident
PTE. P TURNER	28/08/92:	IRA sniper, Crossmaglen

3rd Battalion

PTE. P K EASTAUGH	23/03/71:	Shot accidentally in the Ardoyne area of Belfast
CPL. I R MORRILL	28/08/72:	IRA sniper, Belfast (Att from RGJ)
LCPL. A KENNINGTON	28/02/73:	IRA sniper, Ardoyne area of Belfast
LCPL. C R MILLER	18/09/73:	Shot in West Belfast
PTE. R D TURNBULL	29/06/77:	Ambushed and shot West Belfast
PTE. M E HARRISON	29/06/77:	Killed in same incident
PTE. L J HARRISON	9/08/77:	IRA sniper, New Barnsley, Belfast
CPL. D P SALTHOUSE	7/12/82:	IRA bomb Droppiin' Well pub, Ballykelly

Light Infantry (Bn unknown)

L/CPL TERENCE WILSON	1/07/78:	RTA
PTE KEVIN MCGOVERN	3/07/78:	RTA

North Irish Militia

RANGER SAMUEL M. GIBSON.	24/10/74:	Abducted and murdered off duty (TA)
CPL WESLEY REA		RTA (TA)

Parachute Regiment

PTE PETER DOCHERTY	21/05/70:	Accidental death
PTE VICTOR CHAPMAN	24/06/70	Drowned
SGT. M WILLETTS GC.	25/05/71:	Killed saving civilians in IRA bomb blast, Springfield Road, Belfast
PTE. R A BARTON	14/07/71:	Shot protecting comrades, Andersonstown, Belfast
FATHER GERRY WESTON, MBE	22/02/72:	Killed in IRA bomb outrage, Aldershot
PTE. A KELLY	18/03/72:	Killed in accident, Holywood, Co Down
PTE. C STEPHENSON	24/06/72:	IRA landmine, Glenshane Pass, Londonderry
PTE. F T BELL	20/10/72:	DoW after being shot on Ballymurphy Estate, Belfast
CPL. S N HARRISON	7/04/73:	IRA landmine, Tullyogallaghan
L/CPL. T D BROWN	7/04/73:	Killed in same incident
L/CPL. D A FORMAN	16/04/73:	Accidentally shot, Flax Street Mill, Ardoyne
WO2. W R VINES	5/05/73:	IRA landmine, Crossmaglen
A/SGT. J WALLACE	24/05/73:	IRA booby trap, Crossmaglen
PTE. R BEDFORD	16/03/74:	Shot in IRA ambush, Crossmaglen
PTE. P JAMES	16/03/74:	Killed in same incident
PTE. W SNOWDON	28/06/76:	IRA bomb, Crossmaglen
PTE. J BORUCKI	8/08/76:	IRA booby trap, Crossmaglen
L/CPL. D A JONES	17/03/78:	Shot in gun battle, Glenshane Pass, Londonderry
PTE. J FISHER	12/07/78:	IRA booby trap, Crossmaglen
CPL. R D ADCOCK	2/12/78:	Killed in helicopter accident

MAJ. P J FURSMAN	27/08/79:	Killed in IRA double bomb blast, Warrenpoint. One of 16 Paras and 2 other soldiers killed
WO2. W BEARD	27/08/79:	Killed in same incident
SGT. I A ROGERS	27/08/79:	Killed in same incident
CPL. N J ANDREWS	27/08/79:	Killed in same incident
CPL. J C GILES	27/08/79:	Killed in same incident
CPL. L JONES	27/08/79:	Killed in same incident
L/CPL. CG IRELAND	27/08/79:	Killed in same incident
PTE. G I BARNES	27/08/79:	Killed in same incident
PTE. D F BLAIR	27/08/79:	Killed in same incident
PTE. R DUNN	27/08/79:	Killed in same incident
PTE. R N ENGLAND	27/08/79:	Killed in same incident
PTE. R D U JONES	27/08/79:	Killed in same incident
PTE. T R VANCE	27/08/79:	Killed in same incident
PTE. J A VAUGHAN-JONES	27/08/79:	Killed in same incident
PTE. A G WOOD	27/08/79:	Killed in same incident
PTE. M WOODS	27/08/79:	Killed in same incident
PTE. P S GRUNDY	16/12/79:	IRA booby trap, Forkhill
LT. S G BATES	1/01/80:	Shot accidentally, OP at Forkhill
PTE. G M R HARDY	1/01/80:	Killed in same incident
A/SGT. B M BROWN	9/08/80:	IRA booby trap, Forkhill
L/CPL. P HAMPSON	25/12/81:	Violent or unnatural causes
L/CPL. M C MAY	26/07/82:	RTA
SGT. A I SLATER MM	2/12/84:	Killed in anti-IRA operation, Fermanagh
SGT. M B MATTHEWS	29/07/88:	DoW, IRA landmine, Cullyhanna
PTE. R SPIKINS	25/03/89:	RTA, Belfast
L/CPL. S WILSON	18/11/89:	IRA landmine, Mayobridge (3 soldiers killed)
PTE. D MACAULAY	18/11/89:	Killed in same incident
PTE. M MARSHALL	18/11/89:	Killed in same incident
PTE. A HARRISON	19/06/91:	Murdered by IRA in fiancée's home, East Belfast
L/CPL. R COULSON	27/06/92:	Drowned crossing a river
L/CPL. P H SULLIVAN	27/06/92:	Drowned trying to rescue his friend
PTE. M B LEE	20/08/92:	Violent or unnatural causes
PTE PETER F.J. GROSS	13/03/93:	RTA
PTE. P F J GROSS	13/05/93:	Accidental death at Holywood
PTE. C D KING	4/12/94:	Violent or unnatural causes
PTE. M A RAMSEY	21/08/97:	Died in an accident

Prince Of Wales' Own Regiment of Yorkshire

S/SGT ARTHUR PLACE	18/05/73:	Booby trap bomb, Knock-na-Moe Hotel, Omagh
PTE DAVID WRAY	10/10/75:	DoW after being shot Creggan area, Londonderry

Princess Of Wales' Royal Regiment

MAJOR JOHN BARR	26/11/92:	Helicopter crash, Bessbrook Mill

Queen's Lancashire Regiment

SGT JAMES SINGLETON	23/06/70:	Died on duty
PTE MICHAEL MURTAGH	6/02/73:	Killed in rocket attack Lower Falls area, Belfast

PTE EDWIN WESTON	14/02/73:	IRA sniper Divis Street area, Belfast
PTE STEPHEN KEATING	3/03/73:	IRA sniper, Manor Street, West Belfast
PTE GARY BARLOW	4/03/73:	Gun battle, Lower Falls area, Belfast
PTE JOHN GREEN	8/03/73:	Shot whilst guarding school in Lower Falls area, Belfast
L/CPL WILLIAM RIDDELL	6/01/76:	RTA
PTE IAN O'CONNER	3/03/87:	Grenade attack, Divis Street flats, Belfast
PTE JOSEPH LEACH	4/06/87:	IRA sniper, Andersonstown, Belfast
L/CPL ANTONY HALTON	25/10/99:	RTA

Queen's Own Highlanders

PTE WILLIAM MCINTYRE	11/10/72:	DoW IRA landmine, Dungannon. Killed with 2 other Soldiers from Argyll & Sutherlands
PTE JAMES HESKETH	10/12/73:	Shot dead on Lower Falls, Belfast
PTE ALAN JOHN MCMILLAN	8/07/79:	Remote-controlled bomb in Crossmaglen
L/CPL D. LANG	24/08/79:	Killed in helicopter crash with another soldier
L/CPL D.A. WARES	24/08/79:	Killed in same accident
LT/COL DAVID BLAIR	27/08/79:	Killed in IRA double bomb blast, Warrenpoint (one of 18 soldiers killed in same incident)
L/CPL VICTOR MACLEOD	27/08/79:	Killed in same incident
CPL R.D. TURNER	27/02/90:	Accidentally shot

Queen's Regiment

PTE DAVID PITCHFORD	27/06/70:	RTA
PTE PAUL CARTER	15/09/71:	DoW after being shot at Royal Victoria Hospital, Belfast
PTE ROBERT BENNER	29/11/71:	Abducted & murdered by IRA off duty at Crossmaglen
PTE RICHARD SINCLAIR	31/10/72:	IRA sniper New Lodge, Belfast
PTE STANLEY EVANS	14/11/72:	IRA sniper Unity Flats complex, West Belfast
PTE PETER WOOLMORE	19/03/79:	Mortar bomb attack, Newtownhamilton, Co Armagh
PTE ALAN STOCK	15/10/83:	Remote-controlled bomb, Creggan, Londonderry
PTE NEIL CLARKE	24/04/84:	IRA sniper, Bishop Street, Londonderry
CPL ALEXANDER BANNISTER	8/08/88:	IRA sniper, New Barnsley, Belfast
SGT CHARLES CHAPMAN	16/07/90:	IRA booby trap, Army recruiting office, Wembley, London
PTE ROBERT BRIMBLECOOMBE		RTA

Queen's Royal Irish Hussars

TROOPER HUGH MCCABE	15/08/69	Killed by friendly fire, Divis Street, Belfast

Royal Air Force

FLT SGT JOHN WILLOUGHBY	7/12/69:	Natural Causes
LAC ROBERT CALDERBANK	10/07/71:	RTA
SAC STEPHEN HENSELER	12/03/80:	RTA
JNR TECH DAVID GILFILLAN	13/10/81:	RTA
SGT DAVID RIGBY	25/10/85:	Killed in Helicopter crash at Forkhill

CPL ISLANIA MAHESHKUMAR	26/10/89:	Shot by IRA in Wildenrath, West Germany and killed alongside baby daughter, Nivruti (6 months old)
SQN LDR MICHAEL HAVERSON	26/10/92:	Helicopter crash, Bessbrook Mill base, Armagh
FLT LT SIMON S.M.J. ROBERTS	26/10/92:	Killed in same accident
FLT SGT JAN PEWTRESS	26/10/92:	Killed in same accident

RAF Regiment

AIRMAN JOHN BAXTER	1/05/88:	IRA booby trap, at Nieuw-Bergan, Holland
AIRMAN JOHN MILLER	1/05/88:	Killed with his friend in the same incident
AIRMAN IAN SHINNER	1/05/88:	Killed by IRA sniper in Roermond, Holland
CPL IAN LEARMOUTH	30/08/89:	Unlawfully killed at VCP

Royal Anglian Regiment

MAJOR PETER TAUNTON	26/10/70:	Violent or unnatural causes
PTE BRIAN SHERIDAN	20/11/70:	RTA
PTE ROGER WILKINSON	11/10/71:	DoW after being shot on Letterkenny Rd, Londonderry
L/CPL IAN CURTIS	9/11/71:	IRA sniper Foyle Road, Londonderry
2/LT NICHOLAS HULL	16/04/72:	IRA sniper Divis Street flats, Belfast
PTE JOHN BALLARD	11/05/72:	IRA sniper, Sultan St. Lower Falls, Belfast
L/CPL MARTIN ROONEY	12/07/72:	IRA sniper Clonnard St., Lower Falls, Belfast
CPL KENNETH MOGG	13/07/72:	IRA sniper Dunville Park, Belfast
L/CPL JOHN BODDY	17/08/72:	IRA sniper, Grosvenor Road area of Belfast
CPL JOHN BARRY	25/09/72:	DoW after gun battle Lower Falls, Belfast
PTE IAN BURT	29/09/72:	IRA sniper Albert Street, Lower Falls, Belfast
PTE ROBERT MASON	24/10/72:	IRA sniper Naples St, Grosvenor Rd area, Belfast
PTE ANTHONY GOODFELLOW	27/04/73:	Shot manning VCP Creggan Estate, Londonderry
PTE N MARWICK	12/09/73:	Cause of death unknown
PTE PAUL WRIGHT	8/10/79:	Killed on covert operation , Falls Road area
PTE KEVIN BREWER	29/09/81:	RTA
PTE ANTHONY ANDERSON	24/05/82:	Killed by vehicle in confusion after petrol bomb attack Butcher Street, Londonderry
PTE MARTIN PATTEN	22/10/85:	Murdered off duty Limavady Rd Waterside,Londonderry
MAJOR ANDREW FRENCH	22/05/86:	Killed by remote-controlled bomb, Crossmaglen
PTE MITCHELL BERTRAM	9/07/86:	Remote-controlled bomb Glassdrumman, Crossmaglen
PTE CARL DAVIES	9/07/86:	Killed in the same incident
PTE DAVID J. KNIGHT	26/07/86:	RTA
PTE NICHOLAS PEACOCK	31/01/89:	Remote-controlled bomb Falls Road area, Belfast

Royal Army Dental Corps

SGT RICHARD MULDOON	23/03/73:	Murdered by the IRA whilst off duty.

Royal Army Medical Corps

PTE 'TAFFY' PORTER	21/04/72:	Violent or unnatural causes
WOII PHILLIP CROSS	2/11/91:	IRA bomb planted at Musgrave Park Hospital (killed with one other soldier)
CAPTAIN HARRY MURPHY	15/03/73:	Violent or unnatural causes
PTE BRIAN ARMSTRONG (TA)		RTA

Royal Army Pay Corps

PTE MICHAEL PRIME	16/02/72:	Shot in ambush at Moira roundabout near Lisburn
L/CPL HENRY M. MCGIVERN		RTA

Royal Army Ordnance Corps

CAPTAIN D A STEWARDSON	9/09/71:	Defusing IRA bomb Castlerobin, Antrim
WO2. C J L DAVIES	24/11/71:	Killed by IRA bomb in Lurgan
PTE T F McCANN	14/02/72:	Abducted and murdered by the IRA, Newtownbutler
SSGT. C R CRACKNELL	15/03/72:	IRA booby trap, Grosvenor Road, Belfast
SSGT. A S BUTCHER	15/03/72:	Killed in same incident
MAJOR B C CALLADENE	29/03/72:	IRA car bomb outside Belfast City Hall
CAPTAIN J H YOUNG	15/07/72:	Defusing IRA bomb, Silverbridge near Forkhill
WO2. WJ CLARK	3/08/72:	Defusing IRA bomb at Strabane
SGT. R E HILLS	5/12/72:	Attempting to make live shell safe Kitchen Hill
CAPTAIN B S GRITTEN	21/06/73:	Killed inspecting explosives, Lecky Road, Londonderry
SSGT. R F BECKETT	30/08/73:	Killed pulling bomb out of a post office Tullyhommon
CAPTAIN RONALD WILKINSON:	23/09/73:	Defusing IRA bomb, Edgbaston, Birmingham
2ND LT L. HAMILTON DOBBIE	3/10/73:	IRA bomb, Bligh's Lane post, Londonderry
SSGT. A N BRAMMAH	18/02/74:	Examining IRA road side bomb, Crossmaglen
SSGT. V I ROSE	7/11/74:	IRA landmine, Stewartstown, Tyrone
WO2. J A MADDOCKS	2/12/74:	Examining milk churn bomb Gortmullen
WO2. E GARSIDE	17/07/75:	Killed with 3 other soldiers IRA bomb nr Forkhill
CPL. C W BROWN	17/07/75:	Killed in same incident
CPL DOUGLAS WHITFIELD	13/03/76:	RTA
SGT MICHAEL G. PEACOCK	13/03/76:	Killed in same incident
SGT. M E WALSH	9/01/77:	Killed dismantling IRA bomb Newtownbutler
L/CPL MICHAEL DEARNEY	31/05/77:	RTA
SIG. P J REECE	2/08/79:	IRA landmine near Armagh
GNR. R .A .J. FURMINGER	2/08/79:	Killed in same incident
WO2. M O'NEIL	31/05/81:	Examining IRA bomb near Newry
PTE IAN ARCHIBALD	15/02/83:	RTA
L/CORPORAL DEREK W GREEN	15/06/88:	One of 6 soldiers killed by IRA booby trap, Lisburn
WO2. J R HOWARD	8/08/88:	IRA booby trap, Falls Road, Belfast

Royal Army Veterinary Corps

CPL BRIAN CRIDDLE, BEM	22/07/73:	DoW after being wounded whilst defusing IRA bomb
CPL. TERENCE O'NEIL	25/05/91:	Killed by hand grenade, North Howard St, Belfast

Royal Artillery

GUNNER ROBERT CURTIS	6/02/71:	Shot by IRA gunmen, New Lodge area, Belfast
L/BOMB JOHN LAURIE	15/02/71:	DoW after same incident
BOMBARDIER PAUL CHALLENOR	10/08/71:	IRA sniper, Bligh's Lane post, Londonderry
GNR CLIFFORD LORING	31/08/71:	DoW after being shot at VCP, Belfast
SGT MARTIN CARROLL	14/09/71:	IRA sniper Creggan, Londonderry
GNR ANGUS STEVENS	27/10/71:	IRA bomb attack, Rosemount RUC station, Belfast
L/BOMB DAVID TILBURY	27/10/71:	Killed in same incident
GNR IAN DOCHERTY	31/10/71:	DoW after being shot in Stockmans Lane, Belfast
GNR RICHARD HAM	29/12/71:	Shot dead in the Brandywell area of Londonderry
L/BOMB ERIC BLACKBURN	10/04/72:	Killed in bomb attack, Rosemount Avenue,
L/BOMB BRIAN THOMASSON	10/04/72:	Killed in same incident
GNR VICTOR HUSBAND	2/06/72:	IRA landmine, Rosslea, Co Fermanagh
GNR BRIAN ROBERTSON	2/06/72:	Killed in the same incident
SGT CHARLES COLEMAN	7/06/72:	IRA sniper, Andersonstown, Belfast
GUNNER WILLIAM RAISTRICK	11/06/72:	IRA sniper Brooke Park, Londonderry
BOMBARDIER TERRENCE JONES	11/06/72	Shot in the back by IRA, Londonderry
GNR LEROY GORDON	7/08/72:	IRA landmine, Lisnaskea, Co Fermanagh
L/BOMB DAVID WYNNE	7/08/72:	Killed in same incident
MAJOR DAVID STORRY	14/08/72:	Booby trap, Casement Park base, Andersonstown
GNR ROBERT CUTTING	3/09/72:	Accidentally shot, New Lodge area of Belfast
S/SGT CRAIG J. GARDNER	19/09/72:	RTA
GNR PAUL JACKSON	28/11/72:	Hit by bomb shrapnel, Strand Road, Londonderry
SGT IVOR W. SWAIN	23/03/73:	RTA
GNR IDWAL EVANS	11/04/73:	IRA sniper Bogside area of Londonderry
GNR KERRY VENN	28/04/73:	IRA sniper Shantallow Estate, Londonderry
SGT THOMAS CRUMP	3/05/73:	DoW after being shot in Londonderry
GNR JOSEPH BROOKES	25/11/73:	Shot in IRA ambush in Bogside area of Londonderry
BOMBARDIER HEINZ PISAREK	25/11/73:	Killed in same incident
SGT JOHN HAUGHEY	21/01/74:	Remote-controlled bomb, Creggan Estate, Londonderry
GNR LEONARD GODDEN	4/02/74:	Killed by IRA bomb on M62 in Yorkshire
BDR TERRENCE GRIFFIN	4/02.74:	Killed in same incident
GNR DAVID FARRINGTON	13/03/74:	Shot by IRA gunmen at Chapel Lane Belfast city centre
LT/COL JOHN STEVENSON	8/04/74:	Murdered by IRA gunmen at his home in Northumberland
GNR KIM MACCUNN	22/06/74:	IRA sniper New Lodge, Belfast
SGT BERNARD FEARNS	30/07/74:	IRA sniper New Lodge area of Belfast

GNR KEITH BATES	4/11/74:	RTA: Central Belfast
GNR RICHARD DUNNE	8/11/74:	IRA bomb in Woolwich, London pub bombings
GNR GEOFFREY B. JONES	9/06/75:	RTA
GNR CYRIL MACDONALD	18/12/75:	IRA bomb attack at Guildhall Square, Londonderry
GNR MARK ASHFORD	17/01/76:	Shot at checkpoint, Great James Street, Londonderry
GNR JAMES REYNOLDS	13/03/76:	RTA
GNR WILLIAM MILLER	3/07/76:	IRA sniper at checkpoint Butcher Street, Londonderry
GNR ANTHONY ABBOT	24/10/76:	Ambushed and killed by IRA, Ardoyne, Belfast
GNR MAURICE MURPHY	22/11/76:	DoW from same incident
GNR EDWARD MULLER	11/01/77:	IRA sniper at VCP in Old Park area of Belfast
GNR GEORGE MUNCASTER	23/01/77:	IRA sniper Markets area, Belfast
GNR PAUL SHEPPARD	1/03/78:	Shot in gun battle Clifton Park Avenue, Belfast
GNR RICHARD FURMINGER	02/08/79:	Killed in IRA landmine attack with RAOC comrade Cathedral Road, Armagh
GNR ALAN AYRTON	16/12/79:	Killed with 3 others in landmine explosion, Dungannon
GNR WILLIAM BECK	16/12/79:	Killed in same incident
GNR SIMON EVANS	16/12/79:	Killed in same incident
GNR KEITH RICHARDS	16/12/79:	Killed in same incident
GNR PETER A. CLARK	9/08/80	RTA
L/BOMB KEVIN WALLER	20/09/82:	Remote-controlled INLA bomb Divis St flats, Belfast
GNR LYNDON MORGAN	26/04/88:	IRA booby trap Carrickmore
GNR MILES AMOS	8/03/89:	IRA landmine, Buncrana Road, Londonderry
L/BOMB STEPHEN CUMMINS	8/03/89:	Killed in same incident
MAJOR MICHAEL DILLION-LEE	2/06/90:	Murdered outside his quarters in Dortmund, Germany
L/BOMB PAUL GARRETT	2/12/93:	IRA sniper Keady, Co Armagh
2 LT JAMES C. FOX	21/01/95:	Violent or unnatural causes
L/BOMB STEPHEN RESTORICK	12/02/97:	IRA sniper at VCP at Bessbrook Mill Army base
GNR JON COOPER	22/02/97:	Violent or unnatural causes

Royal Corps Signals

L/CPL MICHAEL SPURWAY	13/09/69:	Accidentally shot, Gosford Castle
SIGNALMAN PAUL GENGE	7/11/71:	Shot by IRA whilst off-duty in Lurgan
CPL JOHN AIKMAN	6/11/73:	Shot by IRA gunmen Newtownhamilton
SIGNALMAN MICHAEL E. WAUGH	4/02/74:	Killed by IRA bomb, M62, Yorkshire
SIGNALMAN LESLIE DAVID WALSH	4/02/74:	Killed in same incident
SIGNALMAN PAUL ANTHONY REID	4/02/74:	Killed in same incident
SIGNALMAN DAVID ROBERTS	13/03/76:	RTA
CPL AK FORD	7/01/76:	Aircraft accident
L/CPL RICHARD DAVIES	25/02/79:	RTA
SIGNALMAN PAUL J REECE	2/08/79:	IRA landmine, Armagh
SIGNALMAN BRIAN RICHARD CROSS	4/07/81:	Killed in road traffic accident, Lisburn

CPL MICHAEL WARD	1/04/82:	Shot with REME soldier by IRA in Bogside, Londonderry
SGT LESLIE MCKENZIE	24/05/83:	RTA
SIGNALMAN KENNETH ROYAL	28/03/85:	RTA
CPL DEREK T WOOD	19/03/88:	Beaten by mob, shot by IRA, Penny Lane, Belfast
CPL DAVID HOWES	19/03/88:	Killed in same incident
L/CPL GRAHAM P LAMBIE	15/06/88:	Killed by IRA bomb, Lisburn (1 of 6 soldiers killed)
SGT MICHAEL JAMES WINKLER	15/06/88:	Killed in same incident
SIGNALMAN MARK CLAVEY	15/06/88:	Killed in same incident
CPL WILLIAM J PATERSON	15/06/88:	Killed in same incident
S/SGT KEVIN A FROGGETT	16/09/89:	Shot by IRA repairing radio mast Coalisland RUC station
SGT MICHAEL NEWMAN	14/04/92:	Shot by INLA at Army Recruiting office, Derby, England
CPL PAUL SMITH	22/09/94:	RTA
CPL IAN BIBBY	23/11/99:	Violent or unnatural causes
SIGNALMAN THOMAS C. KANE		RTA
S/SGT DAVID CLARKE		RTA
SIGNALMAN LEONARD TURNER		RTA
SIGNALMAN BRIAN CROSS		RTA
SIGNALMAN NICHOLAS BREWER (TA)		RTA

Royal Corps Transport

MAJOR PHILIP COWLEY	13/01/70:	Died on duty
DRIVER STEPHEN BEEDIE	26/03/72:	RTA
DRIVER LAURENCE JUBB	26/04/72:	Killed in vehicle crash after mob attack, Armagh
L/CPL MICHAEL BRUCE	31/05/72:	IRA sniper Andersonstown, Belfast
S/SGT JOSEPH FLEMING	9/07/72:	Shot dead by IRA in Grosvenor Road area of Belfast
DRIVER PETER HEPPENSTALL	14/07/72:	IRA sniper Ardoyne area of Belfast
DRIVER STEPHEN COOPER	21/07/72:	IRA car bomb on 'Bloody Friday' Belfast bus depot
DRIVER RONALD KITCHEN	10/11/72:	IRA sniper at VCP in Old Park Road, Belfast
DRIVER MICHAEL GAY	17/03/73:	IRA landmine, Dungannon
SGT THOMAS PENROSE	24/03/73:	Murdered off-duty with 2 others, Antrim road, Belfast
CPL ANDREW GILMOUR	29/08/73:	RTA
L/CPL EDMOND CROSBIE	23/11/73:	RTA
DRIVER NORMAN MCKENZIE	11/04/74:	IRA landmine, Lisnaskea, Co Fermanagh
DRIVER HAROLD J. KING	19/04/75:	RTA
DRIVER WILLIAM KNIGHT	17/05/76:	RTA
SGT WILLIAM EDGAR	15/04/77:	Abducted and murdered by IRA whilst on leave in Londonderry
DRIVER STEVEN ATKINS	29/11/80:	RTA
DRIVER PAUL BULMAN	19/05/81:	Killed in IRA landmine attack along with 4 RGJs at Camlough, South Armagh
L/CPL NORMAN DUNCAN	22/02/89:	Shot by IRA waterside area of Londonderry
DVR C PANTRY	2/11/91:	Killed by IRA bomb at Musgrave Park hospital, Belfast
CPL KENNETH YOUNG (TA)		RTA

PTE MAURICE CARSON (TA)   RTA

Royal Dragoon Guards
TROOPER GEOFFREY KNIPE   7/08/72: Armoured vehicle crashed after mob attack, Armagh

Royal Electrical & Mechanical Engineers
CFN CHRISTOPHER EDGAR   13/09/69: Violent or unnatural causes
SGT S C REID   24/06/72: IRA milk churn bombs at Glenshane Pass, Londonderry
L/CPL D MOON   24/06/72: Killed in same incident
CFN BRIAN HOPE   14/08/72: IRA booby trap Casement Park, Andersonstown, Belfast
L/CPL COLIN HARKER   20/12/72: IRA sniper Lecky Road, Londonderry
SGT M E SELDON   30/06/74: Violent or unnatural causes
L/CPL ALISTER STEWART   9/10/74: RTA
CFN COLIN MCINNES   18/12/75: IRA bomb attack on Army base in Londonderry
CPL PETER BAILEY   5/04/80: RTA
CFN ALAN COOMBE   16/02/81: RTA
SGT MICHAEL BURBRIDGE   1/04/82: IRA sniper Rosemount barracks, Londonderry
SGT RT GREGORY   22/10/82: Died of natural causes on duty
WO1 (ASM) JAMES BRADWELL   11/10/96: DoW after car bomb attack by IRA on Army base Lisburn

Royal Engineers
SAPPER JOHN CONNACHAN   27/06/71:
SAPPER DEREK AMOS   28/12/71: RTA
SAPPER RONALD HURST   17/05/72: IRA sniper whilst working on base in Crossmaglen
S/SGT MALCOLM BANKS   28/06/72: Shot by IRA Short Strand area of Belfast
SAPPER EDWARD STUART   2/10/72: Shot whilst working undercover Dunmurry, Belfast
WO2 IAN DONALD   24/05/73: IRA bomb Cullaville, Co Armagh
MAJOR RICHARD JARMAN   20/07/73: IRA booby trap Middletown, Co Armagh
SAPPER MALCOLM ORTON   17/09/73:
S/SGT JAMES LUND   19/01/74:
SAPPER JOHN WALTON   2/07/74: IRA booby trap Newtownhamilton
L/CPL IAN NICHOLL   15/05/74: RTA
SGT DAVID EVANS   21/07/74: IRA booby trap Army base, Waterside, Londonderry
WO1 JOHN NEWTON   24/06/75:
SERGEANT ROBERT MCCARTER   17/07/75: IRA bomb, Forkhill
SAPPER HOWARD EDWARDS   11/12/76: IRA sniper, Bogside area of Londonderry
SAPPER DAVIS THOMPSON   13/01/77:
SAPPER MICHAEL LARKIN   10/02/77:
CPL JOHN HAYNES   28/07/77:
SAPPER STEPHEN WORTH   1/08/77:
SAPPER JAMES VANCE   14/11/77: RTA
CPL JAMES ANDREWS   4/09/78:
SAPPER FRASER JONES   3/02/80: RTA
COLONEL MARK COE   16/02/80: Murdered by IRA gunmen at Army home in Bielefeld Germany

SGT KJ ROBSON	18/02/80:	Aircraft accident
CPL THOMAS PALMER	8/02/83:	RTA
L/CPL DAVID HURST	6/10/86:	RTA
L/CPL MICHAEL ROBBINS	1/08/88:	Killed by IRA bomb at Mill Hill Army camp, London
L/CPL PAUL CASSIDY	15/03/88:	RTA
S/SGT DAVID HULL	22/08/89:	RTA
S/SGT JAMES H. HARDY	12/06/90:	RTA
L/CPL CM MONTEITH	5/08/91:	RTA
CPL MD IONNOU	15/04/95:	RTA
S/SGT SJ THOMPSON	30/06/95:	Natural causes
SAPPER ROBERT MOORE		RTA

The Royal Gloucestshire, Berkshire and Wiltshire Regiment.

| CPL GARY LLEWELLYN FENTON | 22/06/98: | Run down and killed by lorry at VCP, Crossmaglen Posthumous Mention in Dispatches |

Royal Green Jackets

L/CPL MICHAEL PEARCE	24/09/69:	Violent or unnatural causes
RFN MICHAEL BOSWELL	25/10/69:	RTA
RFN JOHN KEENEY	25/10/69:	RTA
CPL ROBERT BANKIER	22/05/71:	IRA sniper Markets area of Belfast
RFN DAVID WALKER	12/07/71:	IRA sniper, Northumberland Street, Lower Falls, Belfast
RFN JOSEPH HILL	16/10/71:	Shot by gunman during riots in Bogside, Londonderry
MAJOR ROBIN ALERS-HANKEY	30/01/72:	DoW after being shot in Bogside area of Londonderry
RFN JOHN TAYLOR	20/03/72:	IRA sniper, William Street, Londonderry
RFN JAMES MEREDITH	26/06/72:	Shot in Abercorn Road, Londonderry
L/CPL DAVID CARD	4/08/72:	Killed by IRA gunman in Andersonstown, Belfast
CPL IAN MORRILL	28/08/72:	IRA sniper in Beechmount Avenue, Belfast
RFN DAVID GRIFFITHS	30/08/72:	IRA sniper, Clonnard Street, Lower Falls, Belfast
L/CPL IAN GEORGE	10/09/72:	
RFN RAYMOND JOESBURY	8/12/72:	DoW after being shot whilst in Whiterock area of Belfast
RFN NICOLAS ALLEN	26/11/73:	Death by violent or unnatural causes
RFN MICHAEL GIBSON	14/12/74:	Shot along with RUC constable at Forkhill on joint patrol
CPL WILLIAM SMITH	31/08/77:	IRA sniper, Girdwood Park Army base, Belfast
LT/COL IAN CORDEN-LLOYD	17/02/78:	Helicopter crash near Bessbrook
RFN NICHOLAS SMITH	4/03/78:	IRA booby trap Crossmaglen
MAJOR THOMAS FOWLEY	24/04/78:	
RFN CHRISTOPHER WATSON	19/07/80:	Shot and killed off-duty in Rosemount, Londonderry
RFN MICHAEL BAGSHAW	19/05/81:	Killed along with 4 others IRA landmine at Camlough
RFN ANDREW GAVIN	19/05/81:	Killed in same incident
RFN JOHN KING	19/05/81:	Killed in same incident
L/CPL GRENVILLE WINSTONE	19/05/81:	Killed in same incident

L/CPL GAVIN DEAN	16/07/81:	IRA sniper near Crossmaglen
RFN DANIEL HOLLAND	25/03/82:	Killed with 2 others in gun attack on Springfield Road, Belfast
RFN NICHOLAS MALAKOS	25/03/82:	Killed in same incident
RFN ANTHONY RAPLEY	25/03/82:	Killed in same incident
WO2 GRAHAM BARKER	20/07/82:	Killed in IRA bomb outrage, Regents Park, London
BANDSMAN JOHN HERITAGE	20/07/82:	Killed in same incident
BNDSMN ROBERT LIVINGSTONE	20/07/82:	Killed in same incident
CPL JOHN MCKNIGHT	20/07/82:	Killed in same incident
BANDSMAN GEORGE MEASURE	20/07/82:	Killed in same incident
BANDSMAN KEITH POWELL	20/07/82:	Killed in same incident
BANDSMAN LAURENCE SMITH	20/07/82:	Killed in same incident
RFN DAVID GRAINGER	10/04/83:	
RFN DAVID MULLEY	18/03/86:	IRA bomb, Castlewellan, Co Down
L/CPL THOMAS HEWITT	19/07/87:	IRA sniper, Belleek, Co Fermanagh
CPL EDWARD JEDRUCH	31/07/87:	
SGT THOMAS ROSS	18/09/91:	RTA
L/CPL WAYNE HARRIS	8/11/91:	RTA. Hit a bridge in Armagh
RFN CHRISTOPHER WILLIAMS	8/11/91:	Killed in same incident
CPL MATTHEW MADDOCKS	14/11/91:	Helicopter crash, Gortin Glen, Omagh
CPL LARRY WALL	12/12/91:	Death by violent or unnatural causes
RFN JAMIE SMITH	10/08/92:	RTA
RFN RICHARD DAVEY	29/10/72:	Death by violent or unnatural causes
RFN DAVID FENLEY	17/02/93:	Death by violent or unnatural causes
WO2 KEITH THEOBOLD	2/10/95:	Death by violent or unnatural causes

Royal Hampshire Regiment

PTE JOHN KING	13/03/73:	IRA booby trap, Crossmaglen
PTE ALAN WATKINS	3/08/73:	INLA sniper, Dungiven, Co Londonderry
CPL JOHN LEAHY	3/08/73:	DoW following IRA bomb, Mullaghbawn, Forkhill
DRUMMER FRANK FALLOWS	10/11/76:	Died in accidental shooting, Magaheralin, Co Armagh
SGT MICHAEL P. UNSWORTH	2/06/77:	Drowned after helicopter accident River Bann
PTE COLIN CLIFFORD	30/04/82:	IRA landmine Belleek, Co Fermanagh

Royal Highland Fusiliers

FUSILIER JOHN B. MCCAIG	10/03/71:	Abducted and murdered by the IRA at Ligoniel, Belfast
FUSILIER JOSEPH MCCAIG	10/03/71:	Murdered in the same incident
FUS. DOUGALD P. MCCAUGHE	10/03/71:	Murdered in the same incident
L/CPL DAVID HIND	2/01/77:	Shot by IRA, Crossmaglen
CPL ROBERT M THOMPSON	20/07/80:	IRA car bomb, Moy Bridge, Aughnacloy
FUSILIER S G WELLS.	25/06/01:	Road traffic accident

Royal Hussars

S/SGT CHARLES SIMPSON	7/11/74:	IRA booby trap, Stewartstown, Co Tyrone
LT ROBERT GLAZEBROOK	14/11/76:	RTA

Royal Horse Guards

L/COH KEITH CHILLINGWORTH	14/06/72:	RTA

Royal Irish Rangers

SGT THOMAS MCGAHON	19/01/71:	RTA
CPL JAMES SINGLETON	19/01/71:	Killed in same incident
RANGER WILLIAM J. BEST	21/05/72:	Abducted and murdered when on home leave
RANGER THOMAS MCGANN	26/05/72:	RTA
RANGER H THOMPSON	6/12/77:	RTA
RANGER DAVID LANHAM	10/01/83:	RTA
RANGER CYRIL J. SMITH QGM.	24/10/90:	Killed saving colleagues during bomb attack at Newry
RANGER JOHN MCCELLAND		RTA

Royal Irish Regiment

L/CPL MICHAEL W.A. PATTERSON	6/09/92:	RTA (HOME SERVICE FORCE)
SGT ROBERT IRVINE	20/10/92:	Shot by IRA in his sister's home, Rasharkin
PTE BRIAN MARTIN	20/10/92:	RTA (HOME SERVICE FORCE)
L/CPL IAN WARNOCK	19/11/92:	Shot by IRA as he met his wife in Portadown
PTE STEPHEN WALLER	30/12/92:	Shot by IRA when on home leave, Belfast
L/CPL MERVYN JOHNSTON	15/02/93:	Shot by IRA at his in-laws house West Belfast
PTE CHRIS WREN	31/05/93:	Killed by IRA bomb under his car in Moneymore
CPL ROBERT ARMSTRONG	21/11/93:	RTA
PTE SEAN MAIR	17/04/94:	RTA
PTE REGGIE MCCOLLUM	21/05/94:	Abducted and murdered by the IRA whilst off-duty
PTE SIMON LECKY	31/07/94:	RTA
CPL TRELFORD T. WITHERS	8/08/94:	Shot in his shop, Downpatrick Street, Crossgar
PTE WILLIAM MCCREA	10/10/95:	RTA
PTE ALAN MCCORMICK	1/06/96	RTA
L/CPL STEVE RANKIN	23/09/96:	Death by violent or unnatural causes
PTE WILLIAM WOODS	3/09/97:	Violent or unnatural causes
WOII ROBERT BELL	9/01/98:	Natural causes
PTE MATTHEW FRANCE	1/05/98:	Violent or unnatural causes
PTE RONALD MCCONVILLE	30/06/98:	Natural causes
CPL JACKY IRELAND	13/07/98:	RTA
PTE JOHN MURRAY	28/08/98:	RTA
L/CPL STUART ANDREWS	16/09/98:	Natural causes
CPL GERALD BLAIR	21/10/98:	Natural causes
PTE KAI JENNINGS		RTA
RANGER WILLIAM MORTON		RTA
RANGER PAUL TUNLEY		RTA

Royal Irish Regiment (V)

WO2 HUGH MCGINN	28/12/80:	Killed by INLA in his own home in Armagh
SGT TREVOR A. ELLIOT	13/04/83:	Killed by IRA at his shop in Keady
CPL TREVOR MAY	9/04/84:	IRA bomb under his car in Newry outside his work

Royal Logistic Corps

L/CPL DAVID WILSON	14/05/94:	Killed by bomb attack at VCP at Keady, Co Armagh
L/CPL RICHARD FORD	30/10/98:	Natural causes

Royal Marines

BAND CPL DEAN PAVEY	22/09/89:	Killed in IRA bomb outrage Marine Barracks, Deal
BAND CPL TREVOR DAVIS	22/09/89:	Killed in same incident
BAND CPL DAVE McMILLAN	22/09/89:	Killed in same incident
MUSICIAN RICHARD FICE	22/09/89:	Killed in same incident
MUSICIAN BOB SIMMONDS	22/09/89:	Killed in same incident
MUSICIAN MICK BALL	22/09/89:	Killed in same incident
MUSICIAN RICHARD JONES	22/09/89:	Killed in same incident
MUSICIAN TIM REEVES	22/09/89:	Killed in same incident
MUSICIAN MARK PETCH	22/09/89:	Killed in same incident
MUSICIAN ANDY CLEATHEROE	22/09/89:	Killed in same incident
MUSICIAN CHRIS NOLAN.	18/10/89:	DoW from same incident

Royal Marine Commandos

40 Cdo

MARINE L ALLEN	26/07/72:	Shot by IRA, Unity Flats, Belfast
MARINE ANTHONY DAVID	17/10/72:	DoW after being shot by IRA on Falls Road
MARINE JOHN SHAW	26/07/73:	RTA in highly controversial circumstances *
MARINE ANDREW GIBBONS	28/05/83:	Died Camlough Lake, Co Armagh

42 Cdo

MARINE IVOR SWAIN	23/03/73:	RTA: North Belfast
MARINE GRAHAM COX	29/04/73:	IRA sniper, New Lodge, Belfast
MARINE JOHN MACKLIN	28/03/74:	DoW after being shot in the Antrim Rd, Belfast
CPL ROBERT MILLER	17/08/78:	IRA bomb attack, Forkhill
MARINE GARY WHEDDON	12/11/78:	DoW after bomb attack, Crossmaglen
MARINE ADAM GILBERT	15/06/89:	Shot in friendly fire incident, New Lodge Road

45 Cdo

MARINE ROBERT CUTTING	28/08/72:	Killed in friendly fire incident, Turf Lodge
CPL DENNIS LEACH	13/08/74:	IRA bomb, Crossmaglen
MARINE MICHAEL SOUTHERN	13/08/74:	Killed in same incident
MARINE NEIL BEWLEY	21/08/77:	IRA sniper Turf Lodge, Belfast
SGT WILLIAM CORBETT	23/08/81:	Accidentally shot, Musgrave Park Hospital, Belfast
MAJOR JOHN R. COOPER	16/02/82:	RTA
CPL MARK LAZENBY	21/02/95:	RTA

Royal Military Police

L/CPL WILLIAM G. JOLLIFFE	1/03/71:	Killed in crash in Londonderry after petrol bombing
CPL RODERICK LANE	20/05/73:	RTA
CPL STUART MILNE	20/02/74:	RTA
L/CPL PAUL MUNDY	20/02/74:	Killed in same incident

CPL THOMAS F. LEA	21/01/75:	DoW 8 months after IRA bomb attack, Belfast
CPL GEORGE MIDDLEMAS	8/11/77:	RTA
SGT DAVID ROSS	27/03/84:	Killed in Londonderry after explosion
CPL RICHARD ROBERTS		RTA

Royal Navy

NA (AH) DAVID SHIPLEY	11/01/87:	RTA
AB MARK CARTWRIGHT	11/01/87:	Killed in same incident
LT. A. R. SHIELDS.	22/08/88:	IRA bomb in Belfast; was Naval recruiter
CK1 THOMAS GILLEN		RTA
L/SMN GAVIN STEWART		RTA
STWD ROBERT STEWART		RTA
L/WREN ANNIE BYRNE		RTA
MEM ALAN BALMER		RTA

Royal Pioneer Corps

PTE I. BOWEN	2/08/72:	RTA
SGT J. W. ROBINSON	8/02/73:	Died of natural causes whilst on duty
PTE PHILIP DRAKE	26/08/74:	IRA sniper, Craigavon, Co Armagh
PTE DAVID P. BONSALL	29/03/75:	RTA
PTE L. ROTHWELL	25/10/76:	Cause of Death unknown
L/CPL GRAHAM LEE	22/08/80:	RTA
PTE SOHAN VIRDEE	5/08/81:	Murdered by the IRA whilst off duty
PTE S HUMBLE	26/08/81:	Killed in shooting accident
CPL DEREK HAYES	21/06/88:	IRA booby trap, Crossmaglen

Royal Regiment Fusiliers
1st Battalion

FUSILIER. A SIMMONS	15/11/74:	Shot by IRA at Strabane
CPL. B BARKER	25/01/81:	Shot at VCP in Belfast
CPL. T H AGAR	18/05/84:	Killed by IRA bomb under car at Enniskillen
L/CPL. R V HUGGINS	18/05/84:	Killed in same incident
L/CPL. P W GALLIMORE	18/10/84:	Died of heart attack after bomb attack, Enniskillen

2nd Battalion

MAJOR. J J E SNOW	8/12/71:	DoW after being shot by IRA in New Lodge area
FUSILIER. K CANHAM	14/07/72:	IRA sniper in Lenadoon
FUSILIER. A P TINGEY	23/08/72:	IRA sniper, West Belfast
CPL. D NAPIER	9/03/73:	RTA
FUSILIER. G W FOXALL	16/06/80:	Violent or unnatural causes
FUSILIER. A J GRUNDY	1/05/92:	IRA bomb at VCP at Killeen
L/CPL. M J BESWICK	9/02/93:	DoW after IRA bomb in Armagh

3rd Battalion

CPL. J L DAVIS	15/09/72:	Shot by IRA in Bogside, Londonderry
FUSILIER. C J MARCHANT	9/04/73:	Shot in ambush at Lurgan
CPL. D LLEWELLYN	28/09/75:	RTA
CPL. E GLEESON	9/10/75:	IRA landmine, Lurgancullenboy
SGT. S J FRANCIS	21/11/75:	IRA booby trap, Forkhill

FUSILIER. M J SAMPSON	22/11/75:	Killed in major gun battle with IRA at Drumuckaval
FUSILIER. J D DUNCAN	22/11/75:	Killed in same incident
FUSILIER. P L McDONALD	22/11/75:	Killed in same incident
CPL. D TRAYNOR	30/03/76:	IRA booby trap, Ballygallan
L/CPL. W T MAKIN	3/01/83:	Violent or unnatural causes
L/CPL JAMES J MCSHANE	4/02/74:	Killed in IRA bomb outrage, M62, Yorkshire
FUSILIER JACK HYNES	4/02.74:	Killed in same outrage
CPL CLIFFORD HAUGHTON	4/02/74:	Killed in same outrage
FUSILIER STEPHEN WHALLEY	4/02/74:	Killed in same outrage

Bn Unknown

CPL DEREK NAPIER	9/03/73:	RTA

Royal Regiment of Wales

PTE ALAN ROY ROGERS	13/03/71:	RTA
L/CPL JOHN HILLMAN	18/06/72:	IRA sniper Flex Street Mill, Ardoyne, Belfast
L/CPL ALAN GILES	12/06/72:	Shot in gun battle with IRA, Ardoyne, Belfast
PTE BRIAN SODEN	19/06/72:	IRA sniper in Ardoyne, Belfast
PTE DAVID MEEK	13/07/72:	IRA sniper, Hooker Street, Ardoyne, Belfast
PTE JOHN WILLIAMS	14/07/72:	Killed in gun battle with IRA, Hooker St., Ardoyne
PTE GARY CHANNING	21/11/86:	Accidental death at VCP in Omagh
PTE GEOFFREY JONES	5/01/87:	Death by violent or unnatural causes
WO1 (RSM) MIKE HEAKIN	12/08/88:	Murdered at traffic lights by IRA, Ostende, Belgium
PTE WILLIAM DAVIS	1/06/90:	Murdered in Lichfield railway station by IRA

Royal Scots

PTE RODERICK D W C. BANNON	31/03/76:	IRA landmine explosion, Co Armagh
PTE DAVID FERGUSON	31/03/76:	Killed in same incident
PTE JOHN PEARSON	31/03/76:	Killed in same incident
COL SGT N REDPATH	2/02/81:	Died of heart attack
PTE P J MCKENNA	15/03/81:	Accidentally shot
PTE A BRUCE	17/09/82:	RTA
L/CPL LAWRENCE DICKSON.	17/03/93:	IRA sniper at Forkhill

Royal Scots Dragoon Guards

TROOPER IAN CAIE	24/08/72:	IRA landmine attack at Crossmaglen

Royal Tank Regiment

L/CPL JOHN WARNOCK	4/09/71:	IRA landmine attack, Derrybeg Park, Newry
TROOPER JAMES NOWOSAD	3/03/78:	Shot by gunmen in 'Rag Day' killing, Belfast city centre; also killed was a civilian searcher.
L/CPL NICHOLAS BUSHWELL	2/10/80:	RTA
CPL STEVEN SMITH	2/07/89:	IRA bomb under his car, Hanover, Germany

Royal Welsh Fusiliers

CPL GERALD BRISTOW	16/04/72:	IRA sniper Bishops Street, Londonderry
FUSILIER KERRY MCCARTHY	21/06/72:	IRA sniper Victoria RUC station, Londonderry
CPL DAVID SMITH	21/06/73:	IRA booby trap, Strabane
CPL ALAN COUGHLAN	28/10/74:	Van bomb attack at Ballykinler Army camp
FUSILIER ANDREW CROCKER	24/11/76:	Killed by IRA at Post Office robbery, Turf Lodge
LIEUTENANT STEVEN KIRBY	14/02/79:	IRA sniper Abercorn Road, Londonderry
CORPORAL DAVID WRIGHT	16/12/93:	RTA whilst on duty

Royal Yeomanry (TA)

TROOPER MARK JOHNSTON		RTA
TROOPER ROBERT E. SEWWLL		RTA

Scots Dragoon Guards

TROOPER ANTHONY SUTTON	6/12/77:	RTA

Scots Guards

GUARDSMAN JOHN EDMUNDS	16/03/70:	Drowned
GUARDSMAN BRIAN HALL	4/10/71:	IRA sniper, Creggan heights base, Londonderry
GUARDSMAN GEORGE HAMILTON	17/10/71:	Ambushed and killed by IRA, Cupar Street, Lower Falls
GUARDSMAN NORMAN BOOTH	30/10/71:	Killed in same incident
GUARDSMAN STEPHEN MCGUIRE	4/11/71:	IRA sniper Henry Taggart base, West Belfast
GUARDSMAN PAUL NICHOLS	27/11/71:	IRA sniper, St James Crescent, Falls Road, Belfast
GUARDSMAN JOHN VAN-BECK	18/09/72:	DoW after being shot by IRA, Lecky Road, Londonderry
GUARDSMAN GEORGE LOCKHART	26/09/72:	DoW after being shot by IRA, Bogside, Londonderry
L/SGT THOMAS MCKAY	28/10/72:	IRA sniper, Bishop Street, Londonderry
GUARDSMAN ALAN DAUGHTERY	31/12/73:	IRA sniper, Beechmount Avenue, Falls Road, Belfast
GUARDSMAN WILLIAM FORSYTH	5/10/74:	Killed in IRA bomb outrage, Guildford (with 4 others)
GUARDSMAN JOHN HUNTER	5/10/74:	Killed in same outrage
COL/SGT DAVID NADEN	7/06/78:	RTA
L/CPL ALAN SWIFT	11/08/78:	Killed on covert ops, Letterkenny Rd, Londonderry
COL/SGT EDWIN MURRISON	9/04/80:	RTA
MAJ DONALD NICOL/ ARDMONACH	21/10/86:	Died of natural causes whilst on duty
L/SGT GRAHAM STEWART	5/05/90:	Killed on covert ops, Cullyhanna, Co Armagh
GUARDSMAN PAUL BROWN	2/08/90:	RTA
GUARDSMAN ALEX IRELAND	11/09/90:	Death by violent or unnatural causes
GUARDSMAN DAMIAN SHACKLETON	3/08/92:	IRA sniper, New Lodge, Belfast
GUARDSMAN ANDREW WASON	3/09/92:	Death by violent or unnatural causes

Staffordshire Regiment

S/SGT JOHN MORRELL	24/10/72:	DoW after IRA booby trap, Drumargh, Armagh

2ND LT MICHAEL SIMPSON	23/10/74:	DoW after being shot by IRA sniper, Londonderry
PTE CHRISTOPHER SHENTON	20/01/81:	IRA sniper whilst in OP Bogside, Londonderry
L/CPL STEPHEN ANDERSON	29/05/84:	IRA landmine, Crossmaglen
PTE WAYNE G. SMITH	1/07/95:	RTA

Territorial Army (Unclear to which Regt he was linked)

Thomas Gibson	20/10/89:	Murdered by IRA as he waited for lift in Kilrea

Ulster Defence Regiment
2nd Battalion

SERGEANT HARRY D. DICKSON	27/02/72:	Murdered by the IRA at his home
PTE SIDNEY W. WATT	20/07/73:	Ambushed by the IRA at a friend's house
PTE KENNETH HILL	28/08/73:	Shot in Armagh City whilst attending an incident
CORPORAL JAMES A. FRAZER	30/08/75:	Killed by IRA at a friend's farm
L/CORPORAL JOE REID	31/08/75:	Murdered at home by IRA
L/CORPORAL D. JOHN BELL	6/11/75:	Killed by IRA as he returned from work
C/SERGEANT JOE NESBITT	10/11/75:	Shot by the IRA on his way to work
PTE JOSEPH A McCULLOUGH	25/02/76:	Shot by IRA
CORPORAL ROBERT McCONNELLl	5/04/76:	Murdered at his home in Tullyvallen, Newtownhamilton
L/CORPORAL JEAN LEGGETT	6/04/76:	Ambushed and shot by IRA on patrol in Armagh
Lt JOE WILSON	26/10/76:	Killed at work by the IRA
PTE MARGARET A. HEARST	8/10/77:	Murdered at home by IRA near Middletown
CAPTAIN CHARLIE HENNING	6/10/78:	Shot by IRA whilst at work
L/CPL THOMAS ARMSTRONG	13/04/79:	Ambushed and killed by IRA on his way home
PTE JAMES PORTER	24/06/79:	Murdered at home by IRA
PTE JAMES H. HEWITT	10/10/80:	Killed by bomb under his car
L/CPL FREDDIE A. WILLIAMSON	7/10/82:	Killed with a women prison officer in INLA-caused crash
SGT THOMAS G. COCHRANE	22/10/82:	Abducted and murdered by IRA
CPL CHARLIE H. SPENCE	10/11/82:	Shot by IRA as he left work in Armagh
CPL AUSTIN SMITH	19/12/82:	Shot by IRA after parking his car near home
MAJOR CHARLIE ARMSTRONG	14/11/83:	Killed by IRA bomb in Armagh City
PTE STEPHEN MCKINNEY	25/09/88:	Murdered by IRA as he arrived home after quitting UDR
L/CPL DAVY HALLIGAN	17/11/89:	Shot by IRA as he drove home
PTE PAUL D SUTCLIFFE	1/03/91:	DoW after IRA mortar attack in Armagh
PTE ROGER J. LOVE	1/03/91:	DoW from same incident
PTE PAUL R. BLAKELY	31/05/91:	Killed in IRA bomb at the Glenane base with 2 others
PTE SIDNEY HAMILTON	31/05/91:	Killed in same incident
L/CPL ROBERT W. CROZIER	31/05/91:	Killed in same incident

3rd Battalion

L/CPL JOE JARDINE	8/03/72:	Shot by IRA whilst working

CPL JIM D. ELLIOTT	19/04/72:	Abducted and murdered by IRA; body then booby trapped by his killers
C/SGT JOHN RUDDY	10/10/72:	Shot by IRA on his way to work
PTE JOHN MCCREADY	17/11/74:	Shot by the IRA on duty
CPL CECIL GRILLS	12/01/78:	Shot by IRA as he drove home from work
PTE JIM COCHRANE	6/01/80:	Killed by IRA bomb at Castlewellen. One of 3 killed
PTE RICHARD SMITH	6/01/80:	Killed in same incident
PTE RICKY WILSON	6/01/80:	Killed in same incident
PTE COLIN H. QUINN	10/12/80:	Shot by INLA as he left work
MAJOR W.E. IVAN TOOMBS	16/01/81:	Shot by IRA in Warrenpoint where he worked
L/CPL RICHARD W.J. MCKEE	24/04/81:	Shot by IRA at Kilcoo whilst on duty
CAPTAIN GORDON HANNA	29/11/85:	Killed when IRA bomb exploded under his car at home
CPL D. BRIAN BROWN	28/05/86:	Killed by IRA bomb when searching after a warning
PTE ROBERT W HILL	1/07/86:	Killed when IRA bomb exploded under his car at home
CPL ALAN. T. JOHNSTON	15/02/88:	Shot by the IRA as he arrived for work
PTE W. JOHN MORELAND	16/12/88:	Shot in his coal lorry at Downpatrick
PTE MICHAEL D. ADAMS	9/04/90:	Killed by IRA landmine with 3 others at Downpatrick
L/CPL J (BRAD) BRADLEY	9/04/90:	Killed in same incident
PTE JOHN BIRCH	9/04/90:	Killed in same incident
PTE STEVEN SMART	9/04/90:	Killed in same incident

4th Battalion

PTE FRANK VEITCH	3/09/71:	Shot by IRA at Kinawley RUC station
PTE JOHNNY FLETCHER	1/03/72:	Abducted and murdered by IRA in front of his wife
L/CPL W. HARRY CREIGHTON	7/08/72:	Murdered by IRA at his house near Monaghan
PTE JIMMY. E. EAMES	25/08/72:	IRA booby trapped car at Enniskillen
L/CPL ALFIE JOHNSON	25/08/72:	Killed in same incident
PTE TOMMY. R. BULLOCK	21/09/72:	Murdered along with his wife at their home
PTE J. ROBIN BELL	22/10/72:	Shot by IRA whilst with his father
PTE MATT LILLY	7/09/73:	Shot by the IRA on his milk round
PTE ALAN .R. FERGUSON	25/06/78:	Killed in IRA landmine and gun attack
CPL HERBIE. G. KERNAGHAN	15/10/79:	Shot by the IRA as he delivered to his school; Witnessed by dozens of children
CPL AUBREY ABERCROMBIE	5/02/80:	Murdered by the IRA on his farm
PTE W. RITCHIE LATIMER	7/06/80:	Shot by the IRA at his hardware store
PTE NORMAN. H. DONALDSON	25/11/80:	Shot by IRA as he collected charity money at RUC Station whilst off-duty
L/CPL RONNIE GRAHAM	5/06/81:	Shot by IRA as he delivered coal; one of three brothers murdered by IRA
PTE CECIL GRAHAM	11/11/81:	DoW after being shot by IRA at his wife's house
CPL ALBERT BEACOM	17/11/81:	Murdered by IRA at his home
PTE JIMMY GRAHAM. BEM	1/02/85:	Shot in front of school children by IRA
PTE JOHN. F. EARLY	3/02/86:	IRA landmine
CPL JIMMY OLDHAM	3/04/86:	Shot by IRA gunmen as he arrived where he worked

CPL WILLIE BURLEIGH	6/04/88:	Killed by IRA bomb under his car

5th Battalion

PTE THOMAS CALLAGHAN	16/02/72:	Abducted and murdered in the Creggan, Londonderry
CAPTAIN MARCUS MCCAUSLAND	4/03/71:	Abducted and murdered by the IRA
PTE SAMUEL PORTER	22/11/72:	Shot and killed by the IRA as he walked home
PTE GEORGE E. HAMILTON	20/12/72:	Shot by the IRA as he worked on repairs at a reservoir
CAPTAIN JAMES HOOD	4/01/73:	Murdered by the IRA at home
SGT DAVID C.DEACON	3/03/73:	Abducted and murdered by the IRA
CPL JOHN CONLEY	23/07/74:	IRA car bomb in Bridge Street, Garvagh
PTE ROBERT STOTT	25/11/75:	Shot by the IRA on the way home from work
PTE JOHN ARRELL	22/01/76:	Shot on board his firm's mini bus
PTE JACK MCCUTCHEON	1/04/76:	Shot at work by the IRA
S/SGT BOBBY H.LENNOX	2/04/76:	Postman – lured to an isolated farm and shot
CAPTAIN W. RONNIE BOND	7/11/76:	Shot outside his home in Londonderry as he got home
L/CPL JIMMY SPEERS	9/11/76:	Shot by the IRA at his garage in Desertmartin
L/CPL WINSTON C. MCCAUGHEY	11/11/76:	Shot by the IRA as he stood outside his house in Kilrea
MAJOR J. PETER HILL	23/02/77:	Shot by IRA as he got home from work, Londonderry
PTE DAVID MCQUILLAN	15/03/77:	Shot by IRA as he waited for a lift to work, Bellaghy
L/CPL GERALD C. CLOETE	6/04/77:	Shot by the IRA as he drove to work in Londonderry
LT WALTER KERR	2/11/77:	DoW after IRA bomb under his car
CPL WILLIAM J. GORDON	8/02/78:	Killed along with daughter (10) after IRA bomb exploded under their car
L/CPL SAMUEL D. MONTGOMERY	10/02/81:	Shot by the IRA as he left work
PTE T. ALAN RITCHIE	25/05/81:	Killed in IRA ambush at Gulladuff near Bellaghy
PTE ALLEN CLARKE	12/09/81:	Shot by IRA as he walked through Maghera
L/CPL BERNIE V. MCKEOWN	17/12/83:	Murdered by the IRA in front of his 13 year old son in their car
SGT BOBBY F. BOYD	18/11/85:	Murdered by the IRA at his front door
SGT TOMMY A. JAMISON	8/03/90:	Ambushed and killed by the IRA at work
PTE MICKEY BOXALL	6/11/91:	Killed in IRA mortar attack at Bellaghy

6th Battalion

PTE WINSTON DONNELL	9/08/71:	1st UDR man killed by the IRA; manning VCP at Clady, Tyrone
SGT KENNETH SMYTH	10/12/71:	Shot whilst off duty by the IRA
PTE TED MEGAHEY	9/06/72:	DoW after IRA shooting
PTE WILLIAM J. BOGLE	5/12/72:	Murdered in his car as he sat with his children
PTE ROBERT N. JAMESON	17/01/74:	Shot by IRA as he got off a bus at Trillick

PTE EVA MARTIN	2/05/74:	Killed by IRA in rocket and gun attack at Clogher
CPL W. DEREK KIDD	18/11/76:	Shot and killed at work
CPL WILLIAM J. MCKEE	14/04/78:	Shot and killed by gunmen as he drove a school bus
PTE JOHN GRAHAM	25/04/79:	Shot by the IRA as he collected milk from farms
PTE JOHN A. HANNIGAN	19/06/79:	Shot by IRA as he came out of a shop in Omagh
PTE JAMES A. ROBINSON	19/10/79:	Shot and killed as he was his milk round
PTE WILLIE J. CLARKE	3/08/80:	Shot in the Republic visiting relatives
L/CPL JOHNNY MCKEEGAN	19/11/81:	Lured to a house in Strabane and shot by IRA
LT J. LESLIE HAMILTON	27/04/82:	Shot whilst delivering to a Londonderry supermarket
PTE H. A. (LEXI) CUMMINGS	15/06/82:	Shot by IRA as he prepared to drive home from work
PTE RONNIE ALEXANDER	13/07/83:	One of 4 men killed by IRA landmine at Drumquin
PTE OSSIE NEELY	13/07/82:	Killed in same incident
PTE JOHN ROXBOROUGH	13/07/82:	Killed in same incident
CPL THOMAS HARRON	13/07/82:	Killed in same incident
CPL RONNIE D. FINDLAY	23/08/83:	Shot by IRA as he left work
PTE GREG ELLIOTT	2/01/84:	Shot as he got into his van at Castlederg
L/CPL THOMAS A. LOUGHLIN	2/03/84:	Killed by IRA bomb planted underneath his works van
C/SGT IVAN E. HILLEN	12/05/84:	Shot and killed at his farm in Augher by IRA
CPL HEATHER.C. J. KERRIGAN	14/07/84:	One of 2 UDR men killed in IRA landmine, Castlederg
PTE NORMAN J. MCKINLEY	14/07/84:	Killed in same incident
PTE W. VICTOR FOSTER	15/01/86	IRA bomb planted under his car at Castlederg
PTE THOMAS J. IRWIN	26/03/86:	Shot and killed by IRA at his work in Omagh
PTE WILLIAM C. POLLOCK	8/04/86:	Killed by IRA booby trap at home in Castlederg
CAPT IVAN R.K. ANDERSON	21/05/87:	Shot by IRA as he drove home from his school
L/CPL MICHAEL DARCY	4/06/88:	Murdered at home by IRA in Castlederg
PTE OLVEN L. KILPATRICK	9/01/90:	Shot by IRA at his shoe shop in Castlederg

7th Battalion

PTE SEAN RUSSELL	27/03/81:	Murdered at home by IRA, Belfast; daughter injured
PTE JOHN B. HOUSTON	29/11/75:	Shot at work by the IRA
PTE PETER MCCELLAND	28/08/79:	Killed at VCP
PTE JOHN D. SMITH	27/03/81:	Shot by IRA as he walked to work in Belfast

8th Battalion

PTE W. DENNIS WILSON	7/12/71:	Murdered at home in Curlough
L/CPL HENRY GILLESPIE	20/05/72:	Shot by IRA patrolling near Dungannon
PTE FRED D. GREEVES	15/12/72:	Shot by IRA as left work in Armagh

CPL FRANK CADDOO	10/05/73:	Shot by IRA at his farm in Rehagey
CAPTAIN CORMAC MCCABE	19/01/74:	Abducted and murdered by IRA in Irish Republic
CPL ROY T. MOFFETT	3/03/74:	IRA landmine on Cookstown to Omagh road
WO2 DAVID SINNAMON	11/04/74:	IRA bomb in house in Dungannon
PTE EDMUND R. L. STEWART	29/04/76:	Lured to relatives house and shot by IRA
L/CPL STANLEY D. ADAMS	28/10/76:	Lured to remote farmhouse as mailman and shot by IRA
PTE JOHN REID	9/03/77:	Ambushed and shot by IRA as he fed his cattle
CPL DAVY GRAHAM	25/03/77:	DoW after being shot at work by IRA, Gortonis
CAPTAIN W. ERIC SHIELDS	29/04/77:	Shot by IRA outside his home in Dungannon
2ND/LT ROBIN SMYRL	13/09/77:	Shot by IRA as he drove to work at Plumbridge
PTE BOB J. BLOOMER	24/09/77:	DoW after being shot at home by IRA in Eglish
SGT JOCK B EAGLESHAM (MID)	7/02/77:	A postman, he was shot by IRA on his rounds
PTE G. SAMMY GIBSON	29/04/79:	Shot by IRA as he cycled to work in Tyrone
CPL FRED H. IRWIN	30/10/79:	Shot by IRA driving to work in Dungannon
PTE W. JACK DONNELLY	16/04/81:	Shot by INLA at his local pub in Moy
L/CPL CECIL W. MCNEILL	25/02/83:	Shot by IRA at his work in Tullyvannon
PTE ANDY F. STINSON	4/06/83:	Killed by INLA booby trap on his digger at work
PTE CYRUS CAMPBELL	24/10/83:	Shot by IRA at Carnteel as he drove to farm
PTE N. JIMMY JOHNSTON	8/05/84:	Shot by IRA disguised as ambulance men at his hospital
PTE ROBERT BENNETT	7/09/84:	Shot by IRA at his work in Pomeroy
PTE TREVOR W. HARKNESS	28/02/85:	Killed by IRA bomb at Pomeroy on foot patrol
PTE MARTIN A. J. BLANEY	6/10/86:	Shot by IRA as he drove home in Eglish
MAJOR GEORGE SHAW	26/01/87:	Murdered by IRA at his home in Dungannon
PTE WILLIE T. GRAHAM	25/04/87:	Shot by IRA at his farm in Pomeroy
CAPT TIM D ARRMSTRONG	16/01/88:	Murdered by unknown gunmen (Falklands veteran)
PTE JOHN STEWART	16/01/88:	DoW after being shot by IRA at his home in Coalisland
PTE NED GIBSON	26/04/88:	Shot by IRA as he worked on dustbins in Ardboe
PTE RAYMOND A. MCNICOL	3/08/88:	Shot by IRA as he drove to work in Desertcreat
PTE JOHN HARDY	14/03/89:	Shot by IRA as he drove his lorry to Granville
WO2 ALBERT D COOPER	2/11/90:	IRA bomb planted in car left at his garage in Cookstown

9th Battalion

SGT MAYNARD CRAWFORD	13/01/72:	Shot as he waited in a car at Newtownabbey
CPL ROY STANTON	9/06/72:	Shot by IRA as he drove home
PTE HENRY J. RUSSELL	13/07/72:	Abducted, tortured and shot by the IRA, Carrickfergus
CPL DAVID W. BINGHAM	16/01/73:	Abducted and killed by the IRA
PTE THOMAS J FORSYTHE	16/10/73:	Killed in a shooting accident
PTE STEVEN CARLETON	8/01/82:	Shot by the IRA at petrol station in Belfast
PTE LINDENCOLIN HOUSTON	20/01/84:	Murdered by the IRA at his home in Dunmurry

10th Battalion

PTE SEAN RUSSELL	8/12/71:	Murdered by IRA at his home, New Barnsley, Belfast
PTE SAMUEL TRAINOR	20/03/72:	IRA bomb, Belfast city centre
PTE ROBERT MCCOMB	23/07/72:	Abducted and murdered by IRA in Belfast
PTE TERENCE MAGUIRE	14/10/72:	Abducted and murdered in Belfast
PTE WILLIAM L. KENNY	16/03/73:	Abducted and murdered on way to UDR barracks
CPL JOHN GEDDIS	10/05/77:	Killed by UVF in explosion in Crumlin Road, Belfast
L/CPL GERALD W. D. TUCKER	8/06/77:	Shot by IRA as he left work at Royal Victoria Hospital
CPL JAMES MCFALL	27/07/77:	Murdered by IRA at his home in Belfast
CPL HUGH A. ROGERS	8/09/77:	Shot by IRA as he left for work in Dunmurry
SGT ROBERT L. BATCHELOR	27/11/78:	Shot by IRA as he left work in Belfast
PTE ALEXANDER GORE	6/06/79:	Shot by IRA at UDR base, Malone Road, Belfast
PTE MARK A. STOCKMAN	29/09/81:	Shot by INLA at work in Belfast
SGT RICKY CONNELLY	21/10/81:	Murdered at his home by IRA, Belfast
PTE BILLY ACHESON	4/09/82:	Death by violent or unnatural causes
PTE ALEC YOUNG	1/10/84:	Death by violent or unnatural causes
PTE FRED GALLAGHER	3/10/84:	Death by violent or unnatural causes
LT DUNCAN CARSON	6/04/85:	Death by violent or unnatural causes

11th Battalion

L/CPL VICTOR SMYTH	6/09/72:	IRA bomb underneath his car, in Portadown
2ND/LT R. IRWIN LONG	8/11/72:	Shot by IRA in Lurgan driving to collect his daughter
SGT ALFIE DOYLE	3/06/75:	He and two friends shot dead by IRA as they returned from a meeting in Irish Republic
PTE GEORGE LUTTON	15/11/76:	Shot by IRA on duty in Edward Street, Lurgan
PTE ROBERT J. MCNALLY	13/03/79:	Killed by INLA bomb under his car, Portadown
PTE S. DAVID MONTGOMERY	8/03/84:	Shot by IRA at his works, Moira on the Airport Road
PTE DAVID CHAMBERS	4/06/84:	Shot by IRA as he arrived for work, Dollingstown
PTE WILLIE R. MEGRATH	23/07/87:	Killed by IRA as he drove home to Lisburn

PTE COLIN J. MCCULLOUGH	23/09/90:	Shot by IRA as he sat in his car with fiancé, Lurgan

4–6th Battalion

L/CPL KENNY A. NEWELL	27/11/91:	Abducted and murdered by IRA at Crossmaglen

7-10th Battalion

SGT DENIS TAGGART	4/08/86:	Shot dead outside his home by IRA in Belfast
PTE JOE MCILLWAINE	12/06/87:	Shot by IRA at his work in Dunmurry
PTE G. JOHN TRACEY	26/06/87:	Shot by IRA at his work in Belfast
PTE STEVEN W MEGRATH	17/09/87:	Shot by IRA at his relatives' house
PTE JAMES CUMMINGS	24/02/88:	Killed by IRA bomb in Belfast city centre
PTE FREDERICK STARRETT	24/02/88:	Killed in same incident
L/CPL ROY W BUTLER	2/08/88:	Shot dead by IRA in front of his family in West Belfast shopping centre
PTE BRIAN M LAWRENCE	17/06/91:	Shot by IRA as he arrived for work, Belfast

UDR (Battalion Unknown)

PTE THOMAS WILTON	22/10/70:	Died on duty
PTE JOHN PROCTOR	24/10/70:	RTA
S/SGT GEORGE GILKESON	11/10/71:	RTA
L/CPL PHILIP THOMPSON	31/12/71:	RTA
PTE ANDREW SIMPSON	18/09/72:	RTA
PTE ROBERT MCKEOWN	13/10/72:	RTA
PTE COLIN MCKEOWN	17/10/73:	RTA
CPL WILLIAM MARTIN	20/11/73:	RTA
PTE DAVID SPENCE	20/11/73:	RTA
PTE ROBERT RAINEY	27/07/74:	RTA
PTE SAMUEL WORKMAN	25/08/74:	RTA
PTE JOHN S. MARTIN	18/11/74:	RTA
PTE JOHN TAYLOR	30/11/74:	RTA
S/SGT IVAN NIXON	31/03/75:	RTA
SGT WILLIAM MILLAR	19/09/75:	RTA
PTE DAVID MOSGROVE	21/11/75:	RTA
L/CPL JOHN NIBLOCK	20/12/75:	RTA
PTE WILLIAM OVENS	27/03/76:	RTA
L/CPL ROBERT MCCREEDY	24/04/76:	RTA
PTE ISAAC STEWART	6/05/76:	RTA
LT JOHN HIGGINS	8/08/76:	RTA
W/PTE ANN GAYNOR	9/08/76:	RTA
CAPT ERIC SCOTT	28/08/76:	RTA
CPL WILLIAM DUNN	27/11/76:	RTA
SGT FREDERICK PULFORD	18/02/77:	RTA
PTE ROBERT PURDY	29/05/77:	RTA
PTE RAYMOND MCFARLAND	31/08/77:	RTA
PTE ALAN MCFARLAND	31/08/77:	RTA
PTE WILSON PENNEY	21/09/77:	RTA
CPL ALISTAIR COOKE	19/09/78:	RTA
PTE TREVOR HERRON	4/12/78:	RTA
PTE WILLIAM MORTON	29/04/79	RTA
L/CPL IVAN MCCORKELL	8/06/79:	RTA
PTE ALAN MCCELLAND	4/09/79:	RTA

PTE ALEXANDER ROWE	12/12/79:	RTA
PTE GEORGE BROWN	27/12/79:	RTA
W/PTE MARY COCHRANE	28/02/80:	RTA
PTE WILLIAM KEITH DONNELL	16/04/81:	RTA
LT DAVID PATTERSON	24/04/81:	RTA
PTE SAMUEL WHITESIDE	20/08/81:	RTA
L/CPL BRENDEN MCKEOWN	26/03/82:	RTA
PTE BRIAN WALMSLEY	1/05/82:	RTA
PTE LEONARD GREER	16/04/83:	RTA
PTE BRIAN KIRKPATRICK	1/10/83:	RTA
PTE ROBERT ALEXANDER IRWIN	21/12/83:	RTA
PTE FRAZER BROWN	22/01/84:	RTA
PTE SAMUEL JOSEPH BRADFORD	21/12/84:	RTA
PTE ALBERT BROWN	21/04/85:	RTA
PTE MERVYN SALMON	28/01/86:	RTA
PTE BRIAN NICHOLL	28/03/86:	RTA
PTE ROY ALLEN	26/06/86:	RTA
PTE ANDREW MONTGOMERY	30/06/86:	RTA
W/CPL CIARA OUSBY	20/07/86:	RTA
LT PAUL MAXWELL	4/08/86:	RTA
PTE JOHN MCKERAGHAN	14/03/87:	RTA
CPL JAMES ANDERSON	25/04/87:	RTA
PTE THOMAS AICKEN	11/08/87:	RTA
PTE CARL PEARCE	11/08/87:	RTA
PTE WILLIAM REILLY	8/11/87:	RTA
PTE FRANCIS GIBSON	26/04/88:	RTA
PTE THOMAS JONSTON	8/05/89:	RTA
PTE ALEXANDER PHOENIX	16/03/90:	RTA
PTE BRIAN CORDNER	4/11/90:	RTA
PTE DAVID WILLIAMSON	15/11/90:	RTA
PTE ALAN C. MCCONNELL	9/09/91:	RTA
SGT GEORGE ROLLINS	27/09/91:	RTA
PTE STEPHEN SCANLON	11/05/92:	RTA
L/CPL THOMAS MCDONNELL	8/06/97:	Violent or unnatural causes
PTE FRANCIS ROBINSON	22/01/99:	Natural causes

The following UDR Soldiers were killed in accidents; places unknown:

WO2 BERNARD ADAMSON	31/05/72	
PTE GEORGE ELLIOTT	26/06/72	
PTE WILLIAM HAMILTON	4/08/72	
PTE KENNETH TWADDELL	5/08/72	
MAJOR JOHN MUNIS	16/11/72	
PTE THOMAS I. MCCELLAND	26/04/87	
L/CPL DAVID GASS	16/06/88	
PTE KEVIN HUTCHINGS	12/07/89	
PTE MATTHEW CHRISTIE	11/09/89:	RTA
W/PTE ELIZABETH SLOAN	13/04/92	

Ex Ulster Defence Regiment Soldiers Killed in Northern Ireland

MR D.J. MCCORMICK	10/12/71:	Shot by IRA on way to work
MR ISAAC SCOTT	10/07/73:	Shot by IRA in Belleek, Co Armagh
MR IVAN VENNARD	3/10/73:	Shot dead by IRA on his postal round, Lurgan

MR GEORGE SAUNDERSON	10/04/74:	Shot by IRA at his school in Co Fermanagh
MR BRIAN SHAW	20/07/74:	Abducted and killed, Grosvenor Road, Belfast
MR WILLIAM HUTCHINSON	24/08/74:	Shot by IRA at work
MR GEORGE MCCALL	2/08/75:	Shot by IRA in Moy, Co Tyrone
MR KENNETH WORTON	5/01/76:	1 of 10 men murdered in Kingsmill Massacre
MR NICOLAS WHITE	13/03/76:	Shot at youth club, Ardoyne, Belfast
MR SIDNEY MCAVOY	12/06/76:	Shot at his shop in Dunmurry
MR JOHN FREEBURN	28/06/76:	Shot in Lurgan
MR NORMAN CAMPBELL	15/12/76:	Joined RUC and shot in Portadown
MR ROBERT HARRISON	5/02/77:	RUCR: shot by IRA Gilford, Co Down
MR JOHN LEE	27/02/77:	Shot by IRA in club in Ardoyne, Belfast
MR JAMES GREEN	5/05/77:	Shot by IRA whilst working as Taxi driver, Belfast
MR GILBERT JOHNSTON	19/08/78:	Shot by IRA at his shop in Keady, Co Armagh
MR MICHAEL RILEY	7/06/78:	Shot at his home by IRA in Shankhill Rd Belfast
MR ROBERT LOCHART	17/04/79:	RUCR: killed by IRA bomb at Camlough
MR JACK MCCLENAGHAN	19/05/79:	Shot by the IRA whilst delivering bread in Fermanagh
MR DAVID STANLEY WRAY	20/05/79:	Shot by IRA on his way to church in Claremont
MR DAVID ALAN DUNNE	2/06/79:	RUCR: shot by INLA in Armagh
MR GEORGE HAWTHORNE	5/10/79:	Shot by IRA in Newry
MR JAMES FOWLER	16/12/79:	Shot by IRA as he drove his fish van in Omagh
MR CLIFFORD LUNDY	2/01/80:	Shot at work by IRA near Bessbrook, Co Armagh
MR HENRY LIVINGSTONE	6/03/80:	Shot by IRA at his farm at Tynan, Co Armagh
MR VICTOR MORROW	17/04/80:	Shot by IRA at Newtownbutler, Co Fermanagh
MR JOHN EAGLESON	1/10/82:	RUCR: shot by IRA on way to work
MR WILLIAM ELLIOT	28/06/80:	Shot by IRA at cattle market in Ballybay, Co Monaghan
MR JOHN ROBINSON	23/04/81:	Shot by IRA driving works van in Armagh
MR PTE JOHN PROCTOR	14/09/81:	Shot by IRA at hospital after visiting his wife and newborn baby at Magherafelt
MR HECTOR HALL	5/10/81:	Shot by IRA outside Altnagelvin hospital
MR CHARLES NEVILLE	10/11/81:	Shot by IRA at work in Co Armagh
MR JAMES MCCLINTOCK	18/11/81:	Shot by IRA on his way home from work, Londonderry
MR NORMAN HANNA	11/03/82:	Shot by IRA at his works in Newry
MR THOMAS CUNNINGHAM	12/05/82:	Shot by IRA whilst working in Strabane
MR WILFRED MCILVEEN	27/08/82:	IRA bomb underneath his car in Armagh
MR CHARLES CROTHERS	5/10/82:	Shot by IRA at Altnagelvin
MR ROBERT IRWIN	16/11/82:	RUCR: shot by INLA at Markethill
MR SNOWDEN CORKEY	16/11/82:	RUCR: killed in same incident
MR JAMES GIBSON	2/12/82:	Shot by IRA driving school bus at Coalisland

MR JOHN TRUCKLE	20/09/83:	IRA bomb underneath his car in Portadown
MR RONALD FUNSTON	13/03/84:	Shot by IRA on his farm at Pettigoe, Co Fermanagh
MR HUGH GALLAGHER	3/06/84:	Taxi driver; he was lured by IRA to Omagh and shot
MR MELVIN SIMPSON	8/10/84:	Shot by IRA at work in Dungannon
MR DOUGLAS MCELHINNEY	25/02/85:	Shot by INLA at friend's house in Londonderry
MR GEOFFREY CAMPBELL	25/02/85:	RUCR. One of nine killed IRA mortar attack, Newry
MR HERBET MCCONVILLE	15/05/86:	Shot dead by IRA whilst delivering in Newry
MR HARRY HENRY	21/04/87:	Murdered by IRA at his home in Magherafelt
MR CHARLES WATSON	22/05/87:	Murdered by the IRA at his home, Clough, Co Down
MR NATHANIEL CUSH	15/06/87:	IRA bomb underneath his car in Belfast
MR WINSTON G FINLAY	30/08/87:	Shot by IRA at his home in Ballyronan
MR JOHN GRIFFITHS	4/05/89:	IRA bomb underneath his car
MR ROBERT J GLOVER	15/11/89:	IRA bomb underneath his car near Dungannon
Mr DAVID STERRITT	24/07/90:	RUCR: killed with 4 others by IRA landmine, Armagh
MR DAVID POLLOCK	20/10/90:	Shot by an IRA sniper in Strabane
MR NORMAN KENDALL	10/11/90:	Murdered with 3 others by IRA, Castor Bay, Lurgam
MR HUBERT GILMORE	1/12/90:	Shot by IRA Kilrea, Co Londonderry
MR ERIC BOYD	5/08/91:	Shot by IRA as he left work Cappagh, Co Tyrone
MR RONALD FINLAY	15/08/91:	Shot at work by the IRA, Co Tyrone
MR DAVID MARTIN	25/04/93:	IRA bomb underneath his car, Kildress, Co Tyrone
MR JOHN LYNESS	24/06/93:	Shot by IRA at his home in Lurgan
MR JOHN ALEXANDER BURNS	30/10/93:	Shot by UFF at Eglington
MR ALAN SMYTH	25/04/94:	Shot by IRA in Garvagh
MR ERIC SMYTH	28/04/94:	Shot by IRA at his home in Co Armagh
MR DAVID CALDWELL	1/08/02:	Working on Army camp in Londonderry; killed by 'Real' IRA booby trap

Welsh Guards

SGT PHILIP PRICE	21/07/72:	IRA car bomb on 'Bloody Friday' Belfast bus depot
GUARDSMAN PAUL FRYER	13/11/79:	IRA bomb, Fords Cross, South Armagh
L/CPL MARK HOWELLS	12/07/92	RTA
GUARDSMAN DAVID ROBERTs	24/11/73	Killed by IRA bomb, South Armagh

Worcester & Sherwood Foresters

PTE MARTIN ROBINSON	16/04/72:	Killed in gun battle at Brandywell base, Londonderry
PTE MARTIN JESSOP	20/09/82:	Killed in rocket attack, Springfield Road RUC station
CPL LEON BUSH	27/09/82:	IRA booby trap, West Circular Road, Belfast

CPL STEPHEN MCGONIGLE	4/05/89:	IRA landmine, Crossmaglen
L/CPL STEPHEN KENT	2/02/90:	RTA
CPL GARY KIRBY	2/02/90:	Killed in same accident

Women's Royal Army Corps

W/PTE ANN HAMILTON	5/10/74:	Killed with 4 others in IRA bomb outrage, Guildford
W/PTE CAROLINE SLATER	5/10/74:	Killed in same outrage
L/CPL ROBERTA THAIN	25/03/75:	Accidentally shot dead in Shipquay Street, Londonderry
W/SGT ALISON STRYKER	4/06/76:	RTA
W/PTE KATHRYN WATERLAND	16/08/79:	RTA
W/CPL ELAINE MARRISON	14/02/83:	RTA
W/PTE MARIA HORNSBY	11/12/84:	RTA
W/PTE KAREN R. COWAN	10/11/85:	RTA

Civilian Searchers

NORMA SPENCE	3/03/78:	Shot by IRA in Belfast City centre by IRA
BRIAN RUSSELL	28/09/78:	Shot by IRA Waterloo Place, Londonderry

Security Services (Dates and causes of death withheld by MOD)
MICHAEL G. DALTON DALT
JOHN ROBERT DEVERELL
ANNE CATHERINE MACDONALD
MICHAEL BRUCE MALTBY
STEVEN LEWIS RICKARD
JOHN STUART HAYNESL

Although on the ROH, the following people are *not* included in the *total* number of SF Deaths.

The following Army Women and Children were also killed as a result of terrorism.

MRS LINDA HAUGHTON	4/02/74:	M62 Coach Bomb outrage
MASTER LEE HAUGHTON	4/02/74:	Killed in same outrage
MASTER ROBERT HAUGHTON	4/02/74:	Killed in same outrage
MISS LESLEY GORDON	8/02/78	Murdered with her Daddy by IRA
NIVRUTI MAHESKKUMAR	26/10/89	Murdered with her Daddy, Wildenrath, Germany

Army Personnel Killed in Aldershot IRA bomb outrage 22/02/72
THELMA BOSLEY
JOAN LUNN
MARGARET GRANT
JILL MANSFIELD
JOHN HASLAR
CHERIE MUNTON

Former Army Personnel Killed as a Direct Consequence of the Troubles

Brian Shaw (ex-RGJ)	21/07/74 :	Murdered by IRA in Lower Falls area

Army Civilian Workers Killed in Separate Incidents

Noor Baz Khan	26/06/73:	Murdered by the IRA in Londonderry
Mohammed Abdul Khalid	22/04/74:	Murdered by the IRA at Crossmaglen
Patsie Gillespie:	24/10/91:	Killed by IRA at Coshquin

* Marine John Shaw's death is recorded by the Royal Marines as 'killed in action'

Other soldiers and Civilian workers were killed or died during their time in Northern Ireland and the Author invites anyone with further knowledge of these people with Regiments, dates, or causes of death, to contact him on: ken_wharton@hotmail.co.uk

I gratefully and wholeheartedly acknowledge the incredible services of Emma Beaumont without whom, the compiling of this comprehensive Roll of Honour could never have happened. Great assistance by individual Regimental Associations was also given and I would like to mention Norman Brown of the Royal Pioneer Corps, Kevin Gorman of the Scots Guards and Kevin Stevens, Royal Green Jackets.

Poetry from the Troubles

TO THE MEMORY OF TED MEGAHEY

He has gone from us now; we will miss him so much
Never more will he walk through Drumquin;
He was ambushed near Derry while out on patrol,
Shot down by an IRA gun.

I cried when I heard it like everyone else,
For his life we did fervently pray;
But it was not to be, all our prayers proved in vain,
Why had he to die in this way?

A more generous kind-hearted man never lived,
And he proved it again and again;
May the dark cloud of sorrow that blankets Drumquin
As a mark of respect long remain.

He gave all his spare time, as few men would do
For the good of his parish and town;
And he did what he could to help those in distress -
He never did let a friend down.

The horror and shock that was felt by us all
When the sad news came through he was dead;
Was shown at his funeral by the vast crowd who came
To pay their respects to poor Ted.

As the lone piper played out a haunting lament,
As the Last Post rang out through the dell;
As the last parting volley was fired o'er the grave,
We murmured a final farewell.

In the shade of the church which he worked for so hard,
Just outside his native Drumquin;
He sleeps now in peace in the House of the Lord
Knowing justice will one day be done.

Then the fascists of Ireland will murder no more
And the trouble will come to an end;
But we will remember while we still have life
Ted Megahey, our neighbour and friend.

This poem was published in a local newspaper, the *Tyrone Constitution*, soon after the death in June 1972 of Pte Edward Megahey, of the 6th (Co Tyrone) Battalion of the Ulster Defence Regiment. It is reproduced here by kind permission of the newspaper and its editor Mr Wesley Acheson.

Pte Edward Megahey, a single man of 45 years, died two days after being shot, on June 2, 1972 by a sniper at Buncrana Road, Londonderry. He was on his way in a multiple vehicle patrol to relieve Victor Two border checkpoint. He was in the front passenger seat of the rear vehicle and the shot was fired from a housing estate on higher ground to the left.

Pte Megahey was a part-time soldier of the 6th (Co Tyrone) Battalion and would not normally have been near Londonderry. However elements of his Bn had been deployed to relieve the 5th (Londonderry) Bn who were attending annual training in Ballykinlar. But for this he would have been on some rural patrol near his County Tyrone home - not necessarily any safer of course.

THE UDR SOLDIER

AS POPPY PETALS GENTLY FALL

Remember us who gave our all
Not in the mud of foreign lands
Nor buried in the desert sands.

In Ulster field and farm and town,
Fermanagh's lanes and Drumlin'd Down
We died that violent death should cease
And Ulstermen might live in peace.
We did not serve because we hate
Nor bitterness our hearts dictate.

But we were they who must aspire
To quench the flame of terror's fire.
As buglers sound and pipers play
The proud battalions march away
Now may the weary violence cease
And let our country live
in peace

© John Potter

BENEATH A DIAMOND SKY

A crisp and clear late summer night, my mind is drifting far,
Back nearly forty years or so, to the fields of South Armagh.
Back to the time when I was young, when life was new,
And death was, too.
And in my mind, I catch the smells, of new cut grass, and late night dew.
Of whispering trees, and whispering grass, and all those sounds of night,
The sudden run of unseen hare, the sounds that gave us all a fright.
Then on we'd walk, with silken step, between the hedgerows, body's forced,
Avoiding gaps that may be wired, avoiding paths where streams once coursed.
Skirting round abandoned farms, with mouldy smells of rotting wood,
To venture into unseen ruins would not be wise, would not be good.
And slowly, as the night progressed, we made our torturous route,
Stopping every now and then, on haunches sat, adjusting straps, re-hanging kit,
Tightening up a loosened boot.
Until at last we find our way, to our new 'home' of many a day.
Just fallen stones, where in the past, a wall once stood, but now collapsed,
And here we'll stay, to watch and wait, the 'shuftyscope' hums low and green,
Watching deep into the night, for distant cars, for men unseen.
And as the dawn comes from the East, the pale light bathes the breeze bent grass,
The blood drenched fields of South Armagh revealed now to all who pass.

And so, in age, my head lifts up, a tear of memory fills my eye,
And I remember friends who died, so long ago, beneath a diamond sky.

VON SLAP

The Soldier stood and faced God
Which must always come to pass
He hoped his shoes were shining
Just as bright as his brass.

Step forward you Soldier,
How shall I deal with you?
Have you always turned the other cheek?
To My Church have you been true?

The Soldier squared his shoulders and
said
No, Lord, I guess I ain't
Because those of us who carry guns
Can't always be a saint.

I've had to work on Sundays
And at times my talk was tough,
And sometimes I've been violent,
Because the world is awfully rough.

But, I never took a penny
That wasn't mine to keep.
Though I worked a lot of overtime
When the bills got just too steep,

And I never passed a cry for help
Though at times I shook with fear,
And sometimes, God forgive me,
I've wept unmanly tears.

I know I don't deserve a place
Among the people here.
They never wanted me around
Except to calm their fears.

If you've a place for me here,
Lord, It needn't be so grand,
I never expected or had too much,
But if you don't, I'll understand.

There was silence all around the throne
Where the saints had often trod
As the Soldier waited quietly,
For the judgment of his God.

Step forward now, you Soldier,
You've borne your burden well.
Walk peacefully on Heaven's streets;
You've done your time in Hell.
Author Unknown

I leave the last words, fittingly, to a UDR man, Mark 'C' and to an Artillery man.

Lastly to all the servicemen and women who served in my country and especially to the approx 1300 who made the supreme sacrifice I salute you and thank you for helping bring peace, if it was not for us there would be no peace, please let the public acknowledge that. I add the first and last verse of the UDR Soldiers' Poem, but it is for everyone in every unit. (*I make no apologies for the repetition.*)

AS POPPY PETALS GENTLY FALL
REMEMBER US WHO GAVE OUR ALL
NOT IN THE MUD OF FORIEGN LANDS
NOR BURIED IN THE DESERT SANDS

AS THE BUGLERS SOUND AND PIPERS PLAY
THE PROUD BATTALLIONS MARCH AWAY
NOW MAY THE WEARY VIOLENCE CEASE
AND LET OUR COUNTRY LIVE IN PEACE

Bibliography

Unpublished material

Material for the Rolls of Honour supplied by the Northern Ireland Veterans Association and 'Britain's Small Wars'.

Printed sources

Arthur, M., *Northern Ireland: Soldiers Talking*, Sidgwick & Jackson, London, 1987

Barzilay, D., *The British Army in Ulster*, Century Books, Belfast, 1973–81, 4 vols

Barzilay, D. & M. Murray, *Four Months in Winter*, 2nd Battalion Royal Regiment of Fusiliers, Belfast, 1972

Curtis, N., *Faith and Duty: the True Story of a Soldier's War in Northern Ireland*, Andre Deutsch, London, 2003 (new edition)

Dewar, M., *The British Army in Northern Ireland*, Arms & Armour Press, London, 1985

Doherty, R., *The Thin Green Line: The History of the Royal Ulster ConstabularyGC*, Barnsley, Pen & Sword, 2004

Gamble. R., *The History of E Company 5 UDR: The Last Coleraine Militia?* Regimental Association of the UDR, Coleraine Branch, Coleraine, 2007

Gilpin, D., *Weekends in Uniform*, Write Lines in Print, n.p., 2005

Hammill, D., *Pig in the Middle: The Army in Northern Ireland 1969–84*, Methuen, London, 1985

Lindsay, J., *Brits Speak Out: British Soldiers' Impressions of the Northern Ireland Conflict*, Guild hall Press, Derry, 1998

McKittrick, D., *Lost Lives: The Stories of the Men, Women and Children who died through the Northern Ireland Troubles*, Main stream, London, 2004 (second revised edition)

McKittrick, D. & D. McVea, *Making Sense of the Troubles*, Penguin, London, 2001 new ed.

Morton, Brig. P., *Emergency Tour: 3 PARA in South Armagh*, William Kimber, London, 1989

Nettleton, R.L., *Tales From the Less Darker Side*, privately published by the author, n.p., 2007 reprint

Potter, J., *A Testimony to Courage: The Regimental History of the Ulster Defence Regiment*, Barnsley, Leo Cooper, 2001

Restorick R., *Death of a Soldier: A Mother's Search for Peace*, Blackstaff Press, Belfast, 2000

Silkstone, J.A., *You Two: Fall In – In Three Ranks*, Lulu.com, 2007

Taylor, P., *Brits: The War Against the IRA*, Bloomsbury, London, 2001

Taylor, P., *The Provos: IRA and Sinn Fein*, Bloomsbury, London, 1997

Internet sources

Britain's Small Wars: www.britains-smallwars.com/ni/RM.html
CAIN Index of the Troubles: http://cain.ulst.ac.uk/sutton/alpha/S.html / http://cain.ulst.ac.uk/ni/secu rity.htm#04
Glosters: http://www.rgbw-association.org.uk
Green Howards: www.ex-greenhowards.com
Guardian News Archive: http://www.guardian.co.uk/fromthearchive/story
Light Infantry: www.lightinfantryreunited.co.uk
Northern Ireland Veterans Association: http://nivets.org.uk//index.php
Palace Barracks, Belfast: http://www.palacebarracksmemorialgarden.org/Roll of Honour.htm
RUC Roll of Honour: http://www.policememorial.org.uk/Forces/RUC/RUC_Roll.htm
The music of Terry Friend (written about the Troubles): http://www.anothercountrysong.com
Wesley Johnston: http://www.wesleyjohnston.com/users/ireland/past/troubles/major_killings.html

Photographs

Reproduced by kind permission of:
Eddie Atkinson
Alex Boyd
Dave Bradwell
Mark Campbell
Steve Corbett
Tim Francis
Dave Henley
Joe Harris
Joe Jurkiewicz
Barrie Lovell
Phil Morris
Mo Norton
Royal Regiment of Wales Museum
Richard Smith
John Swaine
Ken Wharton
Arfon Williams
Tony Yarwood

Related titles published by Helion & Company

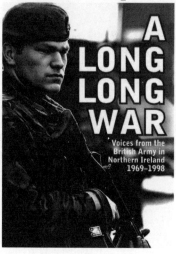

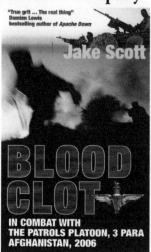

A Long Long War: Voices from the British Army in Northern Ireland 1969-98	*Blood Clot: In Combat with the Patrols Platoon 3 Para Afghanistan 2006*
Ken Wharton	Jake Scott
544pp Hardback	224pp Hardback
ISBN 978-1-906033-18-7	ISBN 978-1-906033-31-6

A selection of forthcoming titles

*Diary of a Red Devil: by Glider to Arnhem with the
Seventh King's Own Scottish Borderers*
A. Blockwell
ISBN 978-1-906033-20-0

*An Active Service: The Story of a Soldier's Life in the
Grenadier Guards and SAS, 1935-58*
R. Dorney
ISBN 978-1-906033-48-4

*The Silent General: Horne of the First Army. A Biography
of Haig's Trusted Great War Comrade-in-Arms*
D. Farr
ISBN 978-1-906033-47-7

HELION & COMPANY
26 Willow Road, Solihull, West Midlands B91 1UE, England
Telephone 0121 705 3393   Fax 0121 711 4075
Website: http://www.helion.co.uk